Children and young people who sexually abuse

New theory, research and practice developments

Edited by

Martin C. Calder

RHP

Russell House Publishing

First published in 2005 by:
Russell House Publishing Ltd.
4 St George's House
Uplyme Road
Lyme Regis
Dorset DT7 3LS

Tel: 01297-443948
Fax: 01297-442722
e-mail: help@russellhouse.co.uk
www.russellhouse.co.uk

British Library Cataloguing-in-publication Data:
A catalogue record for this book is available from the British Library.

ISBN: 1-903855-50-0

Typeset by TW Typesetting, Plymouth, Devon
© Front cover artwork by Stacey Laura Calder
Printed by Antony Rowe, Chippenham

Russell House Publishing
is a group of social work, probation, education and
youth and community work practitioners and
academics working in collaboration with a professional
publishing team.
Our aim is to work closely with the field to produce
innovative and valuable materials to help managers,
trainers, practitioners and students.
We are keen to receive feedback on publications and
new ideas for future projects.
For details of our other publications please visit our
website or ask us for a catalogue. Contact details are
on this page.

Contents

By your children you'll be taught!

Dedication

This book is dedicated to the memory of David O'Callaghan (1959–2004)

I am very honoured to have been asked to write a short piece to dedicate this book to the memory of David O'Callaghan. Dave was one of the founding Directors of the G-MAP organisation and had championed work with young people who had sexually abused since the late 1980s. His untimely death in March 2004 robbed our field of one of its most important leaders and, just as significantly to all those who knew Dave, of a dear friend. His work in respect of young people with learning disabilities who display harmful sexual behaviours was especially influential. The energy, commitment and warmth that Dave showed to all the young people with whom he worked remains an inspiration. Dave had a gift of being able to make a connection with the most rejected and rejecting young people. In a difficult field, Dave was also an exceptionally funny person. On a personal level, I feel truly fortunate to have worked with Dave as a colleague and to have counted him as a friend. Although it will be impossible to fill the gap that Dave's death leaves, the generosity and humility which underpinned Dave's approach remain as a beacon which should light the way for the further development of our field.

Simon Hackett
Durham. July 2004

Acknowledgements

Leigh library for all the material they continue to supply for me.

To the staff at Russell House Publishing for their perseverance with lengthy and frequent manuscripts and for their continuing belief in me.

To all the contributors for producing manuscripts of such high quality.

To frontline workers and managers for their dedication to a demanding and emotive task.

Profiles of contributors

Jack A. Apsche has a doctorate from Temple University. He is board certified by the American Board of Professional Psychology in clinical, behavioural and group psychology. He is a Fellow in the American Academy of Behavioural Psychology and the Academy of Clinical Psychology. He is currently designing a sexually violent predictor's programme for Liberty Healthcare in Bala Cynwyd, PA. Dr Apsche has published numerous articles, book chapters and books on a variety of topics including sex offenders, borderline personality disorders and conduct disorders in adolescents.

Serene R. Ward Bailey MA earned her master's degree in psychology at Texas A & M University and her bachelor's degree in psychology at Virginia Wesleyan College. She is licensed as a professional counsellor (LPC) and certified as a sex offender treatment provider (CSOTP) in the state of Virginia. Ms Bailey is co-developer of mode deactivation therapy (MDT). She has published numerous articles on effective treatment for adolescents, sex offenders, personality disorders, and conduct disorders. She is currently in private practice in Virginia, where she provides cognitive behavioural psychotherapy to children, adolescents and adults with a variety of Axis 1 disorders and personality disorders.

Ann Brady is a Social Worker at the Halt Project where she is involved in assessment and therapeutic services for children, young people and their Carers. She has developed and delivered training to a wide range of professionals. Prior to this she worked with children and young people who had been traumatised. The Halt project is a community resource working with children and young people who display a wide range of problem sexual behaviours. It was established nine years ago by Glasgow City Council. The project is located within child protection and offers a range of services to children, families and professionals.

Gerald L. Brown MD is Professor of Psychiatric Medicine at the University of Virginia. He was a Clinical Director at NIAAA with over 20 years in the Intramural Program. While at NIH, Dr Brown and co-investigators made significant contributions to the study of the relationships between low 5HT and violence/aggression in several populations, including prisoners and children and adolescents. Dr Brown has authored or co-authored over 80 publications in biological psychiatry of which many have focused on impulsivity/aggression, suicidality, hyperactivity/conduct disorders or alcohol and substance abuse.

David L. Burton MSW, PhD has worked in the field of sexual aggression for over 15 years, primarily with adolescents and children. He is a resident faculty member at Smith College School for Social Work in Massachusetts. He researches the trauma and etiology of child, adolescent and adult sexual abusers (current research interests include attachment, cognitive behavioural theory and treatment, effectiveness of treatment for adolescent sexual abusers, racial discrimination of sexual abusers and personality as an etiological factor for sexually abusive behaviour). He has been published in several journals including *Child Abuse and Neglect, Victims and Violence, Sexual Aggression, Evidenced Based Social Work*, and *Sexual Abuse: A Journal of Research and Practice*. Since 2001, Dr Burton has been the Chair of the Association for the Treatment of Sexual Abusers (ATSA) Education and Training Committee and a member of ATSA' executive board.

Martin C. Calder MA, CQSW is a Team Manager of the Child Protection Unit in the City of Salford Community and Social Services Directorate. He has written extensively in the area of sex offenders and is driven to provide accessible, evidence-based frameworks for operational use. He also acts as an independent social work trainer and consultant and is contactable at *martinccalder@aol.com*

Julie Carpentier is a PhD candidate at the School of Criminology at the University of Montreal. She is a clinical criminologist at the Philippe Pinel Institute of Montreal, a maximum-security psychiatric institution. Her research interests are criminal career parameters and recidivism in adolescent sexual aggressors.

Rosalind E.H. Catchpole MA is a doctoral student in child-clinical psychology at Simon Fraser University, and an assistant in the Program Evaluation and Research Department at Youth Forensic Psychiatric Services in British Columbia, Canada. Ms Catchpole's research interests include developmental trajectories to adolescent aggression and psychopathic traits.

Toni Cavanagh-Johnson PhD is a licensed clinical psychologist in private practice in South Pasadena, California. She has been working in the field of child abuse for 24 years as a researcher, trainer and clinician. She has written five books, two booklets, two therapeutic games, published numerous articles in refereed journals, and book chapters on child sexual abuse and children with sexual behavior problems. Her treatment model for conjoint therapeutic group interventions with children and protective parents who have lived together in violent homes has been presented at many national conferences. As chairperson of a task force of the California Professional Society on the Abuse of Children (CAPSAC), Dr Johnson assisted in the development of Guidelines for Monitored (Supervised) Visits. She is a member of the American Psychological Association, the American Professional Society on the Abuse of Children, as well as many other professional organisations. Dr Johnson has lectured on child abuse and domestic violence in Australia, New Zealand, South America, Europe, Africa, Hong Kong, Great Britain, Canada and throughout the United States. She provides consultation to protective service workers, mental health professionals, attorneys, the police, probation and the courts in the area of sexual victimisation, sexual perpetration and domestic violence.

Kevin Creeden MA, LMHC is the Director of Assessment and Research at the Whitney Academy in East Freetown, MA. Mr Creeden has over 25 years of clinical experience with children, adolescents, and their families working extensively with physically and sexually aggressive youth. He trains and consults throughout the United States to school systems, youth service and mental health agencies.

Cynthia Cupit Swenson PhD is Associate Professor at the Department of Psychiatry and Behavioral Sciences Medical University of South Carolina, Charleston. Dr Swenson is the Associate Director of the Family Services Research Center (FSRC) within the Medical University of South Carolina. She has conducted research at the FSRC for the past eight years, focusing on the treatment of child victims of abuse and neglect and their families.

Ronda L. Doonan PsyD is a graduate of the California School of Professional Psychology, Los Angeles. Currently working in the area of Family Therapy.

Lesley French is a clinical psychologist and lead for forensic under 21 provisions at the Bracton Centre, Oxleas NHS Trust. On completing doctoral training at University College London, Dr French provided assessment and treatment work for three years to child and adolescent sex offenders at the Young Abusers Project, a national referral centre for children with serious sexually harmful behaviour. Research work includes a Home Office funded study examining early developmental factors linked to the onset of juvenile sexual offending. A well-established community group work programme for adolescent sex offenders provided by the Bracton Centre is in the process of evaluation.

Jane F. Gilgun PhD, LICSW is a professor in the School of Social Work at the University of Minnesota. She has done research on how persons overcome adversities, the meanings of violence to perpetrators, the development of violent behaviours, and strengths-based assessment of children, youth, and families when the children and youth have adjustment issues, and has published and lectured widely on these topics. She was a public child welfare social worker for several years before she studied for her master's in social service administration at the University of Chicago and her PhD at Syracuse University and also has a licentiate in family studies and sexuality from the Catholic University of Louvain in Belgium. She can be contacted at School of Social Work, University of Minnesota, Twin Cities, 404 Gortner Avenue, St. Paul, MN 55108 USA. Phone: 612/925-3569; Fax: 612/624-3744; email: *jgilgun@umn.edu*; website: *http://ssw.che.umn.edu/faculty/jgilgun.htm*

Heather M. Gretton PhD is a Clinical Psychologist and Chair of the Program Evaluation and Research Department at Youth Forensic Psychiatric Services in British Columbia, Canada. Dr Gretton has spent her career studying the nature and long-term outcomes of adolescents involved in the criminal justice system. Her research over the past twelve years has focussed on the longitudinal study of youths with psychopathic traits.

Robert Hare is Emeritus Professor of Psychology, University of British Columbia, where he has taught and conducted research for some 35 years, and President of Darkstone Research Group Ltd., a forensic research and consulting firm. He has devoted most of his academic career to the investigation of psychopathy, its nature, assessment, and implications for mental health and criminal justice. He is the author of several books and many scientific articles on psychopathy, and is the developer of the *Psychopathy Checklist-Revised* (PCL-R) and a co-author of its derivatives, the *Psychopathy Checklist: Screening Version*, the *Psychopathy Checklist: Youth Version*, the *P-Scan*, and the *Antisocial Process Screening Device*.

Alan Jenkins has worked in statutory and therapeutic settings to develop fair, respectful and accountable intervention practices for people who have engaged in violence and abusive behaviour. Alan is a director of Nada Counselling, Consulting and Training, an independent agency concerned with intervention with abuse, violence and workplace harassment. He is also director of Mary St. Adolescent Program, the South Australian intervention program for young people who have sexually offended. Nada Counselling, Consulting and Training. PO Box 773, Stirling. South Australia. 5152.

Danette Jones AAMFT, LICSW is a therapist in private practice in St. Paul MN. A licenced family therapist and social worker, she has consulted and lectured widely on her approach to therapy and has published in her specialty area. Her master's in social work and in marriage and family therapy are from the University of Wisconsin, Madison. She can be contacted at 2375 University Avenue W., Suite 160, St. Paul, MN 55114 USA. Phone: 651/642-1709; fax: 651/642-0150.

Dr Ian Lambie is a Senior Lecturer in Clinical Psychology from the University of Auckland, New Zealand where he has an ongoing research programme. He has been providing treatment for adolescent sexual offenders for over 14 years and is Clinical Consultant to the SAFE Programme which provides community treatment to adolescent sexual offenders. His specialist clinical and research interests are youth forensic psychology and in particular severe conduct disorder, adolescent sexual offending and arson.

Elizabeth J. Letourneau PhD is Assistant Professor at the Department of Psychiatry and Behavioral Sciences Medical University of South Carolina Charleston. Dr Letourneau has conducted research on sex offenders for the past 15 years. For the past four years, she has worked at the Family Services Research Center (FSRC) within the Medical University of South Carolina. The 10 faculty members that comprise the FSRC all conduct research on juvenile delinquency. Dr Letourneau's area of focus has been the treatment of juvenile sexual offenders and their families.

Robert E. Longo MRC, LPC, is an independent clinician, consultant, trainer, and author dedicated to sexual abuse prevention and treatment, with a focus on sexual abuse prevention and treatment with youth. He has consulted and presented internationally in the field of sexual abuser assessment, treatment, and program development, and is co-founder and first President of the Association for the Treatment of Sexual Abusers. Robert was previously Director of the Safer Society Foundation, Inc. and the Safer Society Press from 1993 through 1998. He is a member of the *National Offense-Specific Residential Standards Task Force*, an Advisory Board member of the *National Adolescent Perpetrator Network*, a national committee member of the *Center for Sex Offender Management*, a national advisory committee member to the *National Center on Sexual Behavior of Youth*, an advisory team member to *From Darkness to Light*, an associate of the *Academy Group* based in Manassas, Virginia, and publisher for NEARI Press. Rob was the director of the Sex Offender Correctional Treatment Program; Mental Health Division, State of Oregon; Oregon State Hospital, Salem, Oregon from April 1983 through August 1989. He was formerly the Director of the Sex Offender Unit; North Florida Evaluation and Treatment Center; Gainesville, Florida and consultant to the sex offender programs for the State of Florida. Rob has trained professionals in law enforcement, mental health, protective service agencies, victim advocate programs, criminal justice, and the judicial system internationally. He has been a consultant and trainer for the National Institute of Corrections and has helped develop sexual abuser treatment programs throughout the United States, and in Australia, Canada, and New Zealand. In addition, Rob has published four books, five workbooks, more than forty chapters and articles in the field of sexual abuse treatment, and pioneered the adult sexual offender workbook series formerly published by the Safer Society Press and now published by NEARI Press. He is the author of the books *New Hope Exercises for Youth: Experiential Exercises for Children and Adolescents and Paths To Wellness*, and co-author of *Who am I and Why am in Treatment?*, *Why Did I Do it Again and How Can I Stop?*, *Enhancing Empathy, Men and Anger: Understanding and Managing Your Anger*, and *Sexual Abuse in America: Epidemic of the 21st Century*. Rob has specialised in the sexual abuse field and has worked with victims, and with juvenile and adult sex abusers in residential hospital, prison, and community-based settings since 1978.

Patrick Lussier is a PhD candidate at the School of Criminology at the University of Montreal. He has been involved in research and clinical activities at the Philippe Pinel Institute of Montreal, a maximum-security psychiatric institution. His research interests are the developmental course of offending, the criminal career in adulthood, interpersonal violence, and quantitative research methods. Some of his work has been published in *International Journal of Offender Therapy and Comparative Criminology*, *Journal of Interpersonal Violence*, and *Sexual Abuse: A Journal of Research and Treatment*. He received a postdoctoral fellowship to pursue his research at the University of Cambridge examining developmental factors linked to the male propensity to use violence against women using a prospective longitudinal framework.

Michelle McBride, PhD is a Clinical Psychologist at Youth Forensic Psychiatric Services in British Columbia, Canada. Dr McBride graduated from the University of British Columbia in 1998 with a doctorate degree in clinical psychology. Her doctoral research examined the childhood histories of adolescents exhibiting psychopathic traits.

Christine McCarlie is a senior social worker and manager of the Halt Project. She has been managing the project since it was established and has helped the project move from using adult informed models to adopting a holistic approach. She is an associate member of The Scottish Institute for Residential Child Care and has developed and delivered training to a wide range of professionals including Glasgow Council's Social Work Services Child Protection Training. The Halt project is a community resource working with children and young people who display a wide range of problem sexual behaviours. It was established nine years ago by Glasgow City Council. The project is located within child protection and offers a range of services to children, families and professionals.

Elizabeth McGarvey EdD has a doctorate in educational psychology and is an Associate Professor and Director of the Division of Prevention Research in the Department of Psychiatric Medicine at the University of Virginia School of Medicine. She is also a Faculty Associate of the Institute of Law, Psychiatry and Public Policy at the university. She has been principal investigator on NIH funded studies in the incarcerated juvenile population. Dr McGarvey has numerous publications on the incarcerated population in Virginia. With Dr Waite, she has also published on the mental health needs of incarcerated adolescents and has participated in the design of educational, prevention and intervention programs. Dr McGarvey can be contacted at *rel8s@virginia.edu*

William Meezan DSW, ACSW is the Marion Elizabeth Blue Professor of Children and Families at the University of Michigan School of Social Work, Ann Arbor, MI. In 1984–85 he served as a Congressional Science Fellow sponsored by the Society for Research in Child Development, while in 1994–95 he was a senior Fulbright scholar in Lithuania. He has been involved in research along the entire continuum of child welfare services. He has written extensively; his work includes five co-authored books, four co-edited books, numerous monographs and over 40 refereed articles and book chapters. He serves on the editorial boards of seven journals and is the recipient of the Society for Social Work Research's Outstanding Research Award. He can be reached at (734) 214-1553 or at *meezan@umich.edu*

Roy O'Shaughnessy is a clinical professor in the Department of Psychiatry and Head of the Division of Forensic Psychiatry at the University of British Columbia and. He is Clinical Director at Youth Forensic Services, Province of British Columbia. He is past president of the American Academy of Psychiatry and Law.

Relana Pinkerton PhD is an Assistant Professor in the Division of Prevention Research in the Department of Psychiatric Medicine at UVA. Dr Pinkerton is a developmental psychologist who plans to focus her research career in the area of the proposed study. She can be contacted at *RCP3W@hscmail.mcc.virginia.edu*

Jean Proulx received his PhD in Psychology from the University of Montreal in 1992. During the last 15 years, he published more than 60 papers or book chapters (in French and English) in the field of sexual aggression. His research interests include the following: phallometric assessment, offending process in child molesters, rapists and sexual murderers, predictors of recidivism, treatment compliance and criminal career parameters in sexual aggressors. In addition, since 1987, he has worked as a clinical psychologist at the Philippe Pinel Institute of Montreal, a maximum-security psychiatric institution. Since 1993, he is a professor at the School of Criminology at the University of Montreal and since 2003 has been co-director of the International Centre for Comparative Criminology.

Katherine V. Regan, MA is a doctoral student in social psychology at Simon Fraser University in British Columbia, Canada. Ms Regan was a research assistant in the Program Evaluation and Research Department at Youth Forensic Psychiatric Services in British Columbia, Canada at the time of the study. Her research interests include the study of violence in domestic relationships.

Kay Rice LICSW, ACSW is a therapist in private practice specialising in children, youth, and their families where the young people are experiencing serious adjustment issues. She has consulted and lectured widely on her approach to therapy and has published in her specialty area. A licensed social worker, her master's in social work is from the University of Iowa. Her address is 2375 University Avenue W., Suite 160, St. Paul, MN 55114 USA. Phone: 651/642-1709; fax: 651/642-0150.

Susan L. Robinson LCSW is a licensed clinical social worker who works in a private mental health agency in Denver, Colorado. She specialises in working with juvenile and adult sexual offending females. She is the author of Growing Beyond: A Workbook for Teenage Girls published by NEARI Press. She has presented on the treatment of sexually abusive girls and women at numerous conferences. Susan can be contacted through email: *surobin@hotmail.com*

Dr Stephen Smallbone is a senior lecturer in criminology and forensic psychology at Griffith University in Queensland, Australia. He has been working with adult sexual offenders for the past 15 years, and with adolescent sexual offenders for the past four years. His main research and professional interests are in developmental, systemic, and situational aspects of sexual crime.

Charlene Steen PhD, JD is a licensed psychologist and retired attorney, who has directed a family sexual abuse treatment program, evaluated sexually violent predators for the State of California, provided outpatient treatment for sex offenders, and currently evaluates sex offenders for the courts and presents workshops throughout the US, Canada and Europe. She has written *The Adult Relapse Prevention Workbook*, *The Relapse Prevention Workbook for Youth in Treatment*, *Treating Adolescent Sex Offenders in the Community*, 'The Expert Witness in the Sex Offender Case' in *The Sex Offender* 'Case Management of Sexual Abuse Victims' in *The Handbook of Forensic Sexology* and a number of articles, including 'Treating Denying Offenders' and 'Sex

Offender Laws: A Need for More Intelligent Solutions' in the *California Coalition on Sex Offending Newsletter*. She has just completed a workbook for female sex offenders.

Jerry D. Thomas MEd is an independent consultant who specialises in work with sexually abusive youth and their families. A member of the National Task Force on Juvenile Sexual Offending, she participated in the development of The Task Force Report published by the National Counsel of Juvenile and Family Court Judges in Reno, Nevada. As a member of the National Task Force on Offense Specific Residential Programs, she participated in the development of standards of practice, published by the NEARI Press in Massachusetts. J Thomas Consulting and Training Services Memphis, Tennessee.

Cindy Tyo LISW-AP, LISW-CP is the lead therapist for the Waypoint Program of New Hope Treatment Centres in South Carolina. She received her Master's Degree in Social Work from Syracuse University and went on to be the Director of a Sexual Abuse Intervention Program for Hillside Children's Centre in Rochester, NY. Cindy joined the Waypoint team in February of 1998 after 12 years of work with Hillside. Cindy has extensive experience in working with victims and offenders of sexual crimes. She is trained as a play therapist and uses this in conjunction with other experiential therapy training in her work with the adolescent boys at Waypoint.

C. Wilson Viar III is an independent research and writing consultant focusing primarily upon problematic social issues and creative efforts to solve them. Since 1996 he has co authored a wide variety of articles, chapters, handbooks, seminars and training materials with Ms Thomas on topics spanning the field. Viar Services Memphis, Tennessee.

Dr Dennis Waite PhD is the Chief Psychologist for the Behavioural Services Unit in the Virginia Department of Juvenile Justice. He is a Licensed Clinical Psychologist, Certified Forensic Evaluator, Certified Sex Offender Treatment Provider, and Clinical Assistant Professor in the Department of Psychiatric Medicine at the University of Virginia and Affiliate Assistant Clinical Professor in the Department of Psychology at Virginia Commonwealth University. Dr Waite has served on numerous legislative task forces, and has been a consultant to the US Department of Justice, Civil Rights Division investigating the conditions of confinement within juvenile justice facilities across the United States. He can be contacted at *waitede@djj.state.va.us*

Ineke Way PhD, ACSW is an Assistant Professor at the School of Social Work, Western Michigan University. She has treatment experience with children who have been sexually abused, non-offending parents, adolescents with sexual offending behaviours, and adult survivors of incest. She co-authored two books on treatment with adolescents with sexually abusive behaviours, and co-developed a cycle of offending behaviours. Her current research focuses on developing an instrument to measure alexithymia in children. The project is funded through a grant awarded to the Southwest Michigan Children's Trauma Assessment Centre (CTAC) as a part of the National Child Traumatic Stress Initiative's Collaborative Response to

Traumatised Children. The initiative is funded by the Substance Abuse and Mental Health Services Administration (SAMHSA). Dr Way can be contacted at the School of Social Work, 1903 W Michigan Ave., Western Michigan University, Kalamazoo, MI 49008-5354, 269/387-3195, or *ineke.way@wmich.edu*

Edward Wieckowski MA, CSOTP is the Co-ordinator of Sex Offender Services for the Virginia Department of Juvenile Justice. He previously worked as a psychologist with juvenile sex offenders for 12 years. He is experienced in sex offender treatment, and program development and implementation. He has served on legislative committees, published articles on the treatment of juvenile sex offenders, and has presented at numerous international conferences on issues related to sex offending. He can be contacted at *wieckoe@djj.state.va.us*

Introduction
Martin C Calder

This book represents a sequel to the jigsaw puzzle text published in 1999 and the development of an evidence-base in 2002 both detailed below and endeavours to build on the growth of research material and practice developments in the intervening period. This book does not replace these texts, rather it attempts to build on the foundation blocks that they set down. This book is organised into several sections to help the reader in being able to relatively easily access the particular information they need. These sections include research and theoretical developments, the engagement of young people, assessment issues, treatment issues, management issues and outcomes. Whilst the book can be read alone, it is best read in conjunction with my other works: *Juveniles and children who sexually abuse: a guide to risk assessment* (Calder, 1997), *Working with young people who sexually abuse: new pieces of the jigsaw puzzle* (Calder, 1999), *Juveniles and children who sexually abuse: frameworks for assessment* 2nd edn. (Calder, 2001) and *Working with young people who sexually abuse: building the evidence-base for your practice* (Calder, 2002). In this way, the reader will be able to grasp the individual and tailored responses now being advocated by referring back to where we started and why we have reached our current state. The books aim to stimulate thought and discussion and identify areas where further research is needed and hopefully will guide practice, policy and procedure development.

In an attempt to meet the above objectives, I have assembled contributions from England, Scotland, Australia, New Zealand, America and Canada and the authors draw from a combination of practice experience, research, programme evaluation and academic review. A couple of issues arise as an editor from such a wide audience. Firstly, there is a wide range of terms used to refer to young people who sexually abuse, and I have not standardised those chosen to highlight why we continue to have basic obstacles to evidence-based practice in this field, especially comparative work. The varying vocabulary reflects that used in the source material which is referred to.

I am very clear about the choice of the term young people who sexually abuse and Simon

Hackett (2001) has articulated this especially well. He recognises that the term 'young person who has sexually abused' is quite clumsy and long, but he avoids using the shorter 'young abuser' or 'adolescent offender' as these terms describe the child only by what they have done wrong. They are terms that do not offer much hope to the young person concerned. It is important not to downplay what a young person has done or make it seem less serious by using language which does not fit with the abuse. However, we should always consider the messages that might be communicated beneath the words we use. Consder the following statements, for example:

The terms	The messages that might be communicated beneath the terms to a young person:
'You are a sexual abuser'	• All you are is an abuser • You are still an abuser • You will always be an abuser • I am only interested in you as an abuser
'You are a young person who has sexually abused'	• You are a young person first and foremost • You have done something wrong in the past but this doesn't mean to say that you will always be an abuser • You could change • I am taking your behaviour seriously – it is abuse but I am interested in you as a young person as well

Secondly, there are some clear differences in spelling between the UK and America and I have chosen to keep the vocabulary as set down by the author. In doing so, I hope that this does not detract from its appeal and use.

In Chapter 1, Stephen Smallbone explores attachment insecurity as a predisposing and precipitating factor in young people who sexually abuse. He summarises the evolution of theoretical views and empirical findings thus far in this area and identifies key limitations in securing a direct causal link between attachment problems and sexual behaviour. Drawing on a broad evidence-base, he then moves into offering a new attachment-conceptual model for understanding sexually abusive behaviour by young people, utilising the theoretical associations between the attachment, caregiving and sexual behaviour systems. This clearly extends the earlier theoretical work in this area and indeed departs from it. He indicates that further refinement work and testing of his hypotheses are required.

In Chapter 2, Heather Gretton and colleagues reported on the second follow-up to their longitudinal investigation into the relationship between psychopathy, treatment completion and criminal outcome in adolescent male sex offenders. Their earlier work had identified psychopathic young people as a unique subgroup of adolescent sex offenders with a propensity to high rates of generalised offending and violence than sex offender per se. Accordingly their sexual misbehaviour is not so much a reflection of specific factors related to sexual recidivism but a more general propensity to impulsive, violating, and self-gratifying behaviour. The chapter goes on to consider how young people with many psychopathic traits differ from other sex offending young people in the course of their criminal behaviours and what impact treatment completion had on their long-term outcomes. They conclude by considering the implications of their findings in relation to the development and organisation of appropriate intervention programmes.

In Chapter 3, Cavanagh Johnson and Doonan review what we have learned about children with sexual behaviour problems in the last two decades and make a series of useful points about how we continue to inappropriately judge children's behaviours through adult behaviours and expectations.

Carpentier and her colleagues in Chapter 4 report on a study to ascertain possible links between developmental and pre-crime factors and two criminal activity parameters, the level of coercion and the number of victims, in a sample of young people who sexually abuse. Their findings highlight the relevance of static and dynamic factors with the criminal activity of young people who sexually abuse and they also embrace factors from wider research that influences the criminal activity of this group.

In Chapter 5, Burton and Meezan review the available research to test the usefulness of

adopting social learning theory with this group. They conclude by making some recommendations for future research.

In Chapters 6 and 7, Alan Jenkins provides us with two thought provoking considerations for engaging young people in the intervention process and the challenges this presents for professionals. In so doing, the young person can be encouraged to develop their sense of identity, self-respect and respect for others. Several case studies are used to maximise the impact of the points being made. Following the theme of engagement, Ian Lambie reviews the relevant literature in relation to interviewing strategies with young people who sexually abuse. In doing this, he offers four psychotherapeutic factors that play a part in assisting change within the young person.

In Chapter 9, Dr Lesley French explores the assessment and treatment strategies for children with sexually abusive behaviours. She addresses the contribution of integrating developmental and cognitive-behavioural perspectives to thinking about this group of children. This is essential if we are to move away from the importation of ideas from work with adults. She also identifies a need to explore how mechanisms of a particular treatment intervention achieve therapeutic change. At present it is difficult to conclude that empirically supported treatments work through the mechanisms specified in the theories of intervention. As such, the importance of moderators could greater influence application of treatment with better identification of those children most likely to respond to specific interventions. This area requires considerably more attention.

In Chapter 10 Ineke Way reviews the literature on empathy and two associated elements – emotional intelligence and alexithymia. In a thought provoking and fascinating chapter she draws together what we know into a helpful structure and supports the need for further research in all these areas.

In Chapter 11 Susan Robinson reviews the available literature on young females who sexually abuse, including the developmental differences across gender, risk assessment, structures on offer and their applicability to females. She provides us with a suggested framework for undertaking core assessments with this group that will allow us to further understand their needs, issues and risk factors.

In Chapter 12, Kevin Creeden presents an overview of the research and writings from the fields of attachment and trauma and describes how this has been translated into treating children and young people with sexual behaviour problems. The integrated treatment approach is premised on the goal that the treatment should not be restricted to the absence of abuse in relationships, but also as the increased capacity to engage and maintain stable, mutual, and intimate relationships with others.

In Chapter 13, Cindy Tyo reports on her work as a play therapist and experiential therapist with young prople who sexually abuse.

In Chapter 14, Charlene Steen provides us with a conceptual overview of relapse prevention and cognitive behavioural treatment and some useful examples for practice applications. It is also useful to refer to the work of Rob Longo (2002) who has provided us with some excellent materials that allows relapse prevention to be located within a more holistic approach for young people who sexually abuse.

In Chapter 15 Jane Gilgun and her colleagues argue on the centrality of emotional expressiveness in the treatment of children 5-10 with problematic sexual behaviours. They review a wide range of theory: on the development of sexually abusive behaviours, emotional development and expression and resilience to support this assertion. They offer us a typology of emotions children present with at the beginning of treatment and move on to explore emotion-focused therapy as an essential addition to our treatment armoury. They conclude by exploring strategies and treatment guidelines for emotion-focused work with children and their families, including some useful indicators of change.

In Chapter 16, Letourneau and Swenson explore MST with children and young people who sexually abuse. They present a view/ overview of the correlates of sexual behaviour problems in these groups before reviewing the treatment outcome literature.

In Chapter 17, Apsche and Ward Bailey provide a conceptually innovative addition to the treatment repertoire for those working with young people who sexually abuse: mode deactivation therapy. Using a case study they show us how we can effect change with young people who sexually abuse with personality disorders or traits. Some useful appendices provide workers with preliminary tools to approach any work with young people who sexually abuse and their families. The workbooks referred to are hopefully to become available in the UK in the near future.

In Chapter 18, McCarlie and Brady report on their evolving risk management framework which has encouraged them to reconsider the interface between the child and their environment and recognise the huge impact the environment can have on making risk more manageable.

In Chapter 19, Rob Longo and myself explore the use of sex offender registration for young people who sexually abuse and compare the issues across the US and the UK.

In Chapter 20 Thomas and Viar consider the necessary prerequisites and process for considering family reunification where sexually abusive behaviour within the sibling group has taken place. Offering a detailed incremental approach to this task, we are provided with a number of useful checklists to guide safe treatment planning.

In the final chapter Wieckowski and his colleagues describe the programme and the outcomes from a nine-year study within a correctional treatment facility measured by recidivism rates. Their findings support the emerging consensus that young people who sexually abuse are not destined to become adult sex offenders and the reality that Sex Offender Treatment Programmes (SOTP) do not make much impact in reducing general criminal behaviour.

Overall, this book is an attempt to:

- Acknowledge the excellent work going on in this area.
- Report and thus share the emerging research, theory and practice necessary to building evidence-based practice.
- Stimulate discussion and debate.
- To identify what we do know and what we do not know and what this means for practice.

I hope this book achieves these aims and you find the material available stimulus for your work.

References

Calder, M.C. (1997) *Juveniles and Children Who Sexually Abuse: A Guide to Risk Assessment.* Lyme Regis: Russell House Publishing.

Calder, M.C. (Ed.) (1999) *Working With Young People Who Sexually Abuse: New Pieces of the Jigsaw Puzzle.* Lyme Regis: Russell House Publishing.

Calder, M.C. (2001) *Juveniles and Children Who Sexually Abuse: Frameworks for Assessment.* 2nd edn. Lyme Regis: Russell House Publishing.

Calder, M.C. (Ed.) (2002) *Working With Young People Who Sexually Abuse: Building the Evidence-Base for Your Practice.* Lyme Regis: Russell House Publishing.

DoH (1999) *Working Together to Safeguard Children.* London: HMSO.

Hackett, S. (2001) *Facing the Future: A Guide for Parents of Young People Who Have Sexually Abused.* Lyme Regis: Russell House Publishing

Longo, R. (2002) A Holistic Approach to Treating Young People Who Sexually Abuse. In Calder, M.C. (Ed.) (2002) op cit.

Part I

Research and theoretical developments

Attachment Insecurity as a Predisposing and Precipitating Factor for Sexually Abusive Behaviour by Young People

Stephen W. Smallbone

Introduction

In view of the sheer volume and diversity of attachment-related research since Bowlby (1969, 1973, 1980) first articulated his comprehensive theory of attachment, it is perhaps easy to lose sight of the fact that Bowlby's original ideas about attachment arose, at least in part, from his observations of '44 juvenile thieves' referred to a London Child Guidance Clinic. Bowlby's (1946) hypothesis concerning the effects of maternal separation and the 'emotional attitude' of parents on the development of antisocial behaviour clearly foreshadowed current attachment-related analyses of delinquency and crime. In his later and better-known trilogy, Bowlby (1969, 1973, 1980) expanded his ideas about attachment into a comprehensive theory of human development, within which, incidentally, little emphasis was given to delinquent behaviour. Nevertheless, attachment theory and its sociological derivatives have subsequently been widely used to explain the now well-established empirical links between adverse parent-child relationships and subsequent involvement in delinquency and crime (see e.g., Fonagy, Target et al., 1997; Gottredson and Hirschi, 1990; Hirschi, 1969; Rankin and Kern, 1994; van Ljzendoorn, 1997; van Ljzendoorn, Feldbrugge et al., 1997; Wilson and Herrnstein, 1986).

Arising in somewhat similar circumstances to Bowlby's early observations of his young offender clients, the application of attachment theory more specifically to understanding **sexual** delinquency and crime originated with Marshall's (1989) clinical observations that adult sexual offenders typically failed to achieve secure childhood and adult attachment bonds. Marshall's observations soon led to further theoretical commentary on the implications of attachment theory for understanding sexual offending behaviour (Marshall, 1993; Ward, Hudson, Marshall, and Siegert, 1995). Both Marshall's (1989) original formulation and Ward et al.'s (1995) extrapolated model identified

possible developmental pathways from insecure childhood attachment to adult sexual offending behaviour. In summary, these authors proposed that insecure childhood attachment may result in deficits in interpersonal skills, self-confidence and empathy, in turn leading to deficiencies in the acquisition of skills required to engage successfully in courtship behaviours and to achieve sexual intimacy. Numerous empirical studies on adult sexual offenders' attachment experiences followed. In general, these have concentrated on investigating differences between sexual and nonsexual offenders, and between different subtypes of sexual offenders, on self-report measures of adult and childhood attachment styles (Jamieson and Marshall, 2000; McCormack, Hudson, and Ward, 2002; Smallbone and Dadds, 1998, 2000, 2001; Smallbone and McCabe, 2003; Ward, Hudson, and Marshall, 1996). Thus far there is insufficient evidence to confirm or disconfirm specific elements of Marshall's (1989, 1993) or Ward et al.'s (1995) models, other than perhaps in the most general sense that sexual offenders on the whole appear to have experienced less secure attachment than adult non-offenders.

The potential application of attachment theory even more specifically to understanding **young** people who have committed sexual offences has also been recognised. Two rather similar models have been proposed, and both in turn are quite similar to Marshall and his colleagues' original formulations concerning adult sexual offenders. First, Marshall, Hudson, and Hodkinson (1993) reviewed empirical evidence linking adverse developmental experiences, including insecure attachment, to general delinquency, noting that young sexual offenders tend to report similar developmental experiences and also tend to have been involved in nonsexual offending. More specific links between insecure attachment and sexual offending behaviour by young people were proposed on the basis of complex interactions between attachment problems and other dispositional factors such as hormonal disturbances, intimacy deficits, and deviant fantasies, and situational factors such as exposure to pornography.

Santry and McCarthy (1999) extended Marshall et al.'s (1993) formulation to consider the interactions between insecure attachment and problems with peer relationships and psychosexual development. They argued that while in many cases insecure attachment itself produced difficulties in peer relationships and psychosexual development, significant developmental events such as peer rejection or sexual abuse may exacerbate the vulnerability already established through early attachment problems, thus 'priming' the vulnerable youth, for example, to engage in excessive sexual self-stimulation or to confuse intimacy with sexuality.

Very recently, Burk and Burkhart (in press) have proposed another model, which considers implications of attachment theory for both adult and adolescent sexual offending. These authors argue that attachment disorganisation results in the failure to internalise self-regulatory skills. In short, their model suggests that sexual offending behaviour can in part be conceptualised as an attempt to ameliorate aversive attachment-related emotions through repeated efforts to exert control in interpersonal, especially sexual, interactions. Marshall et al. (1993), Santry and McCarthy (1999), and Burk and Burkhart (in press) have all made important contributions by delineating and applying established concepts and knowledge from the much broader attachment literature to the newer and more specialised literature on adolescent sexual offending. There are several important limitations, however, that are common to all three formulations. First, none of the models accounts satisfactorily for the link between attachment behaviour and sexual behaviour, and thus for the specific relevance of attachment theory for understanding sexual offending behaviour over and above its relevance for understanding offending behaviour in general. Instead, each model suggests only indirect links between attachment and sexual behaviour, most notably through the influence of early attachment experiences on the development of the social and interpersonal skills needed to achieve emotional and physical intimacy. Second, these previous models do not elaborate on the implications of attachment theory for understanding the relevance of specific interpersonal contexts in which adolescent sexual offending behaviour

typically occurs, for example the sexual exploitation of younger children with whom nonsexual relationships have already been established. Again only indirect links are suggested, mainly involving problems with social isolation and concomitant difficulties with establishing close peer relationships. Finally, although all three models to some extent imply the importance of situational factors, they do not make clear exactly how attachment-related vulnerability might interact with immediate situational factors, and no mechanism is identified by which this interaction might occur. Moreover, the previous models do not account for how sexual offending could occur in young people whose developmental history suggests no particular attachment-related vulnerability.

In this chapter, I aim to describe a new and more parsimonious attachment-theoretical model for understanding the commission of sexual offences by adolescents. The proposed model draws particularly on one of the fundamental principles of attachment theory that has been effectively overlooked in previous formulations, namely the theoretical associations between the attachment, care giving and sexual behavioural systems. I begin by describing the development of the attachment behavioural system from infancy to early adulthood, with particular emphasis on the implications of attachment for empathy and perspective-taking, moral development, affect regulation, and adopting co-operative versus coercive strategies for influencing others. Next, I attempt to explain how the attachment, care giving and sexual behavioural systems are inter-related. Specifically, I consider on one hand the developmental challenge of integrating the three behavioural systems, and highlight on the other hand the importance of establishing and maintaining appropriate functional independence of these behavioural systems. I then consider how attachment-related vulnerabilities may constitute an important predisposing factor for sexual offending behaviour, and how immediate situational factors may precipitate sexual aggression and sexual exploitation of younger children in circumstances where the functional independence of the attachment, caregiving and sexual behavioural systems is compromised. Finally, empirical studies of attachment problems in adolescent and adult sexual offenders are briefly reviewed.

Development of the attachment behavioural system

Bowlby (1969) proposed that the principal evolutionary function of attachment behaviour is protection of infants from harm by predators through maintaining proximity to a caregiver. One condition under which the proximity-seeking behaviour of infants is most reliably and intensely elicited (activation of the attachment behavioural system) is that of subjective distress. Termination of proximity-seeking behaviour (de-activation of the attachment behavioural system) is achieved when felt security is re-established. At first, this is likely to require physical contact with the caregiver, but as the child's cognitive abilities develop, mere knowledge of the proximity of the caregiver, or even confidence in her availability, may suffice. Confidence in the availability of a caregiver is thought to facilitate autonomy with regard to emotional regulation. Lack of confidence in the availability of a caregiver, resulting from repeated lack or inconsistency of caregiver responsiveness, will lead to difficulties in regulating emotions, especially negative emotions. Insecure attachment is therefore thought to lead to difficulties in managing distress and anger, and thus in constraining anger-mediated aggression.

With the development of cognitive perspective-taking in the third or fourth year, a child's strategies for interacting with his caregiver become organised on the basis of what Bowlby termed a goal-corrected partnership. Within a secure attachment relationship, attempts by the child to influence the behaviour of his attachment figure come to be based on a degree of co-operation and mutual interest. Within insecure attachment relationships, however, children have been observed to adopt coercive and noncompliant strategies. These behavioural strategies both influence and are influenced by the attachment figure's behaviour. Clearly, co-operative strategies require some accurate estimation by the child of the desires and experience of the attachment figure, and by the attachment figure of the child. Thus the development of a more general capacity for empathy and perspective-taking may over time be facilitated, or in less favourable circumstances inhibited, in large part depending on the quality of the primary attachment relationships within the first few years of childhood. Importantly, it is this capacity for empathy and perspective-taking that is thought to underpin moral development (Kohlberg and Diessner, 1991). Of particular importance is the possibility that secure attachment representations facilitate the extension of moral reasoning to moral action (Van Ljzendoorn, 1997).

Bowlby (1969) proposed that primary attachment experiences lead to the construction of internal working models of self and other – essentially mental representations concerned with a) perceptions of oneself as the kind of person that others will respond to in certain ways, and b) expectations of others in terms of their availability and reliability. These internal working models are proposed as the mechanism by which dispositions toward close relationships are carried forward into subsequent stages of development. While by no means immutable, primary attachment relationships are thought to lead to relatively stable expectations about close relationships in general, and are thought to have particular significance for patterns of orientation toward later intimate and sexual relationships.

By middle childhood, the range of potential affiliative and social relationships is increased substantially beyond the primary caregivers and the family. While there is some disagreement concerning the kinds of relationships that are considered to constitute attachment relationships, there is substantial evidence that the quality of primary attachment experiences affects interpersonal behaviour in a broad range of relationships. For example, Sroufe (1988) has described differences among socially disadvantaged children whose attachment as infants had been classified as secure, anxious, or avoidant. Secure children were observed to be more empathic, more popular with other children, more resourceful, and more resilient than insecure children. By contrast, anxious children were observed to be more impulsive, more easily frustrated in social settings, and more likely to engage in attention-seeking behaviours than secure children. Avoidant children were observed to be more hostile, unempathic, and antisocial. The link between attachment status and externalising behaviour problems has not been found to be as strong in more socially advantaged groups. Moreover, while harsh parental treatment and stressful life events have been linked to aggression in both boys and girls, avoidant attachment has been shown to be more strongly related to aggressive antisocial behaviour in boys than in girls (Lyons-Ruth, 1996).

Insecure attachment in adolescence and adulthood has been theoretically and empirically linked to a variety of psychopathological outcomes, some of which may be construed as extensions of the patterns of behaviour seen in middle childhood. In general terms, avoidant adult attachment has been associated with conduct and substance abuse disorders, and with narcissistic and antisocial personality disorders. Anxious attachment has been found to be associated with affective, histrionic, and borderline personality disorders. Disorganised attachment has been found to be a significant risk factor for aggressive behaviour problems, and for severe adolescent psychopathology.

There is some disagreement about the role and purpose of the attachment behavioural system in adolescence. Social psychological researchers appear to implicate the attachment system directly in 'romantic love' (Hazan and Shaver, 1987) and 'romantic infatuation' (Hazan and Diamond, 2000). Within this research tradition, romantic love is seen as an overarching construct involving the integration of attachment, care giving, and sexuality (Feeney and Noller, 1996), the purpose of which is ultimately to establish enduring pair bonds that in turn will serve to generate offspring in which resources can be co-operatively invested. This perspective clearly draws upon evolutionary concepts of reproductive fitness, and seems, at least in part, to assume a natural concordance between evolutionary purpose and 21st century social mores. However, as Bowlby (1969) himself pointed out, the environment of evolutionary adaptedness in which the attachment behavioural system was originally selected is very different from the technological age of the present day. Current patterns of social behaviour may therefore at best represent weak indicators of the evolutionary purpose of those behavioural systems.

It is perhaps more likely that clues will be found in the more stable biological systems that underpin social behaviour. In fact, as will be elaborated in a little more detail in the next section, neurobiological analyses of social behaviour suggest that sexual drive, romantic attraction, and attachment, are each mediated by different neurobiological systems, and thus each appears to serve a distinct evolutionary purpose (Fisher, 1998; Fisher, Aron, Mashek, Li, and

Brown, 2002). According to this perspective, attachment behaviour is biologically most closely related to care giving behaviour. The reciprocal nature of the relationship between attachment and care giving in social terms suggests that the evolutionary purpose of this attachment-care giving system is "to co-operate with a reproductive mate until species-specific parental duties have been completed" (Fisher et al., 2002, p413). Thus, while sexual drive and romantic attraction may facilitate the formation of enduring pair bonds, from an evolutionary perspective they may be adaptive without doing so. Moreover, positive socialisation in terms of current environmental demands, and in particular secure attachment experiences, may be critical in constraining the divergence of these behavioural systems. Insecure childhood attachment, then, may fail to constrain this biological potential for sexual drive, romantic attraction, and attachment-care giving to diverge.

Finally, the continuity of the attachment behavioural system from childhood to adolescence has been the subject of considerable debate and empirical inquiry. Recent accounts suggest that the degree of stability of attachment orientation into adolescence and adulthood is considerably less than was once assumed, and that within individuals, patterns of attachment behaviour itself may change according to particular immediate circumstances (Pietromonaco and Feldman Barrett, 2000). Thus, new interpersonal experiences may to some extent alter an individual's general attachment orientation, such as may occur when an insecure individual becomes involved in an enduring, secure intimate relationship. Moreover, although an individual's attachment orientation may in general predict relatively stable patterns of attachment behaviour in interpersonal settings, it is likely that particular attachment-related responses will also vary according to certain features of a given interpersonal context.

In summary, secure childhood attachment has been theoretically and empirically linked to the capacity for autonomous emotional regulation, the development of capacities for empathy and perspective-taking, moral reasoning and moral action, resourcefulness, popularity, co-operative and prosocial behaviour, and enduring, mutual intimate relationships. By contrast, insecure childhood attachment has variously been associated with difficulties in regulating negative emotion, the development of poor empathy and perspective-taking, withdrawn or coercive interpersonal styles, aggressive and antisocial behaviour, and relatively unstable close relationships. Severe disruptions to childhood attachment have been implicated in serious adolescent and adult psychopathology, including personality disorders, substance abuse, and aggression. The purpose of attachment behaviour in adolescence remains uncertain, but biological evidence suggests that attachment and care giving are biologically related and may serve the primary social purpose of co-operating with reproductive mates. The biological bases of related social behaviour systems, notably involving sexual drive and romantic or sexual attraction are thought to be distinct from the attachment-care giving system. Secure childhood attachment may be required to constrain the social divergence of these systems. Finally, some, but by no means absolute, continuity has been observed in attachment styles from childhood to adolescence and adulthood. Patterns of attachment orientation are therefore subject to the influence of new attachment-related experiences, and attachment behaviour itself may be subject to environmental cues present in the immediate social (and especially interpersonal) environment.

The Attachment, care giving, and sexual behavioural systems

For Bowlby (1969), the attachment system is the primary behavioural system, naturally selected in the environment of evolutionary adaptedness, whose ultimate function is to ensure individual survival. Two other behavioural systems – the sexual and parenting systems – need to function sufficiently well in a sufficient proportion of individuals in order to ensure species survival. While much work has been done to elucidate the nature of the relationship between attachment and parenting, surprisingly little work has been done to investigate the relationship between attachment and sexuality, or indeed between sexuality and care giving.

There is a general consensus among attachment researchers that parenting behaviour is organised as a complementary system to attachment behaviour. That is, whereas attachment behaviour may be triggered by distress and de-activated by physical contact with or proximity to the caregiver, parental care giving behaviour in turn is triggered by signals initiated by the child (including efforts to establish

proximity) and may be temporarily de-activated when the child signals a return to emotional equilibrium.

The parenting behavioural system is considered to share its evolutionary basis with the more generalised form of care giving behaviour. Thus, patterns of behaviour directed toward the care and protection of one's own children are seen as analogous to patterns of behaviour directed toward the care and protection of significant others, including other children, and particularly of mates within sexual pair bonds. Among affiliated adults, attachment and care giving behaviour are considered to function reciprocally, such that by turns 'each partner . . . looks to the other as stronger, wiser, or more competent, and the other reciprocates by providing care, comfort, reassurance, and thus feelings of security' (Ainsworth, 1991: p42).

Adult attachment research has more or less implied the importance of the relationship between attachment and sexuality, but this work has tended to deal only indirectly with sexual behaviour, concentrating instead on the associations between attachment and adult romantic, marital, or intimate relationships (Hazan and Shaver, 1987; Feeney and Noller, 1990). It is of course clear that human sexual behaviour can and does occur in the absence of romance, marriage and intimacy, usually without being considered deviant or illegal.

Several contributions to the adult attachment literature are nevertheless noteworthy. Hazan and Zeifman (1994) have highlighted the unique behavioural similarities, briefly alluded to by Bowlby himself, between infant-caregiver interactions and adult sexual interactions. Prolonged skin-to-skin, face-to-face contact, extended mutual gazing, mutual embracing and kissing, and even genital contact, all first occur virtually exclusively within infant-caregiver interactions. The re-emergence of these intimate interpersonal behaviours is then not seen until adolescence, once again tending to occur exclusively, now within romantic and especially sexual interactions. The place given by these authors to care giving is restricted to the reciprocal behaviours of intimate partners; the more complementary aspects of parent/child interactions are not central to their model.

Similarly, Shaver (1994) has described a model of romantic love which aims to integrate the attachment, care giving, and sexual behavioural systems. While recognising the important theoretical links between the three behavioural systems, this model also restricts discussion of care giving to reciprocal behaviour between intimate partners. Shaver investigated empirical relationships between adult attachment and specific sexual behaviours. The data showed, for example, that secure adults tended to be open to a relatively broad range of sexual behaviours (including oral and anal sex, talking dirty etc.) tending to do so within the context of a continuing committed relationship. Avoidant adult attachment tended to be associated with sexual behaviours in the context of diminished interpersonal commitment, such as one-night-stands, sex without love, and extramarital sex. Thus a link between adult attachment and sexual behaviour has been found not so much in terms of particular kinds of sexual behaviours, but in terms of the interpersonal context in which these sexual behaviours are performed.

Returning to an evolutionary theme, Belsky, Steinberg, and Draper (1991) have considered the links between attachment, sexuality and parenting from a behavioural ecology perspective. These authors have argued that childhood attachment experiences signal the availability and predictability of resources required for successful reproduction. In environments where resources are readily available (e.g., close relationships are seen as reliable and enduring), reproductive effort is likely to be directed toward establishing and maintaining few high-quality sexual pair bonds, and toward high levels of parental investment. Conversely, in primary attachment environments where resources are scarce (e.g., close relationships appear to be self-serving and unreliable) reproductive effort is likely to be biased toward sexual promiscuity and low parental investment. Thus, insecure childhood attachment is theoretically linked with opportunistic sexual behaviour, short-term, unstable pair bonds, and limited parental investment – a reproductive strategy that in present-day social terms may be problematic, but that in evolutionary terms may be especially viable in adverse social environments.

Finally, as mentioned in the preceding section, the neurobiological bases of the attachment, sexual and care giving behavioural systems have also been examined. Nelson and Panksepp (1998) have proposed the existence of a 'social motivation circuitry' involving the activity of

oxytocin, vasopressin, endogenous opioids and catecholamines in a wide variety of affiliative behaviours, including childhood attachment. Fisher (1998) has suggested more specifically that while the estrogens and androgens are primarily responsible for sexual arousal, the catecholamines are involved specifically in sexual or romantic attraction, implying that sexual arousal and the selection of potential sexual partners are mediated by different neurobiological systems. Fisher et al. (2002) has illustrated the social implications of this with reference to studies in which adult men and women were administered testosterone to increase sexual desire. In such cases, increased sexual thoughts and sexual activity tend to occur, but without concomitant increases in romantic passion or attachment to sexual partners. Fisher et al. (2002) has further proposed that attachment and care giving behaviour are mediated by common neurobiological systems, specifically involving the activity of the neuropeptides oxytocin and vasopressin. In female nonhuman mammals, oxytocin has been experimentally implicated in the development of partner preference in the absence of mating. Similarly, administering vasopressin to male nonhuman mammals has been shown to evoke preferential mate selection directed toward sexually unreceptive females. Oxytocin is thought to be activated in human females during copulation, parturition, and nursing (Insel, 2000).

Thus, Fisher et al. (2002) argues that sexual drive, sexual attraction, and attachment/care giving have evolved to become increasingly independent of one another, allowing considerable flexibility in human mating and reproductive strategies. As these authors explain:

> . . . men and women can express deep attachment for a long-term spouse or mate, while they express attraction for someone else, while they feel the sex drive in response to visual, verbal, or mental stimuli unrelated to either partner. And men and women can copulate with individuals with whom they are not 'in love'; they can be 'in love' with someone with whom they have had no sexual contact; and they can feel deeply attached to a mate for whom they feel no sexual desire or romantic passion.
>
> (p414).

Rather than the concordance between evolutionary purpose and present-day social mores implied by social psychological analyses of attachment, care giving and sexuality, then, neurobiological perspectives suggest a fundamental tension between biological preparedness for behavioural diversity on the one hand, and socialisation processes directed toward behavioural conformity and constraint on the other. To the extent that sexual offending behaviour by young people can be conceived of as a failure of constraint, it is to the developmental processes of socialisation, and in particular to the developmental implications of attachment insecurity, that we should look for explanations of how such a failure may emerge. However, given the underlying biological potential for sexual impropriety, I hope to also show how attachment theory might explain how sexual offending behaviour can emerge even in circumstances where there is no particular developmentally-based vulnerability.

Attachment insecurity as a predisposing factor for sexual offending behaviour

The link between attachment insecurity and aggression has been observed from the earliest stages of development. Specifically, coercive and aggressive behaviour directed toward the primary caregiver has been associated with avoidant and disorganised attachment patterns (Main and Solomon, 1986). By three or four years of age, opportunities for developing the capacity for empathy and perspective-taking may be missed, again especially for avoidant and disorganised children. By middle childhood, anxious boys have been observed to be more impulsive, and avoidant boys more hostile and aggressive, than have securely attached boys (Sroufe, 1988). Of particular significance are difficulties in the autonomous regulation of emotion, especially subjective distress, which are key features of insecure attachment (Ainsworth et al., 1978; Bowlby, 1969).

From the earliest opportunities for peer socialisation, established patterns of coercive and aggressive behaviour appear to generalise to a broader interpersonal and social context. Thus, attachment theory postulates that patterns of infant-caregiver interaction are carried forward, via internal working models of self-in-relation-to-other, to give rise to relatively stable patterns of interpersonal behaviour. In adverse circumstances, avoidant and especially disorganised attachment may lead to overt antisocial behaviour. This is exemplified in studies of pre-school children, among whom avoidant children have been observed to be more antisocial than secure and anxious children. Anxious children have been observed to be more frustrated in social settings, but are more likely to be victimised than they are to victimise others (Carlson and Sroufe, 1995).

Extending these aggressive and antisocial patterns in childhood to delinquent behaviour in adolescence may be facilitated by a number of factors which are themselves associated with insecure attachment, including poor empathy development, a reduced capacity to regulate subjective distress, negative social expectations, and attribution of hostile intent to others. More broadly, association with similarly aggressive and antisocial peers and the failure to establish attachments to prosocial institutions (e.g., schools; churches; sporting clubs) may serve further to reduce control of antisocial behaviour (Gottredson and Hirschi, 1990).

With the arrival of puberty, goal-directed sexual behaviour will generally involve attempts to engage others for the purposes of sexual union. If previously established patterns of interpersonal behaviour involve either overt or covert aggressive or antisocial dispositions, it is likely that these will be further generalised to include patterns of sexual behaviour. Thus, insecure early attachment experiences may be linked to aggressive and opportunistic sexual behaviour through the incorporation of sexual behaviour into a broader repertoire of interpersonal behaviour. This link between attachment and sexual offending is somewhat similar to that proposed by Marshall et al. (1993) and Santry and McCarthy (1999). However, the links between attachment and sexual behaviour may also be considered in terms of the more fundamental inter-relationships among the attachment, care giving, and sexual behavioural systems. This may provide some more specific clues as to the circumstances in which attachment-related vulnerabilities are likely to become manifest in sexual impropriety, including sexual offending. Specifically, when the attachment, care giving and sexual behavioural systems are poorly integrated, or worse still when they are disorganised, sexual behaviour may be cued by subjective distress (e.g., loneliness or anger), and/or by physical proximity, especially to vulnerable others, including children. Moreover, and especially during adolescence, it is plausible that the attachment behavioural system may be implicated in the commission of sexual offences even in circumstances where no particular developmentally-based vulnerabilities exist.

Attachment instability as a precipitating factor for sexual offending behaviour

Attachment theory suggests that the biological bases for attachment, sexual and care giving behaviour provide for considerable flexibility and diversity in their potential expression, and there is now some evidence to support this view. Attachment theory also suggests that each of these three behavioural systems share a common cognitive, affective and behavioural blueprint – namely patterns of subjective experience and interpersonal behaviour established on the basis of early attachment experiences. Thus, whereas the underlying biological systems provide for behavioural diversity, processes of socialisation provide for the development of the mechanisms of behavioural constraint, namely empathy and perspective-taking, emotional regulation, moral reasoning, and a co-operative interpersonal style. It is important for social adaption that the three behavioural systems are appropriately integrated. On one hand, this is likely to require the acquisition of prosocial attitudes and skills (e.g., recognition of the importance of mutual and consensual interpersonal relations, and the capacities for perspective-taking and autonomous emotional regulation) that provide a common basis upon which all three systems can effectively function. On the other hand, each system needs to be directed toward somewhat different goals, and so a degree of functional independence between the three systems needs to be established and maintained.

Even under the most favourable of circumstances, it would be expected that a degree of functional overlap may occur among the three systems. Within committed adult intimate relationships, for example, spouses will typically provide attachment, care giving, and sexual functions in relation to their intimate partner. The relative activation of one or more of these three behavioural systems is likely to depend both on the extent to which the three systems are integrated and guided by prosocial themes (a dispositional factor), and on the specific cues present in a particular interpersonal setting (a situational factor). For example, proximity-seeking (attachment) behaviour, which may be activated by a subjective state of distress

or discomfort, may result in intimate physical contact with an intimate partner, in turn activating the sexual behaviour system. Similarly, care giving behaviour, activated by the presence of a distressed intimate partner, may activate sexual behaviour through intimate physical contact. The situation is perhaps a little less clear with regard to physical contact with children, but it is conceivable that some confusion concerning care giving behaviour and sexual behaviour may arise in circumstances where sexual responsiveness to children is not adequately inhibited. Maintaining the culturally appropriate separation of these three behavioural systems is likely in part to be dependent on an individual's capacity for perspective-taking, and may work best when co-operation and mutuality are preserved. It would also require some recognition of and identification with cultural norms. In most cultures, special care is demanded in maintaining appropriate sexual boundaries between adults and children and to ensure mutuality in adult sexual interactions. Indeed, it is the laws prohibiting sexual contact with children and non-consensual adult sexual relations that define the construct of sexual offending.

In less favourable circumstances, earlier disorganisation of childhood attachment and/or powerful situational influences may lead to less functional independence between the three systems than would otherwise be expected to occur. In such circumstances, rather than activating the attachment behavioural system, distress may instead readily activate the sexual behaviour system, resulting in inappropriate and possibly coercive attempts to engage sexually in order to restore affective stasis. If all three systems are disorganised, proximity to a child (which might normally activate the care giving behaviour system) when distressed (which might normally activate the attachment behaviour system) may lead to inappropriate activation of the sexual behaviour system, resulting in sexualised interactions with the child. Inhibitory mechanisms that may otherwise have protected against sexual impropriety may be over-ridden by more pressing affective forces, such as loneliness, anger, or sexual arousal.

The tension between the biological demands for diversity of sexual expression and the social demands for sexual constraint is likely to be at its most pressing during adolescence. On one hand, powerful sexual impulses are relatively new, and may be at their most urgent. On the other hand, social conformity is arguably at its weakest point, since stable social and sexual identities are not yet fully established. We would therefore in normal circumstances expect adolescent sexual behaviour to be highly experimental and somewhat disorganised. For adolescents who have already developed an insecure attachment orientation, a great potential thus exists for patterns of coercive, rule-breaking, sensation-seeking, self-serving, under-controlled and/or opportunistic behaviour to be extended to the domain of sexual attitudes and behaviour. However, in the biological, psychological and social maelstrom of adolescence, the functional independence of the three behavioural systems may be compromised even in circumstances where earlier attachment experiences have been relatively unproblematic. Thus we would expect some young people to commit sexual offences largely as a function of situational influences (e.g., unsupervised physical contact with a child, precipitating disorganised attachment-care giving-sexual responses), whereas for others, sexual offences may be part of a broader pattern of antisocial conduct. In the latter case, situational factors that serve to precipitate disorganised attachment-care giving-sexual responses may still be relevant. In either case, more stable patterns of sexual deviance, and especially deviant sexual preferences, may emerge, largely depending on how the initial sexual offence incident was experienced, interpreted, and perhaps followed by further similar incidents.

Evidence for the role of attachment insecurity in sexual offending

There is an extensive body of evidence that adverse developmental experiences are relatively common in the background of adolescent sexual offenders. Although little direct investigation of attachment insecurity in young sexual offenders has yet been attempted, available evidence provides some basis upon which we might infer that attachment-related vulnerabilities play some role in their sexual offending behaviour. First, like adolescent nonsexual offenders, adolescent sexual offenders have been reported to commonly experience parental divorce and separation (Blaske, Borduin, Hengeller, and Mann, 1989; Fehrenbach, Smith, Monastersky, and Diesher, 1986), parental conflict (Ford and Linney, 1995), sexual victimisation (Vizard, Monck, and Misch, 1995), and exposure to physical violence

(Spaccarelli, Bowden, Coatsworth, and Kim, 1997). Differences between adolescent sexual and nonsexual offenders have been observed in the relative extent of attachment-related problems. For example, adolescent sexual offenders have been observed to experience more troubled family relationships (Vizard, Monck, and Misch, 1995), less family cohesion (Bischof, Stith, and Whitney, 1995), greater levels of parental violence (Ford and Linney, 1995), and more exposure to physical abuse (Spaccarelli, Bowden, Coatsworth, and Kim, 1997) than their nonsexual offending counterparts.

In a more direct investigation of attachment problems among young people referred to a New Zealand clinic because of their coercive sexual behaviour, Lightfoot and Evans (2000) too reported a similarly high prevalence of family disruption, physical and verbal abuse, and family violence, in both their sexually coercive group and a matched sample of conduct disordered youngsters. However, the sexually coercive group was twice as likely as the conduct disordered comparison group to have experienced multiple disruptions to their primary attachment relationships prior to age seven. These disruptions themselves were the result of adverse circumstances such as family conflict, abandonment, and maternal depression.

Apart from Lightfoot and Evans' (2000) study, most of the empirical research relating directly to attachment problems in sexual offenders has been conducted with adults. In general, while adult sexual offenders tend to report less secure adult attachment than non-offenders, no consistent differences between different types of sexual offenders or between sexual and nonsexual offenders have emerged (Jamieson and Marshall, 2000; Smallbone and Dadds, 1998; Ward, Hudson and Marshall, 1996). In two studies of adult non-offenders, Smallbone and Dadds (2000, 2001) found positive associations between insecure adult attachment and aggression, antisociality, and coercive sexual behaviour, although findings with respect to different types of insecure attachment were inconsistent.

Childhood attachment experiences of adult sexual offenders have also been investigated, employing retrospective cross sectional designs. Smallbone and Dadds (1998) found that their combined sexual offender group reported significantly less secure maternal and paternal attachment than non-offenders, and less secure maternal attachment than property offenders.

However, Marshall, Serran, and Cortoni (2000), using the same childhood attachment measure, found no significant differences between sexual offenders, nonsexual offenders and nonoffenders on maternal or paternal childhood attachment. Marshall et al.'s (2000) null findings with respect to their sexual offender group – all nonfamilial offenders – may not be as inconsistent with Smallbone and Dadds' (1998) findings, though, as they first seem to be. Nonfamilial child molesters have consistently been found to report more secure parental attachment than other sexual offender groups (see, e.g., Smallbone and Dadds, 1998; Smallbone and Wortley, 2000). Nevertheless, and again using a mixed sexual offender sample, Smallbone and McCabe (2003) found that written autobiographies of sexual offenders were more likely to indicate secure than insecure maternal and paternal attachment. Finally, Smallbone and Dadds (2000, 2001) found insecure childhood attachment to predict coercive sexual behaviour in two separate samples of non-offenders. In both cases childhood avoidant attachment was the best predictor of coercive sexual behaviour after aggression and antisociality were statistically controlled. However, in one study paternal avoidant attachment was the most important predictor, and in the other study maternal avoidant attachment was the most important predictor.

It is perhaps surprising that these studies of childhood and adult attachment have produced such mixed findings, given the consistent findings elsewhere that both adult and adolescent sexual offenders tend to report a broad range of adverse developmental experiences. One explanation may of course lie in the imprecision of the attachment measures thus far employed. Another obvious limitation is in the retrospective designs typically employed. Perhaps the most important limitation, though, is that almost all attachment research with sexual offenders has been based on conceptions of attachment insecurity as a stable, trait-like feature. As discussed earlier, attachment researchers are increasingly questioning the stability of attachment 'style'. Particularly in terms of the attachment model of sexual offending proposed in this chapter, it is important to consider whether there is evidence that attachment insecurity plays a much more proximal role in sexual offending behaviour.

First, the interpersonal context in which both adult and adolescent sexual offending typically occurs is itself suggestive of a proximal link with attachment insecurity of the kind outlined earlier in this chapter. In particular, it is well known that most sexual offences occur in circumstances where a close relationship already exists between the offender and victim. So-called 'grooming' behaviour, in which sexual engagement with children typically follows a period of emotional and nonsexual physical contact (Kaufman, Hilliker, and Daleiden, 1996; Smallbone and Wortley, 2000), suggests some connection between care giving and sexual behaviour, even in extra familial contexts. Second, although it is often assumed that extrafamilial offenders actively join child-related organisations for the purpose of accessing potential victims, there is some evidence that, at least in some cases, the close involvement with children precedes the deviant sexual interests. For example, in their confidential self-report study, Smallbone and Wortley (2000) found that while 20% of a group of adult extra familial child molesters said they had offended within a child-related organisation, only 2% said they had joined that organisation for the express purpose of having access to children for sexual purposes. Similarly, while 45% of extra familial offenders said that they had formed close relationships with the parents of their victims, considerably fewer (29%) said they had ever befriended a parent to gain access to the child.

Third, a link between attachment behaviour and sexual behaviour is suggested by findings that both adult and adolescent sexual offenders commonly report heightened state anger, anxiety, and loneliness immediately preceding the sexual offence incident (Hoghughi, Bhate and Graham, 1997; Pithers, Beal, Armstrong and Petty, 1989), and by experimental studies showing for example that anger arousal increases sexual arousal to depictions of rape (Yates, Barbaree, and Marshall, 1984). Moreover, there is some evidence that negative mood states precipitate deviant fantasy in adult rapists (Proulx, McKibben, and Lusignan, 1996). In Lightfoot and Evans' (2000) study of sexually coercive young people, the sexually coercive incidents were in all cases preceded by an emotionally distressing event. In each case, the young person reported this distressing event in terms that suggested difficulties in emotional regulation.

Finally, although there is little doubt that at least some sexual offenders over time establish stable deviant sexual preferences, the biological basis for these preferences is unclear. With very few exceptions, sexual offenders have been found not to have elevated levels of b lood testosterone or any other particular biological abnormality (Grubin and Mason, 1997; Hucker and Bain, 1990). Indeed, clinical observation suggests that some preferential child molesters continue to desire relationships with children even when their blood testosterone level has been drastically lowered by pharmacological agents. This begs the question whether it is sexual arousal **per se** that is at the heart of the problem, or whether instead it is confused desires related to attachment-care giving, or even romantic passion, that motivate some sexual offenders.

Summary and conclusions

In this chapter I have attempted to outline a new, and I hope parsimonious, attachment-theoretical model of sexual offending. Although the model may have relevance for understanding both adult and adolescent sexual offending, I have tried where possible to highlight particular points of relevance to sexual offending by young people. The model seeks to extend earlier theoretical work in this area, notably by Marshall (1989), Marshall et al. (1993), Santry and McCarthy (1999), and more recently Burk and Burkhart (in press).

The present model represents a significant departure from this earlier work in two ways. First, I have drawn upon one of the key principles of attachment theory that has been effectively overlooked in earlier attachment formulations, namely the theoretical associations between the attachment, care giving, and sexual behavioural systems. Second, I have proposed that attachment insecurity may be conceived of as both a predisposing and precipitating factor in the commission of sexual offences.

In developing the present model, I have tried to draw upon a broad evidence-base involving clinical, social psychology, behavioural ecology, and neurobiological perspectives. With respect particularly to the specialised sexual offender research literature, I have argued that there is substantial indirect evidence, and some limited direct evidence, to support the attachment theoretical model that I have attempted to articulate here. This evidence supports both the possibility that attachment-related vulnerabilities are an important predisposing factor, and that disorganisation of the attachment, care giving and sexual behavioural systems may constitute an important precipitating factor, in the

commission of sexual offences by both adults and adolescents.

In conclusion, much work is needed to further refine the attachment model of sexual offending described in this chapter, and to test some of the hypotheses that may be derived from the model. I hope that the present work will at least serve to promote discussion of some of the many questions it raises, and in particular of the theoretical and applied implications of these questions.

References

Ainsworth, M.D.S. (1991) Attachments and Other Affectional Bonds Across The Life Cycle, in Parkes, C.M. Stevenson-Hinde, J. and Marris. P. (Eds.) *Attachment Across The Life Cycle*. London: Routledge. 33–51.

Ainsworth, M.D.S., Blehar, M.C., Waters, E. and Wall, S. (1978) *Patterns of Attachment: A Psychological Study of The Strange Situation*. Hillsdale, NJ: Erlbaum.

Belsky, J., Steinberg, L. and Draper, P. (1991) Childhood Experience, Interpersonal Development, and Reproductive Strategy: an Evolutionary Theory of Socialisation. *Child Development*, 62, 647–70.

Bischof, G.P., Stith, S.M. and Whitney, M.L. (1995) Family Environments of Adolescent Sex Offenders and Other Juvenile Delinquents. *Adolescence*, 30, 157–70.

Blaske, D.M., Borduin, C.M., Henggeler, S.W. and Mann, B.J. (1989) Individual, Family, and Peer Characteristics of Adolescent Sex Offenders and Assaultive Offenders. *Developmental Psychology*, 25, 846–55.

Bowlby, J. (1946) *Forty-Four Juvenile Thieves: Their Characters and Home Life*. London: Bailliere, Tindall and Cox.

Bowlby, J. (1969) *Attachment and Loss: Vol 1. Attachment*. New York: Basic Books.

Bowlby, J. (1973) *Attachment and Loss: Vol 2. Separation: Anxiety and Anger*. New York: Basic Books.

Bowlby, J. (1980) *Attachment and Loss: Vol 3. Loss*. New York: Basic Books.

Burk, L.R. and Burkhart, B.R. (In Press) Disorganised Attachment as A Diathesis for Sexual Deviance: Developmental Experience and The Motivation for Sexual Offending, *Aggression and Violent Behaviour*.

Carlson, E.A. and Sroufe, L.A. (1995) Contribution of Attachment Theory to Developmental Psychopathology. In Chiccetti,

D. and Cohen, D.J. (Eds.) *Developmental Psychopathology, Vol 1: Theories and Methods*. New York: Wiley. 581–617.

Feeney, J.A. and Noller, P. (1990) Attachment Style as A Predictor of Adult Romantic Relationships. *Journal of Personality and Social Psychology*, 58, 281–91.

Fehrenbach, P.A., Smith, W., Monastersky, C. and Deisher, R.W. (1986) Adolescent Sexual Offenders: Offender and Offence Characteristics. *American Journal of Orthopsychiatry*, 56, 225–33.

Finkelhor, D. (1984) *Child Sexual Abuse: New Theory and Research*. New York: Free Press.

Fisher, H.E. (1998) Lust, Attraction, and Attachment in Mammalian Reproduction. *Human Nature*, 9, 23–52.

Fisher, H.E., Aron, A., Mashek, D., Li, H. and Brown, L.L. (2002) Defining The Brain Systems of Lust, Romantic Attraction, and Attachment. *Archives of Sexual Behaviour*, 31, 413–9.

Fonagy, P., Target, M., Steele, M., Steele, H., Leigh, T., Levinson, A. and Kennedy, R. (1997) Morality, Disruptive Behaviour, Borderline Personality Disorder, Crime, and Their Relationships to Security of Attachment, in Atkinson, L. and Zucker, K.J. (Eds.) *Attachment and Psychopathology*. New York: Guilford Press.

Ford, M.E. and Linney, J.A. (1995) Comparative Analysis of Juvenile Sexual Offenders, Violent Nonsexual Offenders, and Status Offenders. *Journal of Interpersonal Violence*, 10, 56–70.

Gottredson, M. and Hirschi, T. (1990) *A General Theory of Crime*. Stanford, CA: Stanford University Press.

Grubin, D. and Mason, D. (1997) Medical Models of Sexual Deviance, in Laws, D.R. and O'Donohue, W. (Eds.) *Sexual Deviance: Theory, Assessment, and Treatment*. New York: Guilford Press. 434–48.

Harlow, H.F. (1961) The Development of Affectional Patterns in Infant Monkeys. In Foss, B.M. (Ed.) *Determinants of Infant Behaviour*. London: Methuen.

Harlow, H.F. and Harlow, M.K. (1965) The Affectional Systems. In Schrier, A.M. Harlow, H.F. and Stollnitz, F. (Eds.) *Behaviour of Nonhuman Primates, Vol 2*. New York: Academic Press. 75–97.

Hazan, C. and Diamond, L.M. (2000) The Place of Attachment in Human Mating. *Review of General Psychology*, 4 (2) 186–204.

Hazan, C., and Shaver, P. (1987) Romantic Love Conceptualised as an Attachment Process. *Journal of Personality and Social Psychology*, 52, 511–24.

Hazan, C. and Zeifman, D. (1994) Sex and The Psychological Tether. In Bartholomew, K. and Perlman, D. (Eds.) *Attachment Processes in Adulthood*. London: Jessica Kingsley. 151–78.

Hirschi, T. (1969) *Causes of Delinquency*. Berkeley, CA: University of California Press.

Hoghughi, M.S., Bhate, S.R. and Graham, F. (1997) *Working With Sexually Abusive Adolescents*. Thousand Oaks, CA: Sage.

Hucker, S.J. and Bain, J. (1990) Androgenic Hormones and Sexual Assault. In Marshall, W.L. Laws, D.R. and Barbaree, H.E. (Eds.) *Handbook of Sexual Assault: Issues, Theories, and Treatment of The Offender*. New York: Plenum. 93–102.

Insel, T.R. (2000) Toward A Neurobiology of Attachment. *Review of General Psychology*, 4(2) 176–85.

Jameison, S. and Marshall, W.L. (2000) Attachment Styles and Violence in Child Molesters. *Journal of Sexual Aggression*, 5, 88–98.

Kaufman, K.L., Hilliker, D.R. and Daleiden, E.L. (1996) Subgroup Differences in The Modus Operandi of Adolescent Sexual Offenders. *Child Maltreatment*, 1(1) 17–24.

Kohlberg, L. and Diessner, R. (1991) A Cognitive-Developmental Approach to Moral Attachment, in Gerwitz, J.L. and Kurtines, W.M. (Eds.) *Intersections With Attachment*. Hillsdale, N.J: Lawrence Erlbaum. 229–46.

Lightfoot, S. and Evans, I.M. (2000) Risk Factors for A New Zealand Sample of Sexually Abusive Children and Adolescents. *Child Abuse and Neglect*, 24, 1185–98.

Lyons-Ruth, K. (1996) Attachment Relationships Among Children With Aggressive Behaviour Problems: The Role of Disorganised Early Attachment Patterns. *Journal of Consulting and Clinical Psychology*, 64, 64–73.

Main, M. and Solomon, J. (1986) Discovery of an Insecure Disorganised/Disoriented Attachment Pattern. In Yogman, M. and Brazelton, T.B. (Eds.) *Affective Development in Infancy*. Norwood, NJ: Ablex. 95–125.

Marshall, W.L. (1989) Intimacy, Loneliness and Sexual Offenders. *Behaviour Research and Therapy*, 27, 491–503.

Marshall, W.L. (1993) The Role of Attachments, Intimacy, and Loneliness in The Aetiology and Maintenance of Sexual Offending. *Sexual and Marital Therapy*, 8, 109–21.

Marshall, W.L., Hudson, S.M. and Hodkinson, S. (1993) The Importance of Attachment Bonds in The Development of Juvenile Sex Offending. In

Barbaree, H.E., Marshall, W.L. and Hudson, S.M. (Eds.) *The Juvenile Sex Offender*. New York: Guilford Press. 164–81.

Marshall, W.L., Serran, G.A. and Cortoni, F.A. (2000) Childhood Attachments, Sexual Abuse, and Their Relationship to Adult Coping in Child Molesters. *Sexual Abuse: A Journal of Research and Treatment*, 12, 17–26.

McCormack, J., Hudson, S.M. and Ward, T. (2002) Sexual Offenders; Perceptions of Their Early Interpersonal Relationships: an Attachment Perspective. *Journal of Sex Research*, 39, 85–93.

Nelson, E.E. and Panksepp, J. (1998) Brain Substrates of Infant Mother Attachment: Contributions of Opioids, Oxytocin and Norepinephrine. *Neuroscience and Behavioral Review*, 22: 437–52.

Pietromonaco, P.R., and Feldman Barrett, L. (2000) Attachment Theory as an Organising Framework: A View From Different Levels of Analysis. *Review of General Psychology*, 4(2) 107–10.

Pithers, W.D., Beal, L.S., Armstrong, J. and Petty, J. (1989) Identification of Risk Factors Through Clinical Interviews and Analysis of Records. In Laws, D.R. (Ed.) *Relapse Prevention With Sex Offenders*. New York: Guilford Press. 77–87.

Proulx, J., McKibben, A. and Lusignan, R. (1996) Relationships Between Affective Components and Sexual Behaviours in Sexual Aggressors. *Sexual Abuse: A Journal of Research and Treatment*, 8, 279–89.

Rankin, J.H. and Kern, R. (1994) Parental Attachments and Delinquency. *Criminology*, 32, 495–515.

Santry, S. and McCarthy, G. (1999) Attachment and Intimacy in Young People Who Sexually Abuse. In Calder, M. (Ed.) *Working With Young People Who Sexually Abuse*. Lyme Regis: Russell House Publishing.

Shaver, P. (1994) *Attachment, Care Giving, and Sex in Adult Romantic Relationships*. American Psychological Association Invited Address, California.

Smallbone, S.W. and Dadds, M. (1998) Childhood Attachment and Adult Attachment in Incarcerated Adult Male Sex Offenders. *Journal of Interpersonal Violence*, 13, 555–73.

Smallbone, S.W. and Dadds, M.R. (2000) Attachment and Coercive Sexual Behaviour. *Sexual Abuse: A Journal of Research and Treatment*, 12, 3–16.

Smallbone, S.W. and Dadds, M.R. (2001) Further Evidence for A Relationship Between Attachment Insecurity and Coercive Sexual Behaviour. *Journal of Interpersonal Violence*, 16, 22–35.

Smallbone, S.W. and McCabe, B. (2003) Childhood Attachment, Childhood Sexual Abuse, and Onset of Masturbation Among Sexual Offenders. *Sexual Abuse: A Journal of Research and Treatment*, 15, 1–10.

Smallbone, S.W. and Wortley, R.K. (2000) *Child Sexual Abuse in Queensland: Offender Characteristics and Modus Operandi (Full Report)* Brisbane, Australia: Queensland Crime Commission.

Smallbone, S.W. and Wortley, R.K. (2001) Child Sexual Abuse: Offender Characteristics and Modus Operandi. *Australian Institute of Criminology, Trends and Issues in Crime and Criminal Justice*, 193.

Spaccarelli, S., Bowden, B., Coatsworth, J.D. and Kim, S. (1997) Psychosocial Correlates of Male Sexual Aggression in A Chronic Delinquent Sample. *Criminal Justice and Behaviour*, 24, 71–95.

Sroufe, L.A. (1988) The Role of Infant-Caregiver Attachment in Development. In Belsky, J. and Nezworski, T. (Eds.) *Clinical Implications of Attachment*. Hillsdale, N. J: Erlbaum. 18–38.

Van Ljzendoorn, M.H. (1997) Attachment, Emergent Morality, and Aggression: Toward A Developmental Socio-emotional Model of Antisocial Behaviour. *International Journal of Behavioural Development*, 21, 703–27.

Van Ljzendoorn, M.H., Feldbrugge, J.T.T.M., Derks, F.C.H., De Ruiter, C., Verhagen, M.F.M., Philipse, M.W.G., Van Der Staak, C.P.F. and Riksen-Walraven, J.M.A. (1997) Attachment Representations of Personality-Disordered Criminal Offenders. *American Journal of Orthopsychiatry*, 67, 449–59.

Vizard, E., Monck, E. and Misch, P. (1995) Child and Adolescent Sex Abuse Perpetrators: A Review of The Research Literature. *Journal of Child Psychology and Psychiatry*, 36, 731–56.

Ward, T., Hudson, S. M. and Marshall, W.L. (1996) Attachment Style in Sex Offenders: A Preliminary Study. *The Journal of Sex Research*, 33, 17–26.

Ward, T., Hudson, S.M., Marshall, W.L. and Siegert, R.J. (1995) Attachment Style and Intimacy Deficits in Sexual Offenders: A Theoretical Framework. *Sexual Abuse: A Journal of Research and Treatment*, 7, 317–35.

Wilson, J.Q., and Herrnstein, R.J. (1985) *Crime and Human Nature*. New York: Simon and Schuster.

Yates, E., Barbaree, H.E., and Marshall, W.L. (1984) Anger and Deviant Sexual Arousal. *Behaviour Therapy*, 15, 287–94.

Chapter Two

The Relationship between Psychopathy, Treatment Completion and Criminal Outcome over Ten Years: A Study of Adolescent Sex Offenders

Heather M. Gretton, Rosalind E. H. Catchpole, Michelle McBride, Robert D. Hare, Roy O'Shaughnessy and Katherine V. Regan

Introduction

Adolescent sexual violence is a serious problem for society. In Canada in 2002 the rate of adolescent males charged with sexual assault was double that of adult males (Statistics Canada, 2003). Moreover, official statistics indicate that one third of sexual assaults against children are committed by youths (Juristat, 1999). In the United States juveniles represented 16% of arrestees for forcible rape and 17% of arrestees for other sex offences in 1995 (US Department of Justice, 1997). In England and Wales, adolescents also commit a disproportionately higher number of sexual offences than do adults (UK Home Office, 1999). Victimisation surveys indicate that approximately 90% of sex offences are not reported to police (Juristat, 1999) suggesting that official rates provide only a small indication of the extent that sexual victimisation impacts individuals, families, and society at large.

Within the adolescent sex offender literature there is general agreement that adolescents initially charged with sexual offences are at considerable risk for other types of offending. Studies that follow adolescent sex offenders report a broad range of criminal outcomes, including non-violent and violent recidivism (e.g., Hagan and Gust-Brey, 1999; Kahn and Chambers, 1991; Långström, 2002; Sipe, Jensen and Everett, 1998; Smith and Monastersky, 1986; Worling and Curwen, 2000).

A meta-analysis of studies on adult sexual offenders has indicated that risk factors identified that consistently predict adult sexual re-offending include general antisocial behaviour, versatility of criminal behaviour, and early onset of offending, in addition to clear evidence of sexual deviancy (Hanson and Bussiere, 1998). These findings have led some researchers to argue that for many sexual offenders, coercive sexual behaviour is part of a larger antisocial and aggressive syndrome (Seto and Barbaree, 1997).

Clearly, the seemingly straightforward 'sex offender' label belies a much more complicated phenomenon; sex offenders are a heterogeneous group of offenders with different antecedents and varied outcomes. Currently there is a tendency to classify and treat offenders according to the type of crimes they commit, assuming homogeneity among types of offenders. This approach ignores the many other domains of functioning that differentiate adolescent offenders and their particular risks. Because of these complexities, it has been argued that greater sophistication in sex offender typology is needed (Caldwell, 2002; Worling, 2001). Well-validated comprehensive typologies will better inform clinicians and researchers as to particular risks and outcomes associated with particular types of offenders. In turn, a more sophisticated understanding of risks will lead to the development of more appropriate interventions to reduce risk for sexual violence and other criminal behaviour.

Personality functioning of sex offenders

One aspect of sex offender typology that may provide important information about risk and intervention is the investigation of the personality functioning of sexual offenders. In a recent study, Worling (2001) examined and categorised the personality characteristics of 112 adolescent male sex offenders. Using cluster analysis, he found four subgroups of personality types, which he labelled antisocial/impulsive, unusual/isolated, over controlled/reserved, and confident/ aggressive. He found that antisocial/impulsive and unusual/isolated groups were significantly more likely to engage in general and violent (sexual and nonsexual) offences during the follow up as compared to the other two groups. He argued that personality pathology is an important differentiating factor among sex offending youth.

In adults, psychopathy is personality pathology with implications for understanding the nature and progression of an individual's antisocial behaviour. The construct of psychopathy is most commonly operationalised by the Hare Psychopathy Checklist-Revised (PCL-R, Hare, 1991, 2003), a 20-item checklist that assesses individuals on the affective, interpersonal, behavioural, and lifestyle components associated with psychopathy. Affectively, psychopaths display shallow and labile emotions. Interpersonally, they are unable to form long-lasting bonds to people, and are lacking in empathy, guilt, and remorse. Behaviourally, they are impulsive, sensation seeking, and irresponsible. Their lifestyles are characterised by violations of social mores and legal norms. Psychopaths are disproportionately involved in a wide spectrum of crime and violence that frequently brings them into contact with mental health professionals and the criminal justice system (Hare, 2003; Millon, Simonsen, Birket-Smith and Davis, 1998). Psychopathy is characterised by early onset and long-term social and interpersonal dysfunction (American Psychiatric Association, 1994; Hare, 1998).

As a group, psychopaths are more violent, commit a wider variety of crimes (including sexual ones) and have higher rates of general and violent recidivism than other sex offenders (Grann, Långström, Tengstrom and Kullgren, 1999; Hanson and Bussiere, 1998; Harris, Rice and Quinsey, 1993; Hemphill, Hare and Wong, 1998; Rice and Harris, 1995; Salekin, Rogers and Sewell, 1996; Tengström, Grann, Långström and Kullgren, 2000). Psychopaths, as defined by the PCL-R, make up about 10–15% of child molesters and 40–50% of rapists and mixed offenders (Brown and Forth, 1997; Firestone, Bradford, Greenberg and Serran, 2000; Porter et al., 2000; Prentky and Knight, 1991; Quinsey, Rice and Harris, 1995). Psychopathic sex offenders are more likely to be violent and sadistic than are other sex offenders (Brown and Forth, 1997) and are more likely to select diverse sexual victims (Porter et al., 2000).

The sexual aggressiveness of young men with psychopathic traits is evident not only in forensic but also in normative samples. In a self-report study of aggressive sexual behaviour in college men, those who reported engaging in more

sexually aggressive or coercive behaviour described themselves as being more manipulative, impulsive, sensation-seeking, aggressive, and less empathic than those who had engaged in mild or no sexual aggression (Hersh and Gray-Little, 1998). Moreover, Kosson, Kelly and White (1997) found that college men with psychopathic tendencies reported more sexual aggression. They found that psychopathic characteristics in the interpersonal/affective domain predicted the use of threats and force in sexual behaviour. Further, Seto, Khatter, Lalumière and Quinsey (1997) found that higher psychopathy scores predicted deception as a sexual strategy in a community sample of heterosexual men.

More recently, researchers have begun to investigate whether the construct of psychopathy may be meaningfully applied to adolescents, through some modifications to the measure used with adults. The Psychopathy Checklist: Youth Version (PCL: YV; Forth, Kosson and Hare, 2003) is a modified version of the PCL-R designed for use with adolescents aged 12–18. While retaining the same core construct as the PCL-R, the PCL: YV has modified the items to reflect the greater involvement of family and peers in the lives of adolescents, and to emphasise the importance of comparing the youth to same-aged peers. This reflects the understanding that adolescence is a time where a greater degree of certain traits (such as irresponsibility) may be present.

Research with the PCL: YV is beginning to find that psychopathy is associated with a greater risk of criminality and violence among adolescents (Brandt, Kennedy, Patrick and Curtin, 1997; Catchpole and Gretton, 2003; Forth, Hart and Hare, 1990; Gretton, Hare and Catchpole, 2004; Gretton, McBride, Hare, O'Shaughnessy and Kumka, 2001; Kosson, Cyterski, Steuerwald, Neumann and Walker-Matthews, 2002; O'Neill, Lidz and Heilbrun, 2003). Adolescents exhibiting many psychopathic traits are at greater risk for ongoing non-violent and violent offending into early adulthood.

Psychopathy in adolescent sex offenders

Very little investigation has been conducted on the role of psychopathy in adolescent sex offenders. Långström and Grann (2000) retrospectively followed 46 young sex offenders (average age 18 years) in Sweden who had been assessed with the PCL-R using file data. They found that, over a five-year follow-up, high PCL-R scores (> 25) were associated with recidivism generally, but not with sexual recidivism in particular. Myers and Blashfield (1997) found higher psychopathy scores among homicidal sexual adolescent offenders who met diagnostic criteria for sadistic personality disorder than among offenders who did not meet criteria for the disorder.

In an earlier phase of this study we examined the five-year criminal outcomes of a sample of 220 youth referred to an adolescent sex offender treatment programme (SOTP). We found that adolescent sex offenders with many psychopathic traits (as measured by the PCL: YV) were more likely to commit non-violent and violent offences and to violate the conditions of their probation, than were those adolescents with few psychopathic traits. Based on our findings, we argued that psychopathy does not appear suddenly in adulthood, but is measurable with identifiable antecedents in adolescence. Our results showed that, as a group, psychopathic offenders are not so much specialised sex offenders as they are general, versatile, and violent offenders. That is, psychopathic youth make up a unique subgroup of adolescent sex offenders with a propensity to high rates of generalised offending and violence rather than sex offending per se. Accordingly, their sexual misbehaviour is not so much a reflection of specific factors related to sexual recidivism but a more general propensity to impulsive, violating, and self-gratifying behaviour (Gretton et al., 2001).

The present study

The present study represents a continuation of the above-described longitudinal investigation of adolescent male sex offenders. Using a combined retrospective-prospective follow up design, we extend the follow-up from our previous study and examine the criminal outcomes of these youths over ten years.

The purpose of this second follow-up is twofold. First, we continue to examine how youths with many psychopathic traits differ from other sex-offending adolescents in the course of their criminal behaviours, extending the follow-up from five to ten years. Second, we examine the impact of treatment completion on the long-term outcomes of these youths. We

investigate differences in criminal outcomes between youth who completed the sex offender treatment programme with those who dropped out of treatment prior to completion. We also specifically address the role that psychopathy plays in treatment response by examining the interplay between psychopathy and treatment completion in predicting non-violent, violent, and sexual outcomes.

Method

Participants

Participants were 253 of a group of 264 adolescent offenders who had been directed by the courts or by their probation officer to attend the sexual offender treatment programme (SOTP), an outpatient treatment programme of Youth Forensic Psychiatric Services (YFPS) located in Burnaby, British Columbia, between 1985 and 1994. Of the 264 youths, we excluded eleven from the analyses because of missing criminal records. In a previous publication (Gretton et al., 2001) we reported five-year follow up findings for 220 youth for whom we had follow up data at that time. Given procedural changes to the access of criminal records, we have since been able to obtain follow up data on an additional 33 youth.

The racial composition of the sample included primarily White (66%) and Aboriginal (22%) youth, with the remaining 12% primarily of Asian and East Indian descent. Participants were on average almost 15 years old at the time they committed their index offence (the offence for which they were referred to YFPS).

The clinical director and the Research Committee at YFPS approved the study, and so did the Behavioural Research Ethics Board of the University of British Columbia.

Procedures

Treatment programme

The YFPS Sex Offender Treatment Programme (SOTP) is a community-based programme that provides specialised assessment, treatment and support to adolescent sex offenders and their families. Youths who attend the programme undergo a clinical and psychometric assessment of their psychological functioning and areas related to their offending behaviour. The treatment model is primarily a cognitive-behavioural and relapse prevention model, with both group and individual components. Treatment groups meet twice weekly for one-and-a-half hours, for approximately eight months. Topics addressed during group sessions include sex education, victim empathy, social skills, dating and dating violence, problem cycles (individual areas of difficulty associated with the youths' sexual offending) and relapse prevention techniques. Youths also attend individual appointments with one of the group leaders to review group material and address personal issues.

Seventy-nine percent of participants completed the treatment group. A number of youths dropped out of treatment within weeks or months of attending. For the purpose of the present study treatment completion was defined as completion of the entire group format and completion of individual sessions lasting at least six months.

Measure

We used the Psychopathy Checklist: Youth Version (PCL: YV; Forth et al., 2003) to assess psychopathy. The PCL: YV is a 20-item clinical rating tool that assesses youths on several behavioural and personality characteristics associated with psychopathy. It has been slightly modified from the adult version of the Psychopathy Checklist – Revised (Hare, 1991, 2003) extending the concept of psychopathy to adolescence. Each item is scored on a 3-point scale. The total score can range from 0 to 40, with higher scores reflecting a greater degree of psychopathic traits. The mean PCL: YV score in the present sample was 21.6 ($SD = 7.1$). For categorical analyses we divided the sample into three groups using the following PCL: YV cut-off scores: Low (0–18.9), Medium (19–29.9) and High (30–40). Using these cut off criteria, 36% ($n = 92$) were in the Low group, 50% ($n = 126$) were in the Medium group, and 13% ($n = 34$) were in the High group.

The PCL: YV is underpinned by two factors: Factor 1, reflecting the interpersonal/affective traits associated with psychopathy, and Factor 2, reflecting the behavioural/lifestyle traits associated with psychopathy.[1] In the present

study, the mean score for Factor 1 was 8.2 ($SD = 3.4$) and Factor 2 was 10.4 ($SD = 4.3$).

The PCL: YV has strong psychometric properties (see Forth et al., 2003). The PCL:YV has high internal consistency (Cronbach's αs of 0.85–0.90) and high interrater reliability (ICCs of 0.82–0.94; Brandt et al., 1997; Catchpole and Gretton, 2003; Gretton et al., 2001). Validity data show that the PCL:YV is a good predictor of recidivism in a sample of adolescent sex offenders (Gretton et al., 2001) in violent offenders (Catchpole and Gretton, 2003) and in general offenders (Brandt et al., 1997). In the present study Cronbach's alpha was 0.85. We computed reliabilities based on a sub-sample of 54 participants. The single rater intra-class correlation (ICC) for the total PCL: YV score was 0.85. The ICC for Factor 1 was 0.77 and for Factor 2 was 0.83.

Recidivism data

Using British Columbia Corrections files we coded criminal charges and convictions from the time of the youths' discharge from the SOTP to December 20, 1999 (an average of almost ten years). Coders of criminal records were blind to PCL: YV status.

The follow-up period ranged from 56 to 166 months ($M = 112$ months, $SD = 23$ months). The mean age of participants at follow-up was 27 years ($Range = 21$–33 years, $SD = 2.6$ years). In the five-year follow-up we were able to obtain both provincial and federal criminal records. In this follow-up, however, we were unable to obtain federal records; thus, the results reflect only those charges and convictions that occurred within British Columbia.

Outcome variables included offences (as indicated by charges and convictions on BC Corrections files) that occurred following the youths' release from the SOTP until the end of the follow-up period. We coded violent offences (including offences such as assaults, robbery, intimidation, and attempted murder), non-violent offences (including property offences and drug offences) and sexual offences (including offences such as sexual assault, incest, sexual interference, and aggravated sexual assault).

---

[1] Factor 1 includes the following PCL:YV items: impression management, grandiose sense of self worth, pathological lying, manipulation for personal gain, lack of remorse, shallow affect, callous or lacking empathy, and failure to accept responsibility for actions. Factor 2 includes the following PCL:YV items: stimulation seeking, parasitic orientation, poor anger control,

early behavioural problems, lacks goals, impulsivity, irrespon-sibility, serious criminal behaviour, serious violations of condi-tional release, and criminal versatility. Two items (impersonal sexual behaviour and unstable interpersonal relationships) do not load on either factor.

Table 2.1: Characteristics of youth by PCL: YV Group

	Psychopathy Checklist: Youth Version Group		
	Low (*N*=92)	Medium (*N*=126)	High (*N*=34)
IQ			
FSIQ (SD)	95.1 (11.9)	93.9 (13.1)	97.0 (13.7)
VIQ (SD)	93.8 (13.2)	90.9 (12.7)	95.0 (13.5)
PIQ (SD)	97.8 (11.5)	99.2 (13.4)	100.1 (14.5)
Learning disability (%)	29.3	39.6	33.3
ADHD (%)	12.8$_a$	33.9$_b$	62.5$_c$
Age at first offence (SD)	15.8 (1.9)	15.6 (1.6)	15.9 (1.9)
Age at first sexually inappropriate behaviour (SD)	13.5 (2.6)$_a$	11.6 (3.3)$_b$	10.7 (3.5)$_b$

Note: FSIQ=Full Scale Intelligence Quotient; VIQ=Verbal Intelligence Quotient; PIQ=Performance Intelligence Quotient; ADHD=Attention Deficit Hyperactivity Disorder. Means with differing subscripts are significantly different, $p<0.01$.

Results

Descriptive information

Descriptive information is presented in Table 2.1. Overall, the youths' IQs fell into the Average range. Approximately one third were diagnosed with a learning disability, and a similar proportion was diagnosed with ADHD. Youth with higher PCL: YV scores were more commonly diagnosed with ADHD (χ^2 (2, N=219)=27.52, $p<0.001$).

Youth committed their first offence at an average age of almost 16 years. Their first recorded sexually inappropriate behaviour (parent report, self-report) occurred at an average age of 12 years. Individuals with higher PCL: YV scores exhibited sexually inappropriate behaviour at a younger age, F (χ^2 (2, N=221)=12.97, $p<0.001$).

Pre-treatment offending

We present data on the proportion of individuals who were charged with sexual, violent, and non-violent offences before their assessment. This gives a picture of how severe the youths' criminal behaviour was at the time they were referred for treatment, and allows us to see the variability within this group of adolescent sex offenders. Overall, 81% of the sample had a recorded pre-assessment sexual offence,[2] whereas only 16% had a pre-assessment violent offence, and 39% had a pre-assessment non-violent offence.

We also examined the proportion of youth in each PCL: YV group who offended sexually, violently, and non-violently before the start of treatment. These data are shown in Table 2.2. Youths in the high PCL: YV group were significantly more likely to have a history of violent (χ^2 (2, N=250)=17.93, $p<0.001$) and non violent (χ^2 (2, N=250)=20.26, $p<0.001$) offences prior to treatment than were those in the lower psychopathy groups. There were no differences in pre-treatment sex offences between PCL: YV groups. These data suggest that those individuals with higher PCL: YV scores, although referred for sexual offender treatment, tended to have more violent and criminal histories than those with lower PCL: YV scores.

Recidivism rates

Over half (61%) of the participants committed at least one known offence during the ten year follow-up period. Seventeen per cent (17%) committed sexual offences, 30% committed violent offences, and half (51%) committed non-violent offences.

We examined different types of outcomes, to determine the extent of overlap that was present in the types of offences committed (sexual, violent, and non-violent) to answer the question: how many individuals commit multiple types of offences, and how many commit only a single type of offence? We found that, in the follow-up period, 61% of participants reoffended. Six per cent (6%) committed only sexual offences, less than 1% committed only violent offence(s), 20% committed only non-violent offences, with the remainder (34%) committing multiple types of

---

[2] The remainder did not have a formal history of sexual offending, but had engaged in sexually inappropriate behaviour to a degree that it was felt that sex offender treatment was warranted.

Table 2.2: Pre-treatment offending by PCL: YV Group

	Psychopathy Checklist: Youth Version Group		
	Low (N=92)	Medium (N=126)	High (N=34)
Pre-treatment offending			
Sexual (%)	82.6	78.4	87.9
Violent (%)**	7.6	16.8	39.4
Non-violent (%)**	22.8	44.8	63.6

**$p<0.001$.

offences. These findings show that the majority of those who reoffended seemed to have become what we would call 'generalised offenders'. There does, however, seem to be a small subgroup of individuals, initially referred for treatment for sexual offending, who go on to become 'exclusive sex offenders' and also a larger subgroup who go on to become purely non-violent, or 'petty' offenders. On the other hand, there did not seem to be a 'pure violent offender' among this group of adolescents; instead, those individuals who committed violent offences in the follow-up also committed other types of offences.

PCL: YV and recidivism[3]

We examined the relationship between the PCL: YV and recidivism. The percentage of youth in each PCL: YV group that offended sexually, violently, and non-violently in the follow-up period is presented in Figure 2.1. Overall, we found that PCL: YV group was related to violent (χ^2 (2, N=252)=16.1, $p<.001$) and non-violent (χ^2 (2, N=252)=39.4, $p<.001$) recidivism, but not to sexual recidivism (χ^2 (2, N=252)=0.68, $p=0.71$). We also examined the predictive ability of the PCL: YV by using Receiver Operating Characteristic Areas under the Curve (AUCs). This is an analytic technique that is commonly used in situations where events have a base-rate that deviates from 50%, something which has been shown to attenuate correlations. AUCs plot the sensitivity of an instrument against its specificity (technically, one minus specificity) in predicting an event (in this case, reoffending). AUCs can range from 0 to 1, with 0.5 being a chance, or worthless prediction, and 0 and 1

being perfect negative and positive predictions, respectively. AUCs above .70 can be considered large effect sizes.

Table 2.3 shows the AUCs for PCL: YV total scores and factor scores for sexual, violent, and non-violent reoffending. These results parallel those with the PCL: YV groups: the PCL: YV (both the total scores and the factor scores) was predictive of violent and non-violent offending but not of sexual offending. Overall, the PCL: YV was a strong predictor of non-violent offending in the present sample, and a moderate predictor of violent offending.

Treatment completion

We examined the effect of treatment completion on recidivism. We had treatment completion information on 246 individuals (information was ambiguous or missing in 7 cases). Overall, 79% of youth completed treatment. There were differences in the offending histories between those who completed treatment and those who dropped out. A greater proportion of treatment dropouts than treatment completers had violent (33% versus 12%, respectively) and non-violent (67% versus 32%, respectively) offending histories.

Those who completed treatment were less likely to sexually recidivate than those who dropped out (14% versus 27%; χ^2 (1, N=246)=4.99, $p=0.03$). This difference remained significant after controlling for history of offending (non-violent, violent and sexual). Treatment completers were also less likely to violently recidivate than those who dropped out (27% versus 42%; χ^2 (1, N=246)=4.70, $p=0.03$) although this difference did not remain significant after controlling for history of offending. The difference in non-violent recidivism between those who completed treatment (49%) and those who dropped out (62%) was not significant ($p=0.11$).

---

[3] We conducted analyses where we controlled for the differences in pre-assessment violent and non-violent offending, with no changes in the results. Thus we have not presented those analyses here.

Figure 2.1: Recidivism by PCL: YV Group

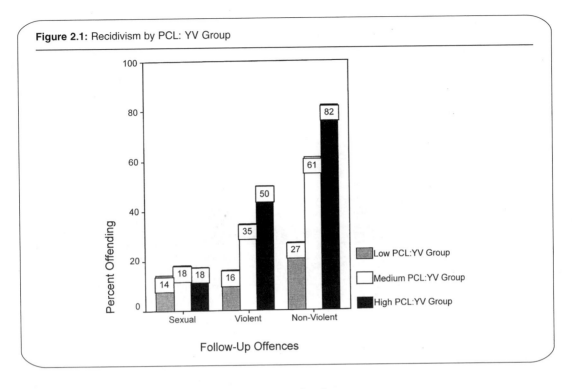

Table 2.3: Areas under the curve (AUCs) for PCL: YV and offending

	AUCs (95% confidence interval)		
	PCL:YV Total Score	PCL:YV Factor 1	PCL:YV Factor 2
Sexual offending	0.51 (0.41–0.60)	0.48 (0.37–0.58)	0.53 (0.42–0.63)
Violent offending	0.67 (0.60–0.74)	0.61 (0.53–0.68)	0.70 (0.62–0.77)
Non-violent offending	0.75 (0.67–0.81)	0.67 (0.60–0.73)	0.76 (0.69–0.82)

Note: AUCs with confidence intervals (CIs) that do not include 0.50 are significant. All AUCs for violent and non-violent offending are significant; none for sexual offending are significant.

PCL: YV and treatment completion

We examined the relationship between treatment completion status and PCL: YV group. Individuals in the high group were less likely to complete treatment than those in the low group (64% versus 82%; χ^2 (1, $N=123$) $=4.7$, $p=0.03$) suggesting that individual with high PCL: YV scores are at increased risk of dropping out of treatment.

The proportion of individuals who recidivated (sexually and violently) are shown by treatment completion status and PCL: YV group in Figures 2.2 and 2.3. These figures illustrate the difference between treatment dropouts and completers

separately for those scoring low on the PCL: YV (<19) and those scoring high (≥ 30).[4]

Treatment completion and sexual recidivism.

Figure 2.2 shows that there was a significant difference in sexual recidivism between treatment dropouts and completers for the Low PCL: YV group only (χ^2 (1, $N=246$) $=13.52$, $p<0.001$). That is, with respect to sexual recidivism, low-scoring PCL: YV youths who completed treatment had a

---

[4] There were no differences in PCL: YV score between treatment completers and dropouts in either the high or low group.

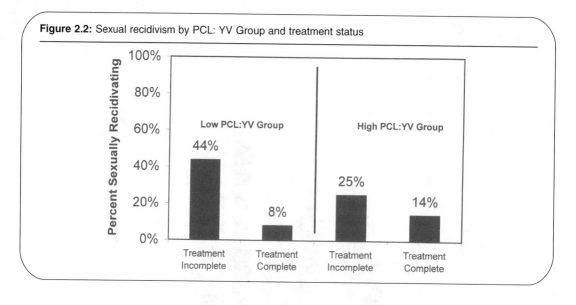

Figure 2.2: Sexual recidivism by PCL: YV Group and treatment status

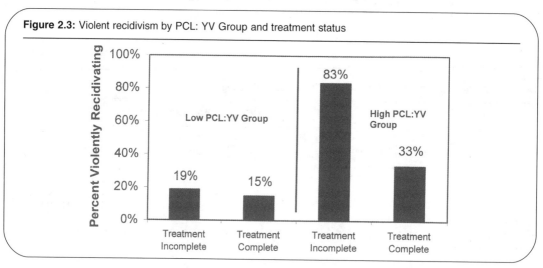

Figure 2.3: Violent recidivism by PCL: YV Group and treatment status

significantly lower sexual recidivism rate than those who dropped out of treatment (8% versus 44%). This difference remained significant after controlling for history of offending. Those in the high group who completed treatment did have a lower sexual recidivism rate than dropouts (14% versus 25%) although this difference was not significant. Low-scoring PCL: YV youth who dropped out of treatment were at the highest risk for sexual recidivism.

Treatment completion and violent recidivism.

Figure 2.3 illustrates the violent recidivism rate, and shows that there was a significant difference in violent recidivism between treatment dropouts and completers for the High PCL: YV group only (χ^2 (1, $N=246$) $=7.64$, $p=.006$). Individuals in the High PCL: YV group who completed treatment showed a large and significant reduction in violent re-offending when compared with those who dropped out of treatment (33% versus 83%). This difference remained significant after controlling for history of offending. In contrast, those in the Low PCL: YV group did not differ significantly in their rates of violent recidivism (19% for treatment completers, 15% for dropouts).

Treatment completion and non-violent recidivism

The differences for non-violent offending were not statistically significant for either high scoring PCL:YV youths (91% for non-completers vs. 81% for completers) or for low scoring PCL:YV youths (44% for non-completers versus 22% for completers).

These findings suggest that completing treatment had the most benefit for low-scoring youth in reducing their rates of sexual re-offending, and for high-scoring youth in reducing their rates of violent re-offending.

Discussion

The present study examined ten-year recidivism rates among adolescent sex offenders referred to a sex offender treatment programme. Over the follow up period, half of the youths studied re-offended non-violently (51%) nearly one third of the sample was charged with a violent offence (30%) and slightly less than one fifth (17%) was charged with a sex offence.

In our sample, half of those who re-offended committed multiple types of offences. These results are consistent with other research findings that youth identified as sex offenders are commonly at risk for a broad range of offences, both sexual and non-sexual (Rasmussen, 1999). In fact, only a small minority, one in twenty youths identified as sex offenders and referred to the sex offender treatment programme went on to become 'exclusive sex offenders', that is, committing only sexual re-offences during the follow up. Similarly, among these youths there did not seem to be a significant subgroup of 'pure violent offenders'. Instead, violent offences in the follow-up were committed alongside a variety of other offences.

These findings have important implications with regard to the development and organisation of appropriate intervention programmes. Many existing programmes are offence-specific. That is, youth are classified and routed into particular

programmes such as sex offender or violent offender treatment programmes according to their referral offence. The present findings suggest that programmes that focus on reducing a single type of offence (like sex offending) may be better designed to systematically address the range of risks among these youth, including risks for general criminality and sexual and non-sexual violence.

One difficulty in developing treatment programmes that are maximally effective is the heterogeneity of offenders who commit certain types of offences, including sexual offences. What is needed is an individualised assessment strategy that characterises the risk areas associated with an offender and that can be used to tailor interventions accordingly. The prevention of high-risk youths from becoming violent and chronic offenders warrants continual efforts and commitment to the early intervention process. Alongside inestimable savings in terms of victim suffering and the prevention of criminality, interventions that reduce rates of re-offending amount to significant long term economic savings.[5] These findings underline, from both a social and economic perspective, the need to better refine our understanding of adolescent sexual violence, and to find methods to assess and reduce youth sexual violence, criminality and violence.

In the present study, we argue that characteristics of the youths' personality are important factors to consider when assessing risk for recidivism and violence. In particular, the constellation of personality characteristics associated with psychopathy provides important information about the long-term risk of sex offending youths for non-violent recidivism and violent recidivism. That is, among adolescent sex offenders, those with many psychopathic traits (including manipulativeness, callousness, impulsivity, and a failure to accept responsibility for their actions) were, expectedly, at higher risk for becoming generalised and violent offenders, rather than sex offenders per se.

Treatment completion and recidivism

One challenge to those designing and providing treatment to young offenders is to keep them in treatment long enough for them to gain benefit

---

[5] Estimated at over a million dollars per youth in the United States (Cohen, 1998) for individuals, society, and the criminal justice system.

from the programme. In the present study nearly 80% of youths completed treatment. Treatment completion was associated with a lower sexual and violence re-offence rate, even after controlling for pre-existing differences related to dropping out of treatment. This finding parallels other studies, which have found that treatment completion reduces the risk for re-offending (Becker and Hunter, 1992; Marshall, Jones, Ward, Johnston and Barbaree, 1991).

Psychopathy and treatment completion

One of the most striking findings in the present study is the relationship between psychopathy and treatment completion. Overall, youths with many psychopathic traits were more likely to drop out of treatment; less than two thirds of youths with PCL: YV scores over 30 completed treatment.

When we examine the impact of treatment completion on specific types of offence outcomes (sexual versus non-sexual violence) based on PCL: YV scores, a striking pattern emerges. For sexual re-offending, treatment completion appears to be critical for low-scoring PCL: YV youths. For individuals with PCL: YV scores below 19, those that dropped out of treatment had a significantly higher sexual recidivism rate (44%) than low-scoring youth who completed treatment (8%). Remarkably, low-scoring PCL: YV dropouts had an even higher sexual recidivism rate (44%) than either high PCL: YV scoring treatment dropouts (25%) or completers (14%). For high-scoring PCL: YV youth, treatment completion was not significantly related to sexual outcomes.

In contrast, when we examine violent recidivism, we see the exact opposite pattern. For high scoring PCL: YV youths, treatment completion was associated with a remarkable reduction in violent recidivism. High-scoring PCL: YV youths who completed treatment had a 50% lower violent recidivism rate than high-scoring PCL: YV youths who dropped out of treatment (33% versus 83% respectively). Conversely, completing treatment had little impact on violent recidivism for low scoring PCL: YV youths. In the case of low PCL: YV scoring youths, their rate of violent recidivism was already much lower than high-scoring PCL: YV youth (either those who completed or dropped out of treatment; 19% and 15% respectively).

In sum, for sexual recidivism, treatment completion was an important factor associated with reduced recidivism among low-scoring PCL: YV youths, whereas dropping out of treatment appeared to be a particularly salient risk indicator. Conversely, for violent recidivism, treatment completion was an important positive prognostic indicator among high PCL: YV youths, while dropping out of treatment was a salient risk factor. In both cases these findings of risk held even after controlling for pre-existing differences among the youths, including age at first offence and history of offending. These findings have important implications in planning interventions for both low and high PCL: YV scoring youths. Once it is established that a given treatment is appropriate and effective for these youths, a key factor for success appears to lie in maintaining them in treatment to completion. For low scoring PCL: YV, more research is needed to understand the factors related to dropping out of treatment and to develop programmes that facilitate treatment completion. For high scoring PCL:YV youth, maintaining them in treatment poses a particular challenge for treatment providers, given their greater impulsivity, irresponsibility, and disruptiveness, which puts them at greater risk for dropping out of treatment.

The findings of treatment completion and psychopathy are interesting when considered in the context of the debate that has arisen about the treatment amenability of psychopathic adults. Some researchers have argued that adult psychopaths are resistant to treatment. In a ten-year treatment outcome study, Rice, Harris and Cormier (1992) found that adult psychopaths who received treatment in a therapeutic community programme violently recidivated at a higher rate than matched (psychopathic) controls who did not receive treatment. Further, Seto and Barbaree (1999) found that individuals scoring high on psychopathy (>20) who received good ratings of treatment behaviour (motivated, completed homework, good behaviour in treatment) were more likely to re-offend than those who received poor ratings of treatment behaviour were. Ogloff, Wong and Greenwood (1990) found that psychopathic individuals in a therapeutic community setting dropped out of treatment sooner than non-psychopaths, and showed less improvement, effort and motivation than non-psychopaths.

On the other hand, others (e.g., Hemphill and Hart, 2002) have pointed out that the vast majority of studies on treatment amenability do not meet minimum standards with regard to methodological rigour, and moreover are often based on out-dated models of treatment, now known to have little impact on recidivism. They argue that the conclusion that one is unable to treat psychopaths is not yet warranted by the literature (Hemphill and Hart, 2002).

In the present study we found that treatment whose content was geared towards sex offending was associated with a reduction in violent offending for more psychopathic adolescents. These findings lend to the argument that high PCL: YV youths are better understood according to their propensity for generalised criminality and violence, rather than necessarily sex offending per se. With this understood, interventions may be more appropriately planned to reduce this generalised and violent risk.

In adolescence, concerns over the perceived treatment amenability of individuals exhibiting many psychopathic traits has led some to caution against the use of the label of psychopathy at all before adulthood. In adolescence, when psychopathy seems to be emerging in a behaviourally adult-like form, there is no literature examining treatment efficacy. Developmentally, it is arguable that youths are likely to be more malleable, and thus more likely to respond to intervention efforts. It should be noted that in the present study, neither high- nor low-scoring PCL: YV youth got worse by completing treatment. This finding is in contrast to fears, in particular for high-scoring PCL: YV youths that adolescent exhibiting many psychopathic traits may be "untreatable" or may be necessarily made worse by completing treatment. While certain types of treatment may be associated with greater recidivism among (adult) psychopaths this was not the finding in the present study.

Further research is needed to elucidate the outcomes of high-PCL: YV youths following intervention and factors that contribute to reducing recidivism and violence among this high risk group. Along with more data examining outcomes, more research is needed investigating the process by which change takes place to reduce risk for violence. Does the mechanism of change for reducing risk in high PCL: YV scoring youths lie in the specific content of a programme, is it related to the intensive *process*, and what is the role of the therapist? As investigations continue into the impact of treatment on outcomes for high PCL: YV scoring youths, study into the mechanisms for change in this group of youths will become paramount.

References

American Psychiatric Association (1994) *Diagnostic and Statistical Manual of Mental Disorders* (4th Edn.) Washington, DC: Author.

Becker, J.V. and Hunter, J.A. (1992) Evaluation of Treatment Outcome for Adult Perpetrators of Child Sexual Abuse. *Criminal Justice and Behaviour*, 19, 74–92.

Brandt, J.R., Kennedy, W.A., Patrick, C.J. and Curtin, J.J. (1997) Assessment of Psychopathy in A Population of Incarcerated Adolescent Offenders. *Psychological Assessment*, 9, 429–35.

Brown, S.L. and Forth, A.E. (1997) Psychopathy and Sexual Assault: Static Risk Factors, Emotional Precursors, and Rapist Subtypes. *Journal of Consulting and Clinical Psychology*, 65, 848–57.

Caldwell, M.F. (2002) What We Do Not Know About Juvenile Sexual Reoffence Risk. *Child Maltreatment*, 7, 291–302.

Catchpole, R.E.H. and Gretton, H.M. (2003) The Predictive Validity of Risk Assessment With Violent Young Offenders: A 1-Year Examination of Criminal Outcome. *Criminal Justice and Behaviour*, 30, 688–708.

Cohen, M.A. (1998) The Monetary Value of Saving A High Risk Youth. *Journal of Quantitative Criminology*, 14, 5–33.

Douglas, K.S. and Webster, C. (1999) The HCR-20 Violence Risk Assessment Scheme: Concurrent Validity in a Sample of Incarcerated Offenders. *Criminal Justice and Behavior*, 26, 3–19.

Firestone, P., Bradford, J.M., Greenberg, D.M. and Serran, G.A. (2000) The Relationship of Deviant Sexual Arousal and Psychopathy in Incest Offenders, Extra Familial Child Molesters, and Rapists. *Journal of The American Academy of Psychiatry and The Law*, 28, 303–8.

Forth, A.E., Hart, S.D. and Hare, R.D. (1990) Assessment of Psychopathy in Male Young Offenders. *Psychological Assessment: A Journal of Consulting and Clinical Psychology*, 2, 342–4.

Forth, A.E., Kosson, D.S. and Hare, R.D. (2003) *The Psychopathy Checklist: Youth Version (PCL: YV)* Toronto, Ontario: Multi-Health Systems.

Grann, M., Langström, N., Tengström, A. and Kullgren, G. (1999) Psychopathy (PCL-R) Predicts Violent Recidivism Among Criminal Offenders With Personality Disorders in Sweden. *Law and Human Behaviour*, 23, 205–17.

Gretton, H.M., Hare, R.D. and Catchpole, R.E.H. (2004) Psychopathy and Offending From Adolescence to Adulthood: A Ten Year Follow

Up. *Journal of Consulting and Clinical Psychology,* 72, 636–45.

Gretton, H M., McBride, M., Hare, R D., O'Shaughnessy, R. and Kumka, G. (2001) Psychopathy and Recidivism in Adolescent Sex Offenders. *Criminal Justice and Behaviour,* 28, 427–49.

Hagan, M. and Gust-Brey, K. (1999) A Ten-Year Longitudinal Study of Adolescent Rapists Upon Return to The Community. *International Journal of Offender Therapy and Comparative Criminology,* 43, 448–58.

Hanson, R.K. and Bussiére, M.T. (1998) Predicting Relapse: A Meta-Analysis of Sexual Offender Recidivism Studies. *Journal of Consulting and Clinical Psychology,* 66, 348–62.

Hare, R.D. (1991) *The Hare Psychopathy Checklist-Revised (PCL-R)* Toronto, Ontario: Multi-Health Systems.

Hare, R.D. (1998) The Hare PCL-R: Some Issues Concerning Its Use and Misuse. *Legal and Criminological Psychology,* 3, 99–119.

Hare, R.D. (2003) *The Hare Psychopathy Checklist-Revised (2nd Edn)* Toronto, Ontario: Multi-Health Systems.

Harris, G.T., Rice, M.E. and Quinsey, V.L. (1993) Violent Recidivism of Mentally Disordered Offenders: The Development of A Statistical Prediction Instrument. *Criminal Justice and Behaviour,* 20, 315–35.

Hemphill, J.F., Hare, R.D. and Wong, S. (1998) Psychopathy and Recidivism: A Review. *Legal and Criminological Psychology,* 3, 139–70.

Hemphill, J.F. and Hart, S.D. (2002) Motivating The Unmotivated: Psychopathy, Treatment, and Change, in McMurran, M. (Ed.) *Motivating Offenders to Change: A Guide to Enhancing Engagement in Therapy.* New York, NY: Wiley. 193–219.

Hersh, K. and Gray-Little, B. (1998) Psychopathic Traits and Attitudes Associated With Self-Reported Sexual Aggression in College Men. *Journal of Interpersonal Violence,* 13, 456–71.

Juristat. (1999) Youth Court Statistics 1997–1998 Highlights. *Statistics Canada,* 19(2).

Kahn, T.J. and Chambers, H.J. (1991) Assessing Reoffence Risk With Juvenile Sex Offenders. *Child Welfare,* 70, 333–45.

Kosson, D.S., Cyterski, T.D., Steuerwald, B.L., Neumann, C.S. and Walker-Matthews, S. (2002) The Reliability and Validity of The Psychopathy Checklist: Youth Version (PCL: YV) in Nonincarcerated Adolescent Males. *Psychological Assessment,* 14, 97–109.

Kosson, D.S., Kelly, J.C. and White, J.W. (1997) Psychopathy-Related Traits Predict Self-Reported Sexual Aggression Among College Men. *Journal of Interpersonal Violence,* 12, 241–54.

Långström, N. (2002) Long-term Follow-up of Criminal Recidivism in Young Sex Offenders: Temporal Patterns and Risk Factors. *Psychology Crime and Law,* 8, 41–58.

Långström, N. and Grann, M. (2000) Risk for Criminal Recidivism Among Young Sex Offenders. *Journal of Interpersonal Violence,* 15, 855–71.

Marshall, W.L., Jones, R., Ward, T, Johnston, P. and Barbaree, H.E. (1991) Treatment Outcome With Sex Offenders. *Clinical Psychology Review,* 11, 463–85.

Millon, T., Simonsen, E., Birket-Smith, M. and Davis, R.D. (Eds.) (1998) *Psychopathy: Antisocial, Criminal, and Violent Behaviour.* New York, NY: Guilford.

Myers, W.C. and Blashfield, R. (1997) Psychopathology and Personality in Juvenile Sexual Homicide Offenders. *Journal of The American Academy of Psychiatry and The Law,* 25, 497–508.

Ogloff, J.R.P., Wong, S. and Greenwood, A. (1990) Treating Criminal Psychopaths in A Therapeutic Community Programme. *Behavioural Sciences and The Law,* 8, 181–90.

O'Neill, M.L., Lidz, V. and Heilbrun, K. (2003) Adolescents With Psychopathic Characteristics in A Substance Abusing Cohort: Treatment Process and Outcomes. *Law and Human Behaviour,* 27, 299–313.

Porter, S., Fairweather, D., Drugge, J., Herve, H., Birt, A. and Boer, D.P. (2000) Profiles of Psychopathy in Incarcerated Sexual Offenders. *Criminal Justice and Behaviour,* 27, 216–33.

Prentky, R.A. and Knight, R.A. (1991) Identifying Critical Dimensions for Discriminating Among Rapists. *Journal of Consulting and Clinical Psychology,* 59, 643–61.

Quinsey, V.L., Rice, M.E. and Harris, G.T. (1995) Actuarial Prediction of Sexual Recidivism. *Journal of Interpersonal Violence,* 10, 85–105.

Rasmussen, L. (1999) Factors Related to Recidivism Among Juvenile Sexual Offenders. *Sexual Abuse: A Journal of Research and Treatment,* 11, 69–85.

Rice, M.E. and Harris, G.T. (1995) Psychopathy, Schizophrenia, Alcohol Abuse, and Violent Recidivism. *International Journal of Law and Psychiatry,* 18, 333–42.

Rice, M.E., Harris, G.T. and Cormier, C.A. (1992) An Evaluation of A Maximum Security Therapeutic Community for Psychopaths and Other Mentally Disordered Offenders. *Law and Human Behaviour*, 16, 399–412.

Salekin, R.T., Rogers, R. and Sewell, K.W. (1996) A Review and Meta-Analysis of The Psychopathy Checklist and Psychopathy Checklist-Revised: Predictive Validity of Dangerousness. *Clinical Psychology: Science and Practice*, 3, 203–15.

Seto, M.C. and Barbaree, H.E. (1997) Sexual Aggression as Antisocial Behaviour: A Developmental Model, in Stoff, D.M. and Breiling, J. (Eds.) *Handbook of Antisocial Behaviour*. Toronto, Ontario: Wiley. 524–33.

Seto, M.C. and Barbaree, H.E. (1999) Psychopathy, Treatment Behaviour, and Sex Offender Recidivism. *Journal of Interpersonal Violence*, 14, 1235–48.

Seto, M.C., Khatter, N.A., Lalumiere, M.L. and Quinsey, V.L. (1997) Deception and Sexual Strategy in Psychopathy. *Personality and Individual Differences*, 22, 301–7.

Sipe, R., Jensen, E.L. and Everett, R.S. (1998) Adolescent Sexual Offenders Grown Up: Recidivism in Young Adulthood. *Criminal Justice and Behaviour*, 25, 109–24.

Statistics Canada (2003) *Persons Charged by Type of Offence*. Downloaded August 13, 2003 From http://www.statcan.ca/english/Pgdb/legal14a.htm

Smith, W. and Monastersky, C. (1986) Assessing Juvenile Sex Offenders' Risk for Reoffending. *Criminal Justice and Behaviour*, 13, 115–40.

Tengström, A., Grann, M., Langström, N. and Kullgren, G. (2000) Psychopathy (PCL-R) as A Predictor of Violent Recidivism Among Criminal Offenders With Schizophrenia. *Law and Human Behaviour*, 24, 45–58.

UK Home Office (1999) Aspects of Crime: Young Offenders 1999. Downloaded August 12, 2003 From http://www.homeoffice.gov.uk/rds/pdfs/aspects-youngoffs.pdf

US Department of Justice (1997) Sex Offences and Offenders: an Analysis of Data On Rape and Sexual Assault. Bureau of Justice Statistics. Downloaded August 6, 2003 From http://www.ojp.usdoj.gov/bjs/pub/pdf/soo.pdf

Worling, J. (2001) Personality-Based Typology of Adolescent Male Sexual Offenders: Differences in Recidivism Rates, Victim-Selection Characteristics, and Personal Victimisation Histories. *Sexual Abuse: A Journal of Research and Treatment*, 13, 149–66.

Worling, J. and Curwen, T. (2000) Adolescent Sexual Offender Recidivism: Success of Specialised Treatment and Implications for Risk Prediction. *Child Abuse and Neglect*, 24, 965–82.

Chapter Three

Children With Sexual Behaviour Problems: What have we Learned in the Last Two Decades?

Toni Cavanagh Johnson, PhD and Ronda Doonan, PsyD

Introduction

While this chapter talks about the 'sexual behaviours' of children, this term could be misleading. The behaviours that most of these children engage in are behaviours that are related to sex and sexuality but are not 'sexual' behaviours in the same way we conceive of adult sexual behaviours. The behaviours of young children often mimic the behaviours of adults, as they touch their own and others' genitals and explore adult gender roles and the pairing/coupling behaviours of adults ('dating,' 'marrying,' 'playing house,' 'playing doctor,' 'dirty dancing,' and/or 'humping'). Unlike adults, children are generally not seeking emotional connections and intimate relationships in their 'sexual' behaviours. Most of the 'sexual' behaviours engaged in by young children are not driven by the desire for sexual arousal, physical gratification, and orgasm. Yet, children's bodies are equipped from birth for arousal and pleasure, and infants can experience orgasms even in utero. Generally, children experience pleasurable sensations from genital touching. Some children experience sexual arousal while others experience orgasm. Sexual arousal and orgasm are more frequently found in older children entering puberty. Therefore, the term 'sexual behaviour' is used for the sake of brevity; otherwise the phrase that is more apt is 'behaviours related to sex and sexuality.'
(Johnson, 2000).

Nomenclature

At this time in the United States the term 'children with sexual behaviour problems' is used frequently, but different people use it differently. Some use the term when referring to children who are sexually offending, some use it to refer to children who are engaging in problematic sexual behaviour of far less seriousness, and some use it to refer to the whole range of sexual behaviour problems in children. This lack of precision can lead to confusion. For instance, someone may refer to the 'victim' of a child with a sexual behaviour problem. If the language (victim) were being used precisely, this would mean that a child has been 'sexually abused' by another child. Yet, upon questioning, it may be that the person uses the language of

victimisation but is talking about a sexual behaviour that was mutually agreed upon but developmentally advanced for children of their age.

Due to the lack of definitions, some people equate all children with sexual behaviour problems as offenders or on a trajectory to sexual offending. When definitions and language are not precise and clearly delineated, children labelled as having problems with sexual behaviours can receive serious legal consequences that can affect their entire lives. Unfortunately, with the advent of sex offender registries and Megan's Law, the stakes have become very high. There are states that register children as sex offenders, even as young as seven years of age. The lack of agreement in the use of terminology and definitions is a problem that needs further work.

Beginning in 1987, Johnson (1993) developed a continuum of sexual behaviours to better delineate the children being referred to Children's Institute International. There are four groups along the continuum. The first group, which is by far the largest, includes children with 'natural and healthy sexual behaviours'; the next three groups pertain to children with problematic sexual behaviour. These three groups are as follows: 'sexually-reactive,' 'children engaged in extensive mutual sexual behaviours,' and 'children who molest.' Johnson uses the term 'children with sexual behaviour problems' to refer to all three groups of children who are not engaging in natural and healthy sexual behaviours. The three groups of children with sexual behaviour problems engage in increasingly disturbed sexual behaviours. Only one group, children who molest engage in sexually abusive behaviour. (See section Identifying the Seriousness of the Child's Problematic Sexual Behaviour below for further information.) These groups were conceptualised based on the first author's clinical experience and have never been subjected to empirical verification. Interestingly, typologies developed by Hall using complex statistical methods derived very similar groups (Hall, Mathews et al., 1998; Hall, Mathews et al., 2002).

The confusion in language and group designation can be seen in Schwartz's 1995 book. She uses 'abuse-reactive' synonymously with 'perpetrator' and 'children who sexually assault.' 'Another population of perpetrators, which has only recently been identified, are children who sexually assault other children. These perpetrators, who have themselves been victims of sexual abuse, are now being referred to as 'abuse-reactive' children' (Schwartz et al., 1995: pp3–4). The implication is that all abuse-reactive children are perpetrators and all have themselves been victims of sexual abuse. In the first author's designation the 'abuse-reactive' child may or may not be a victim of abuse and has no intention of harming another child when engaging in sexual behaviours with them. Sometimes the term 'inappropriate' is used to designate children who are offending (Adams, McClellan et al. 1995). The term 'sexually intrusive' is used by some to indicate interpersonal but unplanned, impulsive and non-aggressive behaviour (Bonner, Walker et al., 1999). Others use 'sexually intrusive' as more synonymous to perpetration behaviours by adult and adolescent sex offenders (Friedrich, Davies et al., 2003). The term 'sexually intrusive' is used in Canada with no consensus as to its definition.

It is the belief of the authors that it is important for the field to develop a consensus of some subsets of 'children with sexual behaviour problems' or develop terminology that defines levels of seriousness. This will aid mental health professionals, child protective services (CPS), law enforcement, and the judiciary to communicate with one another in a meaningful way regarding the level of severity of the sexual behaviour(s) in question, thus allowing for effective case management, treatment, placement and safety planning for each child.

Are all children with sexual behaviour problems victims of sexual abuse?

In the mid-1980s there was a belief that the major etiological factor for children with sexual behaviour problems was that they had been sexually abused. This belief was based on the incorrect notion that virtually all adult sex offenders had been sexually abused, and that the abuse was the cause for their sexual offending.

Several articles were published in the late 1980s about children who molest other children. This

category represents the most seriously disturbed of all children with sexual behaviour problems. A study of 14 boys and 4 girls (Friedrich and Luecke, 1988) found that 75% of the 'sexually-aggressive' boys and 100% of the 'sexually-aggressive' girls had been sexually abused. A study of 47 boys (Johnson, 1988) found that overall, 50% of the 'children who molested' had been sexually abused, with a higher percentage of the younger children being sexually abused and 30% of the children between 11–12 years old being sexually abused. Virtually all of the boys had sustained pervasive harsh physical punishment. In an article on 13 girls who molest, Johnson (1989) found that all of the girls had been sexually abused and they had sustained pervasive harsh physical punishment. Early studies did not confirm a history of sexual abuse in all male and female children who molested.

Even after the above studies, the belief persisted that the reason for children sexually offending other children was a recapitulation of their own sexual abuse. As more children who were molesting other children were brought into treatment, it was found that many did not disclose sexual abuse. As most of the children who did not disclose sexual abuse were boys, a belief developed that the reason more sexual abuse was not being found in their history was due to it being difficult for boys to disclose sexual abuse.

While the samples of children who molest were small, the lower than expected incidence of sexual abuse in boys was corroborated by information gathered on adult sex offenders. Murphy and Peters (1992) state:

There is a good deal of clinical lore that a history of being sexually victimized is predominant in the back-grounds of sex offenders. However, there are a number of problems when extrapolating the clinical lore to the legal arena. First, one must realize that estimates currently suggest that somewhere between 1 in 9 children to 1 in 10 young males will be sexually abused before the age of 18 (Finkelhor, Hotaling et al., 1990). The vast majority of these children do not grow up to be sex offenders and therefore one could not classify someone as a sex offender based on the fact that they have been sexually abused. In addition, reviewed data on 1,717 offenders included in 18 different studies found that the average rate of sexual abuse across studies was 28%.

(Hanson and Slater, 1988).

Although the empirical literature indicates that not all children who molest other children are themselves victims of sexual abuse, this belief has persisted in the minds of the general public, and in some police, CPS workers and mental health professionals (Friedrich and Chaffin, 2000). As with children who sexually offend, it is also true of the entire range of children with sexual behaviour problems that sexual abuse is not pervasive in their history. Drach (Drach, Wientzen et al., 2001) found no significant relationship between being a victim of sexual abuse and the presence or absence of sexual behaviour problems in a sample of children referred for sexual abuse evaluation. Silovsky (2002) likewise found that in a sample of children with sexual behaviour problems, 65% had no history of sexual abuse. In this study the percentage of children who had been physically abused was 47%, and 58% had witnessed domestic violence.

It is important to counteract this belief in professionals, as some may influence children with sexual behaviour problems to make a disclosure of sexual abuse when there has been none. Children may believe that there is only one acceptable explanation for their worrisome sexual behaviour and move to satisfy the belief of the therapist by fabricating a history of sexual abuse. It is also important that children who have been molested and are now engaging in problematic sexual behaviour do not think that being molested is the sole reason for their problematic sexual behaviour. This could act as a reason, a justification, or provide a lessening of resolve to curtail problematic sexual behaviours. It could make them feel less competent to cease from engaging in this behaviour. This belief can also dishearten parents who may feel that their children who have been sexually abused are destined to engage in problematic sexual behaviour.

The belief that sexually abused children will molest others has the effect on many in the general public of seeing child sexual abuse victims as potential threats to other children. Children who have been sexually abused are unjustifiably seen as at substantial risk to molest (Friedrich and Chaffin, 2000, Johnson, 1998a). In schools, foster homes and even in the child's biological home, sexual behaviour by a sexually abused child is often seen as far more disturbed than the same sexual behaviour by a child who has not been sexually abused. (See section below, How Many Victims of Childhood Sexual Abuse Will Sexually Offend in Adulthood)

What are the factors that come together to bring forward sexual behaviour problems in children?

Understanding the etiological factors for the wide range of children who engage in problematic sexual behaviour is still developing. Early studies (Gomes-Schwartz, Horowitz et al., 1985; Friedrich, Beilke et al., 1988; Gale et al., 1988; Gomes-Schwartz, Horowitz et al., 1990; Kendall-Tackett, Williams et al., 1993) found the area that differentiated nonsexually abused children from sexually abused children who were all receiving mental health services was their reported sexual behaviours. Friedrich (Friedrich, Gramsch et al., 1992) found that parents of children with a history of sexual abuse report on the Child Sexual Behaviour Inventory (CSBI) that their children engage in more frequent and intrusive sexual behaviours when compared to children without a history of sexual abuse. In 1995, after reviewing many studies of sexually abused children in an effort to identify indicators that could be used to help determine when a child had been sexually abused, Slusser (1995) states, 'These studies empirically support the growing impression among clinicians that overt sexual behaviour, inappropriate for their age, is an indication of sexual abuse.'

Due to the confluence of research that found a strong relationship between sexual abuse and sexual behaviour, Dr Friedrich analysed his data from the Child Sexual Behaviour Inventory (CSBI) to determine if certain sexual behaviours in which children engaged could distinguish between children who had been sexually abused and children who had not been sexually abused. Dr Friedrich indicated certain sexual behaviours were highly correlated with a history of sexual abuse and developed a system of scoring the reported sexual behaviours, together with data from other sources that could be helpful in pointing to a diagnosis of sexual abuse. Yet, he stressed in the manual (Friedrich, 1997) that the sexual behaviours of a child *are not* sufficient to make a diagnosis of sexual abuse.

As research on the sexual behaviours of sexually abused and non-abused children continued, alternate findings emerged. While sexual abuse is in the history of some children with sexual behaviour problems, there are other demographic and environmental factors that are more pervasive and which may be more instrumental in providing fodder for the development of sexual behaviour problems in children.

Recent research points out that sexually abused children cannot be distinguished from children in outpatient psychiatric clinics based on their sexual behaviours. Dr Friedrich (2002) used data gathered on the Child Sexual Behaviour Inventory (CSBI) to attempt to distinguish between a population of children with no known history of sexual abuse, a non-abused psychiatric population and a clinical sample of sexually abused children. The non-abused psychiatric sample and the sexually abused sample could not be differentiated based on their sexual behaviours. Additionally, Dr Friedrich found that many of the factors in the backgrounds of the non-abused psychiatric population of children, such as poverty, poorly educated single parents and stressful life events, were also factors in the lives of the sexually abused children. He concluded, 'Sexual abuse may be only one of several significant stressors in the life of the typically sexually abused child.' (Friedrich, 2002).

This finding led to further exploration of the backgrounds of sexually abused children. 'Recent data suggest that sexually abused children who are symptomatic are significantly more likely than nonsymptomatic sexually abused children to have experienced more overall life stress, come from more troubled and disrupted families, and have experienced more maternal rejection.' (Friedrich and Fehrer).

Understanding that sexually abused children who engage in problematic sexual behaviours have similar backgrounds to symptomatic nonsexually abused children led to further study. In a 2003 article, Friedrich took three sexual behaviours ('Touches another child's sex parts,' 'Tries to have sexual intercourse with another child or adult,' and 'Puts mouth on another child/adults' sex parts') from the CSBI and called them 'Sexually Intrusive Behaviour' (SIB). Using two large samples, one sexually abused and one non-abused, he determined statistically that the highest correlation to SIB are the Child Behavior Check List externalising and internalising subscales, followed by (in order of statistical significance) low family income, low education, single parent, domestic violence, physical abuse, and sexual abuse. Sexual abuse was defined as involving penetration, being incestuous, occurring when the child was very young or

including multiple perpetrators, consisting of a long duration, and including physical abuse.

Friedrich also found that SIB is inversely correlated with age and has no significant correlation to gender. He notes that the young age of the children likely indicates that the behaviour may be related to immaturity and reactivity to the environment. He notes that this population of children with intrusive sexual behaviour is 'not similar to adults or adolescents with intrusive sexuality as those are mainly male.'

Summarising his findings regarding the etiology of 'sexually intrusive behaviours' in children, Friedrich (Friedrich, Davies et al., 2003) states, 'It does appear that a four-component model has heuristic validity. As demonstrated with the current data, the elements are family adversity, modelling of coercion, modelling of sexuality, and a vulnerable/predisposed child substrate.'

Although children who sexually offend do not necessarily engage in the types of sexual behaviours Friedrich describes as SIB, his model is consistent with the clinical findings of the first author who, over the last 20 years, has studied the etiology of children who molest. Regarding the modelling of coercion and sexuality in Friedrich's model, not only have the majority of the children who molest been physically abused, but they have almost universally witnessed domestic violence between their caretakers. It is hypothesised (Johnson, 1999) that some children who live in homes with domestic violence believe that sex and aggression are complementary. Children who live in homes with partner violence often hear intense arguments in which one partner accuses the other of sexual misconduct, attempts to control all of the behaviours of that partner and emotionally and/or physically hurts the other partner as a payback for alleged or real infidelity. These children often hear angry sexual language and witness violent interactions between parental figures in which one parent violates the other's sexual rights. These children do not learn that sex is an expression of love between two people. Constant fighting and jealousy by parents relating to sex, teaches children that people use sex to hurt other people and that violence in relation to sex is natural. Often, sexual contact appears to be a caring act only after violence has occurred. This pairing of sex and aggression may cause confusion for the child's developing template for sexual relationships. In the homes of children who molest, the children are very aware of the trauma and violence in the parents'/caretakers' lives and often become part of the drama as one or the other parent pulls them in as an ally or a scapegoat. It is not infrequent that when one parent does not have a partner, or when the partner explodes and leaves, the child is used for emotional sustenance for the remaining parent. The child feels overwhelmed by the parent's needs but feels he or she needs to take care of the parent. When the other parent returns, the child is generally thrust aside to feel abandoned, jealous, angry and confused.

Ralph, age 10, is a good example of a boy whose aggressive sexual behaviours led his therapists, teachers and CPS to search for who sexually abused him. They thought that if they found out, this would help him stop the behaviours. When he denied being sexually abused they were stymied. After several years of therapy working with both Ralph and his mother it became clear that Ralph's aggressive sexual behaviours emanated not from being directly (hands-on) sexually abused, but from his anxiety over witnessing his mother having sex many times with men he did not know, seeing her beaten up by these men, being physically and emotionally abused himself by many of his mother's boyfriends and by her, and living in a continual atmosphere of boundariless sexuality.

It should be stressed that many children live in homes with this level of dysfunction and do not start molesting others. Yet, children who sexually offend have almost always lived in these chaotic homes with multiple forms of abuse, neglect and violence.

How many victims of childhood sexual abuse will sexually offend in adulthood?

The belief that sexual abuse was the major etiological factor for sexually abusive behaviour in children spawned the alternate belief that children who were sexually abused were likely to sexually abuse other children. This belief persists, in spite of literature to the contrary. As Kaufman and Zigler (1987) have observed:

The findings of the different investigations are not easily integrated because of their methodological variations. Nonetheless, the best estimate of intergenerational transmission appears to be 30% plus or minus

5%. This suggests that approximately one-third of all individuals who were physically abused, sexually abused, or extremely neglected will subject their offspring to one of these forms of maltreatment, while the remaining two-thirds will provide adequate care for their children ... The rate of abuse among individuals with a history of abuse (30% plus or minus 5%) is approximately six times higher than the base rate for abuse in the general population (5%). Being maltreated as a child puts one at risk for becoming abusive but the path between these two points is far from direct or inevitable. In the past, unqualified acceptance of the intergenerational hypothesis has had many negative consequences. Adults who were maltreated have been told so many times that they will abuse their child that for some it has become a self-fulfilling prophecy. Many who have broken the cycle are left feeling like walking time bombs. In addition, persistent acceptance of this belief has impeded progress in understanding the etiology of abuse and led to misguided judicial and social policy interventions. The time has come for the intergenerational myth to be put aside and for researchers to cease asking, 'Do abused children become abusive parents?' and ask, instead, 'Under what conditions is the transmission of abuse most likely to occur.'
(p192)

In Widom's 1994 article, entitled 'Criminal Consequences of Childhood Sexual Victimization,' she states that compared to other types of child abuse and neglect, childhood sexual abuse does not uniquely increase an individual's risk for later delinquent and adult criminal behaviour. As adults, child sexual abuse victims are at increased risk of arrest for sex crimes, although they are no more likely than victims of nonsexual abuse to have such an arrest. That is, all three of the abuse groups (physical abuse, sexual abuse and neglect) are significantly more likely to commit a sexual offence than the controls. (Those who had been abused or neglected as children are more likely to be arrested as juveniles [27% versus 17%], adults [42% versus 33%], and for a violent crime [18% versus 14%]). Thus, the criminogenic effect associated with sexual offending may not result from sexual abuse uniquely, but rather may be associated with the trauma and stress of these early childhood experiences or society's response to the event. Additionally, childhood sexual abuse victims in this longitudinal study are not at increased risk of arrest for a violent sex crime (rape and/or sodomy). Rather, the findings suggest an association between childhood physical abuse and later arrests for violent sex crimes (rape and/or sodomy) in males. In

Widom's (Widom and Maxfield, 2001) update on this longitudinal study of the effects of abuse and neglect she found that victims of neglect, as well as victims of physical abuse, are likely to develop later violent criminal behaviour.

Johnson (Johnson, 1998a) estimated that less than 0.5% of sexually abused children would go on to sexually abuse other children during childhood. In fact, specialised residential treatment programmes for children who molest are generally unable to find sufficient numbers of children with the severest level of sexual behaviour problems to fill their beds (Johnson, 1998). Unable to fill all of their beds with children who sexually offend, these facilities accept children with a lesser degree of sexual problems. This can present a danger to children who are sexualised but who are not offending.

'Not normal' sexual behaviour is not necessarily abusive

Delineating what is 'normal' sexual behaviour for children has been the subject of much concern and research (Friedrich, Grambsch et al., 1991; Johnson, 1991; Friedrich, Grambsch et al., 1992; Friedrich, Fisher et al., 1998; Johnson, 1998a; Johnson, 1999). Friedrich asked mothers to fill out the Child Sexual Behaviour Inventory and subsequently defined certain behaviours as 'normative' based on at least 20% of mothers observing this behaviour in their children (Friedrich, 1997; Friedrich, Fisher et al., 1998). Defining this has helped us to know what are the most expected behaviours in children as per parent report.

Johnson (1998a) stated that:

*Natural and healthy sexual exploration during child-hood is an **information gathering process** wherein children **explore** each other's bodies, by looking and touching (e.g., playing doctor), as well as explore **gender roles and behaviours** (e.g., playing house). Children involved in natural and healthy sexual play are of **similar age, size and developmental status** and participate on a **voluntary** basis. While siblings engage in **mutual** sexual exploration, most sexual play is between children who have an ongoing mutually enjoyable play and/or school **friendship**. The sexual behaviours are **limited in type and frequency** and occur in **several periods** of the child's life. The child's interest in sex and sexuality is **balanced** by curiosity about other aspects of his or her life. Natural and healthy sexual exploration may result in **embar-rassment** but does not usually leave children with deep feelings of anger, shame, fear or anxiety. If the children*

*are discovered in sexual exploration and instructed to stop, the behaviour generally **diminishes, at least in the view of adults**. The feelings of the children regarding the sexual behaviour is generally **light-hearted and spontaneous**. Generally, children experi-ence pleasurable sensations from genital touching, some children experience sexual arousal, while some children experience orgasm. Sexual arousal and orgasm are more frequently found in older children entering puberty.*

A behaviour that is not expected or considered 'normative' in children cannot necessarily be defined as abusive. There has been a tendency to label developmentally advanced behaviours as abusive. For instance, Burton (Burton, L. et al., 1997) 'defined 'simulated intercourse' between any children 12 and younger as 'sexually abnormal behaviour' and then equated this with 'sexually-aggressive' behaviour.' Whereas this behaviour by young children may not be acceptable, engaging in it does not necessarily mean that one child is forcing the other. It means that it is more advanced than the adults discovering it would like to find.

This transformation of developmentally advanced sexual behaviours into abusive behaviours happens with some regularity in everyday practice. Oral-genital contact is certainly not a behaviour that is considered 'normal' for children. Yet because it occurs between two children does not mean one of the children is abusing the other. A startled preschool teacher who finds two boys in the corner of the classroom with their pants down and one child approaching the genitals of the other with his mouth may describe the approaching child as a 'perpetrator.' If the teacher discovers that both children have put their mouths on the penis of the other, the teacher may describe the more outspoken or bold, older, or larger child as a 'perpetrator.' This immediate reaction has led to serious consequences for children and families. While suspected child abuse is a mandatory reporting issue, a thoughtful approach will allow for some assessment of the circumstances surrounding the discovered events.

Johnson (1998, 2003) encourages examining the characteristics (See Part IV of the Child Sexual Behaviour Checklist in section below on Assessment) of the sexual behaviour being engaged in between children (not the behaviour itself), when trying to determine if sexual abuse has occurred. Young children look at and touch each other's body parts, genital or nongenital, by way of exploration. They also tend to re-enact what they have seen and are not as good, nor diligent, as older children in hiding their behaviour. It has been found that oral-genital contact between children is found more frequently in younger children and that boys and girls both engage in the behaviour (Friedrich, Davies et al., 2003)

Any sexual behaviour can be abusive, not only developmentally advanced behaviours. Some children find it fun to tell dirty jokes, touch each other's bottoms, and use scatological language, while other children may not like it at all. If one child persists in these types of behaviours while the other child feels very uncomfortable and consistently requests the child stop, this can feel like abusive behaviour. If the child doing the behaviours to another child is aware of the child's discomfort, and after repeated requests to stop by the child and adults, does not care what the other child wants or feels and gets pleasure (not necessarily sexual) out of being mean to the other child, this is sexually abusive behaviour.

Another issue of great concern is the situation in which a teacher sees an advanced, developmentally inappropriate sexual behaviour between children. If the teacher is aware that one of the children is a victim of child sexual abuse, this may lead directly to the sexual abuse victim being called a perpetrator. In the late 1990s, the highly pejorative term 'predator' began being used referring to young children, usually sexually abused children, who had engaged in problematic sexual behaviour.

This delineation of a developmentally advanced or inappropriate behaviour being seen as abusive also happens in the criminal justice system. In late 2003 the first author was seeing an 11-year-old girl in therapy who was charged with lewd and lascivious behaviour with a minor. This is a felony offence. This young girl asked a five-year-old boy she knew from her daycare to go with her into a toilet stall in the girl's bathroom. She wanted to see his penis. She had seen some male genitals on the Internet (including multiple advertisements for increasing the size of the male penis) and wanted to see a real penis. When the young boy said he didn't want to take down his pants, she asked him again and he did. There was no force, anger or yelling. She touched his penis one time with her hand. Nothing else happened. There were no previous incidents. Her charges were as follows: On 03/03/03 within the County of Los Angeles, the

crime of LEWD ACT UPON A CHILD, in violation of PENAL CODE 288(A), a Felony, was committed by said minor, who did willfully, unlawfully, and lewdly commit a lewd and lascivious act upon and with the body and certain parts and members thereof of (name withheld), a child under the age of 14 years, with the intent of arousing, appealing to, and gratifying the lust, passions, and sexual desires of the said minor or the said child. Because she was not incarcerated in the California Youth Authority, she is not subject to taking her DNA or sex offender registration.

Legal implications for children labelled as sexual offenders

On July 29, 1994 in New Jersey, a seven-year-old named Megan Kanka was brutally raped and murdered by a previously convicted sex offender living in her neighbourhood. At the time of Megan's death, New Jersey law did not allow the release of information on registered sex offenders to the public. In response to overwhelming public outcry, on October 31, 1994, New Jersey enacted Megan's Law. This law requires sex offenders who are convicted, adjudicated delinquent, or found not guilty by reason of insanity to register with local law enforcement agencies for the remainder of their lives. Under Megan's law, notification for moderate- and high-risk offenders consists of a recent photograph, a physical description of the offender, a description of the offence, the name of the offender, the name of the offender's work or school, and a description and the license plate of the offender's vehicle. Sex offenders must verify their address periodically.

A federal statute known as the Jacob Wetterling Crimes Against Children and Sexually Violent Offender Registration Program (1994) was passed requiring all states to create registration programmes for convicted sex offenders. On May 17, 1996 the federal Megan's Law amendment was signed by President Clinton requiring the release of information on sex offenders for the purpose of community notification and safety. This law, which amended the Wetterling Act, requires that registrant information be available to the public but allows states to set their own criteria for disclosure.

All 50 States, and the District of Columbia, have sex offender registration and some form of community notification. Each state can set its own standards regarding who registers and for how long and what type of notification will be made to the public. In at least 22 states (as of 2003), juveniles (which can include children under 12) are subject to registration as sex offenders. Some states offer public access to their registries over the internet while others require individuals to go into a law enforcement agency to view the information via intranet or CD-ROM.

The registration and notification statutes in some states fail to differentiate the severity of the offence. For example, a juvenile who has been convicted of multiple rapes would appear no differently than a juvenile who had touched the breast of a female schoolmate (Trivits and Repucci, 2002). In Texas, 1,389 of the 26,769 sex offenders posted on the state's Internet registry in the fall of 2000 were between 11 and 16 years old (Williams, 2000), including offenders with relatively minor crimes. For instance, one of the postings is a 12-year-old boy who mooned a group of 5- and 6-year-old children (Trivits and Repucci, 2002).

In California, if a child 12 years old or younger is adjudicated on a serious sex charge, he can be sent to the California Youth Authority, which houses adolescents. After the child's term is up, his DNA is taken for forensic purposes; he has to check in regularly with his probation officer. The child can be registered for life as a sex offender.

In some states in the United States, if a child is registered for life, there is no mechanism for him or her to get off the list. Until July 2001 this was true in New Jersey. In a bold action the State Supreme Court of New Jersey ruled unanimously that offenders found guilty before their 14th birthday should have a chance to escape those sanctions at 18 by presenting evidence that they do not pose a risk of committing another sex crime. Justice Stein wrote that the court was troubled by the lack of evidence to support the charge that J.G., as a 10-year-old, had committed an act of sexual penetration on his cousin. Although J.G. admitted to the crime in 1996, when he was 11, the justice noted that a detective who investigated the case was not convinced that penetration had occurred. In addition, a therapist for J.G. testified in a lower-court hearing that the boy had a learning disability and had difficulty reading and spelling simple words, and that she did not believe that he understood the terms 'sex,' 'rape' or 'penetration' when he admitted the crime.

The New Jersey case is very instructive of the errors in assessment of children's sexual

behaviours. Not only is there is a lack of understanding of children's cognitive, emotional, and sexual development, but there are no good criteria to define what is sexual offending by children.

Since there is no empirical evidence, either longitudinal or retrospective, to indicate that when children molest (or engage in developmentally advanced sexual behaviour) at a young age they will continue to sexually offend, and there are no guidelines for assessment of children with sexual behaviour problems, it is cruel and unusual punishment to condemn them to a lifetime stigma as a sex offender.

Children should not be judged by adult standards regarding their sexual behaviours

Defining sexual abuse between children

Some of the confusion experienced by professionals working with young children with sexual behaviour problems has occurred due to a reliance on standards for adult sexual offending. It is a great deal more clear-cut when defining what is sexually abusive when one of the persons involved in the sexual activity is an adult and the other is a child, rather than two children twelve and younger engaging in sexual behaviour together. An adult being sexual with a child is clearly sexual abuse. This is largely not the case when children twelve and younger behave in a sexual manner with other children. While the greater the age difference between the children, the more concern there is about the sexual behaviour, it is very infrequently sexually abusive when a child engages in sexual behaviour with children younger than themselves. Unfortunately, if adult laws are applied to children's sexual contact, misinterpretations can be made and nonabusive sexual contact between children can be criminalised. When children are experimenting and trying to gather knowledge about sex and sexuality, they are not thinking about the adult laws regarding sexual contact and they are not trying to conform their exploration to this unknown set of restrictions.

Consider the eight-year-old brother who wants to see what a vagina looks like and asks his only sister to show him hers. She is three and willingly shows him while she is taking a bath. He looks and then touches between the labia with his finger to see what it feels like. For the three seconds it takes place they both giggle and that is the end of it. Is it legitimate to call this a sexual offence, as it would be construed if an adult engaged in the same behaviour? No, but it could be construed this way in the current climate in some jurisdictions in the United States. The data on a police charge sheet might look like this, '8-year-old male digitally penetrates vagina of 3-year-old sister.'

When the police or a Child Protective Services worker believes, based on the sexual behaviour, that a child has sexually abused another child, the child often has little or no ability to explain what he or she was thinking or what his or her motivation was for engaging in the sexual behaviour. If the boy in the example above tried to explain, if he were allowed, it might be perceived as a rationalisation, or trying to lie to get out of trouble, or that the child is denying or minimising (terms used with adolescent and adult sexual offenders) the behaviour. Because police, CPS and mental health professionals tend to believe they only know the 'tip of the iceberg,' the child may be continually questioned about additional sexual behaviours. If the child acknowledges further behaviours, this can further cement the CPS or police officer's perception that the child is a sexual offender. In some cases, the term 'sexual predator' may be used if multiple children or multiple acts are discovered. The child's reality is often not taken into account. The adult demands that the child see the behaviour from the adult's perspective while the adult refuses to see the behaviour from the child's perspective. Many practitioners, following the belief that 'all sex offenders lie' do not listen to the children and develop their own picture of events.

Sexual arousal and sexual offending

Some penal codes that deal with sexual offending require that the individual have the 'intent of arousing, appealing to, and gratifying the lust, passions, and sexual desires of that person or the child.' (California Penal Code 288(a).[1] This code

section is frequently used when dealing with children's interpersonal sexual behaviours. While it is possible that a child is seeking pleasant sexual feelings, or even sexual arousal, most of the sexual behaviours engaged in by young children are not for the purpose of sexual arousal. Sexual stimulation (as an adult might feel), was reported by 5.3% of adults recalling their sexual experiences at 6–10 years of age and 17.4% recalling their sexual experiences at 11–12 years of age (Johnson, Huang et al., under review).

If it can be proved, and this is difficult in young children, that the child who engaged in a sexual behaviour has experienced sexual arousal while engaging in the behaviour, is that adequate to label the behaviour an offence? Consider the five-year-old child, Jeannie, who likes the genital sensations she feels when she is masturbating. As she is trying to sleep, Jeannie frequently overhears her alcoholic father and his drug addicted girl friend having intercourse in the living room while they talk about the sexual pleasure they feel and describe the pleasuring they want from the other. Jeannie, listening to this night after night, gets in bed with her older or younger brother and simulates intercourse with him trying to recreate what she thinks is going on in the other room. She feels sexual arousal while she is engaging in the behaviour. Is this sexual offending?

There have been several appellate decisions dealing with young children that relied upon PC 288(a). In Jerry M. (1997) 59 Ca.App. 4th 289, the California Court of Appeal ruled an 11-year-old touching three different girls' breasts on four separate occasions cannot be convicted of PC 288 (a), where there was no evidence that the minor had reached puberty or that any of the touching was intended to accomplish sexual arousal. The appellate court relied on: there was no evidence of sexual arousal, or of whether the minor had reached puberty; the victims each knew the minor; the conduct was in public, during the daytime, and occurred in the presence of others, without any attempt or opportunity to avoid detection; there was no clandestine activity preceding the touching; 'There was no attempt to prolong the touching beyond the initial momentary contact; there was no caressing. The record shows Jerry was a brazen 11-year-old whose conduct was more consistent with an intent to annoy and obtain attention than with sexual arousal. Under these circumstances Jerry was perhaps guilty of battery (242), but the

---

[1] 288. (a) Any person who willfully and lewdly commits any lewd or lascivious act, including any of the acts constituting other crimes provided for in Part 1, upon or with the body, or any part or member thereof, of a child who is under the age of 14 years, with the intent of arousing, appealing to, or gratifying the lust, passions, or sexual desires of that person or the child, is guilty of a felony and shall be punished by imprisonment in the state prison for three, six, or eight years.

record does not support a true finding beyond a reasonable doubt of conduct intended sexually to exploit a child – the 'gist' of section 288, subdivision (a).'

Billie Y. (1990) 220 Cal. App. 3d 127 states that there must be lewd and lascivious intent proven, as well as knowledge of its wrongfulness.

Motivation and sexual offending in children

Whereas the motivation for a sexual behaviour is not a valid way of discriminating when sexual behaviours between an adult and a child are sexually abusive, it is very important when two children are involved. If a child is engaging in the sexual behaviour due to curiosity, desire for knowledge, experimentation, anxiety, confusion, or if the child is replaying something he or she has seen or heard about or something that was done to him or her, and there is no element of anger, revenge, payback or desire for harm, then the behaviour generally should not be categorised as an offence. Instead of trying to figure things out by reading about them or directly asking for help, children often play out their concerns, worries and confusion. Children are concrete thinkers and learn most effectively when it is experiential. This is also the case for learning about their sexual selves.

Consider the sexually abused child who touches the penis of another child in a re-creation of what was done to him. He does not force the child or hold the child down. He finds a child who will allow the behaviour and does it in an attempt to make sense of what was done to him. If he tries the behaviour on a child who says 'no' he will not force that child, he will go and try it with another child. Is this sexual abuse?

Children's knowledge of legal standards

Whereas it is assumed that an adult knows that acting in a sexual way with a child is wrong and illegal, this cannot be assumed with young children. Trying out sexual behaviours with other children has been going on throughout history. Eighty-four per cent of adults reporting about their sexual behaviours when they were 12 or younger said they engaged in solitary sexual behaviours, and 81% said they engaged in sexual behaviours with other children (Johnson, Huang et al., under review).

In a culture with extensive sexually explicit public media and advertising which encourages children to explore sex and sexuality, adults' messages to children are generally punitive if they see children mimic the sexual behaviours they see. Even young children who engage in sexual behaviours with other children learn that grownups get uncomfortable when they mimic adult sexual behaviours. For this reason, children usually hide when they engage in sexual conversations or sexual behaviour with one another. Hence when being questioned by the police (Gladys R) or Child Protective Services, children will acknowledge that they know it is wrong to engage in sexual behaviours with another child. Yet, the wrong to which they refer is not morally wrong or legally wrong.

Children do not think in terms of age differences and legal standards. They are almost never aware that their behaviour could lead to criminal prosecution. Most children engage in sexual behaviours with their friends who are of a similar age, size and developmental status (Johnson, 1991; Johnson, 2000; Johnson, 2004). Yet, some children who have no same age children available, or are developmentally delayed, or socially inadequate, or have neurological disorders may play with substantially younger children and hence might choose to sexually experiment with them. There are frequently cases of children with ADD or ADHD who get caught up in the criminal justice system or CPS because they touch younger children. It is frequently not taken into account that younger children are the play-mates of children with ADD and ADHD because children their own age will not play with them due to their immaturity and impulsiveness. Children do not know about laws that declare a three, four or five year age difference illegal sexual behaviours. Children who engage in natural and healthy sexual behaviours do so with available children who are friendly with them and seemingly interested, regardless of their age. It is implausible to think that a child would ask the age of a play-mate to see if he or she fit within the legally accepted ages for consensual sexual behaviour. Adults and adolescents, unless intellectually impaired, know that sex with children is illegal. This is not the case with children 12 and younger. Knowledge that their behaviour is illegal should not be taken for granted.

Children and consent

Whereas agreement between people engaged in sexual behaviours is an essential ingredient when defining consensual sexual behaviour between adults, it is a developmentally advanced concept for young children. Children understand that physical force is not acceptable in any behaviours. They know that if they purposely hit someone and hurt her or him, this is never acceptable. But one child may not pay close attention to whether the other child really wants to do something with them (consents) that he or she wants to do. Children tend to be more self-focused than other-focused. This is particularly true of children with ADD or ADHD or children who are developmentally delayed or poorly socialised. For instance, two children have water guns and are shooting at each other. After some time one wants to stop and the other does not. The one child may continue, semi-oblivious to the protestations of the other. The child would generally not be thinking they are harming the other child, just that they are having fun and want to continue. This can also be true with sexual behaviours between children. Children do not necessarily differentiate between one kind of play behaviour and another.

When an adult sexual offender provides children with toys or special privileges, these bribes create an atmosphere that leads the child to want to please the grownup. These bribes are an indirect form of manipulation and subtle coercion. Children also use bribery and coercive techniques to get their way. For example, if one child wants to play catch and the other wants to play soccer, one child may say he will not play with the other child ever again, if the other child does not play soccer. Or, one child may bribe the other child by saying he will give him extra time on a video game, if he plays soccer. We must be careful not to over interpret these persuasive methods as sexually coercive or grooming behaviour when it comes to sexual behaviour between children. This would be using concepts derived from adult sex offender behaviour to interpret children's behaviour. This potentially leads to false conclusions.

Miranda Rights

Before children are queried by the police regarding their sexual behaviour they are often read their Miranda rights, just as an adult offender would be read his or her Miranda Rights. This warning, originally written for use with adults, is frequently not understood by children, and they can become entrapped by it. Children believe they have to do what grownups say and, if they do not, they will get in trouble. This is particularly true of children and police officers in uniform.

> Timothy, age 10, had been caught six months previously humping his six-year-old cousin. He had been in therapy for five months regarding this behaviour.
>
> Timothy was in class when a person from the attendance office came and took him to the main office. There he met a woman who said she needed to speak to him. She took him into a separate area. At that time she read him his Miranda Rights. Six months after this event Timothy described his feelings at that time. 'I wasn't sure what was happening. I didn't have time to think. I didn't know that this woman was from the police. I thought she was a therapist. I was in therapy, and I thought it was just another therapist. I didn't think anything bad would happen if I did what she wanted. I've always been told it's better to tell the truth then be caught in a lie. I wasn't sure, so I agreed to everything'.
>
> Timothy did not realise that he was talking to a police officer until well into the interview. During the interview, after Timothy had told the detective what he had done, the detective asked Timothy what he thought his adult cousins would do if they found out. Timothy responded that maybe the cousins would go to the police and press charges. At that point, the detective said, 'I am the police.' Timothy said he kept talking because he thought she might take him to jail if he didn't, and that would make it worse for him. He said, 'I felt like I wanted to tell her to stop, but I thought maybe I would get arrested. Like if I said something about her, like she was rude, she might tell that in court.' At no point did he think he could stop talking, even after he realised that it was the police.
>
> In reviewing the actual phrases used in Miranda six months later, Timothy was still unclear what they meant. When asked to paraphrase the first two Miranda questions (1. You have the right to remain silent. Do you understand? 2. Anything you say may be used against you in a court of law. Do you understand?) Timothy said, 'If I said something she didn't like, she could use it against me in court or if you say anything wrong, it can be used against you in court.' Timothy did not comprehend at all that he had a choice at any time to simply say, 'No, I don't want to answer your questions.' Regarding having an attorney present Timothy said, 'But I didn't have an attorney, and I didn't have time to think about what it all meant.'

A recent decision by the US Supreme Court says, 'The police need not always warn a teenage crime suspect of his rights before formally questioning him, the Supreme Court said Tuesday. The 5–4 ruling gives police a bit more leeway to question suspects without warning them of their Miranda rights, and it says that a suspect's youth is not reason enough to treat him with more caution.' (Savage, 2004)

Once a sex offender always a sex offender

An additional problem with assuming that information about adult sex offenders fits for children who sexually abuse is that most people believe that adults who sexually offend will always sexually offend. This static approach to a developing child's sexuality is unwarranted. There is no empirical evidence to support that once a child has engaged in sexually abusive behaviours, the child will continue to engage in sexually abusive behaviour throughout his or her lifetime. Likewise, it is untrue that adults and adolescents who sexually abuse will all continue to sexually abuse others. (See section in this chapter, Misinformation on the Recidivism Rates of Adult and Adolescent Sex Offenders Taints Perception of Children Who Sexually Abuse.)

Less guilty by reason of pre-adolescence

Juvenile offenders are held to answer for their crimes in Juvenile Court and are not generally tried as adults. Steinberg and Scott, (Steinberg et al., 2003) argue in *Less Guilty by Reason of Adolescence* that emerging knowledge about cognitive, psychosocial, and neurobiological development in adolescence supports the conclusion that juveniles should not be held to the same standards of criminal responsibility as adults. 'Under standard, well-accepted principles of criminal law, the developmental immaturity of juveniles mitigates their criminal culpability and, accordingly, should moderate the severity of their punishment.' Steinberg and Scott (2003, p1010) distinguish between an 'excuse for bad behaviour' and 'mitigation'. 'In legal parlance, *excuse* refers to the complete exculpation of a criminal defendant; he or she bears no responsibility for the crime and should receive no punishment.' 'Unlike excuse, which calls for a binary judgment – guilty or not guilty – *mitigation* places the culpability of the guilty actor somewhere on a continuum of criminal

culpability and, by extension, a continuum of punishment. They continue'. . . we argue that the developmental immaturity of adolescence mitigates culpability and justifies more lenient punishment, but that it is not, generally, a basis for excuse – except in the case of *very* young, pre-adolescent offenders.' (p1010) Pre-adolescent offenders, in the case of this article, are children who sexually offend.

When discussing mitigation, Steinberg and Scott (2003) report, 'In general, factors that reduce criminal culpability can be grouped roughly into three categories. The first category includes endogenous impairments or deficiencies in the actor's decision-making capacity which affect his or her choice to engage in criminal activity. 'Under the second category, culpability is reduced when the external circumstances faced by the actor are so compelling that an ordinary (or "reasonable") person might have succumbed to the pressure in the same way as did the defendant.' 'The third category of mitigation includes evidence that the criminal act was out of character for the actor and that, unlike the typical criminal act, his or her crime was not the product of bad character.'

The major impetus of the Steinberg and Scott (2003) article is to persuade against the use of the death penalty for juveniles. Yet, these categories that reduce culpability for adolescents are salient to an argument for not using adult criteria and laws to adjudicate pre-adolescents regarding their sexual behaviours and are certainly strong reasons for mitigating their culpability regarding punishment.

Regarding Steinberg's (2003) first mitigating factor, the ability to engage in reasoning and sound decision-making regarding sexual behaviours is only rarely developed in pre-adolescents in general, and virtually never in children who sexually offend. Children who sexually offend model their behaviour from the adult role models with whom they live, as well as television, music videos, song lyrics, their friends, the Internet and printed material, often of a questionable nature, found around their homes. It has been found that the vast majority of children who engage in sexual offending live in families with poor emotional, physical and sexual boundaries and have generally observed domestic violence. These children have frequently been exposed to explicit adult sex in vivo and given little, if any healthy education regarding sexual mores and values. Their role models are their parents' whose lives are generally fraught with marital break-ups, a history of abuse, incarcerations, drug and alcohol addiction, and overall poor social and emotional adjustment. The problem-solving ability of the parents is often as deficient as that of the children.

Regarding heightened vulnerability to coercive circumstances, Steinberg's (2003) second mitigating factor, the psychosocial immaturity of pre-adolescents makes them extremely vulnerable to being led into bad behaviour. Being surrounded by sexual confusion and sexual tension provides a premature sexualisation of the child and an impetus to problematic sexual expression. While pre-adolescents who sexually offend are not generally coerced into engaging in abusive behaviour, most are surrounded in their families by people who violate the law and others' rights on a consistent basis. These children's caretakers provide coercive and aggressive role models. Generally there have been a series of males who have been sexually, physically and emotionally abusive to the child's mother, which the child has witnessed on an ongoing basis. Steinberg (2003) states, 'Adolescents' claim to mitigation on this ground is particularly compelling in that, as legal minors, they lack the freedom that adults have to extricate themselves from a criminogenic setting'. This is even truer of children 12 and under.

The third category of mitigation includes evidence that the criminal act was out of character for the individual and that it was not the product of bad character. The criminal law implicitly assumes that harmful conduct reflects the person's bad character, but if there is evidence that this assumption is not accurate this can mitigate culpability believes that most adolescents identity is not formed into a developed *self* until late adolescence or early adulthood, therefore their crimes are less culpable than those of typical adult criminals. Pre-adolescents' character is by nature of their age, unformed. There is no data to support that all or most pre-adolescents who engage in sexual offending behaviour will continue to engage in the behaviour into adolescence. In fact, studies of criminal or delinquent behaviour in adolescents' indicate that the majority desist from criminal activity as they mature into adulthood.

Misinformation on the recidivism rates of adult and adolescent sex offenders taints perception of children who sexually abuse

There has been an ongoing misperception by the public, as well as many professionals who work in the field of sexual offending, about the recidivism rates of adult and adolescent sex offenders. While accurate recidivism rates are extremely difficult to calculate due to the element of secrecy in both victims and offenders (Schwartz et al., 1995) even if the true rates are 200% higher than the published rates, they are still lower than most people believe.

The general perception has been, 'Once a Sex Offender, Always a Sex Offender.' This has severely affected children with sexual behaviour problems. Because so many people do not differentiate between the levels of seriousness of sexual behaviours in children, many schoolteachers, day care providers and foster parents will not care for a child who has engaged in problematic sexual behaviour. If the behaviour by the child has been labelled 'sexual offending,' many children are totally separated from other children for years based on the presumption that they will soon 'strike' again.

The reported recidivism rates for adult sex offenders vary depending on whether the offender has or has not received treatment. A recent meta-analytic study by Hanson (Hanson, Gordon et al., 2002) that examined the effectiveness of treatment for sex offenders revealed sexual recidivism rates of 17.3% for untreated offenders, compared with 9.9% for treated offenders. There was also a large difference in general recidivism from 51% for untreated sex offenders and 32% for treated sex offenders. A Wisconsin study (Alexander, 1999) suggests a dramatic decrease in sexual recidivism rates when child molesters are treated. Overall, in an analysis of 11,350 sex offenders from 79 treatment outcome studies, recidivism for child molesters in most categories was less than 11%.

A meta-analytic study of eight studies (Alexander, 1999) totalling over 1000 juveniles who participated in offence-specific treatment in a variety of settings found the combined recidivism rate for all of these youths was 7.1% in 3–5 year follow-up.

A comparison study of juveniles treated in an offence-specific, multi-systemic treatment versus non-specific traditional counselling found that the multi-systemic approach resulted in an 83% reduction in the rate of sexual offence recidivism (as well as a 50% reduction in non-sexual recidivism), compared to that of youth who received traditional non-specific therapy. Sexual recidivism was 12.5% in the specialised treatment.

James Worling (Worling and Curwen, 2000) reports that his programme in Canada obtained records from all Canadian jurisdictions of any new (juvenile or adult) charges filed against two groups of sexually abusive youth, an average of six years after they were identified and assessed. One group had successfully completed offence-specific group treatment along with treatment aimed at enhancing family and peer relationships, and the second group had been assessed for treatment due to similar sexual offences, but had either not entered treatment or had dropped out of treatment prematurely. They found that the treated group had a 72% reduction in sexual recidivism, along with a 41% reduction in non-sexual violence charges and a 59% reduction of non-violent/non-sexual charges. In comparing the treated and untreated samples, 18% of the untreated boys had new charges, compared to 5% of those who had successfully completed treatment.

It is assumed that sexual recidivism rates among juveniles are very high. Yet, the studies that have been conducted on re-offence behaviour indicate that official recidivism rates for sexual offences are actually lower than anticipated. The official sexual recidivism rates for juveniles (even when followed into early adulthood) appear to range from 2% to 14%. Most juvenile sex offenders do not go on to become adult sex offenders. However, there may be a subset of chronic sex offenders who need to be identified. The key concern should be how to identify these high risk offenders, as opposed to assuming that all sex offenders are at high risk to reoffend (Milloy, 1998).

Are we damaging children's sexual development?

Many children who are not molesting children but who have problematic sexual behaviours are given the label of 'perpetrator,' 'abuser,' 'sex offender,' or 'molester.' This can seriously affect the life of the child and family. There are children who have been mislabelled throughout the world. When a child is continually told he or she is a 'sex offender,' and it is not accurate, the child will likely have extreme difficulty in understanding not only what constitutes offending behaviour but also what constitutes healthy sexual behaviour. Healthy sexual development for children includes natural curiosity about their bodies, others' bodies, finding out the differences between the genders, trying to discover how babies are made, experiencing genital feelings, etc. We must guard against making children feel it is wrong to exercise their interest in this natural experience of childhood.

In a study that asked mental health and child protective services professionals to report on their sexual experiences when they were 12 and younger, 33.9% said when they were engaging in sexual behaviour they felt 'good' about it, 39.5% said they felt 'silly, giggly', and 22.7% said they felt excited (not sexually) (Johnson, Huang et al., under review). It is possibly very damaging to children's natural exploration of their sexual selves to have this behaviour made 'bad.' The same study by Johnson et al. indicates that 11.8% of the respondents felt 'bad' when they were engaging in sexual behaviours, 19.1% felt 'scared,' 37.8% felt 'guilty,' and 31.6% felt 'confused.' It would be extremely unfortunate for the children of today to grow up and report significantly higher percentages of negative feelings about their childhood sexual behaviours.

It has become increasingly clear that children in therapy for sexual issues are beginning to believe that all contact with the genitals is bad and that they are bad if they do it. The responses to vignettes, which were given as part of a pilot study of an instrument to understand children's thinking about interpersonal sexual behaviour, are indicative of this problem. The first author created six vignettes that describe different scenarios related to genital touching or other sexual behaviours between children, between children and adults, and between adolescents and children. The answers of 49 children in four different residential facilities were tabulated. Each child who was in therapy for sexual behaviour problems was asked by her or his therapist to respond to the series of vignettes. The therapist read the vignette and made sure the child understood it. The age of the child in the vignette was changed to correspond to the child's age that was being asked the questions. Each question was asked following the vignette, and a response was received before the next question was asked. The answers to the first vignette are illustrative of the children's thinking about mutual versus victimising sexual behaviours.

Vignette: Johnny (use the age of the child you are asking) has always wanted to see a girl's private parts. Suzie has always wanted to see a boy's private parts. They are good friends and agree to go in Suzie's bedroom and look at each other's private parts. A friend of theirs sees them.

1. What do you think the friend does? Will the friend who sees them tell anyone? Why? Why not?
2. Is what Johnny and Suzie did okay? Why? Why not?
3. If two good friends agree to look at each others' private parts would that ever be considered sexual abuse? If so, who is the abuser and who is the victim?

Virtually all children said the friend would tell because what the children were doing was 'not right,' 'bad,' 'wrong.'

The vast majority of children said that Johnny and Suzie were both abusers. A few said they were both 'victims and abusers.' Only two said they had not hurt one another.

The first author evaluated a child (10 years old) in November 2003 who was just entering into individual therapy. He was living at home with his grandmother. He had been removed from his mother for neglect. As part of the evaluation he responded to a series of vignettes. He had been in group therapy for sexual behaviour problems.

Vignette: Two children (10 years old) agreed to kiss. The teacher caught them on the far side of the playground.

1. What will the teacher do?
2. Will the teacher tell anyone else?

The child said that the teacher would call the police and the boy would be taken to jail for sexual harassment. When he was reminded they had agreed to kiss and was asked if this made a difference in his answer he said 'no.' 'He sexually abused her.' This young boy had little or no concept of consensual sexual behaviours between two children. The boy's saying the boy is the abuser is consistent with a gender bias ascribing abusive behaviour to males more often than to females.

It is of great concern that children's experiences of sex and sexuality are being pathologised

(Krivacska, 1991; Okami, 1992). The concepts of 'good touch' and 'bad touch' have become equated in many children's minds as 'good touch' is 'healthy touch' and 'bad touch' is 'sexual touch.' Many children see everything that has to do with sex as being 'bad,' 'dangerous,' and/or 'harmful.' Some programmes for children with sexual behaviour problems have 'sexual behaviour rules' that the children learn. Children who are in the groups have broken a rule and need to talk about this and listen to other children talk about the rules they broke. These rules often leave the children feeling that anything that has to do with sex and sexuality is 'wrong' or 'rule breaking.' Healthy sexual behaviours are generally not discussed.

An additional concern about the treatment process for children with sexual behaviour problems is that many programmes have 'no touch' policies. This is sometimes true in group treatment, day treatment and residential care. In these programmes there is to be no physical contact at any time between the children. In a very few programmes this policy relaxes as the child learns how to have healthy and nonintrusive physical contact. Other programmes, perhaps the majority, never allow touch. Some programmes tell children they are in a bubble and their bubble is not to touch the bubble of any other child. Some use a hula-hoop analogy in much the same way. One programme said that the children could not come within an arm's length of any other child. What are we teaching the children about themselves? Touching is dangerous? They are dangerous? All touching is sexual touching, which is dangerous? They cannot control themselves and so they cannot touch anyone? They will never control themselves, so they can never touch anyone? Once you engage in a 'bad touch' you will remain dangerous? The negative self-percepts are endless.

There are also elementary schools with 'no touch' policies in the United States where children are literally not to touch one another. Many schools have sexual harassment prevention programmes that are taught to all of the students. Students can be suspended or expelled for sexually harassing another child. In a book entitled *STOP IT NOW-A Guide For the Prevention of Sexual Harassment* the following behaviours are given as examples of sexual harassment: (Davis, 1998)

For K-2nd grade

'I am in second grade. I like school but I don't like it that two of the girls in my class keep trying to hug me and tell me that I am 'cute.' One of them kissed me in the hall. I want them to stop it!'

For grades 3–6

Jamal picks up the phone and hears a girl giggling. The girl says, 'I want to kiss you.' This is the sixth call Jamal has gotten from the girl today, even though he has asked her to leave him alone.

Behaviours such as in the above examples have been happening in schools forever. While they may need to stop, examples such as these trivialise and over generalise the term sexual harassment. Just as with using the term 'perpetrator' for a young child with sexual behaviour problems, using the term 'sexual harassment' for normal childhood behaviours is problematic. Children's behaviours related to sex and sexuality are not the same as adults' sexual behaviours. The intent, motivation and pleasure seeking are not the same as adults. It is essential to understand children's thinking about sex and sexuality and not confuse it with adult sexuality. When a young girl calls a boy and says she wants to kiss him, or tells a boy he is cute and hugs him, she is not intending any harm, nor would she think that any harm could come to him. She is not thinking about sex in a negative or hurtful way. She (and likely her friends) is having fun. They are giggling as they engage in the childhood games between the genders. We must not pathologise behaviours that have occurred over the centuries and for which there is no evidence of harm. The behaviour should not be encouraged but the child should not be made to feel stigmatised as a bad person.

Assessment

This section will not instruct the reader 'how to' do an assessment but rather discusses issues that have arisen over the last 20 years that modifies the focus of previous assessments.

Data gathering

All children with behaviour problems require a thorough assessment of their early life history, prenatal care, prenatal drug exposure, developmental milestones, day-care, school history including performance both academically and interpersonally, any behavioural or psychological problems and when they arose, child and family's strengths and weaknesses, primary caretakers, attachment figures, problems with siblings, deaths, divorces and incarcerations of parents or parental figures, out-of-home placements, etc.. Checklists such as the Child Behaviour Checklist and the Trauma Symptom Checklist are very good normed instruments for gathering additional behavioural information. These can be used to establish a baseline and used again later in treatment.

Previously it was believed that being a victim of sexual abuse was the main determinant for developing sexual behaviour problems. Consistent with recent research (Friedrich, 2002; Friedrich, Davies et al, Silovsky and Nice, 2002) on children with sexual behaviour problems, Kordich-Hall (Hall, Mathews et al., 1998) found a significant relationship between children with interpersonal sexual behaviour problems and multiple forms of abuse (sexual, physical and emotional), single parent (mother), high stress, and poor boundaries regarding privacy and sexuality.

Based on our current understanding, assessment of a child with sexual behaviour problems should investigate all forms of abuse and neglect. Domestic violence should be investigated as this is almost universal in the histories of children who sexually abuse (Johnson, 1998a). The assessor should no longer feel that the answer has been found to the child's troubles, just because the child has disclosed sexual abuse. This is particularly true if the sexual abuse happened many years previously. If a child, 12 and under, is going to show problematic sexual behaviours, it is more likely to happen in close proximity to the sexual abuse rather than years later.

For instance, if a foster mother complains that her eight year old foster child who was sexually abused at three has just started masturbating excessively, there are more plausible explanations to pursue than the sexual abuse five years earlier. While all avenues should be explored, including any lingering issues related to sexual abuse, environmental, emotional and physical issues in the child's current circumstances should not be excluded. For instance, what is 'excessive' masturbation to the foster mother? Is the boy masturbating in public? Is he trying to be discrete? When did this start? Are there older children in the foster home? What is the sexual environment in the foster home? Has he been evaluated for any medical conditions? Does he have other behaviours that are impulsive and unplanned? Is the masturbation planned to annoy someone? How long has he been in this foster home? Did he do this in previous foster homes?

There are endless circumstances in the present that may be coming into play with newly discovered masturbatory behaviour that might have something to do with the early sexual abuse or nothing to do with it. Since the problem is in the present, it is best to look for the solution in the present. If the behaviour is linked emotionally with the past, the child can learn that later. Telling a child (or adult) she is doing something today because of something that happened when she was three provides no relief. If the events are connected, we learn the present precipitants, help the child get them under control and then deal with latent emotional issues.

Recent research points us to the parents' and the child's environment as important in the etiology of the child's problems. This is particularly salient if the child is living with biological parents who may have a history of abuse, neglect or domestic violence that is making them less able to deal with their child's problems. Some parents had a history of sexual behaviour problems themselves that may impinge on their ability to help their children. Since the parents will need to provide a stable environment for the children to heal, assessment and remediation of issues for the parents will be important (Johnson, 1998a).

Research findings also point us to a thorough evaluation of the child's environment. There are several instruments that have been developed for this purpose. The Family Practices Questionnaires (Johnson, 1998b) ask parents/caregivers of the child up to what age they believe children and parents should sleep, shower, bathe, and change clothes together; kiss on the mouth, give full body hugs, etc. The Family Roles, Relationships, Behaviours and Practices Questionnaire (Johnson, 1998b) is four pages of items regarding emotional, physical and sexual boundary violations from the fairly benign to more egregious. For both questionnaires each parent is separately asked to indicate which of these occurred in the home in which they grew up. In subsequent clinical interviews, the parents are told that most parents parent the way they were brought up. It is very usual for parents to bring into their own home, the same practices that were engaged in their family of origin. Each parent is then asked which of the boundary violations occur in their present home.

The first two pages of the Family Roles, Relationships, Behaviours and Practices Questionnaire (Johnson, 1998b) is used with children eight and older. These can be used to check on the parent's veracity. Most children are more truthful than their parents. The items on the questionnaire were developed through work with the families of children with sexual behaviour problems and can be used throughout treatment. These boundary violations are often the substrata for the anxiety and confusion that the children are acting out in their worrisome sexual behaviours.

There are two instruments that have been developed specifically to assess children's sexual behaviours: the Child Sexual Behaviour Inventory (CSBI) (Friedrich, 1997) and the Child Sexual Behaviour Checklist (CSBCL) (Johnson, 1998c). The CSBI was initially developed to try to distinguish between sexually abused and nonsexually abused children. It has approximately 34 items. There is normative data that indicates from the sample of mothers of nonsexually abused children the frequency with which they saw each of the sexual behaviours listed. There is also data that indicates which behaviours are developmentally unexpected.

The CSBCL offers a descriptive history or summary record of a child's sexual behaviours from the perspective of the parents or caregivers. Part I of the CSBCL contains over 150 behaviours of children related to sex and sexuality ranging from natural and healthy childhood sexual exploration to behaviours of children experiencing severe difficulties in the area of sexuality. Part II asks about aspects of the child's life which might increase the frequency of sexual behaviours, e.g., access to pornography, the Internet, nudity, abuse history, sleeping and bathing arrangements and whether the child has seen violence between people he or she knows. Part III provides a more detailed description of sexual behaviours engaged in with other children. Part IV should be completed by the therapist/evaluator with the parent/caregiver if it appears the child may have a sexual behaviour problem. This section is comprised of 26 characteristics of children's sexual behaviours that raise concern. The seriousness of the child's sexual behaviour problems increases in direct proportion to the number and type of the characteristics that fit the child's sexual behaviours. The 26 characteristics fall into nine factors that indicate where the child's problems are, if the child has problem sexual behaviour. The factors are as follows:

1. Child's sexual development is different than same age peers.
2. Child shows anxiety, guilt, and/or shame about sex.
3. Child has a greater than expected emphasis on sex and sexuality.
4. Child does not respond to limit setting.
5. Child is confused regarding sexual boundaries.
6. Child shows adult-like sexual behaviours.
7. Child disregards or objectifies others.
8. Child has angry feelings about sex.
9. Child uses coercion or hurts others with sex.

Part IV of the CSBCL was developed to assist the evaluator to use more than the advanced nature of the sexual behaviour to determine if the behaviour is abusive. The nine factors on the CSBCL can be used to help distinguish the type, frequency, range and level of severity of the child's sexual problems.

There are projective tests such as the Roberts Apperception Test (Roberts, 1982) and the Projective Storytelling Cards (Caruso, 1987) that can be useful in understanding how the child sees relationships between adults and children, parents, boyfriends and girlfriends, siblings, and play-mates. The child's world-view often arises out of the stories given in response to the projective cards. Issues of violence, sexuality, love, hatred, vengeance, and jealousy often arise. While these stories cannot be taken at face value, repeated themes can form the basis of hypotheses to explore with the child.

It is also important to gather information on the siblings or children living in the home with the child with sexual behaviour problems. It may be that the identified child was caught engaging in problematic sexual behaviours with a neighbour but is also engaging in problematic sexual behaviours with siblings or relatives. It is possible that there is a sibling with sexual behaviour problems who initiated the present behaviour with this child. Older siblings may be exposing younger siblings to sexual material or experiences that are too advanced for the child. Interviewing all of the siblings of a child always provides a good balance of information about the child, parents and home-life.

Every effort should be made to get accurate information about the other children involved in the sexual behaviours, their social and sexual history with the identified child, any sexual or behavioural problems they have, their account of what happened leading up to the known behaviours and their detailed account of the actual behaviours that brought the identified child for evaluation. It will be important to know where the behaviours occurred, why they occurred there, who decided on the behaviours, who else was present, had the children done these before at any one else's suggestion, etc. (Johnson, 1992).

Assessment techniques such as the polygraph and plethysmograph sometimes used with adult and adolescent offenders are not suitable for use with children. There is inadequate base-line data on children to determine what is normal and not normal responding.

Interviewing clinicians about what they have learned in working with children with sexual behaviour problems always brings forth the exclamation, 'don't rely on the referral information!' This caveat is exceptionally important when working with young children and sexual issues. Initial investigators have very little time when sent out on a call about a child engaging in sexual behaviours. They determine what they need for their agency and send the matter on. Some children look very frightening and highly pathological on paper. This may occur because as adults we fill in the gaps in information the way we would if the child were an adult doing the sexual things noted. It is also possible that the facts that were available were misconstrued and the investigator saw everything from the point of view of an adult offender and did not take into account child sexuality. There are many, many cases where the facts are wrong, the previous history of the children is not known, the child's motivation for the behaviour is not understood, and a child is named a perpetrator or predator based on the type of behaviour attempted or engaged in. Each person doing an assessment of a child with sexual behaviour problems should try to get as many source documents as possible and talk to as many people who know the child well over as long a period as possible, and get people who are in every day contact with the child for extended periods to fill out (with proper authorisation) the CSBI or the CSBCL.

Each data gathering instrument should be completed by as many people who know the child as possible (with proper authorisation). It is helpful if people outside the family, including the schoolteacher fills out the CSBI or CSBCL and the CBCL. Different people report different things depending on when and under what circumstances they see the child, and their input provides perspective. The greater the number of informants, the broader the perspective. It is possible that some behaviours, including sexual behaviour, only occur under certain circumstances. This will be important for understanding the child's sexual behaviour and treatment planning.

Identifying the seriousness of the child's problematic sexual behaviour

After detailed assessment, it is helpful to have some framework in which to conceptualise the child and family so that a treatment plan can be developed. While empirically derived typologies have not been successful to date (Chaffin, Letourneau et al., 2002), a clinically derived continuum of sexual behaviours has provided a rudimentary template for understanding the myriad of different sexual behaviours of young children. This continuum attempts to categorise the sexual behaviours of children, 12 and younger, into four large groups. The first group is 'natural and healthy sexual behaviours' (see definition under section above entitled, 'Not Normal' Sexual Behaviour is not Necessarily Abusive) that is by far the largest group; the next three pertain to children with problematic sexual behaviour. These three groups are: 'sexually-reactive,' 'children engaged in extensive mutual sexual behaviours,' and 'children who sexually abuse.' Children, if they move from group one where each child starts, first move to being 'sexually-reactive.' No child goes from group one to being sexually abusive, group four. If there is movement out of group one, it is to group two. If children's behaviour becomes more serious, generally due to a lack of attachment and a feeling of abandonment to caring adults, children can move to group three or group four.

Most children who engage in problematic sexual behaviours fall into the category of 'sexually-reactive.' 'Sexually-reactive' children engage in self-stimulating behaviours and also engage in sexual behaviours with other children and, sometimes, with adults. Generally, this type of sexual behaviour is in response to environmental cues that are overly stimulating or reminiscent of previous abuse or feelings that reawaken traumatic or painful memories. The child may respond directly by masturbating or engaging in other sexual behaviours alone or with others. Hiding the sexual behaviours or finding friends to engage in the behaviours in private may not always be possible as the sexual behaviour is a way of coping with overwhelming feelings of which they cannot make sense. The behaviours are often impulsive but are sometimes planned. Sexually reactive behaviour is often not within the full conscious control of the child. In some situations children are trying to make sense of something sexual done to them by doing it to someone else. These children do not coerce others into sexual behaviours but act out their confusion on them. Many of these children do not understand their own or others' rights to privacy. While there is no intent to hurt or be mean to others, receiving sexual behaviours can be confusing for the other child and may feel like a violation or abuse (Johnson, 1998a).

Because 'sexually-reactive' children may impulsively act out on other children, they are often confused with children who sexually abuse. Yet, the 'sexually-reactive' child has no ill feelings toward the other child, and does not think he can or will hurt the other child. The 'sexually-reactive' child is trying to work out his own premature sexualisation or confusion about sexual matters. (It can occur that a child with whom a 'sexually-reactive' child acts out can feel victimised, based on his or her history; where the 'sexually-reactive' child had no intention to harm the child.)

Consider the boys, ages nine and seven, whose mother is an alcoholic and drug addict and leaves the boys alone frequently. One night she leaves them with a four-year-old girl cousin while she is 'partying.' The children find a pornographic video and watch it. Later that night the boys hump the little girl and each tries to put his penis inside her. A neighbour who can see the children from his window reports to the police that all the children were laughing and giggling while this went on. It lasted about 2–3 minutes. After interviews and testing, no history of other sexual problems was found for any of the children. They were doing relatively well at school and had no problems with peers at home or at school. There was a history of ADHD for the nine-year-old. The little girl was not traumatised, said she thought it was fun and had no after effects that could be noted. The major problem was the mother's neglect and lack of supervision with pornographic videos readily available. The initial evaluator agreed with the facts, as just stated, but encouraged adjudication based on the advanced nature of the sexual behaviours.

The second group of children with sexual behaviour problems that is seen in clinical populations is 'children who engage in extensive, mutual sexual behaviours.' Often distrustful, chronically hurt and abandoned by adults, they relate best to other children. In the absence of close, supportive relationships to adults, the sexual behaviours become a way of making a connection to other children. They use sex as a way to cope with their feelings of abandonment, hurt, sadness, anxiety, and often despair. These children do not coerce other children into sexual behaviours but find other similarly lonely children who will engage with them. Almost all of these children have been emotionally abused and neglected. All have lived in sexualised environments with no real parental supervision and love. They look to other children to help meet their emotional needs and their need for physical contact (Johnson, 1998a). All of these children have previously been 'sexually reactive' children who are now using sexual behaviour as a coping mechanism to cope with their overwhelming fears of abandonment and potential annihilation.

John, a ten-year-old, and Jim, an eleven-year-old, are both boys at a residential treatment facility. Jim and John became friends at the residential unit. Both were emotionally needy and confused. Late one night a staff member caught Jim and John in the bathroom with Jim applying Vaseline to his penis while standing behind John. Jim was a year older than John, much bigger, more aggressive, and was standing in a position to insert his penis in John's rectum. It was for these reasons that it was decided that Jim was an offender and John was the intended victim.

Before entering the facility, John lived with his mother and stepfather. John's mother had been physically, emotionally, and sexually abused as a child and had given birth to John when she was seventeen and unmarried. She worked hard to keep John and his sister at home and safe but eventually married a man who was physically and emotionally abusive.

Child protective services removed John and his sister from their mother and stepfather because

the children were engaging in sexual behaviour with one another. The social workers were unaware of any emotional, sexual, or physical abuse the children might have endured when they removed them from their home. The children were placed in separate institutions for fear that they would continue to engage in sexual behaviours if they remained together. John was very depressed, anxious, and fearful when he entered the residential centre. John missed his sister and asked to see her frequently. His requests were denied. John didn't ask about his mother or stepfather. He wasn't actively aggressive toward staff or other children and although superficially compliant, at most times he was distrustful and emotionally disconnected from staff.

Jim was brought to the residential centre after being hospitalised for severe depression and suicidal ideation. He alternated between being physically aggressive with his peers, and being totally withdrawn. He'd been abandoned as a young child by his mother and father and lived off and on in foster care for many years. On several occasions Jim was returned to his mother only to be removed due to her drug and alcohol problems. Jim was emotionally and physically neglected by his mother and often left alone for long periods when his mother went on binges. In the last four foster homes Jim had engaged in sexually reactive behaviours with other foster children. When they were caught, they were punished. In one of his foster homes, Jim's hands had been tied to the sides of his bed to stop him from masturbating when he was falling asleep at night.

When interviewed about the incident in the bathroom with the vaseline, both John and Jim said it was the other one's idea, both said they wanted to do it, both denied being forced, and both said it made them feel better. Jim, the 11-year-old, was not believed and it was felt that John, the 10-year-old, was intimidated into silence. Jim was removed to a sexual offender treatment programme.

Both John and Jim are examples of children engaged in extensive but mutual sexual behaviours. Jim started out as a sexually reactive child, but moved into group three as he became more alienated from his family and more despairing about adults. Sex had become an important part of his life. The only close and comforting relationship he had had was with an adult neighbour who sexually abused him at one of his foster homes; he did not share this fact with anyone. Confusing sex with caring and love, he sought out John as a source of emotional and physical comfort. John and his sister had been physically and sexually abused on a regular basis by their stepfather. Their stepfather frequently accused John of having sexual thoughts about his mother. John had already engaged in a sexual relationship with his sister before he left home. He and his sister clung to each other in a sexual way to overcome the abandonment feelings in the highly charged sexual environment of their home.

Both John and Jim had engaged in many problematic sexual behaviours alone and with other children before seeking each other out. Their sexual contact was being used as a coping mechanism for the depression, disconnectedness, and despair they both felt. Both boys denied any homosexual feelings. Yet when living in a dorm full of boys, they felt temporary relief while engaging in the sexual behaviours. John and his sister and then John and Jim are examples of children engaged in extensive, mutual sexual behaviours who use sex to cope with their intense alienation and feelings of abandonment and aloneness in a scary world.

The third group of children who have sexual behaviour problems are children who molest (Johnson, 1998a).There has been difficulty with an over identification of children engaging in problematic sexual behaviours being labelled as sexual abusers. There are only a small number of children who engage in sexually abusive behaviour. To reduce confusion about the criteria used to define a child who is sexually abusive, the following definition is provided.

Children, eleven years and under who sexually abuse and meet all of the following criteria:

1. A child, eleven years or younger, who intentionally touches the sexual organs or other intimate parts of another person, or orchestrates other children into sexual behaviours.
2. The child's problematic sexual behaviours have occurred across time and in different situations.
3. The child has demonstrated a continuing unwillingness to accept 'no' when pressing another person to engage in sexual activity.
4. The child's motivation for engaging in the sexual behaviour is to act out negative emotions toward the person with whom he or

she engages in the sexual behaviour, to upset a third person (such as parent of a sibling), or to act out generalised negative emotions using sex as the vehicle. There are a few children who are cut off from their own and other's emotions and orchestrate children into sexual behaviours to control them.
5. The child uses force, fear, physical or emotional intimidation, manipulation, bribery, and/or trickery to coerce another person into sexual behaviour.
6. The child's problematic sexual behaviour is unresponsive to consistent adult intervention and supervision. (See number four below.)

The following are important points related to children who molest:

1. When children are asked if they know if it is right or wrong to engage in sexual behaviours, they universally say it is wrong. By this statement, they do not mean that sexual behaviour is wrong because it is abusive or against the law. They mean that children are not supposed to engage in sexual behaviour. Children almost universally receive negative reactions from adults when they use bad words, tell dirty jokes, try to watch others engaged in sexual behaviours, look at R-rated movies or magazines with naked pictures, or touch their own or others' genitals. Even children who are not castigated consistently for these types of behaviours know they are 'wrong' for children to do.

   The response by adults to children's sexual expression is complicated by adults' apparent acceptance of sexual messages via the media that bombard children and enter virtually every home. In the homes of children who sexually abuse, there are almost always sexual, physical and emotional boundary violations that impinge directly on them propagated by the adults with whom they live.
2. Sections in laws about sexual offences written for adolescents and adults refer to touching that is done with the specific intent to arouse, appeal to, or gratify the lust, passions, or sexual desires of either person. Sexual arousal and/or sexual pleasure may or may not be involved when children engage in behaviours related to sex and sexuality. Most frequently, it is not involved. A child can sexually abuse another child without any intention for sexual arousal.
3. Any sexual behaviours from kissing to penetrative acts can constitute abusive

behaviour. Sexual abuse is not defined by the sexual behaviour alone. For instance, oral-genital contact or humping by young children does not necessarily constitute sexual abuse, whereas it would be sexual abuse if done by an adult with a child. Oral-genital contact or humping by young children is sexual abuse, if it fits all of the criteria of the definition.

4. Many children who engage in abusive sexual behaviour will stop the behaviour after they are placed in a stable environment and learn healthy emotional, physical and sexual boundaries. Therefore, it is important to reassess the child prior to each court report to determine if the child remains at risk for aggressive sexual behaviour, and whether the intervention plan, including placement, is the least restrictive and the most health producing.

5. Children sexually abuse children as well as people older than themselves. The age and size differential are not definers of whether or not a child has molested.

Treatment of children with sexual behaviour problems

There has been a tendency in all realms of working with children with sexual behaviour problems to equate them with adult and adolescent sexual offenders. Because the sexual behaviours are similar, there is a temptation to use treatment techniques with children akin to those used with older clients. Even as late as 1995, professionals were suggesting 'a modified version of adult offender treatment' for children and adolescents (Cashwell and Bloss, 1995). As late as 2000, assessment and treatment of adolescents and children were considered to be so similar that separate sections were not written to describe them (Shaw, 2000).

It has become crystal clear that children with sexual behaviour problems are not just miniature versions of adult and adolescent sexual offenders. In the first place, the variation in the severity of the problems is much greater. Most importantly, only one subset of children with sexual behaviour problems, children who molest, engages in abusive sexual behaviours. The majority of children with sexual behaviour problems are not coercing other children into sexual behaviours. Hence, therapy that is based on reducing sexual offending completely misses the mark for most children with sexual behaviour problems. Even

when working with children who sexually abuse, the strong confrontation used with adult offenders is not justifiable. There is no evidence that it will work with children (Marshall, Serran et al., 2002; Marshall, Fernandez et al., 2003; Marshall, Serran et al., 2003).

The first published group treatment approach (Johnson and Berry, 1989) proposed parallel treatment of the children who molested and their parents. Based on a cognitive-behavioural model, the children were grouped by age and gender with structured experiential exercises aimed at increasing their self-management skills (problem-solving, anxiety reduction, self-soothing, etc.) and gaining a cognitive understanding of their problematic sexual behaviour and interpersonal problems. The parallel parents' group focused on boundary issues, parenting skills, parent-child relationships and healthy sexuality. Issues of all forms of abuse were addressed in both the parents' and the children's groups. A great deal of attention was paid to integrating the group work with the child and family's home, school life and day-care.

There have been two randomised clinical studies of children (ages 6 to 12) with sexual behaviour problems funded by the National Center on Child Abuse and Neglect (NCCAN). One was in Oklahoma (Bonner, Walker et al., 1999; Bonner, Walker et al., 1999) and the other in Vermont (Gray, Busconi et al., 1997; Pithers, 1998). Each programme tested two different treatment methods on randomly assigned children and parents. In the Bonner study (http://w3.ouhsc.edu/ccan/CSBP) 12 sessions of either a structured cognitive-behavioural approach or an unstructured psychodynamic play therapy approach was used for both the children and in parallel groups for the parents/caretakers. In the cognitive-behavioural approach sexual behaviours were mentioned frequently; in the unstructured approach, sexual behaviours were only discussed if brought up by the clients. Both had approximately the same success in decreasing problematic sexual behaviours.

In the Pithers' study (Pithers, Gray et al., 1998; Pithers, 1998) 32-week group treatment programmes were compared: a structured relapse prevention programme and a sexual behaviour focused expressive therapy programme. Parallel caregiver groups were provided. There were no appreciable differences in the results based on reduction of sexual behaviours. Pithers did conclude that relapse prevention treatment is not useful for children with generic sexual behaviour problems. He thought it might be useful, with many modifications, for some severely traumatised and/or sexually aggressive children.

Four different treatment methodologies were used between the two programmes with no significant differences in rate of reoccurrence of the problematic sexual behaviours. Therefore, there are no research-based guidelines that can be offered as far as the best theoretical framework on which to base treatment. The one thing that was consistent between the programmes was the presence of at least one parent in parallel treatment groups. As has been found in the work of Johnson (Johnson and Berry, 1989; Johnson, 1998), the work with the parents was very important (Chaffin, Letourneau et al., 2002).

Unfortunately, this co-ordination of the treatment of children with their parents is not always done. Some practitioners attempt to treat children with sexual behaviour problems in isolation from their parents or caregivers. This may be due to their conceptualisation of the problem. If the clinician believes that the problem resides within the child or because of an event that has happened to him/her, and believes that the child has the strength to overcome the problem with help of the therapist alone, the work may proceed without the child's parents or caretakers. The problems of young children with sexual behaviour problems generally emanate not from within, but from circumstances in their lives. Because the home environment, including the parents and others they bring into the home, are often a significant factor in precipitating and sustaining the sexual behaviour, working with the parents/caretakers is essential.

Young children with sexual behaviour problems are generally trying to solve feelings of confusion, anxiety, shame, or anger about sex and sexuality through their acting out. It takes the form of sexual behaviour due to sexualised circumstances that have occurred in their young lives. These children need adults who understand them and to whom they can talk who will help solve their problems. Fundamental to the problem is generally a lack of close attachment of the children to the parents/caregivers. The parents are not attuned to the children's needs and worries. As the children become more overwhelmed by the circumstances in their lives and do not feel that their parents will take care of them, they attempt to solve their problems on

their own. Unable to do this, they escalate and eventually come to the attention of the authorities.

If the children live with their biological parents and have grown up with them, the parents and the environment they provide will likely be a significant part of the problem and therefore, a major part of the solution. Young children's sexual behaviour problems evolve from what has happened to them, as well as from what they have learned and seen when growing up. The children need a healthy sexual environment with good boundaries and parents who support their growth to overcome sexual behaviour problems. Working with the parents to determine the elements in the child's relationship to them and boundary issues in the environment that may be fundamental to the child's problems will be essential. The parents will be needed to help the child decrease the problematic sexual behaviours. A modified behaviour management approach with the target behaviours, reinforcers, and substitute behaviours decided on by the parents and the child together has been found to be highly effective in decreasing problematic sexual behaviours. If the children's sexual problems have arisen out of confusion due to extra familial sexual abuse or other inappropriate sexual exposure outside the home, the child's parents will need to be active agents in the child's learning to change.

If the child lives in a foster home, it is important to involve the foster parents. Children need to learn skills and be supported by their caregivers in modifying problematic sexual behaviours. A plan will need to be developed with the child and foster parents to assist the child in achieving their treatment goals. If there are problems in the foster home that are causing or exacerbating the child's sexual behaviour problems, these problems need to be assessed and changes put in place. Even if there are no problems in the foster home, a plan will need to be developed with the child and foster parents to decrease the sexual behaviours.

If the child lives in a residential facility with rotating staff, it is important to have the same caregiver transport the child to therapy and take a strong interest in the child's development. Fostering an attachment between the caregiver and the child will assist the child in understanding relationships and help her or him feel less isolated and alone. In some cases the sexual behaviour with another child is an attempt to feel attached to someone (Johnson, 1998a). This attachment should be to adults, not children.

Placement in residential care that is specifically focused on the sexual behaviour problems will only be appropriate for a very few children. The problems in young children who exhibit problematic sexual behaviours are very broad. In only a few cases will the sexual behaviours be a central issue. Focusing too much attention on the sexual aspect may put too much emphasis where it is not needed and fixate the child on that aspect of his or her development.

A problem that frequently arises with the placement of children in programmes specifically focused on sexual behaviours is that children are placed with adolescents who sexually offend. Due to developmental differences and differences in types and severity of sexual problems, the younger children are exposed to pathology that is far beyond their own and developmentally too advanced. Children who are not sexually offending but have less serious problems should never be placed with adolescents who sexually offend. Even children who are sexually abusing should never be put with older adolescents. Some residential facilities house 9–14-year-olds together. The developmental differences from a social/emotional perspective and differences in sexual feelings, attitudes and behaviours between 9–10-year-olds and 13–14-year-olds are too great. The younger children will be negatively affected.

Whereas many people feel that once a child has sexual behaviour problems he or she will continue, this is not the case. The sexual behaviour problems of most children are very amenable to treatment. As demonstrated in the programmes funded by NCCAN, only about 15% of the children engaged in the problematic sexual behaviours after the 12-week treatment. Some children's problems require greater assistance and always in combination with their parents/caregivers.

The level of seriousness of the child's sexual behaviours and the strengths and weaknesses of the child's family are essential in determining the treatment. Treatment will need to be fashioned for the child and family. When children are grouped together for treatment it is advised that children who sexually abuse not be in the same groups as children who do not abuse. The thinking, emotional problems, level of severity of other behaviour problems and complexity of the family's problems are generally far greater than those of children with lesser sexual behaviour problems.

Whether the child and parents need individual, group or family therapy and in what combination will depend on the assessment of the child and family's problems. All children with sexual behaviour problems will need family work during the treatment process. When there are other children in the family, or sibling incest occurs, the safety of all of the siblings using the support of the parents will be a significant part of the family work. Whereas some providers recommend not telling the other children in the family, whether it be a biological or foster family, about the events that have occurred is ill-advised. Openness, with sensitivity, compassion and objectivity is far better than secrecy. It helps the child with the sexual behaviour problem know that others are there to help him or her stop engaging in problematic sexual behaviour.

When children with serious sexual problems may cause a risk to other children, the treatment will need to be co-ordinated with the school, day care and other locations. It is generally most helpful to develop a plan about how to manage the behaviours that can be operationalised in these other settings. It is not advisable to call a school principal or school counsellor and say a child is acting in sexual ways with other children without suggesting a safety plan based on the one developed in the overall treatment plan for the child. Some school officials will ask for the child to be removed from the school unless the treatment provider details a plan, and sometimes even if there is a detailed plan. This is likely due to schools being held liable in the United States based on the US Supreme Court decision (1999) Davis v. Monroe County if they allow a hostile learning environment to occur. One of the definitions of a hostile learning environment is not providing students with reasonable protection from sexual harassment from other students.

Safety planning should be based in a developmental context. The plan should meet the child's needs at the time and change as the child develops better self control, understands the parameters around sexual contact, and is capable of more freedom. Some plans leave children completely isolated from other children with no chance to develop the social skills they need as they grow and develop. The children then feel as if they are dangerous and pariahs.

When selecting treatment providers for children with sexual behaviour problems, the major criteria should be that they understand and relate to 'the child' in these children. For far too long, treatment providers have come from a background of working with adult or adolescent offenders and look for the 'offender' not 'the child.' It is far better to come to the work with an openness to learn and understand the children's problems from their perspective with no basic assumptions based on sexual offending in adults and adolescents.

Conclusion

Children with sexual behaviour problems are not miniature adult or adolescent sexual offenders. Only a very small number of these children are sexually offending; most are engaging in sexual behaviours which are developmentally too advanced and need to be curtailed. Not only is children's sexuality different than adults and adolescents, their emotional, social, and cognitive awareness and relationship to the world is different. It is dangerous to children that we do not recognise the differences and treat the child, not our projections onto the child.

References

Achenbach, T.M. (1983) *Manual for the Child Behavior Checklist and Revised Behavior Profile*. Burlington, University of Vermont.

Adams, J., McClellan, D. et al. (1995). Sexually Inappropriate Behaviours in Seriously Mentally Ill Children and Adolescents. *Child Abuse and Neglect*. 19: 5, 555–68.

Alexander, M. (1999). Sexual Offender Treatment Efficacy Revisited. *Sexual Abuse: A Journal of Research and Treatment*. 11: 2, 101–16.

Bonner, B., Walker, C.E. et al. (1999). *Treatment Manual for Cognitive-Behavioural Group Treatment for Parents/Caregivers of Children with Sexual Behaviour Problems*. Washington, D.C., National Clearinghouse on Child Abuse and Neglect Information.

Bonner, B., Walker, C.E. et al. (1999). *Treatment Manual for Dynamic Group Play Therapy for Children with Sexual Behaviour Problems and their Parent/Caregivers*. Washington, D.C, National Clearinghouse on Child Abuse and Neglect Information.

Burton, D.N.L. et al. (1997). Clinician's Views on Sexually Aggressive Children and Their Families: A Theoretical Exploration. *Child Abuse and Neglect*. 21: 2, 157–70.

Caruso, K. (1987). Projective Storytelling Cards. Redding, California, Northwest Psychological Publishers, Inc.

Cashwell, C. and Bloss, K. (1995). From Victim to Client: Preventing the Cycle of Sexual Reactivity. *School Counselor*. 42: 3, 233–40.

Chaffin, M., Letourneau, E. et al. (2002). Adults, Adolescents, and Children Who Sexually Abuse Children. *The APSAC Handbook on Child Maltreatment*. Myers, J., Berliner, L., Briere, J. et al. Thousand Oaks, Sage.

Davis, D. (1998). *STOP IT, NOW – A Guide for the Prevention of Sexual Harassment for Elementary School Children*. Seattle, Washington, Help Yourself Books.

Drach, K., Wientzen, et al. (2001). The Diagnostic Utility of Sexual Behaviour Problems in Diagnosing Sexual Abuse in a Forensic Child Abuse Evaluation Clinic. *Child Abuse and Neglect* 25: 489–503.

Finkelhor, D., Hotaling, G. et al. (1990). Sexual Abuse in a National Survey of Men and Women: Prevalence, Characteristics, and Risk Factors. *Child Abuse and Neglect* 14: 19–28.

Friedrich, W. (1997). *Child Sexual Behaviour Inventory Professional Manual*. Odessa, Florida, Psychological Assessment Resources, Inc.

Friedrich, W. (2002). Child Sexual Behaviour Inventory: Normative, Psychiatric and Sexual Abuse Comparisons. *Child Maltreatment* 6(1): 37–49.

Friedrich, W., Beilke, R. et al. (1988). Behaviour Problems in Young Sexually Abused Boys. *Journal of Interpersonal Violence* 3(1): 21–27.

Friedrich, W. and Chaffin, M. (2000). *Developmental-Systemic Perspectives on Children with Sexual Behaviour Problems*. Association for the Treatment of Sexual Abusers, San Diego.

Friedrich, W. and Fehrer, E. *Correlates of Behaviour Problems in a Clinical Sample of Sexually Abused Children*.

Friedrich, W., Fisher, E. et al. (1998). Normative Sexual Behaviour in Children: A Contemporary Sample. *Paediatrics* 101: 4.

Friedrich, W., Grambsch, P. et al. (1991). Normative Sexual Behaviour in Children. *Paediatrics* 88(3): 456–64.

Friedrich, W., Grambsch, P. et al. (1992). The Child Sexual Behaviour Inventory: Normative and Clinical Comparisons. *Psychological Assessment* 4(3): 303–11.

Friedrich, W. and Luecke, W. (1988). Young School-Age Sexually Aggressive Children.

Professional Psychology Research and Practice 19(2): 155–64.

Friedrich, W. N., Davies, W. et al. (2003). Sexual Behaviour Problems in Preteen Children: Developmental, Ecological, and Behavioural Correlates. *Annals of the New York Academy of Sciences* 989: 95–104.

Gale, J., Thompson, R.J., Moran, T., and Sack, W.H. (1988). Sexual Abuse in Young Children: Its Clinical Presentation and Characteristic Patterns. 12: 163–70.

Gomes-Schwartz, B., Horowitz, J. M. et al. (1990). *Child Abuse: The Initial Effects*. Newbury Park, CA, Sage.

Gomes-Schwartz, B., Horowitz, J.M. et al. (1985). Sexual Abuse in Young Children. Its Clinical Presentation and Charateristic Patterns. *Child Abuse and Neglect* 12: 163–70.

Gray, A., Busconi, A. et al. (1997). Children with Sexual Behaviour Problems and Their Caregivers: Demographics, Functioning, and Clinical Patterns. *Sexual Abuse: A Journal of Research and Treatment* 9(4): 267–90.

Hall, D. K., Mathews, F. et al. (1998). Factors Associated with Sexual Behaviour Problems in Young Sexually Abused Children. *Child Abuse and Neglect* 22(10): 1045–63.

Hall, D. K., Mathews, F. et al. (1998). *Problematic Sexual Behaviour in Sexually Abused Children: A Preliminary Typology*. National Adolescent Perpetrator Network International Conference, Winnipeg.

Hall, D. K., Mathews, F. et al. (2002). Sexual Behaviour Problems in Sexually Abused Children: A Preliminary Typology. *Child Abuse and Neglect* 26: 289–312.

Hanson, K., Gordon, A. et al. (2002). First Report of the Collaborative Outcome Data Project on the Effectiveness of Psychological Treatment for Sex Offenders. *Sexual Abuse: A Journal of Research and Treatment* 14(2).

Hanson, R. K. and Slater, S. (1988). Sexual Victimization in the History of Sexual Abusers: A Review. *Annals of Sex Research* 1: 485–99.

Johnson, T. C. (1988). Child Perpetrators – Children Who Molest Other Children: Preliminary Findings. *Child Abuse and Neglect* 12: 219–29.

Johnson, T. C. (1991). Understanding the Sexual Behaviours of Young Children. *SIECUS Report* August/September.

Johnson, T. C. (1992). *Investigating Allegation of Sexual Behaviours Between Children*. 1101 Fremont Ave. South Pasadena, CA 91030, Author.

Johnson, T. C. (1993). *Sexual Behaviours: A Continuum*. Sexualized Children :Assessment and Treatment of Sexualized Children and Children Who Molest. Gil, E. and Johnson,T. C. Rockville, MD., Launch Press: 41–52.

Johnson, T. C. (1998b). *Treatment Exercises for Abused Children and Children With Sexual Behaviour Problems*. South Pasadena, CA, Author.

Johnson, T. C. (1998d). *Children Who Molest. Sourcebook of Treatment Programs for Sexual Offenders*, in Marshall, W., Hudson, S., Ward, T. and Fernandez, Y. New York, Plenum Press.

Johnson, T. C. (2004). *Understanding Children's Sexual Behaviours – What's Natural and Healthy*. South Pasadena, CA, Author.

Johnson, T. C. (1999). *Understanding Your Child's Sexual Behaviour*. Oakland, California, New Harbinger Publications.

Johnson, T. C. (2000). Children With Sexual Behaviour Problems. *SEICUS* 29(1): 35–39.

Johnson, T. C. (2003). *Assessment Packet for Children With Sexual Behaviour Problems*. 1101 Fremont Avenue, Suite 101, South Pasadena, California 91030.

Johnson, T. C. and Berry, C. (1989). Children who Molest Other Children: A Treatment Program. *Journal of Interpersonal Violence* 4(2): 185–203.

Johnson, T. C.,Huang, E. et al. (under review). A Retrospective Analysis of Children's Sexual Behaviours.

Kaufman, J. and Zigler, E. (1987). Do Abused Children Become Abusive Parents? *American Journal of Orthopsychiatry* 57(2): 186–92.

Kendall-Tackett, K., Williams, L. et al. (1993). Impact of Sexual Abuse on Children: A Review and Synthesis of Recent Empirical Studies. *Psychological Bulletin* 113(1): 164–80.

Krivacska, J. J. (1991). Child Sexual Abuse Prevention Programs; The Need for Childhood Sexuality Education. *SIECUS Report* 19(6): 1–7.

Marshall, W., Fernandez, Y. et al. (2003). Process Variables in the Treatment of Sexual Offenders: A Review of the Relevant Literature. *Aggression and Violent Behaviour: A Review Journal* 8(2): 205–34.

Marshall, W., Serran, G. et al. (2003). Therapist Characteristics in the Treatment of Sexual Offenders: Tentative Data on Their Relationship with Indices of Behaviour Changes. *Journal of Sexual Aggression* 9: 25–30.

Marshall, W., Serran, G. et al. (2002). Therapist Features in Sexual Offender Treatment: Their Reliable Identification and Influence on

Behaviour Change. *Clinical Psychology and Psychotherapy* 9: 395–405.

Milloy, C. (1998). Specialized Treatment for Juvenile Sex Offenders: A Closer Look. *Journal of Interpersonal Violence* 13(5): 653–56.

Okami, P. (1992). Child Perpetrators of Sexual Abuse: The Emergence of a Problematic Deviant Category. *The Journal of Sex Research* 29(1): 109–30.

Pithers, W., Gray, A. et al. (1998). Caregivers of Children with Sexual Behaviour Problems: Psychological and Family Functioning. *Child Abuse and Neglect* 22(2): 129–41.

Pithers, W. D., Gray, A., Busconi, A., Houchens, P. (1998). Children with Sexual Behaviour Problems: Identification of Five Distinct Child Types and Related Treatment Considerations. *Child Maltreatment* 3(4): 384–406.

Roberts, G. (1982). *Roberts Apperception Test.* Los Angeles, Western Psychological Services.

Savage, D. G. (2004). Teens' Miranda Rights Redefined. *New York Times.* New York.

Shaw, J. (2000). Summary of the Practice Parameters for the Assessment and Treatment of Children and Adolescents who are Sexually Abusive of Others. *Journal of the American Academy of Child and Adolescent Psychiatrists* 39(1): 127–30.

Silovsky, J. and Nice, L. (2002). Characteristics of Young Children with Sexual Behaviour Problems: A Pilot Study. *Child Maltreatment* 7(3).

Slusser, M. (1995). Manifestations of Sexual Abuse in Preschool-Aged Children. *Issues in Mental Health Nursing* 16: 481–91.

Steinberg, L. and Scott, E. (2003). Less Guilty by Reason of Adolescence. *American Psychologist* 58(12): 1009–18.

Widom, C. and Maxfield, M. (2001). *An Update on the Cycle of Violence.* National Institute of Justice Research in Brief, NCJRS: 14.

Worling, J. and Curwen, T. (2000). Adolescent Sexual Offender Recidivism: Success of Specialized Treatment and Implications for Risk Prediction. *Child Abuse and Neglect* 24(7): 965–82.

Chapter Four

Predictors of Criminal Activity in a Sample of Juvenile Sexual Aggressors of Children

Julie Carpentier, Jean Proulx and Patrick Lussier

Abstract

The aim of this study was to ascertain possible links between developmental and pre-crime factors and two criminal activity parameters, i.e., the level of coercion and the number of victims, in a sample of juvenile sexual aggressors of children. One hundred and two juvenile sexual aggressors who had committed offences against children were included in this study. According to hierarchic multiple regression and logistic regression analyses, the best predictors for the level of coercion were:

- The age of the victim.
- Aggressiveness during adolescence.
- Deviant sexual fantasies.

The best predictors for the number of victims were:

- The age of the subject.
- Physical abuse in childhood.
- Loneliness in adolescence.

In Canada, about 25% of sexual offences against children are committed by juvenile offenders (Health Canada, 1997). In the United States these rates are even higher, with juveniles committing almost half of all sexual offences against children each year (Becker and Kaplan, 1993). Socio-demographic, developmental, and clinical characteristics of juvenile sexual offenders have been studied for two decades, some of which are consistent over time and place.

Sexual abuse

Juvenile sexual offenders frequently have a history of sexual abuse in childhood. (Fehrenback et al., 1986). In fact, different studies observed rates between 40% and 80% (Becker and Hunter, 1997; Kahn and Chambers, 1991). Hunter and Figueredo (2000) attempted to explain why some sexually abused children become sexual offenders and others do not. They found that early victimisation, a high rate of abusive incidents, a long period between the first event and its report,

a lack of support after the disclosure of the abuse, as well as exposure to domestic violence are all negative factors positively associated with the development of a propensity to sexually abuse during adolescence.

Physical abuse and neglect

In a sample of 564 adult sexual offenders, Knight and Prentky (1993) found that sexual offenders of children who began their sexual criminal career in adolescence, had more often been sexually and physically victimised than those who began in adulthood. Fehrenbach et al. (1986) reported similar results and concluded that physical abuse and exposure to family violence contribute to the development of sexual violence in adolescence. Moreover, findings from a comparative study conducted with juvenile sexual offenders and juvenile non-violent, non-sexual offenders indicated that physical abuse rates were higher in the first group (Ford and Linney, 1995). However, a history of physical abuse did not differentiate juvenile sexual offenders from violent, non-sexual juvenile offenders.

Poor social skills

Several studies found that juvenile sexual offenders possess poor social skills (Becker, 1990; Cortoni and Marshall, 2001; Fehrenbach et al., 1986; Hunter and Figueredo, 2000; Jacob, McKibben and Proulx, 1993; Kahn and Chambers, 1991; Kenny, et al., 2001; Knight and Prentky, 1993; Laforest and Paradis, 1990; Långström and Grann, 2000). According to Cortoni and Marshall (2001), social isolation and poor attachment are correlated with a tendency to experience negative emotional states. In addition, sexual offenders of children, peers or adults engaged in sexual activities (deviant or not) following stressful situations more frequently than non-sexual, non-violent delinquents or violent, non-sexual delinquents. Finally, those with serious skill deficits used sexual behaviour as a prominent strategy to cope with their emotional distress. These offenders reported that sexual activity provided them with a pleasant experience, temporarily evacuating negative emotions. Thus, it would appear that juvenile offenders with deficits in social competence use sexuality to cope with intimacy and attachment problems.

Behaviour problems and personality disorders

Jacob (2000) reported that several juvenile sexual offenders suffered from psychopathologies, such as behaviour disturbance, hyperactivity, oppositional disorder, conduct disorder, Tourette's disorder, etc. Accordingly, Becker, Kaplan, Cunningham-Rathner and Kavoussi (1986) found that 55% of their juvenile sexual offender study group suffered from at least one personality disorder. Knight and Prentky (1993) observed that early onset sexual offenders distinguished themselves from late onset offenders by having committed a higher number of offences. Furthermore, Carpenter, Peed and Eastman (1995), using the MCMI (Millon Clinical Multiaxial Inventory), found that juvenile sexual offenders usually presented a high score on the antisocial scale. They concluded that sexual offenders were impulsive and tended to engage in antisocial behaviours.

Gretton et al. (2001) carried out a study on recidivism in a sample of juvenile sexual offenders (n = 220). Their results showed that a high score on the Hare Psychopathy Checklist: Youth Version (PCL: YV) was associated with sexual recidivism. Moreover, they found that offenders scoring high on the PCL: YV frequently escaped from carceral institutions, often broke probation rules, and recidivated within five years of the initial sexual assault. Finally, high scores on the PCL: YV were significantly associated with non-sexual criminal recidivism.

Deviant sexual fantasies

Hunter and Becker (1994) noted that studies investigating the link between deviant sexual fantasies and sexual abuse by adolescents are relatively scarce. Although not all juvenile sexual offenders have deviant sexual fantasies, those having them tend to deny or minimise having such fantasies, leading to frequent underreporting. A retrospective analysis carried out with 306 adult sexual offenders showed that

42% of the sample had fixed deviant sexual fantasies, i.e., since adolescence, their preferred sexual fantasies included children (Abel, 1984). In an attempt to explain the development of deviant preferences, Marshall and Eccles (1993) suggested that certain males were more vulnerable to deviant sexual scripts due to their personal history. According to classical conditioning theories, juveniles who pair deviant fantasies with masturbation may develop a deviant preferential pattern and acquire cognitive distortions leading to their first sexual offence. The authors proposed a second hypothesis, namely that the first offence is in fact a response to particular circumstances and opportunities. According to the Pavlovian theory, the conditioning process leading to the development of deviant sexual fantasies is the result of repeated sex offending.

Using phallometry, Murphy, DiLillo, Haynes and Steere (2001) investigated factors related to deviant sexual preferences in 71 juvenile sexual offenders. The best predictor of deviant sexual preferences was the interaction between the history of sexual abuse and the selection of a male victim. These results are in agreement with the finding that juveniles with frequent deviant sexual fantasies almost exclusively commit their offences on young boys (Marshall, Jones, Ward, Johnston and Barbaree, 1991).

Other characteristics of the offender

Among the characteristics reported in juvenile sexual offenders are: problems at school (Awad et al., 1984; Fehrenbach et al., 1986; Kahn and Chambers, 1991; Kenny et al., 2001; Laforest and Paradis, 1990) use of pornography (Hunter, 2000; Knight and Prentky, 1993) cognitive distortions supporting sexual offending against children (Becker and Kaplan, 1988; Kahn and Chambers, 1991; Knight and Prentky, 1993; Laforest and Paradis, 1990); and substance abuse (Campbell and Lerew, 2002; Epperly-Trudel, 1991; Hunter, 2000).

Characteristics of the victim

The majority of victims of juvenile sexual aggressors are female (Awad et al., 1984; Carpenter et al., 1995; David and Leitenberg, 1987; Dozois, 2000; Fehrenbach et al., 1986; Hunter and Figueredo, 1999; Laforest and Paradis, 1990; Rasmussen, 1999; Smith and Monastersky, 1986) while less than 25% are male

(Carpenter et al., 1995; Dozois, 2000; Rasmussen, 1999; Smith and Monastersky, 1986). However, as underlined above, the proportion of sexually victimised boys increased as the age of the victim decreased (Hornick et al., 1994; Becker et al., 1986; Murphy et al., 2001).

Relationship between offender and victim

In Fehrenbach et al.'s (1986) sample, 75% of sexual aggressions were committed by a person known to the victim or by a member of the family. However, only 4% of Prentky et al.'s (2000) subjects did not previously know their victim. Although rates varied across samples, juvenile offenders tended to commit their offence on children they knew (David and Leitenberg, 1987; Dozois, 1994; Fehrenbach et al., 1986; Hunter et al., 1994; Jacob et al., 1993; Prentky et al., 2000; Rasmussen, 1999; Ryan, Miyoshi, Metzner, Krugman and Fryer, 1996; Wieckowski, Hartsoe, Mayer and Shontz, 1998; Worling, 2001).

Use of force or coercion

According to Becker (1998), juvenile sexual offenders of peers or adults tended to use more physical force than juvenile sexual offenders of children. The same conclusion was reported by Fehrenbach et al. (1986). Moreover, abuses towards children are often perpetrated in a context of babysitting or against a family member, which could explain the scarcity of violent acts. Stermac and Mathews (1987) also suggested that physical force and threats are more commonly used with older victims.

Certain studies concluded that sexual aggression against female victims is more violent. In a sample of 514 Canadian juvenile offenders (Hornick et al., 1994), more than 39% used coercion (physical or verbal) during their offence. Moreover, 46% of the offences perpetrated against young girls were violent, compared to 28% against boys. Also, a study carried out by Lafortune (1996) showed that 33% of juvenile sexual offenders (n = 30) used physical violence (constraint, blows) during the offence. A study carried out with juvenile sexual offenders (n = 23) imprisoned at a maximum security psychiatric institution (Institut Philippe Pinel de Montréal) indicated that 44% of the subjects used violence, i.e., striking, injuring or using a weapon to attack the victim (Jacob et al., 1993). Finally, Johnson and Knight (2000) found two developmental

paths leading to sexual coercion. In the first path, sexual abuse and peer aggression favours sexual compulsivity. Physical abuse, alcohol abuse and peer aggression led to hypermasculinity, outlined in the second path. Both sexual compulsivity and hypermasculinity were related to sexual coercion through the presence of misogynist fantasies.

Number of victims

Juvenile sexual offenders usually commit several sexual offences before being denounced to authorities (Fehrenbach et al., 1986; Hornick et al., 1994). Out of a total of 297 subjects, Fehrenbach et al. (1986) found that more than 57% (n = 171) had committed more than one offence. Similarly, Mathews (1987) indicated that 64% of his sample had previously committed sexual crimes. However, Carpenter et al. (1995), in a sample of 36 sexual offenders, found that only 31% (n = 11) had committed at least one previous sexual offence.

The number of victims per offender varied according to different studies. The Institut Philippe Pinel de Montréal's sample of juvenile sexual offenders (Jacob et al., 1993) revealed an average of five victims and 35 offences per offender. Prentky et al.'s (2000) study established 132 known victims for 96 offenders, 20% (n = 25) of whom had more than one victim. Oakland Family Services in the United States estimated the average number of victims of a juvenile sexual offender during his criminal career to be seven. This average increased to 380 victims once the offender reached the age of 30 (Oakland Family Services, 2003).

Characteristics associated with recidivism

Certain characteristics of juvenile sexual offenders are associated with sexual recidivism (Kenny et al., 2001). For instance, learning difficulties at school (Kenny et al., 2001), as well as poor social skills (Hudson and Ward, 2000; Hunter and Figueredo, 2000; Kenny et al., 2001; Långström and Grann, 2000) were associated with a higher rate of sexual recidivism. Moreover, juvenile sexual offenders who experienced deviant sexuality (e.g., sexual abuse, exposure to inadequate sexual models) had more frequent deviant sexual fantasies, as well as a higher rate of sexual recidivism compared to those who did not (Kenny et al., 2001). In addition, cognitive distortions supporting sexual aggression

(Hudson and Ward, 2000; Kenny et al., 2001) and deviant sexual fantasies (Kenny et al., 2001) are related to sexual re-offending. As to personality disorder variables, Gretton and his colleagues found that juvenile sexual offenders who sexually recidivated scored higher on the Hare Psychopathy Checklist than non-recidivists (Gretton et al., 2001). Långström and Grann (2000), in a mixed sample of juvenile sexual offenders, however, concluded that psychopathy is associated with criminal re-offending, but not sexual re-offending.

Some researchers investigated links between recidivism rates and sexual offence characteristics. They found that recidivism rates were higher for offenders with male victims (Kahn and Chambers, 1991; Långström and Grann, 2000; Smith and Monastersky, 1986) unknown to the offender (Smith and Monastersky, 1986). Also, Rasmussen (1999) found that juvenile sexual offenders were more likely to sexually relapse if they had several previous female victims, compared to a single female victim or several boys. In the same way, Långström and Grann (2000) suggested that the rate of sexual recidivism was higher among juveniles with a higher number of victims. The authors concluded that predictive factors of non-sexual re-offending are not the same as those associated with sexual re-offending. For example, they found that the use of a weapon or threats during sexual aggression was not a predictor of sexual recidivism, but of criminal recidivism.

It is difficult, however, to draw firm conclusions from existing studies on recidivism. Variations in recidivism rates could be due to methodological differences, such as the definition of recidivism, the duration of the follow-up period, and the nature and the validity of the information source. Prentky et al. (2000) noted that juvenile studies are frequently subject to additional problems, such as difficulties obtaining juvenile files, significant rates of non-official sexual offending committed by minors, as well as a large number of subjects missing recidivism information. In our view, 'recidivism' is but one aspect characterising the criminal career of juvenile sexual offenders, and there are important shortcomings emphasising this component alone. Not only does this parameter not indicate the total number of victims, but it does not tell us anything about the level of coercion either. Consequently, the aim of this study was to verify which variables were associated with two

criminal activity parameters in juvenile sexual aggressors of children: the number of victims and the level of coercion. Predictors included in this study were developmental, pre-crime, and crime factors.

Methodology

Subjects

Our sample included 102 subjects evaluated at the Centre de psychiatrie légale de Montréal (CPLM) an outpatient clinic affiliated to the Institut Philippe Pinel de Montréal, between 1992 and 2000. In this study, a juvenile sexual offender of children is defined as a male aged between 12 and 17 who had sexual contact with a child at least three years younger than himself. The victim was under the age of twelve.

The mean of age of our subjects at the time of evaluation was 15 years old (S.D. = 1.54; range = 12-17) and the mean number of victims was two (S.D. = 1.64; range = 1–10). A total of 47 subjects had more than one victim, and 28 more than two. The mean age of victims being six years old (S.D. = 2.58; range = 1-12) and the majority of victims were female (62% versus 38% males). 44% of subjects had committed their last aggression against an immediate family member (i.e., brother, sister, step-brother, step-sister, brother or sister from recomposed family), 54% had abused a child without a close family tie (e.g., neighbour, friend, cousin, or babysitting) and only two subjects had abused a child unknown to them.

Procedure

Data were collected from clinical files obtained at the Centre de psychiatrie légale de Montréal. Files provided information such as psychiatric and psychological assessments, victim statements, and police reports. Data were gathered for each subject during the risk assessment procedure. Conclusions from these assessments were used by a judge to determine the judicial response in order to reduce the risk of offending (e.g., inpatient programme, Youth Centre). Data were analysed using the SPSS 10.0 package.

Construction of scales

Developmental factors (prior to the age of 12) were dichotomised (yes/no). Offenders with a history of sexual abuse, both intra and extra-familial, were defined as previously sexually abused. Items of sexual victimisation were defined as follows: victim of sexual touching; victim of sexual aggression with coercion; victim of sexual aggression with fondling; victim of sexual aggression, details unavailable; and prostitution.[1] A total of 38% of subjects were sexually abused prior to the age of 12. The physical violence and negligence factor was defined as any form of such abuse in childhood. A single experience of negligence or physical violence was sufficient to be recorded. Only 18% of subjects had been physically victimised prior to age 12. Finally, psychological abuse included the following items: exposure to family violence; victim of verbal threats, intimidation, or terror; social isolation; and, repeated unreasonable demands by parents. A total of 40% of offenders had experienced at least one of the above forms of psychological violence prior to age 12.

As for developmental factors during adolescence, two scales were built following principal component analyses. Aggressiveness and loneliness scales were calculated by adding variables. Each subject obtained a score for the two scales. The higher the score, the more negative and serious the factor. The aggressiveness scale included ten items: aggressiveness with male peers; two measures of verbal violence: from age 12 to six months prior to the aggression; and, from six months prior to the aggression itself; two measures of physical violence (defined in the same way as the measures of verbal violence); defiance of authority figures in school; physical violence towards peers; disruptive behaviour in class. Scale reliability (Cronbach' alpha) was 0.94 (see Annexe A). Since this scale showed an asymmetric distribution without the possibility of conclusive transformations, we recoded it into four categories using quartiles cut-off scores (group 1 = 25%; group 2 = from 25 to 50%, and so on).

The loneliness scale included four items: few or no leisure activities; individual leisure activities; lack of intimacy with male peers; and, lack of intimacy with female peers. The Cronbach' alpha score was 0.83. Since this scale showed an asymmetric distribution without the possibility of

conclusive transformations, loneliness was transformed into a dichotomic variable (Farrington and Loeber, 2000). Finally, deviant sexual behaviour factors included the following items: exhibitionism; voyeurism; bestiality; frotteurs; fetishism; use of deviant pornography; compulsive masturbation; transvestic fetishism. Only 21.6% of the sample revealed deviant sexual behaviours. We further reduced this factor to two categories: presence or absence of at least one deviant sexual behaviour in adolescence.

Pre-crime factors referred to the inner world of the offender prior to the most recent sexual aggression. The decision to study only the most recent offence was based on two considerations: Firstly, it was usually the most documented in the files available to us. Furthermore, the subject was often referred for evaluation following his most recent offence. Secondly, the theory of the criminal career continuum suggests that the most recent offence is most representative of the sexual offending process of an offender (Proulx, Perreault, Ouimet, Guay, 1999).

Considering there are few elements available to measure pre-crime factors, we considered them in a dichotomic manner. Presence of negative emotions included one of the following items: anger; sadness; anxiety, jealousy or revenge. A total of 54% of subjects acknowledged having felt negative emotions prior to their last offence, whereas 46% acknowledged having felt sexual excitement or any kind of positive emotion. The cognitive distortions factor refers to justifications used by the aggressor to acquit himself of the responsibility of the offence. For example, he might have said that the victim was agreeing, that the aggression was educational for the victim, or that the victim deserved to be attacked. Half (48%) the subjects presented cognitive distortions related to their last offence. Finally, the deviant sexual fantasies factor refers to the presence of deviant sexual fantasies towards the victim or any other child 48 hours prior to the last sexual offence. A total of 52% of our sample admitted the presence of this type of fantasy, compared to 41% who did not.

Dependent variables

The total number of victims for each subject was calculated from information available on file. This variable fluctuated between one and ten, with an average of two victims per subject. Initially, the second dependent variable, the level of force, was

---

[1] We considered prostitution as sexual victimisation considering the incapacity of the subject at the time, i.e., being under the age of 12, to consent to any form of sexual activity with an older person.

composed of three categories, according to Avery-Clark and Laws' criteria (1984): no force, minimal force to initiate the offence, more than necessary force. This last category refers to 'an excess of force used by the offender, whose force exceeds that necessary to control the victim'. (Ouimet, Guay, Proulx, 2000: p161). The concept of minimal force refers to the use of coercion when the victim tried to resist the aggression. For the more recent offence, the variable level of force was recoded into two categories, due to the low number of subjects having used a level of force greater than necessary (n=2). The distribution of the new categories was almost equivalent, with 52% using no force compared to 48% using either minimal force or more than necessary.

Data analysis

To verify the relationship between developmental, pre-crime, and criminal activity, path analyses were performed. This statistical method allows the verification of direct and indirect relationships between exogenous variables (developmental factors prior to age 12) and endogenous variables (developmental factors in adolescence, pre-crime, and crime factors). Hierarchical multiple and logistic regression analyses were used to perform a path analysis with chronological data entry. Firstly, we verified the relationship between developmental factors prior to age 12 and developmental factors in adolescence. Secondly, we verified the relationship between the two developmental blocks and pre-crime factors. Finally, the relationship between the first three blocks (developmental factors prior to age 12, developmental factors in adolescence, pre-crime factors) and two criminal career parameters (level of coercion and number of victims) were verified.

Results

Table 4.1 shows descriptive statistics for all variables included in our model. Complete information was available for all variables. Table 4.2 shows a correlation matrix between developmental factors, pre-crime factors and dependent variables. Level of coercion used during the offence was positively related to aggressiveness in adolescence. Among pre-crime factors, only deviant sexual fantasies were positively correlated with the level of coercion. Age of the victim was also positively and

significantly related to the level of coercion. Physical abuse in childhood and loneliness in adolescence was positively correlated with the number of victims.

A hierarchical logistic regression analysis regarding the level of force used during the offence is presented in Table 4.3. Two outliers were removed from the equation. The number of subjects used for the analysis was 100. Values showed in Table 4.3 are odds ratios (Exp (B)). Variables were entered by block, according to their chronological order. In the control variable block, age of the victim (Exp (B) =1.375) was predictive of the level of force used during the offence (p<0.01). The probability of using violence during the offence increased by 1.4 when the age of the victim increased by a year. Among block 2, none of the developmental factors in childhood were significant. The addition of the developmental factors in adolescence (block 3) in the equation increases the percentage of the variance explained by the model from 15% to 23% (R^2 adjusted =0.233, p<0.01). Aggressiveness in adolescence predicts significantly the use of coercion (Exp (B) =1.673; p<0.05). As for pre-crime factors (block 4), only deviant sexual fantasies (Exp (B) =5.117; p<0.01) was predictive of the level of coercion. The presence of deviant sexual fantasies increased the probability of using force during the offence. The addition of pre-crime factors to the equation increased the percentage of correctly classified subjects from 66% to 73% and the model reached a total of 37% of explained variance (p<0.01).

In Table 4.4, we display the results of a hierarchical multiple regression analysis on the total number of victims. Two outliers were removed from the equation. Values showed in Table 4.4 are beta coefficients (β). This standardised coefficient was used to compare each variable's contribution to the prediction of the dependant variable (number of victims). Variables were entered by block, according to their chronological order. In the control variables' block, the age of the subject was significantly related to the number of victims ($\beta = -0.247$, p=0.01). The older the subject, the lower the number of victims. Among developmental factors in childhood (block 2), physical and psychological abuses were predictive of the number of victims. The number of victims increased if subjects were abused or physically neglected ($\beta = 0.463$, p<0.01). On the other hand, this number decreased if subjects were

Table 4.1: Descriptive data[1]

	N	Mean	Med.	S.D.	Skewness	Kurtosis	Frequency	%
Control variables								
Age of subject (12–18)	102	15.66	15.64	1.54	0.1	−1.0		
Age of victim (1–12)	102	6.42	6.0	2.59	0.5	0.4		
Developmental factors prior to age 12								
Physical abuse or neglect	102						0 No: 84	82.4%
							1 Yes: 18	17.6%
Psychological abuse	102						0 No: 61	59.8%
							1 Yes: 41	40.2%
Sexual abuse	102						0 No: 63	61.8%
							1 Yes: 39	38.2%
Developmental factors in adolescence								
Aggressiveness (0–3 Scale)	102	1.39	1.0	1.05	0.84	−1.2		
Loneliness	102						0 No: 59	57.8%
							1 Yes: 43	42.2%
Deviant sexual behaviour	102						0 No: 80	78.4%
							1 Yes: 22	21.6%
Pre-crime factors								
Negative emotions	102						0 No: 47	46.1%
							1 Yes: 55	53.9%
Deviant sexual fantasies	102						0 No: 42	41.2%
							1 Yes: 60	58.8%
Cognitive distortions	102						0 No: 53	52.0%
							1 Yes: 49	48.0%
Dependent variables								
Presence of coercion	102						0 No: 57	55.9%
							1 Yes: 43	44.1%
Number of victims (1–10)	102	2.07	1.0	1.64	2.1	6.1		

[1]Control variables (1 – age of subject, 2 – age of victim) are all continuous variables, as is aggressiveness and total number of victims.

psychologically abused ($\beta = -0.312$, p<0.01). To verify the relation between psychological abuse and the number of victims, analyses of multilevel correspondence were performed.[2] Psychological abuse was related to the number of victims only by virtue of its relationship with physical abuse, which was strongly associated with the number of victims.[3] Among the developmental factors related to adolescence (block 3), only loneliness was positively correlated with the number of victims ($\beta = 0.187$, p<0.05). The number of victims increased if subjects were lonely. The

addition of pre-crime factors (block 4) to the model was not significant. Once all blocks were entered into the model, the total of explained variance reached 30% (p<0.01). Finally, physical abuse or neglect (developmental factor in childhood) was the strongest predictor of the total number of victims.

Additional analyses were performed to investigate relationships between independent variables. With regression analysis, we verified whether the variables from the last two blocks (developmental factors in adolescence and pre-crime factors) could be explained by factors preceding them. First, we established the relationship between the developmental factors in childhood and those in adolescence, controlling for variables first entered into the equation. Only one marginally significant relationship was found, namely between psychological abuse in childhood and

[2]To carry out the correspondence analysis , we used the median as a cut-off point.
[3]Correspondence analysis showed a positive, non-significant relationship between psychological abuse and the number of victims for subjects who were not physically abused [$\chi^2(1) = 0.78$, $p=0.38$, phi=0.10], whereas the relationship became negative and non-dignificant for subjects who were physically abused [$\chi^2(1) = 2.29$, $p=0.13$, phi $= -0.36$].

Table 4.2: Intercorrelations matrix (Pearson R correlation)

	(1)	(2)	(3)	(4)	(5)	(6)	(7)	(8)	(9)	(10)	(11)	(12)	(13)
(1) Age of subject		0.09	−0.07	−0.24**	0.11	−0.24**	0.07	0.01	0.07	−0.11	0.06	0.02	−0.17
(2) Age of victim			0.06	−0.08	−0.09	0.08	−0.12	0.03	−0.03	−0.03	0.06	0.28**	0.01
(3) Physical abuse or neglect				0.41**	0.11	0.02	0.02	0.06	−0.19*	−0.03	0.17	−0.10	0.28**
(4) Psychological abuse					0.14	0.13	0.15*	0.06	0.10	−0.03	−0.07	−0.01	0.00
(5) Sexual abuse						−0.03	0.19*	0.10	−0.04	0.00	0.01	−0.13	0.15
(6) Aggressiveness							0.06	−0.05	0.14	−0.01	−0.01	0.25**	0.16
(7) Loneliness								−0.08	−0.01	−0.01	0.01	0.04	0.21*
(8) Deviant sexual behaviour									−0.11	0.02	−0.10	−0.15	0.14
(9) Negative emotions										−0.01	−0.10	0.07	−0.11
(10) Deviant sexual fantasies											0.04	0.22*	0.07
(11) Cognitive distortions												−0.06	0.20
(12) Level of coercion													−0.10
(13) Number of victims													

Note: * = $p<0.05$; ** = $p<0.01$ (2-tailed).

Table 4.3: Logistic regression analysis regarding the level of coercion used during the offence[1]

	Block 1		Block 2		Block 3		Block 4			
	Exp(B)	P	Exp(B)	P	Exp(B)	P	Exp(B)	P	C.I. <	C.I. >
Control variable — Age of the victim	1.286**	0.005	1.287**	0.005	1.282**	0.008	1.375**	0.003	1.11	1.70
Developmental factors prior to age 12										
Physical abuse or neglect			1.519	0.414	1.251	0.689	1.954	0.272	0.59	6.45
Psychological abuse			0.821	0.834	0.784	0.652	0.610	0.401	0.19	1.93
Sexual abuse			0.493	0.126	0.549	0.228	0.430	0.123	0.15	1.26
Developmental factors in adolescence										
Aggressiveness					1.613*	0.032	1.673*	0.036	1.04	2.70
Loneliness					1.030	0.952	1.164	0.768	0.43	3.19
Deviant sexual behaviour					0.444	0.149	0.365	0.099	0.11	1.21
Pre-crime factors										
Negative emotions							1.344	0.549	0.52	3.54
Cognitive distortions							0.415	0.084	0.15	1.12
Deviant sexual fantasies							5.117**	0.002	1.79	14.65
Nagelkerke R square	R^2 0.117**	P 0.002	R^2 0.149*	P 0.019	R^2 0.233**	P 0.008	R^2 0.367**	P 0.005		

[1]Area under the Roc curve = 0.79.

Note: * = $p<0.05$; ** = $p<0.01$. $N=100$.

Table 4.4: Hierarchical multiple regression analysis regarding the number of victims (Beta)

		Block 1		Block 2		Block 3		Block 4	
		β	P	β	P	β	P	β	P
Control variable	Age of the subject	−0.224*	0.025	−0.263**	0.006	−0.253**	0.008	−0.247*	0.010
Developmental factors prior to age 12	Physical abuse or neglect			0.455**	0.000	0.468**	0.000	0.463**	0.000
	Psychological abuse			−0.260*	0.010	−0.320**	0.002	−0.312**	0.004
	Sexual abuse			0.075	0.415	0.046	0.615	0.044	0.637
Developmental factors in adolescence	Aggressiveness					0.147	0.112	0.149	0.115
	Loneliness					0.188*	0.041	0.187*	0.046
	Deviant sexual behaviour					0.090	0.315	0.092	0.321
Pre-crime factors	Negative emotions							−0.004	0.964
	Cognitive distortions							0.025	0.785
	Deviant sexual fantasies							0.060	0.504
Model		R^2 0.050* R^2adj. 0.040*	P 0.025	R^2 0.234** R^2adj. 0.202**	P 0.000	R^2 0.293** R^2adj. 0.239**	P 0.000	R^2 0.297** R^2adj. 0.218**	P 0.000

Note: * = $p<0.05$; ** = $p<0.01$. N=100

aggressiveness ($\beta=0.20$, $p=0.06$). Thereafter, we verified how the two blocks of developmental variables were related to pre-crime factors. Logistic regression analyses showed that physical abuse was positively correlated with cognitive distortions (Exp (B) =0.26, $p<0.05$) and with negative emotions (Exp (B) =6.62, $p<0.01$). Moreover, psychological abuse in childhood was also correlated with negative emotions (Exp (B) =0.32, $p<0.05$).

Figure 4.1 shows significant relationships between developmental and pre-crime factors and criminal career parameters (the level of coercion used and the total number of victims). It should be noted that factors with no significant relationship with other factors were excluded from the model. Moreover, we included significant relationships between independent variables.

Among developmental factors in childhood, only psychological abuse was related to a developmental factor in adolescence. Psychological abuse in childhood may lead to aggressiveness in adolescence. Among the developmental factors in childhood related to pre-crime variables, psychological abuse was negatively related to negative emotions, whereas physical abuse may support the emergence of negative emotions. Moreover, physical abuse was negatively related to cognitive distortions. Physical abuse was the only developmental factor in childhood related to the number of victims; psychological abuse was only related by virtue of a suppression effect (registered in brackets). Among developmental factors in adolescence, aggressiveness is positively related to the use of coercion during the offence. Loneliness was positively related to the number of victims. Finally, deviant sexual fantasies were the only pre-crime factor related to the level of coercion.

Discussion

Level of coercion

According to Canadian studies, between 33% and 44% of juvenile sexual offenders admitted having used violence during their offence (Hornick et al., 1994; Jacob et al., 1993; Lafortune, 1996). Our results appear to be congruent with these studies, with 48% of our subjects having used violence during their last offence. Kaufman, Orts and colleagues (1996) found that juvenile sexual offenders used threats and physical force more

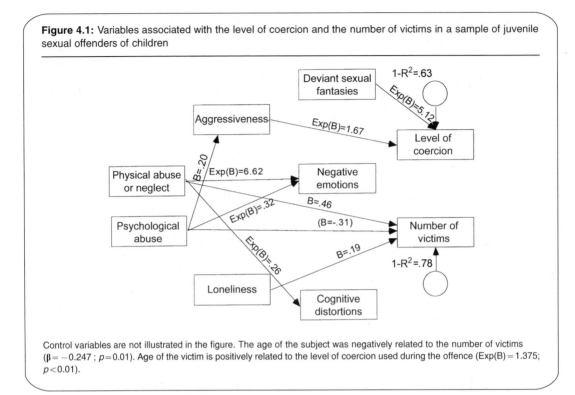

Figure 4.1: Variables associated with the level of coercion and the number of victims in a sample of juvenile sexual offenders of children

Control variables are not illustrated in the figure. The age of the subject was negatively related to the number of victims ($\beta = -0.247$; $p = 0.01$). Age of the victim is positively related to the level of coercion used during the offence (Exp(B) = 1.375; $p < 0.01$).

often than adults. Compared to adolescents, adult sexual offenders applied refined modus operandi strategies, using seduction and trickery to control their victim.

We found a positive relationship between aggressiveness in adolescence and the level of coercion used during the offence. This result is in agreement with those of Knight and Sims-Knight (in press) who showed that aggressiveness during adolescence was related to the level of coercion used in a sexual context, in a sample of adolescent sexual offenders.

The only pre-crime factor significantly related to the level of coercion was the presence of deviant sexual fantasies; subjects who admitted having deviant sexual fantasies had committed more violent sexual offences. Johnson and Knight (2000) showed a positive relationship between coercive sexual aggression and the presence of deviant sexual fantasies in a sample of juvenile sexual offenders of peers. These results suggest that the presence of deviant fantasies prior to a sexual offence is related to the likelihood of using force during the offence. Proulx and his colleagues found different results in a sample of adult sexual offenders: the presence of deviant

sexual fantasies was related to coercive sexual aggression for sexual offenders of women, but was related to non-coercive sexual aggression for sexual offenders of children (Proulx, St-Yves, Guay and Ouimet, 1999; Proulx, Perreault, Ouimet and Guay, 1999). Rapists associated deviant sexual fantasies with anger, whereas adult child molesters had positive affects (e.g., joy, tenderness) related to their fantasies. In adult sexual aggressors of children, self-confidence during sexual aggression, gained through experience, may explain the lower level of coercion used compared to adolescent offenders.

Several authors observed that the age of the victim is a significant factor related to the use of coercion during the offence (Fehrenbach et al., 1986; Hornick et al., 1994; Stermac and Mathews, 1987). According to their reports, physical coercion is more likely to be used with older victims. That conclusion is in accordance with our results. Older children, being less vulnerable, may offer more resistance than their younger counterparts.

Our results also indicate that 46% of sexual aggressions perpetrated against young girls were violent, compared to 47% against boys. Hornick et al. (1994) found a congruent rate for girl victims. Also, they suggested that the assault is more violent if the victim is female, which was not observed in our results. Discrepancies between rates can be explained by methodological differences. While we used official and self-reported information, Hornick et al. (1994) only gathered information on the juvenile's accusation.

Factors included in our multivariate model of coercive sexual aggression explained 37% of the variance. Although our model was developed for sexual offenders of children, it shares certain characteristics with the model developed by Johnson and Knight (2000) for sexual aggressors of peers or adults. Indeed, Johnson and Knight showed that physical abuse was indirectly related to the level of coercion by two mediating variables: aggressiveness towards peers and sexual compulsivity. In our study, aggressiveness in adolescence was directly related to the level of coercion, as was deviant sexual fantasies. Johnson and Knight also observed a relationship between deviant sexual fantasies and coercive sexual aggression. However, they also found a relation between sexual abuse and coercive sexual aggression, which was not confirmed by our model. Finally, the present model included a variable not considered by Johnson and Knight (2000), that is, the age of the victim. It was directly and positively related to the level of coercion used during the sexual aggression.

Number of victims

In the present study, 47% of subjects admitted having assaulted more than one victim, a rate slightly lower than those observed by Fehrenbach et al. (57%) or by Mathews (64%). However, it was twice the rate found by Prentky et al. (2000). These differences can be explained by the context of the assessment and the sources of information (official files versus self-reported information). In our study, even though both official and non-official data were considered, the subjects could have minimised the number of sexual aggressions they admitted to, considering the potential legal consequences of the evaluation.

Our participants had an average of two victims and 21 offences, which is relatively low compared to the sample of the Institut Philippe Pinel de Montréal (an average of five victims and 35

offences). This difference may be explained by the type of setting and the nature of the sexual aggression. The sample of the Institut Philippe Pinel included juveniles who were incarcerated at a maximum-security institution due to the severity of their criminal activities.

Fehrenbach et al. (1986), as well as Ford and Linney (1995) found a positive relationship between physical abuse in childhood and sexual aggression in adolescence. In our sample, physical abuse or neglect during childhood was the best predictor of the number of victims. This result suggests that family violence or neglect is a significant developmental factor in the risk assessment of juvenile sexual offenders.

Our results showed that loneliness was positively associated with the number of victims. To explain this relation, we turned to the attachment model proposed by Marshall (1989; Marshall, Hudson and Hodkinson, 1993). If the adolescent is unable to establish significant relationships with peers, sexuality (e.g., masturbation, sexual fantasies) is used to cope with negative feelings or fear of rejection. Also, the offender attempts to fulfil his intimacy needs through sexuality.

Moreover, our results indicate that the youngest subjects had more victims than the older ones. Originally, the decision to introduce the age of the subject as a control variable was based on the opposite assumption. One might expect the number of victims to increase with age. However, the nature of our sample might have influenced this logic. The subjects referred to the CPLM at 12 or 13 years of age already presented serious sexual problems, whereas the older ones did not necessarily begin their sexual criminal career as early and intensively.

Variables associated with the number of victims were analysed using a hierarchical multiple regression analysis. This analysis showed that none of the pre-crime factors were associated with the number of victims. In contrast, Kenny et al. (2001), as well as Hudson and Ward (2000), found that the presence of deviant sexual fantasies and cognitive distortions were related to sexual recidivism. However, our results are in agreement with studies indicating that socially isolated juveniles are more likely to recidivate than those who do not present this type of difficulty (Becker and Kaplan, 1988; Långström and Grann, 2000).

Conclusion

Our study showed that a combination of static and dynamic factors is related with criminal activity of juvenile sexual offenders of children. Other authors also reported such findings, in spite of sample and methodological differences. Physical abuse was a significant predictor of the number of victims per aggressor. Early onset of offending is also a significant variable for predicting recidivism. The youngest offenders had more victims than the older ones. The best predictors of the level of violence were aggressiveness in adolescence and presence of deviant sexual fantasies prior to the offence. Moreover, the level of violence was higher the older the victim.

The presence of negative developmental factors, however, should not be considered a necessary fate leading to a career as a sexual offender. As underlined by Becker and Hunter (1997), negative developmental characteristics are common to several juvenile offenders, sexual offenders or not. Thus, antecedents of physical violence or neglect, as well as aggressiveness or loneliness, should not be regarded as direct causes for deviant sexual behaviour in juveniles, but rather as risk factors contributing to the development of such behaviour.

Apart from factors included in our model, there are other elements influencing the sexual criminal activity of juveniles. For example, Hunter and Figueredo (2000) suggested investigating the context of childhood victimisation (i.e., the number of incidents, the duration, age at first victimisation, the circumstances of the disclosure, the reaction of his environment, etc.). Opportunities are other elements, which can influence the sexual criminal activity of a juvenile. Hunter (2000) mentioned that juveniles are more opportunistic than adults, who seem to be more structured. Finally, other victim characteristics must be considered in order to explain sexual offences perpetrated by juveniles, such as their relationship with the offender (Fehrenbach et al., 1986) the sex of the victim (Hornick et al., 1994) and their reaction to the offence.

Few researchers have studied the sexual criminal activity of juveniles. The majority of studies are limited to a general descriptive portrait of this population. Our study, however, suffered from some methodological limits. Firstly, the evaluation interview was carried out in a legal context. Participants might have omitted or minimised some information for fear of reprisal or due to social desirability. Secondly, our sample included juvenile sexual offenders of children who were referred to the Centre de psychiatrie légale de Montréal for a psychiatric evaluation and possible therapeutic treatment. It is conceivable that these particular adolescents had more sexual problems than the majority of juvenile sexual offenders of children.

In conclusion, other exploratory studies with various samples of juvenile sexual offenders of children, peers and adults should be performed in order to compare their respective criminal activity. Moreover, longitudinal studies should be carried out to analyse variables associated with recidivism, as well as factors associated with other criminal activity parameters.

References

Abel, G.G. (1984) Adolescent Sexual Offences: Serious Problem Ignored. *Sexuality Today*, 7 (3)

Avery-Clark, C.A. and Laws, D.R. (1984) Differential Erection Response Patterns of Sexual Child Abusers to Stimuli Describing Activities With Children. *Behaviour Therapy*, 15, 71–83.

Awad, G.A., Saunders, E. and Levene, J. (1984) A Clinical Study of Male Adolescent Sexual Offenders. *International Journal of Offender Therapy and Comparative Criminology*, 28, 105–15.

Becker, J.V. (1990) Treating Adolescent Sexual Offenders. *Professional Psychology: Research and Practice*, 21, 362–65.

Becker, J.V. (1998) What We Know About The Characteristics and Treatment of Adolescents Who Have Committed Sexual Offences. *Child Maltreatment*, 3 (4), 317–29.

Becker, J.V., and Hunter, J.A. (1997) Understanding and Treating Child and Adolescent Sexual Offenders. In Ollendick, T.H. and Prinz, R.J. (Eds.) *Advances In Clinical Child Psychology*. New York, NY: Plenum Press. 177–97

Becker, J.V. and Kaplan, M.S. (1993) Cognitive Behavioural Treatment of The Juvenile Sex Offender. In Barbaree, H.E., Marshall, W.L. and Hudson, S.M. (Eds.) *The Juvenile Sex Offender*. New-York, NY: Guilford Press. 264–77.

Becker, J.V. and Kaplan, M.S. (1988) The Assessment of Adolescent Sexual Offenders. *Advances In Behavioural Assessment of Children and Families*, 4, 97–118.

Becker, J.V., Kaplan, M.S., Cunningham-Rathner, J. and Kavoussi, R. (1986) Characteristics of Adolescent Incest Sexual Perpetrators: Preliminary Findings. *Journal of Family Violence*, 1 (1), 85–97.

Cambell, J.S. and Lerew, C. (2002) Juvenile Sex Offenders In Diversion. *Sexual Abuse: A Journal of Research and Treatment*, 14 (1), 1–17.

Carpenter, D., Peed, S. and Eastman, B. (1995) Personality Characteristics of Adolescent Sexual Offenders: A Pilot Study. *Sexual Abuse: A Journal of Research and Treatment*, 7 (3), 195–203.

Cortoni, F. and Marshall, W.L. (2001) Sex as A Coping Strategy and Its Relationship to Juvenile Sexual History and Intimacy In Sexual Offenders. *Sexual Abuse: A Journal of Research and Treatment*, 13 (1), 27–43.

David, G.E. and Leitenberg, H. (1987) Adolescent Sex Offenders. *Psychological Bulletin*, 101 (3), 417–27.

Dozois, J. (1994) Adolescent Et Agresseur Sexuel: Bilan D'une Recherche. *Criminologie*, 27 (2), 71–84.

Dozois, J. (2000, August) *Trajectoire Des Adolescents Agresseurs Sexuels Aux Centres Jeunesse De Montréal De 1993 À 1998*. Paper Presented At The VIIeme Colloque De L'association Internationale Des Criminologues De Langue Française. Montreal, Quebec, Canada.

Epperly-Trudel, B.A. (1993) *Personality Variables of Adolescent Sex Offenders*. Doctoral Dissertation, UMI Dissertation Abstracts Database. Vanderbilt University, Michigan.

Farrington, D.P. and Loeber, R. (2000) Some Benefits of Dichotomisation In Psychiatric and Criminological Research. *Criminal Behaviour and Mental Health*, 10, 100–22.

Fehrenbach, P.A., Smith, W., Monastersky, C. and Deisher, R.W. (1986) Adolescent Sexual Offenders: Offender and Offence Characteristics. *American Journal of Orthopsychiatry*, 56 (2), 225–33.

Ford, M.E. and Linney, J.A. (1995) Comparative Analysis of Juvenile Sexual Offenders, Violent Nonsexual Offenders, and Status Offenders. *Journal of Interpersonal Violence*, 10, 56–70.

Gretton, H.M., Mcbride, M., Hare, R.D., O'Shaughnessy R. and Kumba, G. (2001) Psychopathy and Recidivism In Adolescent Sex Offenders. *Criminal Justice and Behaviour*, 28, 427–49.

Hornick, J.P., Bolitho, F.H. and Leclaire, D. (1994) *Young Offenders and The Abuse of Children:*

Technical Report. Direction Générale De La Recherche Et De La Statistique, Ministère De La Justice Du Canada.

Hudson, S.M. and Ward, T. (2000) Interpersonal Competency In Sex Offenders. *Behaviour Modification*, 24 (4), 494–527.

Hunter, J.A. and Becker, J.V. (1994) The Role of Deviant Sexual Arousal In Juvenile Sexual Offending: Etiology, Evaluation and Treatment. *Criminal Justice and Behaviour*, 21 (1), 132–49.

Hunter, J.A. and Figueredo, A.J. (1999) Factors Associated With Treatment Compliance In A Population of Juvenile Sexual Offenders. *Sexual Abuse: A Journal of Research and Treatment*, 11, 49–68.

Hunter, J.A. and Figueredo, A.J. (2000) The Influence of Personality and History of Sexual Victimisation In The Prediction of Juvenile Perpetrated Child Molestation. *Behaviour Modification*, 29 (2), 259–81.

Hunter, J.A. (2000) *Understanding Juvenile Sex Offenders: Research Findings and Guidelines for Effective Management and Treatment*. The Virginia Department of Criminal Justice Services.

Jacob, M., Mckibben, A. and Proulx, J. (1993) Étude Descriptive Et Comparative D'une Population D'adolescents Agresseurs Sexuels. *Criminologie*, 26 (1), 13–163.

Johnson, G.M. and Knight, R.A. (2000) Developmental Antecedents of Sexual Coercion In Juvenile Sexual Offenders. *Sexual Abuse: A Journal of Research and Treatment*, 12, 165–78.

Kahn, T.J. and Chambers, H.J. (1991) Assessing Reoffense Risk With Juvenile Sexual Offenders. *Child Welfare*, 70, 333–45.

Kaufman, K.L., Orts, K., Holmberg, J., Mccrady, F., Daleiden, E.L. and Hilliker, D. (1996, November) *Contrasting Adult and Adolescent Sexual Offenders' Modus Operandi: A Developmental Process*. Paper Presented At The 15th Annual Conference of The Association for The Treatment of Sexual Abusers. Chicago, Illinois, USA.

Kenny, D.T., Keogh, T. and Seidler, K. (2001) Predictors of Recidivism In Australian Juvenile Sex Offenders: Implications for Treatment. *Sexual Abuse: A Journal of Research and Treatment*, 13, 131–48.

Knight, R.A. and Prentky, R.A. (1993) Exploring Characteristics for Classifying Juvenile Sex Offenders. In Barbaree, H.E., Marshall, W.L. and Hudson, S.M. (Eds.) *The Juvenile Sex Offender*, New-York, NY: Guilford Press. 45–83.

Knight, R.A. and Sims-Knight, J.E. (In Press) *The Developmental Antecedents of Sexual Coercion Against Women In Adolescents.*

Laforest, S. and Paradis, R. (1990) Adolescents Et Délinquance Sexuelle. *Criminologie*, 23 (1), 95–116.

Lafortune, D. (1996) *Antécédents Et Caractéristiques Psychologiques De L'adolescent Ayant Commis Un Abus Sexuel.* Thèse De Doctorat Inédite, Université De Montréal.

Långström, N. and Grann, M. (2000) Risk for Criminal Recidivism Among Young Sex Offenders. *Journal of Interpersonal Violence*, 15, 855–71.

Marshall, W.L. (1989) Intimacy, Loneliness and Sexual Offenders. *Behaviour Research and Therapy*, 27, 491–503.

Marshall, W.L. and Eccles, A. (1993) Pavlovian Conditioning Processes In Adolescent Sex Offenders. In Barbaree, H.E., Marshall, W.L. and Hudson, S.M. (Eds.) *The Juvenile Sex Offender.* New York: Guilford Press, 118–42.

Marshall, W.L., Hudson, S.M. and Hodkinson, S. (1993) The Importance of Attachment Bonds In The Development of Juvenile Sex Offending. In Barbaree, H.E., Marshall, W.L. and Hudson, S.M. (Eds.) The *Juvenile Sex Offender.* New York, NY: Guilford Press. 164–81.

Marshall, W.L., Jones, R., Ward, T., Johnston, P. and Barbaree, H.E. (1991) Treatment Outcome With Sex Offenders. *Clinical Psychology Review*, 11, 463–85.

Mathews, F. (1987) *Adolescent Sex Offenders: A Needs Study.* Toronto, ON, Central Toronto Youth Services.

Murphy, W.D., DiLillo, D., Haynes, M.R. and Steere, E. (2001) An Exploration of Factors Related to Deviant Sexual Arousal Among Juvenile Sex Offenders. *Sexual Abuse: A Journal of Research and Treatment*, 13 (2), 91–103.

Ouimet, M., Guay, J.-P. and Proulx, J. (2000) Analyse De La Gravité Des Agressions Sexuelles De Femmes Adultes Et De Ses Déterminants. *Revue Internationale De Criminologie Et De Police Technique Et Scientifique*, 2, 157–72.

Prentky, R., Harris, B., Frizzel, K. and Righthand, S. (2000) An Actuarial Procedure for Assessing Risk With Juvenile Sex Offenders. *Sexual Abuse: A Journal of Research and Treatment*, 12, 71–87.

Proulx, J., St-Yves, M., Guay, J-P. and Ouimet, M. (1999) Les Agresseurs Sexuels De Femmes: Scénarios Délictuels Et Troubles De La Personnalité. In Proulx, J., Cusson, M. and Ouimet, M. (Eds.) *Les Violences Criminelles.* Les Presses De l'Université Laval, Québec. 157–85.

Proulx, J., Perreault, C., Ouimet, M. and Guay, J.-P. (1999) Les Agresseurs Sexuels D'enfants: Scénarios Délictuels Et Troubles De La Personnalité. In J. Proulx, M. Cusson, and M. Ouimet (Eds.) *Les Violences Criminelles.* Les Presses De l'Université Laval, Québec. 187–216.

Rasmussen, L.A. (1999) Factors Related to Recidivism Among Juvenile Sexual Offenders. *Sexual Abuse: A Journal of Research and Treatment*, 11, 69–86.

Ryan, G., Miyoshi, T.J., Metzner, J., Krugman, R.D. and Fryer, G.E. (1996) Trends In A National Sample of Sexually Abusive Youths. *Journal of The American Academy of Child and Adolescent Psychiatry*, 35 (1), 17–25.

Smith, W.R. and Monastersky, C. (1986) Assessing Juvenile Sexual Offenders' Risk for Reoffending. *Criminal Justice and Behaviour*, 13, 115–40.

Stermac, L. and Mathews, F. (1987) *Adolescent Sex Offenders: Toward A Profile.* Toronto, ON, Central Toronto Youth Services.

Wieckowski, E., Hartsoe, P., Mayer, A. and Shontz, J. (1998) Deviant Sexual Behaviour In Children and Young Adolescents: Frequency and Patterns. *Sexual Abuse: A Journal of Research and Treatment*, 10 (4), 293–303.

Worling, J.R. (2001) Personality-Based Typology of Adolescent Male Sexual Offenders: Differences In Recidivism Rates, Victim-Selection Characteristics, and Personal Victimisation Histories. *Sexual Abuse: A Journal of Research and Treatment*, 13, 149–66.

Electronic Documents

Health Canada, National Clearinghouse on Family Violence Publication (1997) *The Sexual Abuse of Children.* [On Line].Http://Www.Hc-Sc.Gc.Ca/Hppb/Familyviolence/Html/Nfntsxagrsex_E.Html. (2003–06–27)

Jacob, M. (Novembre 2000) *Les Différentes Pathologies Sexuelles À L'adolescence.* In Institut Philippe Pinel De Montréal. Psychiatrie Et Violence. *Site De L'institut Philippe Pinel De Montréal*, [On Line]. Http://Www.Pinel.Qc.Ca/Psychiatrie_Violence/Archives.Htm. (2001–09–10)

Oakland Family Services (2003) *Sex Offender Treatment Program: Facts About Sex Offending.* [On Line]. Http://Www.Ofs-Family.Org/Programs/Sexoffend.Htm. (2003–06–27)

Appendix A: Descriptive statistics of developmental factors' scales

Scale	Factors[1]	Correlation	Alpha
Aggressiveness	Aggressiveness with male peers	0.63	0.94
	Verbal violence from age 12 to 6 months prior to aggression	0.57	
	Verbal violence 6 months or less prior to aggression	0.57	
	Physical violence from age 12 to 6 months prior to aggression	0.60	
	Physical violence 6 months or less prior to aggression	0.58	
	Arrogance towards peers	0.39	
	Defiance of authority figures in school	0.22	
	Violence towards teachers	0.54	
	Violence towards peers	0.54	
	Disruptive behaviour in class	0.68	
Loneliness	Lack of intimacy with male peers	0.68	0.83
	Lack of intimacy with female peers	0.65	
	Individual leisure activities	0.58	
	Few or no leisure activities	0.57	

[1]Scales are composed of dichotomous variables (0 = no; 1 = yes).

Chapter Five

Revisiting Recent Research on Social Learning Theory as an Etiological Proposition for Sexually Abusive Male Adolescents

David L. Burton and William Meezan

This article first appeared in the *Journal of Evidence-Based Practice* and is reproduced by kind permission of David Burton, William Meezan and the Haworth Press.

Abstract

This chapter examines social learning theory as a construct that is applicable to adolescent sexual abusers based upon recent published research. Bandura's (1986) work is used to outline the theory and then research on victimisation, aggression, criminality, pornography and personality is reviewed to assess the theory as a reasonable fit for adolescent sexually abusive behaviour. Research implications are offered that argue for rigorous research methods in the field to allow for further test of this theory.

Masculine pronouns will be used throughout this paper, since it focuses on the application of this model to sexually aggressive adolescent males.

Introduction and background

Sexual abuse by adolescent males continues to be a serious public health issue (Association for the Treatment of Sexual Abusers, 2000). Recent statistics from the Federal Bureau of Investigation demonstrate that males under 18 account for 19.7% (n = 8,969) of arrests for sexual crime that do not include rape or prostitution and 16.4% (n = 2,312) of rape arrests (Federal Bureau of Investigation, 2001). Research on juvenile sexual assault is not plentiful, but one of the primary etiological assumptions in the research is that sexual aggressivity is a learned behaviour.

Historically social learning theory has held prevalence over all other proposed etiological models for sexual aggression in both adults and juveniles. For example, in 1888 Binet wrote that sexual deviation was learned behaviour (as cited in McGuire, Carlisle and Young, 1965), and later

Freud considered sexual deviancy or 'perversion' that began in childhood a response '. . . to social conditioning and educational pressures' (Howells and Cook, 1981: 57).

While these two respected theorists seemed to be discussing sexual aggression by adults, other early writers applied these ideas to adolescent males. Waggoner and Boyd (1941), for example, discussed aberrant juvenile sexual behaviour as being '. . . moulded pre-eminently by psychological factors and emotional influences including 'psychic trauma' (p275), while Bandura and Walters (1963) stated that '. . . deviant sexual responses appear to be sometimes the result of parental encouragement and reinforcement of inappropriate sexual behaviours' (p154). Recently, research has been conducted that has been grounded in individual components of this theory, but there has been little writing that ties these components together in an attempt to form a comprehensive model that might explain sexually aggressive behaviour.

This paper reviews some of the basic concepts of observational learning as a subset of social learning theory, and proceeds to review the available literature on adolescent sexual aggressors to assess the usefulness of this theory as an explanatory model for sexual aggression among juveniles. Other theoretical explanations for sexual aggression among youth are then explored, as are the research implications of the material presented.

Social learning theory

In Bandura's most recent text on social learning theory, or as he now calls it, social cognitive theory (1986), he reviews its various theoretical components and the empirical evidence that supports each component. The underpinning of the theory is the concept of learning through modelling (observational learning), which is summarised below.

Observational learning[1]

Observational learning starts with witnessing a behaviour, which is then imprinted in memory and modelled by the youth. Along with the behaviours that are learned in this way, youth incorporate the patterns of verbalised thoughts and the expressed and interpreted emotions of the person modelling the behaviour. Bandura hypothesised that four processes determine successful observational learning: attentional processes, retention processes, production processes, and motivational processes. Each of these processes is affected by a youth's developmental progress.

Attentional processes refer to how much attention is paid to a modelled event and to the person modelling a particular behaviour. Attentional processes are altered, enhanced, or detracted from based on the characteristics of the model or the modelled event. For example, if an event is particularly salient to a youth, then he may be more likely to learn the behaviour. Salience may be increased by the evocativeness of the delivery of the modelled behaviour, or by unique, unusual or conspicuous characteristics of the event (e.g., an event that is more severe in its occurrence, such as violence that is more severe). Increased prevalence or frequency of exposure to a modelled behaviour may also increase salience and learning. Additionally, if a youth sees that the model is rewarded (e.g., emotionally, physically or socially), the youth's attention to the event may be heightened and increase his likelihood of learning from it.

Similarly, models who are attractive or more important to a youth (e.g., parents, siblings), and models who are able to strongly engage a youth (e.g., friends), are likely to be stronger models for the youth, and they will therefore pay more attention to their behaviours than to the behaviours of others. Furthermore, those people with whom the youth spends more time will provide stronger behavioural models for the youth simply because of the frequency of exposure to their behaviours.

In addition, Bandura argues that if a youth is in a chaotic environment he may have the opportunity to witness inappropriate behaviours more often, more clearly, and in greater detail; in structured and well-controlled environments, the number of behaviours available for observation will be more limited.

Attentional processes change as the child or youth develops. Older children and youths have greater ability to pay attention to complex behaviours and incentives, and social behaviours may have more meaning to them. Additionally, the salience of events may increase as a child matures and has a greater ability to recognise subtle differences in behaviours. Thus, more mature youth may be able to pay attention to smaller, less directly observable, parts of an event.

Retention processes refer to the factors involved in incorporating information from a modelled event. Bandura discussed the need for acquisition and use of a comparison template in order to later reproduce the initially observed behaviour. In other words, if a youth learns information he must store it in his memory so that he can compare his own behaviour to the observed behaviour when trying to replicate it. This process occurs through a cognitive symbolic representation of the initial behaviour. These symbols may be understood through visual, oral, or other types of memories that, when put together, allow a person to recall a behaviour they have witnessed. Bandura (1986) discussed research in which, after multiple exposures to similar events (e.g., repeated violence in the family), youths are more likely to remember a prototype of the behaviour rather than the separate events witnessed.

While cognitive rehearsal (e.g., cognitive replaying of the event) or enactment or potential re-enactment of the behaviour (e.g., via fantasies) strengthens the memory of an event, behavioural rehearsal of the event is a more effective way of accurately retaining and acting upon an observed behaviour. Similarly, incentives for learning (i.e., rewards) may increase the accuracy of retention processes. Reinforcement for a cognitive rehearsal of an event (e.g., pleasant feelings from daydreams, masturbatory pleasure, orgasm) may also further the chance that a youth will recall a prototypical or even a specific modelled event.

Memory and abilities to retain access and understand modelled events clearly improve as children age. Furthermore, as children gain more language and acquire greater skills in symbolic representation, their ability to accurately retain information increases. Thus, as they age, children acquire increased ability to symbolically code more information and to understand the

---

[1] Masculine pronouns will be used in this chapter since it focuses on the application of this model to sexually aggressive adolescent males.

complexities of, and apparent incentives for, behaviour. Alternatively, social cognitive deficits may reduce a child's ability to store information completely and accurately. Youth may misinterpret social cues in their environment or misunderstand modelled events due to such deficits, creating poor storage of the event and, later, poor reproduction of the modelled behaviour.

After an event is witnessed and retained, it may then be re-enacted through *production processes*. A youth must somehow organise his memories into a step-by-step set of behaviours, and then compare what he has done with what he has experienced in order to understand if he has produced the initial behaviour properly. Bandura believes that the constituent sub-behaviours, and the order of the sub-behaviours, are learned and retained symbolically as a whole. Production of the behaviour is then a matter of attempting to match what one is doing with the prototype of the behaviours one has stored.

Inability to make an accurate match between what one has experienced and what one does may occur if someone has not seen the behaviour often enough to encode a clear set of memories. It may also occur if they have not understood the behaviour due to developmental limitations or an inability to interpret the event. Similarly, motor deficits or differences between the person who modelled the behaviour and the youth may reduce the youth's ability to match the behavioural sequence and reproduce the behaviour. However, these deficits or differences can be overcome with age, as children develop the additional cognitive and motor abilities needed to reproduce behaviours.

Finally, Bandura discusses *motivational processes* in which three types of incentives for behaviour are described: direct, vicarious, and self-generated or self-produced. Direct incentives are those that a youth receives for undertaking the previously modelled behaviour. Vicarious incentives are rewards that a youth sees another person receive for the behaviour, and assumes that he will receive for behaving in the same way. Self-generated incentives may be affect-based, such as feelings of greater self-efficacy, which may act as an incentive for further behavioural reproduction. Bandura believes that '. . . observational learning occurs through cognitive processes during exposure to modelled events before any responses have been performed and does not necessarily require any intrinsic reward'

(p76). He also argues that both observational learning and modelling of behaviours may occur without any immediate extrinsic reward. He discusses this at length in his ongoing research and writing on self-efficacy (Bandura and Locke, 2003) which indicates that those with greater self-efficacy will continue to work towards their goals even in the light of failure and negative social feedback. This will clearly be the case if a youth anticipates rewards for his behaviour.

Naturally, a youth's perception of anticipated consequences may be accurate – the youth may actually receive the rewards he observed someone else receiving if he behaves in the same fashion. Therefore, a youth may anticipate a set of consequences (e.g., pleasure) for a given behaviour and repeat it based on that anticipated consequence. Alternatively, a youth's perceptions may be inaccurate – he may misperceive or misinterpret the consequences of behaviour he has observed or its long-term consequences. However, since he believes the consequences of the behaviour are positive, he may modify a modelled behaviour in the anticipation that he will ultimately receive the positive consequence. Once a behaviour is performed, further reinforcements (physiological, cognitive or affective) may occur, leading to further behavioural reproduction.

Finally, as children mature they are better able to understand complex rewards, subtle rewards, and delayed gratification. This suggests that youth may be able to understand that rewards do not always come with early awkward attempts at new behaviours, or that rewards may take time (i.e., delayed gratification) or be subtle (e.g., emotional rather than material). With such understanding, the ability to learn complex behaviours is enhanced.

Common learning events for sexually abusive youth

Based on Bandura's theory, several learning paths to sexual aggression can be hypothesised. Sexually aggressive behaviour should increase if one has experienced or witnessed sexual abuse. One might expect that the more severe the sexual abuse experienced or witnessed, the higher the probability that one will abuse, and the severity of the experiences should be related to the type of abuse one commits. Finally, exposure to pornography, criminality, chaotic environments, and other forms of aggression should be related to the development of sexually aggressive behaviour. How well are these hypotheses borne out?

Sexual abuse

One of the first apparent facts that supports social learning theory as being viable for explaining sexually abusive behaviour in adolescent males is their higher than normal rates of childhood sexual victimisation (Cooper, Murphy and Haynes, 1996; Hunter and Figueredo, 2000; Fehrenbach, Smith, Monastersky, and Deisher, 1986; Groth, 1977; Ryan, 1989). This fact supports the theoretical presumption that a learning event occurred from which the youth modelled their own sexually abusive behaviour; that is, they were either sexually victimised or saw others being sexually victimised (Ryan, 1989; Bandura and Walters, 1963).

The literature reports a broad range of statistics on the sexual victimisation of adolescent sexual victimisers. While findings indicate that not all sexually abusive youth have been sexually victimised, reported rates of sexual victimisation for adolescent sexual abusers range from 0% to 86% (Adler and Schulz, 1995; Awad, Saunders and Levene, 1984; Becker, 1990, Benoit and Kennedy, 1992; Burton, 2000; Cooper, Murphy and Haynes, 1996; Fagan and Wexler, 1988, Fehrenbach, Smith, Monasterky and Deisher, 1986; Hunter and Figueredo, 2000; Moody, Brissie and Kim, 1994; Worling, 1995). One reason for the wide diversity of these reports may be the variety of methodologies used in these studies. For example, while some of these samples are from residential facilities (e.g., Burton, 2000); others are from community-based treatment facilities (e.g., Worling, 1995). Presumably, there are differences between these two groups of offenders, which results in their differential placements. For example, residentially based youth typically have more severe victimisation histories (e.g., Burton, 2000; Moody, Brissie and Kim, 1994) and also commit more severe crimes (e.g., Burton, Miller and Shill, 2002) when compared to community-based samples (e.g., Smith, Monastersky and Deisher, 1987; Worling, 2001).

Timing of the data collection may also alter findings across studies. Youths may vary in their willingness to disclose a history of sexual victimisation depending upon their progress through, or time in, treatment. For example, by the end of treatment, youths may have learned more about how to define sexual abuse, may be

more honest about their victimisation history, or may be hoping for leniency from judges or treatment staff (Worling, 1995).

To try and resolve these methodological differences, preliminary research from a recent study combining data from over 50 studies with a combined sample of 8,135 adolescent sexual abusers indicated an overall sexual victimisation rate of 40.28% (Burton and Schatz; 2003). This sexual victimisation rate is almost three times the rate that is found among non-sexually offending delinquents (14.80% of 5,811) in the same analysis. It is also three to four times higher than the sexual victimisation rate of non-abusive youth or community samples of non-delinquent youth, whose sexual victimisation rates are reported to range from 10–15% (Crouch, Hanson, Saunders, Kilpatrick and Resnick, 2000; Finkelhor, Hotaling, Lewis, and Smith, 1990).

All of these figures may represent an under-reporting of sexual victimisation for several reasons. For example, older male youth typically do not disclose as much as younger males (Campis, Hebden-Curtis, and Demaso, 1993). In addition, many males may not disclose sexual victimisation due to fears of being called 'gay' (Johnson and Shier, 1987). Non-disclosure may also be due to the lack of societal permission for males to express feelings or their possessing the skills needed to do so (Mathews, 1986). Finally, boys may not disclose their sexual victimisation because they may feel that they should have been able to protect and defend themselves or that they were weak or somehow unmanly in their responses (Peluso and Putnam, 1996).

For sexually abusive youth who report sexual victimisation, research indicates that the presence of a history of victimisation is related to certain characteristics of their victims. For instance, Worling (1995) investigated the relationship between the presence of sexual victimisation and the gender of victims. He reported that 75% of the male youth that sexually assaulted a male child reported sexual victimisation compared to 25% of those youth that assaulted a female child. Similarly, Cooper, Murphy, and Haynes (1996) reported that youth who had been sexually victimised were more likely to abuse male children than those who had not been sexually victimised. These findings corroborate, in part, Kaufman, Hilliker and Daleiden (1996) who found that sexually victimised adolescent sexual abusers were more likely to victimise males (or both males and females), and younger children.

Severity of sexual victimisation

Severity of the youth's sexual victimisation, which conceptually increases the salience of the modelled event for the youth, seems to affect the youth's own sexual aggression in several ways. Several authors have proposed that adolescent male sexual abusers may have suffered more severe sexual victimisation than non-sexual abusers (Freeman-Longo, 1986; Garland and Dougher, 1990; Burton, 2000). Severe sexual victimisation may result in greater salience of the modelled event, in increased memory of the event, and in greater anxiety and symptomatology from the trauma of the event, including acting sexually inappropriately (Kendall-Tackett, Williams, and Finkelhor, 1993) or aggressively (Burton, 2000). Therefore, more severe victimisation should predict more severe sexually abusive behaviour.

There is some support for this idea in the empirical literature. For example, severity of sexual victimisation is related to the age at which the youth begins to sexually abuse others; youth who begin to aggress at an earlier age have more severe sexual victimisation histories than those whose aggression begins later in life (Burton, 2000; Cooper, Murphy, and Haynes, 1996; Wieckowski, Hartsoe, Mayer and Shortz, 1998). Additionally, the severity of sexual victimisation is a predictor of the severity of youth's later sexual abuse of others. For example, Burton (2003) found that severity and complexity of a youth's sexual victimisation, and the youth's sexual perpetration were significantly correlated, with severity of victimisation accounting for 25.4% of the variation in the severity of perpetration.

Pornography

Pornography may be another medium of learning sexually abusive behaviour, and may help explain why some youth who are sexually aggressive do not have a sexual victimisation history. Many researchers have found frequent use of pornography, early exposure to pornography, and exposure to violent pornography in adult and juvenile sexual abusers (Carter, Prentky, Knight, Vanderweer, and Boucher, 1987; Demare, Lips, and Briere, 1993; Ford and Linney, 1995; Malamuth, Addison, and Koss, 2000; Zolondek, Abel, Northey, and Jordan, 2001). For example, Ford and Linney (1995), in comparing juvenile sexual offenders, violent nonsexual offenders, and status offenders found that exposure to pornographic material differed among the groups, with sexual abusers having more exposure. Moreover, Leguizamo (2000) found that sexually abusive youth were significantly more likely to be exposed to hard-core explicit pornography before the age of 10 than non-sexually abusive delinquents.

The nature of the pornography to which one is exposed (e.g., explicit or violent sexual photography) may increase its salience. So, also, may the person who introduced the youth to pornography (e.g. a parent or a victimiser), the verbalisations regarding sexual behaviour that accompany the introduction of pornography, and the use of pornography as stimulation for masturbation.

Malamuth has been the most productive researcher on the relationship between pornography and sexually abusive behaviours. In a recent review of his and others' work, Malamuth, Addison, and Koss (2000) report a consistent and strong relationship between pornography use and sexually aggressive behaviours, particularly for violent pornography and for men at high risk for sexual aggression. Pornography may lead to further aggressive sexual fantasy for victimised youth or non-victimised youth who later become abusive. Orgasm and other physical pleasure accompanying masturbation may reinforce the cognitive rehearsals of sexual behaviour or aggression generated from memories of sexual victimisation. Additionally, masturbatory fantasies stimulated by pornography may lead to cognitive distortions about sex, possible sexual partners, or potential targets for sexually aggressive behaviours.

Yet the role pornography plays in sexual offending is not entirely clear. Drawing firm conclusions from the research is confounded by methodological differences across studies in design, measurement, and operationalised proxies for sexually aggressive behaviour (Seto, Maric and Barbaree, 2000). Nonetheless, it seems that it may be a potent stimulus for some sexually aggressive youth.

Criminality

There may be additional learning paths to sexually abusive behaviour. For example, what if a youth was exposed to and learned criminality or rule breaking from family members or peers? Or what if he learned negative or hostile biases towards children or women from these people?

Research indicates that many sexually aggressive youth have been exposed to significant amounts of criminality in their families, and have siblings, fathers, mothers and other relatives in jail for various crimes (Baker, Tabacoff, Torunusclio and Eisenstadt, 2001; Bagley and Shewchuk-Dann, 1991; Caputo, Frick and Brodsky, 1999; Wieckowski, Hartsoe, Mayer and Shortz, 1998. For studies of delinquents which include sexual abusers see Chung, Hill, Hakwins, Gilchrist and Nagin, 2002; Farrington, Joliffe, Loeber, Stouthamer-Loeber and Kalb, 2001; Herrenkohl, Huang, Kosterman, Hawkins, Catalano and Smith, 2001). It is therefore logical to assume that many of these youth have had the opportunity to learn rule breaking and criminal behaviour, and have been exposed to criminal thinking (e.g., rationalisation and justification for criminal behaviours). Such exposures might make them less sensitive to the plight of their victims and help pave the way for their victimising behaviour. For example, they may have seen those close to them commit crimes (Baker, Tabacoff, Torunusclio and Eisenstadt, 2001; Bagley, Shewchuk-Dann, 1991; Morris, Anderson and Knox, 2002; Zgourides, Monto and Harris, 1994), may have been encouraged by others to commit crimes, been in gangs (Braaten-Antrim, R. and Thompson, K. M, 1998), or been socialised by criminal peers (Cottle, Lee, and Heilbrun, 2001; Blaske, Borduin, Henggeler, and Mann, 1989).

In fact, it is evident that many sexually abusive youth have committed serious non-sexual crimes. In 1986, Ferhenbach et al. reported that 44% of their sample of adolescent sexual abusers in treatment had a record of non-sexual offences. More recently, Johnson-Reid and Way (2001) reported that 36.8% of the sexually abusive adolescents in their study had prior juvenile court petitions. Burton, Hedgepeth, Ryan and Compton (2003) reported that 60% of their sample had committed serious crimes, including animal cruelty, arson, assault, burglary, car theft, and drug related crimes or theft. Additionally, the recidivism literature indicates that after treatment for sexual abuse, sexually abusive youth are more likely to be arrested for non-sexual crimes than for sexual crimes (Långström and Grann, 2000; Worling and Curwen, 2002) demonstrating that non-sexual crimes are a serious issue for these youth both before and after treatment for their sexual aggression.

There are a number of explanations of these findings that fit well with a social learning interpretation of behaviour. For some youth it may be that when exposure to criminal behaviour has occurred at an early age, or when they have committed crimes early in life, sexual offending or rule breaking is a logical progression when they become developmentally focused on their sexuality – they see no reason not to break rules, and have been taught that rule breaking is a way to fulfil their desires. For other youth, sexually aggressive behaviour may lead to involvement in other criminal activities such as drug use and socialisation with criminal peers. Thus, the relationship between general criminality and sexually abusive behaviour may be bi-directional; some youth start sexually offending which leads to involvement in non-sexual crimes while other youth's criminal activity precedes their sexual offending.

Substance abuse is a specific area of criminality and rule breaking that may be of concern in studying sexual victimisers, but this relationship is more evident in research on adult sexual abusers than in research on adolescents. For example, in several studies evaluating more than 1,400 adult sexual abusers, between 65% and 72% of each sample reported drug abuse (Abracen, Looman and Anderson, 2000; Peugh and Belenko, 2001; Mio, Nanjundappa, Verleur and De Rios, 1986). Substance abuse may compound already poor decision-making, further distorting social cognitions and social cues, ultimately resulting in more sexually abusive behaviour.

Aggression

A similar path might be the learning of aggressive behaviour through witnessing domestic and other violence. If a youth witnesses violence they may learn to be violent. This may then combine with their own sexual victimisation, or may be an independent occurrence that when combined with sexual development or other factors (e.g., exposure to pornography, personality traits, social skills deficits) lead to coercive sexual behaviour or sexual aggression. For example, research has indicated that many sexually abusive youth have witnessed domestic violence and thus have had the opportunity to learn about the mistreatment and instrumental use of others through violent means (Baker, Tabacoff, Torunusclio and Eisenstadt, 2001; Caputo, Frick, Brodsky, 1999; Ford and Linney, 1995; Kahn and Chambers, 1991; Skuse, Bentovim, Hodges, Stevenson, Andreou, Lanyado, New, Williams, and McMillan, 1998; Wieckowski, Hartsoe, Mayer and Shortz, 1998).

In addition to exposure to violence, other studies have indicated that sexually abusive youth have been physically victimised at higher rates than non-sexually abusive youth. Using data from over 50 studies, Burton and Schatz (2003) have agreed with others (Fehrenbach, Smith, Monastersky and Deisher, 1986) that the rate of physical victimisation of adolescent sexual abusers is high. They found a rate of 48.62% of residentially placed sexual abusers (n = 1,388) were physically abused, and that 30.90% of community placed sexual abusers had experienced such abuse (n = 1,053).

Experiencing physical victimisation or witnessing physical aggression has probably also exposed the youth to rationalisations and justifications for such behaviours. In such situations the youth not only see and experience the behaviours, but they hear the social cognitions of their models and may take them on as their own.

Cognition

Manifesting sexually abusive behaviour is undoubtedly more complex than the simple expression of a physical behaviour learned by being exposed to sexual abuse or pornography. As Bandura (1986) discussed, youth may not only learn a behaviour, but they may also learn the verbalised thoughts and interpretations of motives associated with the behaviour. Such verbalised thoughts and interpreted motives may then affect, guide, or alter a youth's thoughts and thought processes, which may be a necessary condition for the youth to express the behaviour. In other words, these cognitions and processes are models for the youth's own cognitions and processes which lead to behavioural expression.

Cognitive distortions

Cognition, social cognition, and thoughts of offending are frequently asserted to be, and have been found to be, problematic for adults (Abel, Becker, and Cunningham-Rathner, 1984; Blumenthal, Gudjonsson, and Burns, 1999; Briere,

Malamuth, and Check, 1985; Gore, 1988; Hanson, Gizzarelli, and Scott, 1994; Murphy, 1991; Neidigh and Krop, 1992; Ward and Hudson, 1998; Ward, Keenan, and Hudson, 1999; Ward, Louden, Hudson, and Marshall, 1995) and adolescent sexual abusers (Kaplan, Becker, and Tenke, 1991; Racey, Lopez and Schneider, 2000; Ryan, 1989). Conceptually, if a youth has thoughts that normalise abuse or obviate empathic responses, he may be more likely to abuse others (Anderson and Dodgson, 2002; Bumby, 1999; Lopez and Emmer, 2002; Moulden and Marshall, 2002). Alternatively, if he has thoughts that it is alright to abuse others, that it will feel good, that it will decrease anxiety or that his victims 'deserve' such behaviour or actually 'ask' for it, he may then be more likely to be abusive. Youth may misinterpret social cues either because of an inability to interpret them or because they reinterpret them based on their understanding of violence.

The presence of such distorted cognitions was found by Shahinfar, Kupersmidt and Matza (2001). Using data from 110 violent youths, 46% of whom were sexual abusers, they found that violent victimisation was significantly related to '. . . approval of aggression as a social response, problems with the interpretation of social cues and maladaptive social goals' (p.136). They state that violent youths have a '. . . maladaptive social information-processing mechanism' (p.138). Overall, they argue that violent youth, including sexual abusers, have social cognitive deficits. This corroborates the research of Racey, Lopez, and Schneider (2000), who found that adolescent sexual abusers were less able to identify emotional states as expressed through facial expressions, and were more likely to misinterpret important non-verbal messages.

Sexual fantasies

The process of cognitive rehearsal under pleasurable conditions (e.g. reviewing the modelled events during masturbation), may also enhance the learning of a modelled event. Such rehearsals may increase the likelihood of distorted cognitions and ultimately play a part in the re-enactment of a modelled event.

One cognitive product that has received attention is the sexual fantasies of sexual abusers, which have long been thought to be deviant for some adolescent sexual abusers (Daleiden, Kaufman, Hilliker and O'Neil, 1998; Kahn, 1990;

Malamuth, 1981). However, the question always arises as to what is a 'deviant' sexual fantasy, and how prevalent such fantasies are in the general population (Donnelly and Fraser, 1998; Leitenberg and Henning, 1995; Plaud and Bigwood, 1997). For example, Leitenberg and Henning, (1995) in an analysis of this field of research, reported that the use of force and power in sex are among the most popular fantasies for all adult males.

Males may have forceful sexual fantasies for a number of reasons, including socialisation (e.g., media, social values) (Donnelly and Fraser, 1998) and evolutionary sociobiology (Hyde and Oliver, 2000; Wilson, 1997). However, while many males may have such sexual fantasies, not all males act on them. This may be due to the factors that influence the formation of these fantasies. Sexual fantasies may be aggressive due to societal media and messages for many men. For others, however, aggressive sexual fantasies may be present because they have been abused or been exposed to deviant sexual behaviour through sexual victimisation, sexual aggressiveness, physical victimisation, or violent pornography. Thus, the factors behind the fantasies may relate to whether a youth abuses others. This hypothesis is borne out in a study of adolescent sexually abusive males by Johnson and Knight (2000), who found that sexual victimisation, both directly and through misogynistic sexual fantasies, predicts the degree of sexual coercion used in the youths' offences.

Retention and production processes

A basic proposition of social learning theory, when applied to sexually abusive behaviour, is that sexually aggressive youths may be behaving in ways that indicate that they have learned from their own victimisation (Ryan, 1989; Dicenso, 1992; Veneziano, Veneziano and LeGrand, 2000). According to Bandura (1986), this would occur if the event is accurately stored and the youth anticipates pleasure by enacting it. While having sex for reproduction may be a mammalian instinct, it is hard to argue that a young man knows how to commit sexual crimes without prior information about them. It is difficult to imagine, for example, that a youth would know how to insert his penis into another male's anus or to expect that fellatio might be a pleasurable act without having any knowledge of these behaviours and the possible gratifications that might accrue from them. One test of this part of the model – that the adolescent abuser may have encoded the behaviour in memory and is repeating what he has learned – is to assess if adolescents who have been sexually victimised and who are abusive repeat what was done to them.

The research of Veneziano, Veneziano and LeGrand (2000) supports this hypothesis. They found significant relationships between the victimisation experienced by the youth and the abusive behaviour perpetrated by the youth when assessing fondling and anal intercourse. More recently, Burton (2003) tested four other dimensions of the youth's sexual victimisation and compared these to the same characteristics of the youth's sexually abusive behaviour. He found significant relationships on all dimensions tested: gender, relationship, modus operandi, and severity of acts. For example, if youth were abused by men, they were more likely to abuse males than those not abused by males; if youth suffered from a penetrative act, they were more likely to repeat the behaviour than if they had not experienced penetration during their own victimisation. Thus, youth seem to repeat much of what they learn through their own victimisation.

Other factors that may influence learning

Chaotic environments

Bandura (1986) suggests that another factor that may affect whether a person learns something is whether he has an increased opportunity to see modelled behaviours. He posits that a chaotic home may allow a youth to see more typically adult behaviours than in a well structured home. For sexually abusive youth, the question becomes 'Do these youth have more opportunities to witness sexual, sexually aggressive, and aggressive behaviours than non-abusive youth?'

Research on the families of adolescent sexual abusers typically indicates difficulties within the family constellation, including family relations that are characterised by rigidity and low cohesion, with mothers having many neurotic symptoms (Blaske, Borduin, Henggeler, and Mann, 1989), difficult relationships among family members (Awad, Saunders and Levene, 1984), broken homes (DeMartine, 1989), domestic violence between parents (Fagan and Wexler,

1988), high rates of sexual victimisation of mothers as children (Becker, Cunningham-Rathner and Kaplan, 1987; Kaplan, Becker and Martinez, 1990), and absence of parents in the lives of youth and thus a lack of both nurturance and supervision (Hummel, Thomke, Oldenburger, and Specht, 2000; Prentky et al, 1989).

Additional research indicates that many sexually abusive youth have witnessed criminality, substance abuse, and domestic violence in their homes (Baker, Tabacoff, Torunusclio and Eisenstadt, 2001; Wieckowski, Hartsoe, Mayer and Shortz, 1998; Bagley, Shewchuk-Dann, 1991; Morris, Anderson and Knox, 2002; Zgourides, Monto and Harris, 1994). Based on all these findings, it might be hypothesised that many adolescent sexual abusers have been in homes in which they had more opportunities to observe and learn developmentally inappropriate sexual and violent behaviours than non-sexual abusers.

Personality

The quest for consistent personality patterns among adolescent sexual abusers has been elusive (Carpenter and Peed 1995; Smith, Monastersky and Deisher, 1987; Worling, 2001). However, studies exploring these factors have had disturbing results that have implications for the treatment of these youth. In the few studies that have compared juvenile sexual abusers to non sexually abusive youth, sexual abusers have had clinically concerning scores on multiple scales contained in various instruments. For instance, on Catell's High School Personality Questionnaire, Moody, Brissie and Kim (1994) found that sexual offenders were more detached, intelligent, impatient, indulgent, sensitive to threat, and expectant of affection and attention than the oppositionally defiant non-sexual offending youth. They were also more likely than delinquent youth to be followers in a group and to follow their own urges. Similarly, on the Millon Adolescent Clinical Inventory, Burton (in press) found that sexual abusers scored higher than non-sexual offending youth on the introversive, inhibited, doleful, forceful, egotistic, oppositional and borderline scales.

Such findings may indicate that personality factors play a role in the sexual aggression of some youth, although this role is as of yet unclear – personality may exacerbate or interact with experiences of victimisation. For example, Burton (in press) found that scores on the scales above, when combined with sexual trauma, contributed significantly to explaining group membership (i.e., sexually abusive youth versus non-sexually abusive delinquents).

Protective factors

As stated earlier, many youth who have been sexually victimised do not become sexually aggressive. Recent consideration of the resiliency of youth in general (Fraser, in press; Williams, Ayers, and Arthur, 1997), the application of strengths-based assessment in practice, and the emergence of the concept of protective factors, have led some authors to apply these ideas to their research. For example, Veneziano and Veneziano (1995), in studying a college sample, reported that deterrents to committing crimes in general include an unwillingness to violate moral, ethical and religious principles, feelings of guilt, and the threat of formal sanctions. Hence, having strong ethical, moral, and religious principles, having a healthy sense of guilt, and understanding the formal costs of the violation of the law, may be seen as protective factors that help youth who are at-risk of abusive behaviour avoid aggression.

The notion and application of protective factors are just making their way into the literature on sexually aggressive youth. Specifically, Bremer (1998) has developed a protective factors scale based on the literature and her clinical work to help determine strengths in youth. Her factors fall into seven areas: general behaviour, offence characteristics, offence denial, social adjustment, emotional adjustment, co-operation, and family style. For example, in the area of emotional adjustment, youth with no history of emotional problems, a full range of healthy affect and normative test responses are seen as having more protective factors than a youth with a history of emotional problems, flat affect, and notable emotional disturbance. While this scale has not yet been applied to the etiology of sexual aggression, it may be useful in understanding what factors may be protective of the development of sexually aggressive behaviours. Unfortunately, there is no research using this scale or its constructs. However, knowledge of protective factors and their application in research could further our understanding of the etiology of sexually abusive behaviours, help in the development of preventive interventions, and enhance our treatment of sexual offenders.

Contradictory research

In the research concerning juvenile sexual abusers, only one study is at all contradictory to the set of propositions that emanate from Bandura's model. Skuse et al. (1998) report that in a comparison of two groups of young (11-15 years of age) sexually victimised adolescents (11 who sexually abused others and 14 who did not), characteristics of their own sexual victimisation (e.g., force, duration, evidence of penetration, number of perpetrators) did not differentiate the two groups using either bivariate or multivariate logistic analyses. This would indicate that the severity of abuse did not predict the severity of or the presence of sexually abusive behaviour. The authors did, however, find that exposure to family violence was a predictor of being in the sexually abusive group. Perhaps this group of youth entered sexually abusive behaviour along the aggression pathway described previously.

This study included many other interesting ideas as possible explanations for their findings, but is limited due to its small sample size. Future studies should explore these ideas, including the influences of developmental stage, IQ, and social networks, to further test the viability of social learning theory as a framework for understanding sexually abusive behaviour.

Alternate explanations

Few other theories have been used to explain sexually aggressive behaviour among youth, and none has been empirically supported at this point in time. However much theoretical writing has been done about sexual aggression in adults, and some of the insights derived from these theories might provide new, different, and useful perspectives when they are applied to sexually abusive adolescents.

Feminist theory

Feminist approaches are frequently credited with bringing attention to the problem of sexual aggression (Marshall, Laws and Barbaree, 1990; Stermac, Segal and Gillis, 1990). These approaches discuss normal socialisation processes as a large part of the cause of sexual aggression (Daigle and Harris, 1989; Brownmiller, 1975). Most feminist writers criticise those who would blame women for the abuse they suffer and believe that such views support male dominance in US culture. They see these and related factors as etiologically relevant for sexual abusers and as supportive of continuing sexual aggression.

There is, however, a dearth of research on this theory as an explanation for sexual aggression. The unit of analysis, the difficulty in defining variables that emanate from it, and the empirical support for individualistic theories, have made it difficult to test this theories' derived hypotheses in the etiology of sexual offending. Nevertheless, writers from the feminist perspective raise and clarify issues about the etiology and treatment of sexual offenders, and make us aware of society's culpability for this problem.

Biology

Biology seems to be a potentially important and somewhat neglected variable in this area of research. Data from studies testing the relationship of biological factors to sexual aggression come from samples of adult sexual abusers, and indicates that, at least for some abusers, neurobiology may play a role in their abusive behaviours (Lothstein, 1999). For example, Galski, Thornton and Shumsky (1990) found brain abnormalities and several neurological deficits within their sample.

A superb review of work and theory integration from this perspective is presented by Golden, Jackson, Peterson-Rohn and Gontkovsky (1996). They note that temporal damage, central nervous system degeneration, poor impulse control due to impaired frontal lobe function, global cognitive dysfunction, and other neurological factors are all potential contributors to a small number of adult male sexual abusers' behaviours.

In addition, several neurological factors may also be impacted by sexual victimisation. These include hippocamal change – changes in the locus coerulus and other areas of the brain (Knopp and Benson, 1996) – which may then lead to aggressive behaviour (Bell, 2000; Pincus, 1999). Could it be that those sexual abusers that have neurological damage also have experienced sexual victimisation?

Emerging theories

Two theories have recently been introduced into the literature in this field. The first is attachment theory, which a few studies have incorporated but which has not yet been fully explored in research with sexual abusers (Lyn and Burton, in press; Marshall and Eccles, 1991; Smallbone and Dadds, 1998, 2000, 2001). In the results to date, researchers agree that adult sexual abusers have insecure attachment, usually fearful or dismissing types. However, there is not agreement as to whether non-sexual criminals have similarly poor attachment (Lyn and Burton, in press; Smallbone and Dadds, 1998, 2000 2001; Ward, Hudson and Marshall, 1996), and therefore whether this trait is specific to sexual abusers and important in their etiology. Ward, Hudson, and Marshall (1996) proposed that the influence of insecure attachment upon sex and intimacy may be particularly strong when combined with other factors that may reduce one's control over sexual impulses. Some of these were discussed above, and include alcohol, drugs, deviant fantasies, and cognitive distortions.

The second theory, evolutionary adaptation (Quinsey and Lalumiere, 1995; Thornhill and Palmer, 2000; Thornhill and Thornhill, 1992), has been posited as a way to understand rape committed by adults. While it has been conceptually discussed and extensively argued in the literature (Archer and Vaughan, 2001; Gard and Bradley, 2001; Kennan, 1998; Malamuth and Heilmann, 1998; Segal, 2001; Vega, 2001; Ward, and Siegert), it has not yet been researched and it is unlikely that the technology to do so will be present in the near future – measurement of human evolution is very difficult, the variables contained in this theory may not be able to be operationalised, and the degree of clarity needed for empirical testing of this theory may not be reached.

Multi-factor theories

Theories that take many, and sometimes divergent, factors into account may be labelled multi-factor theories. Factors such as personality, access to victims, loneliness, social isolation, and deviant sexual interests are commonly considered as acting in concert, or along separate pathways, to influence sexual abusing. Multi-factor explanations (Finkelhor, 1986; Marshall and Barbaree, 1990; Hall and Hirschman, 1992) have been explored in only a limited way, and therefore have not yet been either empirically supported or repudiated. While these theories are more difficult to evaluate

empirically given the number of variables that might be involved in testing them, they offer a more holistic and complex view of abusive behaviours and allow for many pathways to sexual aggression. Such views also tend to fit observations from clinical practice. Large-scale research studies, with carefully considered methodologies, may be very useful in exploring these complex conceptualisations.

Knight and Sims-Knight (2001) have recently undertaken a very promising study, which presents a new multi-factor theory of juvenile sexual aggression. In this pathway analysis of several hundred sexually abusive youth, all have been found to experience some sort of trauma. The use of variables from a number of domains, including personality and sexual fantasy, are being used to help explain sexually abusive behaviours. Further research and analysis by these authors and others may help illuminate multi-factor theories for juvenile sexual offending.

Research implications

It is evident that significant progress has been made in testing the usefulness of social learning theory as a way of understanding the etiology of sexually aggressive behaviours among youth. It is also clear, however, that more needs to be done before the field can be comfortable in adapting this theory as its major and empirically validated orientation to this social problem. Attending to the issues outlined below will help to address the current limits of the juvenile sexual abuser literature.

Research questions

Research questions that explore single variable models are currently the most common in the field. This may be appropriate given the age of the field, but available findings from current research now support the need for studies with greater sophistication. The field must move away from testing one independent variable at a time in order to better understand the etiology of sexual aggression.

There are several research questions that can be derived from social learning theory that are currently either unanswered or inadequately answered. These questions need to be explored individually and in combination with each other. For example, is the effect of multiple types of victimisation stronger than the effect of a single type of victimisation (Higgins and McCabe, 2000a, 2000b; Mullen, Martin, Anderson, Romans and Herbison, 1995) in predicting sexual aggression? Is one type of victimisation (i.e., sexual victimisation) more likely to lead a youth to sexual aggression than other types? How do these factors interact with each other and with other variables that concern victimisation to predict sexually aggressive behaviour?

These considerations lead to a second set of questions that deal with the learning processes of sexually abusive adolescents. What are the attentional processes of victimised sexual abusers? What in their experiences is most salient and how does that salience affect their behaviour? How are sexually abused youth's memories affected by trauma and how are their learning processes altered? What sort of behavioural models do sexually aggressive adolescents hold in their minds when they abuse or fantasise about abusing others? Do they compare their own behaviour to their model? How do they react to discrepancies between the current behaviour and the model? What, other than the obvious (e.g., sexual motivations), motivates sexually abusive youth to produce such behaviours? How do these learning factors interact with one another to further explain various patterns of sexually abusive behaviour?

Beyond these individual areas that derive from social learning theory, multivariate models need to be tested that combine questions from the various parts of social learning theory to more fully assess the behavioural pathways of these adolescents. Conceptual areas that need more thorough assessment, both individually through multiple measures and in combination with other areas, include trauma history, family history (e.g., criminality), environmental factors (e.g., sexualisation, pornography, and exposure to violence), individual characteristics (personality, cognitive processes and content, and functioning), and individual criminal (sexual and nonsexual) behaviour. Within each realm, protective factors (Bremer, 1998) should also be assessed.

Measurement

Measurement of the variables involved in this theory can be quite challenging. Even the measurement of the deceptively simple concepts of victimisation and aggression is

underdeveloped. For example, victimisation has typically been measured by simple dichotomous measures, while sexual aggression tends to be measured through nominal categories (e.g., who they perpetrated against, the acts of perpetration, etc). Multi-level variables, that provide more dimensions and capture the complexity of both victimisation and perpetration need to be developed.

Further, measures that are specific to this field must also be developed. For example, while there are some measures for trauma (Bernstein, Ahluvalia, Pogge, and Handelsman, 1997; Bissada, Briere, Damon, and Johnson, 2001; Ryan, Rodriguez, Rowan, and Foy, 1992), there are very few for sexual aggression (Burton and Fleming, 1998). And none of these more specific measures have been thoroughly psychometrically assessed.

As noted above, there are fundamental questions about the cognitive processes of learning that need to be answered in relation to this population. While recent research by Freyd (DePrince, and Freyd, 1999; Freyd, Martorello, Alvarado, Hayes and Christman, 1998) and others using stroop tests and other learning tasks (DePrince and Freyd, 2001) in relationship to memory and trauma may facilitate the measurement of these variables, more needs to be done to understand the trauma based learning and cognitive processes that occur during the production of behaviour for juvenile sexual abusers.

In addition, issues of self-report cloud the reliability and validity of the measurement of salient variables in this field. Currently most studies in the field do not use a social desirability test as part of their battery of measurements. In addition, while such a measure has been developed for adult sexual abusers (Kroner and Weekes, 1996), its usefulness for adolescents has been questioned (Burton, Miller and Shill, 2002), leading to the need for the development of a more age-specific measure. In addition, specific content related measures of dissimulation or physiological measures (e.g., eye startle examination) may help in this area.

Design

There have been few design variations in the research conducted in this field. Most studies have depended on cross-sectional surveys or intake forms to gather data, which pose significant limitations on the depth of information that can be produced. The use of these designs also exacerbate the problems that are always present in doing research with this population – the amount of time that can be spent collecting data, the collection of sensitive data, issues of confidentiality, and the use of simplistic measures such as single crime points (e.g., index crimes for which youth were arrested versus data reflecting the actual range of crimes a youth commits). Qualitative research with juvenile sexual abusers has not been published. Information from such studies may be illuminating and provide a more in-depth understanding of the issue under investigation. If combined with quantitative data from a survey of the same sample, it is likely that a more complete picture of the phenomena will emerge. The adult offender field has seen recent efforts of this sort which has led to dramatic changes in the field (Ward and Hudson, 1998).

Another design issue in the field is the lack of longitudinal studies. Most research, with the exception of a few recidivism studies (e.g., Worling and Curwen, 2000) and research on the long term effects of victimisation (e.g., Widom, 2001) does not collect data over time on the same sample. Yet, longitudinal and prospective studies would allow this field to learn how childhood experiences shape future offending as well as studying the development of sexual aggression over the life course. And such studies would help to sort out which variables are independent and which variables are dependent in the developmental life course of this population, allow researchers to account for the receipt of treatment as an influence on the reliability of data received, and account for time since victimisation in the analysis and reporting of results.

Sampling

Sampling issues are particularly troublesome in research with this population. For the most part, samples in the studies reported in the literature regarding juvenile sexual offenders are not representative, are small, and lack clarity about the sample's location which can affect results. Unlike other fields, large national or even statewide data sets are not available that can adequately address the complex questions that face the field, and data on the variables needed to assess these questions are not systematically collected.

Such sampling issues make rapid knowledge development difficult and generalisation of findings impossible. To address these issues, future research endeavours should include procedures for sharing and pooling data sets, collecting data from larger representative samples, and possibly adding critical questions to collateral, ongoing, longitudinal data sets that might be helpful in advancing knowledge about this population.

While these solutions will take time to implement, some smaller steps can be taken to improve the quality of the samples used in the research in the field. For example, the literature suggests that residential and community-based sexually abusing youth are different (Way, 2000; Burton and Schatz, 2003). Yet these two groups are often treated as if they were the same, both in empirical studies and reviews of the literature. Stratifying samples along these lines might help to shed light on important questions and the differences between these two groups; at the very least, it will stop the combination of data from these two populations, which can lead to findings that are not valid across subjects.

Using multiple age and demographically matched groups (e.g., sexually abusive youth, sexually abusive youth who are delinquent in other ways, delinquent youth who are not sexually abusive and non delinquent youth who have been sexually abused and who have been exposed to aggression and criminality) can also be used to rule out confounding variables. Studies using such samples could compare these groups on critical variables to begin to understand their pathways to different behaviours.

If the field is to build its knowledge base in an efficient manner, it seems obvious that practitioners, who often control access to this population, must be involved in the determination of research questions and the design and execution of studies carried out in the field. Without such buy-in and co-operation, the possibility of improving the samples used in the field is remote. Yet until recently, research in the field has been controlled by those outside of the agencies that serve this population. In this small and relatively new field of research few collaborative efforts for research have been developed. Recent efforts by both the Association for the Treatment of Sexual Abusers (Kaufman, 2003) and the Collaborative for Adolescent Sexual Abuser Research, Mentoring and Advancement, which was started at the 21st annual Association for the Treatment of Sexual Abusers meeting in San Antonio (2002), are working towards this goal.

Analysis

Small, non-representative samples clearly impact the complexity of the analysis that can be undertaken, and thus limit the nature of the questions that can be answered around this population. Because of this, very few projects have been able to undertake path analysis, structural equation modelling or discriminant function analysis, all of which are typically used for the testing of theoretical models.

Missing data has also been problematic for some studies. In order to remedy this situation, which decreases sample size even further, researchers should be encouraged to learn the recently developed techniques for the imputation of missing data and to use them when appropriate in their research (e.g., Schafer and Graham, 2002).

Practice implications

At this time, practice with juvenile sexual abusers is predominantly based upon cognitive behavioural therapy models (Burton and Smith-Darden, 2001). While incomplete, the research evidence seems to suggest that this approach is appropriate and that further development of cognitive methods for juvenile sexual abusers is warranted. Recent texts (Ryan and Lane, 1997; Rich, 2003) offer many components of treatment for adolescent male sexual abusers, and while a full explication of these suggestions is beyond the scope of this chapter, some of the most important of these should be highlighted. For instance, recent writing on cognitive schema (which are larger and more complex than simple cognitive distortions) and ways to ameliorate them, now present in the literature on adult sexual abusers seems appropriate for juveniles. Additional cognitive treatment components that are already being discussed for juvenile sexual abusers and delinquents include social skills training (Allen, Marsh, McFarland, McElhaney, Land, Jodl and Peck, 2002; Worling, 1998; Tarolla, Wagner, Rabinowitz, and Tubman, 2002) and work to increase emotional intelligence, which is frequently damaged as result of trauma (Goleman, 1995, Trinidad, Johnson and Anderson, 2002; McMurran, Egan, Blair and Richardson, 2002).

In addition, interventions that are designed based on our current understanding of the heterogeneous paths to sexual aggression also seem justified by the research literature. For example, youth who develop sexually abusive behaviour because of traumatic incidents may need a different type of treatment than youth who become sexually abusive by learning criminality in their home.

As the field moves to improve its practice with adolescent sexual abusers it is critical that innovative and new approaches to treatment of this population be rigorously evaluated. After all, the literature just reviewed reveals gaps in knowledge, and thus interventions based on it must be viewed sceptically until they are proven effective.

Expanding trauma-based treatment

Based on this model, trauma resolution should be a key component of treatment for many youth, and over 80% of specialised adolescent sexual abuser treatment programmes address this issue (Burton and Smith-Darden, 2001). Yet the effectiveness of these models has not been demonstrated for this population. Nonetheless, a broad range of cognitive techniques for trauma resolution have been shown to be effective with other disorders (e.g. depression, anxiety, PTSD), and thus may be appropriate for these youth. (Foa, Rothblum, Riggs and Murdock, 1991; Foa, Hearst-Ikeda and Perry, 1995; Nishith, Pallavi, Hearst, Mueser and Foa, 1995). Moreover, research indicates that these methods are successful in ameliorating many of the behaviours and issues that characterise delinquent youth, including PTSD with anger (Novaco and Chemtaub, 1998), disassociation (Wagner and Linehan, 1998), substance abuse (Ruzak, Polusny and Abueg, 1998), trauma-related guilt (Kubany and Manke, 1995) and sexual victimisation (Briere, 1997, Brom, Kleber and Defares, 1989; Lanktree and Briere, 1995; McCann and Pearlman, 1990; Meadows and Foa, 1998, 1999, 2000).

Criminality

While specialised treatment has been shown to be very effective in reducing recidivism of sexual crime, the post-treatment rate for non-sexual crimes in this population is quite alarming (Worling and Curwen, 2000). Therefore, interventions that address this possibility need to be tested with this population. Clinical approaches that strive to establish a therapeutic alliance (Horvath and Greenberg, 1994; Horvath and Symonds, 1991; Digiusuppe, Linscott and Jilton,1996; Shirk and Russell, 1996) are empirically supported for work with delinquent youth since it is associated with psychological improvement and decreased recidivism (Florsheim, Shotorbani, Guest-Warnick, Barrat and Hwang, 2000).

A broad survey of the literature on general delinquency indicates that treatment approaches with a broad-based focus on behaviour change, skill-building, and the incorporation of a psychological framework are efficacious (Lipsey, 1995). Lipsey suggests that multi-modal approaches are most effective with delinquent populations, supporting our contention that treatment programmes that go beyond cognitive-behavioural approaches should be designed and tested with adolescent sexual abusers. One approach that incorporates many of these components is Multisystemic Treatment, which has shown to be effective in delinquent populations (Henggeler, Borduin, Melton, Mann, Smith, Hall, Cone, and Fucci, 1991; Henggeler, Rodick, Borduin, Hanson, Watson, and Urey, 1986) and, in a pilot study, with adolescent sexual abusers (Borduin and Schaeffer, in press).

Family treatment

Studies have shown that the number of programmes offering family treatment to adolescent sexual abusers is declining (Burton, Smith-Darden, Levins, Fiske and Freeman-Longo, 2000). Yet these approaches may be important to test with this population given the fact that the model presented in this paper seems to indicate that many of the etiological issues may occur within the family (e.g., exposure to pornography, exposure to criminality and aggression). It might therefore be wise to test specific forms of family treatment in cases of adolescent sexual abuse where abuse by family members and other family issues are present before allowing these interventions to disappear from the treatment repertoire.

Conclusions

The social learning model has been the dominant orientation for studying sexual aggression among adults, and recent studies have illustrated its empirical strength for studying juvenile sexual

abusers. However, more rigorous empirical work needs to be done if we are to have confidence that this theory is indeed robust for this population. Such an expanded research agenda requires the field to develop studies that address new and more complex research questions and to use more rigorous methods to evaluate the theory. Studies that use more appropriate measurement instruments, research designs, samples, and complex analytic techniques can add to our understanding of the usefulness of social learning theory in explaining the behaviours of sexually aggressive youth.

However, no matter how rigorous the research, it is unlikely that social learning theory alone will be able to fully explain the sexually aggressive behaviour of adolescents. Currently, even the most sophisticated study explains only 44% of the variance in the dependent variable in their study (Knight and Sims- Knight, 2001). More rigorous studies using only this theory base may add to these numbers only marginally.

New directions in the field point to the need to include variables from other theories if we are to more fully understand this phenomenon. The inclusion of biological variables and constructs from feminist theory, attachment theory and, if possible, evolutionary theory would probably advance our knowledge significantly. And thus, the call for the use of multi-factorial explanatory theories, that combine these variables with others described in this paper, should be heeded. Only by integrating knowledge from all levels of ecological theory – biological, psychological, and social – can we hope to gather the most complete understanding of sexually abusive behaviour by adolescents.

Practice models already incorporate some strategies developed from social cognition and learning theory approaches. Such interventions are warranted based on the empirical evidence. However, given what is known from the delinquency literature, multimodal treatments, which address a variety of issues through a variety of means, should be developed and tested with adolescent sexual abusers. Just as the explanatory theory for adolescent sexual abuse should test and, when appropriate, incorporate constructs from multiple theories, interventions must also become more complex based on their demonstrated effectiveness. The practice modalities used with adolescent sexual abusers should expand as our empirical understanding of the etiology of this social problem evolves.

Author note

The authors extend appreciation to Anne Polyzou for initial literature searches, Kerry Jo Duty for help with literature searches and editing, Rachel Schatz for work on the practice implications section and to Drs. Raymond Knight, William Friedrich and Janis Bremer for ideas.

References

Abel, G.G., Becker, J.V. and Cunningham-Rathner, J. (1984) Complications, Consent, and Cognitions in Sex Between Children and Adults. *International Journal of Law and Psychiatry.* 7, 89–103.

Abracen, J., Looman, J. and Anderson, D. (2000) Alcohol and Drug Abuse in Sexual and Nonsexual Violent Offenders. *Sexual Abuse: A Journal of Research and Treatment.* 12: 4, 263–74.

Adler, N. and Schultz, J. (1995) Sibling Incest Offenders. *Child Abuse and Neglect.* 19: 7, 811–9.

Allen, J.P., Marsh, P., McFarland, P., McElhaney, K.B., Land, D.J., Jodl, K.M. and Peck, S. (2002) Attachment and Autonomy as Predictors of The Development of Social Skills and Delinquency During Mid-adolescence. *Journal of Consulting and Clinical Psychology.* 70: 1, 56–66.

Anderson, D. and Dodgson, P. (2002) Empathy Deficits, Self-Esteem, and Cognitive Distortions in Sexual Offenders. in Fernandez, Y. (Ed.) *In Their Shoes.* Oklahoma: Wood 'N' Barnes Publishing.

Archer, J. and Vaughan, A. E. (2001) Evolutionary Theories of Rape. *Psychology, Evolution and Gender: Special Issue.* 3: 1, 95–101.

ATSA Executive Board of Directors (2003) *Sexual Abuse as a Public Health Problem.* ATSA.

Awad, G., Saunders, E. and Levene, J. (1984) A Clinical Study of Male Adolescent Sexual Offenders. *International Journal of Offender Therapy and Comparative Criminology.* 28, 105–16.

Bagley, C. and Shewchuk-Dann, D. (1991) Characteristics of 60 Children and Adolescents Who Have a History of Sexual Assault Against Others: Evidence From a Controlled Study. *Journal of Child and Youth Care.* Fall, 43–52.

Baker, A.J.L., Tabacoff, R., Tornusciolo, G. and Eisenstadt, M. (2001) Calculating the Number of Offenses and Victims of Juvenile Sexual Offending: The Role of Post-treatment Disclosures. *Sexual Abuse: A Journal of Research and Treatment.* 13: 2, 79–90.

Bandura, A. and Locke, E. (2003) Negative Self-Efficacy and Goal Effects Revisited. *Journal of Applied Psychology.* 88: 1, 87–100.

Bandura, A. and Walters, R. (1963) *Social Learning and Personality Development.*

Bandura, A. (1986) *Social Foundations of Thought and Action: A Social Cognitive Theory.* Englewood Cliffs, NJ: Prentice-Hall.

Becker, J. (1990) Treating Adolescent Sexual Offenders. *Professional Psychology: Research and Practice.* 21, 362–5.

Becker, J.V., Kaplan, M.S. and Martinez, D.F. (1990) A Comparison of Mothers of Adolescent Incest versus Non-Incest Perpetrators. *Journal of Family Violence.* 5: 3, 209–14.

Becker, J., Cunningham-Rathner, J. and Kaplan, M. (1987) Adolescent Sexual Offenders: Demographics, Criminal and Sexual Histories, and Recommendations for Reducing Future Offenses. *Journal of Interpersonal Violence.* 1: 4, 431–45.

Bell, C. (2000) *Psychiatric Aspects of Violence: Issues in Prevention and Treatment.* California: Jossey-Bass Inc.

Benoit, J. and Kennedy, W. (1992) The Abuse History of Male Adolescent Sex Offenders. *Journal of Interpersonal Violence.* 7, 543–8.

Bernstein, D.P., Ahluvalia, T., Pogge, D. and Handelsman, L. (1997) Validity of the Childhood Trauma Questionnaire in an Adolescent Psychiatric Population. *Journal of the Academy of Child Adolescent Psychiatry.* 36: 3, 340–8.

Bissada, A., Briere, J., Damon, L. and Johnson, K. (2001) The Trauma Symptom Checklist for Young Children (TSCYC): Reliability and Association With Abuse Exposure in a Multi-Site Study. *Child Abuse and Neglect.* 25: 8, 1001–14.

Blaske, D.M., Borduin, C.M., Henggeler, S.W. and Mann, B.J. (1989) Individual, Family, and Peer Characteristics of Adolescent Sex Offenders and Assaultive Offenders. *Developmental Psychology.* 25, 846–55.

Blumenthal, S., Gudjonsson, G. and Burns, J. (1999) Cognitive Distortions and Blame Attribution in Sex Offenders Against Adults and Children. *Child Abuse and Neglect.* 23, 129–43.

Borduin, C. and Schaeffer, C. (2002) Multisystemic Treatment of Sexual Offenders: A Progress Report. *Journal of Psychology and Human Sexuality.* 13: 3–4, 25–42.

Braaten-Antrim, R. and Thompson, K.M. (1998) Youth Maltreatment and Gang Involvement. *Journal of Interpersonal Violence.* 13: 3, 328–45.

Bremer, J. (1998) Challenges in the Assessment and Treatment of Sexually Abusive Adolescents. *The Irish Journal of Psychology.* 19: 1, 82–92.

Briere, J. (1997) Treating Adults Severely Abused as Children: The Self-Trauma Model. in Wolfe, D.A. (Ed.) *Child Abuse: New Directions in Prevention and Treatment Across The Lifespan.* Thousand Oaks, CA: Sage Publications.

Briere, J., Malamuth, N. and Check, J.V. (1985) Sexuality and Rape-Supportive Beliefs. *International Journal of Women's Studies.* 8, 398–403.

Brom, D., Kleber, R.J. and Defares, P.B. (1989) Brief Psychotherapy for Post-traumatic Stress Disorders. *Journal of Consulting and Clinical Psychology.* 57: 5, 607–12.

Brownmiller, S. (1975) *Against Our Will: Men, Women and Rape.* New York: Simon and Schuster.

Bumby, K. (1999, September) *Selective Empathic Inhibition and Cognitive Distortion.* Presentation at The Annual Meeting of The Association for The Treatment of Sexual Abusers, Orlando, FL.

Burton, D.L. (2000) Were Adolescent Sexual Offenders Children With Sexual Behaviour Problems? *Sexual Abuse: A Journal of Research and Treatment.* 12: 1, 37–48.

Burton, D.L. (2003) The Relationship Between the Sexual Victimisation of and the Subsequent Sexual Abuse by Male Adolescents. *Child and Adolescent Social Work Journal.* 20: 4, 277–96.

Burton, D.L. (In Press) an Exploratory Evaluation of the Contribution of Personality and Childhood Sexual Victimisation to the Development of Sexually Abusive Behaviour. *Sexual Abuse: A Journal of Research and Treatment.*

Burton, D.L. and Fleming, M. (1998) Psychometric Examination of the Sex Offender Evaluation Instrument. Poster for the Annual National Association for the Treatment of Sexual Abusers Conference, Vancouver, CA.

Burton, D.L. and Schatz, R. (2003, July) *Meta-Analysis of the Abuse Rates of Adolescent Sexual Abusers.* Paper Presented at The 8th International Family Violence Conference, Portsmouth, NH.

Burton, D.L. and Smith-Darden, J. (2001) *North American Survey of Sexual Abuser Treatment and Models Summary Data.*

Burton, D.L. and Smith-Darden, J., with Levins, J., Fiske, J. and Freeman-Longo, R. (1999) *The 1996 Safer Society Survey of Sexual Offender Treatment*

Programs. Brandon, VT: Safer Society Foundation.

Burton, D.L., Hedgepeth, M.A., Ryan, G. and Compton, D. (2003) The Relationship of Trauma to Non-Sexual Crimes Committed by Adolescent Sexual Abusers. Submitted for Publication.

Burton, D.L., Miller, D.L. and Shill, C.T. (2002) A Social Learning Theory Comparison of the Sexual Victimisation of Adolescent Sexual Offenders and Nonsexual Offending Male Delinquents. *Child Abuse and Neglect.* 26, 803–907.

Campis, L.B., Hebden-Curtis, J. and Demaso, D.R. (1993) Developmental Differences in Detection and Disclosure of Sexual Abuse. *Journal of the American Academy of Child and Adolescent Psychiatry.* 32, 920–4.

Caputo, A.A., Frick, P.J. and Brodsky, S.L. (1999) Family Violence and Sexual Offending: The Potential Mediating Role of Psychopathic Traits and Negative Attitudes Toward Women. *Criminal Justice and Behaviour.* 26: 3 338–56.

Carpenter, D. and Peed, S.E. (1995) Personality Characteristics of Adolescent Sexual Offenders: A Pilot Study. *Sexual Abuse: A Journal of Research and Treatment.* 7: 5, 195–203.

Carter, D.L., Prentky, R.A., Knight, R.A., Vanderweer, P.L. and Boucher, R.J. (1987) Use of Pornography in the Criminal and Developmental Histories of Sexual Offenders. *Journal of Interpersonal Violence.* 2, 196–211.

Chung, I.J., Hill, K.G., Hawkins, J.D., Gilchrist, L.D. and Nagin, D.S. (2002) Childhood Predictors of Offense Trajectories. *Journal of Research in Crime and Delinquency.* 39: 1, 60–90.

Cooper, C.L., Murphy, W.D. and Haynes, M.R. (1996) Characteristics of Abused and Nonabused Adolescent Sexual Offenders. *Sexual Abuse: A Journal of Research and Treatment.* 8, 105–19.

Cottle, C.C., Lee, R.J. and Heilbrun, K. (2001) The Prediction of Criminal Recidivism in Juveniles: A Meta-Analysis. *Criminal Justice and Behaviour.* 28: 3, 367–94.

Crouch, J.L., Hanson, R.F., Saunders, B.E., Kilpatrick, D.G. and Resnick, H.S. (2000) Income, Race/Ethnicity, and Exposure to Violence in Youth: Results From the National Survey of Adolescents. *Journal of Community Psychology.* 28: 6, 625–43.

Daigle, M. and Harris, D. (1989) Attitudes Towards Child Sexuality. *Medicine and Law.* 8, 379–90.

Daleiden, E., Kaufman, K., Hilliker, D. and O'Neil, J. (1998) The Sexual Histories and Fantasies of Youthful Males: A Comparison of Sexual Offending, Non-sexual Offending, and Non-offending Groups. *Sexual Abuse: Journal of Research and Treatment*. 10: 3, 195–209.

Demare, D., Lips, H.M. and Briere, J. (1993) Sexually Violent Pornography, Anti-Women Attitudes, and Sexual Aggression: A Structural Equation Model. *Journal of Research in Personality*. 27, 285–300.

DeMartino, R.A. (1988) *School Aged Juvenile Sexual Offenders: A Descriptive Study of Self-Reported Personality Characteristics, Depression, Familial Perceptions and Social History*. State University of New York at Albany.

DePrince, A.P. and Freyd, J.J. (1999) Dissociative Tendencies, Attention, and Memory. *Psychological Science*. 10, 449–52.

DePrince, A.P. and Freyd, J.J. (2001) Memory and Dissociative Tendencies: The Roles of Attentional Context and Word Meaning in a Directed Forgetting Task. *Journal of Trauma and Dissociation*. 2: 2, 67–82.

Dicenso, C. (1992) The Adolescent Sexual Offender: Victim and Perpetrator. in Viano, E. (Ed.) *Critical Issues in Victimology: Interpersonal Perspectives*. New York: Springer.

Digiuseppe, R., Linscott, J. and Jilton, R. (1996) Developing the Therapeutic Alliance in Child-Adolescent Psychotherapy. *Applied and Preventive Psychology*. 5: 85–100.

Dodge, K.A. (1980) Social Cognition and Children's Aggressive Behaviour. *Child Development*. 51, 162–70.

Dodge, K.A. and Frame, C.L. (1982) Social Cognitive Biases and Deficits in Aggressive Boys. *Child Development*. 53, 620–35.

Dodge, K.A. and Price, J.M. (1994) on The Relation Between Social Information Processing and Socially Competent Behaviour in Early School-Aged Children. *Child Development*. 65, 1385–97.

Dodge, K.A. and Somberg, D.R. (1987) Hostile Attributional Biases Among Aggressive Boys Are Exacerbated Under Conditions of Threats to The Self. *Child Development*. 58, 213–24.

Dodge, K.A. and Tomlin, A.M. (1987) Utilization of Self-Schemas as A Mechanism of Interpretational Bias in Aggressive Children. *Social Cognition*. 5, 280–300.

Donnelly, D. and Fraser, J. (1998) Gender Differences in Sado-Masochistic Arousal Among College Students. *Sex Roles*. 39: 5–6, 391–407.

Fagan, J. and Wexler, S. (1988) Explanations of Sexual Assault Among Violent Delinquents. *Journal of Adolescent Research*. 3: 3–4, 363–85.

Farrington, D.P., Jollliffe, D., Loeber, R., Stouthamer-Loeber, M. and Kalb, L.M. (2001) The Concentration of Offenders in Families, and Family Criminality in the Prediction of Boys' Delinquency. *Journal of Adolescence*. 24: 5, 579–96.

Federal Bureau of Investigation. (2001) *Crime in The United States: Persons Arrested 2001*. Washington, DC: Author.

Fehrenbach, P.A., Smith, W., Monastersky, C. and Deisher, R. (1986) Adolescent Sexual Offenders: Offender and Offense Characteristics. *American Journal of Orthopsychiatry*. 56, 225–33.

Finkelhor, D. (1986) *A Sourcebook on Child Sexual Abuse*. Newbury Park, CA: Sage.

Finkelhor, D., Hotaling, G., Lewis, J.A. and Smith, C. (1990) Sexual Abuse in a National Survey of Adult Men and Women: Prevalence, Characteristics, and Risk Factors. *Child Abuse and Neglect*. 14, 19–28.

Florsheim, P., Shotorbani, S., Guest-Warnick, G., Barratt, T. and Hwang, W. (2000) Role of the Working Alliance in the Treatment of Delinquent Boys in Community-Based Programs. *Journal of Clinical Child Psychology*. 29: 1, 94–107.

Foa, E.B., Hearst-Ikeda, D. and Perry, K.J. (1995) Evaluation of a Brief Cognitive-Behavioural Program for the Prevention of Chronic PTSD in Recent Assault Victims. *Journal of Consulting and Clinical Psychology*. 63: 6, 948–55.

Foa, E.B., Rothblum, B.O., Riggs, D.S. and Murdock, T.B. (1991) Treatment of Post-traumatic Stress Disorder in Rape Victims: A Comparison Between Cognitive-Behavioural Procedures and Counseling. *Journal of Consulting and Clinical Psychology*. 59: 5, 715–23.

Ford, M.E. and Linney, J.A. (1995) Comparative Analysis of Juvenile Sexual Offenders, Violent Nonsexual Offenders, and Status Offenders. *Journal of Interpersonal Violence*. 10: 1, 56–70.

Fraser, M. (In Press) *Risk and Resilience in Childhood: an Ecological Perspective*. Washington DC: NASW Press.

Freeman-Longo, R.E. (1986) The Impact of Sexual Victimisation on Males. *Child Abuse and Neglect*. 10, 411–4.

Freeman-Longo, R.E. (1998) *Sexual Abuse in America: Epidemic of the 21st Century*. Brandon, VT: Safer Society Press.

Freyd, J.J., Martorello, S.R., Alvarado, J.S., Hayes, A.E. and Christman, J.C. (1998) Cognitive

Environments and Dissociative Tendencies: Performance on the Standard Stroop Task for High Versus Low Dissociators. *Applied Cognitive Psychology.* 12, S91–S103.

Galski, T., Thornton, K.E. and Shumsky, D. (1990) Brain Dysfunction in Sex Offenders. *Journal of Offender Rehabilitation.* 16: 1–2, 65–80.

Gard, M. and Bradley, B. (2000) Getting Away With Rape: Erasure of the Psyche in Evolutionary Psychology. *Psychology, Evolution and Gender.* 2: 3, 313–9.

Garland, R.J. and Dougher, M.J. (1990) The Abused/Abuser Hypothesis of Child Sexual Abuse: A Critical Review of Theory and Research. In Feierman, J.R. *Pedophilia: Biosocial Dimensions.* New York: Springer-Verlag.

Golden, C.J., Jackson, M.L., Peterson-Rohne, A. and Gontkovsky, S.T. (1996) Neuropsychological Correlates of Violence and Aggression: A Review of the Clinical Literature. *Journal of Aggression and Violent Behaviour: A Review Journal.* 1, 3–25.

Goleman, D. (1995) *Emotional Intelligence.* Bantam Books.

Gore, D.K. (1988) *Measuring the Cognitive Distortions of Child Molesters: Psychometric Properties of The Cognition Scale.* A Dissertation. Georgia State University.

Groth, A.N. (1977) The Adolescent Sexual Offender and His Prey. *International Journal of Offender Therapy and Comparative Criminology.* 21, 249–54.

Hall, G.C. and Hirschman, R. (1992) Sexual Aggression Against Children: A Conceptual Perspective of Etiology. *Criminal Justice and Behaviour.* 19, 8–23.

Hanson, R.K., Gizzarelli, R. and Scott, H. (1994) The Attitudes of Incest Offenders: Sexual Entitlement and Acceptance of Sex With Children. *Criminal Justice and Behaviour.* 21, 187–202.

Hawkins, J.D., Herrenkohl, T.I., Farrington, D.P., Brewer, D., Catalano, R.F., Harachi, T.W. and Cothern, L. (2000) *Predictors of Youth Violence.* Washington DC: OJJDP.

Henggeler, S.W., Borduin, C M., Melton, G.B., Mann, B.J., Smith, L., Hall, J.A., Cone, L. and Fucci, B.R. (1991) Effects of Multisystemic Therapy on Drug Use and Abuse in Serious Juvenile Offenders: A Progress Report From Two Outcome Studies. *Family Dynamics of Addiction Quarterly.* 1, 40–51.

Herrenkohl, T.I., Huang, B., Kosterman, R., Hawkins, J.D., Catalano, R.F. and Smith, B.H.

(2001) A Comparison of Social Development Processes Leading to Violent Behaviour in Late Adolescence for Childhood Initiators and Adolescent Initiators of Violence. *Journal of Research in Crime and Delinquency.* 38: 1, 45–63.

Higgins, D.J. and McCabe, M.P. (2000a) Relationships Between Different Types of Maltreatment During Childhood and Adjustment in Adulthood. *Child Maltreatment.* 5: 3, 261–72.

Higgins, D.J. and McCabe, M.P. (2000b) Multi-Type Maltreatment and the Long Term Adjustment of Adults. *Child Abuse Review.* 9, 6–18.

Horvath, A.O. and Greenburg, L.S. (1994) *The Working Alliance: Theory, Research, and Practice.* New York, NY: John Wiley and Sons.

Horvath, A.O. and Symonds, B.D. (1991) Relation Between Working Alliance and Outcome in Psychotherapy: A Meta-Analysis. *Journal of Counseling Psychology.* 38: 2, 139–49.

Howells, K. and Cook, M. (1981) Adult Sexual Interest in Children: Considerations Relevant to Theories of Aetiology. In Anonymous, *Personality and Psychopathology.* London: Academic Press.

Hummel, P., Thomke, V., Oldenburger, H.A. and Specht, F. (2000) Male Adolescent Sex Offenders Against Children: Similarities and Differences Between Those Offenders With and Those Without a History of Sexual Abuse. *Journal of Adolescence.* 23, 305–17.

Hunter, J.A. and Figueredo, A.J. (2000) The Influence of Personality and History of Sexual Victimisation in the Prediction of Juvenile Perpetrated Child Molestation. *Behaviour Modification.* 24: 2, 241–63.

Hyde, J.S. and Oliver, M.B. (2000) Gender Differences in Sexuality: Results From A Meta-Analysis. in Travis, C.B. and White, J.W. (Eds.) *Sexuality, Society, and Feminism.* American Psychological Association.

Johnson, G.M. and Knight, R.A. (2000) Developmental Antecedents of Sexual Coercion in Juvenile Sexual Offenders. *Sexual Abuse: A Journal of Research and Treatment.* 12: 3, 165–78.

Johnson, R.L. and Shrier, D. (1987) Past Sexual Victimisation by Females of Male Patients in an Adolescent Medicine Clinic Population. *The American Journal of Psychiatry.* 144, 650–2.

Johnson-Reid, M. and Way, I. (2001) Adolescent Sexual Offenders: Incidence of Childhood Maltreatment, Serious Emotional Disturbance, and Prior Offenses. *American Journal of Orthopsychiatry.* 71: 1, 120–30

Kahn, T.J. (1990) *Pathways: A Guided Workbook for Youth Beginning Treatment.* Orwell, VT: Safer Society.

Kahn, T.J. and Chambers, H.J. (1991) Assessing Reoffense Risk With Juvenile Sexual Offenders. *Child Welfare.* 70, 333–45.

Kaplan, M.S., Becker, J.V. and Tenke, C.E. (1991) Assessment of Sexual Knowledge and Attitudes in an Adolescent Sex Offender Population. *Journal of Sex Education and Therapy.* 17, 217–25.

Kaufman, K.L., Hilliker, D.R. and Daleiden, E.L. (1996) Subgroup Differences in The Modus Operandi of Adolescent Sexual Offenders. *Child Maltreatment.* 1: 1, 17–24.

Kaufman, K. (2003) Personal Communication, April 25.

Keenan, T. and Ward, T. (2000) A Theory of Mind Perspective on Cognitive, Affective, and Intimacy Deficits in Child Sexual Offenders. *Sexual Abuse: A Journal of Research and Treatment.* 12: 1, 49–60.

Kendall-Tackett, K.A., Williams, L.M. and Finkelhor, D. (1993) Impact of Sexual Abuse on Children: A Review and Synthesis of Recent Empirical Studies. *Psychological Bulletin.* 113, 164–80.

Kennan, B. (1998) Evolutionary Biology and Strict Liability for Rape. *Law and Psychology Review.* 22, 131–77.

Knight, R.A. and Sims-Knight, J.E. (2001) *The Developmental Antecedents of Sexual Coercion Against Women in Adolescents.* Submitted for Publication.

Knopp, F. and Benson, A. (1996) *A Primer on The Complexities of Traumatic Memory of Childhood Sexual Abuse: A Psychobiological Approach.* Vermont: Safer Society Press.

Kroner, D.G. and Weekes, J.R. (1996) Balanced Inventory of Desirable Responding: Factor Structure, Reliability, and Validity With an Offender Sample. *Personality and Individual Differences.* 21, 323–33.

Kubany, E.S. and Manke, F.P. (1995) Cognitive Therapy for Trauma-Related Guilt: Conceptual Bases and Treatment Outlines. *Cognitive and Behavioural Practice.* 2: 1, 27–61.

Langström, N. and Grann, M. (2000) Risk for Criminal Recidivism Among Young Sex Offenders. *Journal of Interpersonal Violence.* 15: 8, 855–71.

Lanktree, C.B. and Briere, J. (1995) Outcome of Therapy for Sexually Abused Children: A Repeated Measures Study. *Child Abuse and Neglect.* 19: 9, 1145–55.

Laws, D.R., Hanson, R.K., Osborn, C.A. and Greenbaum, P.E. (2000) Classification of Child Molesters by Plethysmographic Assessment of Sexual Arousal and A Self-Report Measure of Sexual Preference. *Journal of Interpersonal Violence.* 15: 1, 1297–312.

Leguizamo, A. *Juvenile Sex Offenders: an Object Relations Approach.* Unpublished Doctoral Dissertation, University of Michigan.

Leitenberg, H. and Henning, K. (1995) Sexual Fantasy. *Psychological Bulletin.* 117: 3, 469–97.

Lipsey, M.W. (1995) What Do We Learn From 400 Research Studies on the Effectiveness of Treatment With Juvenile Delinquents? McGuire, J. (Ed.) *What Works: Reducing Reoffending: Guidelines From Research and Practice.* New York, NY: John Wiley and Sons.

Lopez, V.A. and Emmer, E.T. (2000) Adolescent Male Offenders: A Grounded Theory Study of Cognition, Emotion, and Delinquent Crime Contexts. *Criminal Justice and Behaviour.* 27: 3, 292–311.

Lothstein, L. (1999) Neuropsychological Findings in Clergy Who Sexually Abuse. In Plante, T. (Ed.) *Bless Me Father for I Have Sinned: Perspectives on Sexual Abuse Committed by Roman Catholic Priests.* Westport, CT: Praeger Publishers/Greenwood Publishing.

Lyn, T. and Burton, D. (In Press) Adult Attachment and Sex Offender Status. *American Journal of Orthopsychiatry.*

Malamuth, N.M. (1981) Rape Fantasies as A Function of Exposure to Violent Sexual Stimuli. *Archives of Sexual Behaviour.* 10, 33–47.

Malamuth, N.M. and Heilmann, M.F. (1998) Evolutionary Psychology and Sexual Aggression. In Crawford, C.B. (Ed.) *Handbook of Evolutionary Psychology: Ideas, Issues, and Applications.* Mahwah, NJ: Lawrence Erlbaum Associates.

Malamuth, N.M., Addison, T. and Koss, M. (2000) Pornography and Sexual Aggression: Are There Reliable Effects and Can We Understand Them? *Annual Review of Sex Research.* 11, 26–91.

Mann, R. and Beech, A. (2003) Cognitive Distortions, Schemas and Implicit Theories. In Ward, T., Laws, D.R and Hudson, S. (Eds.) *Sexual Deviance: Issues and Controversies.* Thousand Oaks. CA: Sage.

Marshall, W.L. and Eccles, A. (1991) Issues in Clinical Practice With Sex Offenders. *Journal of Interpersonal Violence.* 6, 68–93.

Marshall, W.L., Laws, D.R. and Barbaree, H.E. (1990) Issues in Sexual Assault. In Marshall,

W.L., Laws, D.R. and Barbaree, H.E. (Eds.) *Handbook of Sexual Assault: Issues, Theories, and Treatment of The Offender*. New York: Plenum.

Mathews, F. (2003) *The Invisible Boy: Revisioning The Victimisation of Male Children and Teens*. National Clearinghouse on Family Violence. Health Canada.

McCann, I.L. and Pearlman, L.A. (1990) *Psychological Trauma and the Adult Survivor: Theory, Therapy, and Transformation*. Philadelphia, PA: Brunner/Mazel.

McGuire, R.J., Carlisle, J.M. and Young, B.G. (1965) Sexual Deviations as Conditioned Behaviour: A Hypothesis. *Behaviour Research and Therapy*. 2, 185–90.

McMurran, M., Egan, V., Blair, M. and Richardson, C. (2001) The Relationship Between Social Problem-Solving and Personality in Mentally Disordered Offenders. *Personality and Individual Differences*. 30: 3, 517–24.

Meadows, E.A. and Foa, E.B. (1998) Intrusion, Arousal, and Avoidance: Sexual Trauma Survivors. In Follette, V.M. (Ed.) *Cognitive-Behavioural Therapies for Trauma*. New York, NY: The Guildford Press.

Meadows, E.A. and Foa, E.B. (1999) Cognitive Behavioural Treatment of Traumatized Adults. In Saigh, P.A. (Ed.) *Posttraumatic Stress Disorder: A Comprehensive Text*. Needham Heights, MA: Allyn and Bacon.

Meadows, E.A. and Foa, E.B. (2000) Cognitive Behavioural Treatment for PTSD. In Shalev, A.Y. (Ed.) *International Handbook of Human Response to Trauma*. New York, NY: Kluwer Academic/Plenum.

Mio, J., Nanjundappa, G., Verleur, D. and De Rios, M. (1986) Drug Abuse and the Adolescent Sex Offender: A Preliminary Analysis. *Journal of Psychoactive Drugs: Special Issue: Drug Dependency and The Family*. 18: 1, 65–72.

Miranda, A.O., Umhoefer, D.L. and Hendrix, S.B. *Differences in Resiliency Indicators and Stress-Coping Resources Between Juvenile and Adult Sex Offenders Against Minors*. 16th Annual Conference of the Association for the Treatment of Sexual Abusers.

Moody, E.E., Brissie, J. and Kim, J. (1994) Personality and Background Characteristics of Adolescent Sexual Offenders. *Journal of Addictions and Offender Counseling*. 14: 2, 38–48.

Morris, R.E., Anderson, M.M. and Knox, G.W. (2002) Incarcerated Adolescents' Experiences as Perpetrators of Sexual Assault. *Archives of Pediatric and Adolescent Medicine*. 156, 831–5.

Moulden, H. and Marshall, W.L. (2002) Empathy, Social Intelligence, and Aggressive Behaviour. In Fernandez, Y. (Ed.) *In Their Shoes*. Oklahoma: Wood 'N' Barnes Publishing.

Mullen, P.E., Marten, J.L., Anderson, J.C., Romans, S.E. and Herbison, G.P. (1995) The Long-Term Impact of The Physical, Emotional and Sexual Abuse of Children: A Community Study. *Child Abuse and Neglect*. 20: 1, 7–21.

Murphy, J.K. (1991) Sexual Contact With Children: Clinician's Cognitions. *Behaviour Therapy*. 22, 125–7.

Neidigh, L. and Krop, H. (1992) Cognitive Distortions Among Child Sexual Offenders. *Journal of Sex Education and Therapy*. 18, 208–15.

Nishith, P., Hearst, D.E., Mueser, K.T. and Foa, E.B. (1995) PTSD and Major Depression: Methodological and Treatment Considerations in a Single Case Design. *Behaviour Therapy*. 26: 2, 319–35.

Novaco, R.W. and Chemtaub, C. (1998) Anger and Trauma: Conceptualization, Assessment, and Treatment. In Follette V.M. (Ed.) *Cognitive-Behavioural Therapies for Trauma*. New York, NY: Guildford Press.

Peluso, E. and Putnam, N. (1996) Case Study: Sexual Abuse of Boys by Females. *Journal of the American Academy of Child and Adolescent Psychiatry*. 35, 51–4.

Peugh, J. and Belenko, S. (2001) Examining The Substance Use Patterns and Treatment Needs of Incarcerated Sex Offenders. *Sexual Abuse: A Journal of Research and Treatment*. 13: 3, 179–95.

Pincus, J. (1999) Aggression, Criminality, and the Frontal Lobes. In Miller, B. (Ed.) *The Human Frontal Lobes: Functions and Disorders*. New York: Guilford Press.

Plaud, J. and Bigwood, S. (1997) The Relationship of Male Self-Report of Rape Supportive Attitudes, Sexual Fantasy, Social Desirability and Physiological Arousal to Sexually Coercive Stimuli. *Journal of Clinical Psychology*. 53: 8, 935–42.

Prentky, R.A., Knight, R.A., Sims-Knight, J.E., Straus, H., Rokous, F. and Cerce, D. (1989) Developmental Antecedents of Sexual Aggression. *Development and Psychopathology*. 1, 153–69.

Quinsey, V.L. and Lalumeire, M.L. (1995) Evolutionary Perspective on Sexual Offending. *Sexual Abuse: A Journal of Research and Treatment*. 7, 301–15.

Racey, B.D., Lopez, N.L. and Schneider, H G.(2000) Sexually Assaultive Adolescents: Cue

Perception, Interpersonal Competence and Cognitive Distortions. *International Journal of Adolescence and Youth.* 8: 2–3, 229–39.

Rich, P. (2003) *Understanding, Assessing and Rehabilitating Juvenile Sexual Offenders.* Hoboken, NJ: John Wiley.

Roesler, T. (2000) Reactions to Disclosure of Childhood Sexual Abuse: The Effect on Adult Symptoms. *Journal of Nervous and Mental Disease.* 182: 1, 618–24.

Ruzek, J.I., Polusny, M.A. and Abueg, F.R. (1998) Assessment and Treatment of Concurrent Post-traumatic Stress Disorder and Substance Abuse. In Follette, V.M. (Ed.) *Cognitive-Behavioural Therapies for Trauma.* New York, NY: Guildford Press.

Ryan, G. (1989) Victim to Victimiser: Rethinking Victim Treatment. *Journal of Interpersonal Violence.* 4, 325–41.

Ryan, G., Miyoshi, T.J., Metzner, J.L., Krugman, R.D. and Fryer, G.E. (1996) Trends in a National Sample of Sexually Abusive Youths. *Journal of the American Academy of Child and Adolescent Psychiatry.* 35: 1, 17–25.

Ryan, S., Rodriguez, J., Anderson, R. and Foy, D. (1992) *Psychometric Analysis of The Sexual Abuse Exposure Questionnaire (SAEQ)* Paper Presented at The American Psychological Association, Washington, DC.

Ryan, L. and Lane, S. (Eds.) (1997) *Juvenile Sexual Offending: Causes, Consequences and Correction.* New York: Jossey-Bass

Schafer, J.L. and Graham, J.W. (2002) Missing Data: Our View of the State of the Art. *Psychological Methods.* 7: 2, 147–77.

Schatz, R., (2003) Personal Communication, May 22.

Segal, L. (2001) Nature's Way? Inventing the Natural History of Rape. *Psychology, Evolution and Gender.* 3: 1, 87–93.

Seto, M.C., Maric, A. and Barbaree, H.E. (2001) The Role of Pornography in the Etiology of Sexual Aggression. *Aggression and Violent Behaviour.* 6: 1, 35–53.

Shahinfar, A., Kupersmidt, J.B. and Matza, L.S. (2001) The Relation Between Exposure to Violence and Social Information Processing Among Incarcerated Adolescents. *Journal of Abnormal Psychology.* 110: 1, 136–41.

Shirk, S.R. and Russell, R.L. (1996) *Change Processes in Child Psychotherapy: Revitalizing Treatment and Research.* New York, NY: Guildford Press.

Skuse, D., Bentovim, A., Hodges, J., Stevenson, J., Andreou, C., Lanyado, M., New, M., Williams,

B. and McMillan, D. (1998) Risk Factors for Development of Sexually Abusive Behaviour in Sexually Victimised Adolescent Boys: Cross Sectional Study. *British Medical Journal.* 317: 18, 175–9.

Smallbone, S.W. and Dadds, M.R. (1998) Childhood Attachment and Adult Attachment in Incarcerated Adult Male Sex Offenders. *Journal of Interpersonal Violence.* 13: 5, 555–73.

Smallbone, S.W. and Dadds, M.R. (2000) Attachment and Coercive Sexual Behaviour. *Sexual Abuse: A Journal of Research and Treatment.* 12: 1, 3–15.

Smallbone, S.W. and Dadds, M.R. (2001) Further Evidence for a Relationship Between Attachment Insecurity and Coercive Sexual Behaviour in Non-offenders. *Journal of Interpersonal Violence.* 16: 1, 22–35.

Smith, W.R., Monastersky, C. and Deisher, R.M. (1987) MMPI-Based Personality Types Among Juvenile Sexual Offenders. *Journal of Clinical Psychology.* 43, 422–30.

Stermac, L., Segal, Z. and Gillis, R. (1990) Social and Cultural Factors in Sexual Assault. In Marshall, W.L. Laws, D.R. and Barbaree, H.E. (Eds.) *Handbook of Sexual Assault: Issues, Theories, and Treatment of The Offender.* New York: Plenum.

Tarolla, S.M., Wagner, E.F., Rabinowitz, J. and Tubman, J.G. (2002) Understanding and Treating Juvenile Offenders: A Review of Current Knowledge and Future Directions. *Aggression and Violent Behaviour.* 7: 2, 125–44.

Thornhill, R. and Palmer, C.T. (2000) *A Natural History of Rape: Biological Bases of Sexual Coercion.* Cambridge, MA: MIT Press.

Thornhill, R. and Thornhill, N.W. (1992) The Evolutionary Psychology of Men's Coercive Sexuality. *Behavioural and Brain Sciences.* 15, 363–421.

Trinidad, D.R., Johnson, C. and Anderson, C. (2002) The Association Between Emotional Intelligence and Early Adolescent Tobacco and Alcohol Use. *Personality and Individual Differences.* 32: 1, 95–105.

Vega, J.A. (2001) Naturalism and Feminism: Conflicting Explanations of Rape in a Wider Context. *Psychology, Evolution and Gender.* 3: 1, 47–85.

Veneziano, C. and Veneziano, L. (1995) Reasons for Refraining From Criminal Activity. *American Journal of Criminal Justice.* 19: 2, 185–96.

Veneziano, C., Veneziano, L. and Legrand, S. (2000) The Relationship Between Adolescent

Sex Offender Behaviours and Victim Characteristics With Prior Victimisation. *Journal of Interpersonal Violence.* 15: 4, 363–74.

Waggoner, R.W. and Boyd, D.A. Jr. (1941) Juvenile Aberrant Sexual Behaviour. *The American Journal of Orthopsychiatry.* 11, 275–91.

Wagner, A.W. and Linehan, M.M. (1998) Dissociative Behaviour. In Follette, V.M. (Ed.) *Cognitive-Behavioural Therapies for Trauma.* New York, NY: Guildford Press.

Ward, T. and Siegert, R. (2002) Naturalism and Feminism: Conflicting Explanations of Rape in a Wider Context. *Aggression and Violent Behaviour.* 7: 2, 145–68.

Ward, T. and Hudson, S.M. (1998) A Model of The Relapse Process in Sexual Offenders. *Journal of Interpersonal Violence.* 13, 700–25.

Ward, T., Hudson, S.M. and Marshall, W.L. (1996) Attachment Style in Sex Offenders: A Preliminary Study. *The Journal of Sex Research.* 33: 1, 17–26.

Ward, T., Keenan, T. and Hudson, S.M. (1999) Understanding Cognitive, Affective, and Intimacy Deficits in Sexual Offenders. *Aggression and Violent Behaviour.* 5: 1, 41–62.

Ward, T., Louden, K., Hudson, S.M. and Marshall, W.L. (1995) A Descriptive Model of The Offense Chain for Child Molesters. *Journal of Interpersonal Violence.* 10: 4, 452–72.

Way, I. (2000) *Adolescent Sexual Offenders: The Role of Cognitive and Emotional Victim Empathy in The Victim-to-Victimiser Process.* Unpublished Doctoral Dissertation. Washington University, St. Louis.

Widom, C.S. (2001) Child Abuse and Neglect. In White, S.O. (Ed.) *Handbook of Youth and Justice.* New York, NY: Kluwer Academic/Plenum.

Wieckowski, E., Hartsoe, P., Mayer, A. and Shortz, J. (1998) Deviant Sexual Behaviour in Children and Young Adolescents: Frequency and Patterns. *Sexual Abuse: A Journal of Research and Treatment.* 10: 4, 293–303.

Williams, J.H., Ayers, C.D. and Arthur, M.W. (1997) Risk and Protective Factors in the Development of Delinquency and Conduct Disorder. In Fraser, M. (Ed.) *Risk and Resilience in Childhood.* Washington, DC: NASW Press.

Wilson, G. (1997) Gender Differences in Sexual Fantasy: an Evolutionary Analysis. *Personality and Individual Difference.* 22: 1, 27.

Worling, J.R. (1995) Sexual Abuse Histories of Adolescent Male Sex Offenders: Differences on The Basis of the Age and Gender of Their Victims. *Journal of Abnormal Psychology.* 104, 610–3.

Worling, J.R. (1998) Adolescent Sexual Offender Treatment at the SAFE-T Program. Marshal, W.L., Fernandez, Y.M., Hudson, S.M. and Ward, T. (Eds.) *Sourcebook of Treatment Programs for Sexual Offenders.* New York: Plenum.

Worling, J.R. (2001) Personality-Based Typology of Adolescent Male Sexual Offenders: Differences in Recidivism Rates, Victim-Selection Characteristics, and Personal Victimisation Histories. *Sexual Abuse: A Journal of Research and Treatment.* 13: 3, 149–66.

Worling, J.R. and Curwen, T. (2000) Adolescent Sexual Offender Recidivism: Success of Specialized Treatment and Implications for Risk Prediction. *Child Abuse and Neglect.* 24, 965–82.

Zgourides, G., Monto, M. and Harris, R. (1994) Prevalence of Prior Adult Sexual Contact in a Sample of Adolescent Male Sex Offenders. *Psychological Reports.* 75, 1042.

Zolondek, S.C., Abel, G.G., Northey, W.F. and Jordan, A.D. (2001) The Self-Reported Behaviours of Juvenile Sexual Offenders. *Journal of Interpersonal Violence.* 16: 1, 73–85.

Part II

Engagement of young people

Making it Fair: Respectful and Just Intervention with Disadvantaged Young People Who Have Abused

Alan Jenkins

Introduction

An invitational model of engagement and intervention is designed to assist young men to find motivation to discover their own preferences and capacities for respectful ways of being and relating. Processes of inquiry are developed to invite adolescents to make choices in relation to undertaking and investing in an ethical journey towards responsibility and respect of self and others. Such a journey promotes the cessation of abusive practices. This model has been previously described and documented (Jenkins, 1990; Jenkins, 1999).

An invitational model is concerned with enabling *readiness* for the young man to:

- Declare his ethics.
- Establish his own goals in relation to these stated ethics.
- Develop his own motivation to achieve them.
- Examine his ethics and actions as expressions of a preferred sense of identity.

The young man is invited to make his *own* decisions, based on his *own* ethics and preferences, whether or not to undertake a journey towards responsibility and respect. I invite a fundamental shift in focus from the initial investments of young people in accommodation to the wishes of workers or parents and adversarial battles centred on resistance to their influence, to the possibility of choosing to embark upon a personal journey. It must be the young man's journey; one which he has chosen for himself.

The invitational model promotes the discovery and co-construction of a sense of identity, which is informed by qualities and practices of responsibility and respect, as opposed to an identity of 'sex offender'. The young man is afforded opportunities to develop a sense of self-respect and respect of others, as he discovers his own sense of justice, courage, honour and integrity.

Principles of intervention

This model of engagement and intervention is informed by five major principles, which relate to notions of social justice.

- The safety and well-being of those that are at risk of abuse and harm is paramount in intervention. Intervention practices must not compromise the safety and well-being of others.
- Individuals who have abused are regarded as fully responsible for their abusive actions. Intervention workers must help provide a safe and accessible passage for the young person to take responsibility for his abusive actions.
- Intervention practices must promote accountability to the experiences and needs of those with least power and privilege, particularly those who have been subjected to abuse. This requires that workers ensure that intervention practices take into account and privilege those experiences and needs. Practices must be made transparent and open to scrutiny and critique by those who have been abused and their advocates.
- Intervention practices must at all times be respectful to those who have abused. Intervention practices should promote the respect of self and others.
- Intervention practices should promote fairness, both with respect to young men who have abused and within their communities. Intervention practices should be experienced as fair and just by all concerned.

The principle of fairness in an unfair world

In recent times I have become increasingly preoccupied with the principle of fairness, particularly when working with young people who have been subjected to disadvantage, oppression or abuse and who have sexually abused others.

In our zealous attempts to challenge the oppressive secrecy, under-reporting and ineffectual community responses to sexual abuse, it is easy to overlook or underestimate the importance of fairness in working with young people. Those who are subjected to abuse are treated in appallingly unjust ways, both prior to and subsequent to disclosure. Most people who perpetrate abuse appear to remain unaccountable for their actions, in the face of their victim's unmitigated suffering and ambivalent or indifferent community responses.

The combination of well-intended efforts to prevent abuse and hold young people accountable for their actions, in a post-September 11th political context with overtones of zero-tolerance and the concept of the pre-emptive strike, have resulted in fairness being the one principle most often overlooked or disregarded in policy and practice. This is especially the case in intervention programmes with disadvantaged young people.

It is extremely challenging to find a balance in intervention practice which privileges safety, responsibility and accountability, on one hand, along with respect and fairness on the other. However, this is a vital balance. Young people are only likely to find their own motivation and make their own investment in a journey towards ceasing abusive practices, if the context of fairness is privileged along with the other important principles.

This chapter (and its companion, 'Knocking on Shame's Door' – Chapter 7) concerns three major dilemmas in intervention, which are at the heart of the principle of fairness:

- How can we intervene with young people who have abused, without reproducing dominant abusive practices?
- How can we respectfully address young people's experiences of disadvantage and victimisation, without sacrificing the priority on responsibility and accountability for their abusive actions?
- How can we work with shame without shaming the young person who has abused?

Political contexts for intervention

When we attempt to assist young people to cease abuse and develop respectful practices, we are conducting our intervention within several contexts which mitigate against a sense of fairness and justice. Dominant cultural ideologies, policies and practices tend to support a form of political colonisation of young people which serves to:

- Ignore or disqualify disadvantaged, young people's respectful ethics or preferences.
- Stifle and suppress young people's legitimate protest against injustice.

The politics of disadvantage

We face a basic dilemma when we attempt to promote fairness in intervention, within a broader socio-cultural context characterised by a dominant ideology which favours notions of individualism, competition and inequality. Can we do more than pay lip service only to concepts of fairness and equity?

I have previously documented the restraining influences of dominant cultural values which support an exaggerated sense of entitlement and an abdication of responsibility by the privileged. This serves to maintain various inequalities and acts as a paradigm for all forms of abuse, in which the more powerful and privileged exploit those with less power and privilege (Jenkins, 1990).

Young disadvantaged men are much more likely to face police and justice consequences for their abusive acts which are much more visible in the community, compared with those perpetrated by the privileged. The privileged have access to a wide range of economic, legal and cultural mechanisms and structures to avoid being held accountable for their actions.

The politics of adult/child relations

Most western cultures allow the interests and well-being of their young people to be sacrificed, in order to maintain economic structures which create high levels of youth unemployment. This maintains a wealth gap which supports adults with greater economic privilege. Young people are then blamed for the inevitable consequences of such oppressive policies. When disadvantaged young people fail to obtain work or when they protest and refuse to co-operate with demeaning social structures, they often face criticism and seen as lazy, stupid or unmotivated.

Young people are generally regarded as requiring protection and support. Attainment of a certain age is required to qualify specific adult rights and privileges, such as voting etc. When it suits adult's needs, they are regarded as children. However, when young people commit serious crimes, many legislatures are empowered to regard them as adults and subject them to adult criminal justice systems and penalties. These shifts in attributed developmental status are arbitrary and are always in the direction of withdrawing the protections of childhood status. Young people are seldom afforded adult privileges when they act responsibly and respectfully. When children offend the powers that be, they may do so at the expense of their childhood.

Often when young people protest or challenge these conventions, their protests are disregarded or disqualified as being ill-informed or even mischievous. Developmental psychology is sometimes employed as a tool to oppress, when young people's protest is regarded as a stage of adolescent development which might later be outgrown. This provides a psychological justification for dismissing and dishonouring legitimate protest.

Disadvantaged young people have even less opportunity for their protest to be heard, let alone taken seriously. For some young people, their only experience of being heard or noticed is when their protest is loud and aggressive, or when it involves violence or 'anti-social behaviour'. In these circumstances, the violence is often responded to, usually with attempts to suppress or punish the young person. However, the protest is frequently overlooked.

In fact, many adults believe that it is their 'god-given duty' to correct young people and teach them ethics; to 'put them on the right track'. Adolescence is often regarded as a wild force that needs to be tamed and civilised, to enable a young person to take their place in the social order.

Joe, aged 16, is a young indigenous man who was court-mandated to attend an intervention programme to address several sexual assaults upon younger children, in a variety of foster placements. Joe had himself been subjected to severe physical and sexual assaults and neglect, in his first nine years of life, after which he endured a series of foster placements where he suffered further sexual assaults on two occasions.

Joe is an intelligent and creative young man. However, his experience at school was characterised by enormous difficulties in fitting with conventional educational and teaching structures and strategies. He also experienced racial harassment on a daily basis through-out his school attendance. At school, Joe was subjected to the usual sifting and sorting processes which serve to separate 'winners' from 'losers' and favour the privileged (Connell, 1993). The myth of equality, which proposes that anyone can succeed if they are bright enough and work hard enough, was inadvertently rubbed in Joe's face.

Joe was initially assessed as 'learning disordered' but 'failed to respond' to remedial intervention strategies. When attempts to help Joe were not helpful, he was described, in assessment reports, as 'possible ADHD' with a suspected 'bad attitude.' The alternative diagnosis suggested that Joe might be 'lazy.' As Joe was relegated to the 'loser' bin and increasingly harassed at school, he lost interest in the curriculum and protested. His protests were at first ignored and later regarded as, 'attention seeking', and 'provocative' and finally 'deliberately disruptive and abusive,' when they were associated with violence towards property and other people. Joe's protests were disqualified but his violence and aggression was noticed resulting in a diagnosis of 'conduct disorder'.

Just prior to my first meeting with Joe, he and two 'whitefellas' had been charged with the offence of stealing a car. The 'whitefellas' were released on bail but Joe was remanded in custody.

Disadvantaged young men such as Joe are constantly confronted with their lack of privilege. Their ethics are often overlooked and their protest disqualified. They are regarded as irresponsible and disrespectful; in effect, as 'losers.' They tend to be defined in their families and communities, with disabling descriptions; 'He doesn't care about anyone but himself'; 'He has no remorse,' etc. Such disabling descriptions may be supported by documented, professional opinions which detail and label conditions and syndromes, such as 'conduct disorder', 'empathy deficit' and disorders of 'impulse control'.

It is hardly surprising that these young men experience a life of 'being done to' and eventually come to believe in judgements that they may be worthless and insufficient. Life becomes a struggle to 'become somebody', through the only culturally prescribed means available; violence and aggression (Wexler, 1992). These young men engage in desperate attempts to avoid all of the pointers and signs which highlight a humiliating sense of identity as 'loser'.

The politics of intervention

In traditional statutory and therapeutic intervention programmes, there has been a tendency to ignore the politics of disadvantage and the politics of adult-child relations, in dominant theory and practice. Confronting, zero-tolerance models which were developed to address the abusive behaviour of adults, have too often been imposed upon adolescents. Their developmental status is denied and they are, in effect, regarded as 'little adults'.

Little attention has been paid to examining the abusive behaviour of adolescents within the developmental context of childhood. The political context of power relations, concerning a child living in an adult-focused world, is often overlooked in psycho-educational curricula which is often developed in adult programmes and then imposed upon young people.

Statutory and therapeutic authorities have tended to develop models of intervention in white, middle class contexts and then proceed to impose psychological assessment and intervention procedures upon young people who may live in extremely disadvantaged circumstances.

This raises a major dilemma:

What does it mean if we expect young people to be respectful and understanding of their victim's experiences and feelings (and refrain from imposing unwanted ideas and practices upon others)
– if we fail to understand or take account of their own experiences of disadvantage and deprivation.

Our intervention can actively serve to promote fairness and provide opportunities for atonement, restitution and restoration. Alternatively we can collude with a kind of 'justice' that masks a form of colonisation which promotes confrontation, correction and retribution. Colonisation practices may be well-intended but always lead to the inevitable consequences of protest and insurrection or passive accommodation. Prolonged patterns of protest and accommodation are, of course, highly restraining for a journey towards responsibility and respect.

If a young person experiences our intervention as a form of colonisation, with accompanying practices of psychological invasion and benevolent bullying, we only serve to provide yet another experience of 'being done to'; one which is very familiar to most disadvantaged young people. The effect on identity is to confirm the young person's marginalised state and a sense of judgement that he really is a worthless 'loser'.

In this context, colonisation generally triggers a survival response of accommodation; of appearing to be satisfying the requirements of the coloniser, in order to ensure that the young

person will get through yet another experience of 'being done to'. Most disadvantaged young people have survived invasions and violations which will have involved much more sinister tactics than those utilised in our interventions. However, each experience of 'being done to' adds to the sense of marginalisation and to a sense of identity which may serve to foster greater risk of harm to self and others.

What is fairness?

The invitational model draws upon Foucault's descriptions of power and Derrida's conceptualisations of justice (Larner, 1999; Ransom, 1997).

Fairness is an idea which is aspired to and regarded as vital in any intervention which seeks to promote respectful relationships which are free of abuse. However, fairness is not sought by appealing to a universal code of human rights which exists as an external truth and which might be applied when we see fit, in various sites of injustice. Fairness is not an outcome but an ongoing ethical responsibility and commitment to critique and reflection which requires considerable investment and commitment.

The idea of fairness aspires to the establishment of 'a non-violative relationship to the other' which:

- Respects and 'sustains the other's difference and singularity.'
- Allows for the hidden interplays of power and resistance, in all forms of interaction, to become visible, articulated and open to critique.
- Respects the other's capacity for thought and action, which is at times complicit with and at times resistant to, dominant power relations.
- Appreciates the creative tension between complicity and resistance in power relations and the opportunities it provides for inspiration by the imagination of new possibilities.
- Fosters ongoing critique of power relations in the relationship with the other.
- Embraces and examines the paradox of taking a position of power in order to subvert dominant power relations.

The major challenge posed by the idea of fairness lies in this paradox. Fairness requires that we take a position on justice and ethics, which is a power relation itself. The construction of such hierarchies of power is, of course, inevitable and unavoidable. We also have power invested in us by society by virtue of our roles and expertise. Our ethical responsibility requires considerable critique and scrutiny in this context, if we are to act ethically and minimise violence towards our clients. If we embrace this paradox, we must aspire to enact 'a power that is non-hegemonic'; one that does not align itself with dominant power relations; one 'that allows the other to 'say everything'... to think their own thoughts, to have their own feelings ... to write their own narrative.' This might be regarded as a 'political 'position taking' towards discourses of power which aligns itself with the voices of the marginalised and the many' (Larner, 1999).

The ethics that inform the concept of fairness, in an invitational model, is based on consideration of others needs and feelings, with recognition of individual differences, particularly those which concern invested power and privilege. These ethics are not based on appeals to universal concepts of 'human rights' or 'equal opportunity.' These concepts still construct life as a competition in acquisition, albeit from an equal start, in which there will inevitably be winners and losers. The invitational ethic is perhaps similar to Derrida's concept of 'hospitality' (Derrida and Dufourmantelle, 2000), and requires those with privilege to recognise it and attend to the needs and feelings of those who may be experiencing disadvantage. Fairness requires an ongoing critique of power relations in which the personal and political are intimately connected.

Establishing a context for fairness – Responsibility overload

What does it mean to talk about fairness when working with a disadvantaged young person who already has a history of marginalisation in a dominant culture which fosters inequality and injustice? We cannot reverse injustices or make the world entirely fair for young people. However, if we begin to privilege fairness in our work and attend to the various political contexts, within which our interventions are situated, we can challenge and subvert the effects of dominant power relations. We can establish safe and enabling environments for our work which will foster responsibility and respect.

Two major themes of inquiry are of vital significance in establishing a context for fairness:

- Attending to ethics in the face of adversity.
- Honouring young people's protest.

I work with many disadvantaged young men who have experienced considerable abuse, oppression and neglect and who feel a strong sense of injustice in their own lives. Most of these young men have never felt that anyone has ever been genuinely interested in understanding their experiences of injustice, abuse and victimisation, let alone appreciate their capacities for survival. Young Aboriginal Australians and other economically disadvantaged youth, in intervention programmes, have experiences of disadvantage and marginalisation which are seldom understood or acknowledged. These young men often experience a profound sense of injustice and may have been subjected to a range of extreme abuses, yet there is an expectation that they will address their own abusive behaviour. This expectation often constitutes a set of unreasonable and unrealistic expectations and, in an invitational model, is referred to as responsibility overload. The following dilemmas relate to responsibility overload:

What does it mean for a context of fairness, if we expect young people to take responsibility for and understand the effects of their abusive behaviours, if others are not prepared to take responsibility for or understand the effects of abuses done to the young person?

To what extent might we expect young people to take steps that others have never been prepared to take on their behalf?

The issue of responsibility overload is pivotal in establishing a context for fairness. Responsibility overload exists whenever we hold unrealistic or unfair expectations of the young man. We may unrealistically:

- Expect him to provide something which has never been provided for him, such as:
  –acknowledging responsibility for his actions.
  –demonstrating consideration or understanding of other's feelings.
  –demonstrating remorse or shame.
- Take ethical actions undertaken by the young person, in the face of extreme adversity, for granted.
- Overlook current or past injustices experienced by the young person, whilst encouraging him to face responsibility for his own unjust actions.
- Overlook or disrespect significant cultural values, relevant to the young person, whilst at

the same time expecting him to adopt our cultural values.

Establishing a context for fairness – Ethics in the face of adversity

I am continually astonished and amazed at the tenacity and determination of my young clients to hold on to respectful ethics and preferences, in the face of what seems to be overwhelming injustice and oppression.

Before I had even met Joe, I was informed that he had sexually assaulted five young children in several foster care families. I was furnished with a history of his violent and abusive actions. This history was accompanied by attributions which included; 'He is bad'; 'He has an evil mind'; 'He doesn't care about anyone but himself'.

Over time I learned about an appalling variety of abuses and injustices to which Joe had been subjected, throughout his sixteen years of life. He had been physically and sexually abused by two of his uncles and some older children, in his first nine years of life. Joe was frequently neglected as a little child and learned to look after his siblings and his mother, while he 'grew himself up'. He had been subjected to racist harassment and taunts throughout his life, in school and a variety of other settings. Joe was removed from his home and community at the age of 10 and placed in a series of non-aboriginal foster placements, in two of which he was further sexually abused. For six years, he was deprived of contact with his own family, community and culture.

However, after only a few conversations with Joe, I discovered that he felt intense shame about his sexual assault of several little children. When I inquired about this, he showed some recognition of the fact that these children had looked up to him and that he had betrayed their vulnerability and trust.

How such realisations could be made, given the descriptions of 'empathy deficit' and 'conduct disorder' which had been documented in his psychological assessments. It occurred to me that perhaps he had never been observed in a context where empathy or compassion might be expressed or noticed.

I began to wonder:

How is it that Joe is able to begin to consider his own abusive actions and their consequences; the hurts he had caused others, when he has felt and continues to feel so much hurt himself?

How was Joe able to care for and protect his mother and siblings, as a little child, when he experienced so little protection and care and so much neglect himself?

What does this say about Joe, in the face of the adversity he has experienced?

I noticed that few others seemed interested in these dilemmas. Most tended either to distrust Joe's expressions of remorse, or to take them for granted; 'Well he damn well should feel ashamed for what he has done, he is a sex offender'; 'Anyway, we don't want him in our school, he has a bad attitude'.

Few opportunities are afforded to enable young men like Joe to find a fair and respectful space to consider, let alone express ethics which might support a capacity for empathy, compassion or caring and concern. These young men lose sight of their ethical beliefs and values and have few means to be able to incorporate them into a sense of respectful identity. When disabling stories and labels concerning empathy deficits, conduct disorder and cycles of abusive behaviour, are privileged in considerations about young men like Joe, *they* become the influences which inform his sense of identity.

Addressing responsibility overload – Individual level

Young people most often present to an intervention programme as the result of external coercion, often following police intervention and with a justice system mandate. Disadvantaged young people, with a history of 'being done to', come to intervention programmes accompanied by a selection of disabling descriptions, labels, diagnoses and stories. The young person may anticipate his time in the intervention programme as yet another chapter in the history of his experience of injustice and marginalisation. In this context, they can appear extremely irresponsible and unmotivated.

However, despite all appearances and suggestions to the contrary, most of these young people are struggling with a pervasive sense of shame, in relation to their abusive actions, and are engaging in desperate attempts to avoid this experience. Attributions of worthlessness, insufficiency and the further entrenchment of a sense of identity as a 'loser,' are at the centre of these struggles.

It is both logical and sensible that the young person is preoccupied with survival and self-defence at this time. We should not be surprised when our initial inquiries, regardless of how much they might be informed by motives of caring and concern, elicit hostile or avoidance reactions.

Jake (aged 15) is attending his first appointment following a court-mandate, after having raped his six-year-old half-sister repeatedly over an 18 month period of time, beaten her up following her disclosures and later beaten up his mother. On introduction, he rolls his eyes upwards and exclaims, 'Whatever!'

Mike (aged 14) exclaims, 'This is all bullshit!' despite having partially acknowledged repeated rape of his five-year-old cousin.

Steve (aged 14) looks sullen and resentful whilst frequently glancing at his watch. He begins to challenge, 'When is this gonna be finished, I've gotta meet my mates in half an hour.'

These responses, when taken at face value, provide a powerful and challenging invitation for a therapist to confirm disabling descriptions and stories about the young person; to regard him as deficient in ethics of empathy, care and concern. In these circumstances, it can be difficult to decline the invitation to adopt coercive practices of confrontation and challenge.

Jake had partially acknowledged the abuse of his half-sister but greatly minimised its nature and impact. 'I dunno what the fuss is about. It didn't hurt her. Why do I have to come here? This sucks!'

Jake's mother is beside herself with worry. She laments, 'He doesn't care; He just goes on like nothing has happened; He's turning out just like his (abusive) step-father.'

We can easily 'prove' the disabling premise that young men like Jake have no remorse, are conduct disordered, and are indeed turning out just like their (abusive) parent by replicating the violence they witnessed, or to which they were subjected. We may even inadvertently encourage these young men to believe such disabling ideas themselves.

In order to address and prevent responsibility overload, it is vital that we maintain openness and curiosity, regarding the possibility that the young person may have and may be open to embrace respectful ethical preferences. This requires that we ensure that we do not expect anything of the young person which we are not prepared to provide for him. To practice fairness, we must, at all times be engaged with the following dilemmas:

● How can we ensure that any of the young person's experiences of injustice are acknowledged and appreciated, before we establish expectations about his own unjust behaviour?
● How can we appreciate and acknowledge the young person's experiences of injustice and marginalisation, without sacrificing the focus

on responsibility whereby these experiences are regarded as excuses or justifications for abusive behaviour?

Confrontation and coercion may have their places in police and some statutory contexts, where arrest, stopping a crime and ensuring the safety of individuals in immediate danger, are primary considerations. However, they have no helpful place in therapeutic intervention and should be regarded as power plays, which reproduce and promote abusive and disrespectful practices.

It is often helpful to respond to hostile or avoiding reactions with inquiries about fairness:

I know you have been told by the court that you have to come here, but has anyone taken the trouble to find out what you think or how you see the whole situation?

You have got people trying to tell you what to do or what to think but is anyone bothering to listen to you or find out what you think?

This type of inquiry may be broadened to a wider context:

I have a hunch that for a lot of your life you have probably had heaps of unfair things pushed on to you, with people trying to tell what to do and think, but nobody taking the trouble to listen to what you think or care about what you feel?

I imagine that coming here probably feels like just another unfair thing that has been pushed on to you?

This can culminate in a formal proposal:

You have to come here. You have no choice in that. But you don't have to put up with being pushed around or made to do things that are unfair.

I have no right to try to make you talk about things you don't want to talk about.

In fact, there is no way I'd even think about talking to you about what happened with (your sister), if I didn't understand what is important to you and where you stand.

You have the right to speak out or refuse to do or talk about anything which feels unfair. I will respect this and butt out if you do speak out. You should not have to put up with anything that is unfair in here.

These inquiries and proposals must be complemented with statements of the purpose of intervention, in order to establish fair and respectful reasons for conducting the interviews in the first place. The broad aims of intervention can be stated in an open and up front manner. I generally make repeated statements of purpose in a general and non-confrontational manner, in the early interviews:

You are here because of what happened with your sister. My job is to try to help find ways to put things right which are fair for you, fair for your sister and fair for your mum.

These statements of purpose can be made increasingly specific with gradual shifts in naming practices from, *'what happened with your sister'*, towards, *'hurting your sister'* and eventually *'abusing your sister'*, as engagement with the young person allows for readiness to assume greater levels of responsibility.

As the purpose of intervention becomes established, the priority of fairness is gradually developed and extended by raising a series of basic fairness dilemmas which expose and highlight potential responsibility overloads:

Other people are worried about what you have done to (your sister). They are expecting you to stop and think about unfair things you have done to her, but;

How much have you had to put up with things that have been heaps unfair to you in your life?

How much has anyone bothered to stop and think about what you have been through and what it has been like for you?

How fair would it be to expect you to face up to what you did and think about (your sister's) feelings, if nobody takes the trouble to stop and think about what you have been through and what it has been like for you?

These forms of inquiry state basic fairness dilemmas and serve to name responsibility overloads which may be active in the context of therapeutic intervention, family and community.

When a responsibility overload is named, potential injustices are anticipated and means can be found to avoid perpetrating further unfairness. The young person can be invited to speak out or protest, if processes are felt to be unfair, thus promoting a form of legitimising and honouring of protest. Workers can unite with the young person to remain vigilant in identifying and taking stands against unfairness.

In this way, the young person's hostile or avoiding behaviour may be regarded as a form of legitimate protest which is respected rather than disqualified or pathologised.

When protest is encouraged in a context of fairness, young people seldom use or take advantage of these inquiries to justify or excuse their own abusive behaviour. Protest becomes directed towards genuine injustices rather than becoming wasted through impotent avoidance

practices. The young person may eventually be invited to protest in ways which are increasingly more direct and less aggressive or harmful to others.

Discovering and naming ethics

At the heart of the context for fairness and respect, is a requirement for us to be open to believe in the young person's capacity to discover his own respectful ethics, evaluate his own behaviour and plan respectful actions which accord with his ethics. If we underestimate this capacity, intervention is likely to become highly colonising and disqualifying of the young person's sense of integrity and agency. Such underestimation serves only to provide yet another example of 'being done to' and an implicit judgement of the young person's insufficiency and worthlessness.

If we remain carefully attuned and vigilant in the anticipation of responsibility overloads, whilst promoting a context for fairness, the young person's ethics readily become evident and accessible.

When disadvantaged young people experience a pervasive sense of injustice, the ethic concerning *protest against injustice* is often accessible for discovery and naming. When the young person has little experience of others being interested in his feelings and needs, a simple inquiry may assist in the respectful naming of and invitation to practice protest:

Do you believe in speaking out/standing up for yourself, when something is unfair?

Will you stand up for yourself if I say or do anything that's unfair?

The young person is invited to engage in a legitimate activity to challenge injustice, rather than submit to suppression or pathologising of his protest. These inquiries may be broadened to a wider context:

Have you had to look out for yourself/stand up for yourself a fair bit in your life?

Have you had to put up with unfair things a lot?

Has anyone stood by you/stood up for you, or have you had to handle this on your own?

Many disadvantaged young people gradually reveal a painful but courageous story of survival in which they learned to 'look out for themselves' or 'grow themselves up,' with little support and in the face of considerable adversity.

The ethic of protest against injustice can be explored in conversation about challenges the young person has faced or is facing. Initial contexts for this inquiry which they may feel safe enough to speak about, can include living out of the family, living in residential care, police intervention and at school. Contexts which relate to being subjected to abuse and exploitation or family betrayal and neglect may require a level of trust in engagement, before they are accessible by inquiry. Opportunities for inquiry often arise quite serendipitously:

Jake was describing an incident at school in which he had observed a teacher hitting a student in a classroom with a steel-edged ruler. Jake walked up to the teacher and took the ruler from his hand. The teacher was outraged and sent Jake to the principal's office. The principal chastised Jake for disrespectful behaviour towards the teacher (and for possessing cigarettes found whilst checking Jake's pockets). It was evident that no one noticed or enquired about Jake's motivation for challenging the teacher.

I was unable to resist; 'Why did you do that, Jake?'
  He looked surprised, perhaps regarding this as a stupid question.
  I persisted until Jake eventually explained; 'A teacher can't do that to a kid.'
  I enquired further as to why not? Jake again looked surprised but eventually explained his actions as being informed by his understanding that the teacher had breached a duty of care and had violated a smaller person who was less powerful and in a vulnerable situation. It was evident that Jake, like many young people, had engaged in few conversations about his ethics, especially with adults.

I obtained Jake's permission to make further inquiries:
  'How much do you believe in sticking up for other people who are being treated unfairly?'
  'How important is it to you to stick up for the little guy, if he is being picked on by a bigger person?'

These inquiries can later be broadened in a wide range of contexts which can include family circumstances, involving abuse and neglect. Many disadvantaged young people have witnessed and experienced severe domestic violence:

How much did your father/stepfather stand by you and how much did you have to look out for yourself?

What sort of things did your family have to put up with?

What sort of things did your Mum have to put up with?

How much did (your stepfather) hurt your Mum and your family?

Did you worry about your Mum?

How much did you worry about your Mum?

These initial inquiries are best focused upon other family members and not the young person himself, who may not feel ready to acknowledge high levels of hurt and fear which he experienced through abuse directed towards him personally. However, when these inquiries do focus upon others within the family, it often emerges that the young person was 'worried sick' about his mother or other family members. He may even have tried to stand up for or protect others in the family. Such experience and action may begin to highlight qualities such as caring, concern, loyalty and protectiveness, as valued ethics.

However, the meaning of his experiences must be canvassed and clarified, in order to avoid the possibility of colonising his ethics with our labels, descriptions and good intentions. This is not an exercise in 'reinforcing the good' in others according to our standards. The young person must be invited to make meaning of his own experience, name the ethics it reflects and decide what value he places upon them:

When did you first try to stick up for your Mum?

How did you manage that when you were only a little guy of (7) years old?

Why do you think you did that?

How did you manage to think about other people's feelings when you were heaps scared and hurt yourself?

When you look back at yourself then, what kind of person do you see?

What does this say about you?

How does it fit with what you believe in?

Inquiries which employ concepts of connection through difference, can help to subvert the oppressive 'inter-generational cycle of violence' ideology which proposes that the young person is acting like (and is perhaps similar to) the older abusive person. These inquiries highlight differences in thinking and action which have previously been developed by the young person but which may have been lost or suppressed along the way:

When you saw (your stepfather) hurting people smaller than him, what did you think?

Do you think (your stepfather) ever took the trouble to stop and think about what he was doing to you guys or how much he was hurting your family?

How did you manage to see what he wasn't seeing, when you were only a little kid?

Who understands that you were trying to stand up against unfairness in your family?

The young person can be gradually invited to clarify and name his ethics:

What is it that you were standing up for in your family?

What is it that you believe in, that you were fighting for, back then?

These initial conversations about protest against injustice can appear somewhat alarming, when a young person begins to describe ways that he has stood up for himself or stood up for other people, which have used violence or unjust behaviour to achieve this goal. Young people will frequently describe terrible acts of vengeance and threaten to enact them upon an abusive adult who has caused considerable hurt and pain towards themselves and their families.

It is helpful to decline the invitation to become alarmed and corrective, in response to these violent descriptions, and to focus instead upon the young person's motivation and intent. Then we can appreciate the ethics that he has been struggling to enact. There will be plenty of opportunity for the young person to discover preferred, respectful means of protest at a later time, if the concepts of fairness and protest are legitimised and honoured in the present.

Exploring injustices without sacrificing responsibility

If intervention is conducted in the spirit of fairness, it can enable a responsible exploration of the nature and impact of injustices and challenges experienced by the young person, as well as the abuse he has perpetrated. If inquiry about injustice and responsibility overload is conducted alongside inquiry about ethics, it is unlikely that the young person will begin or continue to regard injustices as an excuse for his own abusive acts. In fact, minimisation and justification are more likely to proffer when we act coercively or try to impose our ethics upon the young person.

When the young person begins to publicly name injustices that he has experienced, perhaps for the first time, further opportunities to name responsibility overload will arise. For example, a young person who has witnessed or experienced abuse from a parent or trusted adult may experience a strong sense of injustice, particularly when the adult has not been held accountable for their actions. It is vital that we name and highlight such overloads:

Was (your step father) ever expected to face up to what he did to your family?

How fair is it that you are expected to do something that he never had to do?

We may never be able to redress such a fundamental injustice, but what does it mean if we fail to acknowledge its existence and potential impact?

Responsibility overloads can be identified and named and respectful ethics discovered and highlighted. It is amazing and wondrous that these ethics can exist and inform behaviour, despite the effects of extreme injustice and adversity. They have a history which demands exploration. Throughout our inquiries, we can honour ethics in the young person's thinking and behaviour and thus ensure that we do not take their existence for granted. In this way, ethical ideas and practices are co-constructed, developed and strengthened throughout the intervention processes. This form of inquiry is called, ethics/honour in the face of adversity.

Does anyone understand what you were trying to do when you were sticking up for and trying to protect your Mum/your brother?

People are worried about the hurt that you did to (your sister) but do they also realise the ways you tried to care for and protect people in your family?

How have you managed to think about other people's feelings when you have had so much unfairness and hurt done to you?

What does this say about you and what you believe in?

How does this fit with who you are as a person – your true colours?

Appeals to an ethical self

The ethics of fairness and respect are promoted, at times, through appeals to essentialist concepts of self which involve a shift away from relativist notions embraced by post-structuralist traditions. Examples include the 'person-act' distinction (see Chapter 7) and forms of inquiry which suggest personal reference points such as, 'the person you really are'; 'showing your true colours' etc. Ethical ideas and practices may be co-constructed and the young person may be regarded in terms of states of becoming in relation to preferred ways of being. However, these preferences can also be regarded as grounded in ethics which can be thought of as having absolute qualities, in relation to a sense of self. In a sense, these ethics are both there to be discovered and are constructed throughout intervention practice.

Such appeals are made in the service of understandings concerning the politics of faith. Appeals to faith, privilege the ethics of fairness and respect as cornerstones for a sense of identity which is honourable and has integrity. Whilst there are many ethical styles, fairness and respect are regarded as having some primacy in determining faith in oneself and a sense of integrity. These ethics tend to survive despite adversity. They are perhaps never totally destroyed or lost, even in circumstances of invasion and extreme violation. They lie at the heart of survival and constitute the soul of integrity. Ethical appeals implicitly honour and respect these qualities. They also accurately and honestly reflect the ethics which inform intervention practice and become part of the necessary declaration of these ethics which assists transparency and openness.

Establishing a context for fairness – naming abuse

As ethics are highlighted and honoured in the face of adversity and injustices and responsibility overloads are named, the young person will usually begin to experience a great deal of dissonance. On one hand there is a gradual appreciation of ethics but on the other, increasing discomfort in relation to awareness of having engaged in abusive behaviours which do not accord with these ethics. The young person will inevitably experience an increased sense of shame from within, rather than a sense of being shamed. Awareness of shame can serve to create an enabling context for him to begin to address his abusive behaviour. (See Chapter 7).

If the young person has already made a limited or partial acknowledgement of abusive actions, enquiries may be initiated in the spirit of inquiry of, ethics in the face of adversity:

How did you manage to start to face up to what you did to (your sister)?

What were you up against?

What stopped you from running away from it and calling (your sister) a total liar?

What did it take for you to start to face the truth?
How does this direction fit with the person you really are?

When the young person begins to consider that his actions may have hurt others, these inquiries may help to further ethical realisations and create a respectful context for the acknowledgement of abusive actions:

How are you managing to even begin to think abut the hurt you did to (your sister) when you are hurting so much about all the things that have been done to you?

How are you able to care about (your sister's) feelings when you have been through so much hurt yourself?

What does this say about you?

How does it fit with the kind of person you really are?

Such a focus on what the young person is ready and able to acknowledge, whilst clearly labelling it as a beginning, establishes a radically different form of inquiry, compared with traditional attempts to challenge and confront the young person to be completely truthful and make full acknowledgements, right from the beginning.

In fact, we find it more helpful to encourage the young person not to acknowledge full details until he knows that it is safe to do so:

If there is more truth to come out (and there usually is) you would be nuts to face it:
  unless you knew for sure that it would
    – help the kid you did it to
    – and help you.
  unless you knew for sure that
    – it wouldn't be used against you
    – it wouldn't be used to put you down or make you feel small

How would you know whether it was safe to speak out?

A broader context for fairness – caregivers

Caregivers, including parents, extended family members, foster carers, residential care workers and mentors, all have vital responsibilities in assisting young people in their care, cease abusive practices and develop respectful ways of relating. The important roles for caregivers have traditionally been underestimated or overlooked in intervention strategies based upon models designed with adults who have abused.

Caregivers have a major influence on the young person's sense of fairness and justice in their everyday lives. As a result, caregivers make a substantial difference when they participate in helping to establish a fair environment for the young person which promotes respectful behaviour. In fact, it is difficult to establish a context for fairness and address responsibility overloads effectively, without the active participation of caregivers.

When the parents are accessible, it is vital that we attempt to engage their ongoing participation in the young person's intervention programme. Parental attributions concerning the young person's abusive behaviour are often highly restraining for his journey towards respect:

He doesn't care about what he has done.

He is turning out just like his father.

He's made his bed, now he can lie in it.

Such attributions inadvertently contribute to responsibility overloads and underestimate the young person's capacity for ethical actions. They reiterate disabling ideas and promote selective perceptions and the biased collection of evidence to support them. Caregivers can be invited to help in the acknowledgement and naming of injustices and challenges faced by the young person, along with maintaining expectations that he address his abusive behaviour.

Caregivers greatly assist when they notice and honour the young person's early glimmers of ethical ideas and practices and provide an appreciative audience to help him to make his own meaning of the steps that he takes in his journey towards respect.

A great deal of careful attention must be paid to engagement with caregivers. Many parents will feel a degree of culpability in relation to the young person's abusive behaviour. Consequently they may hold fearful expectations that professional people will blame them or hold them responsible for the young person's actions.

Peter, aged 14, made a partial acknowledgement that he had sexually abused his seven year old cousin. However, he was described by police as 'sneaky' and 'evasive' and appeared highly distracted and avoiding of responsibility in our initial interviews. It emerged that Peter's father, Tom, had been and still was acting in a highly abusive manner towards Peter, particularly in his attempts to discipline his son. The implications for responsibility overload were obvious.

What would it mean if we encouraged Peter to address his abusive behaviour but overlooked his father's abusive behaviour?

What would it mean of we expected more of Peter than of his father?

This raised an enormous challenge. Peter's father appeared unwilling to participate, having indicated that he was 'disgusted' with his son, whom he regarded as having 'made his bed and now must lie in it'; 'He's on his own now'.

Careful attempts to engage Tom's participation ran parallel with the process of engagement with Peter. Tom also felt an intense sense of injustice in his own life. However, it became apparent that, whilst Tom practiced a highly controlling and punitive style of parenting, he had held hopes of having a relationship with his son that would be vastly more satisfying than his own relationship with his father. Whist establishing a context for fairness, Tom was invited to reconsider a frustrated desire to 'be mates' with Peter and to acknowledge the possibility of taking on a 'real' leadership role for his son, by demonstrating responsibility in addressing behaviours that had been hurtful to Peter.

What would it mean for Peter to know that his father feels ashamed about hurting his son?

What would it mean for Peter if his father took steps to make amends for the hurtful behaviour?

What example would Tom be setting for Peter in his journey to face his own abuse?

Where might this lead their relationship in terms of 'being mates,' earning his son's admiration and respect as opposed to his fear' etc'.

Once Tom had begun to participate actively and responsibly, by acknowledging and addressing his abusive behaviour, towards both his son and his partner, Peter quickly became more focused and took leaps forward in addressing his own abusive behaviour.

A context for fairness, without the highly restraining and burdening influences of responsibility overloads, greatly frees up the young person to discover his capacity to move forward in his journey.

Once Jake had begun to identify and name ethics relating to caring, loyalty and protectiveness, in his relationships with his mother and siblings, ethics which contrasted greatly with his sexual and physical violence towards these family members, I began to enquire about his readiness to participate in a meeting with his mother which might further address responsibility overload:

'Does your Mum know,
- *how much you're worried about her and your family?*
- *what it was like for you when (your stepfather) was in your family?*
- *how you tried to stand up for yourself and your family?'*

'Do you think she would be interested in learning about what it's been like for you?'

'How fair would it be to expect you to talk about what you did to your Mum and (your step sister) but not talk about what it's been like for you?'

These inquiries were complemented with inquiries about Jake's readiness to let his Mum know about some of his initial realisations regarding his abuses within the family:

'Does your Mum know that,
– you feel bad about what you did to (your sister)?
– you realise you hurt (your sister) heaps?
or would she still think that you think that it wasn't such a big deal?'

'What difference would it make to let her know the truth?'

'Are you ready to let her know?'

'What tells you that you are ready?'

'How does this fit with the kind of person you are?'

Inquiries which establish readiness are vital:

Do you think your Mum made the right decision in refusing to put up with any more of (your step father's) violence?

Do you think she should put up with any more violence from anyone? Even from her son?

Does your Mum know that you feel bad about what you did to her or, does she only know that you think she was unfair?

What difference would it make to let her know the truth?

Are you ready to let her know?

Meetings were also being conducted with Jake's mother, Jill, to engage her participation and determine her readiness to address responsibility overloads which might restrain Jake's progress in his journey. To be ready to assist her son, Jill needed first to reclaim her ethics about parenting, discover the strength and caring she used in surviving and protesting against abuse within her family and recognise her own competence. Jill began to challenge a restraining view of herself as 'weak' and defeated.

She then felt ready to talk with Jake about their survival of years of tyranny within the family and the qualities and strength that each had employed to make it through such ordeals. Jill was then invited to appreciate the potential responsibility overload, from a position of strength rather than insufficiency and guilt:

Does Jake know how much you realise about what he has been through?

What would happen if Jake thought we were expecting him to face his abusive behaviour and the effects on (his sister), but felt that no one had understood or acknowledged the challenges that he has been through himself?

In three emotionally moving meetings, Jill and Jake were able to describe and name terrible injustices perpetrated by Jake's stepfather, along with a variety of loyal and protective actions which were aimed at providing mutual support and survival throughout this time. They were able to provide for each other, some of their realisations about the impact of these injustices and abuses upon each other and they started to acknowledge ways they felt that they had let each other down.

At one point, Jill achieved a clear and spontaneous realisation that she had indeed let Jake down. She told him that she could see how he had been desperately worried and trying to protect her, whilst only a little boy, when it was really her job to protect him. She declared the level of injustice that she perceived in this realisation. In the midst of tears and hugs, Jake was able to express his remorse about having hurt his sister and his mother, in a meaningful way to his mother, for the first time.

Acknowledgements such as this, whilst enabling the young person and his parents to reclaim a sense of connection and closeness, also have a significant effect on relieving the huge burden associated with the responsibility overload, in which he is expected to address injustices he has perpetrated without the benefit of having others address injustices he has suffered. The implications of this freeing up can be substantial.

One week after the third meeting between Jake and his mother, Jake telephoned me to make an urgent time to meet. When we met, he disclosed that he had also sexually assaulted one of his sister's friends who had been in the house for a sleepover, several years back. This was the first time that this abuse had been disclosed. Jake's disclosure could be honoured because it furthered his integrity and enabled appropriate notification and responses to be made for the younger child.

When responsibility overload is effectively addressed, it often results in a sense of liberation or freedom from the burden of unfairness which the young person may have carried for a considerable period of time and which has consistently provided an obstacle in his journey towards respect. His capacity for respectful action will be opened up and become more accessible.

When parents, caregivers, residential care workers etc. are invited to:

- Acknowledge injustices and challenges faced by the young person.
- Acknowledge ethical stances and achievements they have observed.

- Hear further evidence of ethical stances and achievements that others have observed with the young person.
- Make meaning of these stances and achievements, in the face of injustice and in context of the young person's sense of identity.

... they play a vital role in reducing the impact of responsibility overloads and in co-constructing and broadening ethical stances which inform a respectful sense of identity.

> Jake's key residential care worker was invited to participate in such inquiries with Jake:
> What do you think it has taken for Jake to face up to this?'
>
> What do you think he is up against?
>
> How do think he is managing to do it, in the face of (named injustice)?
>
> What do you think this says about Jake?
>
> Did you know that he had this kind of strength and courage?
>
> Have you noticed Jake using this type of courage and strength in other areas of his life?

In this context, caregivers generally feel that they are part of the solution rather than part of the problem. The initial unhelpful attributions give way to respectful efforts to assist the young person to define his own ethical qualities. Caregivers provide an audience for honouring respectful ethics and behaviour.

Developing a broader context for fairness – peer group and culture

The young person's relationships with other young people provide a context in which the nature and influence of power hierarchies and dominant ideologies concerning power can be made open to critique, in the light of fairness and ethics. Dominant recipes for gaining status and the uses and effects of violence in differentiating and determining young men's positions in social hierarchies, can emerge from limited awareness into sharper focus.

For example, a young person who has begun to establish and develop ethics which relate to 'standing up against unfairness; 'protection of other's rights'; 'standing by a friend in need' etc, can be invited to examine dominant ideas and practices which promote disrespectful recipes for gaining status, which include:

- Putting down (members of marginalised groups) to feel tough or strong.
- The use of intimidation to get what you want at the expense of others.
- Strategies of revenge and retribution to 'get even', avenge disrespect by others or reclaim a sense of lost honour.
- The use of sex to obtain status.

He may be encouraged to observe his peer group and critique these ideas and practices; to take a position in the light of his own ethics:

> Is (the other person) turning more towards using his head or using his fists to sort out his problems?
>
> When you talk about respect, what kind of respect are you wanting,
> respect that comes from others being scared of you?
> or respect that comes from others admiring you?
>
> Does this fit with being tough or being yourself?
>
> What do you respect most?
>
> What do you think is fair?

Young men in oppressive school, residential care or detention contexts, can be assisted to examine and critique power relations which are troubling and which often serve to marginalise the young person within the institution.

> Steve's reputation in a detention centre, as a 'trouble-maker' with a 'chip on his shoulder', had resulted in considerable loss of his privileges and escalating cycles of violence. He consistently had 'run ins' with one particular residential care worker. This worker appeared, at times, to act in ways which might provoke an aggressive reaction by Steve. The worker then maintained high levels of vigilance in relation to any indications that Steve might be 'losing it' or breaching centre regulations. As Steve learned to identify and name 'power tactics' in his interactions with the worker, he was able to discover a capacity for new forms of resistance and protest which were consistent with his ethics but better served his interests. Steve came to regard the worker's 'provocations' as opportunities to test himself in new skills and demonstrate an ethical capacity, which at times surprised and impressed other workers in the centre.

Young people can be invited to examine and critique specific, dominant ideas as 'dangerous ideas' which inform violence and abusive practices, through the process of externalisation which enables the idea to be made visible in its historical and cultural contexts and accessible for challenge (White, 1995). Cultural and peer support systems which encourage complicity with 'dangerous ideas' along with patterns of resistance against their influence, can be understood and highlighted by the young person, in the context of his own life experience.

These invitational practices will be documented in a forthcoming publication on young people's violence which is currently a work in progress.

Developing a broader context for fairness – community and culture

The context for fairness can include school, church and other community contexts which impact upon the family.

When Joe, and members of his extended family, began to demonstrate readiness to meet for the purposes of mutual acknowledgement and restitution, a dilemma arose which required consideration. Much of Joe's experience of injustice and victimisation had taken place in a range of inappropriate foster placements which had been sanctioned by the statutory child protection authority.

What would it mean if an expectation was maintained that Joe and members of his extended family acknowledge and take responsibility for abusive or neglectful actions that have harmed one another, their families and their community – but the abusive and neglectful actions which took place under the auspice of the child protection authority, were overlooked or ignored?

This kind of responsibility overload is frequently experienced by members of disadvantaged and marginalised communities.

In this case, representatives of the statutory authority were prepared to meet with Joe and members of his extended family. They were prepared to listen to and review case records which documented well-intended but ignorant and appalling decisions about Joe's placement and connection with his community. They were prepared to acknowledge the impact that this had upon Joe and his community. These acknowledgements contributed to an extremely moving discussion which surprised members of Joe's family who had never before experienced welfare authorities taking responsibility for inappropriate or harmful actions. As a consequence Joe was able to reconnect with his family and community and the family were able, for the first time, to begin to forge a co-operative relationship with welfare authorities.

Developing a broader context for fairness – statutory justice

A major context for responsibility overload and which requires community consideration,

concerns the development of respectful and fair statutory justice processes for young people who have abused. I have been particularly preoccupied with the following dilemmas.

To what extent do our statutory justice processes promote fairness?

To what extent do statutory justice processes promote respectful and ethical actions with young people?

To what extent can we equate justice with fairness?

These preoccupations have assisted the respectful developments in juvenile justice in South Australia.

Statutory justice priorities have tended to focus upon the concept of mitigation of responsibility and the pathologising of young people's behaviour, as sentencing criteria. Inadvertently, these priorities tend to encourage young people to avoid responsibility for their actions and sanction punitive consequences for those who fully acknowledge responsibility. Such concerns have led to a shift in sentencing criteria in the Youth Court of South Australia, which is becoming increasingly attuned to responsibility-based assessment and decision-making criteria which promote and support acknowledgement for abusive behaviour.

The therapeutic intervention programme has established close collaboration with the court and provides ongoing assessments of responsibility and programme goal attainment to enable accountable decision-making in the statutory context. Assessments of goal attainment in relation to levels of responsible and respectful behaviour are documented, with the collaborative participation of the young person and his caregivers, and forwarded to the court on a regular basis. The court may order remands, over significant periods of time, to enable such assessment to be reliably conducted, prior to final sentencing.

The development of Youth Conferencing processes in South Australia, has enabled a majority of young people who commit sexual offences, to engage in a justice process which:

● Provides an incentive for acknowledging responsibility, in the form of a guilty plea.
● Provides a forum in which people affected by the offences, can express their experiences of the nature and affects of the abuse to the young person and others.

- Provides a forum in which the young person and those affected by the abuse can participate in determining consequence of the offences, in the form of undertakings or formal requirements.
- Promotes a commitment, by the young person, to address his abusive behaviour, in the context of accountability to the experiences of those who have been hurt by the abuse.

The nature and theory of conferencing processes and their contributions to fairness and social justice have been documented by Braithwaite (2000). Research regarding the effectiveness of these processes, in the context of adolescent sexual offending in South Australia, is described by Daly and Curtis-Fawley (2001, 2003).

I have found that statutory justice processes which privilege fairness and a sense of social justice greatly facilitate young people successfully addressing and challenging their abusive behaviours and the ideologies which inform these behaviours. When justice processes are fair, they promote genuine desires and efforts by young people, to make restitution to the specific individuals they have hurt and to their communities. (Jenkins et al., 2002)

In this context, we have discovered that 45% of young people attending our intervention programme will eventually make further disclosures of abuse of other children, who have not yet disclosed themselves. These acknowledgements are made freely from the young person's sense of ethics, when he understands that such responsibility and honesty will be respected and will enable the possibility of helpful resolutions and outcomes which enhance a sense of respectful identity.

In this way, statutory justice systems can actually serve to promote fairness and respect, whilst holding a young person accountable for his actions and maintaining a priority on community safety.

References

Braithwaite, J. (2000) Shame and Criminal Justice. *Canadian Journal of Criminology*. July: 281–98.

Connell, R.W. (1993) *Schools and Social Justice.* Philadelphia, Temple University Press.

Daly, K. (2001) *Sexual Assault and Restorative Justice.* Paper Presented at Restorative Justice and Family Violence Conference, Canberra, Australian National University.

Daly, K. and Curtis-Fawley (2003) *Sexual Offence Cases Finalised in Court, by Conference, and by Formal Caution in South Australia.* Presentation to National Practitioner's Forum. Adelaide. May, 2003.

Derrida, J. and Dufourmantelle, A. (2000) *Of Hospitality: Anne Dufourmantelle Invites Jacques Derrida to Respond.* Stanford, CA, Stanford University Press.

Jenkins, A., Hall, R. and Joy, M. (2002) Forgiveness in Child Sexual Abuse: A Matrix of Meanings. *International Journal of Narrative Therapy and Community Work.* Issue 1.

Jenkins, A. (1999) Invitations to Responsibility: Engaging Adolescents and Young Men Who Have Sexually Abused. in Marshall, W. (Ed.) *Sourcebook of Treatment Programs for Sexual Offenders*, New York, Plenum.

Jenkins, A. (1990) *Invitations to Responsibility: The Therapeutic Engagement of Men Who Are Violent and Abusive.* Adelaide, Dulwich Centre Publications.

Larner, G. (1999) Derrida and The Deconstruction of Power as Context and Topic in Therapy. in Parker, I. *Deconstructing Psychotherapy*. London, Sage.

Ransom (1997) *Foucault's Disciplines.* Durham, Duke University Press.

Wexler, P. (1992) *Becoming Somebody: Toward A Social Psychology of School.* London, Farmer Press.

White, M. (1995) *Re-Authoring Lives.* Adelaide, Dulwich Centre Publications.

Chapter Seven

Knocking on Shame's Door: Facing Shame Without Shaming Disadvantaged Young People Who Have Abused

Alan Jenkins

Introduction

Shame presents a problematic issue in the day-to-day lives of those who have abused and in intervention programmes designed to address this abuse. These young people's daily experiences and interactions with their peers tend to be saturated with shame-related events, especially in the context of disadvantage and injustice. The sense of disgrace which accompanies shame can feel toxic to the point of annihilation, so that most young people, who have abused, invest much of their time and energy in desperate strategies to avoid the experience of shame. These can range from practices which produce emotional detachment, including a wide range of sexualised pre-occupations and fantasies, to anti-social activities which include excess drug and alcohol use. Such driven investment in avoidance activities and pre-occupations becomes highly restraining and disabling in young people's lives.

Increasingly desperate practices to avoid the experience of shame and frequent shaming practices by others result in cycles of despair and paralysis, which foster a sense of identity as 'loser', characterised by feelings of worthlessness, insufficiency and self-deprecation (see Chapter 6). When young people engage in these self-paralysing practices of avoidance, they invite further shaming explanations and judgements by family members, members of the community and representatives of the justice system. It is not surprising that they become increasingly trapped in vicious cycles of despair and passivity.

This chapter has been written to complement 'Making it Fair' in Chapter 6, with a focus on addressing shame in intervention with young people who have abused, in ways which might enable their investment in an ethical journey towards respectful relationships in which abuse has no place. This requires ethical practices in intervention which allow for shame (and shame-related practices) to be re-positioned from restraining and disabling concepts and experiences to ones which might be enabling and facilitate reclaiming a respectful sense of self. Facing shame can be experienced as both disabling and enabling. However, it is an inevitable and vital component of the young person's ethical journey and we are obliged to help provide safe passage. In an enabling context, facing shame is often the catalyst for reclamation and restoration with the young person and his community.

What is shame?

Shame can be defined as the experience associated with the realisation that one has acted in a way that is dishonourable. This experience generally involves a pervasive judgement of oneself as dishonourable, unworthy or lacking in integrity.

Thus the experience of shame generally promotes a challenge to personal integrity.

The experience of shame can be distinguished from the act of **shaming**. Shaming (to shame) is the attempt to disgrace or make ashamed; to influence, force or compel through the use or attribution of shame. One is a subjective experience, the other a political act of power. They are, of course, strongly interconnected and interdependent in ways which are often hidden or invisible to the individuals concerned. There is a political paradox in the dilemma posed by the idea of making one's own realisation (attributing shame to the self) which requires a social context in which the behaviour is regarded as shameful. However, the distinctions between shame and shaming can be enlightening and are, in fact, vital to considerations of ethical practice for young people and workers alike.

The problem with shame

The problem with shame lies not so much in the capacities and possibilities for young people facing shame and making judgements of personal dishonour or disgrace, but in widespread and pervasive practices designed to avoid the experience of shame. Shame poses a frightening challenge to the young person's sense of worth and integrity and without supporting and enabling structures he will most likely act to protect himself through practices of avoidance.

Attempts to avoid shame attribution and a sense of worthlessness and personal dishonour can involve:

- Complete or partial denial of the dishonourable action.
- Attempts to minimise, justify or excuse the dishonourable action, including attempts to blame other people or circumstances beyond his sphere of influence.
- Strategies to prevent or distract thinking about the dishonourable action. These can include alternative preoccupations which retreat into a fantasy world of self-aggrandisement and impersonal and objectifying sexualised ideas and activities.
- Withdrawal from family and community life and activities.
- Excessive drug and alcohol use.

And in the extreme:

- Aggression and violence towards others, particularly those regarded as having attributed dishonour or disrespect.
- Self-harm.

Such avoidance practices inevitably lead to increasingly paralysing cycles of detachment, desperation and futility. They become increasingly desperate, ineffective and self-destructive and always serve to hint at or point towards judgements of a sense of identity of 'loser'.

These avoidance strategies are generally interpreted by others as indications that the young person is shameless or lacking in responsibility, empathy or compassion. He may then be regarded as in need of direction from others, usually in the form of confrontation, education and correction. These intervention practices often involve shaming discourses and interactions.

Given that patterns of avoidance involve actions, which in turn invite patterns of shaming by family, community and statutory systems, the young person's sense of identity becomes increasingly disabling and destructive towards self and others.

The problem of avoidance of shame, by young people who have abused, is a reflection of a widespread community or social problem concerning avoidance. Young people who have abused, members of their families and communities and workers in justice and therapeutic intervention programmes, often pay little attention to the nature and meanings attributed to shame and shame-avoidance practices. In intervention programmes, naming the issue of shame is often avoided and can be left entirely off the agenda.

Like any set of experiences and practices which relate to power, shame has both repressive and creative aspects. However, dominant ideas in popular culture and modern psychotherapy, ideas which are generally informed by dominant ideologies concerning enlightenment through individual growth, self-expression and self-actualisation, have emphasised the repressive at the expense of the creative potential of shame (Schneider, 1992). Shame has tended to be regarded as repressive and restrictive; something to be overcome or overthrown along with all oppressive structures; an obstacle to enlightenment and liberation of the self.

Schneider invites us to challenge this conservative view by situating self-development in a context of community and highlighting that, 'shame is not a disease . . . it is a mark of our humanity.' Shame can be valued as, 'a pointer of value awareness', whose 'very occurrence arises from the fact that we are valuing animals.' Shame is vital in social relations because it is 'aroused by phenomena that would violate the organism and its integrity.' 'To extirpate shame is to cripple our humanity'. Shame offers us a means of warning regarding potential violation and can enable the protection of privacy. 'To avoid the witness of shame,' is regarded as akin to removing the brakes on a motor vehicle because they slow it down (Schneider, 1992).

It can be helpful to distinguish between **discretion-shame,** which can enable the anticipation and prevention of a potential shameful act and **disgrace-shame,** which may follow its enactment. Both forms have an adaptive and creative potential in the maintenance of respectful relationships (Schneider, 1992). Effective intervention allows for a young person to appreciate and develop a sense of discretion-shame in future relationships, through facing disgrace-shame regarding his past abusive acts. Most forms of inquiry in intervention, discussed in this chapter, invite the young person to address disgrace-shame.

Shame can only be adaptive, in this way, when certain actions are regarded as shameful within a culture and there are effective and accessible means for evaluating its discretion and disgrace aspects. Here lies the paradox of shame. Despite some ambivalence, sexual assault of children is generally regarded as a shameful conduct in most cultures. However, culturally sanctioned, shaming practices, particularly when they are excluding or marginalising of the young person, frequently result in patterns of avoidance of shame.

Mistakenly-attributed shame

Disadvantaged young people, who have been subjected to injustice and oppression, face an additional challenge, which can result in extreme confusion, through their ongoing and pervasive subjection to shaming discourses. It is one thing to experience shame as the result of realisations about one's own dishonourable actions. In this context, shame might be regarded as appropriately attributed. However, the politics of disadvantage allows for shame to be attributed to disadvantaged young people, when the dishonourable acts have been perpetrated by those with greater privilege in a context of fixed and imbalanced power relations, not by the young person himself.

Disadvantaged young people can, for example, experience a sense of failure in relation to not achieving certain culturally sanctioned life goals, despite unequal access to resources. A sense of shame may be mistakenly attributed with these experiences of disadvantage or failure. Such attributions can be the result of cultural expectations and ideologies (e.g., 'not being man enough') or specific attributions of culpability and worthlessness (as often experienced by those who have been abused by a significant other). This might be referred to as **mistakenly-attributed shame**, in that there is no discernible, dishonourable act, which has been carried out by the young person in this context.

Mistakenly attributed shame is perhaps similar to Nietzsche's concept of 'false shame' which is 'a product of fear and embarrassment, not love and respect,' resulting from 'having mistaken oneself ... having underestimated oneself ... a lack of reverence for oneself,' often as a result of 'wrongful humiliation' (Nietzsche, 1967; Schneider, 1992).

Finding safe passage

Widespread practices of avoidance and confusion, in relation to the issue of shame, can make it difficult for young people, caregivers and workers to find constructive and enabling pathways in their journeys towards respect.

It can be extremely difficult to establish an enabling context, which allows for shame to be understood and addressed in ways which might promote a sense of agency and which might foster realisation, restoration, reclamation and redemption. There appear to be few safe places and few opportunities available, in which a young person can face appropriately attributed shame, in ways that might foster a respectful sense of identity.

A safe environment is required to assist the young person to draw several distinctions so that shame can be repositioned or re-contextualised, from a restraining experience to an enabling experience:

- The capacity to identify and name dishonourable acts and the power relations which determine them, in order to attribute responsibility and shame accordingly. This can enable the young person to address the question, 'Whose shame is it?'; to face shame associated with dishonourable acts he has carried out and define and reattribute the shame he may have mistakenly carried on behalf of others or in the service of unhelpful cultural and gendered expectations.
- The distinctions between the dishonourable *act* and the *person* who has carried out the act. The young person can be assisted to discover new possibilities in means of evaluating himself as a person, through his realisations and the positions he takes in relation to the abusive act. This generally involves a gradual transition from an initial state of dishonour and disgrace in judgements of self, towards judgements of his actions as dishonourable and disgraceful.
- The person-act distinction can enable new understandings about the nature and process of facing appropriately attributed shame. If facing and accepting responsibility for dishonourable actions can be regarded as honourable or virtuous (in accordance with the young person's stated ethics) then the painful processes involved in facing shame might be regarded as significant and worthwhile contributions towards developing a sense of

honour, integrity and inner strength. Facing shame might be regarded as an honourable process concerned with restitution and restoration in relation to a dishonourable action. This can clear the way for potential, alternative judgements of self as honourable, in the light of personal assessment and critique of the significance of courageous steps, willingly taken, to face disgrace-shame which inevitably accompanies responsible acknowledgement and realisation. What becomes possible is the recognition that, '*I committed a terrible act*', together with the understanding, earned through processes of reclamation, that '*I am not a terrible person*'.

- The vital distinction, concerning the initiative or motivation of the young person, in the context of external political expectations for him to address his abusive behaviour. The young person may be invited to face responsibility for his abusive actions and thereby invited to face shame. He may decline or accept such invitations. There is a significant difference in enabling possibilities, when a young person chooses to face shame, as opposed to accommodating to experiences of coercion or shaming by others.

An adaptive sense of shame requires cultural attributions of shame towards the perpetration of abusive acts. However, shaming justice or therapeutic interventions may serve only to further confuse the distinctions between the person and the act and foster accommodation or avoidance strategies. The choice to face shame, with appropriate supports, can enable respectful action, which is likely to be owned by the young person and incorporated into a respectful sense of identity.

The processes involved in addressing and taking responsibility for abusive behaviour require a journey, which entails facing shame. It is not possible to understand the political nature of abuse, to develop empathy and compassion for others or to engage in any meaningful form of restoration or reclamation of self, without facing shame.

Attempts to bypass the issue of shame serve only to promote avoidance or a sense of accommodation, or 'going through the motions' of restorative action. The young person's sense of identity remains based on avoidance strategies and on the edge of 'loser' or self-contempt ideology. It is in this context that popular

formulations which attempt to draw distinctions between 'shame' and 'guilt' have been rejected as being unhelpful for an invitational model. These conceptualisations tend to regard 'guilt' as a developmentally 'mature' feeling of regret which focuses upon the abusive action. The action is judged to be bad or wrong. Thus 'guilt' is privileged and regarded as a more desirable focus than 'shame,' which involves a judgement of the identity of the person who has carried out the action. The person is judged to be bad or wrong. The possibilities of restoration and growth are therefore regarded as greater, in the supposedly more self-enhancing context of 'guilt' (Fossum and Mason, 1986).

I can appreciate the spirit of such formulations in attempting to draw the person-act distinction. However, they can serve to privilege 'guilt' and promote bypassing or attempting to rush the significant developmental journey of transition from a shameful judgement of self to a shameful judgement of the act, and the social role that this gradual transition can serve for all concerned. It might be regarded as 'mature' for a person who has abused to experience shameful judgements of himself; indications that he perhaps is experiencing some understanding of the seriousness and gravity of the act of abuse, along with the potential impact upon the abused person. This level of judgement may be helpful in the context of the principle of accountability and restitution to the abused person, who could feel somewhat affronted by the abuser too readily embracing 'guilt' and bypassing 'shame'. 'Guilt' is a concept which has meaning in a legal context, but little relevance as a reference point in therapeutic intervention, where it can obscure the importance of facing shame in the journey.

If the young person decides to face and address abusive behaviour and make significant efforts towards atonement, restitution and restoration, he cannot do this without facing shame. To address abuse requires embarking on a journey in which the young person is assisted to position himself in relation to shame, so that he can 'look shame squarely in the eye'. This is an inevitable and necessary part of this journey. The therapist's role is to remain highly attuned to windows of opportunity, throughout intervention, in which the young person can be assisted to consider enabling means to address shame and decline means which are likely to be disabling to self and others.

How does shame show its face? – The initial contact

Evidence of shame is generally apparent right from the initial contact with the young person, but generally in the form of avoidance behaviours. The young person may not have the understanding or language in which to name and address the experience of shame and is desperately preoccupied with attempts to avoid its potentially disabling consequences. The therapist, however, is in a position to interpret and respond to indicators or signs of shame.

On introduction to the therapist, Jake (aged 15) roles his eyes upwards and defiantly exclaims, 'Whatever'.

Peter (aged 14) averts his eyes downwards and asserts, 'It didn't hurt her'.

Kevin (aged 14) picks up a pen and begins to tap the arm of the chair loudly and rhythmically.

Keith (aged 15) glances frequently out of the window and then towards his watch and demands, 'When's this going to be finished?'.

Mike (aged 14) responds to all inquiries by looking downwards and responding, 'I dunno'.

A disabling interpretation might underestimate the young person's capacity to experience shame and suggest that this initial behaviour is an indication of 'conduct disorder' or deficits in empathy and compassion. Such an interpretation might then inform confronting responses and a desire to challenge and correct the young person's minimisations and irresponsible attitudes.

Interpretations and responses which are enabling will perhaps be based on recognition that the young person's avoidance responses and reactions may in fact be informed by an underlying sense of shame and anticipation that intervention will most likely be a shaming process.

The young person is not likely to be in any position to be able to address abusive behaviour and face shame, given the politics of intervention, unless we first establish a context for fairness. (See Chapter 6) Any expectation that the young person will show remorse, at this point, will only serve to create a more shaming context, which in turn will lead to avoidance, further minimisations, justifications and denial and even the possibility of aggressive behaviour in the interview:

Jake knows he has forced his little step-sister to submit to practices which have hurt her. He knows his abuse of one of her friends on a sleep over is an undisclosed

secret. He knows that he has recently beaten up his mother. He will be desperate to avoid intense shame associated with these actions. On top of this, he carries unimaginable, mistakenly attributed shame, in relation to a sense of culpability associated with letting his family down, in the context of his step-father's abuse, and feelings of failure and worthlessness regarding his own life goals.

If we inadvertently shame a young man like Jake by attempting to coerce him to demonstrate remorse and then label his resistance to our efforts as pathological or deviant, we are perpetrating abuse in the service of therapeutic intervention. Shame can be rightfully attributed to ourselves.

When we focus on fairness and decline invitations to shame the young person, we pay respect to shame. We allow space for avoidance strategies and try to see them for what they are. Such declined invitations implicitly serve to recognise that the young person's shame may be real and intense and is evidence of or a pointer to, honour and integrity of the young person, despite their dishonourable actions. In this way we begin to respect rather than demonise shame.

Interventions which are based on confrontation and correction tend to intensify shaming discourses. This leads to shame becoming increasingly inaccessible to the young person and avoidance strategies becoming more and more entrenched. The only safe option for a young person, in this context, is to accommodate or 'go through the motions' of submission to the demands of the therapeutic programme, by learning the language and behaving in ways that mimic political correctness, in order to ensure survival. This is not an unfamiliar process for young disadvantaged people who have learnt to submit and accommodate in order to survive a wide range of oppressive circumstances.

However, intervention processes which ignore or attempt to bypass or 'protect' the young person from shame, also serve to distance him from his own sense of shame, whilst simultaneously intensifying shame.

In the service of respectful and accountable intervention, we can only attempt to establish enabling conditions under which shame can be safely and courageously faced. In such a journey, the young person must experience judgements of self, including the initial judgement of dishonour and unworthiness, before moving towards a judgement of the dishonourable action and the recognition of his own capacity to act in honourable ways. It is through facing the painful aspects of shame, learning to draw the distinctions between self and action and recognising honour and integrity in facing abuse, that the young person is able to reclaim himself and further a sense of identity based on respect and integrity.

Young people who engage in patterns of avoidance behaviour are generally used to being cajoled and shamed and will anticipate this kind of interaction in an intervention programme. Many of these young people have been shamed by 'experts' in the past and they will be wary and ready to defend themselves with us. If we can recognise the indications of shame, allow space for avoidance, decline invitations to confront or correct and focus on establishing a context for fairness, we may be able to help to open up an enabling way to face shame.

Naming abuse and naming shame

If we maintain patience and persevere with genuine efforts to promote a context of fairness, a range of windows of opportunity will present for assisting the young person to face shame. As injustices and abuses experienced by the young person are recognised, ethics are named and responsibility overloads are addressed, opportunities will become increasingly frequent. The young person has less need to employ such confrontational methods of avoidance. However, he will continue to be watchful, wary and distrustful of the therapist's motives.

In a fair and ethical context, indications of shame will often be evident, when reference is made to the abuse perpetrated by the young person. These indications are usually non-verbal, e.g., eyes averted downwards, head down, wetness in the eyes, faltering in speech. They afford opportunities to begin to name and make meaning of the experience of shame, perhaps wondering, *'What are they setting me up for?'* This underscores the importance of inviting and legitimising protest in the context of intervention. (see Chapter 6).

Tim (14) had greatly minimised his abuse of his five-year-old, half sister, in interviews with the police and statutory authorities. Despite initial defiance, Tim was eventually able to talk about his experience of watching his stepfather tyrannise and abuse his family, in particular his mother. He had attempted at times to stand by and protect his mother when she was being abused. This conversation led to acknowledgement of

injustice, hurt and betrayal to which Tim and his family had been subjected, along with consideration of ethics of concern and care and a desire to stick up for someone being abused by a bigger person.

A responsibility overload was highlighted:
    'People expect you to face up to what you did to your sister and understand how this affected her, but has anyone stopped and thought about what it was like for you when your dad was running amok in your family?'

'How fair is this?'

Tim was invited to consider his ethic:
    'Who understands how worried you were about your Mum and how much you tried to stick up for her?'
    'Why was it so important for you to try to stand up for your Mum?'
    'What is it that is important to you, that you had to stand up for?'

The naming of overloads and the clarification of ethics promote intense dilemmas for young people like Tim. The dissonance between ethics and abusive actions is felt, as shame comes closer to the surface of awareness.

At this point, it may be appropriate to make direct enquiries about the young person's abusive behaviour. These enquiries are informed by a vigilant appreciation of any evidence of respectful and honourable actions, in the face of adversity. Thus a focus on integrity is maintained.

'Tim, can I ask you something about what you did to your sister?

*'How did you manage to find what it takes, to **start** to face up to what you did to Peta?' (Tim had previously acknowledged to police, that he had touched Peta but denied numerous allegations of penetration and other abusive acts.)*

'What stopped you from running away from it and calling her a total liar?'

A focus on evidence of acknowledgement, rather than denial, can be maintained throughout the process of inquiry.

These initial inquiries may also focus upon the young person's **intent**:

'Tim, did you want to hurt Peta and make her feel bad, or did you not realise that what you were doing would hurt her, when you first started?' 'If what you did has hurt Peta, would that worry you?'

Through these inquiries about intent, the young person is given the opportunity to position himself in relation to his intent regarding his abusive actions. The distinctions between 'cruel intent' and 'self-centred lack of consideration' for the younger child are important in the clarification of ethics and in addressing and challenging disabling attributions by others.

As such inquiries promote increasing dissonance between stated ethics and abusive actions, non-verbal indications of shame are likely to be evident. These signs afford opportunities for naming and making meaning of shame through processes called, **'talking about talking about it'**.

> *Tim declared that he had not intended nor wanted to hurt his sister.*
>
> *When asked 'If Peta was hurt by what you did, would it worry you?', Tim's eyes had began to water and he averted them downwards.*
>
> *I responded, 'Tim, you look like you don't feel proud about what you did?'*
>
> *Tim gave a very brief nod and kept his head down.*
> *I enquired, 'What are you realising Tim?'*
> *Tim tearfully responded, 'She was my sister'.*

Even within the restraining context of a young person's limitations of vocabulary and verbal expression and familiar patterns of avoidance, he can begin to identify and name shame, in relation to his abusive actions. These become named as actions he 'doesn't feel proud of' or 'feels bad about,' because 'she is my sister'. In this way, he can further situate his abusive actions in a context of violation of personal and family ethics, concerning loyalty and standing by those in vulnerable circumstances.

In our impatience to address abuse, we can easily overlook or underestimate the enormous significance of initial acknowledgements and realisations. They may be inadequate as they stand; however, they are substantial beginnings and should be open to recognition, further inquiry and honouring.

It can be tempting to immediately pursue lines of inquiry about what it is that Tim feels bad about, in order to deepen his experience and move him further along the path of facing his abusive actions. However, we run the risk of overwhelming him with attempts to coerce movement at our pace, in accordance with our sense of readiness. If we can assist him instead to develop his own framework and rationale for interpreting these initial steps, he may develop a sense of readiness which enables him to take further steps towards achieving his own goals, because he feels safe enough and is convinced that this is the right direction for him to take.

The process of inquiry called, 'talking about talking about it,' invites the young man to reflect upon and attribute meaning to the step he has just taken, in order to critique this step and determine whether it is a step he would want to own because it fits with his own ethics. The therapist might pursue lines of inquiry like the following :

> *'Tim, would anyone else know how bad you feel about what you did?'*
>
> *'Have you ever told anyone before?'*
>
> *'Would anyone be surprised to learn about how bad you really feel?'*
>
> *'Would anyone realise how hard it is to face up to what you are starting to realise?'*
>
> *'What does it take to begin to speak out about the truth?'*
>
> *'How are you able to begin to think about what you did to Peta, when you've been through such hard times yourself?'* ('honour in the face of adversity')

An opportunity may now exist for young men like Tim to begin to make new meanings out of facing shame:

> *'What does it say about you that you are not only beginning to realise that you hurt your sister, but that you are also beginning to speak out about it?'*
>
> *Tim responded, 'I don't know. I guess I'm stupid'.*

Like most young people, Tim does not yet have an enabling framework for making sense of shame. However, his response does give an indication of the meaning he attributes to shame; one which challenges his entire worth and integrity as a person; 'I'm stupid'. This response is typical for young people when they initially try to make sense of the experience of shame. The therapist might further enquire:

> *'Would a stupid person begin to stop and think about what he put the little guy through, or would he just be thinking about himself?'*
>
> *'What would it say about you, if you didn't feel bad about what you did to Peta?'*

In this way, the young person is invited to consider the meaning of experiencing shame, in relation to his ethics and in the context of what might fit with honour and integrity.

> *After some consideration, Tim decided that it would be 'pretty callous' not to feel 'bad'.*

The therapist might further enquire:

'Does it fit with the kind of person you are, that you do feel bad when you have let a little person in your family down?'

'What things does it fit with that you really believe in?'

'How does it fit with caring? Would a caring person feel bad?'

The young person can be invited to speculate about other people's views regarding his feelings of remorse and shame:

'What would other people in your family think, if they knew you feel bad?'

We can invite the young person to choose names for the ethics he is experiencing:

'Anyone can hurt another person or let them down but maybe it takes real guts to face up to it. Is 'guts' the right word or is it something else that it takes?'
   Tim responded, 'It's because I love her.'

It is vital that we do not colonise a young person's experience by attempting to define and name it for him. It is important that we help to create opportunities for the young person to name the experience and their ethics. In this case, Tim declared that *'love'* was the ethic informing his facing up. This shocked some members of Tim's family, who had not imagined that he might experience feelings of love, let alone declare them. However, other family members felt relief that Tim was reclaiming values in himself that were important for the family.

Patterns of avoidance which accompany the experience of shame can remain quite paralysing for some young people, even when significant efforts have been made to establish a context of fairness through highlighting ethics and responsibility overloads.

Mike (aged 14) has been able to speak openly and frankly about having witnessed abuses by his father and his uncles and about the ethics implicit in the protective stance he took in standing up for his younger siblings. However, attempts to invite Mike to address his abusive behaviour towards two younger cousins, have resulted in distracted behaviour and attempts to change the subject which progress towards a paralysed silence, with his body increasingly slumped, occasionally punctuated with 'I don't know' responses. This pattern of behaviour is familiar to members of Mike's family who generally react with corrective responses whilst labelling him as unco-operative and uncaring, in the face of his abusive behaviour.

Attempts to **externalise** avoidance behaviour or shame itself, may be helpful in this context. Externalisation processes can assist the young

person to separate himself from the avoidance behaviour to enable him to examine the behaviour and take a position in relation to his ethics. This position might involve challenging or standing apart from avoidance practices: (White, 1995).

'Mike, something happens when we start to talk about what you did to Emma and Jeff. You seem to phase out and then you stop talking. Something happens and you slump over and can only say, 'I don't know'. Have you noticed?'

The conversation is kept at a level, which is light and non-blaming. Sometimes humour may disrupt avoidance patterns and prevent bogging down in the familiar paralysis.

'It's kind of like something comes in and shuts you down or spaces you out; like a big hand coming down and switching a computer into sleep mode.' 'What do you reckon it's like?'

'Does it try to get you in other places or at other times?'

The processes of externalisation can lead to conversations about restraining events, in which the young person can participate without a sense of being judged. He can be invited to name the restraining experience. A generic name such as, 'the thing' or 'it', is often chosen. Ways in which 'the thing' operates can be noticed and examined. Others reactions to 'the thing' might also be explored.

Mike established that others in his family regard the presence of 'the thing' as an indication that he doesn't care about his abusive actions.

Processes of externalisation allow 'the thing' to be examined and understood. An invitation may be offered to watch out for any signs that might indicate that 'the thing' is coming. Signals may be agreed upon to announce 'the thing's' presence. Agreements can be made to take a break or check out just what 'the thing' is on about, when it shows its face.

These inquiries may lead to speculation about 'the thing's' purpose or meaning. This involves inquiry about intent:

After some reiteration of Mike's stated ethics about caring and concern for the people he has hurt and his desire to make restitution, I made some inquiries about 'the thing':
   'Mike, is it a mean, ''I don't give a stuff,'' kind of ''thing,'' or is it more like an ''I care but its too hard to think about it'' kind of thing?'

'Does "the thing" care about what happened or not give a stuff about what happened?'

'Is "the thing" worried about the abuse or not worried about the abuse?'

'Does "the thing" worry about you or does it not give a damn about you?'

Such conversation can assist Mike to separate an ethical sense of self from the influence of 'the thing,' whilst paying respect to a possible need for avoidance strategies and the potentially intense impact of shame. It was established that 'the thing' was in fact protective of Mike and concerned about 'not wanting to bring me down'.

Further enquiry established that 'the thing' was concerned that Mike might be 'brought down', if he faced his abusive actions, because people would think,' I'm stupid'.

This inquiry led to jointly agreed upon strategies to 'slow down' when 'the thing' tries to take over. 'The thing' needed to be reassured, 'I did a stupid thing but I'm not a stupid person'; 'I have done a bad thing, but I'm not a bad person'.

Of course, these assertions require an accompanying question, 'What is the proof of this?' Mike needed to constantly reassure 'the thing' that the evidence for his integrity lay in the efforts he was making to face and stop abuse and to make restitution to those he had victimised.

Empathy and compassion are not qualities which are either present or deficient as personality traits in young people. They are context-dependent and require a patient, step by step process to be uncovered, noticed, expressed and valued. When the young person is gradually assisted to find enabling ways to face his abuse and face shame, he can understand the nature of abuse and its impact upon others and engage in meaningful acts of restitution and restoration. The intervention process must establish a context for facing shame, largely through 'talking about talking about it' in relation to ethics. This process establishes meaning and rationale for the whole concept of addressing abusive behaviour. Each step the young person takes must have meaning in relation to his own ethics, if this step is to be owned and incorporated into a respectful sense of identity. Facing shame enables the discovery and strengthening of ethical values and qualities which in turn enables further steps to be taken in acknowledging and understanding abusive behaviour and its effects upon others. The young person is continually invited to understand and appreciate the steps he is taking, in a context of demonstrating to himself and others, his ethics and integrity as a person.

Facing shame – seeing abuse like it really is

The invitational language used by the therapist follows a progression which is attuned to the young person's readiness to name his actions appropriately and face the accompanying shame. If we attempt to encourage the young person to name abusive behaviour accurately and without minimisation prematurely, we only invite protest and denial because the young person does not yet have an enabling context or means for facing shame.

Initial invitations tend to be vague and non-specific; 'Can I ask you about what *happened with* Emma' As the young person engages in therapeutic intervention, these inquiries may progress to; 'People may expect you to face what *you did to* Emma'. Later still, the abuse may be referred to in terms of, acts which *may have hurt* Emma. These acts will eventually be named as *abuse* or *molestation*, when the young person is ready to embrace these labels, understand their significance and face the accompanying shame. The use of such a progression in naming practice is enabling in itself and prevents the young person from initially 'painting himself into a corner' of denial and minimisation, from which he will experience humiliation and a loss of face when feeling compelled to depart.

As the young person is open to or accepting of a new label which is more accurate and direct, he is invited to speculate about the meaning of taking on this new terminology. This is referred to as **'seeing it like it really is'**; a move towards facing shame and acting with integrity.

'What difference does it make, when you start to see it like it really is, rather than pretend that it wasn't so bad?'

'What does it take to start to see it like it really is and tell it like it really is?'

'Is this the right way for you to go or would it be better for you to pretend?'

'Will this make you stronger or weaker as a person?'; 'How will it?'

'Does this fit with who you are and the direction that you want to take?'

'What do you respect more?'

Particular sets of terminology and their meanings can be explored:

'Can you handle calling what you did to Amy by it's proper name; sexual abuse?'

What makes it sexual abuse?'

'How hard is it to use the name sexual abuse?'

'What difference does it make when you call it sexual abuse?'

The young person is invited to examine the differences in power and vulnerability, between the person he has abused and himself and to make meaning of what he is doing, in the contexts of shame and personal integrity:

'How old are you? How old is Amy?'

'How much were you trusted with Amy?'

'How much did Amy trust you/look up to you?'

'Who's idea was it in the first place?'

'What did you say to Amy?'

'Was that fair, or was it a trick or a lie?'

'What makes it a trick or a lie?'

'What difference does it make when you call it a trick?'

These inquiries will of course be accompanied by the 'seeing it like it really is' style of inquiry.

We seldom confront the young person with evidence of minimisation or denial and invite the inevitable protest. The young person is encouraged to refrain from making acknowledgment of or naming abuse, until he has an adequate sense that doing so would not only fit with his own sense of ethics but will have benefit to himself and others.

'If there is more truth to come out (and there usually is), you'd be nuts to face it unless you knew for sure that it would,
- *help the kid you did it to*
- *and help you.*
unless you knew for sure that,
- *it wouldn't be used against you*
- *it wouldn't be used to put you down or make you feel small*

How would you know if it was safe to speak out?'

Facing shame – naming the impact of abuse

As the young person is beginning 'to see the abuse like it really is', name tricks and lies and recognising exploitation in the context of differences in power and vulnerability between the person he abused and himself, evidence of shame will become increasingly apparent.

Inquiries such as, *'What are you realising?'* might lead to responses like, *'She was only a little kid'*; *'He looked up to me, like a father'*. Such realisations invoke deep shame and require careful attention to enable their meanings and significance to be safely explored. For example, if ethics relating to 'courage' have been previously named, realisations may be examined in this context:

'How much courage is it taking to see it like it really is? Like you are starting to do now?'

'What are you up against?'

The young person may be invited to choose a feeling label (from a list provided) which he thinks best describes the 'bad' feeling that is experiencing:

'How big (out of ten) is the ashamed feeling that goes with seeing it like it really is?'

'So how big (out of ten) is the courage you need to face it?'

'Did you know that you had that much courage?'

'Does anyone else know that you have that much courage?'

Inquiries which relate to intent and the person-act distinction may be conducted:

'If you could talk about it and not feel that much shame, what sort of person would you be?'

'What does it say about you that you do feel this much shame?'

'Are you feeling more like you are a terrible person or more like you did a terrible thing?'

'Would a terrible person stop and face up to it, like you are doing?'

'What are you proving, about the kind of guy you really are?'

The '**connections through difference**' style of inquiry can be helpful with young people who have witnessed or been subjected to past abuses:

'Do you think that (your step-father) ever took the time or trouble to stop and think and feel about what he did to you and your family; like you are starting to do now for (your sister)?'

'Do you realise that you are doing something that maybe he never had the guts to do?'

'What does this say about you and the direction you are taking?'

Similarly, inquiry may be conducted in the spirit of '**honour in the face of adversity**':

'Do you think that you are taking the tough path or the easy path?'

'How are you managing to do this when you have been through so many hard times yourself?'

'How are you managing to think about other people's hurt feelings when you have been hurt so much yourself?'

'How is this changing you? What are you learning about yourself?'

'How does it fit with the kind of guy you really are?'

'Can you feel the strength and courage, along-side the shame?'

'Can you feel strength and courage growing or shrinking, as you face up?'

'Is facing up making you stronger or weaker?'

'Is carrying shame on your shoulders making them stronger or weaker?'

'Does facing up or running away, fit best with showing your true colours.'

The young person can be invited to situate facing shame, in the context of a healing journey or journey of reclamation of self:

'Facing up always hurts.'

'How can you make sure you turn shame into strength and not weakness?'

'How can you put shame on your side?'

'What things will you need to remind yourself about to do this?'

In this context a range of affirmative concepts concerning shame, which relate to ethics and integrity, can be documented and referred to when facing up is particularly challenging and painful:

Facing shame and feeling the pain:
- proves I care
- gives me training in mental toughness
- means I'm facing up and not running away
- means I'm not leaving it for (my little sister) to worry about
- means I'm not trying to hide behind the little guy
- means I'm being a big brother
- means I'm being true to myself
- means I'm earning the trust and respect of others

In a respectful, step by step, invitational context, where shame can be safely faced as integrity and honour are affirmed, the young person may eventually be able to consider the enormous significance and potential impact of his abusive actions. He may become ready to face inquiries which expose the terrible effects of sexual exploitation:

Jeff had begun to describe how his little brother, Mick, had never had a father who was there for him and how Mick looked up to him 'as a father.' In response to inquiries about how he introduced sexual abuse to Mick, Jeff described ways in which he pretended to be interested in playing with Mick or pretended to be helping to bathe Mick, in order to subtly introduce sexual touching. When Mick felt uncomfortable and asked, 'What are you doing?' Jeff would reassure his brother and tell him it was a game and great fun. As Jeff described this pattern of deception and exploitation, he was asked:

'What would it be like to look up to your big brother, to see him like the father you never had, to trust that he would look out for you; and then find he set you up and just used you, like you were a magazine, to get off on?'

'What would it do to you?'

'What would it be like to discover that he had tricked you, that he was only pretending to care for you; when what he really wanted was to use you?'

'How would this make you think and feel about yourself?'

Young men, like Jeff, may be invited to imagine themselves, 'in the younger child's shoes' and be interviewed, as though they were the little child, responding as they imagine the little child might respond to inquiry about the development of a pattern of abuse and the nature and effects of deception, betrayal and exploitation.

Each bold step taken by the young person to 'look shame squarely in the eye,' must be critiqued in an ethical context of meaning, in terms of the young person's sense of honour and integrity.

Facing shame – restitution and restoration

Shame is of vital importance in family and community settings, where mutual obligations between the young person and others are required, in order to allow for both personal and community restoration, following abuse.

Sexual abuse must be regarded as shameful in the family and community, if shame is to fulfil its adaptive function in the maintenance of respectful relationships. However, caregivers and community members must avoid shaming practices, especially those which reject, exclude or isolate the young person from the community.

The participation of caregivers and community members in intervention practices is vital in a young person's journey towards respect.

Caregivers are invited to address disabling attributions and shaming interactions, in order to assist the young person to reclaim and restore a sense of honour and integrity, by choosing to face his abusive actions and his sense of shame in accordance with his own ethics.

Parents and family members are frequently restrained by their own avoidance practices which are associated with a sense of shame regarding unsatisfactory parenting, or mistakenly-attributed shame which is linked to a sense of culpability for the young person's abuse and judgements of personal or family dishonour and disgrace. Patterns of denial, blame and disengagement are common, especially when parents have felt shamed in previous encounters with authorities. The young person may then be left unsupported to face his abusive actions or family members may collude in denial of the abuse or of the need to address it. The engagement of caregivers is described in the previous chapter (see Chapter 6).

Caregivers are invited to attribute meaning to significant steps taken by the young person which require facing shame, in a context which is honouring:

'What do you think it is taking for Peter to face up to (specific step)?'

'What do you think he is up against?'

'How do you think he is managing to do it, in the face of (specific challenges or adversities)?'

'What do you think this says about Peter?'

'Did you know that Peter feels ashamed about (specific realisation)?'

'Is this the first time he has let you know?'

'What do you think it is taking for him to let you know?'

'What does it say about him that he does feel ashamed?'

'What would it say about him if he didn't feel ashamed?'

'What difference does it make to know that he feels ashamed?'

'Does it fit with a pathway that you can respect?'

The young person is invited to document his realisations, about the nature and potential impact of his abusive actions upon others and to consider his ethical stance, in relation to providing restitution to those he has hurt. In relation to specific realisations, the young person may be asked:

'Have you let anyone in your family know what you realise you put your sister through?'

'What would it tell them about you?'

'Who would respect it if you did?'

'What would it prove to you about yourself?'

'What would you respect most in yourself, speaking out or keeping quiet?'

Acts of restitution are much more than apologies. They require deep levels of realisation about the exploitative nature of abusive actions and the effects these actions have upon all family and community members.

'What would it mean if you left it for your sister/your family, to sort out on their own?' 'How fair would this be?'

'How much do you owe it to them, to think deeply about what you have put them through?'

'What would saying sorry mean, if you hadn't thought much about what you put them through?'

Restitution can involve sharing realisations or simply respecting other's privacy and staying away from them. Restitution requires consideration of other's feelings and of the destructive effects of abuse upon one's community. It is difficult to imagine any meaningful form of personal restoration (reclaiming of one's own integrity and honour) or meaningful contribution to assisting in the healing of hurts suffered, in the absence of significant steps of restitution. Acts of restitution help to restore a balance or harmony that has been damaged by abuse within communities. Close scrutiny and study of the nature and effects of abuse, along with meaningful restitution practices, enables the development of a sense of discretion-shame and its protective function to be realised in individuals and in their communities.

A more detailed description of theory and practice concerning restitution and restoration in the context of child sexual abuse has been previously documented (Jenkins et al., 2002).

Facing shame – mistakenly-attributed shame

A substantial focus in therapeutic intervention concerns the distinctions between disgrace shame and mistaken shame. These are inevitably confused in the experience of young people and members of their families and communities. The goals are simple, disgrace shame must be faced and mistaken shame must be reattributed, but the processes can be complex and challenging.

Young men are steeped in traditions of shaming as a means of differentiating power relations and determining relative positions in social hierarchies. The art of put down, sarcasm and practices of humiliation in social relations, have generally been practised and honed over years. They are often taken for granted as appropriate and familiar strategies for connection. Every male is faced with the challenge posed by the ubiquity of these dominant shaming traditions, if he is genuinely interested in developing an ethic of care and concern for others which privileges their feelings and needs.

Therapeutic intervention processes which are highly confronting can inadvertently reproduce and support such shaming practices. For example, group processes which encourage young men to develop 'bullshit detectors' in order to challenge minimisations and justifications in other's descriptions of their abuses, can undermine an ethic or care and concern for others and promote hegemonic patterns of relating in the guise of caring.

Invitational practices designed to assist young men to critique aspects of dominant cultural ideology have been discussed in the previous chapter (see Chapter 6).

The effects of past shaming practices require careful attention in intervention practice. We can easily overwhelm young people and under-estimate the effects of shaming, in our enthusiasm to further their journeys towards respect.

John (aged 15) described a pattern of shaming by his father throughout his early childhood. His father would try to encourage him to engage in rituals of humiliation towards his mother; 'Tell your mother she's stupid'; 'Doesn't she cook shit' etc. John would never participate. He would burst into tears and run away to try to hide from his father, whereupon his father would ridicule him, calling him a 'wimp' and 'pathetic'.

In my enthusiasm to highlight ethics, I exclaimed, 'You were really brave!' John looked at me bewildered and annoyed. He regarded himself as 'weak' and this experience proved it. I was attempting to colonise his ethics, to impose my interpretations upon him, just as his father had done to him.

I needed to enquire:
'Why didn't you say those things to your mum?'
'Why didn't you go along with your dad?'
'Wouldn't it have been easier to do what he said than have him put you down?'

'Was it better to cop it yourself, than see your mum suffer?'
'What stopped you from causing hurt to your mum?'
'What is it about you?'
'Do you think your dad ever thought this way?'

I needed to refrain from under-estimating John's capacity to discover and name his ethical stance and establish conditions where he might determine and name this stance and its significance for himself.

Young people, who have been subjected to sexual abuse themselves, can be invited to separate and examine disgrace shame and mistaken shame, in ways which mutually promote responsibility for abuse perpetrated and ameliorate the effects of abuse suffered.

Corey (aged 14 years) disclosed that his uncle had sexually abused him, between the ages of 9 and 11, when he was meant to be providing child care for Corey's parents. Corey had begun to examine the political context of this abuse. Conversation with Corey included inquiries like the following:
'Whose idea was it?'
'How old were you, how old was he?'
'What was his job, what was your job?'
'What did he do to get your trust?'
'How did he set up opportunities?'
'How did he try to convince you that it was OK?'
'How did he try to trick you into thinking that it was a game/friendship?'
'How did he try to get you to keep it secret?'
'How did he try to set you up to feel responsible/like it was your fault?'

'Whose shame is it?
'How did he try to trick you into carrying his shame?'

These inquiries may assist the young person to examine his experience from a perspective of power relations and relative responsibilities, in order to locate ownership of shame appropriately, with the person who perpetrated the abuse. Such inquiries also run parallel with a similar set concerning the abuse perpetrated by the young person. It can be enlightening for the young person to be invited to switch focus from one to the other, especially in the spirit of 'connections through difference' style inquiries. In this way, a deeper sense of empathy and compassion regarding the abused person is reached, through reference to the young person's own experience of exploitation, betrayal and hurt feelings.

'Did your uncle ever stop and think about your feelings, like you are now doing for your little sister?'

'Did he ever try to do anything about the hurt he was causing you?'

'What does this say about the path you are taking?'

Similarly, as the young person is invited to name factors that made it hard for him to speak out about the abuse done to him, for example:

He said he would go to gaol, if I told

I thought that no-one would believe me

People would think I'm gay

I should have stopped it earlier

I brought shame on my family

He is invited to attribute responsibility and shame, in accordance with a developing political understanding of abuse. He may become more able to understand some of the dilemmas faced by the child that he abused. Disgrace shame may be addressed and faced and mistaken shame can be appropriately attributed.

Facing shame – the statutory context

A fair statutory justice process (as described in Chapter 6), will be informed by the concept that sexual abuse is a shameful act. However, it will not rely on shaming as a means of deterrence or promoting respectful behaviour. The young person will be afforded opportunities:

- To choose respectful directions which are accountable to those he has hurt.
- To participate in supportive community networks and intervention programmes which do not serve to marginalise, exclude or isolate him.
- To establish his ethics and make respectful realisations, in his own time frame.

... but in a statutory context which expects that abusive behaviour will be addressed and which monitors and documents responsible goal attainment, thus holding the young person accountable for his actions.

Braithwaite (2000), has proposed theory and reviewed research which supports the use of statutory justice processes which communicate shamefulness of specific behaviours in a respectful manner, as opposed to shaming processes which are degrading, humiliating and rejecting.

The collaborative Youth Conferencing and remand processes, previously discussed, can greatly assist fair, respectful and accountable intervention.

References

Braithwaite, J. (2000) Shame and Criminal Justice. *Canadian Journal of Criminology.* July: 281–98.

Fossum, M.A. and Mason, M.J. (1986) *Facing Shame: Families in Recovery.* New York: WW Norton.

Jenkins, A., Hall, R. and Joy, M. (2002) Forgiveness in Child Sexual Abuse: A Matrix of Meanings. *International Journal of Narrative Therapy and Community Work.* Issue 1.

Nietzsche, F. (1967) *The Will to Power.* New York: Random House.

Schneider, C.D. (1992) *Shame, Exposure and Privacy.* New York: WW Norton.

Chapter Eight

You Can Get an Adolescent to Grunt but You Can't Make Them Talk: Interviewing Strategies with Young People Who Sexually Abuse

Ian Lambie

Introduction

If you think back to a time in your childhood when you did something you knew was wrong, how did you respond? If most of us were honest we'd say that our first desire may have been to lie or at least minimise what we did. Such responses are normal when faced with surmounting pressure to 'cough up' for something that we know we shouldn't have done. The work with young people who sexually abuse is no different really. Young people who have been sexually abusive will often lie and minimise their offending in order for them not to face the consequences or avoid detection. Other reasons why they may not wish to look at what they have done is a fear of the anger and hostility from both their family and the victims, along with the potential rejection they may suffer from their family.

Hence, it is a natural response that many people may at least contemplate when faced with an adverse situation. Namely, to minimise the perceived or actual harm they may face and for many clinicians, this is the reason why they would choose to work with clinical populations that are potentially more 'compliant' and less challenging.

What impacts on the success or failure of an interview?

Despite the treatment of young people who sexually abuse dating back to the early 1980s, there is surprisingly little literature available on treatment modalities that have been shown to work for this group of clients. What is even more surprising is the apparent lack of written material available on the sort of clinical methods that work best with this group of clients. For instance, it is widely accepted that treatment for young people who sexually abuse has been informed by adult sex offender treatment, which in turn has shaped

programmes for younger children. Yet the question remains, are models and methods used for adults appropriate for younger populations?

A decade ago catch phrases like 'breaking down denial' and 'confronting denial' were not uncommon. Thankfully the field has since developed and clinicians are all too well aware of the need to develop more sophisticated and ethical approaches to treatment if they are going to effectively change clients. One of the major concerns of using confrontative approaches is that clients are more likely to be 'compliant' to therapists and that some of the client's cognitions that may have contributed to their offending may actually go 'underground' as the client places their energies in defending themselves 'against the therapist'.

So what affects whether young people do or do not talk about their offending? Like any other psychotherapeutic relationship, it is influenced by the client factors (e.g., presenting problem, gender, age, culture, counter transference, etc.) and also the therapist factors (e.g., experience, personal history, transference, etc.). It is very important that clinicians are aware that these issues impact on a client's ability and receptiveness to therapy. I know that culturally in New Zealand, the way in which psychologists working with adolescents physically present themselves in a professional setting may be very different to how a psychologist in America does. For example, for an interview that I undertook in a maximum security prison once where New Zealand's most dangerous prisoners are held, I purposefully dressed in jeans, a T-shirt and sneakers to make the client feel less intimidated and more able to speak. I wanted the client to feel comfortable and feel that they were in a position to talk freely to me – not to feel that I was someone who had no idea of who they were and what sort of world they came from. Hence, when we are talking about the process of engagement with clients, we must be aware of the cultural differences that exist with our clients.

The process of change

What is apparent in working with any client group is the role that 'psychotherapeutic factors' play in assisting change within the client. A significant body of research indicates that the effectiveness of therapy may in fact have more to do with process issues (e.g., client-therapist relationship), as opposed to therapeutic 'techniques' (Hubble, Duncan and Miller, 1999).

Lambert (1992) proposed that therapy is composed of four therapeutic factors. He called these:

- extra-therapeutic factors
- therapeutic techniques
- relationship factors
- expectancy or placebo factors.

Extra-therapeutic factors

Lambert (1992) argued that extra-therapeutic factors, or client factors, are the most important amongst psychotherapies. Extra-therapeutic factors are what clients bring with them to therapy as well as environmental influences. They may include the client's strengths, social supports, the sense of personal responsibility, the severity and type of problem, and the motivation to change, the strength of social supports and the presence or absence of co-morbidity disorders. Commonly, young people who sexually abuse may present with co-morbid disorders, as in mental health problems that typically may include conduct disorder, attention-deficit hyperactivity disorder, substance abuse, and post-traumatic stress disorder (Bourke and Donohue, 1996; Lightfoot and Barbaree, 1993; Morenz and Becker, 1995; Ryan, Miyoshi, Metzner, Krugman and Fryer, 1996). The presence of these disorders and the aforementioned factors can affect whether there is a positive or negative outcome in psychotherapy. Co-morbid disorders left untreated can lead to significant impairment and distress that are likely to impact negatively on treatment. High levels of trauma reported by these adolescents are also likely to have an adverse effect on the outcome of treatment, possibly through subsequent dysregulation of emotional states and a resulting hyper-arousal to stimulus in their environment.

Research suggests that client factors change at varying rates and may account for as much as 40% of the outcome in psychotherapy (Bergin and Garfield, 1994). For example, motivation may vary quite rapidly as opposed to personality variables that may remain relatively stable over time. What is evident is that clients who show the most improvement believe the results of their gains are primarily due to themselves as opposed to therapist or other external factors.

Therapeutic relationship

A significant factor that contributes to the process of change in clients is the relationship between therapist and client. These include a positive regard towards the client, genuineness, and congruence with the client. Other factors such as being able to express empathy and affirmation towards the client when appropriate also impact on treatment outcome. Relationship factors are thought to account for up to 30% of the treatment outcome in counselling. Some of these factors include warmth, caring, empathy, acceptance, mutual affirmation, and encouragement. Lambert and Bergin (1994) proposed that these probably account for the most gain in psychotherapy.

Bordin (1976) suggested that there are three important components of the therapeutic alliance that impact on the outcome: (a) goals, (b) tasks, and (c) bonds. The goals of therapy are the objectives that both the client and therapist agree on, while the tasks are the nuts and bolts of a therapy session that include both behaviours and processes. For a strong therapeutic alliance to happen, it is important that both therapist and client view these as important. Finally, therapeutic bonds are the positive relationship between a client and therapist that includes trust, confidence and acceptance.

Therapeutic technique

These are factors that are specific to the therapy the client is undergoing. It includes the therapy model (e.g., in treatment for young people who sexually abuse the predominant models are cognitive behavioural and family systems model). Despite many studies being undertaken comparing one model with another, surprisingly little evidence has been found for one model being superior over another (Lambert, 1992). In the field of young people who sexually abuse treatment, the research is still in its infancy and comparative studies of one therapeutic model over another have still to be undertaken. Lambert

(1992) suggested that the therapeutic technique may account for approximately 15% of the outcome in psychotherapy.

Expectancy/placebo factors

The final set of factors is placebo, hope, and expectancy. This involves clients gaining improvement based on their knowledge that they are being treated and their assessment that the therapist is credible. One common factor that influences all medicine and psychotherapeutic outcomes is that treatment in itself offers people hope that change can take place. Lambert (1992) argued that hope and expectancy of change may be as important in producing change as technique. It is thought to account for up to 15% of the variance in client change. Lambert, Weber and Sykes (1993) reviewed studies looking at the effect sizes of psychotherapy, placebo, and no-treatment controls. They found that the average client placed in placebo treatment has a 66% greater improvement compared with no-treatment controls, while an average client undergoing psychotherapy is better off than 79% of clients who do not receive any treatment.

Using motivational interviewing to assist the process of change

An important development in the rehabilitation of sexual offenders has been the work on motivational interviewing by Prochaska and DiClemente (1984), Garland and Dougher (1991) and Miller and Rollnick (2002). Motivational Interviewing is a model of assisting clients who may be experiencing resistance to change through a variety of techniques by which the clinician can increase the internal motivation of client towards change, and assist clients to sustain new behaviours and avoid relapse.

Two key assumptions of motivational interviewing are that a client's 'resistance' typically stems from their environment, and that motivation to change behaviour (or to overcome their resistance), is elicited from within the client rather than being imposed externally. While these issues may arise for adolescents, there are also maturational processes that may be unique to this client population such as anti-authoritarian issues. In addition, engagement in therapy is often dependent upon the client being mandated to attend treatment and over time their motivation often increases.

The role of the clinician is not to persuade or convince the client to change or resolve the client's ambivalence. Rather, the clinician's task is to quietly direct the client towards examining that ambivalence and to develop discrepancy and dissonance in the client about their situation. Arguments with clients are to be avoided; resistance is not to be directly confronted. Instead the clinician is encouraged to argue indirectly – to 'roll with' the client's resistance in much the same way as a martial arts fighter might roll with their opponent's momentum and use it to make their opponent's position less secure. At the same time, clinicians must operate from a position of empathy with their client. They must create for the client a sense that change is both desirable and achievable, and that efforts towards change will be based on a collaborative effort between them rather than be imposed and directed by the clinician.

Six stages of change have been identified through which clients may progress during the progress of change (Miller and Rollnick, 1991). These stages are often referred to as the 'wheel of change'.

1. *Pre-contemplation*
   At this stage in the cycle of change, a person has not yet realised the need for change, though someone else may be aware they have a problem. If pointed out by someone, they may be unaware and surprised and bewildered but not defensive. People at this stage require information and feedback in order to raise their level of awareness.
2. *Contemplation*
   Some clients present with a reasonable understanding of what has brought them to treatment, but may still feel ambivalent about change. They may be weighing up the pros and cons of the status quo as compared to making the required changes. Clients at this stage need gentle challenge in order that any comparisons arrived at are realistic. They also need encouragement to see that change is possible.
3. *Preparation*
   After some time, a client may come to feel as though the reasons for changing their behaviour outweigh the reasons for things staying the same. They become increasingly interested in and ready to change. They may begin to experiment with change, or make plans to change; they may even make some

initial changes. At some point during this stage, they have made a decision to change. Clients at this stage require reassurance and support that they have made the right decision.

4. *Action*

Clients in the action stage are making changes and trying out new ways of behaving. Again, considerable support may be necessary for clients and particularly those who lack the necessary self-esteem or for whom the changes may result in major lifestyle consequences (e.g., leaving a long term relationship).

5. *Maintenance*

This stage involves the client attempting to sustain the changes and beginning to implement strategies that will prevent their relapsing into old behaviours. This may lead to permanent change. However, there may also be occasional 'lapses' back into the old ways. Lapses are temporary slippages and, while they may be frustrating and demoralising, they are not unexpected or unusual. Usually with a lapse, the clients desire to change remains.

6. *Relapses*

'Relapses' are different from these occasional 'lapses'. In addition to the old behaviours returning for a longer period of time, a relapse is usually accompanied by a return to earlier change stages such as pre-contemplation during which the client questions their motivation and rationale for change. Following a relapse, the client will need to re-visit all the stages of the wheel of change rather than simply begin again at the action stage. This is necessary in order to ensure their readiness and motivation to change is as strong as possible.

A number of techniques from the Motivational Interviewing model may be used effectively with young people who sexually abuse and many of these are contained in the strategies outlined below.

Process issues when interviewing adolescents:

An adolescent's developmental stage is one where they are making dramatic changes. What may complicate therapy is a rebellious nature that some adolescents have as they make the transition from dependence to independence. In

the process of assessment and therapy, creative ways need to be employed that not only engage the adolescent but also allow for the important issues in sex offender treatment to be addressed:

1. Make the adolescent feel as comfortable as possible.
2. Enter the client's model of the world (Hayley, 1973).
3. 'Role reverse with our clients' – ask ourselves – 'how would I feel if I was an adolescent and was being interviewed at this moment' – what would help me to talk more, what would help me to talk less?
4. Treat them how you would like to be treated.
5. Be aware of how our behaviour may impact negatively on our clients.
6. Remember the key issues from motivational interviewing that can be useful with adolescents, namely – roll with resistance, the good things – less good things about changing.
7. Get regular supervision – no lets make it video taped – better still if we really want to improve our interview skills.
8. It's not about interrogation – clinicians who are starting out in the field often emphasise that the goal of an interview is to get a full disclosure. Personally my goal when I interview an adolescent is to get them to come back a second time and to talk honestly to you about their offending. In essence I mean – maintain rapport.

Everyday interviewing strategies

1. *Interview Preparation – read the background notes*

Prior to the interview, read all documentation available on the adolescent, their family, and the victim's disclosure, etc. Discuss the referral with your colleagues or supervisor as required.

2. *Establish Rapport and create a context for Honesty*

Putting the client at ease will increase the likelihood of honesty and compliance in counselling. This is the crucial stage of any interview and it is often necessary to talk about everything else but the reason why they are there.

The clinician should state from the beginning of the interview that they have experience with other adolescents who have sexually abused to assist in establishing credibility and control of the interview. The clinician can seem especially credible if they can predict what the adolescent might be thinking and the extent of their behaviour.

3. *Respect the Adolescent*
   The clinician should create a context for respectful behaviour in the interview and model this for the adolescent. For example, only respectful sexually explicit language should be allowed (no sexually aggressive terms for body parts, etc), don't talk down to them. If challenging the adolescent's cognitive distortions, the clinician could say: 'I respect you and believe you deserve a better life than that of continuing your sexually abusive behaviour, so I want to be really honest with you about your offending'. By doing this, the clinician models both respect and honesty. The clinician should take care not to distance the adolescent by showing strong emotional reaction to their disclosures and take any issues that need to be processed to supervision.

   The interview should be prefaced by the clinician talking about the importance of honesty and the consequences for the offender of not being honest. Clinicians should be aware of the importance of not only under but also over disclosing as the young person may want to 'please professionals' and tell them what they think the clinician wants to hear. Remember, more does not necessary equal a more honest disclosure, nor a better one! The clinician should support and reinforce even the smallest admission of offending by the adolescent with praise for being honest. This increases the likelihood that they will be more honest in the future.

4. *Use Open-Ended Questions and Non-Jargon/Down to Earth Language*
   This is especially important in allowing the adolescent to talk about their offending in as much detail as possible and to allow them sufficient time to do this. And remember while we may understand what we are saying, the young person may have no idea. My goal is to use language that is even more straightforward than I feel the young person needs to assist them to understand. Be aware also that adolescents have little respect for people who patronise them.

5. *Anticipate Embarrassment and Shame*
   The adolescent may have their own stereotype of sexually abusive adolescents as

being totally deviant and worthless. The clinician can help facilitate disclosure by downplaying that stereotype. The clinician could also compare the adolescents discomfort now with their likely increased discomfort if their offending was to continue. A strategy I often use is to inform the adolescent that they may change their account later to a more honest one and that I would not be surprised or that it is common for adolescents to remember more details of their offending the more they talk about it. It is also a well-known phenomenon that many offenders feel a sense of relief when they finally disclose their offending.

6. *Offer Hope Through Therapy*
   It can be comforting for the adolescent and their family if therapy is discussed as a positive experience. The clinician must outline the positive aspects of having therapy, as well as the consequences if they refuse help. They could also use examples of other adolescents for whom therapy has been successful. It might be useful to say things such as: 'You're really lucky to have this opportunity to change. Many adult offenders did not have this chance and have led really unhappy lives. You have many positive things going for you and you deserve better than this, while I'm sure its difficult for you to currently see this, your life can be different'.

7. *Predict Cognitive Distortions*
   It is rare that an adolescent is able to be totally honest in the initial interview due to the shame, embarrassment or denial they may have. The adolescent may come to the interview with their story better prepared than the clinician's. The adolescent's stance can be challenged if the clinician is able to predict the kind of excuses the offender will use. The clinician could then say for example; 'if you say to me that you didn't know it was wrong or it was the younger child's fault, then you will be saying the same things that other kids that offend say and what do you think your family would say to that? What do you think I'll think?'

   Face-saving manoeuvres that the clinician may offer include suggesting a second interview at which you predict the adolescent will have remembered more of their offending as this commonly occurs. The clinician may also suggest to the offender some of the excuses they may have used at the time of their offending and allows the young person to make those excuses in the interview e.g., 'You may not have realised that what you did was really abusive . . . but it sounds like you did something to the child'. The clinician 'sidelines' the cognitive distortions in order to get an admission. The distortions should be noted for follow-up later in therapy.

8. *Working with Cognitive Distortions*
Working through cognitive distortions is essential in ensuring that offenders change their behaviour. As we have seen in the earlier section on motivational interviewing, to effect change, the challenging should not be forceful or hostile, but respectful. Creating dissonance by repetition, reframing, rephrasing, interrupting and information-giving are all useful ways in which to challenge the young person's thoughts and offending behaviour. Ways of enabling the challenging to occur while maintaining rapport include; acting more warmly at the time; using plenty of humour and making joining comments; using simple, non-jargon language and reinforcement when appropriate. Remember, if an adolescent goes 'underground' in their story it can increase the difficulty of them successfully completing treatment.

9. *Working with Denial*
The clinician should be careful when directly challenging an offender's account of an offending incident. Often a direct challenge such as; 'you're lying' only serves to place the young person further in denial. It is often more successful to resort to a face-saving manoeuvre or to simply note the discrepancy in the statement and return to it later. Remember the motivational interviewing principal . . . 'roll with resistance'.

10. *The Adolescent Tells 'Their Story'*
Even if the clinician has a good account of the offending incidents, the adolescent should be encouraged to describe the offending rather than the clinician relate what they know of the victim's disclosure. This assists the offender in both being honest and in accepting responsibility for their actions. Telling the adolescent that you know there may be more for them to disclose as talking about it for the first time allows them to think about it in a different way and offences they may not have previously thought about, may be recalled.

11. *Reframing*
Other examples of helpful 'reframing' that the clinician could use are: therapy is an opportunity to make a different life and is not an imposition; therapy does not indicate failure, but a success on which the adolescent is to be congratulated for being brave enough to attend. Reframing can also include ways of working with cognitive distortions such as for those adolescents who may deny planning their offending (e.g., an adolescent saying, 'it just happened', might be challenged by the clinician suggesting that, if they have no control over their sexual behaviour, they need institutional care or why didn't you offend on a busy street?'

12. *Assume the Adolescent may have a History of Offending*
The clinician should take a cautious position and assume that the adolescent has a history of sexually abusive behaviour. It is possible they have been sexually offending for some time prior to getting caught. Rather than ask questions such as; 'Did you do . . .?' the clinician could ask; 'When did you first offend? How many months or years have you been doing this for?' 'How many other children have you sexually abused'?

13. *Check Suicidal Ideation and Depression*
While the clinician should request a mental health assessment if there are genuine concerns for the offender's mental health, it is always useful to at least assess for depression and suicidality. This would include current and past mood level and mental state, detailing any current suicide plans, past attempts, whether there is positive family history and whether they have known someone who has committed suicide. Suicidal ideation or intent should not be downplayed or ignored and clinicians should always seek further specialist assessment.

There is a need to be aware that on very rare occasions, an adolescent **may** use the threat of suicide in an attempt to manipulate the clinician's sympathies in this situation and as a way of taking the pressure off them. An important part of any risk assessment for depression and suicide is case consultation and supervision and this should be routinely undertaken.

14. *Provide Information*
It is useful to offer the young person and their family a prediction, based on the clinical

research and your experience with other adolescents of their likely future and consequent need for therapy. The clinician should always provide information on what help is available to the offender. Even if they are still denying any abusive behaviour at the end of the initial interview, the clinician should take the opportunity to educate both the adolescent and their family or caregivers about the effects of sexually abusive behaviour on both victims and perpetrators.

15. *Addiction as a Metaphor*

For adolescents who deny the need for help on the basis that they will never reoffend, it can be useful to use a practical example of sexual offending being like alcohol addiction (i.e., it may be difficult to stop without professional assistance, needing to learn how to deal with temptation in high risk situations and needing to change lifestyle problems that may have contributed to the problem). However, the addiction metaphor needs always to be used with care in case the adolescent or family is left with the impression that the offending was beyond the adolescent's control or responsibility, or that he has an 'illness' which is 'incurable'.

Interviewing an adolescent's family

An adolescent's family or caregivers can be a powerful force to support them in talking honestly about their abusive behaviour. As a consequence, it is essential that the family are involved in the early stages of interviewing the adolescent.

As a rule, it is advisable to meet briefly first with the adolescent and their family together, then have a period alone with the adolescent and finally bring them all back together.

Frequently, the family will be having great difficulty in accepting the reality of the adolescent's behaviour. If the family and adolescent both strongly deny the offending, despite conclusive evidence to the contrary, it is useful to interview them separately early in the interview process.

Throughout the interview with the family there are a number of strategies that can help prepare the adolescent to disclose offending.

1. *Prepare the Family for the Shock of Disclosure and Create a Context for Honesty*

It is essential that the family is prepared in the event that an adolescent is likely to disclose their offending. This can be facilitated by joining with the family in the first instance and then acknowledging the anger, disbelief, shame and embarrassment of learning that their child has sexually offended. Offer hope, dispel myths, give information, be educational, and particularly be supportive and show compassion. The clinician should constantly be trying to encourage the family to make supportive comments about the adolescent being honest. The type of questions you might ask include: 'Would you rather your son was honest or dishonest about his behaviour? Would you respect your son if he was more honest?' Explain that their reaction will greatly affect the adolescent's ability to be honest. Support the family in respect of their being able to tell the adolescent that they will be able to handle the disclosure. Present to the family the consequences of not getting the necessary help. The clinician might say: 'would you want your son to have a future where he grows up to be an adult sex offender and ends up in jail?' In some situations, the use of some form of leverage may be needed to convince the family to appreciate the seriousness of the issue.

2. *Prepare the Family for Talking Explicitly About Sex*

For many adolescents who sexually offend, their families may be ambivalent about discussing sexuality. By preparing the family for detailed discussion on sexual matters, the clinician is also giving permission for the adolescent to speak explicitly and possibly break the family norms.

3. *Be Sensitive to the potential of other Victims being in the Family*

Often other victims of abuse within the family will be present and understandably may find these sessions extremely difficult. Sometimes their experiences can be helpful in confronting the offender. Their personal stories can begin to create a climate for further honest disclosures from the adolescent. Respect for the feelings of victims must be shown at all times. It would be inappropriate to have both the offender's siblings and victims of abuse at a family interview.

It is important that the family is also offered support. This enables them to continue to see treatment as valuable, to motivate the adolescent towards change, and to more effectively monitor the adolescent's behaviour in the family.

4. *Inform the Family of Potential Relapse*
Always discuss with the family the risk of the adolescent re-offending. If the victim is within the same household, discuss the need for the adolescent to spend some time outside the home. This is especially relevant in the initial stages of counselling and if younger children are living at home. The family must have safety rules in place around the adolescent and these rules need to be discussed with the clinician. It is also important that the family is informed that keeping safe is the *offender's* rather than the family's responsibility and that their role is to support him in carrying this out. Statutory child welfare agencies must be involved to ensure that the safety issues are adhered to.

Conclusion

The purpose of this chapter is not to offer a one size fits all approach when interviewing sexually abusive youth but rather to offer a range of effective and practical techniques that I have found useful in my clinical work.

Adolescents often have relatively simple cognitive distortions (and some will not have any) when compared with adult sexual offenders and consequently they are often more responsive to making changes in counselling than adult offenders. This message should be given to adolescents and their families to increase their hope and motivation for change.

Development and maintenance of the therapeutic relationship with the adolescent is key in ensuring the success of future interventions, and the use of motivational interviewing techniques are part of a 'tool kit' which allow clinicians to systematically work with the adolescent towards increasing their motivation for engaging in therapy, thereby increasing the likelihood of sustained change. Furthermore, by involving the adolescent's family and providing ongoing support, the clinician further sets the scene to assist the adolescent towards making the necessary changes to reduce their level of risk.

References

Bergin, A.E. and Garfield, S. (Eds.) (1994) *Handbook of Psychotherapy and Behaviour Change* (4th Edn.) Washington: American Psychological Association.

Bordin, E.S. (1976) The Generalisability of the Psychoanalytic Concept of the Working Alliance. *Psychotherapy: Theory, Research and Practice*, 16, 252–60.

Bourke, M.L. and Donohue, B. (1996) Assessment and Treatment of Juvenile Sex Offenders: An Empirical Review. *Journal of Child Sexual Abuse*, 5, 47–70.

Garland, R.J. and Dougher, M.J. (1991) Motivational Interviewing In The Treatment of Sex Offenders. In Miller, W.R. and Rollnick, S. *Motivational Interviewing: Preparing People To Change Addictive Behaviour* New York: Guilford Press. 303–13.

Haley, J. (1973) *Uncommon Therapy.* New York: W. W. Norton and Co.

Hubble, M.A., Duncan, B.L. and Miller, S.D. (1999) In Hubble, M.A. Duncan, B.L. and Miller S.D. (Eds.) *The Heart and Soul of Change: What Works in Therapy* Washington: American Psychological Association. 1–32

Lambert, M.J. (1992) Implications of Outcome Research for Psychotherapy Integration. In Norcross, J.C. and Goldstein, M.R. (Eds.) *Handbook of Psychotherapy Integration* New York: Basic Books. 94–129.

Lambert, M.J. and Bergin, A.E. (1994) The Effectiveness of Psychotherapy. In Bergin, A.E. and Garfield S.L. (Eds.) *Handbook of Psychotherapy and Behaviour Change* (4th Edn.) New York: Wiley. 143–89.

Lambert, M.J., Weber, F.D. and Sykes, J.D. (1993) *Psychotherapy Versus Placebo.* Poster Presented At The Annual Meetings of The Western Psychological Association, Phoenix, Az.

Lightfoot, L.O. and Barbaree, H.E. (1993) The Relationship Between Substance Use and Abuse and Sexual Offending In Adolescents. In Barbaree, H.E. Marshall, W.L. and Hudson, S.M. (Eds.) *The Juvenile Sex Offender* New York: Guilford. 203–24.

Miller, W.R. and Rollnick, S. (1991) *Motivational Interviewing: Preparing People to Change Addictive Behaviour.* New York: Guilford Press.

Miller, W.R. and Rollnick, S. (2002) *Motivational Interviewing: Preparing People to Change Addictive Behaviour* (2nd Ed.) New York: Guilford Press.

Morenz, B. and Becker, J. (1995) The Treatment of Youthful Sexual Offenders. *Applied and Preventive Psychology*, 4, 247–56.

Prochaska, J.O. and Diclemente, C.C. (1984) *The Transtheoretical Approach: Crossing the Traditional Boundaries of Therapy*. Malabar, Fl: Krieger.

Ryan, G., Miyoshi, T.J., Metzner, J.L., Krugman, R.D. and Fryer, G.E. (1996) Trends in a National Sample of Sexually Abusive Youths. *Journal of the American Academy of Child and Adolescent Psychiatry*, 35(1), 17–25.

Part III

Assessment issues

Assessment and Treatment Strategies for Children with Sexually Abusive Behaviours: A Review of Cognitive, Developmental and Outcome Considerations

Lesley French

Introduction

The question of what predicts emotional and behavioural disorders in young people is critically linked to the 'what works' debate in considering the outcomes for children and young people undergoing therapeutic interventions for these disorders. While cognitive-behavioural therapy (CBT) has built up a robust evidence base for the treatment of common mental health problems in childhood, the theory explaining the mechanisms for change only partially accounts for treatment success. Much of the evidence base for CBT has been drawn from well-controlled trials, where therapy, adapted from work with adults, has been delivered to children with one major aspect to their presentation, for example, anxiety. For children who have multiple aspects to their difficulties, it is a complex clinical task to identify what aspects of functioning might respond to an evidence-based approach, what might resolve without a specific intervention and what might actually be harmful to the child to attempt to address through therapy. This paper sets out to explore the relationship of cognitive-behavioural theory to practice in child mental health and specifically addresses the contribution of integrating developmental and cognitive-behavioural perspectives to thinking about the needs of children who present with sexually aggressive and abusive behaviours.

Cognitive-behavioural model of change

Cognitive-behavioural therapy for children consists of a variety of techniques that enable children to use cognitive mediational strategies to guide their behaviour and improve their adjustment (Durlak et al., 1991). The term cognitive-behavioural in itself represents the integration of cognitive, behavioural, affective and social strategies for change and treatment

techniques are based on models of learning. These strategies for change in clients share the central assumption that emotions and behaviour are primarily a function of how environmental events are construed (Ronen, 1997). For example, cognitive therapy for depression developed by Beck (Beck et al., 1979) holds that depression results primarily from pervasive, negative misinterpretations of experience that give rise to a negative view of the self, the world and the future. These beliefs are maintained in the face of contrary evidence, in part, because of distortions in information processing, that is, a negative bias in how experience is interpreted. Subsequent behavioural avoidance and withdrawal contributes to the maintenance in depressed mood. In turn, this is linked to the presence of dysfunctional schemata (stable cognitive patterns) including beliefs and attitudes, which construct how a person interprets information from their environment and leads to the development of a pessimistic explanatory style. Cognitive therapy in essence attempts to identify and modify maladaptive thinking patterns. Treatment techniques are administered within a collaborative framework where the clinician and client attempt to uncover and examine maladaptive interpretations of the world (Ronen, 1997).

There has been also important work undertaken to integrate Beck's cognitive model with developmental theory. Leahy (1995) considers that two developmental models are of particular relevance to this integration. The first is Piaget's structural model that emphasises the development of stages of intellectual functioning and in symmetry with Beck's model, focuses on the implications of the individual, unique, structuring of experience. The second is Bowlby's model of the attachment system (Bowlby, 1969) where the experience of early or primary attachment establishes a schema for later secondary attachment experiences. Bowlby went on to describe the development of cognitive avoidance of earlier attachment threats and compensation as an adaptation against further threat. These affect-laden schemas of the self and others, which are formed at the preoperational level in the development of personality disorders, are maintained throughout childhood and into adulthood (Beck et al., 1990).

Cognitive-behavioural therapy

The cognitive-behavioural model is based on the central premise that cognitions, behaviours and emotions are highly interdependent and an intervention that targets one domain of functioning is expected to indirectly affect the other aspects of human functioning. Cognitive skills applicable to CBT include memory, language skills, information and attentional processing, social perception and meta-cognition. The key question remains as to which of these skills is important in which clinical context (Durlak et al., 1991). Cognitive behavioural methods represent an integration of newer techniques that directly target cognitions and emotions with the more well-established and demonstrably effective behavioural techniques. The cognitive-behavioural theoretical model also integrates learning theory, particularly the influence of conditioning, contingencies and models in the environment with the impact of cognitive factors (Kendall, 2000).

In a review of the effectiveness of CBT for children (Durlak et al., 1991) the authors set out to identify the variables that moderate the outcomes of CBT for dysfunctional children. Their hypothesis, that children's cognitive developmental level would be the most important moderator, was confirmed in the meta-analyses undertaken. The effect size (0.92) for children in the cognitive stage of formal operations (ages 11–13) was almost twice the magnitude of the effect obtained for children in less advanced cognitive stages (ages 5–7, 0.57; ages 8–11, 0.55). Critically, the relationship between child characteristics and outcomes is mediated by cognitive developmental level rather than age per se. These findings offer support to the field of developmental psychopathology, which emphasises that the study of normal and abnormal development are complementary and research and practice in one field should inform the other (Kendall et al., 1994).

Cognitive-developmental level was the only

significant moderator to emerge from the analyses. However, as the authors note, evidence for the importance of cognition in CBT is diminished by the failure to find a significant relationship between changes in cognitive processes and behaviour. Therefore the specified connection between cognitive functioning and adjustment is unclear as is the specificity of the underlying mechanism of change in CBT.

A developmental view

Leahy (1995) proposes five issues that developmental models should address.

1. What really develops – cognitive content, structure or defences? Schema-based models suggest that schemas are formed at an early age and persist throughout life with the implication that there are no structural or qualitative changes in the schema as development proceeds. In this sense early schema models are not truly developmental in that schemas remain unchanged or undeveloped. Leahy suggests that the model of early maladaptive schemas might imply it is that defences change with increasing development.
2. Are there stages of development or is development simply an accumulation of experiences, information and learning? Classical developmental theories, for example Freud, Piaget, propose a series of stages which are determined by biological maturation. There is no implication by cognitive theorists that stages progress sequentially or that there is a universal pattern of stages. Is there a fundamental ordering to personality development?
3. Is development progressive, always moving toward something more adaptive as Piaget implies or is it marked along 'deviant pathways' as Bowlby's model implies?
4. What accounts for transition or change? Is it cognitive conflict or learning mechanisms or threat or all of the above?
5. Both Piaget and Bowlby argue for the conservation of schema or limitations on change. Piaget's model is one of a balance of assimilation and accommodation, in effect a readiness for change. Bowlby describes the importance of avoidant and compensatory mechanisms that maintain a schema.

Consideration of these issues should preface any theoretical integration of early experience into cognitive therapy. Leahy (1995) suggested that once the affect or content of early schemas is accessed – through situational stressors, biochemical imbalance or cognitive distortions – the preoperational structure is also accessed. Because cognitive therapy specifically addresses the early structural components of the patient's preoperational thinking errors, it is effective in 'reversing the negativity' embedded with the structure. The subsequent value of cognitive theory remaining consistent with the structural model is that it enables the integration of cognitive-attachment models that share a similar logical structure. In summary, the understanding of development as described by Piaget and Bowlby enhances the scope of Beck's cognitive model to elaborate a cognitive-developmental therapy for adults and children presenting with distorted schemas and subsequent maladaptive behaviours.

Developmental risk factors for sexual offending

Difficulties in providing adequate definitions of sexually abusive behaviour by young people are compounded by the absence of literature regarding 'normal sexual development' and confusion about what is appropriate at different ages. The sexual behaviour of children and young people ranges from exploration and experimentation to serious and violent crimes. Most definitions acknowledge that abusive behaviour involves force or coercion on another child and severity if the behaviour increases with greater disparity between the ages of the children involved. Existing theoretical models in relation to children and young people who sexually abuse are based on work with adults and seldom take into account the physical, emotional and developmental factors which are an integral part of assessing and treating child psychopathology (Vizard et al., 1995). Thus, an integrative developmental model appears critical in the treatment of child patients with multiple aspects to their presentation which include sexual aggression.

Dodge and colleagues have proposed a model linking early child abuse, development of biased social information processing and subsequent violent behaviour in young people (Dodge, Bates and Pettit, 1990). The empirically-based hypothesis is that children, who are prone to aggression focus on threatening aspects of other's

actions, interpret hostile intent in the neutral actions of others and are more likely to select and favour aggressive solutions to social challenges (Crick and Dodge, 1994). Subsequent studies have demonstrated that aggressive children make more encoding errors than non-aggressive controls, or are less accurate in their registering of the facts of a situation (Hill, 2002).

The integration of cognitive and developmental theory also provides a model for understanding the onset and maintenance of sexually aggressive behaviours in abused children. At a basic level, young sexually abused children may imitate abusive language or engage in inappropriate sexual behaviour as a result of observing and modelling the behaviour of the perpetrators of their abuse. Children may use the same coping strategies to suppress memories that may have been adaptive in coping with the abuse, for example, dissociation, denial or avoidance. Use of these strategies may inadvertently strengthen the inappropriate associations made between psychological distress and abuse-related cue that has been generalised, for example, fear of the dark. Continued avoidance of abuse-related thoughts and memories may prevent these children from effectively processing and understanding their abusive experiences, leaving them with misperceptions and inaccurate cognitive schemas related to the abuse (Deblinger and Heflin, 1996). Untreated, such distortions are a core vulnerability to the development of sexualised aggression against others.

A number of theories and models emphasise the role of negative developmental events as precursors to the occurrence of sexually offending behaviour. Harsh coercive or violent parenting is a well-established risk factor for child psychopathology but is specifically hypothesised to contribute to the onset of sexual aggression through insecure attachment and the development of strong resentment and hostility (Marshall and Barbaree, 1990). Various types of childhood adversities, principally, child physical, emotional and sexual abuse has been associated with later arrests for sex crimes (Widom and Ames, 1994) along with high rates of family dysfunction (Dhawan and Marshall, 1996). There is also evidence that different types of childhood adversities may be associated with different types of sexual offending. As noted, childhood sexual abuse is associated with adult sexual offending in general (Langevin et al., 1989), and its prevalence rate is higher for child abusers (paedophiles) than adult rapists (Seghorn et al., 1987). Early findings such as these point to the relationship of childhood sexual abuse with a specific type of sexual offending and more recent work suggests that childhood sexual abuse is uniquely associated with paedophilia (Lee et al., 2002). Childhood emotional abuse is a robust predictor of maladjustment (McGee et al., 1997) and it is likely that the presence of physical and emotional harm to children interacts and enhances the effects of childhood sexual abuse.

Skuse et al. (1998) demonstrated that victimisation experiences were key factors for sexually abused children showing abusive behaviours themselves. Half of this sample of boys had been sexually abused and were considered to have been exposed to a climate of 'pervasive violence' in their families. The implications for development are along with neglect, that key developmental tasks and development of personality are seriously affected. High levels of discontinuity of care and failure to form good attachments were seen as critical factors for the development of childhood abusive behaviours. In specialist services, girls are less frequently identified and referred for assessment, although studies suggest approximately 10% of victims of sexual abuse are molested by women and girls (Saradjian, 1996). At present, there appears to be more similarities than differences between girls and boys who display sexually abusive behaviours in terms of factors contributing to their abusing behaviour, how they abuse and their amenability to treatment (Blues et al., 1999). However, girls tend to have particularly disturbed backgrounds, high levels of sexual abuse, physical victimisation and educational difficulties (Cavanagh-Johnson, 1989).

Lee et al. (2002) showed that childhood emotional abuse was an important developmental risk factor for adult sexual offending and men who were both sexually and emotionally abused as children, not sexually abused alone, display sexual interests involving children (Bagley et al., 1994). However it is important to stress that any predictive power from developmental history regarding subsequent behaviour lies in a particular combination of risk factors in relation to psychopathology. When considering the literature on conduct disorder for example, children with early onset (and poorer prognosis) differ from those with later onset in that they

have lower IQ, more attentional and impulsivity problems, a greater level of neuropsychological deficits, greater peer difficulties and a higher rate of adverse family circumstances (Moffit et al., 1996). Similarly, early onset of sexually aggressive behaviour and the subsequent use of violence are associated with a poor prognosis regarding outcomes for young people who sexually abuse (Butler and Seto, 2002).

Frick and colleagues propose that the presence of callous-unemotional traits in children, such as lack of guilt, absence of empathy and shallow emotions are central to psychopathy in childhood and that these children are a separate cohort within conduct disordered or anti-social young people (Frick, 1998). Strong association has been found between callous-unemotional traits and hyperactivity-attention deficit problems but children with these traits also show fewer verbal deficits, higher IQ, poorer inhibition and there is less association with harsh parenting practices (Lynam, 1996). Hill (2002) argues there should be a broader specification of conduct disorder in that its persistent course and poor prognostic outcome and links with the onset of serious anti-social behaviour approximates to the adult concept of personality disorder. This would at least focus attention on developmental pathways for children most at risk of serious dysfunction in adult life and identify an evidence base for trials of early intervention.

Increasing neuro-biological work is underway linking psychopathy, for example, with a failure to inhibit aggression in response to signs of distress in others, arising from a deficit in processing behavioural evidence of that distress (Blair et al., 1997). If childhood psychopathy proves as stable and predictive of adult psychopathology as the category of conduct disorder, this should mean a greater opportunity to specify treatment interventions rather than anxieties about labelling or conversely 'writing children off' (Hill, 2002). The majority of children presenting with significant emotional and behavioural problems should be conceptualised as children at the greatest level of need of specific therapeutic interventions. Efforts to correctly identify and map the pathway of early origins of serious and persistent sexual offending are underway (Vizard et al., 2004). In relation to intervention imperatives, it should also be noted that untreated harmful behaviours in young people may also be illegal ones for children aged ten and above, with all the implications for entry at a very young age into the criminal justice system.

Treatment implications

Currently there is a broad consensus that treatment of sexually abusive behaviours in young people requires a specialist component addressing this aspect of behaviour (Vizard et al., 1995). It is also critical that such interventions consider social and cultural factors of the presenting child along with their cognitive-developmental level and their own experiences of victimisation. As with all children presenting with significant co-morbidity, treatment provision for more deviant and entrenched behaviours requires significant intensity and duration of delivery (O'Callaghan, 2001). Currently there is some evidence to suggest it is a minority of sexually aggressive children who continue to abuse as adults but studies that attempt to offer predictive pathways have been fraught with methodological problems (Beckett, 1999). It is recognised that sexually abusive children, whose difficulties persist into adolescence are at greater risk of violent offending and general recidivism than specific sexual re-offending (Glasser et al., 2001). There are also clear differences in children who display persistent intense sexualised interest in young children and those children who show coercive behaviours to their peers. Early onset in childhood of persistent sexualised behaviour has been linked to later entrenched paedophilic behaviour in adults (Vizard et al., 1995).

A helpful treatment model based on the range of traumas presenting children are likely to have experienced is based on alleviating untreated symptoms of Post-Traumatic Stress Disorder (PTSD). These symptoms might appear as distress regarding memories of abuse, avoidance of those memories and reminders of the abuse and hyper-arousal symptoms (Deblinger and Heflin, 1996). The child's cognitive schema for understanding the trauma may become a template for cognitively processing problems in the future. Related to the presenting behaviours is the conceptual model that intrusive thoughts and images may be driving other dysfunctional or maladaptive behaviours, both internalising (anxiety, depression) and externalising (physical and sexual aggression). Treatment strategies might then be drawn from the coping skills training literature, graded exposure, systematic

desensitisation, cognitive and affective processing, identifying and challenging maladaptive cognitions, therapist modelling of appropriate adult-child communication and behaviour management skills training for carers of these children. Treatment work with children should ultimately focus on enabling the child to return to a 'normal developmental pathway' (Ryan, 1991).

Child and adolescent interventions – what works?

It has been estimated that over 1500 controlled outcome studies for children and adolescents have been completed (Kazdin, 2000) with increasing attention paid to improving methodological rigour (Durlak et al., 1995). Reviews of this research consistently indicate that child therapy is effective and in some cases that psychological treatments are the treatment of choice for various child and adolescent problems. For example, evidence on behalf of cognitive-behaviour therapy includes several outcome studies (Kendall et al., 1997) where effects of treatment have been evident up to six years after treatment has ended. Parent management training is similarly supported by research evidence. Treatment has been evaluated in multiple randomised controlled outcome trials with children and adolescents varying in age and severity of oppositional, aggressive and antisocial behaviour, along with other systemic derivatives of cognitive-behavioural approaches, such as multisystemic therapy for seriously disturbed delinquent adolescents (Henggeler et al., 1998; and Chapter 16, this volume).

It is however unclear in reviews of psychotherapy outcomes for young people whether the statistically significant effects of therapy in clinical trials translate into clinically significant changes in children's functioning and distress (Weersing and Weisz, 2002). Moreover, when treatment works what are the mechanisms of action that produce therapeutic change? Kazdin and colleagues (1990) reported that less than 3% of published clinical trials of psychotherapy with young people included measures of the processes thought to underlie intervention effects. For example, the theory of psychopathology underlying CBT posits that a major cause of depression is cognitive distortions – faulty information processing that leads young people to take unrealistically negative views of themselves, their world and their future and the causes of significant events in their lives (Beck et al., 1979). CBT techniques, such as cognitive restructuring, are designed to interrupt and 'correct' these distorted ways of thinking and through this mechanism produce changes in the broader syndrome of depression. Meta-analyses of the effects of CBT with depressed adolescents show large effect sizes (e.g., Lewinsohn and Clarke, 1999) and do better than treatments that do not specifically target depressive cognitions. However, it is salutary to note that the only investigation that has directly tested mechanisms of action in a CBT trial found that change in cognitive distortions actually did not mediate the effects of treatment on depression symptoms (Kolko et al., 2000).

However, comparative designs must possess sufficient power for an adequate test of any hypothesised treatment differences. Durlak et el (1991) estimate that attaining 80% power to detect differential treatment effects for two different CBT treatments at the .05 level using a two-tailed test would require a sample size of approximately 170 per group. CBT outcome studies rarely involve sample sizes this large and the danger is then that small but important differences in treatment effects are missed because of insufficient power.

It is in reality difficult to conclude that empirically supported treatments for children and adolescents work through the mechanisms specified in their theories of intervention (Weersing and Weisz, 2002). These authors note that reported treatment results were also limited by conceptual and methodological overlap between mediators and outcomes, a difficulty most apparent in studies that assessed cognitive mediators. Cognitive distortions were typically measured with self-report rating scales as were symptomatic outcomes (Kolko et al., 2000). There has also been increasing interest in developing standardised performance-based measures that do not rely on children's ability to introspect and verbally report on cognitive processes. Alternatively, there may also be value in testing behavioural mediators of CBT effects, for example, the assessment of engagement in pro-social pleasant activities (Lewinsohn et al., 1992) a major skill taught to depressed young people to help them improve their mood.

Historically, participants in outcome research have tended to differ rather markedly from clinical contexts and the effects of treatment models tested under optimal conditions may not generalise well to the wider context of children in need of mental health services and who are referred the most. Children recruited for clinical trials are often screened to limit co-morbid psychiatric problems or to exclude those children with learning disabilities, despite the evidence that co-morbidity is high in children referred to specialist child mental health services (Angold, Costello and Erkanli, 1999). This suggests that clinical trial research that focuses on 'pure' diagnostic samples may be creating and refining treatments for relatively rare groups of children and adolescents. Such research may also risk overlooking commonalities between different disorders and common mechanisms of therapeutic action. For instance, depressed anxious and aggressive children all may overestimate the hostile intent of others, although their behavioural responses to this attribution error may differ markedly, for example, social withdrawal versus aggression (Quiggle et al., 1992).

Kazdin (2002) argues that the greatest single limitation of contemporary research is the inattention to and seeming disinterest in the question of why or how therapy works. Research on the nature of a serious clinical problem is likely to identify sub-types and multiple paths leading to a similar onset and a differential pattern of risk and protective factors. These characteristics are likely to influence treatment outcome and to serve as a basis for using different treatments with different types of children. An example of such research would be efforts to distinguish among conduct disordered children based on the onset of disorder, patterns of co-morbidity and biological and neuropsychological correlates discussed earlier (e.g., Hill and Maughan, 2001). Connections of treatment research with psychopathology research could greatly enrich treatment by suggesting possible intervention targets and moderators of therapeutic change.

The guiding question for therapy research must be how a particular treatment achieves change. Moderators refer to characteristics on which outcome depends (Kazdin, 2002) and theory, empirical findings and clinical experience all can inform the search for moderators. For example, sexually abused children are likely to develop cognitions that the world is a dangerous place, that adults cannot be trusted and that one's own efforts to influence the world are not likely to be effective (Wolfe, 1999). Based on this understanding of the problem, it might be predicted that sexually abused children with these cognitions would respond less well to treatment, as measured by post-treatment pro-social functioning. If these cognitions are not altered in treatment, children may be restricted from participating in a range of activities compared to similar children without these cognitions. Adequate evaluation of treatment depends on including a measurable component of treatment that focuses on these cognitions. The current evidence base does suggest that multiple factors contribute to treatment outcome in the way that risk factors accumulate in predicting onset (Kazdin, 2000). Identifying moderators could greatly influence application of treatment with better identification of those children most likely to respond to specified interventions.

The range of outcomes that are evaluated in research ought to be expanded, beyond the exclusive focus on symptom change. Presently, there is no compelling evidence that symptom change, as opposed to reduced impairment or improvements in pro-social functioning, family interaction or peer relations, is the best predictor of long-term adjustment or functioning. When assessment domains are expanded, treatment of the child has been shown to reduce parental symptoms of psychopathology and stress and to improve family relations (Kazdin and Wassell, 2000). On a pragmatic level, Kazdin (2000) argues that dissemination, costs and acceptability of treatment models are three factors that are likely to influence adoption and use by therapists, clients and third party payers of treatment.

Furthermore, research ought to expand the range of samples included in therapy research. For example, relatively few treatment outcome studies have evaluated children with parents who have severe disorders such as depression or alcohol abuse, children with learning or physical disabilities, children exposed to physical or sexual abuse or neglect or juvenile offenders. All these groups have high rates of clinical dysfunction and represent a high priority for intervention while most do not fit easily in to existing models of child mental health service delivery.

Conclusions

Further work is needed to identify the mediating variables between the established developmental risk factors and the onset of sexually abusive behaviours along with the role of protective factors for children. Returning to the issues summarised by Leahy (1995) that developmental models should address, it seems that an important contribution of cognitive approaches has been to integrate the impact of early experiences in schema-based models which in turn are influenced by external events, biological and genetic processes. The challenge for the cognitive model remains to specify what the common mechanisms of change are across interventions that are accounting for successful outcomes for children and adolescents. This is a critical step toward developing empirically-based approaches that may help the majority of children who present to child mental health services with significant co-morbidity.

In addition to the social policy imperative to develop and refine treatments for 'real world' children and families, Weersing and Weisz (2002) argue that testing mediational models in community samples may end up being better science. Working with co-morbid community populations, not children 'screened' for research purposes, may reveal significant limitations in current models of 'effective' interventions. It is most likely that effective treatment is tapping several domains of functioning, not just the 'symptom' or presenting difficulty and further specification of what accounts for change is needed. Additionally, the cognitive-developmental level of the child has been shown to be a critical factor in outcome and should remain an integral part of the formulation of a child's difficulties, although this is not always apparent in outcome studies. Children and young people who sexually abuse are themselves a highly vulnerable group, who are likely to have undergone significant trauma, have severe emotional and behavioural difficulties and impairments in their ability to learn. Therapeutic consideration needs to be given to developing a system of care that addresses their developmental needs along with the collective capacity to hold in mind the risks they pose to others.

References

Angold, A., Costello, E.J. and Erkanli, A. (1999) Co-morbidity. *Journal of Child Psychology, Psychiatry, and Allied Disciplines*, 40, 57–87.

Bagley, C., Wood, M. and Young, L. (1994) Victim to Abuse: Mental Health and Behavioural Sequels in A Community Survey of Young

Adult Males. *Child Abuse and Neglect*, 18, 683–97.

Beck, A.T., Rush, A.J., Shaw, B.F. and Emery, G. (1979) *The Cognitive Therapy of Depression*. New York: Guilford.

Beck, A.T., Freeman, A. and Associates (1990) *The Cognitive Therapy of Personality Disorders*. New York: Guilford.

Beckett, R. (1999) Evaluation of Adolescent Abusers. in Erooga and Masson (Eds.) *Children and Young People Who Sexually Abuse Others*. London: Routledge.

Blair, R.J., Jones, L., Clark, S. and Smith, M. (1997) The Psychopathic Individual: A Lack of Responsiveness to Distress Cues? *Psychophysiology*, 34, 192–8.

Blues, A., Moffat, C. and Telford, P. (1999) Work With Adolescent Females Who Sexually Abuse: Similarities and Differences. in Erooga and Masson (Eds.) *Children and Young People Who Sexually Abuse Others*. London: Routledge.

Bowlby, J. (1969) *Attachment and Loss: Volume 1 Attachment*. New York, Guilford.

Butler, S. and Seto. (2002) Distinguishing Two Types of Adolescent Sex Offenders. *Journal of The American Academic of Child and Adolescent Psychiatry*, 41, 83–90.

Cavanagh-Johnson, T. (1988) Child Perpetrators: Children Who Molest Other Children: Preliminary Findings. *Child Abuse and Neglect*, 12, 571–85.

Crick, N.R. and Dodge, K.A. (1994) A Review and Reformulation of Social Information Processing Mechanisms in Children's Social Adjustment. *Psychology Bulletin*, 115, 74–101.

Deblinger, E. and Heflin, A.H. (1996) *Treating Sexually Abused Children and Their Non-Offending Parents*. Thousand Oaks: Sage.

Dhawan, S. and Marshall, W.L. (1996) Sexual Abuse Histories of Offenders. *Sexual Abuse: A Journal of Research and Treatment*, 8, 7–15.

Dodge, K.A., Bates, J.E. and Pettit, G.S. (1990) Mechanisms in The Cycle of Violence. *Science*, 250, 1678–83.

Durlak, J.A., Fuhrman, T. and Lampman. (1991) Effectiveness of Cognitive-Behavioural Therapy for Maladapting Children. *Psychological Bulletin*, 110, 204–14.

Durlak, J.A., Wells, A.M., Cotton, J.K. and Johnson, S. (1995) Analysis of Selected Methodological Issues in Child Psychotherapy Research. *Journal of Clinical Child Psychology*, 24, 141–8.

Frick, P.J. (1998) *Conduct Disorders and Severe Antisocial Behaviour*. New York: Plenum.

Glasser, M., Campbell, D., Leitch, I. and Farrelly, S. (2001) Cycle of Child Sexual Abuse: Links Between Being A Victim and Becoming A Perpetrator. *The British Journal of Psychiatry*, 179, 482–94.

Henggeler, S.W., Schoenwald, S.K., Borduin, C.M., Rowland, M.D. and Cunningham, P.B. (1998) *Multisystemic Treatment of Antisocial Behaviour in Children and Adolescents*. New York: Guilford.

Hill, J. (2002) Biological, Psychological and Social Processes in The Conduct Disorders. *Journal of Child Psychology and Psychiatry*, 43, 133–64.

Hill, J. and Maughan, B. (2001) *Conduct Disorders in Childhood and Adolescence*. Cambridge: Cambridge University Press.

Kazdin, A.E. (2000) *Psychotherapy for Children and Adolescents: Directions for Research and Practice*. New York: Oxford University Press.

Kazdin, A.E. (2002) The State of Child and Adolescent Psychotherapy Research. *Child and Adolescent Mental Health*, 7, 53–9.

Kazdin, A.E. and Wassell, G. (2000) Therapeutic Changes in Children, Parents and Families Resulting in Treatment of Children With Conduct Disorders. *Journal of The American Academy of Child and Adolescent Psychiatry*, 39, 414–20.

Kendall, P.C. (1994) Treating Anxiety Disorders in Youth: Results of A Randomised Clinical Trial. *Journal of Consulting and Clinical Psychology*, 65, 100–10.

Kendall, P.C. (2000) *Child and Adolescent Therapy*. New York: Guilford.

Kendall, P.C., Flannery-Schroeder, E., Panichelli-Mindel, S.M., Southam-Gerow, M.A., Henin, A. and Warman, M. (1997) Therapy for Anxiety Disordered Youth: A Second Randomised Clinical Trial. *Journal of Consulting and Clinical Psychology*, 65, 366–80.

Kolko, D., Brent, D., Baugher, M., Bridge, J. and Birmaher, B. (2000) Cognitive and Family Therapies for Adolescent Depression: Treatment Specificity, Mediation and Moderation. *Journal of Consulting and Clinical Psychology*, 68, 603–14.

Langevin, R., Wright, P. and Handy, L. (1989) Characteristics of Sex Offenders Who Were Sexually Victimised as Children. *Annals of Sex Research*, 2, 227–53.

Leahy, R.L. (1995) Cognitive Development and Cognitive Therapy. *Journal of Cognitive Psychotherapy*, 9, 173–85.

Lee, J.K., Jackson, H.J., Pattison, P. and Ward, T. (2000) Developmental Risk Factors for Sexual Offending. *Child Abuse and Neglect*, 26, 73–92.

Lewinsohn, P.M. and Clarke, G.N. (1999) Psychosocial Treatments for Adolescent Depression. *Clinical Psychology Review*, 19, 329–42.

Lynam, D.R. (1996) The Early Identification of Chronic Offenders: Who is The Fledgling Psychopath? *Psychological Bulletin*, 120, 209–34.

Marshall, W.L. and Barbaree, H.E. (1990) An Outpatient Treatment Programme for Child Molesters. *Annals of The New York Academy of Sciences*, 528, 205–14.

McGee, R.A., Wolfe, D.A. and Wilson, S.K. (1997) Multiple Maltreatment Experiences and Adolescent Behaviour Problems: Adolescent Problems. *Development and Psychopathology*, 9, 131–49.

Moffitt, T.E., Caspi, A., Dickson, N., Silva, P. and Stanton, W. (1996) Childhood-Onset Versus Adolescent-Onset Antisocial Conduct Problems in Males: Natural History From Ages 3–18 Years. *Development and Psychopathology*, 8, 399–424.

O'Callaghan, D. (2001) The Interagency Management of Children and Young People Who Sexually Abuse. in Bailey and Dolan (Eds.) *Handbook of Adolescent Psychiatry*. London: Blackwell.

Quiggle, N.L., Garber, J., Panak, W.K. and Dodge, K.A. (1992) Social Information Processing in Aggressive and Depressed Children. *Child Development*, 63, 1305–20.

Ronen, T. (1997) *Cognitive Developmental Therapy With Children*. Chichester: Wiley.

Ryan, G. (1991) Historical Response to Juvenile Sexual Offences. in Ryan and Lane (Eds.) *Juvenile Sexual Offending: Causes, Consequences and Correction*. Massachusetts: Lexington Books.

Saradjian, J. (1996) *Women Who Sexually Abuse Children: From Research to Clinical Practice*. Chichester: Wiley.

Seghorn, T.K., Prentky, R.A. and Boucher, R.J. (1987) Childhood Sexual Abuse in The Lives of Sexually Aggressive Offenders. *Journal of American Academy of Child and Adolescent Psychiatry*, 26, 262–7.

Skuse, D., Bentovim, A., Hodges, J., Stevenson, J., Andreou, C., Lanyado, M., New, J., Williams, B. and McMillan, D. (1998) Risk Factors for Development of Sexually Abusive Behaviour in Sexually Victimised Adolescent Boys: Cross-Sectional Study. *British Medical Journal*, 317.

Vizard, E., French, L., Hickey, N. and Bladon, E. (2004) Severe Personality Disorder Emerging in Childhood: A Proposal for A New Developmental Disorder. *Criminal Behaviour and Mental Health*, 14, 17–28.

Vizard, E., Monck, E. and Misch, P. (1995) Child and Adolescent Sex Abuse Perpetrators: A Review of The Research Literature. *Journal of Child Psychology and Psychiatry*, 36, 731–56.

Weersing, V.R. and Weisz, J.R. (2002) Mechanisms of Action in Youth Psychotherapy. *Journal of Child Psychology and Psychiatry*, 43, 3–29.

Weiss, B.H. and Weisz, J.R. (1995) Relative Effectiveness of Behavioural and Nonbehavioural Child Psychotherapy. *Journal of Consulting and Clinical Psychology*, 63, 317–20.

Widom, C.S., and Ames, J. (1994) Criminal Consequences of Childhood Sexual Victimisation. *Child Abuse and Neglect*, 18, 303–18.

Wolfe, D.A. (1999) *Child Abuse*. Newbury Park: Sage.

Chapter Ten

Empathy, Emotional Intelligence, and Alexithymia: Implications for Research and Practice with Young People with Sexually Abusive Behaviours

Ineke Way

Introduction

There is much interest in learning how sexual offending behaviours develop in adolescents, and in the last ten years theorists have posited multiple theories. Trauma theory suggests that early life experiences of maltreatment may lead to disorganised attachment (Carlson, Cicchetti, Barnett and Braunwald, 1989), and alter brain development (Schore, 2001). Taken together, these dynamics may negatively impact a child's sense of self, empathy, self-esteem, personal control, shame, and emotional regulation (Friedrich, 1995; James, 1994).

Researchers have found a high proportion of adolescents with sexually abusive behaviours who report having been sexually abused, physically abused, or neglected (see Way, 2002 for a review). No prospective studies of maltreated children and later sexual offending could be located. However, prospective studies of maltreated children and delinquent behaviour indicate that they are much more likely than non-maltreated children to offend as adolescents (Kelley, Thornberry and Smith, 1997; Stewart, Dennison and Waterson, 2002). Kelley et al. found that maltreated children later had higher rates of general delinquency of all severity levels, and more violent delinquency than a comparison group of non-maltreated children. Stewart et al. found that a history of physical abuse, and of neglect, predicted later general offending behaviour, while sexual abuse did not.

Clearly, the large majority of children who have been maltreated go on to live healthy productive lives and do not develop delinquent behaviours, including sexual offending. Trauma theory suggests risk and protective factors that may influence developmental paths for children who have been maltreated (Burgess, Hartman and McCormack, 1987; Karr-Morse and Wiley, 1997). This chapter reviews the literature on one protective factor proposed to mediate

development of aggressive behaviour – empathy – and examines two elements associated with empathy – emotional intelligence and alexithymia, or lack of language for feelings. The first section reviews emotional intelligence as a set of abilities that are influenced by early life experience. The remainder of the chapter discusses alexithymia and empathy as two subcomponents of emotional intelligence.

Emotional Intelligence

Gardner (1983) proposed that intelligence may take multiple forms, and that some people may demonstrate high intellectual intelligence, yet have limited skill in understanding themselves or others. Gardner identified additional forms of intelligence, including *intrapersonal* and *interpersonal* intelligence under the umbrella of personal intelligences. He and his colleague (Gardner and Walters, 1993: pp24–5) defined *intrapersonal* intelligence as:

> . . . knowledge of the internal aspects of a person: access to one's own feeling life, one's range of emotions, the capacity to effect discriminations among these emotions and eventually to label them and to draw upon them as a means of understanding and guiding one's own behaviour.

In contrast, *interpersonal* intelligence 'builds on a core capacity to notice distinctions among others; in particular, contrasts in their moods, temperaments, motivations, and intentions' (p23). Gardner and Walters suggest that these intelligences begin as 'raw patterning ability' (p28), develops over time, and may be enhanced by early and intentional intervention.

The two forms of personal intelligence were incorporated by Salovey and Mayer (1989–1990), into the concept *emotional intelligence* (EI). Mayer and Salovey (1997) define emotional intelligence as:

'the ability to perceive accurately, appraise, and express emotion; the ability to access and / or

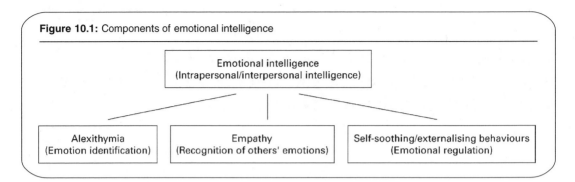

Figure 10.1: Components of emotional intelligence

generate feelings when they facilitate thought; the ability to understand emotion and emotional knowledge; and the ability to reflectively regulate emotions in ways that promote emotional and intellectual growth' (p23)

They further clarify that EI is an ability or mental skill, 'e.g. being able to figure out one's own and others' emotions' (p8), and thus is distinct from *traits*, or 'any fairly consistent behaviour or set of behaviours an individual tends to exhibit such as enjoying being with people, being conscientious, or trying new things' (p23).

There has been debate about whether EI constitutes a distinct intelligence (Roberts, Zeidner and Matthews, 2001). However, Mayer, Caruso and Salovey (1999) argue that EI meets the standard criteria for a form of intelligence, including conceptual, correlation, and developmental criteria. EI may be distinguished from *social intelligence*, which is defined as the capability for 'producing adequate behaviour for the purpose of achieving desired social goals' (Björkqvist, Österman and Kaukiainen, 1999: p192). Social intelligence includes such components as social skills and social competence. Björkqvist et al. (1999) found that when controlling for empathy, greater social intelligence is associated with increasing aggression in adolescents. In contrast, greater empathy is associated with less aggression of all kinds, when controlling for social intelligence (see also Moulden and Marshall, 2002 for further discussion). This suggests that EI (e.g. empathy) may be more critical in helping prevent aggressive behaviour than is social intelligence alone.

Components of emotional intelligence

Goleman (1994) brought Salovey and Mayer's early work on EI into the popular press with his

book by the same name. He details Salovey and Mayer's (1989–1990) three primary domains of EI:

1. 'knowing one's emotions (also termed emotional identification), or 'self-awareness . . . ability to monitor feelings from moment to moment.
2. recognising emotions in others, e.g., 'empathy . . . attuned to the subtle social signals that indicate what others need and want.
3. managing emotions (also termed emotional regulation), or 'capacity to soothe oneself . . . bounce back from setbacks and upsets.'

These primary domains of EI are outlined in Figure 10.1, and are discussed below. Two additional domains of EI, motivating oneself, or 'delaying gratification and stifling impulsiveness . . . in the service of a goal,' and handling relationships, or 'social competence . . . interacting smoothly with others' (pp43–4), are beyond the scope of this chapter.

Emotion identification

The term emotional identification refers to the ability to recognise ones own emotions, also termed emotional awareness. In contrast, the inability to identify emotions, or lack of awareness of emotions, is termed *alexithymia*. As might be predicted, greater alexithymia has been found to be associated with lower emotional intelligence (Parker, Taylor and Bagby, 2001). One consequence of alexithymia, or inability to identify emotions, is subsequent difficulty in managing the effects of strong feelings, or emotional regulation.

Recognition of others' emotions

Empathy for others develops through experiencing empathy from positive role models and through secure attachment to caregivers.

Theorists contend that there is an innate capacity for empathy, and that early life experiences influence how that capacity develops (Brothers, 1989; Williams, 1990; Zahn-Waxler and Radke-Yarrow, 1990). Greater empathy has been associated with greater emotional intelligence in undergraduate students (Ciarrochi, Chan and Caputi, 2000).

Emotional regulation

Brenner and Salovey (1997) argue that emotional regulation, or managing emotions such as sadness or anger, is learned in early childhood through role modelling by caregivers, direct teaching or coaching, and caregivers intentionally providing appropriate activities. The child who has poor role models for emotional intelligence does not learn self-soothing skills that can help manage the painful effects of traumatic experiences. Researchers have found that toddlers who have been maltreated have less language for feelings and are less able to regulate their negative emotions (Friedrich, 1990). These children are thus at the mercy of overwhelming feelings and may numb themselves as a form of self-protection instead of taking action to initiate self-soothing (Karr-Morse and Wiley, 1997). Children who do not have good skills for regulating their emotions may cope in extremes of either internalising (e.g., depression, withdrawing) or externalising (e.g., fighting, breaking things) behaviour patterns (Brenner and Salovey: p181; Goleman, 1994).

Taken together, these domains of emotional intelligence suggest important implications for treatment with adolescents with sexually abusive behaviours. Deficits in knowing one's emotions, or alexithymia, may contribute to difficulties in developing and demonstrating emotional empathy and may lead to increased externalising behaviour problems. Deficits in recognising emotions in others may contribute to lack of cognitive empathy. In contrast, increased empathy is theorised to help reduce aggressive behaviour. Deficits in managing emotions may contribute to difficulties with benefiting from treatment and successfully working to prevent relapse.

Given this relevance to treatment for adolescents with sexual offending behaviours, the remainder of this chapter examines emotional intelligence and two of its major components, alexithymia and empathy. The chapter details

their development, discusses their interrelationships, and outlines implications for treatment with children who have been maltreated and adolescents with sexual offending behaviours.

Development of emotional intelligence

While an infant is born with preliminary brain structures, the child's brain continues to develop during the first five years and evolves through the impact of early relationships with caregivers and early life experiences. Emotional intelligence (EI) is thought to develop through emerging brain structures in the limbic system, whose structures 'are involved in multiple aspects of emotion, including the recognition of emotional expressions on the face, action tendencies, and the storage of emotional memories' (Greenberg and Snell, 1997: p99). Within the limbic system, the amygdala is the primary structure that processes emotion:

> The primary function of the amygdala appears to be the interpretation of incoming sensory information within the context of the individual's survival needs and emotions . . . the amygdala scans experience, examining even minute changes in context. It is asking the question, is there something important here? Something to fear? Something attractive? Another crucial function of the amygdala is the assigning of emotional meaning to memories
>
> (p101).

Goleman (1994: p227) emphasises the importance of healthy development, and argues that 'each (developmental) period represents a window for helping that child install beneficial emotional habits or, if missed, to make it that much harder to offer corrective lessons later in life'.

Effects of maltreatment

Attachment theory contends that the quality of the early relationship between parent and infant exerts a strong influence on the child's ability to develop and maintain intimate relationships later in life (Ainsworth, 1989). Attachment theory emphasises the concept of the child's *internal working model*, or, 'expectations about: a. their own role in relationships (worthy and capable of getting others' attention versus unworthy and incapable of getting needed attention) and b. others' roles in relationships (seeing others as trustworthy, accessible, caring, and responsive versus seeing them as untrustworthy,

inaccessible, uncaring, and unresponsive')
(Alexander, 1992: p186).

These internal working models then serve as
templates for subsequent interactions with others.
Attachment theory proposes that very young
children develop differing types of attachments
based on the internal working models they
incorporate. Children may develop a secure
attachment (characterised by ego resiliency,
empathy, and social competence), an
anxious/ambivalent attachment (characterised by
attention-seeking, impulsivity, and passivity), an
avoidant attachment (characterised by lack of
empathy, detachment from others, and antisocial
thoughts or behaviour), or a disorganised/
disoriented attachment (characterised by
contradictory approach and avoidance
behaviours) (Alexander, 1992).

A baby whose caregiver is attentive, sensitive,
responsive, and empathic learns to connect relief of
pain and discomfort with the presence of a caring
other. However, children who are maltreated
during early childhood not only miss out on the
safe, nurturing attention of a sensitive and caring
caregiver, but that caregiver actually becomes the
source of the infant's distress (Schore, 2001; Siegel,
2000). Theorists propose different impacts of abuse
trauma at different developmental stages
(Kendall-Tackett, 2003). Schore (2001) explains the
effects of 'relational trauma,' or the experience of
an abusive caregiver, on early brain development:

> *This caregiver is inaccessible, and reacts to her infant's
> expressions of emotions and stress inappropriately or
> rejectingly, and shows minimal or unpredictable par-
> ticipation in the various types of arousal regulating
> processes. Such states are accompanied by severe
> alterations in the biochemistry of the immune brain,
> especially in areas associated with the development of
> the child's coping capacities*
>
> (p205, citing Schore, 1996, 1997a)

These brain changes have been associated with
problems in regulating emotions, a key
component of emotional intelligence. Taylor,
Parker and Bagby (1999: p350) emphasise, 'there
is accumulating evidence that emotional
interactions between the infant and caregiver
influence not only the development of
representational and cognitive capacities, but also
the maturation of parts of the brain involved in
emotional awareness and emotional regulation'.
Ito, Teicher, Glod and Ackerman (1998: p305)
found that abused children had deficits in their
left hemisphere. They conclude:

> *... the right hemisphere plays a pivotal role in the
> perception and expression of emotion, particularly
> negative emotion. Deficient right and left hemisphere
> integration could result in the misperception of affect
> and a state of internal confusion or inconsistency.*

In summary, emotional intelligence is thought to
develop through early life experiences. These life
experiences have an effect on the child's
developing capacities and his or her approach to
coping with life experiences. This occurs through
developing brain structures and through
development of skills, abilities, and behaviour
patterns.

Measurement of Emotional Intelligence

In the last 10 years, numerous instruments have
been developed to measure components of
emotional intelligence (see Table 10.1). These
instruments may be categorised as measuring
self-reported traits or abilities/performance
(Mayer, Caruso and Salovey, 2000; Petrides and
Furnham, 2000) and are detailed below.

The *Bar-On Emotional Quotient Inventory* (EQ-i,
1997) is a self-report trait measure developed
with university students. The EQ-i consists of 133
items comprising 13 factors and 4 second-order
factors (intrapersonal, interpersonal, adaptability,
stress management). The EQ-i has adequate
reliability (Cronbach's alphas = 0.81–0.94 for the
second order factors, and 0.96 for the total scale),
and demonstrates convergent and discriminate
validity (Dawda and Hart, 2000).

The *Multifactor Emotional Intelligence Scale*
(MEIS), Student Version (Mayer et al., 1999)
measures ability. The MEIS was developed with
university students, and a shorter version was
tested with high school students and church
youth group members. The MEIS consists of 402
items, related to 12 tasks, which comprise 4
categories of abilities: perceiving emotion,
assimilating emotions, understanding emotions,
and managing emotions.

The *Mayer-Salovey-Caruso Emotional Intelligence
Test* (MSCEIT V2.0) (Mayer, Salovey, Caruso and
Sitarenios, 2003) is adapted from the MEIS
(Mayer et al., 1999). The MSCEIT V2.0 measures
four components, or branches, of emotional
intelligence: 'perceiving emotion correctly, using
emotion to facilitate thought, understanding
emotion, and managing emotion' (p97) with 141
items. These items comprise eight tasks (e.g.,
identifying emotions in a face, identifying the
degree of emotion being portrayed in a face). The

MSCEIT V2.0 uses a unique scoring system which provides two scores – how well a respondent's score matches 'consensus scoring' with scores from other respondents in the sample, and how well the score matches the 'expert scoring' established for the instrument (see also Salovey, Mayer, Caruso and Lopes, 2003). Experts' scores for the MSCEIT were obtained from volunteers attending a national meeting of the International Society for Research on Emotions (2000). The MSCEIT V2.0 was developed with adults, and has been administered in person and on the internet. Test-retest reliability for the total MSCEIT V2.0 is adequate ($r=0.86$), with adequate reliability for the four branch scores (Cronbach's aphas $=0.76$–0.91). The MSCEIT demonstrated discriminate and convergent validity (Salovey et al., 2003).

The *Trait Meta-Mood Scale* (TMMS, Salovey, Mayer, Goldman, Turvey and Palfai, 1995) was developed with undergraduate students, and measures subcomponents of emotional intelligence as traits, with three factors (i.e., attention to feeling, clarity of feelings, mood repair). The TMMS consists of 48 items rated on a five point Likert scale (1 = 'strongly disagree'; 5 = 'strongly agree') the short form has 30 items. Sample items include 'I pay a lot of attention to how I feel' (attention to feeling), 'I always know exactly how I am feeling' (clarity of feeling), and 'When I become very upset, I remind myself of all the little pleasures in life' (mood repair). The TMMS has adequate reliability for both the long and short versions (Cronbach's alpha = 0.82–0.88 for the subscales), and demonstrated convergent and discriminate validity.

The *Emotional Intelligence Scale* (EIS, Schutte, Malouff, Hall, Haggerty, Cooper, Golden and Dornheim, 1998) is a self-report trait measure developed with university students. Schutte et al. contend that the 33 items of the EIS comprise a single factor; however, they identify 13 items related to 'appraisal and expression of feelings,' 10 items related to 'regulation of emotion,' and 10 items related to 'utilization of emotion' (p171). The EIS uses a five point Likert scale (1 = 'strongly disagree'–5 = 'strongly agree'), with higher scores indicating greater emotional intelligence. Sample items include 'I am aware of my emotions as I experience them,' 'I have control over my emotions,' and 'When I am faced with a challenge, I give up because I believe I will fail.' The EIS has adequate reliability (Cronbach's alpha 0.87–0.90) and is rated at grade level 5.68

(Schutte et al., 1998). Schutte et al. grant permission to use the instrument freely, and scale items are provided in their journal article. Petrides and Furnham (2000) conducted confirmatory factor analysis on the EIS with university students, using a seven point Likert response scale. They argue that the scale actually has three factors (with a problematic fourth factor). This four-factor structure was also confirmed by Saklofske, Austin and Minski (2003), using the original five point Likert response scale.

In summary, most instruments that measure emotional intelligence were developed with undergraduate students. The exception is the MEIS, which was also tested with adolescents. Sullivan (1999) developed the *Emotional Intelligence Scale for Children*, modeled on the MEIS (Mayer et al., 1999), but no studies using this instrument could be found. These instruments all measure either self-reported traits or demonstrated abilities. A number of studies have examined EI in adolescents.

Emotional intelligence in adolescents

A number of researchers have examined emotional intelligence in adolescents. Study samples include private high school students (Ciarrochi, Deane, Wilson and Rickwood, 2002), middle school students (Ciarrochi, Chan and Bajgar, 2001, Martinez-Pons, 1998–1999; Mayer et al., 1999; Trinidad and Johnson, 2002), adolescents with sexually abusive behaviours (Moriarity et al., 2001), and adolescents in a military training camp (Charbonneau and Nicol, 2002). These studies are detailed below (see Table 10.2).

Overall, higher EI has been associated with higher functioning in adolescents. Researchers have found that adolescents with higher EI had a stronger orientation toward task accomplishment and were less depressed (Martinez-Pons, 1998–1999), had higher verbal intelligence and empathy for others (Mayer et al., 1999), and reported stronger social support systems (Ciarrochi et al., 2002). Students who rated their parents' EI higher also rated their own EI higher (Martinez-Pons).

Higher EI has been associated with fewer problem behaviours in adolescents, including lower cigarette and alcohol use in middle school students (Trinidad and Johnson, 2002), and a stronger intention to ask for help from both

Table 10.1: Measures of emotional intelligence (EI)

Measure	Developers	Sample	Focus	Method	Measurement	Factorial structure
Bar-On Emotional Quotient Inventory (EQ-i)	Bar-On, 1997	university students (*N* = 243)	self-reported EI traits	self-report questionnaire	5-pt. Likert scale, 133 items	4 second order factors: intrapersonal, interpersonal, adaptation, stress management (including 13 factors)
Emotional Intelligence Scale (EIS)	Schutte et al., 1998	university students (*N* = 346)	self-reported EI trait	self-report questionnaire	5-pt. Likert scale, 33 items	single factor
Emotional Intelligence Scale-Revised (EIS-R)	Petrides and Furnham, 2000	university students (*N* = 260)	self-reported EI traits	self-report questionnaire	7-pt. Likert scale, 33 items	4 factors: optimism/mood regulation, appraisal of emotions, social skills, utilisation of emotions
Mayer-Salovey-Caruso Emotional Intelligence Test, Version 2.0 (MSCEIT V2.0)	Mayer et al., 2003	university students, community adults (*N* = 2,112)	EI abilities	paper and pencil or web-based, varied tasks (e.g., view faces, pictures)	5-pt. Likert scale, multiple choice responses 141 items	4 factors: perceiving emotions, using emotions, understanding emotions, managing emotions (including 2 tasks per factor)
Multifactor Emotional Intelligence Scale (MEIS)	Mayer et al., 1999	community adolescents (*N* = 229); adults (*N* = 503)	EI abilities	paper and pencil or web-based, varied tasks (e.g., view faces, pictures)	varied Likert scales (5-10 pts.) 402 items	4 sets of abilities: perceiving, assimilating, understanding, and managing emotions (including 12 tasks)
Trait Meta-Mood Scale (TMMS)	Salovey et al., 1995	under-graduate students (*N* = 148)	self-reported EI traits	self-report questionnaire	5-pt. Likert scale 48 items (30 item short form)	3 factors: attention to feeling, clarity of feeling, mood repair

informal and formal sources (Ciarrochi et al., 2002: p185). In contrast, adolescents with lower emotional competence were less likely to seek help from informal sources. Ciarrochi et al. summarise; 'those who are likely to need help the most have the lowest intention of seeking it . . . and have the highest intention of not seeking help from anyone'. This finding suggests important implications for adolescents with sexual offending behaviours who are working on relapse prevention. A critical component of most relapse prevention plans is seeking help in times of concern or crisis. Trinidad and Johnson suggest that higher emotional intelligence may help students benefit from drug and alcohol education programmes because those with high levels of EI may be better prepared to process and use information gained during treatment. It may be hypothesised that higher levels of EI would benefit adolescents with sexually abusive behaviours in a similar manner.

A number of researchers have examined between-group differences in EI. Ciarrochi et al. (2001) found that females reported higher emotional intelligence than males on three subscales of the EIS (perception, managing others' emotions, utilising emotions), but found no gender difference for regulating ones own emotions. Charbonneau and Nicol (2002) found no gender difference on the EIS for their adolescent sample. In another study, adolescents scored significantly lower than adults on individual and combined components of emotional intelligence, supporting the hypothesis that EI increases with age (Mayer et al., 1999).

In the single study of EI in adolescents with sexually abusive behaviours, Moriarity et al. (2001) found that the offender group reported greater *attention to feelings* (as measured by the TMMS) than a comparison group of high school students. This study has a small offender sample ($n = 15$), which limits generalisability of the findings, but suggests important direction for further study.

Future research may also do well to account for the effect of asking about socially desirable attributes. Charbonneau and Nicol (2002) found that scores on the EIS scales were highly correlated with a measure of social desirability, indicating response bias (respondents' endorsing responses that presented them in a favourable light). This raises concerns about the transparency of the scale's items.

Summary

In summary, emotional intelligence has been identified as an independent form of intelligence that may assist in understanding self and others, benefiting from treatment, and seeking help. Lower emotional intelligence is theorised to be linked with a number of problems including lack of insight, reduced mindfulness, limited social support, and difficulty with emotional coping. Inadequate emotional intelligence has been associated with alexithymia.

Alexithymia

Lane and Schwartz (1987) proposed a cognitive-developmental theory to explain how emotional awareness develops. They suggest that this process begins with an awareness of bodily sensations, followed by behavioural responses to experiencing strong feelings. The next stage is the ability to identify single emotions, followed by the ability to identify more complex blends of emotions. Lane and Schwartz contend that the highest developmental stage of emotional awareness is the ability to identify combinations of blends of emotions.

Sifneos (1973) proposed the term alexithymia to describe a phenomenon that involves a lack of language for feelings. Individuals with alexithymia do experience strong emotions, but they cannot identify what they are feeling, and they cannot express their feelings in words (Reckling and Buirski, 1996; Schore, 2001; Taylor and Taylor, 1997). Instead, these individuals tend to identify bodily sensations and somatic complaints (e.g., stomach ache, headache, etc.). Alexithymia includes, '1. difficulty in identifying and describing subjective feelings; 2. difficulty distinguishing between feelings and the bodily sensations of emotional arousal; 3. constricted imaginable capacities, as evidenced by a paucity of fantasies; and 4, an externally oriented cognitive style' (Taylor, 2000: p135, citing Nemiah, Freyberger and Sifneos, 1976). Sundararajan (2001) explains that alexithymia may be thought of as the opposite of 'inward sensing,' or insight (citing Gendlin, 1997). Schore (2001: p243) summarises that alexithymia is 'fundamentally an impairment in emotional information processing, specifically a deficit in cognitive processing and regulation of emotions'.

Taken together, these descriptions suggest a person who is out of touch with his or her

Table 10.2: Studies of emotional intelligence in adolescents

Study	Sample	Measurement	Findings
Charbonneau and Nicol, 2002	adolescents in a military training camp ($N=191$)	Emotional Intelligence Scale (EIS, Schutte et al.); Interpersonal Reactivity Index (IRI, Davis, 1980); Weisinger Emotional Intelligence Scale, 8-item desirability scale	no gender difference for EIS scores strong correlation with desirability ($r=0.49$) significant correlation between EIS scores and total empathy ($r=0.22$), empathic concern ($r=0.38$), perspective taking ($r=0.38$)
Ciarrochi et al., 2001	private middle school students ($N=131$) ages 13-15	EIS with 4 factors	females higher total EI ($F(1, 128)=23.7$, $p<0.05$), perceive emotions ($F(1, 128)=16.87$, $p<0.05$), regulate emotions of others ($F(1, 128)=33.3$, $p<0.05$), utilise emotions ($F(1, 128)=4.37$, $p<0.05$) no gender difference in regulating own emotions
Ciarrochi et al., 2002	private high school students ($N=137$)	EIS with 3 factors Beck Hopelessness Scale (Beck et al., 1974) General Help-Seeking Questionnaire (Deane et al., 2001b)	greater intention to seek help for personal issues associated with: higher managing own emotions ($F(10, 115)=2.0$, $p=0.04$) managing others' emotions ($F(10, 115)=3.12$, $p=0.002$), controlling for hopelessness
Martinez-Pons, 1998-1999	junior high school students ($N=109$)	Trait Meta-Mood Scale (TMMS, Salovey et al., 1995), completed by students about their parents, and about themselves Reynolds Adolescent Depression Scale (1997)	parents' EI associated with students' EI ($r=0.44$, $p<0.05$) students' EI associated with higher task orientation ($r=0.70$, $p<0.05$) and lower depression ($r=-0.39$, $p<0.05$) parents' EI not significantly associated with students' social functioning or depression
Mayer et al., 1999	community adolescents ($N=229$), ages 12-16	Multifactor Emotional Intelligence Scale (MEIS, Mayer et al.) 30-item empathy scale similar to Mehrabian-Epstein	EI is correlated with verbal intelligence ($r=0.45$, $p<0.001$) and with empathy ($r=0.37$, $p<0.001$) adolescents have significantly lower EI than adults ($F(1, 709)=22.3$, $p<0.001$)
Moriarity et al., 2001	adolescent males with sexually abusive behaviours (outpatient) ($n=15$); high school students ($n=49$)	TMMS, modified by Heng, 1996	offender group less attention to feelings ($F(1, 62)=6.07$, $p<0.05$)
Trinidad and Johnson, 2002	middle school students ($N=232$)	MEIS	higher total EI associated with lower overall cigarette and alcohol use ($r=-0.19$, $p<0.05$), even when controlling for grades, age, gender higher emotional identification associated with lower tobacco use ($r=-0.18$, $p<0.05$) and alcohol use ($r=-0.18$, $p<0.05$) understanding emotions associated with lower tobacco use ($r=-0.15$, $p<0.05$)

feelings, who experiences strong feelings but does not understand them and cannot describe them, and who has difficulty understanding what is going on internally. This then raises questions about how the presence of alexithymia may influence children's personal development, social relationships, and capacity to benefit from treatment. The presence of alexithymia is of concern because it is hypothesised that if a person has alexithymia and cannot process his/her own feelings, he or she is likely to have somatic symptoms, have difficulty feeling empathy for others, and have increased acting out behaviours (Taylor et al., 1999).

It has been estimated that 10 to 15% of the general population may have alexithymia (Parker, Taylor and Bagby, 1989; Rybakowski, Ziolkowski and Zasadzka et al., 1988, as cited in Keller, Carroll, Nich and Rounsaville, 1995). Furthermore, alexithymia has been identified in 39% of those diagnosed with depression (Honkalampi et al., 2000), 48% to 77% of individuals diagnosed with anorexia, 40% to 60% of those diagnosed with bulimia (reported in Taylor, 2000), and 39% to 50% of those with substance abuse problems (Haviland, Shaw, Cummings and MacMurray, 1988; Keller et al., 1995; Taylor, Parker and Bagby, 1990). More males than females report high alexithymia scores (Honkalampi et al., 2000). Alexithymia has been found to be negatively correlated with emotional intelligence in adults (Parker et al., 2001; Taylor and Bagby, 2000), meaning that people with alexithymia have lower levels of emotional intelligence.

Effect of maltreatment on development of alexithymia

It appears that alexithymia may be either inborn (primary alexithymia), or related to brain changes following trauma (secondary alexithymia). Schore (2001) suggests that alexithymia is strongly related to brain structure. He describes alexithymia as involving a disconnect between the parts of the brain that deal with emotions (right hemisphere) and with verbal expression (left hemisphere).

It is theorised that early life experiences, including poor parent-child relationships, contribute to development of alexithymia (Kleinberg, 1996; Kraemer and Loader, 1995; Schore, 2001; Taylor and Bagby, 2000). Alexithymia has been linked to insecure

attachment (Taylor et al., 1999), and Krystal (1988) was one of the first researchers to suggest that alexithymia may be viewed as an attempt to cope with the trauma of child abuse. An abused child, who experiences strong emotions, yet is not able to understand or express them verbally, may therefore act out physically, either through externalising behaviour or through somatic complaints (Friedrich, 1995; Friedrich and Schafer, 1995; Reckling and Buirski, 1996). Van der Kolk and Fisler (1994: p157) explain, '(abused children) have difficulty putting feelings into words and instead act out their feelings without being able to resort to intervening symbols that would allow for flexible response strategies'. Ito et al. (1998: p298) found that abused children had 'higher levels of left hemisphere coherence' than nonabused children, while their right hemisphere functioning was similar to that of the nonabused children. Reckling and Buirski (1996: p85) emphasise the effects for children who have been abused: 'children who have been abused are often noted to be alexithymic.' They have difficulties desomatising, identifying, and verbally articulating their affective experiences. Rather than communicating feelings with words, the abused child's feelings are frequently expressed through somatic states and physical actions.

Alexithymia is hypothesised to lead to externalising behaviour problems (including aggression, anorexia, bulimia, and substance abuse problems) as an (ineffective) attempt to modulate feelings (Van der Kolk and Fisler). Marohn (1992: p623) contends that many violent and assaultive adolescents may suffer from alexithymia, and summarises, 'they have little awareness of an inner psychological world, cannot name affect, or differentiate one from another, and often confuse thought, feeling, and deed'.

Measurement of alexithymia

The measurement of alexithymia is relatively new in the last 20 years, and there are few standardised instruments (see Table 10.3). The primary instrument used to measure alexithymia in adults and adolescents is the *Twenty-Item Toronto Alexithymia Scale* (TAS-20, Bagby, Parker and Taylor, 1994). TAS-20 questions are rated on a five point Likert scale (1 = 'strongly disagree'–5 = 'strongly agree'), with higher scores indicating greater alexithymia. The TAS-20 has three factors (i.e., difficulty identifying feelings, difficulty expressing feelings, and externally-oriented thinking). The TAS-20 has adequate reliability (Cronbach's alphas ranging from 0.80 to 0.83 for total scale, and from 0.64 to 0.81 for subscale scores) and demonstrates convergent and discriminate validity (Bagby, Taylor and Parker, 1994). Sample items include 'I am often confused about what emotion I am feeling' (difficulty identifying feelings, 'It is difficult for me to find the right words for my feelings' (difficulty describing feelings), and 'I prefer to just let things happen rather than to understand why they turned out that way' (externally-oriented thinking). Because of the strong negative correlations between the TAS-20 and measures of EI, the TAS-20 has also been proposed as an adequate measure of EI (Taylor, Bagby and Luminet, 2000).

In contrast to the TAS-20, which measures self-reported judgements, the *Levels of Emotional Awareness Scale* (LEAS, Lane, Quinlan, Schwartz, Walker and Zeitlin, 1990) measures emotion recognition through demonstrated ability. Respondents read 20 vignettes and answer two qualitative questions for each (i.e., How would you feel?; How would the other person feel?). For each vignette, the 2 responses are scored by the clinician/researcher on a five point Likert scale according to what level of emotional awareness the responses indicate (i.e., 0 = 'non-emotion', 1 = 'physiological cues', 2 = 'undifferentiated emotion', 3 = 'differentiated emotion', 4 = 'multiple differentiated emotion'), using a scoring glossary (interrater reliability = 0.84), and for each vignette, a total score is calculated. The LEAS has been shown to have adequate reliability (Cronbach's alpha = 0.81) and demonstrated discriminate validity.

There is one instrument developed to measure alexithymia in children, the *Alexithymia Scale for Children* (ASC, Fukunishi, Yoshida and Wogan, 1998). The ASC consists of 12 items rated on a three point Likert scale (0 = 'not true'–2 = 'very true or often true'), and is completed by a parent or other caregiver who is familiar with the child. Two subscales measure difficulty expressing feelings and difficulty relating to others. Sample items include 'Able to describe his/her feelings easily' (difficulty expressing feelings) and 'Seems to be sympathetic to others when they are hurt or sad' (difficulty relating to others). The original Japanese-version ASC was translated to English, and back-translated to ensure accuracy of the

wording of questions (I. Fukunishi, personal communication, May 15, 2002). The Japanese-version ASC has been shown to have adequate internal reliability (Cronbach's alpha = 0.84) and demonstrated criterion validity. The psychometric properties of the English version of the ASC have not been tested, and no norms could be located.

Alexithymia in children and adolescents

Research has focused primarily on alexithymia in adults. Alexithymia has been studied in adult substance abusers (e.g., Haviland et al., 1988; Scher and Twaite, 1999) and college students with varying levels of dissociation, i.e., cognitive avoidance (Irwin and Melbin-Helberg, 1997), and adults with eating disorders (Taylor, Parker, Bagby and Bourke, 1996). The few studies of alexithymia in adolescents and children are summarised in Table 10.4.

The majority of studies of alexithymia in young people have been conducted in Japan. Fukunishi and colleagues used the ASC to examine alexithymia in children being treated for refractory hematological diseases (including leukemia). They found that the children's parents rated them as having significantly higher alexithymia than prior to becoming ill (retrospective rating), these scores were higher than for a comparison group of healthy children (Fukunishi and Tsuruta, 2001), they had higher rates of PTSD and alexithymia than children who had experienced a flood disaster, and higher alexithymia and difficulty describing feelings were associated with PTSD (Fukunishi, Tsuruta, Hirabayashi and Asukai, 2001).

In another Japanese study, university students' higher alexithymia scores were negatively correlated with their ratings of their mothers' care as they were growing up. This was true for students who grew up in both nuclear and extended families, indicating that students who scored higher on alexithymia rated their mothers as providing less care (Fukunishi and Paris, 2001). There was a significant correlation between how students rated themselves on alexithymia and how their mothers rated themselves retrospectively (to adolescence). This supports the hypothesis that parents' level of alexithymia influences their children's level of alexithymia.

In the two studies of alexithymia in adolescents, researchers found that a greater intention to ask for help with personal issues was

Table 10.3: Measures of alexithymia

Measure	Developers	Sample	Method	Measurement	Factorial structure
Alexithymia Scale for Children (ASC)	Fukunishi, Yoshida, and Wogan, 1998	Japanese elementary students (N=286)	caregiver-completed questionnaire	3-pt. Likert scale, 12 items	2 factors: difficulty in describing feelings, difficulty in relating to others
Levels of Emotional Awareness Scale (LEAS)	Lane et al., 1990	under-graduate students (N=35)	self-report instrument	qualitative questions, scored on a 5-pt. Likert scale, 20 vignettes	5 levels: bodily sensations, action tendencies, single emotions, blends of emotions, combinations of blends
Toronto Alexithymia Scale (TAS-20)	Bagby, Parker, and Taylor, 1994a	undergraduate students (N=965)	self-report questionnaire	5-pt. Likert scale, 20 items	3 factors: difficulty identifying feelings, difficulty describing feelings, externally-oriented thinking

associated with higher scores on identifying emotions and lower externally-oriented thinking (Ciarrochi et al., 2002). In contrast, the single study of alexithymia in adolescents with sexual offending behaviours found no difference in scores for identifying or describing feelings between the offender group and high school students (Moriarity et al., 2001). However this study's small sample ($n=15$) limits generalisability of the findings.

Summary

In summary, alexithymia refers to a difficulty identifying or expressing feelings, and a tendency to focus on the outer world rather than on internal experience. Alexithymia may contribute to somatic problems, acting out, and reduced empathy.

Empathy

Empathy has been defined as 'the capacity to share, or cognitively interpret, another person's emotional experiences' (Roys, 1997: p55). Research on very young infants indicates that empathy is immediately evident after birth. Within the first days following birth, infants can already discriminate a single adult's varied facial expressions (Scharfe, 2000, citing Field et al., 1982). Scharfe reports that these young infants were able to distinguish their own cry from that of another infant, and that they displayed negative emotions in response to hearing other infants cry (citing Dondi, Simion and Caltran, 1999). Empathy has been found to increase with age (Davis and Franzoi, 1991; Eisenberg and Strayer, 1987) and develops through a secure attachment to adult caregivers and experiencing and observing the empathic interactions of those adults (Feshbach, 1987; Thompson, 1987).

Effects of maltreatment on development of empathy

During the past 20 years there has been increased attention on reduced empathy as a major psychological effect for children who have experienced childhood maltreatment (Cornett, 1985; Eckenrode, Powers and Garbarino, 1997; Feshbach, 1989; Kolko, 1992; Ryan, 1989; Wiehe, 1986). Empathy develops through a secure attachment to adult caregivers, and through experiencing and observing the empathic interactions of those adults (Feshbach, 1987; Thompson, 1987).

Table 10.4: Studies of alexithymia in children and adolescents

Study	Sample	Measurement	Findings
Ciarrochi et al., 2002	private high school students ($N=137$)	Levels of Emotional Awareness (LEAS, Lane et al., 1996) Toronto Alexithymia Scale (TAS-20, Bagby et al., 1994) Social Support Questionnaire (Sarason et al., 1983) Beck Hopelessness Scale (Beck et al., 1974) General Help-Seeking Questionnaire (Deane et al., 2001)	• greater intention to seek help for personal issues was associated with greater identify emotions ($F(10, 116)=2.40$, $p=0.01$) and lower externally oriented thinking ($F(10, 116)=2.29$, $p=0.02$), controlling for hopelessness
Fukunishi and Paris, 2001	university students ($N=428$) and their mothers	TAS-20, Japanese version Parental Bonding Inventory Family Environment Scale	• total alexithymia and factor 1 and 2 scores correlated with ratings of mother's care for students from nuclear families ($r=-0.34$ to -0.48, $p<0.05$) • total alexithymia and factor 2 scores correlated with their ratings of mother's care for students from extended families ($r=-0.34$ to -0.37, $p<0.05$) • total alexithymia and factors 1 and 2 scores for students correlated with mothers' retrospective alexithymia scores ($r=0.39–0.60$, $p<0.05$)
Fukunishi et al., 2001	children with refractory hematological disease ($n=33$); children who experienced flood disaster ($n=215$) healthy children ($n=286$)	Alexithymia Scale for Children (ASC, Fukunishi et al., 1998) Posttraumatic Stress response Scale (Asukai, 1996)	• children with illnesses had higher PTSD than flood survivor children ($\chi^2=11.8$, df$=1$, $p<0.0006$) • children with illnesses had higher alexithymia than healthy children ($F(1,31)=7.1$, p <0.009) • total alexithymia scores and difficulty describing feelings scores were associated with PTSD ($r=0.40$, $p<0.02$)
Fukunishi and Tsuruta, 2001	children with refractory hematological disease ($n=33$); healthy children ($n=102$)	ASC	• subjects' scores more alexithymic than control group (Fisher's PLSD $=1.27$, df $=1$, $p<0.05$); subjects' scores more alexithymic than parent's retrospective pre-illness rating (Fisher's PLSD $=1.65$, df $=1$, $p<0.05$)
Moriarity et al., 2001	adolescents with sexually abusive behaviours, outpatient treatment ($n=15$); high school students ($n=49$)	TAS-20	• no difference in identifying or describing feelings

Maltreatment by a parent negatively impacts children in several related ways. First, the child observes destructive models for relationships when a maltreating parent demonstrates a lack of concern for the child's needs and feelings (Karr-Morse and Wiley, 1997). Second, the child does not experience a nurturing, loving, sensitive caregiver to respond to and soothe the child's painful feelings (Ryan, 1996). Third, the abused child may develop a self-protective stance for self-preservation (Garbarino, 1999). Fourth, the abused child may identify with the abusive parent and take on his or her distorted thought processes. Fifth, the child may blame themselves for the abuse in order to preserve an internal image of a caring and protective parent (Ryan, 1996; Staub, 1996).

Burgess et al. (1987) suggest that children who have not acknowledged and dealt with their own pain will not be able to experience empathy for others. Ryan (1996) describes a sequence of effects of chronic trauma that includes chronic arousal and the child's numbing their own feelings as an attempt to manage this internal state (citing James, 1994). This numbness to one's own feelings may then contribute to lack of empathy for the feelings or experiences of others (Burgess et al., 1987; Way and Spieker, 1997).

Finkelhor and Lewis (1988) suggest that males may have more barriers to empathy for children than do females because they traditionally have had little training for, nor involvement in, care giving. They also note that because males learn to deny or minimise their own emotional vulnerability, they may be less likely to acknowledge or empathise with the emotional needs of the children with whom they come in contact (see also Levinson, 1994).

Garbarino (1999: p138) describes the lack of empathy in violent youths, and argues, '(a) boy who has organised his inner life around the need to protect himself from his feelings of victimisation and unworthiness is unlikely to pay attention effectively to the feelings of others, especially to their feelings as victims'. Garbarino uses the term 'emotional retardation' to describe deficits in empathy for others' feelings. He contends that, '(e)motional retardation is one of the socially expensive side effects of surviving rejection in childhood, particularly in boys whose temperament puts them in jeopardy for emotional compartmentalisation in the first place' (pp53–4).

Types of empathy

While much has been written about empathy, empathy may be conceptualised in a variety of ways (see Figure 10.2). First, discussion about *empathy* may refer to either general (dispositional) empathy or to victim (situational) empathy. Second, empathy may be conceptualised as a single form (i.e., general or victim empathy), or as comprising separate subtypes (i.e., cognitive and emotional victim empathy). These are detailed below.

General empathy. General (dispositional) empathy refers to an individual's general ability to experience empathy for others. Empathy may be distinguished from *sympathy*, defined as, 'a vicarious emotional response to similar external conditions, which consists of feelings of sorrow or concern for others' (Zahn-Waxler and Radke-Yarrow, 1990: p108) and *personal distress*, defined as, 'self-focused, aversive reaction to another's state and experienced as anxiety or distress' (Zahn-Waxler and Radke-Yarrow, 1990: p108). Eisenberg and Strayer (1987) emphasise that the experience of personal distress actually interferes with experiencing empathy because the former results in self-oriented concern.

A growing number of theorists agree that general empathy has both a *cognitive* and

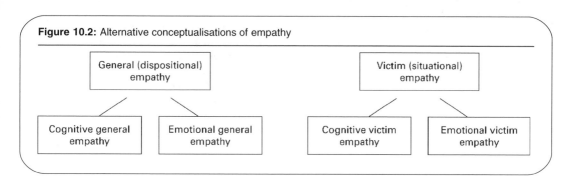

Figure 10.2: Alternative conceptualisations of empathy

emotional component (Davis, 1983a, 1983b; Hilton, 1993; Pecukonis, 1990; Roys, 1997). The cognitive component of empathy refers to the ability to notice and discern emotional cues in others and to put oneself in another person's place, while the emotional component refers to the ability to actually experience these emotions (Feshbach, 1989; Williams, 1990).

Theorists suggest that the relationship between empathy and aggression involves both cognitive and emotional aspects of empathy (Davis, 1996; Hilton, 1993; Miller and Eisenberg, 1988). *Cognitive* empathy serves as a barrier to **initiating** aggressive behaviour because it helps one make sense of, or form an explanation for, another person's behaviour and/or statements (Davis, 1996). In contrast, *emotional* empathy serves as a barrier to **continuing** aggressive behaviour once one can sense what it feels like to be experiencing the other person's distress. Marshall, Hudson, Jones and Fernandez (1995) outlined a four stage process of empathy that includes both cognitive and emotional components, '1. recognition of another person's emotional state; 2. taking the perspective of the other person; 3. experiencing the same or similar emotion as the observed person; and 4. taking some action to ameliorate the other person's distress' (Marshall, 2002: pp13–14).

Empathy has been identified as a critical component of sexual offending behaviour in adolescents (National Task Force on Juvenile Sexual Offending, 1993; Shaw, 2000) and adults (Fernandez, 2002; Marshall, Anderson, Fernandez, Mulloy and Eccles, 1999). In contrast to the earlier focus on general empathy, recent focus has shifted to examining victim empathy as a specific form of empathy.

Victim empathy. In the last ten years, theorists and researchers have emphasised the importance of examining victim-specific empathy rather than general empathy in adult sexual offenders (Hanson and Scott, 1995; Levinson, 1994; Marshall, O'Sullivan and Fernandez, 1996; McGrath, Cann and Konapasky, 1998). This is based on the assumption that, while sexual offenders may be able to experience and demonstrate appropriate empathy for others in general, they may be less able to experience empathy for victims of trauma or the individuals whom they victimised. Proeve and Howells (2002) theorise that the internalised shame that sexual offenders experience may serve as a barrier to experiencing empathy for victims of

abuse. In recent studies, adult sexual offenders reported the lowest empathy for the specific victim they assaulted, followed by greater empathy for victims of abuse in general, with their highest empathy being reported for others in general (Fernandez, Marshall, Lightbody and O'Sullivan, 1999, Marshall, Hamilton and Fernandez, 2001). These findings argue for measuring victim-specific empathy rather than general empathy. Existing studies of both forms of empathy in adolescents with sexually abusive behaviours are reviewed below.

General empathy in adolescents with sexually abusive behaviours

Measurement. General empathy in adolescent sexual offenders has been measured with self-report measures (Arundell, 1991; Monto et al., 1994; Monto et al., 1998), clinician rating and role play ratings. Self-report measures include standardised empathy scales (Interpersonal Reactivity Index, Davis, 1983; Index for Empathy for Children and Adolescents, Bryant, 1982), self-developed scales (Monto, Zgourides, Wilson and Harris, 1994; Monto, Zgourides and Harris, 1998), and related scales (e.g., Loevinger Ego-Development Scale, Loevinger and Wessler, 1970; Rape Myths Acceptance Scale, Burt, 1980).

Some instruments measure cognitive empathy (e.g., Hogan Empathy Test, 1969) and others measure emotional empathy (e.g., Index of Empathy for Children and Adolescents, Bryant, 1982; Questionnaire Measure of Emotional Empathy, Mehrabian and Epstein, 1972). As discussed above, many researchers now emphasise the importance of measuring empathy as a multidimensional phenomenon (Arundell, 1991; Davis, 1983a; 1983b; Hilton, 1993; Pecukonis, 1990).

The most commonly used measure of general empathy is the *Interpersonal Reactivity Index* (IRI, Davis, 1980), which measures cognitive and emotional empathy on two separate scales. The IRI also measures personal distress in social situations and ability to empathise with situations through fantasy. The IRI consists of 28 questions rated on a five point Likert scale (A = 'does not describe me well'–E = 'describes me very well'). Sample items include 'I sometimes try to understand my friends better by imagining how things look from their perspective' (perspective-taking), 'I am often quite touched by things that I see happen' (empathic concern), 'I tend to lose control during emergencies' (personal distress), and 'I really get involved with the feelings of the characters in a novel' (fantasy). The IRI has been shown to have adequate reliability (Cronbach's alphas range from 0.70 to 0.78 for the four subscales for males and females).

Findings. Some studies of adolescents with sexually abusive behaviours have examined general empathy as a unitary construct (see Table 6). For example, Monto et al. (1994) found that adolescent sexual offenders report slightly lower (though nonsignificant) general empathy than a community group of high school students (see also Monto et al., 1998). The measurement used in these studies limits generalisability of the findings due to measurement of empathy as a unitary construct and restricted variance in empathy scores, with using four questions that were rated yes/no.

In contrast, a number of studies of sexually abusive adolescents have distinguished the cognitive and emotional dimensions of general empathy through administration of the Interpersonal Reactivity Index (IRI, Davis, 1983b). Arundell (1991) found that abused sexual offenders reported lower total general empathy than abused nonoffender adolescents. Higher general empathy has been found to be associated with increased age and increased response bias (Curwen, 1997). Other researchers found that sexually abusive adolescents reported: a. cognitive and emotional empathy levels lower than high school students (Burke, 2001), b. lower empathic concern than nonsexual delinquents (Lindsey, Carlozzi and Eells, 2001), and c. personal distress levels similar to nonsexual delinquents but higher than non delinquent youths (Lindsey et al., 2001).

This set of studies of general empathy contributes to knowledge by comparing general empathy in groups of adolescents, but many used small sexual offender samples ($n = 20–30$), which limits generalisability of their findings. The Monto et al. studies had larger samples ($n = 82–84$), but used a coarse measurement of empathy. Only the Lindsey et al. study controlled for demographic characteristics such as age. The Lindsey et al. finding that sexually abusive adolescents reported higher personal distress suggests intriguing implications given that personal distress may serve as a barrier to experiencing empathy for others. More recently, instrument development and research design

have focused on the measurement of victim empathy.

Victim empathy in sexual offenders

Measurement. Although researchers have emphasised the need to measure specific victim empathy in adolescents with sexually abusive behaviours, there are no measures of victim empathy normed with adolescent sexual offenders (see Table 10.5). However, there are a number of instruments developed with adult sexual offenders, including the Child Empathy Test (Hanson and Scott, 1995), the Empat (McGrath et al., 1998), the Levinson Victim Empathy Scale (Levinson, 1994), and the Child Molester Empathy Measure (Fernandez et al., 1999). The Adolescent Empathy Test (Bosley, 2000) measures victim empathy in adolescents with sexually abusive behaviours.

The *Child Empathy Test* (CET, Hanson and Scott, 1995) measures perspective taking (cognitive victim empathy). The measure consists of 16 vignettes which portray non abusive, ambiguous, and clearly sexually abusive situations. Respondents rate each vignette on a seven point Likert scale according to how they believe the child feels (1 = 'very upset or unhappy'–7 = 'very good, happy, cheerful'). The CET has been shown to have low reliability (Cronbach's alphas = 0.30–0.59).

The *Empat* (McGrath et al., 1998) consists of 52 statements that measure unidimensional victim empathy (34 items) and general empathy (18 items), rated on a five point Likert scale. Sample questions include 'If someone was molested 18 years ago, they should be over it by now' (victim empathy) and 'People who fought in the war usually exaggerate the injuries they got' (general empathy). A higher score indicates greater empathy. The Empat has been shown to have adequate reliability (Cronbach's alphas = 0.92, 0.77 respectively). No validity data was provided.

The *Levinson Victim Empathy Scale* (LVES, Levinson, 1994; see also Prentky and Edmunds, 1997) consists of 37 statements that measure cognitive, perspective-taking, and emotional components of empathy for victims of abuse and/or other experiences. The items are rated on a seven point Likert scale (7 = 'always describes me'–1 = 'never describes me'). Scores range from 37 to 259, with a higher score indicating greater victim empathy. The LVES has three factors (empathic response, interpersonal appreciation, and interpersonal sensitivity). Sample items include 'I try to imagine how I would feel when someone tells me how he/she was hurt' (empathic response), 'It's hard for me to understand why someone else gets upset' (interpersonal appreciation), and 'I cannot feel anyone else's pain right now' (interpersonal sensitivity). The LVES has adequate reliability (Cronbach's alphas = 0.80; 0.79; 0.73 respectively; overall alpha = 0.84), and demonstrated convergent validity.

The *Child Molester Empathy Measure* (CMEM, Fernandez et al., 1999) measures unidimensional general empathy and victim empathy. The measure consists of three vignettes describing an accident victim, a victim of sexual abuse, and the child molested by the offender respondent. The respondent rates each child's feelings with 31 feelings rated with a ten point Likert scale (0 = 'not at all'–10 = 'very much'). This scale has been shown to have adequate reliability (Cronbach's alphas = 0.79 to 0.94). No validity data was provided.

For the single instrument developed to measure victim empathy in adolescents with sexually abusive behaviours, Bosley (2000) adapted the *Adolescent Empathy Test* (AET) from the Child Empathy Test (Hanson and Scott, 1995). The AET measures perspective taking (cognitive victim empathy), and uses 19 written vignettes. For each vignette, respondents are asked to select the feeling they believe the child is experiencing on a seven point Likert scale (1 = 'very upset, unhappy or scared'–7 = 'very good, happy and cheerful'), and write an explanation for why they believe the child would feel this way.

In summary, there are a number of new measures of victim empathy developed with and for sexual offenders. Several measure victim empathy as a unitary concept (Empat, CMEM) and two measure cognitive victim empathy (CET, AET). The LVES measures cognitive and emotional victim empathy with three factors. The single empirical study of victim empathy in adolescents with sexually abusive behaviours is summarised below.

Findings. While a number of researchers have examined victim empathy in adult sexual offenders (Fernandez et al., 1999; Marshall et al., 2001; Marshall et al., 1996; Webster and Beech, 2000) only one study of victim empathy in adolescents with sexually abusive behaviours could be located (see Table 10.6). Way (1999)

examined the relationship between self-reported childhood maltreatment history and cognitive and emotional victim empathy in adolescents with sexually abusive behaviours in specialised residential treatment settings ($N = 96$) using a subset of items from the Levinson Victim Empathy Scale (Levinson, 1994). She found that more severe maltreatment was associated with greater emotional victim empathy ($r = 0.24$, $p < 0.05$), while a greater number of maltreatment perpetrators was associated with higher cognitive victim empathy ($r = 0.35$, $p < 0.001$). However, the study has a number of methodological limitations, including small maltreated sample ($n = 85$) use of an unnormed measure of victim empathy, lack of a non-offender comparison group, and limited variability in empathy scores, which limits generalisability of the findings.

In summary, researchers increasingly distinguish general (dispositional) and victim (situational) empathy, and distinguish the cognitive and emotional components of these separate types of empathy. Theorists suggest that enhancement of cognitive and emotional victim empathy may differentially influence the potential for further offending. Research on general and victim empathy provides a foundation for attempting to understand how empathy operates in adolescents with sexually abusive behaviours. One critical issue is exploring the relationships between empathy, treatment for sexual offending behaviours, and potential for relapse.

Enhancement of empathy in treatment

Strengthening victim empathy has been identified as critical to preventing relapse in adolescents (National Task Force on Juvenile Sexual Offending, 1993) and adults (Pithers, 1999). Hanson and Scott (1995: p260) emphasise the intuitive importance of studying empathy in adult sexual offenders:

> . . . *Interest in empathy training for offenders seems to be based primarily on the plausible assumption that victim empathy should inhibit offending and the observation that sexual offenders often appear callous toward their victims.*

Despite the lack of empirical support for treatment methods, nearly all treatment programmes for adolescents with sexually abusive behaviours (97%) and adult sexual offenders (95%) include victim empathy as a treatment component (Knopp, Freeman-Longo

Table 10.5: Measures of empathy

Measure	Developers	Sample	Method	Measurement	Factorial structure
Adolescent Empathy Test (AET)	Bosley (2000)	not provided	19 written vignettes	7-pt. Likert rating of how child in vignette felt	
Child Empathy Test	Hanson and Scott, 1995	adult sexual offenders ($n=149$), community sexual offenders ($n=49$), nonsexual offenders ($n=41$), university students ($n=76$)	16 written vignettes (non abusive – ambiguous – clearly sexual abusive situations)	7-pt. Likert scale rating of how child in vignette felt	cognitive victim empathy
Child Molester Empathy Measure (CMEM)	Fernandez et al., 1999	adult child molesters ($n=29$), community adults ($n=36$)	3 written vignettes (accident victim, sexual abuse victim, offender's 'own victim')	10-pt. Likert rating of how child in vignette felt, 50 items	general empathy, general victim empathy
Empat	McGrath et al., 1998	adult child molesters ($n=30$), nonsexual offenders ($n=30$), university students ($n=30$)	self-report questionnaire	5-pt. Likert scale, 52 items	general victim empathy, general empathy
Levinson Victim Empathy Scale (LVES)	Levinson, 1994	adult child molesters	self-report questionnaire	7-pt. Likert scale, 37 items	cognitive victim empathy, emotional victim empathy, perspective taking
Interpersonal Reactivity Index (IRI)	Davis, 1980	university students ($N=1,344$)	self-report questionnaire	5-pt. Likert scale, 28 items	general empathy: empathic concern, perspective taking, fantasy, personal distress

Table 10.6: Studies of empathy in adolescents with sexually abusive behaviours

Study	Sample	Measurement	Findings
Arundell, 1991	abused adolescents in outpatient/residential treatment, grouped by offender/non offender ($N=60$)	Interpersonal Reactivity Index (IRI, Davis, 1980)	• non offenders had greater empathy ($F(4,55)=3.03$, $p<0.03$) • multiple perpetrators predicted lower empathy ($F=4.81$, $p<0.01$) • treatment following victimization predicted greater empathic concern ($F(2,57)=5.64$, $p<0.006$)
Burke, 2001	adolescents with sexually abusive behaviours, outpatient ($n=23$), high school students ($n=23$)	IRI therapist rating of victim empathy	• adolescents with sexually abusive behaviours lower total empathy ($t(44)=-2.37$, $p<0.02$) • lower cognitive empathy ($t(44)=-2.85$, $p<0.009$) • lower emotional empathy ($t(44)=-2.29$, $p<0.03$)
Curwen, 1997	adolescents with sexually abusive behaviours ($N=123$)	IRI	• empathy positively associated with offender age/response bias • no difference for maltreatment history, victim age, victim gender • no association with therapist rating of victim empathy
Gomes-Schwartz, 1984	adolescents with sexually abusive behaviours in outpatient treatment ($N=18$)	Loevinger Ego-Development Scale	• 86% were rated on low levels of ego development
Lindsey et al., 2001	adolescents with sexually abusive behaviours ($n=27$), nonsexual delinquents ($n=27$), non delinquents ($n=27$)	IRI	• adolescents with sexually abusive behaviours lower emotional empathy than nonsexual delinquents ($F(1,26)=12.62$, $p<0.001$) • greater personal distress than nondelinquent youths ($F(1,26)=7.12$, $p<0.013$)
Monto et al., 1994	adolescents with sexually abusive behaviours ($n=82$), high school students ($n=108$)	4-item self-developed scale	• adolescent sexual offenders rated slightly (non-significant) lower empathy levels
Monto et al., 1998	adolescents with sexually abusive behaviours ($n=84$), high school students ($n=113$)	4-item empathy scale, 5-item scale adapted from Rosenberg Self-Esteem Scale	• no difference in empathy, empathy not related to social desirability; no association between empathy and length of treatment
Schram et al., 1991	adolescents with sexually abusive behaviours in outpatient and residential treatment ($N=197$)	record review	• non-reoffenders exhibited more victim empathy than all reoffenders combined
Way, 1999	adolescents with sexually abusive behaviours (residential/outpatient) ($N=96$), ages 13-20	Levinson Victim Empathy Scale (1994)	• longer time in treatment was associated with higher cognitive victim empathy ($r=0.30$, $p<0.003$); time in treatment and emotional victim empathy was nonsignificant

and Stevenson, 1992). While it appears that this proportion has dropped significantly, as reported in the most recent Safer Society National Survey of Treatment Providers (3%–7% of programmes treating adolescents with sexually abusive behaviours reported they provide a victim empathy component, Burton and Smith-Darden, 2000), enhancement of empathy continues to be identified as an important treatment focus for those who have molested a child (Fernandez, 2002).

Recently, there has also been increased attention to distinguishing treatment for cognitive versus emotional victim empathy. Theorists argue that strengthening *cognitive* empathy, typically addressed in sexual offender treatment for both adolescents and adults, is not adequate to prevent recidivism (Hilton, 1993; Roys, 1997). While *emotional* empathy has been hypothesised as the more critical component of relapse prevention, Hilton (1993: p293) raises caution about potential unintended consequences of increasing cognitive empathy without at the same time strengthening emotional empathy. Hilton suggests that, 'the psychopath, characterised by not only charm and manipulativeness but also shallow affect and callousness, epitomises the combination of well-developed cognitive empathy and absent emotional empathy'. This suggests that increased cognitive empathy may be exploited by sexual offenders so that they become more adept at identifying vulnerability in potential victims and in carrying out the grooming process.

Researchers have found a relationship between empathy training and increased empathy in adult sexual offenders (Marshall et al., 1996; Pithers, 1999). More recently, researchers have examined how treatment may impact empathy in adolescents who have molested a child. Monto et al. (1998) tested the relationship between length of time in treatment and one-dimensional general empathy in sexually abusive adolescents, but found no significant relationship. This null finding may be due to the measurement used for empathy (four questions rated yes/no) in this cross-sectional study.

In another study, Way (1999) examined victim empathy in adolescents with sexually abusive behaviours in cognitive-behavioural treatment programmes in residential and outpatient settings, and found that longer time in treatment was associated with higher cognitive victim empathy. This finding held, even after controlling for demographic characteristics. In contrast, there

was no relationship between the length of time the adolescents had been in treatment and their level of emotional victim empathy. While the treatment programmes were broadly equivalent in treatment philosophy, the specific treatment components were not analysed as a part of this cross-sectional study, which limits generalisability of these findings.

These findings do raise several questions. First, what are the prerequisites to developing emotional empathy, and (how) do they differ from those needed to develop cognitive empathy (Schwartz, 1999)? Second, how does treatment for development of emotional empathy differ from treatment for development of cognitive empathy (Webster and Beech, 2000)? Third, how well do sexual offender treatment programmes currently address emotional empathy as compared to cognitive empathy? Fourth, how is increased empathy related to risk for sexual and other recidivism (Worling, 2002)?

Summary

Development of emotional intelligence has been linked to early childhood experiences, including childhood maltreatment. Two components of EI, alexithymia and empathy, are hypothesised to be related to aggression (though in opposite directions). These relationships suggest important implications for further research and for our practice with maltreated children and adolescents with sexual offending behaviours. The remainder of this chapter focuses in these two areas.

Implications for research

Knowledge in a new area tends to evolve in stages:

1. Identify the concept of interest.
2. Examine its causes/etiology/consequences.
3. Develop effective measures of the concept.
4. Develop treatment protocols and treatment models.
5. Test the effectiveness of alternative treatments.
6. Establish best practice standards.

Knowledge related to EI, alexithymia, and empathy has progressed greatly in the past 25 years, but much remains to be learned. The implications for further research in these three areas are discussed below.

Emotional intelligence. A number of instruments have been developed to measure components of

EI in adults; several of these (i.e., EIS, MEIS, TMMS) have been used in research with adolescents. Of these, only the MEIS (Mayer et al., 1999) measures EI as ability, identified as the more accurate perspective (Mayer et al., 2000; Petrides and Furnham, 2000). The MEIS protocol is lengthy and has a complicated scoring procedure, which may require training. The EIS (Schutte et al., 1998), which measures EI as trait, has most often been used in research with adolescents; it has a brief, self-report format.

Much remains to be learned about how EI operates in the development of sexual offending behaviours and other delinquent behaviours in adolescents. There is currently only one published study of EI in adolescents with sexually abusive behaviours (Moriarty et al., 2001). This study provides important direction for further research, though it used a small offender sample ($n = 15$), which limits generalisability of the findings. Much remains to be learned about how the level of EI in adolescents with sexually abusive behaviours compares to that of non offender comparison groups, and how increased EI is related to successfully completing sexual offender treatment and preventing relapse.

Alexithymia. Measurement of alexithymia in adults has primarily used the TAS-20 (Bagby et al., 1994a), and the two studies with adolescents used this instrument as well (Ciarrochi et al., 2002; Moriarty et al., 2001). While alexithymia in adults and adolescents is measured using a self-report format, the one instrument that measures alexithymia in children (ASC, Fukunishi et al., 1998) is completed by a caregiver familiar with the child. Alexithymia has been hypothesised to be a potential barrier to developing emotional empathy (Way, 1999), but this relationship has not been tested.

Because little is known about alexithymia in adolescents or adolescents with sexually abusive behaviours, there is much need for further research. The one study of alexithymia in adolescents with sexually abusive behaviours (Moriarty et al., 2001) suggests intriguing direction. This research should include developing norms for alexithymia in the general adolescent population, measuring alexithymia in adolescents who have been maltreated, and testing relationships between alexithymia and variables of interest (e.g., emotional/cognitive victim empathy, PTSD, depression, somatic complaints).

Empathy. Of the three concepts discussed in this chapter, empathy has been studied most extensively. However, empathy has proven to be a difficult concept to measure, and much remains to be learned about how to effectively measure general and victim empathy in sexual offenders. For instance, relatively little is known about emotional empathy and how to accurately measure this phenomenon.

Careful attention is needed to develop less transparent instruments, in order to reduce response bias and more accurately measure cognitive and emotional empathy. More accurate measurement could help detect greater variance in levels of empathy. There is no measure of victim empathy normed for adolescents. Recent developments in measuring victim empathy in adult sexual offenders (Fernandez et al., 1999; Webster and Beech, 2000) and adolescent sexual offenders (Bosley, 2000) suggest directions for further research. The one study of victim empathy in adolescents with sexual offending behaviours (Way, 1999) provides some direction but has a number of methodological limitations. Future research needs to compare victim empathy in adolescents with sexually abusive behaviours and general population adolescents and examine the relationship between empathy and variables of interest (e.g., alexithymia, cognitive distortions, shame, and personal distress).

Implications for practice

Bill Marshall has long argued that lack of intimacy skills contributes to sexual offending in adult sexual abusers (Marshall, 1989, 1993, 1998). He describes low-intimacy individuals as characterised by emotional loneliness, poor interpersonal skills, and low empathy for others (1998). It may be that EI and alexithymia, which have only recently been examined in adolescents with sexually abusive behaviours, can provide crucial direction for treatment to help address empathy deficits, increase prosocial behaviour, and reduce the risk for sexual offending and other aggressive behaviour.

Feshbach (1987) contends that empathy requires the capacity for discrimination of cues in others, perspective-taking ability, and ability to experience feelings. Most empathy training focuses on training *cognitive* empathy, and treatment modules have been developed to help adolescents with sexually abusive behaviours develop a cognitive understanding of what others have experienced. *Emotional* empathy is the more complex form of empathy, and it makes intuitive sense that the potential to increase emotional empathy for others may be constrained by clients' skill and ability to experience and recognise their own feelings (e.g., presence of alexithymia, deficits in EI). This suggests the importance of helping adolescents with sexually abusive behaviours strengthen their ability to identify and express their own emotions before expecting them to experience genuine emotional empathy for others.

There has been some initial consideration of these phenomena. For example, Marohn (1992) proposes that violent and assaultive adolescents may suffer from alexithymia and therefore are not able to use their emotions in communication. He argues that their acting out behaviour can be reduced by helping them understand and recognise their feelings, and learn how to modulate and manage their feelings to understand themselves and communicate with others.

Initially, treatment with adolescents would need to draw on the substantial literature detailing treatment for alexithymia in adults, much of it in psychoanalytic and health-related journals. Kleinberg (1996: p78) describes characteristics of people with alexithymia: '(they) describe details instead of feelings . . . use action to avoid conflict . . . associate thought content more with external events than with their feelings . . . are sometimes overwhelmed with undifferentiated affect storms'. Kraemer and Loader describe a bland and boring communication style, with a focus on external matters or physical symptoms, but not about feelings or internal states.

Given these difficulties, people with alexithymia are thought to be poor candidates for insight-oriented therapy (Taylor and Bagby, 2000). Instead, group therapy is recommended in order to provide opportunity for clients to benefit from role modelling provided by other clients (Kleinberg, 1996; Swiller, 1988; Taylor, 2000). The benefit of group therapy supports the practice of using open-ended groups with adolescents with sexual offending behaviours so that new members can learn from others who have made progress in their own treatment (Way and Balthazor, 1990). Active participation in a safe group setting, where trust and relationships are emphasised, provides clients opportunity to receive positive feedback from peers and therapist, and become increasingly aware of how

others experience them (Swiller, 1988). This emphasis on trust and safety raises caution about group modalities that rely heavily on confrontation, which could actually increase clients' defenses rather than assist in reducing them.

A progression of treatment might include increasing internal awareness (Sundararajan, 2001), developing emotional awareness (Taylor, 2000; Taylor, Bagby and Parker, 1997), learning to identify affect 'without first discharging it into soma' (Swiller, 1988: p56), and then expressing the emotion verbally (Swiller, 1988; Taylor, 2000). Sundararajan (2001) describes the therapeutic technique of *focusing* (or inward sensing, with reference to Gendlin, 1997) to help individuals with alexithymia to move their awareness from the external to the internal experience, and from physical states to recognition of feelings. Serran (2002) details a combination of cognitive and emotion-based techniques for developing emotional recognition (citing Carich, Henderson-Odum and Metzger, 2001), including exploring the sexual abuser's family-of-origin experience with expressing emotions, cognitive restructuring, relaxation, and journaling. Swiller (1998: p56) argues that as this work progresses, 'new cognitive structures are developing which permit increasingly differentiated and integrated internal experiences'. Therapy can thus help increase awareness of complexity of feelings, identify hidden feelings, and connect feelings to behaviours.

A critical component of treatment to address alexithymia is that as skills and interactions change, there are also changes in brain structures. LeDoux (1998) contends that one purpose of therapy is strengthening the cortex of the brain by 'getting the cortex to control the amygdala . . . emphasis on conscious insight and conscious appraisals, may involve the control of the amygdala by explicit knowledge through the temporal lobe memory system and other cortical areas involved in conscious awareness' (p. 265).

In addition to the verbal treatments discussed above, nonverbal techniques such as art therapy are also recommended. Heiman, Strnad, Weiland and Wise (1994: p145) report that patients with alexithymia created drawings of their illnesses as richly detailed as those who did not have alexithymia. Heiman et al. recommend art therapy as, 'a richly symbolic means for alexithymics to begin to express, recognise . . . discuss feelings . . . (and) promote exploration of feelings'. Schwartz (1999: p7) outlined a process for helping adolescents with sexual offending behaviours to access feelings and emotional memories using high impact imagery (e.g., photographs, music, and art). He emphasises the importance of this process, 'affect precedes cognition. Ideas (and) beliefs are forms of justification to perpetuate . . . feelings'. Because people with alexithymia tend to have poor memory for dreams, Taylor (2000) recommends helping clients learn to focus on their dreams.

Much of the literature on developing EI in children has focused on family and school interventions. This may include assessing and developing parents' EI skills (Zeidner, Matthews, Roberts and McCann, 2003), providing guidance for parents to enhance their young child's emotional awareness (Shapiro, 1998), and developing school curricula to increase emotional competence (Collaborative for the Advancement of Social and Emotional Learning, Greenberg and Snell, 1997; Salovey and Sluyter, 1997; Stone and Dillehunt, 1978).

Summary

Much remains to be learned about how greater emotional intelligence and empathy and reduced alexithymia may help in treatment with adolescents with sexually abusive behaviours. This chapter has outlined aetiology, and has detailed implications for clinical practice and further research. It is critical that we continue to learn how to prevent sexual abuse of children, assist children in maintaining healthy functioning following childhood maltreatment, and provide meaningful treatment for adolescents with sexually abusive behaviours that helps reduce the risk for relapse. The stakes are high and the potential benefits are many.

Acknowledgements

The author gratefully acknowledges graduate research assistants Tobias Towers and Gail Martin, who helped with the literature search for this chapter. Many thanks also to Curtis McMillen, Ph.D., George Warren Brown School of Social Work, Washington University in St. Louis, who introduced the author to the concept of alexithymia, and to James Henry, Ph.D. and Connie Black-Pond, M.A. of the Southwest Michigan Children's Trauma Assessment Centre, for comments on an earlier version of this manuscript.

References

Ainsworth, M.D.S. (1989). Attachments Beyond Infancy. *American Psychologist*, 44, 709–16.

Alexander, P.C. (1992) Application of Attachment Theory to the Study of Sexual Abuse. *Journal of Consulting and Clinical Psychology*, 60, 185–95.

Arundell, R.M. (1991) The Relationships of Empathy, Social Support, Trauma Symptoms and Family Violence in the Victim to Victimiser Process in Adolescent Males. *Dissertation Abstracts International*, 52 (09), 4965. (University Microforms No. Aat 9205394)

Awad, G.A. and Saunders, E.B. (1991) Adolescent Child Assaulters: Clinical Observations. *Journal Of Interpersonal Violence*, 6, 446–60.

Bagby, R.M., Parker, J.D.A. and Taylor, G.J. (1994) The Twenty-Item Toronto Alexithymia Scale-I. Item Selection and Cross-Validation of the Factor Structure. *Journal of Psychosomatic Research*, 38, 23–32.

Bagby, R.M., Taylor, G.J. and Parker, J.D.A. (1994) The Twenty-Item Toronto Alexithymia Scale-Ii. Convergent, Discriminate, and Concurrent Validity. *Journal of Psychosomatic Research*, 38, 33–40.

Bar-On, R. (1997) *Bar-On Emotional Quotient Inventory. Technical Manual.* Toronto: Multi-Health Systems.

Björkqvist, K., Österman, K. and Kaukiainen, A. (1999) Social Intelligence – Empathy = Aggression? *Aggression and Violent Behaviour*, 5, 191–200.

Bosley, T. (2000, February) *Creating Victim Empathy: The Measurement and Inducement of Empathic Responses.* Presentation at the Annual Meeting of the National Adolescent Perpetration Network, Denver.

Brenner, E.M. and Salovey, P. (1997) Emotion Regulation During Childhood: Developmental, Interpersonal, and Individual Considerations, in Salovey, P. and Sluyter, D.J. (Eds.) *Emotion Development and Emotional Intelligence: Educational Implications.* New York: Basic Books. 168–92.

Brothers, L. (1989) A Biological Perspective on Empathy. *American Journal of Psychiatry*, 146, 10–9.

Bryant, B.K. (1982) An Index of Empathy for Children and Adolescents. *Child Development*, 53, 413–25.

Burgess, A.W., Hartman, C.R. and McCormack, A. (1987) Abused to Abuser: Antecedents of Socially Deviant Behaviours. *American Journal of Psychiatry*, 144, 1431–6.

Burke, D.M. (2001) Empathy in Sexually Offending and Nonoffending Adolescent Males. *Journal of Interpersonal Violence*, 16, 222–33.

Burt, M.R. (1980) Cultural Myths and Supports for Rape. *Journal of Personality and Social Psychology*, 38, 217–30.

Burton, D. and Smith-Darden, J. (2000) *North American Survey of Sexual Abuser Treatment and Models: Summary Data 2000*. Brandon, Vt: Safer Society Press.

Carlson, V., Cicchetti, D., Barnett, D. and Braunwald, K. (1989) Disorganised/ Disoriented Attachment Relationships in Maltreated Infants. *Developmental Psychology*, 25, 525–31.

Charbonneau, D. and Nicol, A.A.M. (2002) Emotional Intelligence and Leadership in Adolescents. *Personality and Individual Differences*, 33, 1101–13.

Ciarrochi, J., Chan, A.Y.C. and Bajgar (2001) Measuring Emotional Intelligence in Adolescents. *Personality and Individual Differences*, 31, 1105–19.

Ciarrochi, J., Chan, A.Y.C. and Caputi, P. (2000) A Critical Evaluation of the Emotional Intelligence Construct. *Personality and Individual Differences*, 28, 539–61.

Ciarrochi, J., Deane, F.P., Wilson, C.J. and Rickwood, D. (2002) Adolescents Who Need Help the Most are the Least Likely to Seek It: the Relationship Between Low Emotional Competence and Low Intention to Seek Help. *British Journal of Guidance and Counselling*, 30, 173–88.

Cornett, C. (1985) The Cyclical Pattern of Child Physical Abuse From a Psychoanalytic Self-Psychology Perspective. *Child and Adolescent Social Work*, 2, 83–92.

Curwen, T. (1997) Utility of the Interpersonal Reactivity Index in Measuring Differences in Empathy Among Adolescent Sex Offenders. *Masters Abstracts International*, 36 (06), 1698. (University Microforms No. Aat Mq28703)

Davis, M. (1983a) Effects of Dispositional Empathy on Emotional Reactions and Helping: A Multi-Dimensional Approach. *Journal of Personality*, 51, 167–84.

Davis, M. (1980) A Multidimensional Approach to Individual Differences in Empathy. *Jsas Selected Documents in Psychology*, 10, 85. Select Press, Pob 37, Corte Madera, Ca, 94976–0037.

Davis, M.H. (1996) *Empathy: A Social Psychological Approach*. Boulder, Co: Westview Press.

Davis, M.H. (1983b) Measuring Individual Differences in Empathy: Evidence for a Multidimensional Approach. *Journal of Personality and Social Psychology*, 44, 113–26.

Davis, M.H. and Franzoi, S.L. (1991) Stability and Change in Adolescent Self-Consciousness and Empathy. *Journal of Research in Personality*, 25, 70–87.

Dawda, D. and Hart, S.D. (2000) Assessing Emotional Intelligence: Reliability and Validity of the Bar-On Emotional Quotient Inventory (Eq-I) in University Students. *Personality and Individual Differences*, 28, 797–812.

Eckenrode, J., Powers, J.L. and Garbarino, J. (1997) Youth in Trouble are Youth Who Have Been Hurt, in Garbarino, J. and Eckenrode, J. (Eds.) *Understanding Abusive Families: An Ecological Approach to Theory and Practice*. San Francisco: Jossey-Bass Publishers. 166–193.

Eisenberg, N. and Strayer, J. (1987) Critical Issues in the Study of Empathy, in Eisenberg, N. and Strayer, J. (Eds.) *Empathy and Its Development*. New York: Cambridge University Press. 3–13.

Fernandez, Y. (2002) *In Their Shoes: Examining the Issue of Empathy and Its Place in the Treatment of Offenders*. Oklahoma City, Ok: Wood 'N' Barnes Publishing and Distribution.

Fernandez, Y.M., Marshall, W.L., Lightbody, S. and O'Sullivan, C. (1999) The Child Molester Empathy Measure: Description and Examination of Its Reliability and Validity. *Sexual Abuse: A Journal of Research and Treatment*, 11, 17–31.

Feshbach, N.D. (1987) Parental Empathy and Child Adjustment/Maladjustment, in Eisenberg, N. and Strayer, J. (Eds.) *Empathy and Its Development*. New York: Cambridge University Press. 271–91.

Feshbach, N.D. (1989) The Construct of Empathy and the Phenomenon of Physical Maltreatment of Children, in Cicchetti, D. and Carlson, V. (Eds.) *Child Maltreatment: Theory and Research on the Causes and Consequences of Child Abuse and Neglect*. Cambridge, Ma: Cambridge University Press. 349–73.

Finkelhor, D. and Lewis, I.A. (1988) An Epidemiological Approach to the Study of Child Molestation, in Prentky, R.A. and Quinsey, V.L. (Eds.) *Human Sexual Aggression: Current Perspectives*. New York: New York Academy of Sciences. 64–78.

Friedrich, W.N. (1995) Attachment: An Overview, in *Psychotherapy With Sexually Abused Boys: An Integrated Approach*. Thousand Oaks, Ca: Sage Publications. 19–38.

Friedrich, W.N. (1990) Developmental Considerations, in *Psychotherapy of Sexually Abused Children and Their Families*. New York: W. W. Norton and Co. 40–63.

Friedrich, W.N., and Schafer, L.C. (1995) Somatic Complaints in Sexually Abused Children. *Journal of Pediatric Psychology*, 20, 661–70.

Fukunishi, I. and Paris, W. (2001) Intergenerational Association of Alexithymic Characteristics for College Students and Their Mothers. *Psychological Reports*, 89, 77–84.

Fukunishi, I. and Tsuruta, T. (2001) Alexithymic Characteristics in Children With Refractory Hematological Diseases. *Psychosomatics*, 42, 276–7.

Fukunishi, I., Tsuruta, T., Hirabayashi, N. and Asukai, N. (2001) Association of Alexithymic Characteristics and Posttraumatic Stress Response Following Medical Treatment for Children With Refractory Hematological Diseases. *Psychological Reports*, 89, 527–34.

Fukunishi, I., Yoshida, H. and Wogan, J. (1998) Development of the Alexithymia Scale for Children: A Preliminary Study. *Psychological Reports*, 82, 43–9.

Garbarino, J. (1999) *Lost Boys: Why Our Sons Turn Violent and How We Can Save Them*. New York: The Free Press.

Gardner, H. (1983) *Frames of Mind: the Theory of Multiple Intelligences*. New York: Basic Books.

Gardner, H. (1993) *Multiple Intelligences: the Theory in Practice*. New York: Basic Books.

Gardner, H. and Walters, J. (1993) A Rounded Version, in Gardner, H. (Ed.) *Multiple Intelligences: the Theory in Practice*. New York: Basic Books. 13–34.

Garland, R.J. and Dougher, M.J. (1990) The Abused/Abuser Hypothesis of Child Sexual Abuse: A Critical Review of Theory and Research, in Feierman, J.R. (Ed.) *Paedophilia: Biosocial Dimensions*. New York: Springer-Verlag. 488–509.

Gibson, J.W. (1992) Compensating for Missing Data in Social Work Research. *Social Work Research and Abstracts*, 28, 3–8.

Goleman, D. (1994) *Emotional Intelligence: Why It Can Matter More Than Iq*. New York: Bantam Books.

Greenberg, M.T. and Snell, J.L. (1997) Brain Development and Emotional Development: the Role of Teaching in Organising the Frontal Lobe, in Salovey, P. and Sluyter, D.J. (Eds.), *Emotional Development and Emotional Intelligence: Educational Implications*. New York: Basic Books. 93–119.

Hanson, R.K. and Scott, H. (1995) Assessing Perspective-Taking Among Sexual Offenders, Nonsexual Criminals, and Nonoffenders. *Sexual Abuse: A Journal of Research and Treatment*, 7, 259–77.

Haviland, M.G., Shaw, D.G., Cumings, M.A. and MacMurray, J.P. (1988) Alexithymia: Subscales and Relationship to Depression. *Psychotherapy Psychosomatics*, 50, 164–70.

Heiman, M., Strnad, D., Weiland, W. and Wise, T.N. (1994) Art Therapy and Alexithymia. *Art Therapy: Journal of the American Art Therapy Association*, 11, 143–6.

Hilton, N.Z. (1993) Childhood Sexual Victimisation and Lack of Empathy in Child Molesters: Explanation or Excuse? *International Journal of Offender Therapy and Comparative Criminology*, 37, 287–96.

Hogan, R. (1969) Development of an Empathy Scale. *Journal of Consulting and Clinical Psychology*, 33, 307–16.

Honkalampi, K., Hintikka, J., Saarinen, P., Lehtonen, J. and Viinamaki, H. (2000) Is Alexithymia a Permanent Feature in Depressed Patients? *Psychotherapy and Psychosomatics*, 69, 303–8.

Irwin, H.J. and Melbin-Helberg, E.B. (1997) Alexithymia and Dissociative Tendencies. *Journal of Clinical Psychology*, 53, 159–66.

Ito, Y., Tiecher, M.H., Glod, C.A. and Ackerman, E. (1998) Preliminary Evidence for Aberrant Cortical Development in Abused Children: A Quantitative E.G. Study. *Journal of Neuropsychiatry*, 10, 298–307.

James, B. (1994) *Handbook for Treatment of Attachment-Trauma Problems in Children*. New York: Lexington Books.

Karr-Morse, R. and Wiley, M.S. (1997) *Ghosts From the Nursery: Tracing the Roots of Violence*. New York: The Atlantic Monthly Press.

Keller, D.S., Carroll, K.M., Nich, C. and Rounsaville, B.J. (1995) Alexithymia in Cocaine Abusers: Response to Psychotherapy and Pharmacotherapy. *American Journal on Addictions*, 4, 234–44.

Kelley, B.T., Thornberry, T.P. and Smith, C.A. (1997, August) In the Wake of Childhood Maltreatment. *Juvenile Justice Bulletin*. Order Ncj 165257

Kendall-Tackett, K. (2003) *Treating the Lifetime Health Effects of Childhood Victimisation*. Kingston, Nj: Civic Research Institute.

Kleinberg, J.L. (1996) Working With the Alexithymic Patient in Groups. *Psychoanalysis and Psychotherapy*, 13, 76–85.

Knopp, F.H., Freeman-Longo, R. and Stevenson, W.F. (1992) *Nationwide Survey of Juvenile and Adult Sex-Offender Treatment Programs and Models*. Brandon, Vt: The Safer Society Press.

Kolko, D.J. (1992) Characteristics of Child Victims of Physical Violence: Research Findings and Clinical Implications. *Journal of Interpersonal Violence*, 7, 244–76.

Kraemer, S. and Loader, P. (1995) 'Passing Through Life': Alexithymia and Attachment Disorders. *Journal of Psychosomatic Research*, 39, 937–41.

Krystal, H. (1988) *Integration and Self-Healing: Affect-Trauma-Alexithymia*. Hillsdale, Nj: The Analytic Press.

Lane, R.D., Quinlan, D.M., Schwartz, G.E., Walker, P.A. and Zeitlin, S.B. (1990) The Levels of Emotional Awareness Scale: A Cognitive-Developmental Measure of Emotion. *Journal of Personality Assessment*, 55, 124–34.

Lane, R.D. and Schwartz, G.E. (1987) Levels of Emotional Awareness: A Cognitive-Developmental Theory and Its Application to Psychopathology. *American Journal of Psychiatry*, 144, 133–43.

LeDoux, J. (1998) *The Emotional Brain: the Mysterious Underpinnings of Emotional Life*. New York: Touchstone Books.

Levinson, B.S. (1994) The Development and Validation of an Instrument to Measure Victim Empathy in a Male Sex Offender Population. *Dissertation Abstracts International*, 55(06), 2434. (University Microforms No. Aat 9428589)

Lindsey, R.E., Carlozzi, A.F. and Eells, G.T. (2001) Differences in the Dispositional Empathy of Juvenile Sex Offenders, Non-Sex-Offending Delinquent Juveniles, and Nondelinquent Juveniles. *Journal of Interpersonal Violence*, 16, 510–22.

Loevinger, J. and Wessler, R. (1970) *Measuring Ego Development: 1. Construction and Use of a Sentence Completion Test*. San Francisco: Jossey-Bass.

Marohn, R.C. (1992) Management of the Assaultive Adolescent. *Hospital and Community Psychiatry*, 43, 622–4.

Marshall, W.L. (2002) Historical Foundations and Current Conceptualisations of Empathy, in Fernandez, Y. (Ed.) *In Their Shoes: Examining the Issue of Empathy and Its Place in the Treatment of Offenders*. Oklahoma City, Ok: Wood 'N' Barnes Publishing and Distribution. 1–15.

Marshall, W.L. (1998, June) *Impact of Attachment Bonds in the Development and Treatment of Sexual Offending*. Paper Presented At the Meeting of the National Adolescent Perpetration Network, Winnipeg, Canada.

Marshall, W.L. (1989) Intimacy, Loneliness, and Sexual Offenders. *Behaviour Research and Therapy*, 27, 491–503.

Marshall, W.L. (1993) The Role of Attachments, Intimacy, and Loneliness in the Etiology and Maintenance of Sexual Offending. *Sexual and Marital Therapy*, 8, 109–21.

Marshall, W.L., Anderson, D., Fernandez, Y., Mulloy, R. and Eccles, A. (1999) Empathy, in *Cognitive Behavioural Treatment of Sexual Offenders*. New York: John Wiley and Sons, 73–92.

Marshall, W.L., Hamilton, K. and Fernandez, Y. (2001) Empathy Deficits and Cognitive Distortions in Child Molesters. *Sexual Abuse: A Journal of Research and Treatment*, 13, 123–30.

Marshall, W.L., Hudson, S.M., Jones, R. and Fernandez, Y.M. (1995) Empathy in Sex Offenders. *Clinical Psychology Review*, 15, 99–113.

Marshall, W.L., O'Sullivan, C. and Fernandez, Y.M. (1996) The Enhancement of Victim Empathy Among Incarcerated Child Molesters. *Legal and Criminological Psychology*, 1, 95–102.

Martinez-Pons, M. (1998–1999) Parental Inducement of Emotional Intelligence. *Imagination, Cognition, and Personality*, 18, 3–23.

Mayer, J.D., Caruso, D.R. and Salovey, P. (1999) Emotional Intelligence Meets Traditional Standards for an Intelligence. *Intelligence*, 27, 267–98.

Mayer, J.D., Caruso, D.R. and Salovey, P. (2000) Selecting a Measure of Emotional Intelligence, in Bar-On, R. and Parker. J.D.A. (Eds.) *The Handbook of Emotional Intelligence: Theory, Development, Assessment, and Application At Home, School, and in the Workplace*. San Francisco: Jossey-Bass. 320–41.

Mayer, J.D. and Salovey, P. (1997) What Is Emotional Intelligence? In Salovey, P. and Sluyter, D.J. (Eds.) *Emotional Development and Emotional Intelligence: Educational Implications*. New York: Basic Books. 3–31.

Mayer, J.D., Salovey, P., Caruso, D.R. and Sitarenios, G. (2003) Measuring Emotional Intelligence With the MSCEIT V2.0. *Emotion*, 3, 97–105.

McGrath, M., Cann, S. and Konopasky, R. (1998) New Measures of Defensiveness, Empathy, and Cognitive Distortions for Sexual Offenders Against Children. *Sexual Abuse: a Journal of Research and Treatment*, 10, 25–36.

Mehrabian, A. and Epstein, N. (1972) A Measure of Emotional Empathy. *Journal of Personality*, 40, 525–43.

Miller, P.A. and Eisenberg, N. (1988) The Relation of Empathy to Aggressive and Externalizing/Antisocial Behaviour. *Psychological Bulletin*, 103, 324–44.

Monto, M., Zgourides, G. and Harris, R. (1998) Empathy, Self-Esteem, and the Adolescent Sexual Offender. *Sexual Abuse: a Journal of Research and Treatment*, 10, 127–40.

Monto, M., Zgourides, G., Wilson, J. and Harris, R. (1994) Empathy and Adolescent Male Sex Offenders. *Perceptual and Motor Skills*, 79, 1598.

Moriarty, N., Stough, C., Tidmarsh, P., Eger, D. and Dennison, S. (2001) Deficits in Emotional Intelligence Underlying Adolescent Sex Offending. *Journal of Adolescence*, 24, 743–51.

Moulden, H. and Marshall, W.L. (2002) Empathy, Social Intelligence, and Aggressive Behaviour, in Fernandez, Y. (Ed.) *In Their Shoes: Examining the Issue of Empathy and Its Place in the Treatment of Offenders.* Oklahoma City: Ok: Wood 'N' Barnes Publishing and Distribution. 53–72

National Task Force on Juvenile Sexual Offending. (1993) The Revised Report From the National Task Force on Juvenile Sexual Offending, of the National Adolescent Perpetrator Network. *Juvenile and Family Court Journal*, 44, 1–120.

Parker, J.D.A., Taylor, G.J. and Bagby, R.M. (2001) The Relationship Between Emotional Intelligence and Alexithymia. *Personality and Individual Differences*, 30, 107–15.

Parker, J.D.A., Taylor, G.J., and Bagby, R.M. (1989) The Alexithymia Construct: Relationship With Sociodemographic Variables and Intelligence. *Comprehensive Psychiatry*, 30, 434–41.

Pecukonis, E.V. (1990) A Cognitive/Affective Empathy Training Program As a Function of Ego Development in Aggressive Adolescent Females. *Adolescence*, 25, 59–76.

Perry, B. (2003, April) *Early Investment, Long-Term Gain: Foundations for a Strong Community.* Presentation At Kresa, Kalamazoo Regional Educational Service Agency, Kalamazoo, Michigan.

Petrides, K.V. and Furnham, A. (2000) On the Dimensional Structure of Emotional Intelligence. *Personality and Individual Differences*, 29, 313–20.

Pithers, W.D. (1999) Empathy: Definition, Enhancement, and Relevance to the Treatment of Sexual Abusers. *Journal of Interpersonal Violence*, 14, 257–84.

Prentky, R. and Edmunds, S.B. (1997) *Assessing Sexual Abuse: a Resource Guide for Practitioners.* Brandon, Vt: The Safer Society Press.

Proeve, M. and Howells, K. (2002) Shame and Guilt in Child Sexual Offenders. *International Journal of Offender Therapy and Comparative Criminology*, 46, 657–67.

Reckling, A.E. and Buirski, P. (1996) Child Abuse, Self-Development, and Affect Regulation. *Psychoanalytic Psychology*, 13, 81–99.

Richburg, M. and Fletcher, T. (2002) Emotional Intelligence: Directing a Child's Emotional Education. *Child Study Journal*, 32, 31–8.

Roberts, R.D., Zeidner, M. and Matthews, G. (2001) Does Emotional Intelligence Meet Traditional Standards for an Intelligence? Some New Data and Conclusions. *Emotion*, 1, 196–231.

Roys, D.T. (1997) Empirical and Theoretical Considerations of Empathy in Sex Offenders. *International Journal of Offender Therapy and Comparative Criminology*, 41, 53–64.

Ryan, G. (1989) Victim to Victimiser: Rethinking Victim Treatment. *Journal of Interpersonal Violence*, 4, 325–41.

Ryan, K. (1996) The Chronically Traumatised Child. *Child and Adolescent Social Work Journal*, 13, 287–310.

Saklofske, D.H., Austin, E.J. and Minski, P.S. (2003) Factor Structure and Validity of a Trait Emotional Intelligence Measure. *Personality and Individual Differences*, 34, 707–21.

Salovey, P. and Mayer, J.D. (1989–1990) Emotional Intelligence. *Imagination, Cognition, and Personality*, 9, 185–211.

Salovey, P., Mayer, J.D., Caruso, D. and Lopes, P.N. (2003) Measuring Emotional Intelligence As a Set of Abilities With the Mayer-Salovey-Caruso Emotional Intelligence Test, in Lopez, S.L. and Snyder, C.R. (Eds.) *Positive Psychological Assessment: A Handbook of Models and Measures.* Washington, D.C.: American Psychological Association. 251–65.

Salovey, P., Mayer, J.D., Goldman, S.L., Turvey, C. and Palfai, T.P. (1995) Emotional Attention, Clarity, and Repair: Exploring Emotional Intelligence Using the Trait Meta-Mood Scale, in Pennebaker, J.W. (Ed.) *Emotion, Disclosure, and Health.* Washington Dc: American Psychological Association. 125–54.

Scharfe, E. (2000) Development of Emotional Expression, Understanding, and Regulation in

Infants and Young Children, in Bar-On, R. and Parker, J.D.A. (Eds.) *The Handbook of Emotional Intelligence: Theory, Development, Assessment, and Application At Home, School, and in the Workplace.* San Francisco: John Wiley. 244–62.

Scher, D. and Twaite, J.A. (1999) The Relationship Between Child Sexual Abuse and Alexithymic Symptoms in a Population of Recovering Adult Substance Abusers. *Journal of Child Sexual Abuse*, 8, 25–40.

Schore, A.N. (2001) The Effects of Early Relational Trauma on Right Brain Development, Affect Regulation, and Infant Mental Health. *Infant Mental Health Journal*, 22, 201–69.

Schutte, S.N., Malouff, J.M., Hall, L.E., Haggerty, D.J., Cooper, J.T., Golden, C.J. and Dornheim, L. (1998) Development and Validation of a Measure of Emotional Intelligence. *Personality and Individual Differences*, 25, 167–77.

Schwartz, C. (1999, September) *Increasing Empathy of Adolescent Offenders With High Impact Imagery.* Presentation At the Annual Meeting of the Association for the Treatment of Sexual Abusers, Orlando.

Serran, G. (20020. Emotional Expression and Recognition, in Fernandedz, Y. (Ed.) *In Their Shoes: Examining the Issue of Empathy and Its Place in the Treatment of Offenders.* Oklahoma City, Ok: Wood 'N' Barnes Publishing and Distribution. 91–109.

Shapiro, L.E. (1998) *How to Raise a Child With a High EQ: A Parent's Guide to Emotional Intelligence.* Scranton, Pa: Harper-Collins.

Shaw, J.A. (2000) Summary of the Practice Parameters for the Assessment and Treatment of Children and Adolescents Who are Sexually Abusive to Others. *Journal of the American Academy of Child and Adolescent Psychiatry*, 39, 127–30.

Siegel, D.J. (2000) Toward an Interpersonal Neurobiology of the Developing Mind: Attachment Relationships, Mindsight, and Neural Integration, in Osofsky, J.D. and Schore, A.N. (Eds.) *Contributions From the Decade of the Brain to Infant Mental Health.* New York: John Wiley and Sons, Inc. 1–25.

Sifineos, P.E. (1973) The Prevalence of Alexithymic Characteristics in Psychosomatic Patients. *Psychotherapy and Psychosomatics*, 22, 255–62

Staub, E. (1996) Cultural-Societal Roots of Violence: the Examples of Genocidal Violence and Contemporary Youth Violence in the United States. *American Psychologist*, 51, 117–32.

Stewart, A., Dennison, S. and Waterson, E. (2002) Pathways From Child Maltreatment to Juvenile Offending. *Trends and Issues in Crime and Criminal Justice*, 241.

Stone, K.F. and Dillehunt, H.Q. (1978) *Self Science: the Subject Is Me.* Santa Monica, Ca: Goodyear Publishing Co.

Sullivan, A.K. (1999) The Emotional Intelligence Scale for Children. *Dissertation Abstracts International*, 60(01), 68. (University Microforms No. Aat 9916408)

Sundararajan, L. (2001) Alexithymia and the Reflexive Self: Implications of Congruence Theory for Treatment of the Emotionally Impaired. *Humanistic Psychologist*, 29, 223–48.

Swiller, H.I. (1988) Alexithymia: Treatment Utilising Combined Individual and Group Psychotherapy. *International Journal of Group Psychotherapy*, 38, 47–61.

Taylor, G.J. (2000) Recent Developments in Alexithymia Theory and Research. *Canadian Journal of Psychiatry*, 45, 134–42.

Taylor, G.J. and Bagby, R.M. (2000) An Overview of the Alexithymia Construct, in Bar-On, R. and Parker, J.D.A. (Eds.) *The Handbook of Emotional Intelligence: Theory, Development, Assessment, and Application At Home, School, and in the Workplace.* San Francisco: Jossey-Bass. 40–67.

Taylor, G.J., Bagby, R.M. and Luminet, O. (2000) Assessment of Alexithymia: Self-Report and Observer-Rated Measures, in Bar-On, R. and Parker, J.D.A. (Eds.) *The Handbook of Emotional Intelligence: Theory, Development, Assessment, and Application At Home, School, and in the Workplace.* San Francisco: Jossey-Bass. 301–19.

Taylor, G.J., Bagby, R.M. and Parker, J.D.A. (1997) Treatment Considerations, in *Disorders of Affect Regulation: Alexithymia in Medical and Psychiatric Illness.* New York: Cambridge University Press.

Taylor, G.J., Parker, J.D.A. and Bagby, R.M. (1999) Emotional Intelligence and the Emotional Brain: Points of Convergence and Implications for Psychoanalysis. *Journal of the American Academy of Psychoanalysis*, 27, 339–54.

Taylor, G.J., Parker, J.D.A. and Bagby, R.M. (1990) A Preliminary Investigation of Alexithymia in Men With Psychoactive Substance Dependence. *American Journal of Psychiatry*, 147, 1228–30.

Taylor, G.J., Parker, J.D.A., Bagby, R.M. and Bourke, M.P. (1996) Relationships Between Alexithymia and Psychological Characteristics Associated With Eating Disorders. *Psychosomatic Research*, 41, 561–8.

Taylor, G.J. and Taylor, H.L. (1997) Alexithymia, in McCallum, M. and Piper, W.E. (Eds.) *Psychological Mindedness: A Contemporary Understanding.* Mahwah, Nj: Lawrence Erlbaum Associates. 77–104.

Thompson, R.A. (1987) Empathy and Emotional Understanding: the Early Development of Empathy, in Eisenberg, N. and Strayer, J. (Eds.) *Empathy and Its Development.* New York: Cambridge University Press. 119–45.

Trinidad, D.R. and Johnson, C.A. (2002) The Association Between Emotional Intelligence and Early Adolescent Tobacco and Alcohol Use. *Personality and Individual Differences,* 32, 95–105.

Van Der Kolk, B.A. and Fisler, R.E. (1994) Childhood Abuse and Neglect and Loss of Self-Regulation. *Bulletin of the Menninger Clinic,* 58, 145–68.

Way, I.F. (1999) Adolescent Sexual Offenders: the Role of Cognitive and Emotional Victim Empathy in the Victim-To-Victimiser Process. *Dissertation Abstracts International,* 61(01), 367. (University Microforms No. Aat 9959970)

Way, I. (2001) Childhood Maltreatment Histories of Male Adolescents With Sexual Offending Behaviours: Review of the Literature, in Calder, M.C. (Ed.) *Young People Who Sexually Abuse: Building the Evidence Base for Your Practice,* Lyme Regis: Russell House Publishing. 26–55.

Way, I.F. and Balthazor, T.B. (1990) *A Manual for Structured Group Treatment With Adolescent Sexual Offenders.* Notre Dame, In: Jalice Publishers.

Way, I.F. and Spieker, S.D. (1997) *Cycle of Offence: A Framework for Treating Adolescent Sexual Offenders.* Notre Dame, In: Jalice Publishers.

Webster, S.D. and Beech, A.R. (2000) The Nature of Sexual Offenders' Affective Empathy: A Grounded Theory Analysis. *Sexual Abuse: A Journal of Research and Treatment,* 12, 249–61.

Wiehe, V.R. (1986) Empathy and Locus of Control in Child Abusers. *Journal of Social Service Research,* 9, 17–30.

Williams, C.A. (1990) Biopsychosocial Elements of Empathy: A Multidimensional Model. *Issues in Mental Health Nursing,* 11, 155–74.

Worling, J. (2002, November) Risk Assessment and Treatment Issues for Sexually Aggressive Youth. Presentation At the Michigan Sharing Conference, Windsor, Ontario.

Zahn-Waxler, C. and Radke-Yarrow, M. (1990) The Origins of Empathic Concern. *Motivation and Emotion,* 14, 107–30.

Zeidner, M., Matthews, G., Roberts, R.D. and McCann, C. (2003) Development of Emotional Intelligence: Towards a Multi-Level Investment Model. *Human Development,* 46, 69–96.

Information on emotional literacy courses:
The Collaborative for the Advancement of Social and Emotional Learning (Casl), Department of Psychology (M/C 285), University of Illinois At Chicago, 1007 W. Harrison St., Chicago, Il, 60606–7137.

Chapter Eleven

Considerations for the Assessment of Female Sexually Abusive Youth

Susan L. Robinson

Assessment is an art; unfortunately there is no unique formula.

Saradjian and Hanks, 1996: p207.

Overview

Sexually abusive behaviour committed by girls is an existing problem that has received insufficient attention. Consequently, there have been few treatment programmes or assessment tools specifically designed to meet the needs of this population. The existing models of treatment and assessment are based on working with males. These models originated from working with adult male incarcerated sex offenders and subsequently were adapted to meet the needs of residential and outpatient sexually abusive male youth. Because there were relatively few girls entering the system for sexual offending behaviour, few perceived a need to tailor programming to girls. Others assumed that the treatment and assessment would be the same. This belief, although slowly changing, remains prevalent today, despite the increased number of arrests for female juvenile sexual offending behaviour (Poe-Yamagata and Butts, 1996). In 1997, female juveniles accounted for 2% of the 5,500 juvenile arrests for forcible rape and 9% of the 18,500 juvenile arrests for other sex offences (excluding prostitution) in the United States alone (Snyder and Sickmund, 1999). This amounts to 1,775 female juvenile arrests for sexual offending behaviour in one year. Given the increase in girls entering the judicial system for sexual offending behaviour, the development of assessment and treatment models are necessary, ones that take into account female development and the dynamics of female juvenile sexual aggression.

While it is true that there are many commonalities among juvenile males and females who sexually abuse, there are gender differences that need to be considered. Because the development and socialisation process of females and males differs, the questions asked and information gleaned from the assessment process

will, at times, be different. This chapter focuses on the development of a differential assessment for sexual offending female youth with the idea that such an assessment will further an understanding of the needs, issues, and risk factors unique to this population. In an effort to determine how the assessment process may diverge from one geared towards male sexual offending juveniles, this chapter examines the differences between male and female development, and juvenile male and female sexual offending behaviour. The literature on female adolescent sexuality and aggression are also discussed in order to augment awareness of the areas warranting consideration in the assessment process of these girls. Furthermore, the current risk assessments and their applicability to juvenile females are explored. Suggestions are then offered for the development of a future risk assessment specific to sexually abusive female youth. The chapter concludes with an assessment guideline and a listing of some assessment tools that can be useful for this population.

Literature review

Although a body of literature exists on female juvenile sexual aggression (Bumby and Bumby, 1997; Fehrenbach and Monastersky, 1988; Higgs, Canavan, Meyer, 1992; Hunter et al., 1993; Johnson, 1989; Mathews, Hunter and Vuz, 1997; Ray and English, 1995; Scavo, 1989; Turner and Turner, 1994) there is an absence of information about assessment as it applies to this population. For example, in one chapter on female sexual abusers, the need for a comprehensive assessment of sexually abusive female adolescents is underscored, but it does not state how this comprehensive assessment should be conducted (Minasian and Lewis, 1999). The chapter further maintains the necessity for the development of assessment tools specific to females. Johnson (1989) also noted a need to develop specific tools and risk criteria for assessing sexually abusive girls. Bumby and Bumby (1997) suggested that risk factors, which should be considered in the assessment and treatment of sexually abusing girls, include depression, suicidal ideation, anxiety, poor self-concept, and childhood sexual victimisation. Finally, Hunter and Mathews (1997) conclude that the assessment of both female sexual offending adults and young people should be conducted knowing that female sexual offending behaviour often occurs in a broader context of psychiatric and psychosocial impairments. They continue to note the lack of gender-specific assessment tools; there are none that are standardised or normed on the female sexual offending population.

The literature available on non-sex offending adjudicated female young people also offers relatively little to guide the assessment process. Acoca and Dedel (1998) advocate for a comprehensive needs based assessment for girls involved with the juvenile justice system which takes into account of their physical and mental health, substance use and abuse related needs, educational and vocational needs, and needs related to their involvement in gangs and the juvenile justice system. Acoca's (1995) Interview Protocol (as included in Acoca and Dedel, 1998) is a tool utilised to broadly assess these girls. Other tools are also available (Ereth and Gramling, 2003; National Council on Crime and Delinquency, 1999), however, because they are not specific to sexual offending female juveniles, they have limited use for the assessment of this population.

Developmental considerations

In order to conduct a thorough assessment of a female who sexually abuses, it is important to understand some of the differences between male and female development. Female development is a relational development; that is, females derive their identity through their relationships and connections with others (Brown and Gilligan, 1992; Gilligan, 1982; Gilligan, Lyons, Hammer, 1990; Jordan et al., 1991; Miller and Stiver, 1997). Surrey (1991) describes this development as 'self-in-relation'. Comparatively, research on male development indicates males tend to develop their identities through independence, separation, and autonomy (Erikson, 1950, 1968; Kohlberg, 1981; Levinson, 1978). Girls tend to be interpersonally oriented due to their relational

development; boys have more of an instrumental orientation geared towards action and achievement. This relational development is important to nurture with girls for their overall mental health and sense of identity.

Another area where juvenile males and females tend to differ is in the way they manage their feelings. Girls are socialised to internalise their feelings more than boys. Harris, Blum and Resnick (1991) discuss how adolescent girls engage in behaviours of 'quiet disturbance', i.e., eating disorders or suicide attempts, whereas boys tend to externalise their feelings, which can lead to more overt aggressive behaviours and diagnoses that are consistent with an externalisation process, i.e., Conduct Disorder, Oppositional Defiant Disorder, Attention Deficit and Hyperactivitiy Disorder (Harris, Blum and Resnick, 1991; Leschied et al., 2000; Loeber and Stouthamer-Loeber, 1998; Perry, 1995; Perry et al., 1996). Given this internalisation process, it is not surprising that depression is significant in the lives of female adolescents. Approximately one in four girls experience symptoms of depression (Commonwealth Fund, 1997), a rate that is 50% higher than seen in adolescent boys. Problems with body image are also markedly higher for adolescent girls than boys (Commonwealth Fund, 1997).

Anger is one emotion that tends to be processed and manifested differently in males and females (Brown, 1998; Lamb, 2001; Lerner, 1988; Simmons, 2002). The cultural script teaches girls that anger is not acceptable. Girls are 'supposed' to be 'sugar and spice and everything nice'. Because of this unrealistic expectation, many girls learn to deny, suppress, and hide their anger. Simmons (2002) maintains that because our culture disallows the overt expression of conflict for girls, they learn to release anger in alternative ways. For some girls, their internalised anger results in depression.

For other girls, their anger is expressed through relational aggression. Relational aggression (also referred to as indirect or social aggression) is defined as a covert form of aggression that uses relationships as weapons (Simmons, 2002). It is aggression that is harming to others by damaging relationships. Research indicates that adolescent girls are more likely to adopt this form of aggression than adolescent boys (Bjorkqvist, Lagerspetz and Kaukianen; Owens and MacMullin; Pakaslanhti and Keltikangas-Jarvinen, as cited in Leschied et al., 2000). Forms of this aggression include rumour spreading, the silent treatment, name-calling, backbiting, exclusion, manipulation, and nonverbal gesturing.

Male aggression is often physical in nature; relational aggression is more psychological and threatens what is most important to girls and their development-relationships. It threatens affiliation and connection and it is effective because of girls' fears of abandonment, rejection, and isolation.

Self-confidence is another area of gender difference. As girls mature into their high school years, their self-confidence decreases; yet for boys, it increases (American Association of University Women [AAUW], 1995; Orenstein, 1994). In the Commonwealth Fund Survey of the Health of Adolescent Girls (1997), only 39% of girls demonstrated a high level of confidence. Those at greatest risk for this self-confidence loss are Caucasian, Hispanic and Asian-American girls. African-American girls are more likely to sustain their confidence as they mature (Sadker and Sadker, 1994).

A loss of voice, the loss of a pre-adolescent authentic self, and the development of a false self are discussed in the literature on female adolescence (Brown and Gilligan, 1992; Gilligan, 1982; Hancock, 1984; Pipher, 1994; Shandler, 1999; Stern, 1991). Pipher (1994) regards female adolescence as a time when girls 'crash and burn in a social and developmental Bermuda Triangle' (p19). Stern (1991) refers to a 'disavowing' of the self that occurs during this life stage. Freud (as cited in Stern, 1991) observed female adolescence as a 'fresh wave of repression.' It is from this loss of self and voice that girls develop a chameleon identity as a result of sociocultural scripts that direct them to be desirable, liked, and fit in; girls acting in this manner can easily become what they perceive others want them to be. This is one way girls protect themselves from relationship loss and rejection. The unfortunate result, however, is that they may eventuate weakly constructed identities since their identities change depending upon who they are with and what environment they are in.

Additionally, substance abuse differs among adolescent males and females. Among 12–17-year-olds, females surpass males in the use of cigarettes, cocaine, crack, inhalants, and non-medical use of prescription drugs (The National Clearinghouse for Alcohol and Drug Information, 2001). Girls who regularly smoke marijuana are at a higher risk for infertility problems and raised testosterone levels. Alcohol abuse also causes menstrual and fertility problems for girls, and may impede adolescent maturation. Substance abusing girls are at greater risk for unwanted pregnancies, unwanted and unprotected sex, and sexually transmitted diseases (The National Clearinghouse for Alcohol and Drug Information, 2001).

Assessing the cultural sexual script

Perhaps one of the greatest areas of difference between female and male adolescence has to do with the sociocultural scripts each gender receives pertaining to sexuality. The literature on adolescent female sexuality speaks of rigid gender constructions, societal pressures, and the silencing of female sexuality (Fine, 1988; Lamb, 2001; Thompson, 1990, 1995; Tolman, 1991, 1994, 1999, 2001, 2002; Wolf, 1997). The overwhelming conclusion emanating from this work is that adolescent girls are largely unaware of, and unsure about, their sexuality. However, attaining sexual subjectivity is an adolescent developmental task (Tolman, 2002). Sexuality for teenage girls is often hidden and ignored; it becomes buried underneath scripts of how girls are taught to behave. Girls often learn how to pleasure boys before they learn how to pleasure themselves. A girl's body remains her own unexplored territory; she learns the topography of her body largely through her interactions with the opposite sex (Farber, 2002). In this respect, learning about her sexuality becomes an afterthought, secondary to pleasing her partners. As Wolf (1997) writes, during female adolescence sex becomes a 'performance for the benefit of boys' (p70). In other words, female adolescents become sexually accommodating. Girls become objects and fail to be the sexual subjects of their own lives. They want to be wanted (Young-Eisendrath, 1999) and are willing to become objects because their self-worth may become dependent upon the degree they are successful at being objects for the opposite sex.

Additionally, it is through an unawareness of their own anatomy and arousal that girls subordinate their needs and act dishonestly (i.e., by feigning pleasure) to please their partners. Many teenage girls sacrifice their right to achieve an orgasm or their right to request further exploration and stimulation to learn what feels good (Tolman, 2002). It is incongruent that many girls do not learn to take ownership over their sexual selves and desires, yet they perceive themselves as responsible for what occurs in their sexual relationships, and will blame themselves for not performing sexually 'good enough' to keep their boyfriends interested. One client of this author recently demonstrated this responsibility by stating, 'Girls must know how to do everything while having sex or it is their fault.'

Our culture also teaches girls that to be 'good,' they should be sexually passive. This sanctioned script purports that girls should not appear sexually demanding or too knowledgeable; rather, they should be desirable, not desiring (Tolman, 2002). This pressure to act inexperienced and naïve prevents girls from developing negative reputations. Girls who show sexual initiative, drive, and confidence are often viewed as 'sluts,' whereas the same attributes for males are seen as acceptable, expected, and normal. The script that girls should be inexperienced makes it difficult for girls to navigate their own desires. They have no compass guiding their sexual rights. Masturbation, for example, is still something that is rarely discussed among girls; consequently, many girls are left feeing guilty, abnormal, or dirty after masturbating, which results in diminished pleasure. Not only is female adolescent sexuality dampened due to fears of negative labelling, but also because of fears of male sexual aggression; if they hide their sexuality, girls believe they may be able to protect themselves from becoming possible targets of male sexual violence.

The final result of the silencing of female adolescent sexuality is that a girl, who has desire, may perceive herself as deviant (Lamb, 2001). And as Lamb (2001) concludes, 'Sexual shame drives girls to do such things in closets and behind closed doors' (p58). By examining the literature on female adolescent sexuality, clues may be rendered to explain how these gendered pressures and expectations relate to female sexual aggression. The question is: What can female adolescent sexuality tell us about female adolescent sexual aggression, and what implications does this have for the assessment of a sexually abusive female adolescent? This will be discussed in the section addressing juvenile females' motivations for sexual offending behaviour.

The pathway to female aggression

Another important area to understand for assessment purposes is the developmental pathways to female aggression. Assessment includes determining the pathway for each sexually abusive female juvenile; the underlying pathway is then considered in the development of individualised treatment needs and goals. One of the risk factors for psychopathology in females may be early maturation (Stattin and Magnusson, as cited in Loeber and Stouthamer-Loeber, 1998), especially when there are other risk factors present (Caspi and Moffit, as cited in Loeber and Stouthamer-Loeber, 1998). As Levene et al. (2001) describe, early maturation can lead to sexualised behaviours; these girls may enter, through their affiliations with older boys, situations for which they are not developmentally prepared (sexual activity and intimate relationships).

Also important in the development of female aggression is the gender paradox that has been described by Loeber and Keenan (1994). Although boys are more often diagnosed with conduct disorder and attention deficit and hyperactivity disorder (ADHD), a girl who is diagnosed with either has a poorer prognosis in terms of psychiatric outcomes. Szatmari, Boyle and Offord (as cited in Loeber and Stouthamer-Loeber, 1998) found that girls diagnosed with attention deficit disorder were more likely than boys to develop conduct disorder. Similarly, Cohen (as cited in Loeber and Stouthamer-Loeber, 1998) found that a diagnosis of conduct disorder in girls was more likely to lead to the development of personality disorders.

Given the importance of this gender paradox in the pathway of female aggression, it is imperative to be cognisant of the different manifestations of ADHD and conduct disorder in girls and boys for assessment purposes. Researchers argue that girls with ADHD have been under identified because the symptom presentation in girls typically reflects inattention rather than the overt behavioural problems more often exhibited among boys (Biederman et al., 1999; Brown et al., as cited in Levene et al., 2001). Peer rejection, social isolation, difficulties with forming and maintaining relationships, and a lack of involvement in activities have also found to be problematic in girls having ADHD. Biederman et al. (1999) found that 45% of girls with ADHD also exhibit co-morbid diagnoses such as disruptive behaviour disorders, mood disorders, anxiety disorders, and substance abuse. Moreover, males with conduct disorder will exhibit confrontational behaviours such as fighting and stealing, yet girls with this diagnosis, are more likely to engage in less confrontational behaviours such as lying, prostitution, substance abuse, running away, and truancy (American Psychiatric Association, 2000).

Two other prominent pathways for the development of female delinquent behaviour are depression and victimisation. Depression is viewed as a more significant pathway for girls than it is for boys (Obeidallah and Earls, 1999). Leschied et al. (2000) found that young, depressed girls were nearly four times more likely to be aggressive than boys. A lower level of Serotonin, which occurs with depression, is also linked to addiction and aggression. Likewise, Acoca and Dedel (1998) maintain, 'victimisation is *the* critical dynamic underlying girls' involvement in crime and other problem behaviours' (p116). In their study, 92% of the girls reported experiencing emotional, physical, and/or sexual abuse. Trauma can lead to compromised self-regulation and increased aggression. A diagnosis of posttraumatic stress disorder (PTSD) further leads to high distress levels and low self-restraint (Cauffman et al., 1998) and therefore, increases the risk of behavioral problems and offending behaviors. Not surprisingly, the rate of PTSD is higher for incarcerated female delinquents than incarcerated male delinquents. Cauffman et al. (1998) found that their sample of incarcerated juvenile females were 50% more likely to exhibit current PTSD symptomatology than incarcerated juvenile males.

Research further indicates that the presence of criminal behaviours among family members and extended family members has a greater influence on the development of a negative trajectory and antisocial values in girls than boys (Cloninger, Christiansen, Reich and Gottesman, 1978; Funk, 1999). Additionally, poor relationships with parents (Funk, 1999), particularly mothers (Pakashlahti et al., as cited in Levene et al., 2001), and a lack of caregiver continuity (Levene et al., 2001), also appear to correlate more to female delinquency than boys. Further, Levene et al. (2001) note that disliked girls are at high risk for developing antisocial behaviours. Aggressive girls, given their lack of compliance with gender norms and stereotypes, are even more likely to experience peer ostracism. Because female development is relationally based, the impact of interpersonal difficulties (i.e., social isolation and peer rejection) is more likely to be negative for girls. When the relational development of girls is compromised, psychopathology can develop.

There are also studies indicating that girls require a higher number of risk factors for aggression to develop (Cloninger, Christiansen, Reich and Gottesman, 1978; Mannuzza and Gittelman, as cited in Loeber and Stouthamer-Loeber, 1998). Regarding female adolescent sex offending behaviour, Mathews, Hunter and Vuz (1997) conclude, 'biological and socialisation factors create a higher threshold for the externalisation of experienced developmental trauma in females than males' (p194).

Protective factors for girls

Many protective factors for girls relate to their relational development. Levene et al. (2001) note, through examining various studies, that a positive relationship with an adult outside a girl's immediate family, i.e., a teacher-child relationship, is a significant protective factor for girls. Flansburg (1991) also noted that a girl's self-esteem could increase given one non-exploitive relationship with an adult. A healthy relationship with one's mother is a protective factor for girls (Harris, Blum and Resnick, 1991) as is having close friends (Werner and Smith, as cited in Levene et al., 2001). As Gilgun (1990) states, 'The underlying factor of protective mechanisms is human relationship' (p180). Interestingly, girls have the advantage with protective factors given their socialisation: Girls learn to identify and express their feelings more so than boys; adults support the expression of feelings in girls; and, emotional expressiveness is the single most important protective factor (J. Gilgun, personal communication, June 15, 2003).

Problem-solving abilities have also been noted to be protective for girls (Keltikangas-Jaervinen and Pakaslahti, as cited in Levene et al., 2001). Additionally, academic success has a positive impact on girls' self-esteem and protects them from engaging in negative behaviours (Flansburg, 1991; Mazorell, as cited in Levene et al., 2001). Finally, in citing studies by Heimer and Perry et al., Levene et al. (2001) note that the acceptance of gender normative beliefs and definitions is a protective factor specific to girls. It may also be that girls who do not lose their ability to voice and assert themselves during adolescence, when so many girls forfeit their voice for passive social constructions, are also better protected from developing negative trajectories because they are true to themselves and their self-esteem stays intact. Other protective factors to be aware of in the assessment of juvenile females are those also noted in the literature to be helpful for males: resilience, an ability to self-soothe (self-regulation), a positive sense of self, and the capacity to envision a positive future (Gilgun, 2001).

Differences between juvenile male and females with sexual offending behaviour

Although there have been a few comparative studies conducted on female and male sexual offending juveniles, it is important to understand that these findings are preliminary and should not be considered conclusive due to the limitations of these studies (i.e., small sample sizes, a reliance on self-reporting, possible clinician bias, and the use of non-randomised sampling procedures). Nevertheless, evaluators and treatment providers should be aware of these suggested differences during the assessment process, otherwise they may fail to recognise dynamics that are unique and important to female juvenile offending behaviour. Perhaps the most consistent and striking finding for sexually abusive female juveniles, is the high rates of victimisation they have experienced compared to sexually abusive juvenile males (Bumby and Bumby, 1997; Mathews, Hunter and Vuz, 1997; Miccio-Fonseca, 2000; Ray and English, 1995). Sexually abusive girls are also more likely to be abused at younger ages (Mathews, Hunter and Vuz, 1997; Miccio-Fonseca, 2000), by more than one perpetrator (Bumby and Bumby, 1997; Mathews, Hunter and Vuz, 1997) and experience more severe abuse (Mathews, Hunter and Vuz, 1997; Ray and English, 1995). Ray and English (1995) found that girls exhibited higher rates of sexual abuse histories than boys (94% versus 85%), and were more likely to have experienced multiple types of abuse (94% versus 86%). Mathews, Hunter and Vuz (1997) found from their sample that 77.6% of sexually abuse girls reported sexual abuse histories, compared to 44.3% of sexually abusive boys.

Furthermore, the negative sequalae of experienced trauma, leads to the development of co-morbid diagnoses. Females, more so than males, are more likely to develop mental health disturbances as a result of trauma (Breslau et al., Dembo et al., Horowitz et al., Dessler et al., as cited in Cauffman et al., 1998), and are six times more likely to develop PTSD (Giaconia et al., as cited in Cauffman et al., 1998). In the Commonwealth Fund Survey of the Health of Adolescent Girls (1997), girls with abuse histories were approximately twice as likely to drink alcohol as non-abused girls. They were more likely to have used drugs, and more likely to have engaged in behaviours characteristic of eating disorders, i.e., binging and purging (32% versus 12%). They were twice as likely to have low self-confidence (57% versus 27%). Girls with abuse histories also tend to be psychosomatic and have issues about their body (Commonwealth Fund, 1997). Perry (1995) and Perry et al. (1996) have found that girls will adapt to trauma by resorting to dissociation, whereas boys adapt to trauma through hyper arousal. Thus, males develop more externalising symptoms; females develop more internalising ones. Because many sexually abusive girls have extensive trauma histories, diagnoses such as posttraumatic stress disorder, depression, anxiety, and eating disorders are more the norm than not. Likewise, self-destructive behaviours, especially cutting and suicidal gestures are common. On the other hand, boys who sexually abuse may display a wider variety of criminal behaviour and defiance.

Another important negative impact of trauma to be aware of during the assessment of a juvenile female is the development of attachment disturbances. Bartholomew (1990) developed a four-category model of attachment styles based on a positive and negative view of self and others. Although adolescents, given their identities are still developing, may not clearly fit into one of these categories, traits can be discerned and for some, attachment styles appear to be in place. Two of these four attachment styles seem particularly relevant to sexually abusive juvenile females: preoccupied and fearful. These two styles can culminate into destructive relational patterns. The preoccupied attachment style is characterised by a negative view of self and a positive view of others. Female over-dependency and abusive relationships are possible outcomes for those possessing this attachment style. This author has found that female juveniles who sexually abuse tend to be more dependent in their relationships than boys. They are more likely to enter dysfunctional, chaotic, and abusive intimate peer relationships where they are victimised. Moreover, their dependency keeps them from leaving abusive relationships because of their fear of abandonment and loneliness. For some sexually abusive girls, as is true for adult females who sexually offend, their dependency may also be linked to their sexual offending behaviour because of an inability to assert themselves for fear of losing a relationship. Likewise, a negative view of self and others denotes a fearful attachment style whereby the person is socially avoidant and fearful of intimacy. Because females are more often the victims of abuse (i.e., sexual), female juveniles seem more likely to adopt a fearful attachment style than males. It is also from these two attachment styles that females frequently act as chameleons. Although the chameleon presentation often occurs among female adolescents for reasons described earlier, chameleon identities also develop as a result of trauma. A chameleon presentation reflects hyper vigilance, a symptom of posttraumatic stress disorder, and is a coping strategy utilised to optimise survival. It is a means of ensuring safety by blending into abusive environments rather than standing out or 'rocking the boat,' so to speak.

Girls that sexually abuse often lack positive female role models (Mathews, Hunter and Vuz, 1997). It is not coincidental that many mothers of sexually abusive girls have a history of displaying poor sexual boundaries and discussing their sexual problems with their daughters. Johnson (1989) found that many of the mothers of girls in her sample had been victims of domestic violence and sexual abuse, and/or had substance abuse issues. Over dependency, enmeshment, and role reversals were common in the mother-daughter relationships. Turner and Turner (1994) found that the mother-daughter relationships in their sample were characterised by enmeshment, malevolent attachments and abandonment. In some cases, the girl was in a parentified role and was her mother's caretaker. In this author's experience, few female sexually abusing females display healthy relationships with their mothers. Instead, the girls have typically experienced real abandonment or have perceived their mothers as having emotionally abandoned them. In some cases, the mother sacrifices her own daughter to maintain an unhealthy relationship with a male partner who is sexually perpetrating on her daughter. Given the importance of the same sex parent to role model for their child and the significant deficits apparent in many of these

mother-daughter relationships, the mother-daughter relationship is an important facet of the assessment process.

Sexually abusive female juveniles are also viewed differently than sexually abusive male juveniles. Whereas male juvenile sexual aggression is seen as more 'typical,' (because male adolescents are often viewed as being overpowered by their sexual impulses), females who commit sexual offences have often been regarded as victims who were acting out their own victimisation and therefore in need of help for their victimisation issues, or as psychiatrically ill requiring psychiatric intervention (Allen, 1990). Furthermore, girls are less likely than boys to enter the criminal justice system for sexual offending behaviour (Ray and English, 1995). This is due, in part, to an overall denial of the criminal justice system to acknowledge that juvenile female sexual offending behaviour exists because it defies the traditional belief that females are protectors, not abusers. This gender bias is particularly prevalent with sexual offences perpetrated on peers: Although girls may sexually harass or abuse peers, they are far less likely than boys to be adjudicated for sexual offending on peers. The lack of programmes available to meet the needs of these girls also results in fewer sentencing options for the adjudicated female juvenile. Conversely, female juveniles who are labelled as 'bad' girls for defying sociocultural scripts that espouse how 'good' girls ought to sexually behave, may be punished for overt defiance. Historically, female juveniles have more often been adjudicated for status offences for sexual transgressions than boys (Chesney-Lind, 1997); one explanation for this is so girls are pressured to comply with the sociocultural script. Girls committing sexual offences are not only violating victims, but are violating the traditional female sexual role as nurturers and caretakers; this may result in stiffer sentences for some girls who are made examples of by the criminal justice system.

Additionally, because there is more documented sexual abuse committed by males and more sexually abusive boys are involved in the criminal justice system, girls with sexual offending behaviours often feel isolated and alone. A sexually abusive girl may initially believe she is the only girl that has offended. She may perceive herself as 'bad' because she has not acted in a manner consistent with how girls are taught to behave. Because of this, the internalisation of shame appears higher for girls who sexually offend (Robinson, 2002). Similarly, parents of a sexually abusive girl may experience more shame and embarrassment over their daughter's behaviour and are less likely to understand how their daughter could have engaged in such behaviour. Accepting sexual abuse has occurred can be a greater difficulty for these parents. Parents of sexually abusive girls are also more likely to blame their daughter's behaviour as a result of known or unknown sexual victimisation.

There are other notable differences. Girls are more likely to sexually abuse someone they know, most often in the context of caretaking (Bumby and Bumby, 1997; Fehrenbach and Monastersky, 1998; Margolin, 1991), and are, therefore, less likely to abuse strangers (Mathews, Hunter and Vuz, 1997). Additionally, girls appear more likely to resort to caretaking and altruistic cognitive distortions to justify their behaviour and will explain their offending behaviour as an act of altruism due to their caretaking nature. For example, one girl reported that her reason for offending was to prepare her sister for being sexually abused by their stepfather. Another girl stated her sexual contact with her sister was her way of fulfilling a motherly role by helping her sister overcome masturbation: 'I thought if she lays on top of me, I can ask her why. I wanted to help the situation and that's why I put her on top of me.' A few studies also indicate that females tend to use less force or violence than males when sexually abusing (Matthews, 1993; Ray and English, 1995) and are less likely to perpetrate the act of rape (Ray and English, 1995). Girls, however, appear more likely to steal and engage in temper tantrums (Ray and English, 1995). Moreover, it is rare for female juveniles to force others to sexually abuse with them. This is a dynamic that occurs more often with male offenders and many adult female offenders fit into the typology of a male coerced (Mathews, Matthews and Speltz, 1989, 1990) or male accompanied offender (Syed and Williams, 1996). Finally, a few studies indicate that girls will sexually abuse at younger ages than boys (Johnson, 1989; Ray and English, 1995).

Juvenile females' motivations for sexual offending behaviour

The reasons for and motivations behind sexual offending among males and females may also

differ. Traditionally, the male model of sex offending behaviour has viewed sexual aggression as stemming from a need to have power and control and/or be sexually gratified. However, research on adult and juvenile sex offending females indicates that females do not abuse as often for sexual reasons as males (Connor et al., as cited in Hunter and Mathews, 1997; Davin, 1999; Dunbar, 1999; Finkelhor and Russell, 1984; Johnson, 1989; Saradjian and Hanks, 1996; Turner and Turner, 1994).

Although sexually abusive males may abuse as a reaction to their own sexual victimisation (or at least in part), the correlation between victimisation and sexually abusive behaviour appears stronger for sexually abusive females. This seems to reflect the fact that sexually abusive females tend to have more extensive sexual abuse histories than males. Furthermore, it is important to assess the outcome of the disclosure of a girl's own sexual abuse history (if it was previously disclosed). Johnson (1989) found that all the girls in her sample had sexual abuse histories and none of these girls had supportive and positive experiences disclosing their own histories of abuse. The development of female juvenile sex offending behaviour often appears to stem from an environmental context unsupportive and disbelieving of a girl's own sexual victimisation. For some girls, sex offending may be a way to get someone to notice that they have been sexually abused as a response to a caretaker's failure to protect and believe them. For example, one client described her offence as a cry for help; she wanted someone to stop her mother's boyfriend from sexually assaulting her. Although she had previously told her mother, her mother failed to intervene because she did not believe her daughter's disclosure.

Given the relational development of females, female sex offending may be a form of relational aggression (Lamb, 2001; Leschied et al., 2000; Loeber and Stouthamer-Loeber, 1998; Simmons, 2002). Although by definition sexual offending behavior is not the kind of conduct categorised as relational aggression, it is aggression, and it is relational in that the behaviour may be a way to attempt to connect with a particular person (not necessarily the victim), or disconnect from a relationship (Robinson, 2002). Turner and Turner (1994) viewed juvenile female sexual aggression as a way to maintain relationships and noted that all the girls in their sample were 'striving to establish relationships' (p17). They additionally stated, 'It is from the relationship aspect of victimisation that a female may commit abuse. That is, identifying with one's aggressor, taking on his or her characteristics, is a way of staying in the relationship' (p16). They also hypothesised that girls sexually abused as one avenue to differentiate themselves from their enmeshed, victim-identified mothers. Johnson (1989) and Turner and Turner (1994) both found that for some girls, their sexual offending behaviour appeared to be a reaction to their mothers' victimisation stance and over dependency on their daughters. Other girls simply describe sex offending as a means of finding a connection with someone. For example, one client maintained, 'I was lonely and wanted someone to be sexual with me. I wanted to feel close to someone and be touched.' Another stated, 'I felt lonely and angry . . . If I did this then I would be closer to them and less lonely.' Additionally, a different client said, 'I abused so . . . I could feel that someone cared and loved me.'

This author has found a strong correlation between real or perceived maternal loss and offending behaviour. In some instances, the girl's offending is a way to express anger towards her mother. One client stated that part of her motivation to sexually abuse her younger siblings was because of 'not feeling loved by mother . . . I chose them because they were taking all the attention away from my mom. I was jealous of them.' Howley (2001) also found anger to be a motivating factor in approximately 60% of her sample of 66 juvenile females; consistent with this author's experience, Howley found the anger was primarily directed towards the girls' main caretakers. Similarly, other girls offend to elicit the attention they believe has been insufficient from their mothers; consequently, offending becomes a tool to re-establish the mother-daughter relationship. One client said, 'I wanted my mom to pay more attention to me than the boys.' Another one stated, 'I wasn't getting enough attention . . . If I get these kids alone and I do something bad with them then maybe my mom will pay more attention to me instead of her boyfriend'. This is not to negate the role or attachment to fathers, however, the attachment or lack of attachment to the mother appears much more significant in the lives of these girls because of the importance these attachments have in the development of their identities. Likewise, for boys, the attachment and relationship to their fathers may play a more crucial role as an antecedent variable to sexual aggression.

It is important to note that the language used for describing the motivations behind sex offending has historically neglected attachment and relational dynamics despite the research that has been conducted in this area (Marshall, Hudson and Hodkinson, 1993; Ward et al., 1995). It may be that male sex offending is significantly more relational than clinicians have previously believed, however, because treatment providers have traditionally looked through a lens of power and control, other explanations have been overlooked. Although relational dynamics are present in male sexual aggression, perhaps due to their relational orientation, females are better able to describe their behaviour in relational terms.

Because one of the primary differences between juvenile males and females has to do with the different sociocultural scripts and subsequent pressures they receive, it is important to assess for each sexually abusive girl, if and to what extent these sociocultural influences relate to her offending behaviour. Is female adolescent sexual aggression a reaction to, and rejection of, the cultural script that teaches girls to suppress and hide their own sexuality, and place the sexual needs of males above their own? How many sexually abusive girls reject the current constructions of female adolescent sexuality and adopt alternative avenues (i.e., sexual abuse) to explore their sexuality or sexual orientation? This author proposes that for some girls, sexually abusive behaviour may be a rejection of cultural norms that teach girls to be silent and unaware of their own sexuality.

For example, a girl who sexually offends may be claiming experiential knowledge of her own body, needs, and desires, on her own terms. She may be defying the passive construction of female sexuality, refusing to subordinate her desires, trying to take ownership of her sexuality and find her own pleasure, and rejecting the compulsory heterosexuality script (Rich, 1984), albeit at the expense of a victim. One client described her reason for offending by stating, 'I could learn more about sex in my own terms.' Another client described her reason for sexual offending as a means to explore her sexual identity. Peers at school were referring to her as a lesbian and teasing her. She was not sure if she was at the time, but she certainly did not want to have sexual contact with female peers, leaving her more open to ridicule and exclusion. Her decision to sexually abuse two boys for whom she babysat, was a way for her to see if she could be sexually aroused by males. Moreover, many girls are worried about being labelled a slut if they appear too sexually desiring, therefore, for some sexually abusive girls who victimise a younger child, they may be engaging in such behaviour to avoid getting labelled a slut by their peers. Furthermore, since many girls learn to be submissive in their interpersonal relationships, perhaps sexual abuse for some is a means for them to attain the more traditional view of sexual aggression: power and control. It can also become a means for girls to protect themselves from exploitation, particularly for those with sexual victimisation histories. For example, one client described her sexual aggression by stating: 'I will not be a victim or place myself in a position to be victimised.' Her choice was to be the victimiser instead; that way she did not have to worry about being used or treated as an object.

The assessment of any girl with sexual offending behaviour should include asking her about her motivation to offend and what it was a means to achieve, for example, a means to: establish or injure a relationship, express buried anger, learn about her sexuality and be in control over her body, protect herself from being victimised, or a combination of the above. Remembering that sexual abuse rarely occurs from a single motivation but instead a combination of various factors is important so that each one can be adequately addressed in treatment.

Considering preliminary typologies

Typologies can be useful to determine the aetiology of and motivations underlying sexual aggression. Further, typologies assist in the identification of treatment needs and goals. Therefore, distinguishing which typology may be applicable to a sexually abusive juvenile female is one aspect of the assessment process. But given the lack of research conducted on girls, this is a difficult task. Research has been conducted to classify adult and adolescent sexually abusive males (Hunter et al., 2003; Knight and Prentky, 1990, 1993). There have also been categories developed for adult female offenders (Faller, 1995; Mathews, Matthews and Speltz, 1989; McCarty, 1986; Saradjian and Hanks, 1996), however, these categories are primarily based on descriptive data and have lacked the scientific rigor of studies conducted on males. Even fewer studies have attempted to develop typologies for

sexually abusive juvenile females (Mathews, Matthews and Speltz, 1990; Mathews, Hunter and Vuz, 1997). Mathews, Matthews and Speltz (1990) describe female adolescents as falling into three basic groups: intergenerational predisposed offenders, experimenters and exploiters, and male coerced offenders. The intergenerational predisposed offender was a typology initially generated from working with adult females (Mathews, Matthews and Speltz, 1989). These girls tend to have extensive sexual and physical abuse histories. They most often abuse relatives. The abuse tends to be repetitive and compulsive. Their reason for offending is significantly linked to their abuse histories and is abuse reactive in nature. These girls are often re-enacting their childhood sexual abuse trauma; their offending behaviour is similar to the behaviour perpetrated on them, and the age of their victims may be similar to the age they were when sexually victimised. Girls fitting into this typology have a multitude of deficits including poor boundaries, weak ego strength, and low self-esteem. They are described as more likely to abuse females; however, the gender of the victim is often determined by opportunity. Intergenerationally predisposed girls comprise the majority of sexually abusive juvenile females. The second group, experimenters and exploiters, are girls that offend often while babysitting on a male child on one occasion. They tend to be naïve and have not yet engaged in sexual behaviours with peers, nor do they feel safe to explore their sexuality with peer-aged males. They lack social skills and confidence in social settings.

Like the intergenerationally predisposed offender, their third typology, the male-coerced offender, was developed through their work on adult females (Mathews, Matthews and Speltz, 1989). In their 1990 study, only three adolescent females fit into this typology from their sample of 20 adolescent girls and one of those three was actually coerced to offend by a female peer, not a male. Similar to male-coerced adult females, girls fitting into this typology may be dependent, lacking self-esteem, and unassertive. Caution should be used in applying this typology to an adolescent female given the few numbers of girls falling into this group making the reliability of this subgroup more questionable than the others described. Second, by definition, the notion of a male-coerced offender diminishes a girl's responsibility in sex offending; it may be that she was not coerced but rather an equal participant who maintains she was forced in order to minimise or justify her culpability. The study conducted by Mathews, Hunter and Vuz (1997) consisting of 67 adolescent sexually abusive females did not identify any girls fitting into this category. This author, having worked with and evaluated approximately 80 sexually abusive juvenile females, has identified a few girls who sexually offended due to peer-influence. They most likely would not have sexually abused on their own accord; instead, they needed the influence of others in a specific situation to offend. For example, one client was dared by two peer-aged males to perform oral sex on a younger male. She was not coerced into doing so, nor did she describe complying to their wishes; she made a choice to abuse and was a willing participant in this offence.

Mathews, Hunter and Vuz (1997) did not develop typologies but rather, described three subgroups of girls in their sample from outpatient and residential treatment settings based on offence dynamics, background variables, and psychological profiles. Girls fitting into the offence dynamic subgroup (a small subgroup), most closely resemble those girls in the experimenter/exploiter typology in the former study. These girls offended on a single or few occasions with non-related children most often while babysitting. Their behaviour was motivated by sexual curiosity. They exhibited many strengths and lacked individual psychopathology. These girls did not have abuse histories or come from disturbed family backgrounds. From this author's perspective, girls fitting into this subgroup would also consist of those described earlier as defying sociocultural scripts; these are girls that are attempting to learn about sex and their sexuality without the pressure to behave in accordance with sexual norms. Blockage may be a motivating factor for their offending behaviour (Finkelhor, 1984).

The subgroup of girls based on background variables in Mathews, Hunter and Vuz's study (1997), consisted of approximately one-third of the outpatient girls in their sample. These girls are described as having mild to moderate levels of individual psychopathology. Additionally, histories of maltreatment and impaired family systems were noted. Most of these girls displayed personality strengths and appropriate social skills for their age, but they lacked sexual experiences with peers. They offended due to being triggered by their own sexual abuse histories; their offending was similar to the manner in which they were abused.

The final subgroup of girls, based on psychological profiles, were girls with moderate to severe levels of individual or family psychopathology (approximately half of their sample). The girls in this subgroup endured severe abuse and neglect. The abuse they perpetrated was often extensive and repetitive. Many of them had co-morbid diagnoses of depression, anxiety, conduct disorder, or posttraumatic stress disorder. They exhibited attachment and empathy deficits. These girls also had a tendency of coping with their abuse histories through their own sexualised presentations and behaviours. Some had deviant sexual arousal patterns.

Girls fitting into these last two subgroups are similar to the predisposed girls described in Mathews, Matthews and Speltz (1990). This author has also found a similar subgroup in her work and would add that many of these girls have an inchoate or disorganised identity. Additionally, this author has also worked with some girls who appear to fit into the experimenting/exploiting typology but also have a history of sexual abuse; however, their sexual abuse histories are not as severe or extensive as girls fitting into a typology of predisposed offending. Furthermore, their primary motivation to offend appears to be sexual curiosity. Their sexual offence does not seem to be triggered by their own victimisation; their abuse history may be one contributing factor, but it is not the most significant.

In conclusion, there is far more research needed in the development of female adolescent typologies. What can be discerned thus far is that the majority of young females who sexually abuse appear to be predisposed in some way due to extensive histories of abuse. They tend to have significant interpersonal and individual deficits and will have co-morbid diagnoses. A second subgroup reflects girls who are experimenting on or exploiting younger children due to their own naïveté, peer blockage, and lack of sexual confidence. Opportunity is the key to their offending behaviour, which often occurs in the context of babysitting. There may also be another subgroup of girls who are influenced by their peers and would not sexually offend without this situational influence.

When assessing a sexually abusive juvenile female, it is important to remember sexually abusive girls (like boys) are a heterogeneous group and clinicians should not be over eager to classify them, nor should typologies be used to label adolescents. Given that there needs to be far more research conducted in order to develop valid and reliable typologies for juvenile females, listening to the narratives these girls share during the assessment process, can help further an understanding of their behaviour and be beneficial in the future development of typologies.

Considerations for risk assessment

There is no risk assessment validated on female adult or juvenile offenders at this time. Studies done thus far on the recidivism of young people who sexually abuse have either not included females (Hagan and Cho, 1996; Sipe, Jensen and Everett, 1998; Smith and Monastersky, 1986), or have included relatively few (Kahn and Chambers, 1991; Lab, Shields and Schondel, 1993; Rasmussen, 1999; Worling and Curwen, 2000). Lab, Shields and Schondel's study (1993) included 151 males and 1 female. Rasmussen's study (1999) was based on 167 males and 3 females. The ratio of males to females in Kahn and Chambers's study (1991) based on 221 participants, was 20 to 1. In Prentky, Harris, Frizzell and Righthand's study (2000) of 96 juvenile sexual offenders, there was no mention of females being included in their sample or the possible differences in risk among females and males who offend. Because of the under-representation of female juveniles in the studies of juvenile sexual re-offence, the current juvenile risk assessment tools, such as the J-SOAP (Prentky et al., 2000) and ERASOR (Worling and Curwen, 2001) have been developed based on studies primarily consisting of male participants. The fact female juveniles have been underrepresented is understandable given the higher numbers of males adjudicated for sexual offending behaviour, however, in developing risk assessments it may not be accurate to presume that the risk factors correlated with male sex offending recidivism are the same for females. It stands to reason that the differences in male and female sexual aggression need to be considered when designing a risk assessment protocol.

It is concerning, then, that clinicians are left utilising risk assessments based on male offending to females. Although many of the risk factors for males appear to be applicable to females, such as having numerous victims, this author contends we do not yet have enough information on female juvenile offending to assume these factors equally apply to both sexes. For example, as Prentky et al. (2000) discuss, a history of sexual victimisation as a risk factor has, thus far, been inconclusive. However, as noted in the literature (Bumby and Bumby, 1997; Mathews, Hunter and Vuz, 1997; Miccio-Fonseca, 2000; Ray and English, 1995), females with sexually abusive behaviour are more likely to have been sexually abused in their childhoods than their male counterparts. Their histories often reflect severe abuse at young ages by multiple perpetrators. In some studies on adolescent females, all the girls had histories of sexual abuse victimisation, many quite severe (Bumby and Bumby, 1997; Hunter et al., 1993; Johnson, 1989). Therefore, it seems reasonable to conclude that a history of significant sexual trauma may be a risk factor for females. Sexual victimisation by a female aggressor may also be a factor worth examining for risk. In Mathews, Hunter and Vuz (1997), girls were three times more likely than boys to have been sexually abused by a female. In Hunter et al. (1993), 60% of the girls that offended were sexually abused by females. Howley (2001) also found that many girls in her sample had been molested by females. Perhaps girls who are sexually abused by females are at a heightened risk to repeat the behaviour due to the impact that the modelling of such behaviour has on their burgeoning identity.

Additionally, sexually abusive girls may also have higher levels of non-sexual victimisation in their childhoods. As previously noted, Ray and English (1995) found that girls outnumbered boys as having experienced multiple forms of abuse in their childhoods. Similarly, in Mathews, Hunter and Vuz (1997), more girls than boys had physical abuse histories. The extensive role modelling of aggression and the impact sustained from numerous trauma insults may make the offending behaviour even more intractable for girls with these histories. Therefore, a history consisting of high levels of multiple forms of abuse (sexual and non-sexual) could be a risk factor for girls.

Perhaps another risk factor that should be taken into account for juvenile females is the presence of co-morbid diagnoses. Leschied et al. (2000) found that aggressive girls often have co-morbid psychiatric diagnoses of depression, anxiety, and adjustment disorders, and have higher rates of suicidal ideation than boys. Many girls who sexually offend have histories of suicidal ideation or attempts (Bumby and Bumby, 1993; Hunter et al., 1993; Miccio-Fonesca, 2000). In Bumby and Bumby (1997) 58% of their female sample attempted suicide. In Hunter et al. (1993), 60% of their girls had a history of suicide attempts or ideation. Mathews, Hunter and Vuz (1997) also noted suicidal behaviours in a subgroup of girls. Furthermore, since many girls who offend have sexual abuse histories and meet the criteria for PTSD (Hunter et al., 1993; Bumby and Bumby, 1997), perhaps female sexual offending is associated with trauma re-enactment more so than boys and therefore, a diagnosis of PTSD would increase their risk level. Finally, because depression for girls leads to antisocial behaviour more so than it does for boys, it should be viewed as a risk factor for girls (Obedidallah and Earls, 1999). (Depression and anxiety were common in Johnson's sample (1989) of pre-adolescent girls.) Yet the only diagnosis viewed as a risk factor on the J-SOAP is conduct disorder, even though girls receive this diagnosis much less often than boys (American Psychiatric Association, 2000).

Although it is the case that many girls who sexually offend will meet the criteria for conduct disorder, and it appears likely that those who do will be at a higher risk to reoffend (given the negative outcomes associated with conduct disorder in females), it is also evident that conduct disorder does not capture risk for females as well as it does for males. Criteria for conduct disorder, i.e., use of a weapon, physical cruelty to animals, armed robbery, fire setting, and mugging (American Psychiatric Association, 2000), are behaviours more commonly associated with males. In summary, many sexually abusive girls may not have conduct disorder but be at a high risk to re-offend because of other interplaying co-morbid diagnoses. Further research is needed to examine to what extent the presence of several co-morbid diagnoses and the combination of certain diagnoses (i.e., conduct disorder with PTSD) would raise a girl's risk level.

Another risk factor worth examining for girls is early maturation. Levene et al. (2001) describe sexual development as a risk factor specific to girls. As they describe, girls with early sexual maturation are predisposed to negative body image, concerning social affiliations and involvements with older boys, and substance abuse. Precocious sexual behaviour may occur leading to sexual victimisation or a tendency for these girls to define themselves through their sexuality and success at attracting the opposite sex. Although early sexual maturation appears to correlate to the development of negative behaviours, the role it plays specifically in girls' sex offending behaviour has not yet been studied. Nevertheless, early maturation may correlate to female juvenile sex offending behaviour. Many girls who mature early experience peer ostracism and rejection, and their peer group may not be developmentally ready to engage in sexual exploration. Although young physically mature girls are also most likely not developmentally prepared for sexual involvements, because their bodies are already developed, they often inappropriately believe that they are emotionally ready (or at least should be) for sexual contact. Therefore, the lack of sexual opportunities with their peer group, could lead to developing their own opportunities to explore their sexuality. Many girls go to older boys or adult men, other girls may explore their sexuality given access to younger children.

Furthermore, given the relational development of girls, if the avenues to engage in the normal course of relational development are blocked and impaired, it is hypothesised that girls would be at greater risk for negative behaviours. Another factor that possibly pertains to a girl's risk to re-offend is an absence of a healthy same sex role model or parent. Like many boys who sexually offend, many sexually abusive girls tend to lack a functional and stable same sex parent. Since a healthy relationship between a girl and her mother is a protective factor for developing some forms of mental health disturbances (Harris, Blum and Resnick, 1991), the lack of a healthy relationship with a girl's mother or female guardian, could increase risk. In this regard, negative female role modelling is a compromising influence that provides a catalyst for the development of disturbing behaviours. Levene et al. (2001) further substantiate the importance of the mother-daughter relationship in the development of an antisocial trajectory for girls. The caregiver-daughter interaction is a risk factor identified for girls (Levene et al., 2001) and is a distinguishing difference from the risk factors noted for boys (Augimeri et al., 2001).

General delinquency and antisocial behaviour are re-offence risks noted in the literature (Ageton, 1983; Becker, Kaplan, et al., 1986; Knight and Prentky, 1993), however, females with sexual behaviour problems appear to be less often delinquent and antisocial than their male counterparts. For example, Fehrenbach and Monastersky (1988) found that other forms of delinquency for sex-offending girls in their sample were uncommon. Even though there are other studies on juvenile female sexual aggression that have found behavioural problems such as physical fighting and stealing present amongst these girls (Bumby and Bumby, 1993; Ray and English, 1995), it is questionable whether or not general delinquency and antisocial behaviour is as valid a risk factor for girls. In developing their risk assessment for young girls, Levene et al. (2001) removed authority contact, an item present in their risk assessment for boys (Augimeri et al., 2001); this was due to the fact that girls had a lower occurrence of authority contact than boys. This lower occurrence reflects the gender differences with the manifestation of aggression. Historically, delinquency and antisocial behaviour have not included the relational aggression found in females. Accordingly, it is recommended that relational aggression be included in the continuum of delinquent and antisocial behaviours. A better risk factor for girls may be a history of relational aggression. Henington et al. (as cited in Leschied et al., 2000) suggest that assessment procedures identifying girls at risk should include relational aggression. This was taken into account in the development of the EARL-21G for pre-adolescent girls (Levene et al., 2001) and also appears necessary for adolescent females.

Both the J-SOAP and ERASOR include impulsivity as a risk factor. The EARL-21G (Levene et al., 1991) lists Hyperactivity/ Impulsivity/Attention Deficits (HIA) as a risk factor for young girls, and this risk factor should be considered in the development of a risk instrument for sexually abusive juvenile females. The rationale for incorporating this as a risk factor is due to the gender paradox present with this diagnosis; that is, although boys are diagnosed more frequently with ADHD, girls receiving such diagnoses are at a greater risk than boys to develop conduct disordered behaviours (Szatmari et al., as cited in Loeber and Stouthamer-Loeber, 1998). Additionally, as discussed earlier, girls with ADHD tend to exhibit different symptomatolgy than boys and are more likely to be inattentive than impulsive. Therefore, HIA appears to be a better construct as

a female risk factor than merely listing impulsivity. Inattentiveness can lead to risky behaviours. A sexually abusive girl who is inattentive may not pay attention to cues that she is in a high-risk situation; she may also not pay attention to important triggers that need to be managed to prevent re-offence.

In developing risk factors for girls, one factor may need to reflect that most girls offend while in caregiving situations and are less likely to abuse strangers. (Bumby and Bumby, 1997; Fehrenbach and Monastersky, 1988; Margolin, 1991). Yet a risk factor for the ERASOR is 'ever sexually assaulted a stranger.' While it is true that a girl who abuses a stranger may be at a higher risk to re-offend because it is atypical of female sex-offending and demonstrates a willingness to engage in higher risk taking behaviour, this risk factor is based on the dynamics of male sex-offending and does not capture the dynamics of female sexual aggression. Because females appear to be less predatory, this risk factor does not correlate well to females. Instead, a more appropriate risk factor for females appears to be continued caregiving opportunities (prior to the completion of offence-specific treatment).

Another risk factor of questionable applicability to juvenile females is the selection of a same sex victim. A static risk factor on the ERASOR is 'ever sexually assaulted a male victim.' This risk factor is coded only for sex offending juvenile males due to studies on adult male sexual offenders and two studies on adolescent males concluding that males with same sex victims were more likely to re-offend. However, there is insufficient information to conversely state that females who have a same sex victim are at a higher risk to re-offend. There is not yet enough research to verify that this is the case.

Evidence of sexual preoccupation is a risk factor on the J-SOAP. Examples of this include: 'preoccupation with sexual fantasies and gratification of sexual needs, compulsive masturbation, excessive use of pornography, reports frequent uncontrollable sexual urges, multiple paraphilias' (Prentky et al., 2000, p88). Similarly, the ERASOR (Worling and Curwen, 2001) notes deviant sexual interests and obsessive sexual interests/preoccupation with sexual thoughts as risk factors. However, as noted earlier, research suggests that female sex offending is less about deviant sexual interests, arousal, and sexual preoccupation (Davin, 1999;

Dunbar, 1999; Finkelhor and Russell, 1984; Turner and Turner, 1994). In their work with adult female offenders, Sardajian and Hanks (1996) concluded that the use of sexual fantasy was 'less extensive and universal' than for male sex offenders (p144). Moreover, paraphilias are not as common among females. The sex ratio among paraphilias is estimated to be 20 males for each female; the one exception is sexual masochism (American Psychiatric Association, 2000). In addition, females are less likely to use pornography, especially in an excessive manner. Marshall and Eccles (1993) discuss the fact that deviant sex and pornography remain a male domain and suggest the difference in socialisation is the reason: Western culture promotes values and stereotypes that lead to the development in adolescent males to adopt a 'sexualised view of the world,' thereby leading to predatory and sexually aggressive behaviour towards females (p133). Consequently, these risk factors (sexual preoccupation, deviant sexual interests, or multiple paraphilias) do not appear to be as valid for sexual offending female juveniles.

Despite these concerns about the present risk factors, many of them appear to be congruent with female sexual aggression. For example, a history of school suspensions or expulsions, a risk factor noted in the J-SOAP, is a static variable that seems applicable to females (however, most likely not to the same extent as males). In Bumby and Bumby (1997) two-thirds of their female sample had been suspended or expelled for physical aggression towards peers or teachers, or for other causes. Similarly, alcohol abuse, also included in the J-SOAP, appears to be an accurate risk factor for both sexes. Bumby and Bumby (1997) found 75% of the females who sexually offended abused alcohol. In addition, the J-SOAP lists the quality of peer relationships as a risk factor and the ERASOR includes a lack of intimate peer relationships/social isolation as a risk factor. Given female relational development, these risk factors have great significance for girls. Bumby and Bumby (1997) found that 75% of girls in their sample were socially isolated and all but one girl had peer difficulties at school. In Johnson's (1989) sample, the girls had few, if any, peer relationships. Finally, high levels of familial dysfunction and an absence of environmental supports are consistent factors present in the lives of females with sex offending behaviour (Bumby and Bumby, 1997; Mathews,

Hunter and Vuz, 1997). The ERASOR notes high-stress family environment as a risk factor, whereas the J-SOAP includes caregiver instability as a risk factor.

Since the development of juvenile risk assessments remains in the infancy stage, developing a risk assessment specific to females will be even more difficult considering the limitations of research conducted on juvenile female sex offending and the small sample sizes of juvenile female abusers from which to glean actuarial data. Because the existing tools have not yet been proven to predict sexual recidivism (Caldwell, 2002) and these are tools developed largely on males, caution should be exercised when applying these tools to female juveniles. For a summary of factors that appear applicable to sexually abusive female juveniles, refer to the appendix.

Assessment suggestions

Towards a guideline for female assessment

Because there is a lack of assessment tools that have been developed for female juveniles with sexual abuse behaviours, there is a greater reliance on self-report (Hunter and Matthews, 1997). When assessing sexually abusive juvenile females, much of the assessment process will reflect similar questions posed to juvenile males. However, below are questions that may help guide the assessment process of a juvenile female. These questions are based on the literature on female adolescent development and sexual offending and can help to identify a girl's clinical needs. This is by no means an exhaustive list and is a guideline to alter as desired:

1. Offending behaviour:
(a) What was her victim selection: stranger, family member, acquaintance? How many victims?
(b) What was her relationship to her victim? If she knew her victim, how would she describe their relationship (i.e., close, distant)?
(c) How did she gain access to her victim(s)? Was she in a position of trust, i.e., caretaking, or other?
(d) What was her motivation for offending? Examine cultural scripts which may influence offending motivation, offending behaviour as a form of relational aggression,

dependency issues, trauma re-enactment, or sex as a means of attachment (sex=love). Was it an expression of anger or a way to learn about her sexuality?

(e) What are her cognitive distortions? Does she exhibit altruistic/caretaking justifications for offending?

(f) Does she exhibit guilt, remorse, shame, or empathy for her offending behaviour? Is there evidence that she is feigning empathy?

(g) What is her pathway to offending behaviour (i.e., depression, victimisation, early maturation, criminal activity among family members, etc.)?

(h) Which typology seems to match her behaviour (i.e., predisposed, experimenting/exploiting, peer influenced)?

As with the assessment of boys, other areas to pay attention to include: the degree of premeditation or impulsivity; the relationship of offending to sexual arousal; the level of coercion; the severity of the offence and duration of behaviour; and the level of denial.

2. History of maltreatment (physical, sexual, emotional abuse or neglect):

(a) What kind of maltreatment did she experience?

(b) Has she witnessed marital violence?

(c) Has she been raised in an environment of criminal activity and/or substance abuse?

(d) Is there role modelling of aggression by a female perpetrator in her history?

(e) Are there multiple perpetrators?

(f) What was her relationship to her perpetrators? What words does she use to describe the relationships (i.e., close, damaged, untrusting, loving, and caring)?

(g) How young was she when abused? What was the duration?

(h) Did she disclose abuse? If so, was there a positive or negative outcome to disclosure?

(i) How has the abuse affected her? What negative messages has she incorporated into her identity (i.e., thinking the abuse was her fault; thinking she is damaged goods; believing she deserved to be abused; or, believing she must have liked the abuse since her body became sexually aroused)?

3. History of conduct disordered behaviour and/or relational aggression:

(a) Does she have a history of lying? About what types of things?

(b) Does she have a history of stealing? If so, what would she steal?

(c) What other forms of negative behaviours have occurred, i.e., fighting, vandalism, or false reporting.

(d) Has she engaged in relational aggression, i.e., backbiting, gossiping, hurtful rumours, shunning previous friends, and malicious behaviour towards female peers? To what extent?

4. Relational development, female identity, and attachment styles:

(a) Are relationships important to her?

(b) Is there evidence of healthy and supportive relationships (reciprocity, mutuality)?

(c) What are her current peer and intimate relationships like?

(d) Is she in or has she been in any abusive relationships?

(e) What is her family constellation?

(f) What are the family dynamics?

(g) What are the strengths and weaknesses of the family system?

(h) Does she have close relationships with extended family members?

(i) What are the dynamics of the mother-daughter relationship? What is her previous and current relationship like with her mother?

(j) Does she have healthy or unhealthy female role models?

(k) What is her view of females?

(l) What is her view of self?

(m) Is her identity inchoate, formulated and stable, or disorganised and incoherent? Does she easily change her identity based on whom she is with and what she perceives others want her to be? ('Chameleon' Identity)

(n) What is her attachment style (negative or positive view of self and others)?

(o) Is she overly dependent? Or, does she refuse to depend on anyone?

(p) Is her ability to trust impaired?

(q) What kind of boundaries does she have (non-existent, walled, or healthy)?

(r) To what extent does she use others to get her needs met?

(s) Is her external presentation congruent with her internal presentation? (i.e., does she protect herself from vulnerability by acting tough?)

5. Sexual functioning, body image, and health:

(a) Does she describe herself as having low or high sexual desire?

(b) Is she sexually experienced, promiscuous, sexually naïve, or inexperienced?

(c) Is there evidence of a trauma bond pairing sexual victimisation and arousal, or other deviant sexual interests and behaviours?

(d) Does she take ownership of her sexuality or is she sexually passive and allow herself to be the object of others?

(e) Is she aware of her sexuality/sexual orientation?

(f) How does she feel about her sexuality? Is there evidence of sexual shame? Does she perceive herself as sexually inadequate?

(g) Does she define herself by her sexuality and desirability?

(h) Is she sexually knowledgeable? (For example, does she know where to find her clitoris? Does she know about female sexual response and orgasms? Is she informed about birth control?)

(i) What is her sexual experience? What kinds of sexual exploration has she engaged in? For example, while it is often not spoken about, it is fairly common for girls to practice having sex with other girls; it provides them with a 'rehearsal' in preparation for contact with boys. Has she engaged in practicing behaviours with other girls? How did it feel?

(j) What is her reproductive health? Has she had any pregnancies, abortions, or miscarriages? Has she had any sexually transmitted diseases?

(k) Does she have any sexual dysfunctions?

(l) Does she place herself in unsafe sexual situations where she is victimised? Has she done so previously?

(m) Does she engage in unprotected sex? If so, why?

(n) Does she own and use birth control?

(o) Does she have a desire to get pregnant? Has she previously lied about being pregnant? If so, why?

(p) When did she begin menstruating? What stages of puberty has she reached?

(q) What is her body image? Does she feel positively or negatively about her body? Does she view herself as overweight?

(r) Does she have any history of medical problems? Any current problems?

6. Mental health issues/internalisation:

(a) Has she received any prior mental health treatment and/or been psychiatrically hospitalised?

(b) Are there current or prior mental health problems, such as, depression, dissociation, anxiety, low self-esteem, suicidal ideation/attempts, self-mutilation, substance abuse, eating disorders, hypercriticism, perfectionism, post-traumatic stress disorder, hygiene, recklessness, or compulsive exercise?

(c) Does she meet the criteria for ADHD or conduct disorder? (Be mindful that the manifestation of these disorders can be different in girls).

(d) How does she manage her anger? Was she taught that anger was not an acceptable feeling to have or express?

(e) How does she manage other difficult feelings, i.e., shame, sadness, fear? Pay attention to forms of internalisation as well as externalisation.

As with boys, other areas to assess include: the kinds of defence mechanisms utilised (primitive or highly adaptive); level of self-esteem; degree of ego strength; and, the ability to self-regulate and self-soothe.

7. Academic functioning:

(a) Does she have a history of school behavioural problems? Suspensions or expulsions?

(b) Does she have a history of truancy?

(c) Has school been an area of success?

(d) What is her attitude toward learning?

(e) Does she have any diagnosed or possibly undiagnosed learning problems?

(f) Does she have difficulties with concentration and/or inattention?

8. Assets and protective factors:

(a) Is she able to voice herself and assert herself appropriately?

(b) Does she have healthy support systems and relationships in place?

(c) Does she have a positive relationship with her mother? Is there another positive female role model?

(d) What are her problem-solving abilities?

(e) Does she have close friendships? Does she engage in relational reciprocity?

(f) Does she accept gender normative definitions and beliefs?

9. Risks and deficits:
(a) Is there unprocessed trauma and PTSD reactivity?
(b) Is there caregiver loss or abandonment?
(c) Does she exhibit an inability to voice and assert herself?
(d) Is there evidence of relationship instability/disconnection?
(e) Has she experienced social rejection and peer exclusion?
(f) Are there negative peer and family relationships?

Many other strengths, protective factors, risks, and deficits are similar for male and female youth. These facets can be determined by examining whether or not a youth has the following: secure attachment, resilience, intellectual abilities, areas of competence, affect regulation, impulse control, an ability to delay gratification, emotional expressiveness, pro-social interests or talents, self-soothing and self-care strategies, an ability to foresee a positive future, and, a sense of hope.

Finally, the assessment process for any sexually abusive youth would not be complete without a review of offence reports and the victim's account; a thorough sexual history (i.e., number of consensual sexual experiences, access to pornography, experience with sex education, etc.); other pertinent aspects of a developmental history (prenatal care, developmental milestones, brain injuries, etc.) treatment amenability; and, the evaluation of sexual offending risk.

Existing tools

The following are some of the existing tools that may be helpful during the assessment process for a sexually abusive female juvenile.

1. *Adolescent Dissociative Experiences Scale* (A-DES; Armstrong, Putnam and Carlson, 1997): This 30-item scale for 10–21 year olds, measures an adolescent's use of dissociation which is helpful given the extent and severity of sexual abuse in the histories of girls with sexually abusive behaviours. Available from: Sidran Institute, 200 E. Joppa Rd., Suite 207, Towson, MD, 21286. Online: *www.sidran.org*

2. *Clinical Assessment Package for Client Risks and Strengths* (CASPARS; Gilgun, 1999): The CASPARS includes five instruments that are used to assess a child's assets and risks in different domains: Emotional Expressiveness, Family Relationships, Peer Relationships,

Sexuality, and Family's Embeddedness in the Community. The instruments have been found to have high reliability and validity. Although these tools are not gender specific, the benefit of these tools is that they determine the client's strengths needing to be increased and risks needing to be decreased throughout treatment. Information and instruments available online at *ssw.che.umn.edu/faculty/jgilgun/caspars.htm*

3. *Child Behaviour Checklist and Youth Self-Report* (CBCL/6–18 and YSL; Achenbach, 1999): The Child Behaviour Checklist, consisting of 118 items, is designed to assess social competence and behaviour problems for children ages 6–18. There is a profile specific to girls. The Youth Self-Report is for ages 11–18. Information available online at *www.aseba.org*.

4. *Cook County's Individual Girl Strengths and Needs Assessment/Reassessment* (Ereth and Gramling, 2003). This is a tool for adjudicated juvenile females. It examines family relationships, peer relations, social supports, emotional stability/mental health, substance abuse, history of abuse/neglect, motherhood, physical health, basic needs, physical safety, life skills, and school/employment status. The assessment identifies a girl's top three priority needs and top three strengths. Available from: National Council on Crime and Delinquency, 426 S. Yellowstone Dr., Suite 250, Madison, Wisconsin, 53719. Phone #: 608–831–8882.

5. *Cook County Juvenile Female Risk Assessment* (1999). This tool assesses the following risk factors: the number of prior arrests, number of arrests for drug offences, number of prior findings of delinquency, the age at first juvenile arrest, prior out-of-home placements, peer relationships, number of schools enrolled in during past two years, and alcohol abuse. The assessment is in *Cook County's Structured Decision Making Model for Girls in the Juvenile Justice System: Training Manual*. Available from: National Council on Crime and Delinquency, 426 S. Yellowstone Dr., Suite 250, Madison, Wisconsin, 53719. Phone #: 608–831–8882.

6. *Early Assessment Risk List for Girls* (EARL-21G; Levene et al., 2001). This tool was specially designed for girls up to the age of 12. The purpose is to assess a girl's risk for future antisocial behaviour. Available from: Earls Court Child and Family Centre, 46 St. Clair

Gardens, Toronto, Ontario, M6E, 3V4, Canada. Phone #: 416–654–8981. Online: *www.earlscourt.on.ca.*

7. *Massachusetts Youth Screening Instrument* (MAYSI-2; Grisso and Barnum, 2000): This self-report instrument is designed to identify adjudicated 12-17-year-old youths who may have mental health needs. It is a quick, user-friendly instrument consisting of 52 questions. This is a gender sensitive tool: There are 7 scales for boys and 6 scales for girls. Available online from Professional Resource Press: www.prpress.com.

8. *Multiphasic Sex Inventory* II JF (adolescent female form) (MSI II JF; Nichols and Molinder): This instrument is specifically geared to sexual offending girls and is used to examine their sexual characteristics. It can also be utilised to assess treatment progress. It has not yet been standardised on juvenile females. It is a paper and pencil test that takes approximately 90 minutes to complete and requires a 7th grade reading level. Available online at *www.nicholsandmolinder.com.*

9. *Personal Sentence Completion Inventory* (Miccio-Fonseca, 1997): A flexible tool to assess sexual development that consists of open-ended sentence stems. Available through Safer Society Press, PO Box 340, Brandon, Vermont, 05733. Phone: 802–247–3132. Online: *www.safersociety.org.*

10. PHASE *Sexual Attitudes Questionnaire* (O'Brien, 1994): A 50-item questionnaire useful for girls and boys to examine their sexual knowledge and beliefs about sex. Available from: Michael O'Brien, 1600 University Ave., W., Suite 305, St. Paul, Minnesota, 55104.

11. *Piers Harris Self-Concept Scale* (Piers-Harris 2; Piers, Harris and Herzberg): This scale is used for children ages 7–18. It is a 60-item measure that can be completed in 10–15 minutes. Available online from Psychological Assessment Resources: *www.parinc.com*

12. *Relationship Questionnaire* (Bartholomew and Horowitz, 1991): This self-report instrument is used for adolescents and adults. Clients rate themselves on a 7-point rating scale in response to four short paragraphs depicting attachment styles. Available in: Bartholomew, K. and Horowitz, L.M. (1991). Attachment styles among young adults: A test of a four-category model. *Journal of Personality and Social Psychology*, 61(2), 226–244.

13. *Reynolds Adolescent Depression Scale* (RADS-2; Reynolds). This is a 30-item self-report measure for 11–20-year-olds that can be completed in 5–10 minutes. Available online from Psychological Assessment Resources: *www.parinc.com.*

14. *Sexual Attitudes Scale* (Craig, Follingstad, Franklin and Kalichman, 1988). A measure initially designed for men, the wording was changed so it could be used for females. It may be appropriate for older adolescent females. This 19-item scale was designed to differentiate sexually coercive from non-coercive individuals. Available in: Anderson, P.B. and Struckman-Johnson, C. (Eds.) (1998). *Sexually Aggressive Women: Current Perspectives and Controversies*. New York: The Guilford Press.

15. *Trauma Symptom Checklist for Children* (TSCC; Briere). This checklist for 8-16-year-olds includes 54 items to measure post-traumatic stress and other psychological sequelae of traumatic events. It takes 15–20 minutes to complete. There are *female profile forms.* Available online from Psychological Assessment Resources: *www.parinc.com.*

Conclusion

The purpose of this chapter has been to increase awareness of the needs and issues specific to female sexually abusive young people. It is through an awareness of the differences between male and female juveniles, that a thorough assessment on juvenile females can be conducted thereby informing and guiding the treatment of sexually abusive girls. The assessment process should be guided by an understanding of female development and sexual behaviour; without this, the assessment procedure may miss important dynamics and characteristics specific to females requiring treatment attention. Since assessment has historically been conducted through the lens of male sex offending behaviour, it is time to assess through the lens of female development and sexual behaviour. It is from such an approach that specific tools and treatment methods will be developed for these girls. This is a work in progress. And much work is needed in the development of assessment tools for sexually abusive girls. It is this author's hope that further research on sexually abusive juvenile females will be conducted to promote our understanding of this population and improve current treatment approaches to better suit this growing and unique population.

Appendix
Risk Factors Specific to Female Juveniles

Factors that appear to necessitate further investigation for the development of a risk assessment for sexually abusive juvenile females:

Static factors:

1. A history of sexual abuse (Acoca and Dedel, 1998; Bumby and Bumby, 1997; Mathews, Hunter and Vuz, 1997; Miccio-Fonseca, 2000; Ray and English, 1995). The following factors may further increase risk: sexual abuse perpetrated by a female (due to the same-sex role modelling); the presence of multiple perpetrators; sexual abuse beginning at an early age; and, an extended period of abuse.
2. A history of other forms of maltreatment (Funk, 1999; Ray and English, 1995). It is well documented that girls with delinquent behaviours often experience multiple forms of abuse and neglect in their histories (Acoca and Dedel, 1998) and girls witnessing marital violence are more likely to adopt more externalising behaviours than boys (O'Keefe, as cited in Levene et al., 2001). Therefore, a history of emotional and physical abuse, and neglect should also be considered as a risk factor. Theoretically (and as with boys), the more forms of abuse present in these girls' histories, the more difficult it would be to counter the role modelling they received, which would potentially increase risk levels.
3. A history of relational aggression (Leschied et al., 2000). It is hypothesised that since girl's development is relational, when they are on a healthy developmental course, they are less likely to engage in behaviours that would negatively impact or destroy their relationships (Brown and Gilligan, 1992; Jorden et al., 1991; Miller and Stiver, 1997). Relational aggression needs to be viewed as aggression that is conduct disordered given the degree of harm that can be done to the victim. It may be less overt than forms of aggression more commonly used by boys, but it does not mean it is less significant.

4. Impaired attachment. Approximately half of the girls in Mathews, Hunter and Vuz (1997) had significant attachment disturbances. Furthermore, girls with attachment disturbances are more likely than those without, to act out sexually (Salzman, 1990).
5. Early maturation (Levene et al., 2001). There is evidence to suggest that premature sexual development leads to negative affiliations, peer blockage, and inappropriate sexual behaviours. The EARL-21G (Levene et al., 2001) lists sexual development (i.e., early menarche, early physical development) as a risk factor for the development of antisocial behaviour in young girls. It may also be an appropriate risk factor for older girls.

Stable and dynamic factors:

1. Current co-morbid diagnoses: The presence of more than one diagnosis and certain combinations of diagnoses may increase risk.

    (a) Depression: In Leschied et al. (2000) depressed girls were nearly four times more likely to be aggressive. Obeidallah and Earls (1999) also found depression to be a risk factor for female aggressive behaviour.
    (b) Posttraumatic Stress Disorder: A diagnosis of PTSD is common among sexually abusive girls (Hunter et al., 1993; Mathews, Hunter and Vuz, 1997) and if untreated, could correlate to continued offending behaviours due to a drive towards sexual re-enactment.
    (c) Hyperactivity/Impulsivity/Attention Deficits (HIA): Levene et al. (2001) incorporate this in their risk assessment for the development of antisocial behaviour in young girls; it also appears to have utility for older girls.
    (d) Conduct Disorder: Girls diagnosed with this disorder have poorer outcomes than boys (Szatmari et al., as cited in Leschied et al., 2000) therefore, girls with this diagnosis appear more likely to reoffend.

2. An absence of a stable and supportive female role model (Harris, Blum and Resnick, 1991; Mathews, Hunter and Vuz, 1997). A ruptured or damaged relationship with one's mother also appears to heighten a girl's risk to engage in negative behaviours. Levene et al. (2000) list

caretaker-daughter interaction as a risk factor for antisocial behaviours in young girls, and this factor also seems applicable for adolescent girls.

3. Disconnection from family (Harris, Blum and Resnick, 1991). Given the relational orientation of girls, familial connection (if healthy) can provide girls with a stable base that will lesson the likelihood of negative behaviours.

4. Continued access to caregiving situations. Since many sexually abusive girls offend while caretaking (Bumby and Bumby, 1997; Fehrenbach and Monastersky, 1998; Margolin, 1991) access to these situations when they have not yet completed treatment would raise their risk.

References

Acoca, L. and Dedel, K. (1998) *No Place to Hide: Understanding and Meeting The Needs of Girls in The California Juvenile Justice System*. Oakland, CA: The National Council on Crime and Delinquency.

Ageton, S.S. (1983) *Sexual Assault Among Adolescents*. Lexington, MA: Lexington Books.

Allen, C.M. (1991) *Women and Men Who Sexually Abuse Children: A Comparative Analysis*. Brandon, VT: Safer Society Press.

American Association of University Women (1995) *How Schools Short-Change Girls – The AAUW Report: A Study of Major Findings on Girls and Education*. New York: Marlowe and Company.

American Psychiatric Association (2000) *Diagnostic and Statistical Manual of Mental Disorders, Text Revision – DSM-IV-TR*. 4th Edn. Washington, DC: American Psychiatric Association.

Armstrong, J.G., Putnam, F.W., Carlson, E.B., Libero, D.A. and Smith, S.R. (1997) Development and Validation of A Measure of Adolescent Dissociation: The Adolescent Dissociative Experiences Scale. *The Journal of Nervous and Mental Disease*, 185 (8) 491–7.

Augimeri, L.K., Koegl, C.J., Webster, C.D. and Levene, K.S. (2001) *Early Assessment Risk List for Boys*, EARL-20B (Version 2) Toronto, ON: Earlscourt Child and Family Centre.

Bartholomew, K. (1990) Avoidance of Intimacy: An Attachment Perspective. *Journal of Social and Personal Relationships*, 7, 145–78.

Bartholomew, K. and Horowitz, L.M. (1991) Attachment Styles Among Young Adults: A Test of A Four-Category Model. *Journal of Personality and Social Psychology*, 61 (2) 226–44.

Becker, J.V., Kaplan, M.S., Cunningham-Rathner, J. and Kavoussi, R. (1986) Characteristics of Adolescent Incest Sexual Perpetrators: Preliminary Findings. *Journal of Family Violence*, 1, 85–97.

Biederman, J., Faraone, S.V., Mick, E., Williamson, S., Wilens, T.E., Spencer, T.J., Weber, W., Jetton, J., Kraus, I., Pert, J. and Zallen, B. (1999) Clinical Correlates of ADHD in Females: Findings From A Large Group of Girls Ascertained From Paediatric and Psychiatric Referral Sources. *Journal of The American Academy of Child and Adolescent Psychiatry*, 38, 966–75.

Brown, L.M. (1998) *Raising Their Voices: The Politics of Girls' Anger*. Cambridge, MA: Harvard University Press.

Brown, L.M. and Gilligan, C. (1992) *Meeting At The Crossroads: Women's Psychology and Girls' Development*. New York: Ballantine Books.

Bumby, K.M. and Bumby, N.H. (1997) Adolescent Female Sexual Offenders, in Schwartz, B.K. and Cellini, H.R. (Eds.) *The Sex Offender: Vol. 2. New Insights, Treatment Innovations and Legal Developments*. Kingston, NJ: Civic Research Institute. 10.1–16.

Caldwell, M.F. (2002) What We Do Not Know About Juvenile Sexual Reoffence Risk. *Child Maltreatment*, 7(4) 291–302.

Cauffman, E., Feldman, F., Waterman, J. and Steiner, H. (1998) Posttraumatic Stress Disorder Among Female Juvenile Offenders. *Journal of The American Academy of Child and Adolescent Psychiatry*, 37(11) 1209–17.

Chesney-Lind, M. (1997) *The Female Offender: Girls, Women, and Crime*. Thousand Oaks, CA: Sage Publications.

Cloninger, C.R., Christiansen, K.O., Reich, T. and Gottesman, I. (1978) Implications of Sex Differences in The Prevalence of Antisocial Personality, Alcoholism, and Criminality for Familial Transmission. *Archives of General Psychiatry*, 35, 941–51.

Commonwealth Fund (1997) *The Commonwealth Fund Survey of The Health of Adolescent Girls*. [On-Line], Available: *Www.Cmwf.Org/ Programs/Women/Factsheet.Asp*

Davin, P.A. (1999) Secrets Revealed: A Study of Female Sex Offenders, in Davin, P.A., Hislop, J.C. and Dunbar, T. *The Female Sexual Abuser: Three Views*. Brandon, VT: Safer Society Press. 9–134.

Dunbar, T. (1999) Women Who Sexually Molest Female Children, in Davin, P.A., Hislop, J.C. and Dunbar, T. *The Female Sexual Abuser: Three Views*. Brandon, VT: Safer Society Press. 311–93.

Ereth, J. and Gramling, S. (2003, January) *Cook County's GIRLS LINK Gender-Responsive Program Self-Assessment*. Madison, WI: National Council on Crime and Delinquency.

Erikson, E.H. (1950) *Childhood and Society*. New York: W. W. Norton.

Erikson, E.H. (1968) *Identity: Youth and Crisis*. New York: W. W. Norton.

Faller, D.C. (1995) A Clinical Sample of Women Who Have Sexually Abused. *Journal of Child Sexual Abuse*, 4(3) 13–31.

Farber, S.K. (2002) *When The Body is A Target: Self-Harm, Pain, and Traumatic Attachments*. Northvale, NJ: Jason Aronson, Inc.

Fehrenbach, P. and Monastersky, C. (1988) Characteristics of Female Adolescent Sexual Offenders. *American Journal of Orthopsychiatry*, 58(1) 148–51.

Fine, M. (1988) Sexuality, Schooling, and Adolescent Females: The Missing Discourse of Desire. *Harvard Education Review*, 58(1) 29–52.

Finkelhor, D. (1984) *Child Sexual Abuse: New Theory and Research*. New York: The Free Press.

Finkelhor, D. and Russell, D. (1984) Women As Perpetrators: Review of The Evidence, in Finkelhor, D. *Child Sexual Abuse: New Theory and Research*. New York: The Free Press. 171–87.

Flansburg, S. (1991) *Building A Self: Teenaged Girls and Issues of Self-Esteem*. Washington, DC: Women's Educational Equity Act Publishing Centre.

Funk, S. (1999) Risk Assessment for Juveniles on Probation: A Focus on Gender. *Criminal Justice and Behaviour*, 26(1) 44–68.

Gilgun, J.F. (1990) Factors Mediating The Effects of Childhood Maltreatment, in Hunter, M. (Ed.) *The Sexually Abused Male: Vol. 1. Prevalence, Impact, and Treatment*. Lexington, MA: Lexington Books. 177–90.

Gilgun, J.F. (1999) CASPARS: New Tools for Assessing Client Risks and Strengths. *Families in Society*, 80, 450–9.

Gilgun, J.F. (2001, May) Protective Factors, Resilience and Child Abuse and Neglect. *Healthy Generations* [On-Line], 2(1) 4–5. Available: *Www.Epi.Umn.Edu*.

Gilligan, C. (1982) *In A Different Voice: Psychological Theory and Women's Development*. Cambridge, MA: Harvard University Press.

Gilligan, C., Lyons, N.P. and Hammer, T.J. (Eds.) (1990) *Making Connections: The Relational Worlds of Adolescent Girls At Emma Willard School*. Cambridge, MA: Harvard University Press.

Grisso, T. and Barnum, R. (2000) *Massachusetts Youth Screening Instrument-2: User's Manual and Technical Report*. Worcester, MA: University of Massachusetts Medical School.

Hagan, M.P. and Cho, M.E. (1996) A Comparison of Treatment Outcomes Between Adolescent Rapists and Child Sexual Offenders. *International Journal of Offender Therapy and Comparative Criminology*, 40, 113–22.

Hancock, E. (1989) *The Girl Within*. New York: Fawcett Columbine.

Harris, L., Blum, R.W. and Resnick, M. (1991) Teen Females in Minnesota: A Portrait of Quiet Disturbance, in Gilligan, C., Rogers, A.G. and Tolman. D.L. (Eds.) *Women, Girls and Psychotherapy: Reframing Resistance*. Binghamton, NY: Harrington Park Press. 119–35.

Higgs, D.C., Canavan, M.M. and Meyer, W.J. (1992) Moving From Defence to Offence: The Development of An Adolescent Female Sex Offender. *The Journal of Sex Research*, 29(1) 131–9.

Howley, D. (2001, May) *A Descriptive Study of Sexually Abusive Female Juveniles in Residential Treatment*. Workshop Presented At The National Adolescent Perpetration Network Annual Conference, Kansas City, Missouri.

Hunter, J.A., Figueredo, A J., Malamuth, N.M. and Becker, J.V. (2003) Juvenile Sex Offenders: Toward The Development of A Typology. *Sexual Abuse: A Journal of Research and Treatment*, 15(1) 27–48.

Hunter, J.A., Lexier, L.J., Goodwin, D.W., Browne, P.A. and Dennis, C. (1993) Psychosexual, Attitudinal, and Developmental Characteristics of Juvenile Female Sexual Perpetrators in A Residential Treatment Setting. *Journal of Child and Family Studies*, 2, 317–26.

Hunter, J.A. and Mathews, R. (1997) Sexual Deviance in Females, in Laws, R.D. and O'Donohue, W. (Eds.) *Sexual Deviance: Theory, Assessment and Treatment*. New York: The Guilford Press. 465–80.

Johnson, T.C. (1989) Female Child Perpetrators: Children Who Molest Other Children. *Child Abuse and Neglect*, 13, 571–89.

Jordan, J.V., Kaplan, A.G., Miller, J.B., Stiver, I.P. and Surrey, J.L. (1991) *Women's Growth in*

Connection: Writings From The Stone Centre. New York: The Guilford Press.

Kahn, T.J. and Chambers, H.J. (1991) Assessing Reoffence Risk With Juvenile Sexual Offenders. *Child Welfare*, 70, 333–45.

Knight, R.A. and Prentky, R.A. (1990) Classifying Sexual Offenders: The Development and Corroboration of Taxonomic Models, in Marshall, W.L., Laws, D.R. and Barbaree, H.E. (Eds.) *The Handbook of Sexual Assault: Issues, Theories, and Treatment of The Offender*. New York: Plenum. 27–52.

Knight, R.A. and Prentky, R.A. (1993) Exploring Characteristics for Classifying Juvenile Sex Offenders, in Barbaree, H.E. Marshall, W.L. and Hudson, S.M. (Eds.) *The Juvenile Sex Offender*. New York: The Guilford Press. 45–83.

Kohlberg, L. (1981) *The Philosophy of Moral Development*. San Francisco: Harper and Row.

Lab, S.P., Shields, G. and Schondel, C. (1993) Research Note: An Evaluation of Juvenile Sexual Offender Treatment. *Crime and Delinquency*, 39, 543–53.

Lamb, S. (2001) *The Secret Lives of Girls: What Good Girls Really Do – Sex Play, Aggression, and Their Guilt*. New York: The Free Press.

Lerner, H.G. (1988) *Women in Therapy*. New York: Harperperennial.

Leschied, A., Cummings, A., Van Brunschot, M., Cunningham, A. and Saunders, A. (2000) *Female Adolescent Aggression: A Review of The Literature and The Correlates of Aggression* (User Report No. 2000–04) Ottawa: Solicitor General Canada.

Levene, K.S., Augimeri, L.K., Pepler, D.J., Walsh, M.M., Webster, C.D. and Koegl, C.J. (2001) *Early Assessment Risk List for Girls, Earl-21G* Consultation Edition Toronto, ON: Earlscourt Child and Family Centre.

Levinson, D. (1978) *The Seasons of A Man's Life*. New York: Alfred A. Knopf.

Loeber, R. and Keenan, K. (1994) The Interaction Between Conduct Disorder and Its Co Morbid Conditions: Effects of Age and Gender. *Clinical Psychology Review*, 14, 497–523.

Loeber, R. and Stouthamer-Loeber, M. (1998) Development of Juvenile Aggression and Violence: Some Common Misconceptions and Controversies. *American Psychologist*, 53 (2) 242–59.

Margolin, L. (1991) Child Sexual Abuse by Nonrelated Caregivers. *Child Abuse and Neglect*, 15, 213–21.

Marshall, W.L. and Eccles, A. (1993) Pavlovian Conditioning Processes in Adolescent Sex Offenders, in Barbaree, H.E., Marshall, W.L. and Hudson, S.M. (Eds.) *Juvenile Sex Offending*. New York: The Guilford Press. 118–42.

Marshall, W.L., Hudson, S.M. and Hodkinson, S. (1993) The Importance of Attachment Bonds in The Development of Juvenile Sex Offending, in Barbaree, H.E., Marshall, W.L. and Hudson, S.M. (Eds.) *Juvenile Sex Offending*. New York: The Guilford Press. 164–1.81.

Mathews, R., Hunter, J.A., Jr. and Vuz, J. (1997) Juvenile Female Sexual Offenders: Clinical Characteristics and Treatment Issues. *Sexual Abuse: A Journal of Research and Treatment*, 9(3): 187–200.

Mathews, R. Matthews, J.K. and Speltz, K. (1989) *Female Sexual Offenders: An Exploratory Study*. Orwell, VT: Safer Society Press.

Mathews, R., Matthews, J. and Speltz, K. (1990) Female Sexual Offenders, in Hunter, M. (Ed.) *The Sexually Abused Male: Vol. 1. Prevalence, Impact, and Treatment*. New York: Lexington Books. 275–93.

Matthews, J.K. (1993) Working With Female Sexual Abusers, in Elliott, M. (Ed.) *Female Sexual Abuse of Children*. New York: The Guilford Press. 57–73.

McCarty, L. (1986) Mother-Child Incest: Characteristics of The Offender. *Child Welfare*, 65(5) 447–58.

Miccio-Fonseca, L.C. (1997) *Personal Sentence Completion Inventory: User's Guide*. Brandon, VT: Safer Society Press.

Miccio-Fonseca, L.C. (2000) Adult and Adolescent Female Sex Offenders: Experiences Compared to Other Female and Male Sex Offenders. *Journal of Psychology and Human Sexuality*, 11(3) 75–88.

Miller, J.B. and Stiver, I.P. (1997) *The Healing Connection: How Women Form Relationships in Therapy and in Life*. Boston, MA: Beacon Press.

Minasian, G. and Lewis, A.D. (1999) Female Sexual Abusers: An Unrecognised Culture, in Lewis, A.D. (Ed.) *Cultural Diversity in Sexual Abuser Treatment: Issues and Approaches*. Brandon, VT: Safer Society Press. 71–82.

National Clearing House for Alcohol and Drug Information (2001) [On-Line] *Www.Health.Org/ Govpubs*

National Council on Crime and Delinquency (1999, February) *Cook County's Structured Decision Making Model for Girls in The Juvenile Justice System: Training Manual*. Madison, WI: National Council on Crime and Delinquency.

Obeidallah, D.A. and Earls, F.J. (1999, July) Adolescent Girls: The Role of Depression in

The Development of Delinquency. *National Institute of Justice Research Preview*. Washington, DC: US Department of Justice.

O'Brien, M. (1994) *PHASE Treatment Manual*. St. Paul, MN: PHASE Program.

Orenstein, P. (1994) *Schoolgirls: Young Women, Self-Esteem, and The Confidence Gap*. New York: Harper Perennial.

Perry, B.D. (1995) Incubated in Terror: Neurodevelopmental Factors in The 'Cycle of Violence.' in Osofsky, J.D. (Ed.) *Children, Youth and Violence: Searching for Solutions*. New York: The Guilford Press.

Perry, B.D., Pollard, R.A., Blakley, T.L., Baker, W.L. and Vigilante, D. (1995) Childhood Trauma, The Neurobiology of Adaptation and 'Use-Dependent' Development of The Brain: How 'States' Become 'Traits.' *Infant Mental Health Journal*, 16 (4) 271–91.

Pipher, M. (1994) *Reviving Ophelia: Saving The Selves of Adolescent Girls*. New York: Ballantine Books.

Poe-Yamagata, E. and Butts, J.A. (1996, September) *Female Offenders in The Juvenile Justice Systems: Statistics Summary* (NCJ Report No. 160941) Washington, DC: US Department of Justice.

Prentky, R., Harris, B., Frizzell, K. and Righthand, S. (2000) An Actuarial Procedure for Assessing Risk With Juvenile Sex Offenders. *Sexual Abuse: A Journal of Research and Treatment*, 12 (2) 71–93.

Rasmussen, L.A. (1999) Factors Related to Recidivism Among Juvenile Sexual Offenders. *Sexual Abuse: A Journal of Research and Treatment*, 11, 69–85.

Ray, J.A. and English, D.J. (1995) Comparison of Female and Male Children With Sexual Behaviour Problems. *Journal of Youth and Adolescence*, 24 (4) 439–51.

Rich, A. (1982) *Compulsory Heterosexuality and Lesbian Existence*. Denver, CO: Antelope Publications.

Robinson, S. (2002) *Growing Beyond: A Workbook for Sexually Abusive Teenage Girls (Treatment Manual)* Holyoke, MA: NEARI Press.

Sadker, M. and Sadker, D. (1994) *Failing At Fairness: How Our Schools Cheat Girls*. New York: A Touchstone Book.

Salzman, J.P. (1990) Save The World, Save Myself: Responses to Problematic Attachment, in Gilligan, C. Lyons, N.P. and Hammer, T.J. (Eds.) *Making Connections: The Relational Worlds of Adolescent Girls At Emma Willard School*. Cambridge, MA: Harvard University Press. 110–46.

Saradjian, J. and Hanks, H. (1996) *Women Who Sexually Abuse Children: From Research to Clinical Practice*. New York: John Wiley and Sons.

Scavo, R.R. (1989, February) Female Adolescent Sexual Offenders: A Neglected Treatment Group. *Social Casework: The Journal of Contemporary Social Work*, 114–7.

Shandler, S. (1999) *Ophelia Speaks: Adolescent Girls Write About Their Search for Self*. New York: Harperperennial.

Simmons, R. (2002) *Odd Girl Out: The Hidden Culture of Aggression in Girls*. New York: Harcourt, Inc.

Sipe, R., Jensen, E.L. and Everett, R.S. (1998) Adolescent Sexual Offenders Grown Up: Recidivism in Young Adulthood. *Criminal Justice and Behaviour*, 25, 109–24.

Smith, W.R. and Monastersky, C. (1986) Assessing Juvenile Sexual Offenders' Risk for Reoffending. *Criminal Justice and Behaviour*, 13, 115–40.

Snyder, H.N. and Sickmund, M. (1999, September) Juvenile Offenders and Victims: *1999 National Report (NCJ Report No. 178257)* Washington, DC: US Department of Justice.

Stern, L. (1991) Disavowing The Self in Female Adolescence, in Gilligan, C., Rogers, A.G. and Tolman, D.L. (Eds.) *Women, Girls and Psychotherapy: Reframing Resistance*. New York: Harrington Park Press. 105–18.

Surrey, J.L. (1991) The 'Self-In-Relation': A Theory of Women's Development, in Jordan, J.V., Kaplan, A.G. Miller, J.B., Stiver, I.P. and Surrey, J.L. (Eds.) *Women's Growth in Connection: Writings From The Stone Centre*. New York: The Guilford Press. 51–66.

Syed, F. and Williams, S. (1996, December) *Case Studies of Female Sex Offenders in The Correctional Service of Canada* [On-Line]. Available: Http://Www.Csc-Scc.Gc.Ca/Sexoff/Female/English/Female-09.Htm

Thompson, S. (1990) Putting A Big Thing Into A Little Hole: Teenage Girls' Accounts of Sexual Initiation. *Journal of Sex Research*, 27, 341–61.

Thompson, S. (1995) *Going All The Way: Teenage Girls' Tales of Sex, Romance and Pregnancy*. New York: Farrar, Straus and Giroux.

Tolman, D.L. (1991) Adolescent Girls, Women and Sexuality: Discerning Dilemmas of Desire, in Gilligan, C.A. Rogers, G. and Tolman, D.L. (Eds.) *Women, Girls and Psychotherapy: Reframing Resistance*. Binghamton, NY: Harrington Park Press. 55–69.

Tolman, D.L. (1994) Daring to Desire: Culture and The Bodies of Adolescent Girls, in Irvine, J.M.

(Ed.) *Sexual Cultures and The Construction of Adolescent Identities*. Philadelphia, PA: Temple University Press. 250–84.

Tolman, D.L. (1999) Female Adolescent Sexuality in Relational Context: Beyond Sexual Decision Making, in Johnson, N.G., Roberts, M.C. and Worell, J. (Eds.) *Beyond Appearance: A New Look at Adolescent Girls*. Washington, DC: American Psychological Association. 227–46.

Tolman, D.L. (2001) Female Adolescent Sexuality: An Argument for A Developmental Perspective on The New View of Women's Sexual Problems, in Kaschak E. and Tiefer, L. (Eds.) *A New View of Women's Sexual Problems*. Binghamton, NY: Haworth Press. 195–209.

Tolman, D.L. (2002) *Dilemmas of Desire: Teenage Girls Talk About Sexuality*. Cambridge, MA: Harvard University Press.

Turner, M.T. and Turner, T.N. (1994) *Female Adolescent Sexual Abusers: An Exploratory Study of Mother-Daughter Dynamics With Implications for Treatment*. Brandon, VT: Safer Society Press.

Ward, T., Hudson, S.M., Marshall, W.L. and Siegert, R. (1995) Attachment Style and Intimacy Deficits in Sexual Offenders: A Theoretical Framework. *Sexual Abuse: A Journal of Research and Treatment*, 7(4) 317–35.

Wolf, N. (1997) *Promiscuities: The Secret Struggle for Womanhood*. New York: Random House.

Worling, J.R. and Curwen, T. (2000) Adolescent Sexual Offender Recidivism: Success of Specialised Treatment and Implications for Risk Prediction. *Child Abuse and Neglect*, 24, 965–82.

Worling, J.R. and Curwen, T. (2001) *The 'ERASOR' (Estimate of Risk of Adolescent Sexual Offence Recidivism – Version 2.0)* Thistletown Regional Centre: SAFE-T Program.

Young-Eisendrath, P. (1999) *Women and Desire: Beyond Wanting to Be Wanted*. New York: Harmony Books.

Part IV

Treatment issues

Integrating Trauma and Attachment Research into the Treatment of Sexually Abusive Youth

Kevin Creeden

Introduction

Treatment philosophies, assessment protocols, treatment models and interventions for young people who have engaged in sexually abusive or inappropriate behaviour have, for most of the past twenty-five years, reflected thinking and research that has largely been based on adult sexual offenders. This has skewed our perspective about how sexual behaviour problems develop and what motivates such behaviour. It has also strongly influenced the nature of our treatment interventions. In the last five to eight years a few researchers and writers (Ward, Hudson and Marshall, 1995; Friedrich, 1995; Ryan, 1999; Leguizamo, 2002) have begun to develop a different, broader perspective with regard to the dynamics of sexually abusive behaviour. In particular there has been a greater focus on distinguishing different pathways that may lead someone to engage in sexually abusive behaviour and differentiating the treatment of those individuals who persist in committing offences into adulthood from interventions directed toward children and young people whose sexually inappropriate or abusive behaviour has been identified much earlier. While developmental issues such as attachment relationships have received greater attention, there appears to have been little change in the overall treatment approach or in specific treatment interventions directed toward adolescent perpetrators.

In this chapter, I will present an overview of research and writing from the fields of trauma and attachment that appear particularly relevant to the treatment of sexually abusive youth. Then I will briefly describe how we have tried to integrate our reading of this research into a model for treating children and young people with sexual behaviour problems. Presently, we are evolving and applying this treatment approach at Whitney Academy, a residential treatment programme for males ages 10–22. The treatment model stems from a developmental

perspective of working with children and is largely rooted in attachment theory. The model reflects a belief that all types of abusive behaviour (sexual, physical, and emotional) are essentially reflective of a striving to meet basic relational needs. Our treatment approach would assume that sexually abusive behaviour arises in large part (but not solely) from a fundamental, even universal, need that individuals have for safety, attention, acceptance, nurturance, and care. We would suggest that it is only the process that some individuals follow to meet these needs that can become distorted and abusive. Therefore what in the end makes abusive behaviour *abusive* is not that the needs being met are different or perverse but that the process for meeting those needs lacks the attunement, trust, and mutuality that eventually distinguishes positive from negative human relationships.

If one reads the literature which has attempted to identify the aetiology of sexually abusive behaviour certain variables seem to consistently arise. These variables are the presence, in early childhood, of some type of neglect, abuse, or abandonment which might broadly be defined as trauma. The other variables that appear to exist to varying degrees in different types of sexual abusers are their difficulties in developing close, stable relationships with others (at times reflected in social or emotional isolation) and perhaps as a consequence, significant deficits in their capacity for empathy (Finkelhor, 1986; Prentky, Knight, Sims-Knight and Straus, 1989). From our perspective, both the difficulties in stable relationships and the lack of empathy are best understood as problems which offenders experience in their attachment relationships.

Recently research has suggested a common thread that may exist between early experiences of trauma and disruptions in primary attachment relationships. Both trauma and insecure attachment relationships appear to have a significant impact on childhood neuro-development (Perry, 2001; Teicher,

Andersen, Polcari, Andersen and Navalta, 2002; Schore, 2002). In fact Siegel (1999), Schore (1998) and others have suggested that a child's early emotional experiences in relation to their primary caretakers may be the central organising feature in the child's brain development. Many of the structural and functional changes which appear to occur in the brain as a consequence of early trauma and disrupted attachment offer a way of understanding many of the behaviours we see in children and adolescents with significant behavioural difficulties. Understanding the brain's response to both trauma and disorganised attachment experiences also directs us to interventions that are developmental, holistic, humanistic, and strength-based on both an individual and systemic level. The Whitney Academy treatment approach that is outlined here is optimistic in that it proposes that children are remarkably resilient; that regular engagement in caring, consistent relationships can alter attachment styles; and that thoughtful, persistent stimulation of neural pathways can change brain function and possibly brain structure.

Trauma and sexual behaviour problems

Historically, we have been engaged in the process of trying to answer the question of why sexual abusers abuse. The most obvious hypothesis suggested a direct social learning aetiology, i.e., sexual abusers commit offences because they themselves were sexually victimised as children. However, research on the incidence of sexual victimisation among sex offenders has not found a direct correlation between sexual victimisation and subsequent sexually abusive behaviour. What does appear almost universally in the prior histories of adolescent sexual abusers is the experience of some form of trauma, if we define trauma in its broadest terms to include not only incidents of physical or sexual abuse but also experiences of early childhood neglect and abandonment, witnessing domestic violence, and other experiences that the child may view as life threatening (McMackin, Leisen, Cusack, LaFratta and Litwin, 2002).

Two aspects of appreciating the trauma histories of our clients are particularly important in our treatment approach. The first is appreciating the neurological impact that early childhood trauma can have on individuals and the second is effectively utilising non-abuser treatment interventions from the trauma field.

Neurological impact of trauma

Recent research into the neurological consequences of repeated exposure to traumatising experiences has shown both structural and functional neurological differences between traumatised and non-traumatised individuals. Among the most notable of these studies is the work of Martin Teicher and his colleagues (2002). They have shown that individuals exposed to early childhood trauma show significant alterations in the amygdala and limbic irritability which in turn fosters increased fight-flight responses and aggressive behaviours. In addition this research indicates that traumatised individuals suffer from changes in the hippocampus that may facilitate the emergence of dissociation; that these individuals also evidence diminished left hemisphere maturation, corpus callosum size, and left-right hemisphere integration. These problems may markedly impact the ability of the individual to regulate intense affective responses and learn from previous emotionally charged experiences. These traumatised individuals also show diminished development of the cerebella vermis which then serves to maintain their state of limbic irritability, hyper arousal, and sympathetic nervous system activation.

Research by Bruce Perry and his colleagues (Perry, Pollard, Blakely, Baker, Vigilante, 1995; Perry, 2001) highlights Teicher's findings regarding limbic irritability by noting changes in baseline heart-rates for individuals with significant trauma experiences and noting that adaptive physiological responses to traumatic experiences become a central feature of how brain structure and function are organised when individuals endure repeated trauma and trauma cues in childhood.

If these neurological alterations are more simplistically translated into the day-to-day experiences of the young people whom we treat what becomes evident is that early experiences of trauma generate a 'kindling effect' within the limbic systems of many of the adolescents with whom we work. The impact of these neuro-developmental changes can be quite far reaching. They include:

1. The kindling effect or limbic irritability noted primarily in the amygdala can lead to hyper vigilance, a greater tendency to interpret social/environmental cues and interactions as

being threatening, and a stronger tendency to engage in fight-flight responses.

2. As these responses in the amygdala are activated the brain's ability to utilise learned information that might allow the individual to place the social/environmental information in context or to engage more appropriate or effective adaptive responses is diminished.

3. Diminished right-left hemisphere integration and smaller corpus callosum size may also create obstacles to effectively and accurately responding to environmental stimulus, learning and adapting problem solving approaches, and integrating and re-working traumatic experiences.

4. Changes in the hippocampus both as an adaptation to and in conjunction with increased limbic irritability may create difficulties in auditory processing and verbal memory that could have a direct impact on the adolescent's ability to process and respond to compliance commands, to learn academic and life skills, and to participate in and utilise therapy interventions all of which tend to be verbally 'loaded' once the individual reaches adolescence.

5. Since most of these responses are occurring at a sub-cortical level, the individual's ability to consciously recognise and adapt to these limbic, mid-brain, and lower brain level responses may be severely limited at the moment when adaptive responses are demanded by the situation.

Trauma focused treatment

The literature that addresses the treatment of trauma has currently reached a consensus regarding the need for a phase-oriented treatment approach (Allen, 2001; Chu, 1992; Herman, 1992; van der Hart et al., 1998; van der Kolk, McFarlane and van der Hart, 1996). Allen (2001) notes that 'we must foster our client's capacity to work on the trauma before tackling traumatic memories' and this would generally suggest that supportive interventions precede expressive interventions. The term 'phase-oriented treatment' does not suggest a rigid, cook-book like, step-by-step approach. Rather it suggests a shift of focus over time based on client needs, support, tolerance, control, and motivation.

Van der Kolk et al. (1996) writes that phase-oriented treatment should include the following:

1. Stabilisation, including (a) education and (b) identification of feelings through verbalising somatic states.
2. Deconditioning of traumatic memories and responses.
3. Restructuring of traumatic personal schemes.
4. Re-establishment of secure social connections and interpersonal efficacy.
5. Accumulation of restitutive emotional experiences.

These authors suggest that while some clients may be able to move quickly from one phase to the next, many others will require that the stabilisation phase be repeated frequently.

Allen (2001) takes the notion of stabilisation and broadens this phase through the use of the metaphor *containment*. He proposes that containment be given priority in treating trauma and writes of how containment is gained through increasing the client's level of self-regulation, developing a structure for treatment, and developing and sustaining supportive relationships.

The importance of self-regulation appears especially important and problematic in light of the neurological impact of trauma which may lead to either increased levels of hyper-arousal or more frequent triggering of dissociative states. Both of these responses lead to diminished capacities for self-regulation since both occur at a sub-cortical level and are not immediately accessible to more conscious coping responses. While treatment for sexual behaviour problems has often focused on how to modulate sexual arousal to 'deviant' or 'risky' triggers or stimulus there seems to have been far less focus on helping clients regulate the full range of emotional/physiological responses or to understand how sexual arousal fits into the adolescent's broader experiences of overall physiological arousal or dysregulation.

While previously treatment for trauma victims had a more exploratory and expressive focus that either implicitly or explicitly encouraged the client to 'dredge up' their previous traumatic experiences and 'get it all out', a shift has occurred over the past decade that recognises that an emphasis on exploration and expressiveness without adequate support, structure, and containment not only can be unproductive but can actually lead to deterioration in the client. The abuser field, with a focus on taking responsibility and holding the abuser accountable, has typically required the abuser to provide detailed and repeated accounts of their offences, if not their victimisation or trauma histories. When abusers avoided reporting particular offences, fantasies, or details these individuals were viewed as being avoidant, deceptive, and resistant to treatment. An alternative explanation could be that some client's sexually abusive behaviour is closely intertwined with their trauma histories and that discussing their offences triggers both traumatic memories and intense affect that they have difficulty regulating. From this view the client's avoidance or denial may be an appropriate coping response, especially in the absence of acquired containment skills and supportive relationships.

Given the broad range of trauma experiences in our client's backgrounds we may be able to learn from trauma focused treatment approaches which could be adapted to our particular populations.

Attachment theory

Attachment theory's primary assumption is that maintenance of proximity to a secure and trusted figure is needed and sought by humans throughout the lifespan and particularly during periods of perceived danger or stress. The fundamental goals of attachment are safety and affiliation. Developing and sustaining secure attachment relationships has been noted as increasing feelings of security, mastery, self-esteem, and social competence. By contrast the loss, inconsistency, or unavailability of secure attachments can lead to sorrow, anxiety, anger, and confusion (Bowlby, 1969; Bowlby, 1980).

Ainsworth, et al. (1978) in her work with infants, utilising a laboratory based observational method known as The Strange Situation, suggested three types of attachment: secure, anxious/ambivalent, and avoidant. *Secure attachment* develops when the child's parents/caretakers are attuned to the child's needs and respond in a consistent and nurturing manner. *Anxious/ambivalent* attachment develops when the child's caregivers are inconsistent in their atonement and responsiveness to the child. Alexander (1992) noted that these children exhibit higher degrees of attention seeking behaviours ranging from impulsive and tense to passive and helpless. Parents of *avoidantly attached* children are typically emotionally detached, affectively

constricted, and unattuned to the child's emotional needs. These children are also likely to be emotionally constricted and may become 'parentified' or compulsively compliant. In more extreme cases these children grow up to lack empathy, and may engage in hostile, anti-social behaviour (Crittenden, 1995). A fourth attachment category was later added to identify those children who did not fit into the other three categories. These children, who often came from backgrounds of significant maltreatment, were referred to as *disorganised/disoriented* (Main and Hesse, 1990).

Mary Main developed an Adult Attachment Interview (AAI) that sought to examine adults' representations of childhood attachment relationships (Main and Goldwyn, 1994). Adults (largely mothers) were classified into attachment groups that paralleled the identified childhood attachment patterns. Bartholomew and Horowitz (1991) proposed a four group model of adult attachment; secure, preoccupied, dismissing, and fearful. *Secure* adults were identified as those who believed in their own worthiness or 'lovability' and held an expectation that others were generally accepting and responsive. *Preoccupied* adults combined a sense of personal unworthiness (unlovability) with a positive evaluation of others. These individuals strive for self-acceptance by gaining the acceptance of valued others. *Dismissing* adults have a sense of personal worthiness but combine this with a negative view of others as being untrustworthy or responsive. These individuals protect themselves against hurt and disappointment by avoiding close relationships. The *Fearful* individual sees themselves as unlovable and also anticipates rejection from others. Bartholomew's 4 group model has been the one most frequently used in research that has tried to examine the connection between attachment style and sexually abusive behaviour.

Researchers have found a correlation between disorganised attachment patterns in early childhood and aggressive behaviour, depression, and other psychiatric problems in later life (Lyons-Ruth and Jacobuitz, 1999; Van Ijzendoorn et al. 1999; Johnson, Cohen, Kasen, Smailes and Brook, 2001).

Attachment and neurobiology

Attachment theory holds that the primary function of attachment relationships is to provide safety and security to the infant. In infancy, the ability to engage a nurturing, available caretaker is the fundamental coping response to stress. Through the process of infant-caregiver attunement, the caregiver highlights and stimulates positive states of excitement, joy, and pleasure and minimises states of stress and anxiety. The caretaker serves as the infant's affect regulator and in turn this allows the infant to develop the neurological connections that will eventually allow for the child to regulate their own affective states (Siegel, 1999). By regulating the child's affect the caregiver is also affecting the release of stress hormones in the infant's brain (Lott, 1998).

Persistent experiences of threat or stress in the absence of regulation and nurturance from the caregiver results in abnormal secretions of cortical and can have an adverse influence on brain development (DeBellis, 1999; Hart, Gunnar and Cicchetti, 1995). The brain's use-dependent nature means that persistent experiences of stress will lead to the over-development of certain areas of the brain where fear and anxiety responses are processed and can result in under-development in other areas, especially in the cortex (Schore,1997). Schore (2002) has particularly focused attention on the right orbit frontal cortex. He notes research by McEwen (2000) suggesting that chronic levels of stress contribute to fewer neural connections between the prefrontal cortex and the amygdala. Without regulation from the prefrontal cortex, sub-cortical processing of fear, especially through the amygdala, proceeds without conscious, inhibitory control.

Crittenden (1997) has written about attachment styles from the perspective of the individual's capacity for effectively integrating their affective and cognitive experiences of the world. Crittenden takes the three main attachment patterns posed by Ainsworth, et al. (1978) and broadens them to include a variety of sub-patterns in each style. In addition, Crittenden defines *Secure* attachment as the ability to integrate both affective and cognitive experiences. Individuals with *Avoidant* styles are viewed as inhibiting or misconstruing affective responses. Individuals with *Ambivalent* styles are then seen as affectively activated but poorly organised to understand what triggers their affective responses or to appreciate the impact/ consequences of their affectively driven behaviour. Crittenden writes of *Disorganised* attachment as occurring when caregivers are frightened and/or frightening. This places the child in the untenable situation of gravitating to the source of their trauma as a way of coping with their trauma. Other researchers have suggested that these circumstances may lead to the development of dissociative responses in the child.

Crittenden's model of attachment is useful in that it reflects the neurobiological difficulties of cortical regulation and integration highlighted by Schore, Teicher and others by viewing attachment not only as a coping response or a relational process but as a brain based process that has a profound impact on future neurological development.

Attachment theory and sexually abusive behaviour

Various researchers have identified a variety of deficits and difficulties in the social/emotional relationships of sexual abusers. Sexual abusers were seen as being socially isolated or failing to achieve intimacy even when not isolated (Awad, Saunders and Levine, 1984; Saunders, Awad and White, 1986; Fagan and Wexler, 1988). Research also suggests that sexually aggressive males have significantly lower empathy skills than other males, especially in relationship to their victims (Lisak and Ivan, 1995; Marshall, Hudson, Jones and Fernandez, 1995; McGrath, Cann and Konopasky, 1998). Recently, research on empathy deficits in sex offenders has suggested that what has previously been defined as a lack of empathy might more accurately be viewed as a lack of integration between affective and cognitive responses in the offender (cognitive distortions) rather than a broader inability to be emotionally responsive to others (Webster and Beech, 2000; Fernandez and Marshall, 2003).

Baumeister and Leary (1995) suggest that the need for intimacy and connection with others is as fundamental a human need as food and sex. One can argue that the need to develop attachment relationships is a biological imperative for humans since the human infant is incapable of caring for themselves and without the ability to engage a caretaker the infant would die. In addition, Crittenden has pointed to the similarities between anxiety arousal and sexual arousal noting that from a learning and limbic system perspective 'there is considerable overlap in the experiential features of anxiety and sexual arousal and of comfort and sexual satisfaction; these can lead to an overlap of the sexual and attachment behavioural systems' (1997: p40).

Marshall (1989) was the first writer to begin questioning the connection between offender attachment styles and their sexually abusive behaviour. He specifically suggested that it was the offender's lack of secure attachment relationships in childhood that led to deficits in social and relationships skills and ultimately to a lack of intimacy in their personal relationships. Ward, Hudson, Marshall and Siegert (1995) extended Marshall's focus by looking at whether different types of offending behaviour were correlated with different types of insecure attachment, using the Bartholomew and Horowitz (1991) two dimensional, four category typology. Marshall and Marshall (2002) provided support for some of the hypothesis suggested by Ward, et al., when they examined the victim choice and the manner in which victim compliance was gained in a group of offenders with a preoccupied attachment style.

While there is a growing recognition of the need to address attachment issues with the sexual perpetrator population in general and with children and young people with sexual behaviour problems in particular, there is little evidence to suggest that attachment based assessment or treatment interventions are specifically identified in the treatment protocols for these populations. Friedrich (1995) presents a treatment approach for males who have been sexual abuse victims that seeks to integrate attachment theory and attachment based interventions into trauma specific treatment, but this approach has not been expanded or adapted to youth who are engaging in sexually abusive behaviour. In truth, there is little that prevents the direct use of trauma specific treatment approaches with our population except for the belief that allowing a perpetrator to focus on their own trauma history somehow enables or encourages them to avoid taking responsibility for hurting others.

An integrated treatment approach

At Whitney Academy, we have made efforts to evolve an integrated treatment approach starting with the understanding that all of our students have a history of trauma. We also believe that the fundamental goal in treating abusive behaviour should not be defined merely as the absence of abuse in relationships, but as the increased capacity to engage and maintain stable, mutual, and intimate relationships with others. Attachment difficulties are not only seen as a

treatment issue; they are a treatment obstacle in that they interfere with the development of the trust, safety, openness, and attunement which we feel are essential for learning, integration, and change to occur. Likewise, we believe that our client's trauma experiences are inextricably intertwined with their attachment difficulties, learning problems, general behaviour problems, and more specifically their sexually abusive behaviour. As opposed to thinking that addressing the client's trauma history will inhibit or delay their ability to address their own sexually abusive behaviour, we have come to believe that not addressing the impact of the client's own trauma will simply impede the learning and (more importantly) the effective use of skills we are teaching them to control/change their inappropriate and abusive behaviour.

Our own clinical perspective has been reinforced and expanded by the more recent brain-based research that addresses the neuro-developmental impact of trauma experiences and attachment difficulties. Our academic programme had already been moving to implement accelerated learning techniques in the classroom and the utility of translating these approaches into the clinical aspect of the programme became increasingly apparent. Also, while we had been receiving regular training in the use of psychodrama with our students, we struggled with how to regularly implement these techniques into a treatment model that had been developed from the belief that the Relapse Prevention Model and group treatment were the accepted *best practice* approaches in treating young people who sexually abuse. By conceptualising the treatment programme in a more phase-oriented, trauma treatment model the task of incorporating these various treatment *pieces* into a useable treatment protocol became far more manageable.

Assessment

There have been a variety of studies which have consistently reported evidence of receptive and expressive language disorders, significant differences in Verbal and Performance IQ scores, and significant difficulties in verbal learning and verbal memory abilities in children with trauma histories and children with aggressive behaviour problems (Bleker, 1983; Grace and Sweeney, 1986; Moffitt, 1993). In addition, many of the problems that present themselves with our most behaviourally difficult adolescents, organising and structuring activity, planning and anticipating consequences, regulating behaviour and emotions, controlling and inhibiting motor responses, maintaining self-awareness and self-monitoring, and achieving flexibility and adaptability in coping responses, are exactly those 'executive functions' which current neuro-developmental research would indicate as being impacted by early trauma and attachment difficulties (Luria, 1966; Teicher et al., 2002; Schore, 2002; Fago, 2003). Fago (2003) argues that assessment protocols and treatment programming for sexually aggressive youth 'have not been adequately informed or revised according to recent research advances in developmental psychopathology and developmental neuroscience' (p249).

To take this into account, it seemed important to have as part of our assessment protocol instruments which identified strengths and weaknesses in neuro-development and neuro-processing as well as those instruments that have been more typically used to gather information on personality dynamics, psycho-social development, sexual interest, sexual attitudes, and risk to re-offend. We are aware that typically there are neither the resources, nor the time to do a full neuro-psychological test battery for every individual who might enter our treatment programme or most community based treatment settings. We decided on assessment instruments that were time efficient, cost effective, widely utilised, and applicable to a broad age range. Our goal was to have screening tools in our assessment protocol that could *flag* problems and also be used in re-testing to measure progress. Finally, we wanted instruments that could adequately identify (and justify to funding sources) those individuals in need of a more thorough neuro-psychological evaluation.

Since the focus of our treatment has broadened from the narrow view of addressing sexually inappropriate and abusive behaviour to addressing the impact of trauma and attachment issues on behaviour and relationships, having some measure of the client's trauma symptoms is seen as an important part of the assessment. While interviews with the student, family, and involved agencies/providers offered information regarding trauma history, frequency, and the more obvious behavioural impacts; they often failed to gather information relating to more

subtle or internalised cognitions and behaviours that were the consequence of the child's trauma experiences. We found that unless we asked specific questions related to trauma symptoms the child or family might not identify certain issues as problematic. Utilising trauma symptom assessment tools allowed for a more consistent method of gathering information about a wide array of trauma symptomatology.

Our reading of the research suggests that a student's attachment experiences and attachment style not only have an impact on their neuro-development but also on the type of treatment interventions one might seek to utilise with a client and their family. In addition, sex offender specific research on attachment style would imply that perpetrators with different attachment styles might be a greater or lesser risk to engage in different types of sexual offences. While there are few instruments that have been widely utilised with adolescents and young adults to identify attachment style, we felt that it was worthwhile to use an available instrument and then compare these self-reported styles with our own experience of the student's attachment dynamics.

Our assessment protocol in its current form has been chosen with the specific needs of our client's and resources of our programme in mind. While there are a variety of assessment instruments that might be used for each assessment area, our belief is that all evaluations of children and adolescents with sexual behaviour problems should include assessment in these main areas of treatment concern. Instruments used for assessment at Whitney Academy are noted for each assessment area.

Cognitive functioning: Wechsler Intelligence Scale for Children (WISC-III); Wide Range Assessment of Memory and Learning (WRAML); Test of Memory and Learning (TOMAL). *Note: these or similar assessment instruments are typically administered by referral agencies prior to admission.*

Personality and Delinquency: Millon Adolescent Clinical Inventory (MACI); Jesness Inventory.

Trauma Symptoms: Trauma Symptom Checklist for Children (TSCC); Trauma Symptom Inventory (TSI).

Executive Functioning: Wisconsin Card Sort-64.

Visual Processing and Organisation: Bender-Gestalt Test; Rey Complex Figure Test (RCFT).

Auditory Processing: SCAN: A.

Sexual Attitudes, Knowledge, Fantasies: PHASE Sexual Attitudes Scale; Socio-Sexual Knowledge and Attitudes Assessment-Revised (SSKAAT-R); Adolescent Cognitions Scale; Wilson Sexual Fantasies Questionnaire.

Attachment Style: Relationship Style Questionnaire (RSQ).

Adolescent Risk Assessment: Estimate of Risk of Adolescent Sexual Offence Recidivism (ERASOR).

Adapting the treatment

Most treatment programmes for sexually abusive youth continue to use relapse prevention, group treatment model (Pithers et al., 1983, Pithers, 1990). Those treatment models that do focus on individual treatment still often prioritise the importance of the youth reporting all of their sexual inappropriate or abusive behaviours, taking responsibility for this behaviour, and creating a plan to avoid or stop those abusive behaviours in the future. While we agree that these goals are important, utilising current research and theory regarding trauma and attachment can suggest notably different pathways and processes for achieving these goals. Our current treatment model reflects more of a phase oriented, trauma and attachment treatment approach than a cognitive-behavioural, relapse prevention model.

Containment

First, we assume that the young person's own trauma experiences and their abusive behaviour share a variety of similar trauma/anxiety associated cues. It therefore may not be reasonable (or even therapeutic) to expect that a young person would enter a group and immediately be open, honest, and forthcoming with information about either their own trauma histories or their offences. While we do want to acknowledge the reason why the individual is involved in the treatment, it may not be important at this point in the process for an adolescent to provide all the details and incidents of his/her behaviour.

Working from both a trauma based and brain based model we believe that the priority in beginning treatment is to provide what Allen (2001) refers to as 'containment'. This is first

supplied by making clear the structure and expectations of the treatment programme, identifying the resources available to help the child maintain control and safety, and beginning to give the individual (and their family) some practical, hands-on skills that will help them feel capable of regulating affect and being in control. We believe that part of the containment aspect of treatment includes educating the young person and the family about how trauma can impact the regulatory and learning processes of the brain. In this regard we use information gathered through the assessment to highlight the particular strengths or obstacles this specific young person and his family may present.

Along with education, the 'containment' phase of treatment focuses strongly on learning and practicing relaxation skills and developing *attunement*. Trauma research has shown us and we have experienced in our own treatment that many of the young people with whom we work are *out of touch* or *immune* to the internal cues that their bodies generate(van der Kolk, van der Hart and Marmar, 1996). As a result, these youth can not distinguish between being calm or tense. Bruce Perry's work on looking at the standing heart rate of traumatised individuals (Perry, 2001) or Martin Teicher's work noting the increased electrical activity in the amygdala of these individuals (Teicher et al., 2002) would suggest that many of these young people (and their family members) are persistently in a state of increased arousal as compared to a normative (non-traumatised) adolescent population. In these cases, the use of simple biofeedback tools can allow individuals to consciously recognise heightened states of arousal and receive input and reinforcement about those behaviours or interventions which lower those arousal states. By its nature, much of this early work at relaxation and regulation is done on an individual basis.

Extrapolating from Teicher's (2002) findings that trauma victims show a diminished capacity of the cerebellum vermis to regulate limbic irritability we have decided to use slow, structured movement to further stimulate these pathways and develop greater degrees of regulation. To this end we have taught students and staff at our programme movement and poses from yoga. We then seek to incorporate brief periods of these movements into the clinical, academic, and residential settings. Some early research in using yoga as a treatment intervention with sexually abusive youth has shown indications that it increases their capacity for relaxation, focus in school, and impulse control (Derezotes, 2000).

To increase *attunement*, which is a fundamental aspect of secure attachment relationships, we focus on a process that is multi-modal and 'brain based' in terms of its treatment interventions (Jensen, 1995; Jensen, 2000, Kornblum, 2002). These interventions often use music, movement, and rhythms to literally allow individuals in a group or family setting to get *in tune* with one another. Increasing the adolescents' capacity for attunement and stimulating those pathways through largely non-verbal methods is consistent with the fact that early parent/child attunement is not language based and is largely mediated through right hemisphere functions (Schore, 2002). We feel that focusing on attunement is important in this early 'containment' phase of treatment because this primary dynamic in the attachment process is fundamental to giving the child a sense of safety and developing affect regulation. In creating interventions that stimulate and generate attunement we not only want to give our students the experience of being attended to but we are hoping to stimulate the neural pathways that are engaged in the attunement process. In doing so, we are hoping to find that atonement and self-regulation is more readily experienced and accessible to these youngsters.

While many treatment providers of children and young people with sexual behaviour problems teach relaxation skills, our experience has been that this part of the treatment is given scant time and attention. Skills, after being taught, are rarely practiced or integrated into the adolescent's larger life experience outside the therapy hour. Important members of the child's support group (parents, teachers, relatives, coaches, etc.) are unaware of the skills or how to cue them for the child. Typically, the youth has never practiced using the skills in the presence of an anxiety provoking or stimulating environmental cue in the therapy setting before being asked to utilise the skill in a community or residential setting. Finally, there is typically no physiological measure that ensures the clinician or the young person that they have effectively mastered the relaxation skill. This combination of lapses in providing young people, their families, and other supportive individuals with useful, integrated skills in affect regulation typically

results in these skills being under-utilised and ineffective.

Another important aspect of the containment phase of treatment is to help those individuals with impairment in their executive functioning to learn organisational skills, problem solving approaches, and an affective language (how to put feelings into words). Many of these interventions are readily available through treatment approaches available for children with attention deficit disorders, language disorders, and borderline personality disorders and can be easily adapted to different clinical settings for this population (Linnehan, 1993; Barkley, 1998, Greene, 1998; Tanguay, 2001).

As Allen (2001) has noted a phase oriented approach to treatment does not mean that the treatment follows in a linear step-by-step progression. Rather, the treatment process will go through a developmental progression where the client will revisit particular issues and behaviours repeatedly but hopefully with different levels of coping skills, independence, complexity, and integration as the phase's progress. All the different aspects of containment will need to be consistently practiced, refined and reintegrated as different traumatic experiences and triggers are addressed and more adaptive coping responses and social behaviours are developed.

Deconditioning traumatic responses and re-establishing social connection

The process for deconditioning traumatic responses in treatment has often been to have the client repeatedly talk about the trauma and then attempt to reframe for the client their understanding and the meaning they place on the experience. However, the obstacle to this process is that trauma may inhibit the individual's ability to 'mentalise'. Schore (1994: p176) points out that in order to modulate an emotional response with cognitive processes the child has to develop 'objects permanence' or the understanding that something exists continuously and independent of the child. Allen (2001: p308) describes it as the capacity to 'apprehend the behaviour of oneself and others on the basis of mental states-thoughts, beliefs, feelings and intentions'. Fonagy (1995) has argued that treatment must not only aspire to alter the content of mental representations but also to foster the capacity for mentalisation and reflective function. He notes that we must do more than interpret; we must provide developmental help.

Attachment theory would suggest that children develop this capacity to *mentalise* through their social interactions with primary caretakers. It is what Bowlby (1980) referred to as developing an 'internal working model'. Developmentally we also understand that children experiment with, practice, and refine these capacities through active play. Therefore in our treatment we seek to focus on current attachment experiences with primary caretakers and the use of more experiential treatment interventions to facilitate the process of deconditioning trauma experiences and re-establishing social connection.

This framework leads us to place particular emphasis on daily tasks of caring. Attending to the routines of self-care, meals, and wake-up and bedtime rituals as treatment interventions can often make the process more an experience of being nurtured and less of a task that needs to be accomplished. Persistent acknowledgement of the child through greetings, smiles, eye contact, and touch reinforces that the child is being *attended to* rather than *monitored*. We believe in the importance of using *touch* in our daily interactions with children and adolescents because we feel that touch is a fundamental aspect of the process through which children develop attachment and also because the youth's inappropriate use of touch in either an aggressive and/or sexual manner is typically the primary reason that they have been referred to treatment. It is only through the youth's *experience* of touch in the context of daily caring and everyday social interactions that they are going to be able to learn the difference between nurturing touch and sexualised touch, between social touch and aggression. If the young person *sexualises* everyday social contact or presents as being averse to any type of touch, the intervention becomes that the adult educates the youth (at that moment) regarding the social cues and social context surrounding the use of touch. The adult would describe their intent in using the touch and ask the young person about what they felt and thought was being conveyed through the use of touch. In therapeutic terminology they would *process* what occurred in the interaction and then move on. We continue to offer the young person opportunities to experience touch the next time the social situation and the nature of the relationship between the individuals involved suggested that touch could occur in a natural context.

Within the family, group, or individual treatment setting experiential treatment interventions become a significant aspect of early treatment. Role play, psychodrama, family sculpting, art therapy, music, and movement play a central role in the process. We use or adapt a wide range of specific interventions from the numerous experiential therapies and brain based learning workbooks that are currently available. John Bergman, a registered drama therapist who specialises in work with sexual and violent offenders (Schwartz and Bergman, 1997; Bergman and Hewish, 2002) has been particularly helpful in the development and use of experiential treatment with these young people. Through these interventions we can identify many of the traumatic triggers that the youth experience and allow them to increase their tolerance and capacity to cope with these feelings. In the beginning of this process we are not seeking interventions that necessarily *re-enact* the specific details of the trauma. Rather, we are addressing the cues that occur in daily life that trigger traumatic responses. Interwoven into this work is a consistent focus on monitoring and regulating arousal responses and affective states utilising the skills we have been teaching in the *containment* phase of treatment. Practicing these skills repeatedly in the presence of traumatic triggers within the structured and containing environment of the treatment setting makes the skills more available to the individual when needed in their everyday lives.

Experiential therapies can also be geared to address the specific attachment styles of the individuals and families one is treating. If the attachment style tends to be more avoidant, the use of experiential interventions that generate increasingly stronger and more complex affective responses can be chosen. If the attachment style appears to more ambivalent, treatment interventions that are focused on impulse control, attending to non-verbal social cues, and recognising the sequence of events and behaviours may be more appropriate. In the end, to use Crittenden's (1997) model, we are seeking a greater capacity to effectively integrate affective and cognitive experiences.

Re-structuring personal traumatic schemes

Foa (1997) identified three essential components for processing traumatic experiences:

1. Engaging emotionally with the traumatic memories.
2. Organising a coherent narrative of the trauma.
3. Modifying core beliefs about the self and the world.

In treating sexual behaviour problems, we feel that this process is essential in addressing the child's own traumatic experiences and in addressing the child's abusive behaviour toward others. While this process may appear obvious when addressing the young person's own trauma history, it may not be as clear when addressing abusive behaviour. In treating sexually abusive youth we are regularly confronted with individuals who engage in denial, avoidance, and cognitive distortions or *thinking errors* in relation to the specifics of their abusive behaviour. All of these cognitive processes can be broadly thought of as *avoidant* coping responses. Generally, these cognitive processes are confronted by the therapist and/or the treatment group, often on a repeated basis, until the individual stops his expression of these cognitions. Quite frequently, we experience young people in treatment groups who learn to *say* the right thing but never integrate these cognitive lessons into their relational behaviour or belief systems.

Allen (2001) points out that avoidance is problematic in that it blocks more effective coping responses but that avoidance of distress is generally adaptive. Our students generally have a great deal of embarrassment, shame, and negative self-beliefs connected to their abusive behaviours. In turn, their abusive behaviours often are connected to their own trauma histories through anxiety, fear, abandonment, anger and other difficult (frequently overwhelming) affective states. In the same way that we want students to develop a new narrative for how they think and feel about their own trauma, we want them to develop a new narrative about their abusive behaviour. This new narrative seeks to emphasise taking responsibility for the abusive behaviour not as a means of blaming but as a foundation for new, non-abusive coping responses. The narrative seeks to include empathy for the victim as well as compassion for the self. The youth may, in fact, feel a great deal of guilt yet we are seeking to diminish or eliminate feelings of shame. The goal is that the youth will actively engage in changing how they participate in current relationships and also consider the possibilities for active restitution for past abusive behaviours.

As a prelude to this phase of treatment or perhaps as a bridge between deconditioning traumatic responses and restructuring the narrative, specific treatment techniques such as Eye Movement Densensitisation and Reprocessing (EMDR) (Shapiro, 1995) and Sensorimotor Psychotherapy (Ogden and Minton, 2000) may prove to be useful in bringing physiological and affective states into conscious awareness where they can be identified and more effectively regulated.

It is during this re-structuring phase of treatment that the more widely used cognitive-behavioural and cognitive restructuring techniques (Resick and Schnicke, 1992; Meichenbaum, 1994; Pithers, 1990) may prove to be more effective. However, even at this phase of treatment we strongly believe that these techniques should be adapted so that multi-modal treatment interventions (music, movement, art, psychodrama, etc.) are used. Given the language processing and verbal memory deficits in this population, the greater variety of ways in which we can help individuals learn and integrate new information and experiences the greater the possibility that they can access and use this information when triggered by traumatic cues.

Conclusion

There are clear indications that significant, often persistent, traumatic experiences and attachment difficulties are prevalent in the histories of many, if not most, of the young people being treated for sexual behaviour problems. There is also a growing body of evidence that the experience of both trauma and attachment disruptions have a notable impact on the neuro-development of these children. If we look at the neuro-developmental problems, we also can identify the basis for many of the behavioural and learning issues which are often problematic for the young people we treat. Yet to date, there has been little widespread use of either assessment protocols or treatment programmes that specifically focus on neuro-processing or broadly utilise trauma or attachment based treatment approaches.

While at present we can not point to outcome studies that demonstrate the effectiveness of a brain-based, phase-oriented, attachment focused treatment programme, our reading of the current literature and our own clinical experience convinces us that this is the direction in which we should be headed. What the specific assessment protocol should look like is certainly not clear, but the fact that it should include assessment of visual and language processing as well as broader executive functioning does seem apparent. It is also unclear what specific interventions or skills will increase the young person's capacity for affective, and in turn behavioural, regulation but it is also apparent that without developing a greater capacity for regulation little else of what we try to teach these youth can either be learned or effectively utilised. Finally, we agree that increasing the capacity for empathy in the youth we treat is a worthwhile goal that may also decrease their risk for future abusive behaviour. Yet a child does not become genuinely empathic without the benefit of more stable attachment relationships.

We are at the very beginning of answering the questions regarding which assessment and treatment tools can be most effectively utilised with specific children and adolescents. Collaborative research and treatment programmes incorporating approaches from the sexual offender field with those from neurobiology, the trauma and attachment fields, and brain based learning could prove both enlightening and exciting.

References

Allen, J.G. (2001) *Traumatic Relationships and Serious Mental Disorders.* New York: Wiley and Sons.

Ainsworth, M.D.S., Blehar, M.C., Waters, E. and Wall, S. (1978) *Patterns of Attachment: A Psychological Study of The Strange Situation.* Hillsdale, NJ: Erlbaum.

Alexander, P.C. (1992) Application of The Study of Attachment Theory to Sexual Abuse. *Journal of Consulting and Clinical Psychology.* 60, 185–95.

Awad, G., Saunders, E. and Levine, J. (1984) A Clinical Study of Male Sex Offenders. *International Journal of Offender Therapy and Comparative Criminology.* 28, 105–15

Barkley, R.A. (1998) *Attention Deficit Hyperactivity Disorder: A Handbook for Diagnosis and Treatment.* New York: Guilford Press.

Bartholomew, K. and Horowitz, L. (1991) Attachment Styles Among Adults: A Test of A Four Category Model. *Journal of Personality and Social Psychology.* 61, 226–44.

Baumeister, R.F. and Leary, M.R. (1995) The Need to Belong: Desire for Interpersonal Attachments As A Fundamental Human Motivation. *Psychological Bulletin.* 117, 497–529.

Bergman, J. and Hewish, S. (2002) *Challenging Experience: Brief Handbook for Experiential Therapy Exercises With Offenders.* Oklahoma City, OK: Woods & Barnes.

Bleker, E.G. (1983) Cognitive Defence Style and WISC-R P > V Sign in Juvenile Recidivists. *Journal of Clinical Psychology,* 39, 1030–2.

Bowlby, J. (1980) Attachment and Loss. Volume III. New York: Basic Books

Bowlby, J. (1969) *Attachment and Loss. Volume I: Attachment.* New York: Basic Books.

Chu, J.A. (1992) The Therapeutic Roller Coaster: Dilemmas in The Treatment of Childhood Abuse Survivors. *Journal of Psychotherapy: Practice and Research.* 1, 351–70.

Crittenden, P.M. (1995) Attachment and Psychopathology, in Goldberg, S., Muir, R. and Kerr, J. (Eds.) *Attachment Theory: Social, Developmental and Clinical Perspectives.* Hillsdale, NJ: Analytic Press. 367–406.

Crittenden, P.M. (1997) Toward An Integrative Theory of Trauma: A Dynamic-Maturation Approach, in Cicchetti, D. and Toth, S. (Eds.) *Rochester Symposium On Developmental Psychopathology.* Rochester, NY: University of Rochester Press. 33–84.

DeBellis, M.D. (2001) Developmental Traumatology: The Psychobiological Development of Maltreated Children and its Implications for Research, Treatment, and Policy. *Development and Psychopathology.* 13, 539–64.

Fagan, J. and Wexler, S. (1988) Explanations of Sexual Assault Among Violent Delinquents. *Journal of Adolescent Research.* 3, 363–85.

Fago, D.P. (2003) Evaluation and Treatment of Neuro-developmental Deficits in Sexually Aggressive Children and Adolescents. *Professional Psychology: Research and Practice.* 34 (3), 248–57.

Fernandez, Y.M. and Marshall, W.L. (2003) Victim Empathy, Self-Esteem, and Psychopathy in Rapists. *Sexual Abuse: A Journal of Research and Treatment.* 15 (1), 11–26.

Finkelhor, D. (1986) *A Sourcebook On Child Sexual Abuse.* London: Sage.

Foa, E.B. (1997) Psychological Processes Related to Recovery From Trauma and Effective Treatment of PTSD, in Yehuda, R. and McFarlane, A.C. (Eds.) *Psychobiology of Posttraumatic Stress Disorder.* New York: New York Academy of Sciences. 8, 410–24.

Fonagy, P. (1995) Playing With Reality: The Development of Psychic Reality and its Malfunction in Borderline Personalities. *International Journal of Psycho-Analysis, 76,* 39–44.

Friedrich, W. (1995) *Psychotherapy With Sexually Abused Boys.* Thousand Oaks, CA: Sage Publications.

Grace, W.C. and Sweeney, M.E. (1986) Comparisons of P>V Sign On The WISC-R and WAIS-R in Delinquent Males. *Journal of Clinical Psychology,* 42, 173–6.

Greene, R. (1998) *The Explosive Child.* New York: Harper Collins.

Hart, J., Gunnar, M. and Cicchetti, D. (1996) Altered Neuroendocrine Activity in Maltreated Children Related to Symptoms of Depression. *Development and Psychopathology.* 8, 201–14.

Herman, J. (1992) *Trauma and Recovery.* New York, Basic Books.

Jensen, E. (1995) *The Learning Brain.* San Diego, CA: Turning Point Publishing.

Jensen, E. (2000) *Different Brains, Different Learners: How to Reach The Hard to Reach.* San Diego, CA: The Brain Store.

Johnson, J.G., Cohen, P., Kasen, S., Smailes, E. and Brook, J.S. (2001) Association of Maladaptive Parental Behaviour With Psychiatric Disorder Among Parents and Their Offspring. *Archives of General Psychiatry.* 58, 453–60.

Kornblum, R. (2002) *Violence Prevention Through Movement and Pro-Social Skills.* Oklahoma City, OK: Woods & Barnes.

Leguizamo, A. (2002) The Object Relations and Victimisation Histories of Juvenile Sex Offenders, in Schwartz, B. (Ed.) *The Sex Offender, Volume IV.* Kingston, NJ: Civic Research Institute.

Linnehan, M.M. (1993) *Skills Training Manual for Treating Borderline Personality Disorder.* New York: Guilford Press.

Lisak, D. and Ivan, C. (1995) Deficits in Intimacy and Empathy in Sexually Aggressive Men. *Journal of Interpersonal Violence.* 10(3), 296–308.

Lott, D. (1998) Brain Development, Attachment and Impact on Psychic Vulnerability. *Psychiatric Times,* 15(5), 1–5.

Luria, A.R. (1966) *Higher Cortical Functions in Man.* New York: Basic Books.

Lyons-Ruth, K. and Jacobvitz, D. (1999) Attachment Disorganisation: Unresolved Loss, Relational Violence, and Lapses in Behavioural and Attentional Strategies, in Cassidy, J. and Shaver, P.R. (Eds.) *Handbook of Attachment: Theory, Research, and Clinical Application.* New York: Guilford Press. 520–54.

Main, M. and Goldwyn, R. (1994) *Adult Attachment Scoring and Classification Systems (Unpublished Scoring Manual)* Berkeley, CA: Department of Psychology, University of California, Berkeley.

Main, M. and Hesse, E. (1990) Parent's Unresolved Traumatic Experiences Are Related to Infant Disorganised Attachment States: Is Frightened and/or Frightening Parental Behaviour the Linking Mechanism? in Greenberg, M.T., Cicchetti, D. and Cummings, E.M. (Eds.) *Attachment in The Preschool Years: Theory, Research, and Intervention.* Chicago: University of Chicago Press. 161–82.

Marshall, W.L. (1989) Intimacy, Loneliness, and Sex Offenders. *Behaviour Research and Therapy.* 27, 491–503.

Marshall, W.L., Hudson, S.L., Jones, R. and Fernandez, Y.M. (1995) Empathy in Sex Offenders. *Clinical Psychology Review.* 15 (2), 99–113.

Marshall, L.E. and Marshall, W.L. (2002) The Role of Attachment in Sexual Offending: An Examination of Pre-Occupied Attachment Style Offending Behaviour, in Schwartz, B. (Ed.) *The Sex Offender, Volume IV.*

McEwen, B.S. (2000) The Neurobiology of Stress: From Serendipity to Clinical Relevance. *Brain Research.* 886, 172–9.

McGrath, M., Cann, S. and Konopasky, R. (1998) New Measures of Defensiveness, Empathy, and Cognitive Distortions for Sexual Offenders Against Children. *Sexual Abuse: A Journal of Research and Treatment.* 10 (1), 25–36.

McMackin, R.A., Leisen, M., Cusack, J.F., LaFratta, J. and Litwin, P. (2002) The Relationship of Trauma Exposure to Sex Offending Behaviour Among Male Juvenile Offenders. *Journal of Child Sexual Abuse,* 11 (2), 25–40.

Meichenbaum, D. (1994) *A Clinical Handbook/Practical Therapist Manual for Assessing and Treating Adults With Post Traumatic Stress Disorder.* Waterloo, Ontario: Institute Press.

Moffitt, T.E. (1993) The Neuropsychology of Conduct Disorder. *Development and Psychopathology,* 5 (1–2), 135–51.

Ogden, P. and Minton, K. (2000) Sensorimotor Psychotherapy: One Method for Processing Traumatic Memory. *Traumatology,* 6 (3).

Perry, B., Pollard, R., Blakely, T., Baker, W. and Vigilante, D. (1995) Childhood Trauma, The Neurobiology of Adaptation, and 'Use Dependent' Development of The Brain: How States Become Traits. *Infant Mental Health Journal.* 16, 271–91.

Perry, B. (2001) The Neurodevelopmental Impact of Violence in Childhood, in Schetky, D. and Benedek, E. (Eds.) *Textbook of Child and Adolescent Forensic Psychiatry.* Washington, D.C.: American Psychiatric Press.

Pithers, W.D., Marques, J.K., Gibatt, C.C. and Marlatt, G.A. (1983) Relapse Prevention With Sexually Aggressives: A Self-Control Model of Treatment and Maintenance of Change, in Greer, J.G. and Stuart, I.R. (Eds.) *The Sexual Aggressor: Current Perspectives On Treatment.* New York: Van Nostrand Reinhold. 214–34.

Pithers, W.D. (1990) Relapse Prevention With Sexual Aggressors, in Marshall, W.L., Laws, D.R., and Barbaree, H.E. (Eds.) *Handbook of Sexual Assault.* New York: Plenum Press. 343–61.

Prentky, R.A., Knight, R.A., Sims-Knight, J.E., Straus, H., Rokous, F. and Cerce, D. (1989) Developmental Antecedents of Sexual Aggression. *Development and Psychopathology.* 1, 153–69.

Resick, P.A. and Schnicke, M.K. (1992) Cognitive Processing Therapy for Sexual Assault Victims. *Journal of Consulting and Clinical Psychology*, 60, 748–56.

Ryan, G. (1999) Treatment of Sexually Abusive Youth: The Evolving Consensus. *Journal of Interpersonal Violence*, 14, 422–36.

Saunders, E., Awad, G.A. and White, G. (1986) Male Adolescent Sex Offenders: The Offender and the Offence. *Canadian Journal of Psychiatry.* 31, 542–49.

Schore, A.N. (1994) Affect Regulation and the Origin of the Self: The Neurobiology of Emotional Development. Hillsdale, NJ: Lawrence Erlbaum.

Schore, A.N. (1997) Early Organisation of The Nonlinear Right Brain and Development of a Predisposition to Psychiatric Disorders. *Development and Psychopathology.* 9, 595–631.

Schore, A.N. (2002) Dysregulation of the Right Brain: A Fundamental Mechanism of Traumatic Attachment and the Psychopathogenesis of Post-traumatic Stress Disorder. *Australian and New Zealand Journal of Psychiatry*, 36, 9–30.

Schwartz, B.K. and Bergman, J. (1997) Using Drama Therapy to do Personal Victimisation Work With Sexual Aggressors – A Review of the Research, in Schwartz, B.K. and Cellini, H.R. (Eds.) *The Sex Offender, Volume II.* Kingston, NJ: Civic Research Institute.

Shapiro, F. (1995) *Eye Movement Desensitisation and Reprocessing: Basic Principals, Protocols, and Procedures.* New York: Guilford.

Siegel, D. (1999) *The Developing Mind: Toward A Neurobiology of Interpersonal Experience.* New York: Guilford Press.

Tanguay, P. (2001) *Nonverbal Learning Disabilities At Home: A Parent's Guide.* Philadelphia, PA: Kingsley Publishers.

Teicher, M., Andersen, S., Polcari, A., Andersen, C. and Navalta, C. (2002) Developmental Neurobiology of Childhood Stress and Trauma. *Psychiatric Clinics of North America*, 25, 397–426.

Van Der Kolk, B.A., McFarlane, A.C. and Van Der Hart, O. (1996) A General Approach to The Treatment of Post Traumatic Stress Disorder, in Van Der Kolk, B., McFarlane, A.C. and Weisaeth, L. (Eds.) *Traumatic Stress: The Effects of Overwhelming Experience On Mind, Body, and Society.* New York: Guilford Press. 417–40.

Van Der Kolk, B.A., Van Der Hart, O., and Marmar, C. (1996) Dissociation and Information Processing in Post Traumatic Stress Disorder, in Van Der Kolk, B.A., McFarlane, A.C., and Weisaeth, L. (Eds.) *Traumatic Stress: The Effects of Overwhelming Experience On Mind, Body, and Society.* New York: Guilford Press. 303–22.

Van Der Hart, O., Van Der Kolk, B.A., and Boon, S. (1998) Treatment of Dissociative Disorders, in Bremmer, J.D. and Marmar, C.R. (Eds.) *Trauma, Memory, and Dissociation.* Washington, D.C.: American Psychiatric Press. 253–83.

Van Ijzendoorn, M.H., Schuengel, C. and Bakermans-Kranenburg, M.J. (1999) Disorganised Attachment in Early Childhood: Meta-Analysis of Precursors, Concomitants, and Sequelae. *Development and Psychopathology.* 11, 225–49.

Ward, T., Hudson, S., Marshall, W.L. and Siegert, R. (1995) Attachment Style and Intimacy Deficits in Sex Offenders: A Theoretical Framework. *Sexual Abuse: A Journal of Research and Treatment.* 7, 317–35.

Ward, T., Hudson, S. and McCormack, J. (1997) Attachment Style, Intimacy Deficits, and Sexual Offending, in Schwartz, B. and Cellini, H. (Eds.) *The Sex Offender, Vol. II.* Kingston, NJ: Civic Research Institute.

Webster, S.D. and Beech, A.R. (2000) The Nature of Offenders' Affective Empathy: A Grounded Theory Analysis. *Sexual Abuse: A Journal of Research and Treatment.* 12 (4), 249–62.

Test instrument citations

Becker, J. and Kaplan, M. (1988) The Assessment of Adolescent Sexual Offenders. *Advances in Behavioural Assessment of Children and Families,* 4, 94–118.

Bender, L. (1938) *A Visual Motor Test and its Clinical Use.* New York: American Orthopsychiatric Association.

Briere, J. (1995) *Trauma Symptom Inventory.* Odessa, FL: Psychological Assessment Resources.

Briere, J. (1996) *Trauma Symptom Checklist for Children.* Odessa, FL: Psychological Assessment Resources.

Griffith, D. and Bartholomew, K. (1994) Models of the Self and Other: Fundamental Dimensions Underlying Measures of Adult Attachment. *Journal of Personality and Social Psychology,* 67 (3), 430–45.

Griffiths, D. and Lunsky, Y. (2003) *Socio-Sexual Knowledge and Attitudes Assessment Tool-Revised.* Wood Dale, IL: Stoelting.

Jesness, C.F. (1996) *The Jesness Inventory Manual – Revised.* North Tonawanda, NY: Multi-Health Systems.

Keith, R.W. (1994) *SCAN-A: A Test for Auditory Processing Disorders in Adolescents and Adults.* San Antonio, TX: The Psychological Corporation.

Kongs, S., Thompson, L., Iverson, G. and Heaton, R. (2000) *Wisconsin Card Sorting Test – 64 Card Version: Professional Manual.* Odessa, FL: Psychological Assessment Resources.

Meyers, J. and Meyers, K. (1995) *Rey Complex Figure Test and Recognition Trial: Professional Manual.* Odessa, FL: Psychological Assessment Resources.

Millon, T., Millon, C. and Davis, R. (1993) *Millon Adolescent Clinical Inventory.* Minneapolis, MN: Parson Assessments.

O'Brien, M. and Bera, W. (1985) *The PHASE Typology.* Minneapolis, MN: Programme for Healthy Adolescent Sexual Expression.

Reynolds, C. and Bigler, E. (1998) *Test of Memory and Learning.* Austin, TX: PRO-ED.

Sheslow, D. and Adams, W. (1990) *Wide Range Assessment of Memory and Learning.* San Antonio, TX: Psychological Corporation.

Wechsler, D. (1991) *Wechsler Intelligence Scale for Children: Third Edition: Manual.* San Antonio, TX: Psychological Corporation.

Wilson, G. (1978) *The Secrets of Sexual Fantasy.* London: J.M. Dent and Sons.

Worling, J. and Curwen, T. (2001) *Estimate of Risk of Adolescent Sexual Offence Recidivism, Version 2.0.* Ontario: SAFE-T Programme.

Chapter Thirteen

Experiential Therapy: Interactive Interventions for Young People Who Sexually Abuse

Cindy Tyo

Last night I walked into a restaurant with my family while Led Zeppelin's 'Stairway to Heaven' was playing. Those familiar with this song will probably remember an event (wedding, prom, high school dance) in which you experienced this song. I remember 'Stairway to Heaven' being my brother's high school prom theme. The memories I have of that time are good ones and I found myself sharing them with my children as we enjoyed our dinner. A song, sound, smell, or any other stimuli are experiences that can trigger a large range of emotions. Allowing these experiences to be shared and talked about is what experiential therapy is all about. Past life experiences of young people who sexually abuse are the key to discovering the path to success in treating their aggressiveness. The defences built up by the young people helps keep therapists from knowing the experiences in traditional talk therapy sessions.

> Treat them as though they were young adults. Dress them, bath them with care and circumspection. Let your behaviour always be objective and kindly firm. Never hug and kiss them, never let them sit on your lap. If you must, kiss them once on the forehead when they say goodnight. Shake hands with them in the morning. Give them a pat on the head if they have made an extraordinary good job of a difficult task.
> (John B. Watson).

Psychologist John B. Watson believed that children are entirely products of their environment, pieces of clay – or blank slates, moulded by parents and other social forces into a final shape. Watson (1928, 1976) believed that a mother's affection was potentially dangerous to her child's character, that picking up a child when it cried or feeding it on demand were pernicious forms of coddling. Early theories of treating aggressive behaviours did not fall too far from this belief. Adapting treatment from the prison addiction models of treatment created thinking that addressing sexually abusive behaviours was best handled by the use of cognitive behavioural approaches. These approaches were primarily talk therapy with specific assignments. 'Don't touch the clients' – they don't understand the touch in any way other than sexual. 'Don't address or treat the client's own past trauma' – they need to first take responsibility for their own behaviours. 'Remain objective and firm' – mould their thinking by restructuring deviant sexual arousal to appropriate sexual arousal.

The Cognitive Behavioural Approach of listening to commitment offences, autobiographies, and offence cycles can become redundant, creating an unproductive result. The clients quickly learn the routine and are able to recreate what they have heard in an earlier group by one of their peers. Is this recovery or adaptation? I believe this is adaptation and I have yet to see conclusive follow-up studies that support the success of this approach in treating young people who sexually abuse.

Prior to working with young people who sexually abuse, I was the director of a programme that assessed and treated children and families who were dealing with issues of sexual abuse. For years professionals in the field of treating victims and survivors of sexual abuse have been under scrutiny for the use of play therapy in assessing and treating children who disclose sexual abuse. The primary concern is that the therapist may 'lead' a child to report false allegations. MacFarlane et al. (1986) was challenged on her techniques of interviewing children who made allegations of sexual abuse against the day care providers at the McMartin School. MacFarlane believes that talking to children requires an adult to communicate in a way that the child understands.

I had an experience observing the difficulty a Child Protective Services (CPS) worker had in communicating with a young boy. This young boy had disclosed sexual abuse by an older male neighbour during a session with a social worker that was involved with the family. The social worker reported the allegations to CPS. The CPS worker asked me to accompany her on the home visit as the child's family was involved with another programme at my agency. The CPS worker and I went to the home for the interview. I took along my bag of toys and drawing materials that I used for therapy. The CPS worker sat in a chair with a clip board to take notes. The boy was sitting on the floor. This boy's primary language was Spanish although he spoke English pretty clearly. The CPS worker asked the boy to explain to her what had happened with the male neighbour. The boy explained in his best English and at his developmental level what had happened. The CPS worker then asked some questions for some further clarification. One question she asked was 'Did he ejaculate?' The boy responded 'yes, can I go play now'.

I asked the CPS worker if it was possible that the boy didn't know the word 'ejaculate'. She asked him if he knew the word and he said 'no'. It appeared as though he answered 'yes' originally so that he could be done with the interview. Alternatively, young children will answer in the affirmative to please the adult involved or gain to approval of an authority figure. Neither of these scenarios gets at the truth. At this point, the boy spotted my bag of toys and asked if he could play. The CPS worker and I agreed to let him play while he talked. We sat on the floor with him and he started to draw us a picture. The CPS worker put her clip board down and began talking to the boy as he drew. The boy agreed to draw a picture of what happened and was more open to talking as he drew. The boy had become more relaxed and comfortable with both of us on the floor – at his level. Also drawing and playing were the tools he was most comfortable using to communicate with us.

Young children are not the only ones in need of communication styles conducive to their developmental level. Teenagers are also in need of an understanding communication style from adults. What do therapists most hear from teenagers about adults? *'They don't understand me'* or *'They never listen to me'*.

Virginia Satir had observed that all too often people react to a message as if we are being attacked. She further broke down communication into four specific styles:

- **Placater** – eager to please, always apologising, saying yes or sacrificing themselves.
- **Blamer** – always pointing the finger at someone else.
- **Computer** – super rational, calm, cool, composed and very reasonable.

- **Distractor** – always unfocused, usually frantic, can't look you in the eye.

All four of these styles are defensive in nature, designed to repel the attacking message. A fifth communication style, known as the 'Leveller' is seen as an effective communication style by Satir.

- **The 'Leveller'** is the combination of the four other styles presented with warmth, sincerity, sensitivity, and a sense of purpose. The 'Leveller' also uses logic, reason, and assertiveness without aggression. Messages of the 'Leveller' would include statements such as these:
  - 'I understand your problem and I'm here, if you need me.'
  - 'I don't necessarily agree with your point of view, but I respect your right to feel that way.'

Understanding our clients' emotions and their responses to these emotions is an important step in therapy when encouraging change. This level of understanding can only be accomplished in a relationship that allows effective communication. The therapeutic relationship requires the therapist to be genuine, empathetic, and show unconditional positive regard. A therapist needs to be attuned to the client's affect and respond in a neutral, respectful and supportive manner. Introducing experiential therapy into a therapeutic relationship requires the 'Leveller' style of response as it remains respectful, neutral and supportive. Clients must feel safe and open to the use of exercises that will evoke emotions.

Prior to beginning the use of experiential exercises the therapist must first obtain permission from the client. Introducing exercises to a client who hasn't experienced this form of therapy can be intrusive and potentially dangerous. Many clients we treat have experienced past trauma and may even carry the diagnosis of Post Traumatic Stress Disorder (PTSD). PTSD criteria A from the Diagnostic Statistical Manual (DSM) defines a traumatic event as one that involves 'actual or threatened death or serious injury or a threat to the physical integrity of self or others' and a 'response of intense fear, helplessness, or horror'. Many clients develop coping mechanisms such as avoidance due to the intensity of the traumatic event. This often includes avoidance of thoughts, feelings, places, people, and things associated with the trauma. Introducing any of these avoided items could cause a re-experience of the actual event. This would trigger persistent symptoms of increased arousal as noted in Criteria D of the DSM diagnosis – thus creating the response of intense fear, helplessness, or horror.

After the therapist obtains permission, the exercise must be explained to the client(s) prior to beginning and throughout the experience (e.g., 'First, we will . . .', 'Then we are going to . . .', 'Now I'm going to . . .'). If the therapist plans on placing their hand on the client or plans on asking other group members to touch the client, permission for the touch must always be obtained from the client and from the group members (e.g., 'I'm going to place my hand on your shoulder, is this OK?' or 'Is it OK for each of the group members to place one hand on either of your shoulders?')

The direction the exercise goes is determined by the response of the individual and/or the group once the exercise begins. As mentioned above, clients with severe responses to emotional exercises may struggle and resort to the use of defence mechanisms in an effort to avoid emotions too difficult to handle. The clients must be told that they are in control of the exercise and can stop the exercise at any point or time. I often hold my hands in the T shape showing them the sign for timeout. They can use this sign, sit in a safe chair or tell the group to stop the activity.

The comfort level of the therapist is also an important factor in using experiential activities. Directing from your seat shows little effort or investment in the activity. The success of an activity will decrease if the therapist is not comfortable with being a part of the experience or assisting the client in the experience.

The following exercises are examples used in group and individual therapy sessions. The first exercise was developed for our Managing Arousal/Relapse Prevention Groups. This exercise is used to assist clients with exploring issues at an emotional/feeling level.

Experiential exercises

Exercise 1 – Monologue

Group

The purpose of this exercise is to assist individuals in communicating feelings/emotions deeper than the intellectual level most often communicated through the use of traditional talk therapy.

The individual is given 1 minute to stand before the group and freely express inner emotions as if the audience were able to hear the individual's inner voice (as if they are talking to themselves). The 1 minute limit allows the client the security of knowing there is an end. The client may or may not wish to process the monologue immediately following the presentation. On some occasions, individuals may choose to use a journal to write about the experience.

Variations

Some individuals may experience more than one inner voice in conflict with each other and may use the monologue to demonstrate this inner conflict.

Process questions

'What did you notice happening as you spoke?' 'What is the primary theme that plays over and over as you allow yourself to express from the inside?'

Exercise 2 – Alter ego interactive sculpt

Group

The purpose of this activity is to explore the different personality characteristics used by individuals as defence or coping mechanisms.

The client is asked in a group setting to identify four personality characteristics they see as primary in themselves (e.g., sexual seeking, sneaky, aggressive, and vulnerable). The client is then instructed to pick four group members to play each of these roles (the therapist might assist in picking group members to include group members that might identify closely with the characteristic chosen by the client). Once group members are chosen the therapist assists the client to sculpt the individuals into positions based on the role that personality plays for the client (e.g., the strongest role standing in front of the other roles). Once the sculpt is complete the therapist then asks the client to stand in front of the sculpt with their back to the sculpt. Then the group members are asked to verbally encourage the client to take on the characteristics of the personalities identified.

Process questions

'Which personality (alter ego) do you most wish to rid yourself of?' 'What is the motivation in keeping this personality (alter ego)?'

'What would it take to give up this coping mechanism?'

Example

I used this exercise recently in one of my groups with an adolescent boy who presents as the 'perfect patient' primarily around his therapist or other clinical staff. When in the milieu he exhibits extremely aggressive and sneaky with his behaviours with other patients. The four personality characteristics he chose for this exercise were:

1. 'Perfect Patient'
2. Sneaky
3. Aggressive
4. Vulnerable/Victim

The 'Perfect Patient' role was identified by the client as the strongest and most out spoken role. The sculpt was changed a few times as the other personalities appeared to be stronger than the 'Perfect Patient'. The final set up of the sculpt had the client standing in the middle of all of the personalities. With the client's and the group members' permission, the four group members put one hand on the client's shoulders. Each group member was insistent on getting the client to be the personality that they each played. The 'Perfect Patient' role being the loudest and most insistent. The client attempted to respond by using rationale for why being the 'perfect patient' wasn't helping him. As he attempted to walk away from the group the group followed and wouldn't let up. The client quickly resorted to the aggressive approach by trying to push the group members away. I pointed out to the client his use of his aggressive side to resolve this anxiety provoking experience. At this point the patient requested help from the group as he stated a need to explore other ways of coping as 'these' four personalities (the four in the role play) were not productive. Follow-up group discussion allowed group members an opportunity to process insight into either their own comfort with the role they played or the reluctance to give up what is familiar to each of them.

Exercise 3 – Head to toe check

Group or Individual

The purpose of this exercise is to help clients connect thoughts, feelings, and emotions to the physical responses of their bodies to assist in managing impulsive urges.

This exercise is best done quickly and introduced at a time when a client may demonstrate a level of anxiety, frustration, excitement, sadness, or any noticeable emotion. Assist clients during group and/or individual therapy in identifying physical responses to arousal by having the client describe the body's physical reaction to current emotions starting at the head and working the way down the body.

Process questions

'What do you notice happening to your body?'
'Starting at your head and working down the body describe any feelings you may have. Check your heart rate, your breathing, your body temperature, any increase of movement of your arms, legs, hands, etc.'

Exercise 4 – Who am I? Three dimensional collage

Group or Individual

The purpose of this exercise is to facilitate expression of the outer and inner self with a sense of security.

The individual is given a large envelope, scissors, markers, glue, and magazines and is instructed to create a collage of themselves using both the outside and the inside of the envelope. The outside is to represent what other's see and know about the individual. The inside represents what others do not see or know about the individual. The inner contributions should not be glued inside the envelope as the individual may choose to bring them to the outside.

Once the collage is completed, the therapist encourages the individual to begin to share the objects on the outside of the envelope working toward sharing the inside.

Process questions

'Tell me about the person expressed on the outside of your envelope.'
'What do you think keeps the inside contributions on the inside?'

Exercise 5 – Colour body chart

Group or individual

The purpose of this activity is to allow individuals an opportunity to express feelings non-verbally.

Participants are given a piece of paper with the outline of a body and a large selection of crayons.

The participants are then instructed to select four colours to identify four different feelings. Once the colours are selected the participants must draw a colour key on the corner of the page identifying each feeling with a different colour. Next, the participants are instructed to colour the body using the chosen colours. The directive given is 'colour how you feel about yourself' (see variations below). Once the picture is completed, participants may be open to verbally discussing feelings by using the picture to describe.

Variations

The directives for colouring the picture can be a large variety and may be used together in one session. Some of these may include:

'Colour how you feel about (significant person)'

- your father
- your mother
- your brother
- your sister
- someone you have abused or hurt
- someone who has hurt or abused you

'Colour how (significant person) feels about you.'

Process questions

'Would you like to tell me about your drawing?'
'Can you talk about how you were feeling when you were colouring this picture?'

Example

This particular exercise has been helpful in assisting clients to explore emotions by taking away the pressure of talking. Once the drawing is complete, the client often becomes more willing to talk about the experience of the activity. I have asked clients to do this exercise early on in therapy and again later in their treatment. Change in colours and use of the colours may indicate change in thinking. An 18-year-old boy who had sexually abused his 17-year-old sister initially was very angry with his sister for disclosing this. He reported in therapy that he and his sister had an agreement that he would not offend her again if she would not tell what he had done. She did tell her mother and he states he felt betrayed. During this exercise early in his treatment, the primary colour used in the body chart in which he was instructed to colour 'How you feel about your sister' was black. He

identified the black colour as anger. The boy stated he was very angry with her for breaking the promise.

As time went on in his treatment, he began to acknowledge his infatuation with his sister and the need for treatment due to his continued desire to sexually abuse her. His feelings toward her changed as he was no longer angry and appreciated that she had told. When colouring another body chart with the same instruction of 'How you feel about your sister' his primary colour was green. The green colour was identified as pride. He did continue to have a blue line of colour that ran through the body like a vein which was identified as infatuation. Treatment continues to address this.

The therapy does not end following the experience in the group or individual session. Clients are often encouraged to use journal writing, relaxation, self-talk, listening to music, drawing or other management techniques identified by the client to assist in assuring management of arousal. Working in a residential programme allows the therapists to check in with clients later in the day. Our programme schedule allows for patient rounds following morning therapy groups to allow the therapists an opportunity to report to other therapists and staff any concerns about a client following group.

Therapists are also encouraged to use healthy interventions to care for and manage their own arousal. Managing a healthy emotional well being is crucial to working in this field. Collaborating with a co-therapist before and after a group is a healthy way of processing the emotions that may have been triggered. Connecting to peers and family outside of work creates a balance between the therapist's professional and personal life. Enjoy your work with adolescents. They are wonderful human beings waiting to be discovered by caring adults.

References

Crisci, G., Lay, M. and Lowenstein, L. (1997) *Paper Dolls and Paper Airplanes: Therapeutic Exercises for Sexually Traumatised Children.* Charlotte, NC: Kidsrights.

Kahn, M. (1997) *Between Therapist and Client: The New Relationship.* (Revised Edition). New York: W.H. Freeman and Company.

Karen, R. (1998) *Becoming Attached: First Relationships and How They Shape Our Capacity to Love.* New York: Oxford University Press.

Macfarlane, K. and Waterman, J. With Conerly, S., Damon, L., Durfee, M. and Long, S. (1986) *Sexual Abuse of Young Children: Evaluation and Treatment*. New York, NY: The Guilford Press.

Satir, V. (1988) *Peoplemaking*. Mt. View, CA: Science and Behaviour Book Inc.

Yontef, G. and Simkin, J. (1981) *Gestalt Therapy: An Introduction*. Illinois: The Gestalt Journal Press.

Chapter Fourteen

Cognitive-Behavioural Treatment under the Relapse Prevention Umbrella

Charlene Steen

Introduction

Cognitive-Behavioural therapy with sex offenders has generally been found to be the most effective of the 'talk' therapies in the decrease of sexual re-offending (Hall, 1995; Alexander, 1999). Derived from the work of Beck, Meichenbaum (1977), Ellis (1977) and others, it is an action-oriented form of psychosocial therapy that assumes that faulty thinking patterns cause maladaptive behaviour and painful emotions. Treatment focuses on changing thoughts in order to change the individual's behaviour and emotions. Among the techniques used in Cognitive-Behavioural therapy are the challenging of irrational beliefs, self-monitoring, cognitive-behavioural rehearsal, thought stopping, communication skills development, assertiveness training, the increasing of social skills, and homework and reading assignments.

This method of treatment was most prominently applied to criminal thinking and behaviour by psychiatrists Yochelson and Samenow (1976). They focused on changing the criminal's way of life by correcting thinking errors, restructuring the criminal's view of himself and his world, introducing the concepts of choice and will, etc. Pure Rational Emotive therapy, a cognitive restructuring approach developed by Ellis, is also widely used in corrections. It targets beliefs that produce problem behaviours, and is very similar to the Yochelson-Samenow approach.

Relapse Prevention therapy is a form of Cognitive-Behavioural therapy pioneered by psychologists Marlatt and Gordon (1985) and others. Originally designed as a maintenance programme following addiction treatment, it is now widely used independently for behavioural self-control. It teaches individuals to anticipate and cope with risk factors leading to relapse, with intervention strategies including coping skills training, cognitive therapy, and lifestyle modification.

Both cognitive and behavioural techniques are used to help the individual reframe and change

thinking and behaviour. It emphasises self-management. The individual learns to understand the process or stages of relapse, recognise and cope effectively with high risk situations, cope with urges, minimise negative consequences, develop a more balanced life style, and make the process a lifetime endeavour.

Psychologists Marques, Pithers, and others applied Relapse Prevention to the treatment of sexual offenders (for a more scientific description, see Laws, 1989). Among the specific applications of Cognitive-Behavioral therapy to sex offenders are Cognitive Restructuring, Relapse Prevention, The Offence Cycle, and Psycho-Educational Training. Treatment foci usually include:

1. Choices and consequences.
2. Avoidance and escape (relapse prevention).
3. Empowerment through language and self-talk.
4. Needs assessment and refocusing.
5. Connecting with emotions relative to victimisation (own and others').
6. Recognition and diffusion of risk factors.
7. Development of more effective coping strategies.
8. Understanding and using sexuality appropriately.
9. Increasing communication and socialisation skills.
10. Delaying gratification and urges.

Specific techniques may include:

1. Journalling and the sexual autobiography.
2. Correcting thinking distortions.
3. Modelling.
4. Cognitive rehearsal.
5. Conditioning (positive reinforcement and lack thereof).
6. Systematic desensitisation techniques
7. Validity testing.
8. Increasing coping skills.
9. Thought stopping and switching.
10. Using the plethysmograph as a feedback device

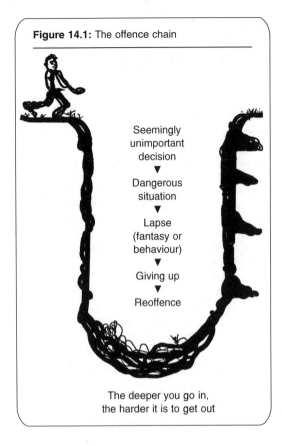

Figure 14.1: The offence chain

Seemingly
unimportant
decision
▼
Dangerous
situation
▼
Lapse
(fantasy or
behaviour)
▼
Giving up
▼
Reoffence

The deeper you go in,
the harder it is to get out

11. Meditation and relaxation techniques.
12. Aversive conditioning.
13. Slow-down techniques.
14. Behavioural homework assignments.

Treatment of young people who sexually abuse has not received the amount of research accorded adult offenders. However, we do know that treatment has decreased the risk of recidivism for sexual offences as much as 72% (Worling and Curwen, 1998) and that it can also effectively reduce the risk of non-sexual recidivism. Most programmes have found Cognitive-Behavioural therapy to be effective for young people, especially when a family component is attached. In addition, according to Alexander's meta-analysis (1999), group treatment appears to be particularly effective for young people.

There is also some evidence that Multi-Systemic Therapy (MST), an approach which involves a broader spectrum than just the young abuser – in particular family, neighbourhood, school, and community, and which has generally been used to prevent general criminal offending, shows promising results with young people who sexually abuse (Borduin, Henggeler et al., 1990). This fits with the many research studies indicating that young people who sexually abuse are more likely to commit other types of criminal offences rather than sexually recidivating. It therefore makes sense to integrate some of the approaches of MST into a Cognitive-Behavioural treatment programme for this population. This includes parent and family as well as offender treatment (see Chapter 15).

Cognitive-Behavioural treatment can take many forms. Since the primary goal of treatment is to prevent further offences, and since healthy all around functioning is critical to the prevention of re-offence, Relapse Prevention serves as a logical umbrella for all of the different Cognitive-Behavioural topics and applications. Relapse Prevention is applied in the most comprehensive manner, reminding the treatment provider of this primary goal while addressing the various dysfunctional aspects of the young offender. It can be utilised effectively in all of the components of treatment – group, individual, family, etc. By incorporating positive family participation and empowerment, utilising collaborative efforts with community entities, evaluating progress regularly, and utilising interventions designed to promote treatment generalisation and long-term maintenance of therapeutic change – basic concepts of MST, under this Relapse Prevention model, effective long term change can be produced.

The first step in treatment: basic relapse prevention

Since re-offence is the most critical concern, it makes sense to begin treatment with basic Relapse Prevention strategies. An easy way for young people to comprehend the steps toward relapse, or offence chain, is to diagramme them in the form of a huge mud hole (Figure 14.1), with each step toward relapse moving deeper into the hole, until the bottom – re-offence, is reached. At each step along the way, however, the young offender has the capability of climbing out of the hole – not re-offending. But the further down the chain toward re-offence, the more difficult it is to climb out.

The steps down the offence chain begin with a *Seemingly Unimportant Decision* (*SUD* for short) – a decision a youth makes which is rational on its face, but propels him/her into the second step –

the *Dangerous Situation*. For example, for a youth who has molested a child in the past, it could be agreeing to baby-sit while a next door neighbour takes an injured child to the hospital. In this second step, the youth has the capacity to re-offend. If the youth has inadequate coping strategies, this may lead to the next step – *Lapse*. A lapse for a young person who sexually abuses is either a fantasy of offending or an action which is dangerously close to offending. Once the youth lapses, the abstinence violation effect comes into play, wherein the youngster basically is *Giving Up*, the simplified term for this stage. At this point the youth either gets caught up in the fantasy or feels they have already gone too far, abrogating the previously held expectation of success (not re-offending). Once the youth gives up this expectation of abstinence from re-offence, it is an easy hop to committing another sexual offence.

It is critical for young people who sexually abuse to understand the concepts which best describe the process of non-offence – *Avoidance* and *Escape*. Avoidance protects the youngsters from getting into dangerous situations where they would have the capacity to re-offend. Escape is how they get out of those situations before re-offending, placing themselves outside of the zone of danger.

Learning and understanding the words *Avoidance* and *Escape*, as well as the terms for the steps down the offence chain (*Seemingly Unimportant Decision* or *SUD, Dangerous Situation, Lapse,* and *Giving Up*) is very important, and can be done in game form, such as by playing the letter game – 'hangman,' with those (and other words they will be learning). Applying these concepts to other problematic behaviours in their lives can also be reminders of the steps and terms.

Making offence chains for their own offences will help the youths see their own processes. By breaking offences into multiple steps, it is easier for them to see how they can intervene at either the outset or at each step to prevent re-offence. Often young persons who sexually abuse will claim they just did the offence, that there was no progression. They must be assisted in such cases in breaking down their actions into these steps (or sometimes many more SUDs and increasingly Dangerous Situations). By doing this, they can see where they can avoid or get out of a potentially dangerous situation at multiple points. It partialises the process of re-offence into small manageable pieces, slowing down the behaviour into stages which can be halted at any time.

Once the young person develops an offence chain of the explicit behaviours which led to the offence, the thoughts which led to those behaviours and the feelings generated by those thoughts must be added in. The way people think about what is happening directly affects what they are feeling and how they behave (Ellis, 1977).

Specifying alternative behaviours, alternative thoughts – changing distorted interpretations of what is happening, and developing strategies for handling painful or non-productive emotions are the next steps in preventing relapse. This is done by looking at each step in the offence chain, finding alternative ways of thinking and behaving at each, and figuring out how those alternatives would change the behavioural outcomes. Likewise, feelings at each step must also be analysed, with their cognitive stimuli recognised and alternative thoughts and behaviours attached.

These same concepts should be taught to parents and siblings. They must learn to identify steps toward their own as well as the youngster's dysfunctional behaviours, develop methods of positive intervention, and utilise them within the everyday living situations.

Choice-based treatment

As is obvious from the prior work on the offence chain, the Relapse Prevention-Cognitive Behavioural approach requires young people who sexually abuse to take responsibility for their thoughts, feelings, and behaviours by making choices along the way in the offence chain and in every aspect of their lives. The treatment provider's responsibility is to give them the tools to make healthy choices – but not to be responsible for the choices the youths make. This is an important concept, because these young people will eventually be going out into life away from treatment and treatment providers. If they have not learned, internalised, and practiced the methods to prevent reoffence, it will be much easier for them to regress to prior dysfunctional thinking and behaviour and eventually to reoffence.

Comprehension of the nature of Choices and Consequences is basic to intelligent, informed choice-making. Choice is under the control of the youngster. There are innumerable possibilities in every given situation, although the young people may not initially realise this. Unlike choices,

Figure 14.2:

Increasing awareness of choices:

Take any situation and list all of the choices you can.
Then list the likely consequences.

Situation: (describe) _____

_____

_____

Choices:	Likely Consequences:
1.	1. 2. 3.
2.	1. 2. 3.
3.	1. 2. 3.
4.	1. 2. 3.

consequences cannot be controlled. They are the natural results of the choices made. But it is possible to figure out or estimate the likely consequences of any given choice. (An exercise to help young people who sexually abuse understand this is shown in Figure 14.2).

By giving them exercises describing various situations and having them brainstorm the multiple choices a person would have in the given situation helps them see the myriad of choices available. It is then necessary to attach the likely consequences to each choice, so they can determine which choices are healthy and practical, and which lead to negative results. It is important for them to realise that every choice made in life has both good and bad consequences. An example is choosing to truant from school. If one decides to truant, the person has the consequences of having fun with friends and not having to do class work. But along with the positive consequences there are the negative consequences of discovery, punishment, poor grades, possible elimination from athletic teams, and even loss of scholarships, etc. Often activities

that are poor choices are initially pleasurable but have many long term negative consequences.

Even their sexually abusive behaviour had both positive and negative consequences. At the time of the offence, they probably had a release of painful emotions and tension, possibly decreasing anger, feelings of helplessness, being out-of-control, etc. They may have enjoyed feelings of power or intimacy. But in the long run, the negative consequences probably prevailed. These include getting caught, shame and guilt, criminal sanctions, having to be in treatment, and sometimes having to leave home and family. Usually the negative consequences in such actions far overshadow the initial positive ones.

In addition, if the youth chooses to stay on the straight and narrow, abstaining from the negative acts, he/she will lose the initial pleasure or release, but in the long run will not have to suffer the adverse results. (See Figure 14.3 for an exercise illustrating positive and negative consequences.)

Through an understanding of the consequences that result from the choices to do and not to do a

Figure 14.3:

Good and bad consequences

Choice	Benefits (positive consequences)	Costs (negative consequences)
DO: **OFFENCE**	1. Immediate gratification 2. Release of anger or other emotions	1. Guilt 2. Social censure 3. Loss of self respect 4. Harm to victim 5. Possibility of getting caught 6. Identity as a pervert 7. Embarrassment of family 8. Being locked up
DON'T DO: **OFFENCE**	1. No harm to others 2. Avoidance of lock-up 3. Increased social approval 4. Increased control 5. Respect of family/peers 6. Freedom from treatment	1. Denial of gratification 2. Frustration 3. No immediate release of emotions

particular act, the young person can make more intelligent and truly self-beneficial choices. Parents and siblings must be taught the same concepts and methodology, so they can assist the young people in making better choices as well as improving the home milieu the young offenders are in or to which they will return.

Correcting distorted thinking (thinking errors)

According to most studies of both adult offenders and young people who sexually abuse, their empathy levels are no different than the non-offending public. Yet they do not seem to understand or care about the effects of their offences on their victims. This is because their thinking has affected their perception of themselves and their victims. Their own needs have somehow encouraged them to fool themselves into denying the harm they are doing or have done.

'She deserved it.' 'He came on to me.' 'I was teaching him about sex.' 'We were just playing.' 'She liked it.' 'I didn't hurt him.' 'She never said no or stop it.' All of these and hundreds more are the distorted thoughts of many young people who sexually abuse, thinking errors which prevent the correct perception of the situation.

By having guest speakers who talk about surviving the types of sex offences committed by the youths in the group, many of the participants can begin to connect with the true pain suffered by their own victims. The speakers can explain why they didn't say no, how they didn't like what was being done to them, how they were afraid of losing someone important to them, how they didn't deserve what was done, and so on. Since one of the reasons for cognitively distorting the painful results of sexual offences is because most offenders really want to be looked at as good, caring, worthwhile people, this can be a powerful motivator for them not to re-offend. Listening to survivors often connects young people who sexually abuse with their own victimisations. Victims who have not adequately processed their own victimisation feelings are more likely to step into the shoes of the aggressor, because they haven't allowed themselves to feel the painful feelings and hence the feelings of their victims. Instead, they act on their experiences, trying to be the powerful one, the one in control. Recognising how powerless or betrayed they felt can help them attach to similar feelings in their own victims. This isn't to shame them. It is to help them think before they act, recognising in advance the hurtful consequences.

Victimisation checklists (what was done to you, how did you feel at the time, what do you feel now, etc.), writing hypothetical letters to themselves from their ostensible victims then reading letters from actual victims (usually much stronger), discussing what victims in particular situations are likely to feel, and acting out scenarios where victims tell, aren't believed, or have to testify, are all ways of correcting thinking errors relative to their victims.

Some young people who sexually abuse may need more work on general emotional recognition and vocabulary. They have never been aware of feelings, nor do they have the words to define them. For these youths, it is important to teach them the terms for emotions and what they represent. Using emotion lists to find words that described how the youths felt in particular situations, storytelling using various emotion words, drawing, painting or using clay to express specific emotions, acting emotions out in little play scenes, playing emotion charade games, writing emotions in poetry, and playing emotion guessing games are all ways of sensitising these youngsters to their feelings and the words that describe them. Awareness of how youths can identify their emotions by their physical manifestations (like tensing up muscles, for example) is another aspect which should be covered.

Also related to the correction of distorted thinking is teaching the youngsters to use words which empower them to change (such as I 'want' or 'don't want' to or 'choose' to rather than I 'can't' 'should' or 'must'), and teaching them to change their self-talk (the messages they tell themselves, which affect their feelings and behaviour). These can be practiced with behavioural assignments in the community.

Parents frequently either rationalise the sexually abusive behaviour their children committed, utilising many of the same thinking distortions about victims, or they generalise the bad acts committed by their children into perceptions of the child as evil. Their thinking needs the same type of straightening out as the young person's in this respect.

Parents may have a hard time recognising or admitting to the victimisations suffered by their abusive behaviour, particularly if it was caused by them, or they may blame the offences committed by their children on the victimisations those children may have experienced, rather than taking appropriate responsibility for their own actions and requiring their children to take responsibility for their actions. This can seriously undermine what the young person is learning in treatment.

Therefore, once again, the families of the young person must be included in the specific treatment modules, learning basically the same things their abusive child is discovering.

Self understanding and needs satisfaction

The previous unit leads naturally into work on increasing self understanding, and especially the awareness of needs. A more positive sense of self is a corollary benefit of this work. This component is based on the premise that those who are healthy, aware of their needs, and have positive coping strategies are less likely to commit socially unacceptable acts.

Autobiographical work, including journalling, is prominent. For those that have problems expressing themselves in writing, check off lists, tape-recorded autobiographies, or comic strip illustrations are effective substitutes.

After looking at or brainstorming needs that everyone has, it is important to zero in on the needs the young abusers were satisfying by committing their offences. Was it loneliness they were assuaging, anger they were expressing, power and control they were gaining, or were they looking for excitement? These and many more specific to the individual must be cited. Then, all of the different ways these needs can be satisfied are examined, with the most positive and successful solutions noted, then used in behavioural assignments. Planning to use these in advance (cognitive rehearsal) of offending can diffuse whatever has led to their genesis.

Viewing how the family satisfies individual and whole family needs ties in with the individual offender work. Often just an awareness of needs can be the impetus for positive changes which can help the young person.

This is also a time to examine roles and power issues within the family, which will also connect with the Communication module below, as family members learn new ways of communicating.

Identifying and diffusing risk factors

Satisfaction of needs ties into an identification of *Risk Factors* which led or could lead to their sexually abusive behaviour. Risk factors are usually painful emotions which cause a dys-equilibrium in the normal, satisfactory functioning of the youngster. The way risk factors are cognitively processed can determine what behaviour will follow. If the youngster has inadequate coping strategies, negative behaviour, such as re-offence, can easily happen. However, with adequate coping strategies which have been practiced and internalised, the risk factors can be diffused without the resort to adverse actions.

Once again, it is important to partialise this process. First, it is important to identify the *Trigger* which causes the risk factor to arise. The trigger is usually something that occurs in the environment, such as the youngster's father angrily calling them good-for-nothing or worthless when a chore has not been done. This leads to the emergence of *Risk Factors*, such as

feelings of depression, hopelessness, and possibly even anger. Without adequate coping skills, the youngster may take the accusation at face value then look for something to make him/her feel better, more powerful or appreciated, or possibly a something or someone to take anger out on. Further sexually abusive behaviour could be that something that could give feelings of power and control, or be a means of expressing anger aggressively.

Adequate coping strategies include some of the past learned techniques of changing self-talk (which in turn reframes the risk factors), finding alternative behavioural choices to cope with the risk factors, as well as delaying tactics (which will be covered more thoroughly later in this chapter).

Work on the steps in the cycle of offence (Figure 14.4) can assist young people who sexually abuse in recognising their prior dysfunctional patterns of behaviour so that they can intervene and change the progression in the future. It should be noted that this goes hand-in-hand with the offence chain, for if the

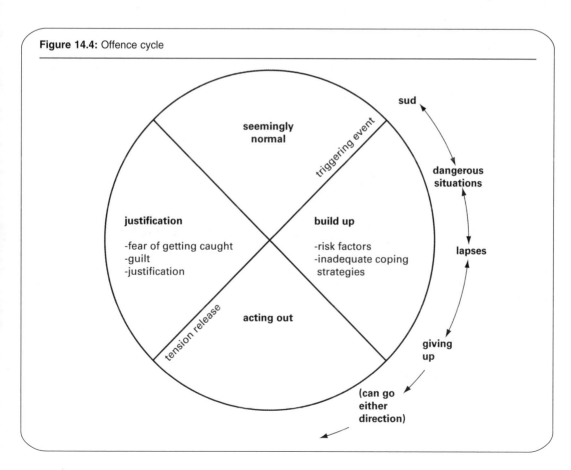

Figure 14.4: Offence cycle

Figure 14.5:

RISK FACTORS

Risk factors are emotions experienced by the offender which lead toward undesirable behaviors, such as sex offending.

Triggers are situations which cause these risk factors to emerge.

Exercise I. List as many triggering situations as you can which you have experienced in the past. Then write down the risk factors which emerge as a result of these situations. Finally write down ways you can diffuse or minimise the risk. For example:

Trigger – my father telling me I am no good.
Risk factors – (I feel) worthless, angry, and unappreciated.
Ways to minimise the risk – (I can) talk with a friend, tell myself my father is really angry with his own life and not me, write a letter saying how I feel.

Triggers	Risk factors	Ways of diffusing my risk factors

Exercise II. Now take a 3 × 5 card and write down you risk factors on the front side and all the ways you can diffuse or minimise them on the back side. Carry this around with you at all times. When you are feeling bad, take it out, read both sides, and do some of the things you wrote down to diffuse or minimise the risk factors.

youth is not in the zone of danger, there is no capacity to re-offend. Thus these two concepts can function together as a protective shield.

Each youth must learn to recognise their own typical triggers and the risk factors they typically elicit, then plan ahead for ways to diffuse the risk factors as another means of preventing re-offence. (See the exercise in Figure 14.5, which can be placed on 3' by 5' card and carried around as a reminder.) Again, practice assignments in the community utilising the diffusing tactics that have been developed help prepare young people who sexually abuse for the situations they are likely to encounter and assist them in making satisfactory coping choices in the future.

Family members can be assisted in modifying some of their own trigger behaviours, changing the way they relate to the young person. While this is very difficult without a total restructuring of each individual's responses and the total family functioning, which is usually not possible, nevertheless small inroads and increased awareness can be of help to the abusive young person. Similarly, with increased awareness, the family can learn to intervene or cue the youngster into effectively intervening into the cycle of offence before re-offence occurs.

Improved communication

Communication is an often overlooked key to successful functioning and coping, which is critical to any intervention with young people who sexually abuse. Communication is often only thought of as talking – expression through words. But half of communication is reception – listening. And communication includes indirect verbal and nonverbal expression – such as a mother's baking cookies for her child expressing love and care, and body language – the way the posture, tension level, vocal tone and production, etc. indicate the mood of the individual.

Receptive communication is a skill important to all of us – the juvenile offenders, treatment providers, teachers, probation officers, family and siblings of the juvenile offender, and others. Awareness of what is being said, what is being omitted, what is being shown through nonverbal behaviour, are all significant.

Listening skills can be taught to the young people in the group setting in a variety of ways. Paired listening is an effective focused listening exercise. Here they are placed into pairs and take turns telling each other about some personal issue, such as a first sexual experience. Only one young person can speak, the other must listen, and then the process is reversed. Afterward they discuss with each other how it felt to listen, what the content made them feel, how they felt about each other afterward, etc. Then the whole group discusses the experience, but not the content of the experience.

Listening games can include 'pass the rock' – where only the person holding the rock can and/or must speak and select the next speaker. Topics of speaking can be everything from open to one topic for all, or picking an unknown topic out of a bowl or bag. How it feels to have to speak on the topic or to have to listen to someone else speak, how it feels to be passed over when one wants to speak, and other communication issues should be aired afterward.

For non-verbal communication, charade type games where one youngster must act out what he is feeling or wanting without words and the other group member must guess what his body language is showing are fun learning tools. This then should be applied to the sexual situation. Young people must learn to listen to and watch the body language of anyone with whom they might be having or want to be having sexual contact. A discussion of what types of non-verbal cues are sent when a person is interested in another person (such as frontal stance, eye contact, lip licking, etc.) is helpful, as are the bodily cues when a person is not interested (such as lack of eye contact, edging away, etc.). They must also listen to verbalisations and learn that even a weak no means no. Discussing how they have felt when they were not listened to when they didn't want to do something is helpful to this concept. As well as listening, young people and their families must also learn how to get someone to listen to them when they have something to say. Brainstorming all the ways one can get another person to listen is a good way to discover various techniques, which should then be discussed regarding their effectiveness. For

example, screaming a person's name and getting in their face may attract their attention, but may not be a positive way of getting the person to listen. However, looking at and speaking to a person directly from a close place, asking the person to set a time to talk, writing a note to let the person know you need to communicate, or going through an intermediary, such as a counsellor if direct methods don't work, are usually effective. Families can even devise codes for listening, such as, when one person puts a hand on the other person's shoulder, the other person agrees to stop and listen.

Assertive rather than aggressive communication must be taught and practiced. The young people learn the difference between the two. This can be done by role playing situations where a person is aggressive and then assertive and distinguishing between the two. Asking for what is wanted or needed, particularly when the want or need is a sensitive one, must be practiced with role plays and behavioural assignments. The importance of speaking up when something is or someone does something uncomfortable must be practiced. The reasons for not speaking up (or speaking up) in these situations should be explored. (Figure 14.6 is an exercise which illustrates this issue. Once again, after the written exercise is completed, it should be discussed with the group or within the family.)

Another aspect of this assertiveness training is learning to say no in a polite but firm way.

Practicing typical situations where a young person usually wants to say no, but has difficulty because of peer pressure or finds aggressiveness easier, are effective training methods. If, how, and when to confront a person in authority, either by giving a refusal, to challenge something unjust, or simply to ask for help must also be examined, practiced in group, practiced at home, and practiced in the community.

Parents should be helped to recognise the importance of communication in the offence chain and cycle of offence. If young persons can talk about things that are bothering them, such as current frustrations, depression, anger, etc. (risk factors) and urges with someone who really listens, this communication becomes a means of diffusing risk factors and of preventing the youths from moving around the offence cycle and down the offence chain. Real communication is an effective means of coping in a functional way which eliminates sexual acting out behaviour.

Figure 14.6:

Touching-assertiveness exercise

1. Think of a time you were touched and didn't like it, and never told the person who touched you how you felt. Who did it and what did he/she/they do?

2. Why didn't you like it?

3. Why didn't you say anything?

4. What could you have said to the person who did it?

5. What effect might that have had on the person who touched you?

6. What effect might that have had on you?.

7. If it, would not have had a positive effect, what does that say to you about yourself?

8. Have you ever touched someone else in a way that person might not have liked? Describe it.

9. If the person did not tell you they didn't like it, can you understand why they didn't? Explain.

Sexuality: education and appropriateness

Many young people who sexually abuse have deficits in sexual knowledge. One young man in our programme thought he had sexual intercourse with a girl he had sodomised, because he did not know female anatomy. Many of the parents have difficulty talking to their children about sexuality, and may even lack sexual knowledge themselves. Having a nurse or sex educator talk about basic sexual functioning and dispel the rampant misinformation is helpful to this problem. It can also help prevent sexual diseases and unwanted pregnancies.

Appropriate sexual behaviour is another matter. What is an appropriate touch in a given situation can be discussed through short vignettes of appropriate and inappropriate behaviour. Many young people who sexually abuse and their families also have poor boundaries and don't understand when sex is

and is not appropriate. Discussions through short vignettes can help to better define these boundaries. For example, necking with a girlfriend in a public place is not appropriate, because it can make other people feel uncomfortable. Nor is a parent giving a child a wet kiss on the lips appropriate. While what is appropriate attire or lack of it in the home varies between homes depending on family attitudes, once a member of the family has molested, more stringent rules must apply regarding clothing. The parents and all family members, including the young person, must understand that this is for the protection of any potential victims.

Related is the differentiation between sex, love, and friendship. While these three elements can be joined together, they are totally separate entities. Just because someone wants to feel close and loved doesn't mean that sex is an appropriate way to attain that closeness, particularly if there is an age discrepancy or the persons involved are close relatives. Just because a person is looking for friendship doesn't mean they want a love or overly intimate relationship nor does it mean they want to have sex. Having the young person come up with situations where one or another of these entities is present without the others help them understand the differences. If they can't come up with such situations, the treatment providers can, often using amusingly extreme situations to make the point. For example, a person may love their dog, but they shouldn't have sex with the dog. Similarly, loving a sibling should not result in sexual activity.

Sexuality should also be detached from negative emotions. Masturbating to either relieve anger or to decrease depression should be stopped, because it reinforces the inappropriate use of sexuality, in particular the similar application in the offenders' sex crimes. It helps to discuss this in group, with each member talking about appropriate sexual experiences and times when sex was used in an unsuitable or potentially dangerous manner.

The use of sexually explicit materials and internet sex are important to discuss, with an emphasis on when they are used inappropriately. If either were used prior to or in connection with any sex offence, then they become risk factors which must be totally avoided. Even if they were not used in connection with an offence, it is important to discuss the depersonalisation that occurs in both. Knowing and building a relationship with a person before having a sexual encounter is important not only to the avoidance of misread signals and re-offence, but also to possible accusation of an offence.

Building relationships

Youngsters in general tend to jump headlong into relationships without adequately knowing the other person. This often results in betrayals and rejections. For young people who sexually abuse who have previously committed sexual offences, betrayal and rejection can be the trigger for painful emotions and hence the genesis of offending behaviour. This cycle can be avoided by encouraging and teaching the young offenders to move more slowly through relationship building – both romantic and general friendship. By breaking relationships down into graduated steps, the youths can see how to protect themselves and with whom they can share sensitive issues without fear of betrayal. These steps can be described like the layers of an onion,

with Acquaintances as the outermost shell, as follows:

1. Acquaintances – persons you may see occasionally (but with whom you do not do anything, such as supermarket checker, mail person, or restaurant server).
2. Casual friends – people with whom you do activities (like work, bowl with, etc.).
3. Good friends – people you do a variety of things with and know beyond the activities.
4. Close friends – the people who you can call on for help, activities, talking, etc., and who you are there for as well when needed.
5. Most Intimate Relationships – usually only one or two people who are always there for you and with whom you share your innermost thoughts and they share theirs.

Sharing innermost thoughts with someone who is not known well is risky behaviour. They may not be trustworthy and keep the confidence. The sharer has also relinquished great power to someone who could use the confidence in a hurtful manner, leaving the sharer vulnerable and helpless – a common risk factor for re-offence.

Within the family structure, the young people who sexually abuse and their family members must realise that although they have had a long time relationship with each other, all family members are not necessarily close or trustworthy. Talking about who in the family is or is not trustworthy and with whom they are or are not close and why helps everyone see the significance of this issue and make behavioural plans that will help themselves.

There are several topics of discussion which further flesh this unit out. They include discussions of the types of communication and actions that are appropriate at each step and why; how to diffuse the hurt when betrayed – such as reframing and depersonalising – which can prevent or lessen the sting of the violation; and how they went beyond the appropriate relationship level and betrayed the expectations of their victims. Role plays of each of these help young people see and feel the results of actions and communications at each step more clearly.

In addition, the importance of healthy pro-social relationships must be stressed and encouraged through behavioural assignments (such as attendance at a recreation department or church youth group or participation on a sports team).

Urge control and delaying gratification

Young people who sexually abuse must learn about their fantasies and urges – their nature, how to direct them toward positive ends, how to intervene to stop dangerous fantasies and urges, and how to delay action when they have a fantasy or urge. Often young people don't know what a fantasy is, or say they don't have any. A fantasy is simply a day dream or mental image. We all have them. They can be about any subject. Sexual fantasies can become a problem when they are deviant, because they can develop into bodily urges which the person may want to fulfil. An urge is a need that propels the person toward action unless certain constraints are present. They can be physical, as when a male becomes tuminescent, or just mental. Sexual urges can be described as waves, which can increase or disperse. They do not have to be satisfied, but can be diffused or waited out. All bodily urges are much like this. For example, hunger pangs come and go whether or not one is fed. It follows that if the juvenile offenders have sexual urges, if they wait long enough or distract themselves, those urges will go away.

Of course, it is better if abusers never have any deviant fantasies or urges. However, it is important that they realise that they have not failed should they have some. It is what they do with the fantasies or urges that is significant. Thought stopping, by yelling stop to themselves, snapping a rubber band on their wrists, smelling a noxious substance, or just thinking about a noxious smell, taste, sight, or touch or about being embarrassed by being arrested in front of friends and family, can drive the deviant fantasy away or give them the opportunity to substitute a positive non-deviant fantasy. The positive fantasies can be planned in advance, so they can be substituted in easily.

If the young people can't seem to divert their deviant fantasies or urges, however, then they must have a plan to protect themselves from acting on them. These can include calling or going to a friend, parent, or counsellor and talking about what they are feeling, reading over an urge control card (see Figure 14.7), keeping themselves out of the zone of danger (not going anywhere where they have the capacity to offend), writing down what has been going on in their lives which triggered the fantasies or urges, doing a relaxation or meditation exercise, forcing themselves to think about or write down all of the likely consequences of their actions, counting to 500, simply waiting a prescribed length of time before acting, or doing any activity which will divert their attention. These slowing down mechanisms can be brainstormed by the young offenders, and the best of them written down and practiced with all types of negative fantasies and urges until they are well assimilated and remembered.

It is important that parents and family members understand that the young people may have deviant fantasies and urges in the future, and that they should not be condemned for these. The parents and other family members must be non-judgemental and open to listening to what is going on, giving support for their avoidance of negative action and helping them contact treatment providers for additional assistance as needed.

Summary

This is just an introduction to the many Cognitive-Behavioural interventions that can be employed to help young people who sexually abuse keep themselves safe. Much more in-depth work, utilising all aspects of cognition, emotions, and behaviour relative to the problematic behaviour is needed.

Work with parents, siblings, extended family if possible, in groups, dyads, triads, etc., both together and separate from other families, will enhance the likelihood of success. Milieu therapy with the families seems to be particularly effective, because the real functioning of the family is clearer than in a neutral setting and interventions can be tailored to fit the environmental situation.

But ultimately it is the young person themselves who must make the decisions in life which will avoid sexual re-offence. The cognitive-behavioural view is a pragmatic one, which realises that the treatment provider cannot change the young person. Treatment providers are just that – providers of the tools which the youngsters can use to prevent re-offence and live a more productive life, and motivators who can encourage them to use those tools.

References

Alexander, M. (1999) Sex Offender Treatment Efficacy Revisited, *Sexual Abuse: A Journal of Research and Treatment*, 11, 2, 101–16.

Figure 14.7:

URGE CONTROL CARD

When I get a strong fantasy, thought, or urge to commit a sex offense, I will sit down and carefully read over the following:

(1) A fantasy, thought, or urge to reoffend is not unusual. It doesn't mean I have lost control or failed. And it doesn't mean I have to offend.

(2) If I feel scared or guilty about my sexual fantasy, thought and/or urge, I will remind myself that I have power over them. I don't have to give in to them. I have other choices. I have other options that can satisfy my needs besides offending.

(3) I will think of this as a learning experience. I will look at my life and try to figure out what has led up to the fantasy, thought, or urge. I will try to figure out what need I am trying to satisfy, and I will brainstorm all the other positive ways I can meet my needs.

(4) If I am still having trouble, I will think about who I can call to talk to. I will look at the phone numbers of these resources on the other side of this card and call until I can talk to one of them.

Name and phone number of friend: *Lee – 555-7913*

Name and phone number of therapist: *Sara Johnson*

555-3629

Name and phone number of probation officer *Mr Frank Jacobs*

5555-4850

Hotline phone number *Suicide Helpline – 555-1111*

Above all, I will remind myself that I am in control.
An urge or fantasy does not make me a sex offender.
I am in control. This urge will pass.

Barbaree, H., Marshall, W. and Hudson, S. (Eds.) (1993) *The Juvenile Sex Offender*. New York: The Guilford Press.

Borduin, C.M., Henggeler, S.W., Blaske, D.M. and Stein, R.J. (1990) Multisystemic Treatment of Adolescent Sexual Offenders. *International Journal of Offender Therapy and Comparative Criminology*, 34, 105–13.

Ellis, A. and Grieger, R. (Eds.) (1977) *Handbook of Rational Emotive Therapy*. New York, Springer.

Greer, J.G. and Stuart, S.E. (Eds.) (1976) *The Sexual Aggressor*. New York, NY: Van Nostrand Reinhold.

Hall, G.C.N. (1995) Sexual offender Recidivism Revisited: A Meta-Analysis of Recent Treatment Studies, *Journal of Consulting and Clinical Psychology*, 66, 2, 348–62.

Laws, D.R. (Ed.) (1989) *Relapse Prevention With Sex offenders*. New York: The Guilford Press.

Marlatt, G.A. and Gordon, J.R. (Eds.) (1985) *Relapse Prevention: Maintenance Strategies in The Treatment of Addictive Behaviours*. New York: Guilford.

Meichenbaum, D. (1977) *Cognitive-Behaviour Modification*. New York: Plenum.

Ryan, G.D. and Lane, S.L. (1991) *Juvenile Sex Offending: Causes, Consequences, and Correction*. Lexington, MA: Lexington Books.

Steen, C. (1993) *The Relapse Prevention Workbook for Youth in Treatment*. Orwell, Vermont: Safer Society Press.

Steen, C. (1989) *Treating Adolescent Sex Offenders in The Community*. Springfield, Il:Charles C. Thomas.

Worling, J.R. and Curwen, T. (2000) Adolescent Sexual Offender Recidivism: Success of Specialised Treatment and Implications for Risk Prediction. *Child Abuse and Neglect*, 24, 965–82.

Worling, J.R. and Curwen, T. (1998) *The Adolescent Sexual Offender Project: A 10-Year Follow-Up Study*. Toronto, ON, Canada: SAFE-T Programme, Thistletown Regional Centre.

Yochelson, S. and Samenow, S.E. (1976 Et Seq.) *The Criminal Personality: A Profile for Change* (3 Volumes) New York: Aronson.

Chapter Fifteen

Emotion-Focused Therapy and Children with Problematic Sexual Behaviours

Jane F. Gilgun, Kay Rice and Danette Jones

Introduction

When Alan (not his real name), eight, and his family entered treatment because of Alan's inappropriate sexual behaviours, the primary emotion he expressed was anger. He did not want to talk about his sexual behaviours. Parents in the neighbourhood warned their children to stay away from him. Children at school either avoided him or taunted him. Alan's parents also were angry. They were quick to blame others for their son's behaviours, reluctant to look at their personal issues that affected Alan, and were unable to deal with their son's sexual behaviours, emotional states, and difficulties in school and with peers. Frustrated, ashamed, and confused, they wanted therapists to fix their son.

At the end of treatment, Alan's parents had begun to manage the difficulties in their relationship and had gained new parenting skills. Alan had developed capacities for appropriate emotional expressiveness, had learned to recognise his emotional states that meant he was at risk to act out sexually, and had demonstrated that he knew what to do when he was at risk to be sexually inappropriate or abusive. In general, he had learned to manage his sexual behaviours through becoming aware of his emotions and through learning how to express his emotions in appropriate ways. He and his parents accepted that Alan was at risk to act out sexually in the future and might require additional interventions as time went on.

Alan's parents were key in how well Alan did after treatment ended. They learned to talk easily and openly about issues related to his sexual acting out. When he needed emotional support, they were there for him. In the years following the end of therapy, Alan and his parents returned periodically to see the therapists. Alan would say, 'It's time for a tune-up,' meaning he needed extra help in managing his sexual behaviours. Usually these return visits were one to two sessions, taking place when Alan was at a transitional point and experiencing emotional turmoil, such as going to a new school and entering puberty.

The purpose of this chapter is to demonstrate the centrality of emotional expressiveness in the treatment of children, aged five to ten, with problematic sexual behaviours. To do so, we pieced together clinical experience, findings from research on the development of sexually abusive behaviours, research and theory on emotional development and expression, and research and theory on resilience. Though there is a vast literature on topics that can shed light on children's emotional development, there is little on the emotional expressiveness of children with issues related to their sexual behaviours. The second and third authors of this paper originated the emotion-focused therapy programme we discuss in this chapter. This paper represents an initial attempt to put to paper ideas that we think are important in child and family therapy when children have sexually inappropriate behaviours.

Sexually inappropriate behaviours

In our view, behaviours are sexually inappropriate when children are pre-occupied with sexual topics to the point where other aspects of their development suffer, when children's sexual behaviours are intrusive, unwanted, and ignore the wishes of others, and when children trick, manipulate, and force others into sexual contact. Like abuse perpetrated by older persons, sexual abuse perpetrated by children often involves an abuse of power where older, stronger, more cognitively developed children take advantage of younger children. We believe the sexual abuse that children and young people perpetrate is as damaging as abuse that adults perpetrate. The younger the children are when sexually inappropriate behaviours begin, the more likely the children were sexually abused themselves.

Some childhood sexual behaviours are normative. Sexual contacts between age peers that are mutually wanted, are of short duration, and where privacy is respected are not inappropriate. A useful guideline that helps to assess for inappropriate sexual behaviours is whether a child stops the behaviour when someone in authority makes the request. For example, a child who masturbates during nap time in preschool is likely doing what comes naturally. If teachers ask the child not to masturbate in public, and he complies, then there is nothing to worry about. If the child persists, then the child and family require professional assessment. Children who engage in sexual activity, even when mutual, but who persist after parents and others ask them to stop would benefit if their parents or others in authority obtain consultation with competent professionals.

An overview of child and family issues

When they began treatment, Alan and his family were typical of families in the early stages of learning to manage children's sexually inappropriate behaviours, and where, family members typically express a restricted range of emotions, primarily displaying defensive anger, possibly covering up their hurt and confusion. Their emotional responses may be under-reactions (flat) or over-reactions (highly emotive), usually with emotions disconnected from conscious thought. The language they use to express emotions lack concreteness, specificity, imagery, and clarity. These qualities are associated with positive change in therapy (Watson, 1996).

Most parents are like Alan's, they come to treatment angry. Their children's behaviours are everyone else's failure. It's hard for them to get beyond their own guilt to their other emotions. Parents usually have their own therapeutic issues. Those who engage in their own therapy are most likely going to 'make it.' For example, when parents had been sexually abused and haven't dealt with the effects, they are unlikely to be effective with children who may have been sexually abused and who have sexually problematic behaviours. Dealing with their own issues clears the way for them to be more emotionally available for their children. Since the pioneering research of social worker Fraiberg (Fraiberg, Adelson and Shapiro, 1975) on infant mental health, researchers and practitioners have recognised the importance of parents' working through their own issues in order to become more effective with their children.

Sometimes parents are willing to examine themselves and their relationships for the sake of

their children. They might not have done so without this motivation. When the parents are engaged in their own therapy, this takes the pressure off the children. Not only may parents function better as a result of therapy, but from children's point of view, everyone in the family is in therapy, not just the children identified with the acting out problems.

Clinically and through research, we have developed a typology of how children display their emotions at the beginning of treatment for sexual behaviour problems. The categories are angry, anxious, hollow, disorganised, blaming, denying, and emotionally expressive. Children typically move back and forth between emotion states, but some display a predominant style. There are likely to be other types of displays of emotions and our list may be incomplete. These styles of presentation sometimes, but not always, mirror how one or both parents and other family member initially display their emotions.

Angry. Typically, when boys begin treatment, they channel their emotions through anger. If they are hurt, they express anger. If they don't get their own way, they are angry. They may express feelings of affection through physically aggressive behaviours such as headlocks or through verbal aggression such as name-calling and put-downs. The impression they give is a desire to show mastery and dominance over others, perhaps in reaction to their own perceived lack of control or their sense of how they are 'supposed' to act, or a combination. To show their vulnerability may be impossible. Many of the boys also have fears of being called gay, especially if they have acted out sexually with other boys or been sexually abused by males. Some boys worry that they may be girls, since they believe that men victimise only girls sexually. Girls, too, may be angry, possibly as a defence against and as a means of managing fear, embarrassment, and shame.

Anxious. Some children display a great deal of anxiety. These children often begin therapy as if they are 'snakes in a can,' but when treatment works, they let go of their anxiety and their personally appealing qualities emerge.

Hollow. Other children appear hollow and disassociated. These children are challenging because therapists find it difficult to connect emotionally with them. Their affect may be flat. Sometimes the term withdrawn fits them. They simply do not want to or cannot discuss their sexual behaviours and usually almost any other emotion-laden topic.

Disorganised. Another typical child presents a picture of emotional disorganisation, often carrying multiple diagnoses including attention deficit hyperactivity disorder, conduct disorder, and oppositional disorder. It is likely that these children have underlying physiological features that are implicated in their emotional disorganisation. They often have experienced multiple adversities, but if parents are willing to engage in therapy and to secure resources needed to facilitate children's development, there is reason to hope that children can learn to manage sexual impulses and develop good peer relationships, do well in school, and look forward to a fulfilling future.

Blaming. Some children appear unable to take responsibility for their behaviours. Typically they blame others, with statements such as 'It's his fault. If he hadn't done this, I wouldn't have done what I did.' Underlying shame and fear of consequences are associated with blaming responses. Still other children may be unable to see that they have any responsibility for their own behaviours.

Denying. Some children outrightly deny their inappropriate sexual behaviours, even when presented with clear evidence. Like children who engage in blaming, they may be full of shame and fear of consequences that they don't want anyone to think they could act in sexually inappropriate or abusive ways.

Emotionally expressive. Not all children and families begin treatment displaying their emotions in these ways. Some children and families can express a range of emotions, their affect and cognitions are interconnected and in balance, and they are accepting of a need for help. This type of family will probably require a less intense form of intervention, perhaps a course of psychosocial education that involves the whole family as well as peer group work for the child with sexual issues.

An overview of emotion-focused therapy

Emotion-focused therapy is based on ideas derived from clinical experience and relevant research and theory. Emotions are a big part of

who we are as human beings. They affect what we perceive, how we perceive, and what we do in response to our perceptions (Isen, 1984; Izard et al., 2002). They influence thoughts and activate internal representations of self, others, and how to behave in particular situations. Children who are emotionally competent can identify and name their own feelings and those of others. They can talk about their negative emotions such as anger, envy, and anxiety, have the presence of mind to consider possible courses of actions, and take into considerations the effects of their behaviours on others (Raver, 2002). They have good peer relationships. Adults find them appealing and engaging. They comply with adult requests, while they also are assertive and express their own wants.

Children with these qualities have positive emotional connections with others. These connections are based on capacities for empathy where children accurately imagine how others are feeling through sensitive interpretations of often subtle clues. Children modify their behaviours in response to these perceptions. Such contingent responsiveness is possible when children identify and understand their own inner states.

Families and emotional expressiveness

Children can't do what their parents can't. Children's emotional development stems from qualities of their attachment relationships to primary caregivers. Sensitive, responsive, reciprocal care giving fosters emotional expressiveness, responsiveness, and empathy in children. When children enter treatment for sexually inappropriate behaviours, therapists obviously cannot observe the quality of attachments that occurred earlier. They can, however, observe parents' interactions with their children as clues to the family's emotion systems.

Children internalise parental behaviours as guidelines for their own. When parents model empathy, consideration for others, and emotional expressiveness that shows integration of thoughts and feelings, children are likely to have similar qualities. For example, when parents take responsibility for their own mistakes, this provides children with important lessons in how to handle emotion-charged situations. An illustration comes from the authors' clinical experience. A mother took responsibility for her inaction when her children first told her their father was molesting them. With no prompting from the therapists, she said in front of the children, 'You told me Daddy was touching you sexually. I thought you were imagining it. I was wrong. I'm so sorry.'

This mother showed balance between powerful emotions of guilt, shame, and regret and her cognitive awareness of the impact of her mistake on her children. In this situation, she neither under-reacted nor over-reacted but provided a balanced and articulate response based on an integration of thoughts and feelings.

Children must feel safe

Another principle in emotion-focused therapy is that children have to feel safe to express their emotions. Sometimes these emotions are unpleasant and may be displayed in ways that trigger in parents automatic responses of guilt, shame, and rage. In such situations parents respond to children's emotion dysregulation with their own. Parents require coaching to rein back their own emotions to give children the space they need to express themselves. Parents' primary job in these situations is to ensure that the children do not harm themselves and others and to provide guidance in constructive management of these powerful inner states.

Gendered emotion expression and display

Parents also may have been socialised to believe gender stereotypes about girls' and boys' display of emotion, where they shame boys for showing 'feminine' emotions such as sadness, shame, compassion, and fear, while they reward boys for being aggressive, stoic emotionally, and in charge. Ironically, the emotions that stereotypic notions stigmatise in boys are those whose expression is important for emotional health.

Effective parenting takes teamwork. In families where there are two parents, the quality of parenting styles reflects the quality of parental relationships. When parents are not getting along, they have difficulty parenting effectively. Children with sexual issues are likely to tax them beyond what they can manage. Children also may misinterpret parents' preoccupation and distraction over their relationship difficulties and think that the parents don't love them or they are to blame for parental difficulties. Therefore, if parents take care of themselves and take care of their own needs, this will help their children. When parents are single, effective parenting requires the help of others: friends, family members, and neighbours. Child care, respite, and organised recreation are integral to providing support to parents.

Family assessments

At intake, therapists assess family members' capacities for the integration of affect and cognitions, whether their emotions are not minimised or overblown, and whether their parents want to come to therapy and genuinely want help. We want to know if they are willing to do what it takes to help their children. Blame, typically, is present. We are most hopeful if the parents blame themselves and not the children or the system. Self-blame is not a huge issue when parents are willing to engage in therapy.

Multi-modal approaches

Typically, children and their families require a multi-modal approach that entails child individual therapy, group psycho-education for the children, family therapy, and couples therapy for two-parent families. We offer this spectrum of services in our emotion-focused therapy programme. Providing individual therapy before entering peer group has important benefits. In emotion-focused therapy, therapists communicate empathy and understanding while at the same time are clear that the sexual behaviours are inappropriate. Therapists speak directly about the children's sexually inappropriate behaviours.

Surprising to some, children and young people often are relieved when therapists speak frankly about sex and expect them to do the same. Far too often, children and young people with sexual issues are raised in families and communities where sexual topics are approached with strain and reluctance, as if there is something naughty, dangerous, and taboo about sexuality. Many adults buy into the myth that children are not sexual beings until some time in adolescence. Thus, individual therapy can communicate acceptance of young people where they are. When children act out sexually, rarely do adults respond appropriately, this is, directly, empathically, and with clear setting of boundaries.

Not only do children gain personally from individual therapy, such work is preparation for group work. The psycho-education groups are 12 weeks long and are small (five to six children) with two therapists required because the children often have attention difficulties and hyperactivity. Group psycho-education provides a place for children to be with other children with similar issues and thus provides opportunities for them to see that they are not the only ones with sexual issues. In peer groups, children learn to manage their sexual behaviours through a series of learning modules that include information and practice in the management of emotion and sexual behaviours. They can learn from other group members. Peers are a primary socialising group for children and adolescents, often as important and sometimes more important to · young people than their families of origin.

Family therapy provides opportunities for therapists to assess family processes that contribute to the children's sexual issues. Rarely is the family atmosphere characterised by emotional balance, where parents model the expression of a range of emotions in appropriate ways, where emotions and cognitions are connected, and where parents coach their children in emotion expression that is balanced and considerate of others. The range of emotions expressed may be restricted and out of balance. Emotions are often suppressed. When expressed, they may be disconnected from conscious thought and thus can be hurtful and counterproductive. Parents may be dismissive of children's attempts at expressions of emotion. Teasing and taunting about displays of emotion are common. Older siblings may be part of an ineffective family emotional system. Gender stereotypes may play out in families where fathers are alternatively distant and harsh and mothers are emotive or distracted and thus emotionally unavailable.

Families in treatment for children's sexually inappropriate behaviours rarely view sexuality as a natural topic of conversation. Few parents provide direct instruction about healthy sexual expression. Rather parents convey information through innuendo and cryptic remarks. Displays of affection may be restrained and awkward. On the other hand, some families have sexualised family atmospheres where ordinary conversation is infused with sexual content, sexual boundaries are routinely violated, and older children and adults in the family perform sexual acts in the presence of children. Children internalise these sexual processes and draw on them as they develop inner representations of ways to express sexuality. Thus, families typically are out of balance in terms of sexuality. On the one hand, they may restrict sexual discussions and appropriate expressions or they may go in the other direction and create a highly sexualised family atmosphere. Children learn what is normal and usual from their families and they bring these assumptions into their relationships with persons outside of the family.

Multiple family therapy and parent groups are beneficial when they are available. Children benefit when they see how other parents interact with their own children. Parents benefit when they have opportunities to interact with other parents in similar situations. In the authors' programme, this type of therapy happens informally, as parents spend time together waiting for the children who are participating in peer group. At the end of each peer group parents are invited in so that their children can show them what they learned during that day's session. A more formal multiple-family and couples group would be desirable but the costs and time commitment for families are often prohibitive.

Significance of emotional expressiveness

In the first author's long-term research on how persons cope with, adapt to, or overcome adversities, she found that the single most important factor distinguishing persons who were resilient from those who harmed others was emotional expressiveness during childhood and adolescence (Gilgun, 1990, 1991, 1992, 1996, 1999c). Aspects of emotional expressiveness include:

- Experiencing, naming and expressing a range of emotions and not just a few.
- Experiencing continuity in emotional states and not switching abruptly from one state to another, such as appearing joyful and an instant later conveying rage.
- Dealing directly with emotions without suppressing them or attempting to relieve them through self-destructive or anti-social means.
- Responding with empathy to the emotional states of others without taking advantage of their vulnerabilities.

Behaviours and activities associated with the acquisition of emotional expressiveness included:

- Confiding to others about personal, painful events and experiencing affirmation.
- Writing out emotions in journals.
- Having outlets for tender feelings, such as caring for younger children and tending to pets.
- Seeking comfort and solace through artistic expression, music, dance, and sports.
- Doing something kind for someone else.

In short, in the first author's research, persons who had capacities for coping with, adapting to, or overcoming risks for harmful behaviours knew what they were feeling, experienced a range of feelings, and managed their feelings so that neither others nor themselves were harmed. When they chose to express their feelings they did so in pro-social ways, certainly not all the time, but they refrained from seriously harmful behaviours to others such as sexual abuse, rape, and physical violence and to themselves such as cutting, chemical abuse, and recklessness.

Persons who had experienced adversities but who also had capacities for emotional expressiveness had at least one long-term close relationship in childhood and adolescence with pro-social persons:

- In whom they confided.
- With whom they identified.
- Whom they admired.
- Whom they emulated because they wanted to be like the persons they admired.
- Whose positive values they internalised and wanted as guidelines for their own lives.

Persons with adversities and who turned out well also had a relationship with persons who actively coached them on appropriate expressions of emotion and modelled it themselves. In childhood and adolescence, these young people consciously studied the behaviours of persons they admired and emulated them. In short, emotional expressiveness develops from positive, long-term relationships during childhood and adolescence. The young people model their own behaviours on persons they admire and work hard at being like them. These relationships typically are with family members, both nuclear and extended, and with peers and families of peers. Appendix 1 lists qualities associated with these positive capacities. Persons who develop these capacities display resilience.

Persons who had experienced adversities and harmed others typically were out of touch with their feelings and the feelings of others; or, if they did have capacities for emotional expressiveness, they also easily disconnected from the emotions and interests of others. They did not confide their personal, painful experiences to others, often because they could not find anyone who they thought was trustworthy. The persons with whom they identified and wanted to emulate typically modelled negative values and behaviours, such as justifications for vengeance when they perceived that others had harmed them. Persons in their environments applauded them when they behaved in ways that lived up to gender stereotypes.

In addition, when they thought about acting out in harmful ways or were in the midst of harming someone, they often felt a tremendous release of strong negative emotions. So powerful was their desire to alleviate this emotional pressure that they disconnected from the humanity of their victims. This release is highly pleasurable. Thus, the act of being sexually abusive can be so strongly pleasurable that young people experience tunnel vision and disconnect from negative consequences for others and for themselves.

Emotional expressiveness and emotion display

Emotional expressiveness is not the same as emotion display. Emotional display is how people choose to show their emotions, through facial expressions, words, tone of voice, and body language (Brody, 2000, 1999; Zeman and Garber, 1996). Persons can express their emotions appropriately without making an obvious display. Some people have muted displays of emotion, often based on cultural practices that enforce limits on emotion displays and encourage stoicism. Many boys and men believe overt displays of emotions are not appropriate in some social situations, but if anyone asked them how they were feeling they could say so. The key idea, then, is awareness and identification of emotions and pro-social expression.

Gender and emotional expression

Most of the persons who acted out against others were male, leading to research for explanations, which can be summarised as related to how males are socialised. All males are exposed to cultural themes and practices that encourage them to be aggressive, in charge, to be stoic and repress displays of most emotions except anger, and to be sexually aggressive (Brody, 1999c, 2000; Gilgun and McLeod, 1999). Males who cope successfully with adversities associated with sexually harmful behaviours somehow bypass these gender-based themes and practices. When pressure builds because of unexpressed emotions, they find release in a range of possible activities, not by harming others. Cultural themes and practices related to being male and that enforce suppression of most emotions, that punish men for emotions associated with being female such as feelings of vulnerability, loneliness, and loss, and that lead men to believe that they can be aggressive and take what they want are strongly implicated in male sexual aggression, apparently even boys and adolescent young men.

In Western cultures, girls and women are less likely to harm others when they have risks to do so because they are socialised to value relationships, to nurture and take care of others, and to express their emotions. In short, being female appears to be a protective factor against sexual acting out while being male is a risk. It's important to state that some girls and women are sexually abusive and most boys and men are emotionally expressive.

Connections between therapy and research

While Gilgun was developing her understandings of the centrality of emotional expressiveness and gender in how persons cope with adversities, the other two authors of this chapter were developing treatment programmes for children and adolescents with sexual behaviour problems. Like Gilgun in her research on resilience, they found gender to be important. Boys were more likely than girls to be their clients and that the boys typically had a great deal of difficulty naming, articulating, managing, and expressing their emotions appropriately. They tended to over-regulate their emotions to the point of suppressing them, sometimes out of fear of appearing unmanly and sometimes because of assumptions about how boys are supposed to handle their emotions. Their sexual acting out, when it involved the safety and well-being of others, is a clear indicator of insensitivity to the emotions and wants of others.

These two authors found that when girls acted out sexually, they usually were flooded with many conflicting emotions and had enormous difficulties managing and regulating their emotions. In brief, boys tended to have a restricted range of emotions and girls tended to be flooded.

Though we arrived at our understanding of emotional expressiveness from different places, there is a great deal of overlap. The three of us view emotional expressiveness in children as developing from a complex web of relationships that have taken place over time. These relationships include those with parents, siblings, peers, extended family, teachers, neighbours, and youth leaders. In addition, children's emotional development, expression, and repression also are influenced by a range of other factors, such as cartoons, films, sports, internet, video and computer games. These various sources provide guidance, rewards, and punishments for how emotions are expressed, with different rules for females and males.

Children absorb messages about appropriate emotional expression for girls and for boys at young ages. Typically by age three, children understand qualities and roles associated with each gender. They emulate those that match their gender and avoid those of the other gender. For boys, to be called a girl or a sissy is an ultimate insult. Appendix 2 is an instrument for the assessment of emotional expressiveness that we developed for use with children and their families where the children had sexual behaviour problems. Appendix 3 is a tool that assesses for healthy child sexuality. These instruments are part of the CASPARS, a set of five assessment tools for children and their families (Gilgun, 1999a, 1999b; Gilgun, Keskinen, Marti and Rice, 1999) and are available at *http://ssw.che.umn.edu/Faculty_Profiles/Gilgun_Jane/Gilgun.pubs.html*.

Applications

In the final pages of this chapter, we address two questions: What fosters therapeutic gains? What are the indictors that children are making gains in capacities for managing sexual behaviours?

Getting There: Fostering Change

The following are strategies and treatment guidelines the second and third authors use in their emotion-focused work with children and families. This, unfortunately, is a partial list, but it is suggestive of directions for treatment professionals to take in emotion-focused work:

● Build relationships with each family member. This will help the children get to the point where the children can manage their sexual behaviours.
● Help children identify and label their feelings. Some kids get angry in therapy and dump on the therapists. When this happens, help them label their feelings. 'I can see you are very angry.' Sometimes children have such powerful fears of abandonment that they do not express their anger. The therapeutic task is to provide a sense of safety in therapy and then in the family so that the children can identify, label, and learn to express these feelings appropriately.
● Provide parents with opportunities to become more emotionally available to their children. As discussed, individual and couples therapy can do this, as well as instruction and information about appropriate ways of dealing with their children's sexuality and other behaviours that are stressing family members and others in the children's environments.
● See the therapist role as multi-faceted including:
  – As a facilitator of emotional development for the children and other family members.
  – As a role model for parents on how to set limits on children's behaviours including sexual behaviours while at the same time creating a sense of safety where no topic is taboo in families; as role models for children and parents in how to talk directly and respectfully about sexuality.
  – As a sex educator for the parents and the children, including preparing parents and children for the kinds of behaviours to expect in the future. In a sense, the toothpaste is out of the tube. The children know what sexual pleasure is, and it is unlikely that they will stop being sexual. Masturbation will probably be an important sexual outlet, even for younger children who have not reached puberty;
  – As an advocate for services children need, from insurance companies, social service agencies, and schools. Be prepared to participate in school conferences to plan how to deal with the children's sexual behaviours in school settings; as honest appraisers of

risks to reoffend. When children do not make progress in their emotional development, treatment professionals typically are required to tell any referral sources and the parents. Red flags for reoffending include having a restricted range of feelings, flat affect when discussing emotion-charged events such as apology and empathy letters, and on-going incapacities for believe there was nothing wrong with their sexual behaviours when there is clear evidence that they violated the rights of others, abused their power, and perpetrated harm.
● Assume that children have capacities in the following areas:
  – for dealing forthrightly with their sexual behaviours and the circumstances under which their sexual behaviours take place.
  – for taking responsibility for their behaviours.
  – for engaging in therapy and becoming competent emotionally including developing empathy for the people they've harmed.
  – for managing their sexuality and the emotions that are associated with their sexual acting out; and have capacities for letting go of gender-based ideologies that stigmatise emotional sensitivity and encourage bravado, aggression, and entitlement.

Specific structured activities build children's capacities for emotional expressiveness. These activities take place in the psycho-education group. The children show their parents their accomplishments at the end of the group. The activities include:

● *Reading the book* Feelings *by Aliki (1987) with the children.* The book is a great help to children who have difficulties identifying and labelling feelings.
● *Presenting children with cartoons*: where the children state what the story is about and identify what the characters might be feeling.
● *Reading Jan Hindman's (1998) 'A very touching book . . . for little people and big people' with the children.* The humour in this book helps children and adults relax about sexual issues and helps them see that sexuality is part of being human from birth to old age.
● *Viewing a video about sexual abuse.* Then the children draw a feeling they saw in the video and discuss a time in their lives when they had that feeling. They also ask questions about

how the child victim might have felt before, during, and after the abuse. This approach gives the children some distance from their own experiences but they are still focusing on a specific person from the video.

- *Feelings charts.* In this exercise, the therapists provide a list of feelings to the children. They ask the children to pick a feeling and pick a colour that stands for the feeling. Then they draw a picture of something that represents the feeling. The children then explain the pictures to other group members. One child drew a black tornado to represent anger. Another child drew a yellow light bulb that shined so hard it exposed everything. The therapists engage children in discussions about the times in the past that they have felt this way, the pros and cons of the various ways to deal with these feelings, and positive ways to deal with these feelings now. In group discussion of the feelings charts, the children present their charts to their parents at the end of the group.

- *Anger pyramid.* The therapists draw a three-foot pyramid with the apex designated as anger. They explain that anger is like the tip of the iceberg that appears above the water line. Underneath the water are all the other feelings that anger covers up such as shame, fear, sadness, loneliness, and rejection. The therapists hope to help the children identify, label, discuss, and identify strategies for the feelings that make them feel vulnerable.

- *Feelings charades.* The therapists present the children with a list of feelings. The children silently choose a feeling and then act out the feeling. The other children yell out their guesses until they guess correctly.

- *Collages.* The therapists provides the children with a list of terms for feelings, magazines, child-safe scissors, glue, and paper and ask the children to pick a feeling and then find a picture in the magazines that represents the feeling.

- *Empathy letters.* When the therapists have evidence that the children have developed emotional competence, they show them how to write an empathy letter to the persons they've acted out on sexually. The children share their letters in group to get the opinions of other group members.

- *Apology letters.* Once the therapists have evidence that the children have developed empathy for the persons they've harmed and

can take responsibility for their behaviours, then they provide guidelines on how to write a letter of apology.

- *Reconciliation sessions.* In these face-to-face meetings, the persons the children harmed tell the children who perpetrated sexual abuse what the abuse meant. The child victims typically go through a period of preparation that is supported by the victim's family. The children who perpetrated go through a long preparation as well, to ensure that they have capacities for empathy and will not even subtly place the blame on victims. Often these reconciliation sessions are between siblings, where an older child sexually abused one or more younger children.

Jan Burton and colleagues (1998) have an extensive set of exercises for children with sexual issues. Each of these strategies requires parental involvement. For example, under the supervision of therapists in family therapy, parents can be helpful in composing and rehearsing empathy letters. This, of course, assumes that the parents have also made gains in their own therapy. For each of the structured activities, parents are involved. They participate in the last ten minutes of every peer group session when the children show them what they did that day in group.

Indicators of change

Indicators that suggest the children are at lower risk to act out in the future come from both the children and their parents. Usually, when the parents make progress in their own therapy, the children's progress is parallel. If the parents don't make progress, any gains the children make are likely to be short-term. The following are some indicators of change. There are many more, but this brief discussion provides:

- *Children show assertiveness.* This quality is complex, but most therapy situations are. The following example will illustrate. Two school age girls were acting out sexually with each other in school. They were unable to stop their behaviours when the teachers told them to. Both girls were referred to treatment and both had single mothers. One mother and daughter engaged in treatment. The other mother refused treatment and did not allow her daughter to. The untreated mother told her daughter, other family members, and friends that the other girl and not her daughter is a perpetrator and should be charged with a crime.

The girl in treatment wrote a letter to the mother stating, 'Dear ——, I'm not a bad kid.' She expressed regret at what had happened between her and the mother's daughter and apologised. In therapy, she took responsibility for her behaviours, became emotionally expressive, and assertive without being aggressive. The child also began doing well in school and behaved appropriately. Her mother showed many therapeutic gains. Thus, with responsiveness to treatment and a mother who also engaged in treatment, this child took the initiative and wrote an assertive and not aggressive letter to the mother of the child with whom she had been inappropriately sexual:

- *Previous taboo topics are on the table.* A family who had completed treatment a few years earlier came back for a tune-up session. The boy who had been the 'target' client in the programme wanted to talk about puberty and masturbation. For almost the entire session, family members told puberty stories and stories about masturbation with humour and respect for boundaries.
- *Children can ask questions that they were too ashamed to ask in the past.* One boy who was approaching puberty asked during group time if it was okay if white stuff came out when he masturbated last week. The therapists said, 'Congratulations. You are growing up.'
- *Children tell on themselves.* Children talk about topics that might have been too painful for them in the past. One boy said he was masturbating in his room and his sister peeked in on him. She told her mother he was masturbating. He was angry at his sister and was embarrassed. Another kid said, 'You got caught white-handed.' The humour allowed the boy to admit that he got in trouble not just because he was masturbating when he saw his sister spying on him, but he chased her with semen on his hand.
- *Humour.* As that story shows, humour often accompanies the development of emotional competence, as well as fostering it.
- *Signs of attachment to others.* Some children feel lonely and isolated and have minimal emotional attachments to others. These children are at high risk to act out sexually if they have been exposed to inappropriate sexual behaviours. One boy, in foster care, formed an attachment to his foster father. He

considers the foster father his father. He said, 'He's the only one I have.' He's also attached to his therapist and to his psycho-education group. He is not attached to his foster brothers and he's doing everything he can to keep everyone else away. Thus, though he's made some progress, he still has more work to do.

- *Affect becomes more animated.* An example will illustrate this point. Another child, who was developmentally delayed, really liked his foster mother and appeared to be attached to her. His affect was less flat than it used to be, and he smiled at jokes, even made jokes himself. He was neater, cleaner, and looked like a different kid. Connection to others is a protective factor. Separateness from others is a risk for sexual acting out in children with these histories.
- *Emotions and cognitions are connected.* When kids are preparing to apologise for their behaviours and express fears and doubts about the apology, this is a more hopeful sign than if they read it by rote.
- *Takes responsibility for their behaviours; empathy for victims.* These two qualities go hand-in-hand. In a reconciliation session, a boy stated that he had had no idea what his sister, whom he had sexually abused, had gone through. He cried for her. He said, 'I took advantage of you.' He admitted that he had exploited her.
- *Parents set limits.* The following is an example. A single-parent family had been in and out of treatment for several years. The son in the family had been molested in pre-school and soon after began grabbing and fondling other children. His mother refused for years to deal with her own childhood abuse. Finally, she agreed to some help with how she was parenting her son. Once she began to manage her own issues, she could start setting limits. She could say to her son, 'Knock it off. I don't want you to behave this way.' The child responded to her limit setting and started showing other signs of making treatment gains, such as handling teasing by age peers with humour. He was in special education and waited at the same bus stop as other children but took a different bus. The other kids picked on him for this. He said, 'I have my own limo to take me to school.' The teasing stopped. He also has become an excellent skate boarder, and when he showed up, the other kids shouted greetings.

Discussion

This chapter pieced together the authors' research and clinical experience as well as research on children's emotional development. Our purpose was to show the significance of emotional expressiveness in the treatment of children and their families where children have sexually inappropriate behaviours. The therapy programme is emotion-focused. Treatment professionals are just beginning to formulate programmes. Rigorous evaluations will take place some time in the future. The approaches we described and the indicators of progress in treatment have not been submitted to randomised clinical trials where children and families are randomly assigned to treatment and control groups. We do not have quantified indicators of treatment effectiveness.

Rather, what we have presented are a set of good ideas, grounded in clinical experience and research and theory. We have recommendations as to how treatment professionals can use this information. We want other professionals to use these ideas to help them think about and identify issues that their own clients might have. We want others to test these ideas for their fit with clients after they have done a thorough assessment of clients' strengths and vulnerabilities. If our ideas don't fit, then modify our ideas. Do not force information from clients into any of the categories that we have offered.

For any of the interventions we've discussed, such as the feelings chart or charades, make sure the children understand what professionals are asking them to do and be sure that how professionals present these exercises is developmentally appropriate. Even children who are about the same age may vary a great deal in terms of their levels of cognitive and emotional development.

If professionals want to do reconciliation sessions and apology and empathy letters, they must have the skills to do so. These are not simple procedures. They require a great deal of skill, experience, and sensitivity to the multiple issues at stake. Be sure to learn from the experiences of other professionals who have expertise in these approaches.

We believe that children's behaviours are adaptations to their life circumstances, filtered through cognitive schemas that shape what they perceive, how they perceive, and what actions they take. The work of Toth and colleagues (2002) provides an in-depth discussion of cognitive schemas and how they affect behaviours. In the long run, effective treatment leads to modification of these adaptive inner representations of self, others, and how the world works. These are not trivial pursuits, nor are they easily accomplished. To do this work, professionals must have highly developed emotional competencies themselves and respect for their own limits.

References

Aliki (1987) *Feelings*. New York: Morrow.

Bargh, J.A. (1997) The Automaticity of Everyday Life, in Robert, S. and Wyer, Jr. (Eds.) *Advances in Social Cognition, Vol. X.* Ahwah, NJ: Erlbaum. 1–61.

Brody, L.R. (2000) The Socialisation of Gender Differences in Emotional Expression: Display Rules, Infant Temperament, and Differentiation. In Fischer, A.H. (Ed.) *Gender and Emotions.* New York: Cambridge University Press. 24–47.

Brody, L.R. (1999) *Gender, Emotion, and the Family.* Cambridge, Ma: Harvard University Press.

Burton, J.E. et al. (1998) *Treating Children With Sexually Abusive Behaviour Problems: Guidelines for Child and Parent.* New York: Haworth.

Fraiberg, S., Adelson, E. and Shapiro, V. (1975) Ghosts in the Nursery: A Psychoanalytic Approach To Impaired Mother-Child Relationships. *Journal of the American Academy of Child Psychiatry,* 14, 387–421.

Gilgun, J.F. (1999a) Caspars: Clinical Assessment Instruments That Measure Strengths and Risks in Children and Families. In Calder, M.C. (Ed.) *Working With Young People Who Sexually Abuse: New Pieces of the Jigsaw Puzzle.* Lyme Regis: Russell House Publishing.

Gilgun, J.F. (1999b) Caspars: New Tools for Assessing Client Risks and Strengths. *Families in Society,* 80, 450–9. Tools Available at *Http://Ssw.Che.Umn.Edu/Faculty/Profiles/Gilgun_Jane/Gilgun_pubs.html*

Gilgun, J.F. (1999c) Mapping Resilience as Process Among Adults Maltreated in Childhood. In Hamilton I., McCubbin, E.A., Thompson, A., Thompson, I. and Futrell J.A. (Eds.) *The Dynamics of Resilient Families.* Thousand Oaks, Ca: Sage. 41–70.

Gilgun, J.F. (1996) Human Development and Adversity in Ecological Perspective: Part 1: A Conceptual Framework. *Families in Society,* 77, 395–402.

Gilgun, J.F. (1992) Hypothesis Generation in Social Work Research. *Journal of Social Service Research*, 15, 113–35.

Gilgun, J.F. (1991) Resilience and the Intergenerational Transmission of Child Sexual Abuse. In Patton, M.Q. (Ed.) *Family Sexual Abuse: Frontline Research and Evaluation.* Newbury Park, Ca: Sage. 93–105.

Gilgun, J.F. (1990) Factors Mediating the Effects of Childhood Maltreatment. In Hunter, M. (Ed.) *The Sexually Abused Male: Prevalence, Impact, and Treatment.* Lexington, Ma: Lexington Books. 177–90.

Gilgun, J.F. and McLeod L. (1999) Gendering Violence. *Studies in Symbolic Interactionism*, 22, 167–93.

Gilgun, J.F., Keskinen, S., Danette Jones, M. and Rice, K. (1999) Clinical Applications of the Caspars Instruments: Boys Who Act Out Sexually. *Families in Society*, 80, 629–41.

Hindman, J. (1998) *A Very Touching Book . . . For Little People and Big People.* (Rev. Edn.) Baker City, Or: Alexandria Associates.

Isen, A.M. (198) Toward Understanding the Role of Affect in Cognition, in Wyer, R.S. Jr. and Srull, T.K. (Eds.) *Handbook of Social Cognition, Vol. 3.* Hillsdale, Nj: Erlbaum. 179–236.

Izard, C.E., Fine, S., Mostow, A., Trentacosta, C. and Campbell, J. (2002) Emotion Process in Normal and Abnormal Development and Preventive Intervention. *Development and Psychopathology*, 14, 761–87.

Raver, C.C. (2002) Emotions Matter: Making the Case for the Role of Young Children's Emotional Development for Early School Readiness. *Social Policy Report*, Xvi (3), 3–18.

Toth, S., Maughan, A., Todd Manly, J., Spagnola, M. and Cicchetti, D. (2002) The Relative Efficacy of Two Interventions in Altering Maltreated Preschool Children's Representational Models: Implications for Attachment Theory. *Development and Psychopathology*, 14, 877–908.

Watson, J.C. (1996) The Relationship Between Vivid Descriptions, Emotional Arousal, and In-Session Resolution of Problematic Reactions. *Journal of Consulting and Clinical Psychology*, 64 (3), 459–64.

Zeman, J. and Garber, J. (1996) Display Rules for Anger, Sadness, and Pain: It Depends on Who is Watching. *Child Development*, 67, 957–73.

Appendix 1: Qualities associated with resilience

At least one long-term relationship with an adult inside or outside the family where:

- The adult models pro-social behaviours and values.
- The young person admires and emulates the adult's positive qualities.
- The adult praises and appreciates the young person's pro-social values and behaviours.
- The young person confides personal and sensitive material to the adult.
- The young person seeks out the adult in times of stress and hurt.
- The young person shares happy news and events with the adult.
- The young person shares with the adult events that occur in peer group.

At least one long-term pro-social friend during childhood and adolescence (longer than five years) who serves a similar role as the pro-social adult described above:

- Has a will to be law-abiding.
- Has a will to engage in pro-social behaviours.
- Is persistent in the face of obstacles.
- Enjoys accomplishing tasks.
- Discusses a sense of inadequacy with others and feels better afterward.
- Views others as deserving of respect.
- Deals directly with persons who are the occasions of anger.
- Makes amends when actions/words hurt others.
- Believes and acts out the idea that negotiating for what you want is respectful.
- Believes and acts out the idea that taking what you want is selfish and wrong.
- Believes that living well is the best revenge.
- Redresses wrongs through negotiation and not through getting back at others.
- Equates masculinity with respect for women.
- Equates masculinity with appropriate expression of emotion.
- Equates being a girl or woman with assertiveness.
- Engages in consensual sexual behaviours with others.
- Goes for a run, a swim, or other physical activity when stressed.

- Uses a wide range of pro-social ways to maintain emotional equilibrium.
- Listens to and learns from criticism.
- Enjoys dating in high school.
- Masturbation is related to sexual desire.
- Has a wide range of sexual fantasies, primarily of age peers.

- Imagines a positive future.
- Takes specific steps toward an imagined positive future.

Appendix 2: Emotional expressiveness

Strength	Risk
3 = High	3 = High
2 = Medium	2 = Medium
1 = Low	1 = Low
0 = Not known/not observed	

	Strength	Risk
1. Child shows a range of feelings	_____	_____
2. Child puts own feelings into words	_____	_____
3. Child's expression of feelings is appropriate to situations	_____	_____
4. Child's feelings and reactions are linked to the events that precipitated them	_____	_____
5. Child can identify a wide range of feelings in others	_____	_____
6. Child sympathises with other people's feelings	_____	_____
7. Child appears to respect the feelings of others	_____	_____
8. Child has a person in family and/or community who facilitates	_____	_____
Appropriate expression of feelings	_____	_____
9. Child's moods are fairly even	_____	_____
10. Child shares emotionally-laden events with others, both positive and hurtful events	_____	_____
11. Child engages emotionally with others	_____	_____
12. Child is sensitive to others	_____	_____
13. Child's emotional responses match demands of the situation	_____	_____
14. Child recognises when her/his emotional responses are inappropriate	_____	_____
15. Child apologises for inappropriate expressions of feelings	_____	_____
16. In general, the child manages his or her emotions well	_____	_____
17. In general, the child is respectful of the emotions of others	_____	_____

Scoring: add scores in each column.	Strength	Risk
	Score _____	Score _____

Appendix 3: Sexuality scale

Strength
3 = High
2 = Medium
1 = Low
0 = Not known/not observed

Risk
3 = High
2 = Medium
1 = Low

	Strength	Risk
1. Parents set limits on child's inappropriate sexual behaviours (e.g., exposing genitals, public masturbation, 'grabbing' others genitals)	_____	_____
2. Child stops sexually inappropriate behaviours when parents set limits	_____	_____
3. Child is appropriately interested in looking at nude or semi-nude pictures in newspapers, magazines, and catalogues, such as lingerie ads	_____	_____
4. Child does not have a known pattern of masturbating while looking at nude or semi-nude pictures in newspapers, magazines, and catalogues, such as lingerie ads	_____	_____
5. Child respects the sexual boundaries of others	_____	_____
6. Child does not have a pattern of attributing sexual behaviours to dolls and other toys	_____	_____
7. Child respects the sexual boundaries of animals	_____	_____
8. Child's sexual interactions with others are appropriate; that is, occur with children about the same age and are mutual	_____	_____
9. Child has a good sense of when to talk about sexual things	_____	_____
10. Child's has appropriate bathroom behaviours (e.g. faeces and urine go into the toilet)	_____	_____
11. Parents have provided child with information about sexuality that is age appropriate	_____	_____
12. Parents respect the sexual boundaries of others, keeping their own sexual behaviours private		
13. Other persons in child's environment keep their sexual behaviours Private	_____	_____
14. Child has witnessed appropriate sexual expressions (e.g., affectionate kissing, hugging, talk, looks, and touching)	_____	_____
15. Child has not witnessed inappropriate sexual expressions (e.g., intercourse, coerced sexual contact such as rape, child sexual abuse, and genital touching, even if between age peers)	_____	_____
16. Family sexual talk is respectful	_____	_____
17. In general, the environments to which the child is exposed is respectful of the child's sexuality and the sexuality of others	_____	_____
18. Materials with sexual content to which child is exposed are age appropriate (e.g., books, magazines, computer games, cable TV, internet information)	_____	_____
19. Child is comfortable with sexual orientation	_____	_____
20. Child is comfortable with gender identity. (e.g., a boy wants to be a boy and a girl wants to be a girl)	_____	_____
21. Overall, child is appropriate sexually	_____	_____

Scoring: add scores in each column.

Strength
Score _____

Risk
Score _____

2003 Jane F. Gilgun

Sexual Offending and Sexual Behaviour Problems: Treatment with Multisystemic Therapy

Elizabeth J. Letourneau and Cynthia Cupit Swenson

In his description of the history of juvenile justice in the United States, Howell (2003) provides a thoughtful and well-defended explanation for the development of myths regarding 'juvenile super-predators'. The idea of young super-predators was driven largely by the media and politicians wanting to demonstrate 'tough on crime' attitudes. Fears about these youths peaked in the late 1990s and remain today, although a belated recognition that rates of juvenile (and adult) violent crimes actually decreased over the past decade seems to have dampened some of the intensity of these fears. However, there remains the widespread perception of juvenile sex offenders as somehow different from, and worse than, other juvenile offenders, despite the fact that sexual crimes decreased over the same time period as other violent crimes (Finklehor and Jones, January, 2004). Beliefs that juvenile sex offenders are at exceptionally high risk to reoffend, are more like adult sex offenders than other juvenile delinquents, and exist in epidemic numbers have led to the most aggressive and invasive legal interventions (i.e., community notification, sex offender registration, and civil commitment) being applied to these youths (Caldwell, 2002; Swenson and Letourneau, in press). These fears have resulted in the institution of highly restrictive, long-term, sex offender-specific treatment being applied to juvenile sex offenders and (increasingly) to younger children with sexual behaviour problems.

The goal of restrictive legal and clinical interventions is to interrupt a progression that begins with child sexual behaviour problems, progresses to juvenile sexual offending, and culminates in a career of criminal sexual misconduct. The desire to interrupt such a progression is understandable and both legal and clinical interventions are appropriate for youth who commit sexual crimes. However, there is no empirical evidence that children who display sexual behaviour problems progress into juvenile sex offenders (Chaffin, Letourneau and Silovsky, 2002; Letourneau, Schoenwald and Sheidow, 2004) and there is ample evidence that most juvenile sex offenders do not progress into adult sex offenders (Alexander, 1999; Caldwell, 2002). Thus, restrictive, long-term, sex offender-specific treatment may represent the misapplication of limited resources to many of these youths.

The present chapter presents an alternative, family and ecologically-focused treatment for juvenile sex offenders and for children with other behavioural problems, including sexual behaviour problems and explains why, in our opinion, that treatment is most effective that addresses empirically validated correlates of sexual misbehaviour, rather than the assumed correlates of such behaviour. There is admittedly little in the way of rigorous outcome research but the extant research supports the efficacy of family and ecologically-focused treatment that specifically targets the known correlates of these problems. Before reviewing the treatment outcome literature, we present a brief overview of the correlates of sexual behaviour problems in youths.

Correlates of sexual behaviour problems in youths

Juvenile sexual offenders

Juvenile sexual offenders are minors who have committed sexual acts defined as crimes by law (Chaffin et al., 2002). Typically, they are teenagers, although over the past decade, the number of younger children adjudicated for sex crimes has increased markedly within the United States (Cauffman and Steinberg, 2001; Griffin, Torbet and Szymanski, 1998). Also, the legal definition of criminal sexual behaviours has expanded and, in some states, includes consensual sex by teenage peers (Cauffman and Steinberg, 2001). The observed prevalence of juvenile sexual offending varies considerably with the method of measurement. Official reports indicate that adolescents account for 17% to 20% of all sex crimes, excluding prostitution (Federal Bureau of Investigation, 1978–1988, as cited in Sipe, Jensen and Everett, 1998; Maguire and Pastore, 1998). Victim-based reports indicate a much higher prevalence rate, with approximately 40% of all sexual assaults committed by minors (Finkelhor and Dziuba-Leatherman, 1994; White and Koss, 1993) and juvenile self-reports confirm higher rates of assaults than are indicated by official reports (Ageton, 1983). Although each source of data has limitations, all suggest that juvenile sexual offending is a significant problem, especially when the psychosocial and financial costs are considered.

The personal and financial costs of sexual offending are well documented (Boney-McCoy and Finkelhor, 1996; Browne and Finkelhor, 1986; Cohen, Miller and Rossman, 1994; Saunders, Villeponteaux, Lipovsky, Kilpatrick and Veronen, 1992; Widom and Morris, 1997). Combined with the prevalence of juvenile sexual offending, these findings clearly suggest juvenile sex offending should be a high priority for treatment. Treatment may prevent further victimisation of others and increase the likelihood that offenders can lead productive, nonoffending lives. However, to reduce the costs to individuals and society treatments must be clinically and cost effective. In designing such treatments, known correlates of offending should serve as an initial guide for treatment targets. Consistent with findings in the general delinquency literature (Loeber and Farrington, 1998), the correlates of juvenile sexual offending tap individual characteristics of the youths as well as characteristics of the social contexts in which they are embedded (i.e., family, peer, school).

Individual characteristics. Research on individual characteristics of juvenile sex offenders suggests some interesting departures from adult sexual offenders. For example, it is often assumed that, like adult offenders, juvenile sexual offenders have deviant sexual arousal patterns and cognitive distortions regarding sex crimes. However, juvenile sexual offenders demonstrate highly variable patterns of sexual arousal (Hunter, Goodwin and Becker, 1994) and sexual interest (Smith and Fischer, 1998) that do not consistently differentiate them from other delinquents and do not correlate with other important clinical characteristics (Becker, 1998).

Likewise, juvenile sexual offenders are not reliably distinguishable from other delinquents and non-delinquents with regards to deviant sexual fantasies (Daleiden, Kaufman, Hilliker and O'Neil, 1998). Finally, in contrast with their adult counterparts, juvenile sexual offenders do not appear to have more cognitive distortions regarding their crimes than other delinquents (Ageton, 1983; Hastings, Anderson and Hemphill, 1997).

On the other hand, several differences have been observed between juvenile sexual offenders and other youths, including higher rates of sexual assault (Awad and Saunders, 1989; Davis and Leitenberg, 1987; Milloy, 1994), and rates of internalising problems (e.g. anxiety, depression) (Blaske, Borduin, Henggeler and Mann, 1989; Kempton and Forehand, 1992). Juvenile sexual offenders report similar or lower rates of alcohol and illicit substance use as compared with other delinquents (Ageton, 1983; Milloy, 1994).

Family relations. Families of juvenile sexual offenders appear to be characterised by less positive communication and warmth (Bischof, Stith and Whitney, 1995) and greater parental violence (Ford and Linney, 1995) than families of other juvenile offenders. Moreover, families of sexual offenders and other offenders had lower rates of positive communication than did families of nonoffenders, although families of juvenile sexual offenders reported higher adaptability and cohesion than did families of other juvenile offenders (Blaske et al., 1989).

Peer relations. It is within the realm of peer relations that the most consistent differences have been reported between juvenile sexual offenders and other delinquent and non-delinquent youth. Specifically, juvenile sexual offenders tend to evidence peer deficits that are more characteristic of youths with internalising problems (e.g. social isolation and low popularity; Blaske et al., 1989; Ford and Linney, 1995; Milloy, 1994). This finding may be more true of juvenile sexual offenders with younger victims than juvenile sexual offenders with peer or adult-age victims. Juveniles who offend against young children tend to be immature relative to same-age peers (Graves, Openshaw, Ascione and Ericksen, 1996) and juvenile sexual offenders who had assaulted peers (versus having younger victims) reported significantly higher rates of association with deviant peers (Ageton, 1983).

School functioning. Several uncontrolled studies indicate that juvenile sexual offenders are at risk for academic deficits (Awad and Saunders, 1989; Fehrenbach, Smith, Monastersky and Deisher, 1986), but controlled studies have not found intellectual or achievement differences between juvenile sexual offenders and other juvenile delinquents (Ford and Linney, 1995; Jacobs, Kennedy and Meyer, 1997).

In summary, with the exception of higher rates of internalising symptoms and deficient relations with same-age peers, research suggests that juvenile sexual offenders have more in common with other juvenile delinquents than is generally assumed. As discussed subsequently, these findings have important implications for the design of effective interventions. Prior to discussing these treatment implications, we next review the correlates of sexual behaviour problems in children.

Children with sexual behaviour problems

Child sexual behaviour problems are defined as behaviours that occur with unexpected frequency, in coercive contexts, or between youth in different age groups, and that resist intervention, interfere with development, and/or are associated with emotional distress (Chaffin et al., 2002). This definition is necessarily modified for older youth and adolescents, who are usually prosecuted for behaviour that occurs in coercive contexts or between youth in different age groups. Rather, non-criminal sexual behaviour problems in older children and adolescents is more likely to include self-directed behaviours (e.g., excessive masturbation) that can interfere with social relationships (Letourneau et al., 2004).

Most research on non-criminal sexual behaviour problems has focused on children between the ages of 6 and 13, with almost no attention given to adolescents (Letourneau et al., 2004; Silovsky and Niec, 2002). Research on these young children reveals a heterogeneous group with just a few distinguishing features relative to children referred for other behavioural or psychiatric problems (Chaffin et al., 2002).

Individual characteristics. Several individual characteristics have been examined, including gender, age, abuse history, and co-morbid psychiatric problems. Few of these characteristics distinguish children with sexual behaviour problems from other groups. Gender, a robust factor for juvenile sex offenders (the large majority of whom are male), does not distinguish groups of children with sexual behaviour problems from comparison groups (Friedrich, Grambsch, Broughton, Kuiper and Beilke, 1991; Silovsky and Niec, 2002). Age is negatively correlated with frequency of inappropriate sexual behaviours and therefore children with sexual behaviour problems tend to be younger, on average, than children referred for other problems (Bonner, Walker and Berliner, 1999; Friedrich et al., 2001; Friedrich et al., 1991).

A prior history of sexual abuse is more characteristic of children with sexual behaviour problems relative to comparison groups (Bonner et al., 1999; Friedrich et al., 1992). Whether physical abuse (a risk factor for sexual offending) is a risk factor for sexual behaviour problems is unclear. One small study of preschool-aged children reported that physical abuse and witnessing domestic violence were both related to sexual behaviour problems (Silovsky and Niec, 2002) but this finding was not reported in a study that compared children (ages 6–12) referred for sexual behaviour problems with a group of children referred for other clinical problems (Bonner et al., 1999). Lastly, children with sexual behaviour problems are more likely than children in comparison groups to exhibit additional internalising and externalising behaviour problems (Bonner et al., 1999; Friedrich et al., 1991, 1992; Langstrom, Grann and Lichtenstein, 2002).

Family relations. One of the most robust correlates of sexual behaviour problems in children is the level of sexuality in their families. Family sexuality, which includes family nudity and opportunities for children to view sexual intercourse, is higher in the families of children with sexual behaviour problems than in children referred for other problems or in normative control groups (Bonner et al., 1999; Friedrich et al., 1991, 1992, 2001).

Peer relations. The influence of peer factors in the development of sexual behaviour problems in children has not been systematically examined.

School functioning. It is unclear whether child sexual behaviour problems are related in any way to school problems. Poor school achievement and the need for specialised school services among children with sexual behaviour problems were suggested by data in one study (Pithers, Gray, Busconi and Houchens, 1998), but this study lacked a comparison group. Further, significant differences in school functioning were not found in a study comparing children with sexual problems with those referred for other problems; both groups had average scholastic achievement (Bonner et al., 1999).

Older children and adolescents with sexual behaviour problems.

To our knowledge, only one study has reported on the characteristics of older youth and adolescents identified by their parents as having sexual behaviour problems (Letourneau et al., 2004). Letourneau and colleagues examined a subsample of youth from a large treatment study of delinquent youth (n = 1522) and found that 11% were rated by their caregivers as having two or more sexual problems in addition to other behaviour problems. Compared with remaining youth whose caregivers indicated one or zero sexual behaviour problems, the group with sexual behaviour problems had a higher proportion of girls, was younger, and had higher rates of both internalising and externalising problems. These characteristics appear more similar to younger children with sexual behaviour problems than to juvenile sex offenders.

In summary, the correlates of non-criminal sexual behaviour problems in children and adolescents and the correlates of juvenile sexual offending provide important clues for the design of effective and appropriate treatment interventions for these youths. As will be seen, however, many of these correlates are overlooked by current treatment practices.

Implications for treatment

As noted above, the correlates of juvenile sexual offending differ from those of non-criminal sexual behaviour problems. However, both sets of correlates result in similar treatment implications. These include the following:

1. Intervention should occur at multiple levels in the youth's ecology (because correlates occur at multiple levels).
2. Intervention should occur in the family's setting (because caregivers have, or can develop, more control over correlates within the family, peer, and school settings than can youth).

3. Interventions should address multiple problems in multiple domains (because there is more than a single cause of these sexual problems).

Treatment outcome research

In this section, we review only those treatment outcome studies that included reasonable comparison groups and that utilised measures of reoffending (or recurrence) of the targeted problem behaviours (i.e., sexual offending or inappropriate sexual behaviour). The best of these studies utilised random assignment to groups. The randomised controlled trial (RCT) is the best research design for the examination of causal relationships. Other designs – even those that involve matching participants within extant groups – are less able to rule out pre-existing differences that might account for some portion of group differences found at post-treatment. Several additional programme evaluation studies have been published that do not include any comparison groups (Barbaree and Cortoni, 1993; Bremer, 1992; Hagan et al., 1994; Hunter and Santos, 1990; Schram, Milloy and Rowe, 1991; Smets and Cebula, 1987). Due to their less rigorous design, these studies are not included in the present review.

Treatment for juvenile sexual offenders

Over the past three decades there has been substantial growth in the number of programmes offering adolescent sex offender treatment (Freeman-Longo, Bird, Stevenson and Fisk, 1995; Knopp, Freeman-Longo and Stevenson, 1992). By far the most common treatment is cognitive-behavioural sex offender-specific (SOS) group treatment (McGrath, Cumming and Burchard, 2003). Juvenile SOS treatment programmes are most often modelled after adult sexual offender treatment programmes and address correlates of offending that have been hypothesised (and, in some cases, empirically validated) for *adult* offending. Thus, common treatment components address (a) deviant sexual arousal; (b) denial and minimisation of sex crimes; (c) cognitive distortions (e.g., regarding misogyny and sex with children); (d) victim empathy; (e) identification of events, moods, thoughts and decisions that preceded offending; (f) relapse prevention plans and targeting of factors that impair relapse prevention (e.g., substance use, anger control); and (g) offenders' own abuse histories, when relevant (Knopp, Freeman-Longo and Lane, 1977; Freeman-Longo et al., 1995). As should be obvious from this list, SOS treatment is largely focused on addressing individual characteristics and, with few exceptions (e.g., Worling, 1998), generally does not include substantial components that address family and almost never addresses peer or school correlates (apart from addressing such correlates solely with the youth). Furthermore, these individual characteristics are either nonspecific to juvenile sex offenders (e.g., most adolescents have underdeveloped empathy) or have not been adequately examined (e.g., there are no studies examining sexual arousal patterns of non-delinquent boys). Furthermore, services are typically delivered in group settings ranging from outpatient clinics to long-term residential treatment centers (Freeman-Longo et al., 1995; Knopp et al., 1992) and frequently last 1 to 2 years (Becker and Kaplan, 1993; Bremer, 1992; Hagan, King and Patros, 1994; Jacobs et al., 1997; Worling, 1998). This treatment delivery format is potentially problematic given research findings that grouping delinquent youth together may result in iatrogenic effects (Arnold and Hughes, 1999; Dishion, McCord and Poulin, 1999; Dishion, Patterson, Stoolmiller and Skinner, 1991).

Despite the proliferation of SOS treatment for juveniles, there are few well-controlled outcome studies (Letourneau, 2004). In fact, a recent meta-analysis (Hanson et al., 2002) identified only three studies that examined this prevailing treatment modality and that included comparison groups and measures of recidivism. Of these three studies, only two were used by Hanson and his colleagues to determine a treatment odds ratio (OR) for juvenile sexual offender treatment in the meta-analysis, with the third study (Lab, Shields and Schondel, 1993) excluded due to potentially biased group assignment at pre-treatment.

Neither of the two SOS outcome studies (Guarino-Ghezzi and Kimball, 1998; Worling and Curwen, 1998) employed randomised assignment. Rather, the authors used pre-existing groups and examined them for pre-existing group differences. Authors of both studies concluded that such differences were not significant. At one-year follow-up, Guarino-Ghezzi and Kimball (1998) found that 0 of 33 (0%) youth treated with the SOS treatment had sexually reoffended compared with 1 of 25

(4%) youth treated with a non-specific treatment protocol. Overall, 30.3% of the youth in the sex offender-specific group reoffended (sexually or non-sexually) versus 48% of youth in the comparison group. At an average of 6-years follow-up, Worling and Curwen (1998; see also Worling and Curwen, 2000) reported that 5% (3 of 58) of youth treated with SOS had sexually reoffended compared with 17.8% (16 of 90) of youth in the comparison group. Overall, 35% of youth in the SOS reoffended (sexually or non-sexually) versus 54.4% of youth in the comparison group.

In combination, the evidence from these two studies examining the effectiveness of SOS treatment appears promising. However, the results are also inconclusive. As noted by Letourneau (2004), without random assignment to groups, both studies lack the methodological rigor necessary for drawing firm conclusions about treatment effectiveness. Furthermore, each study suffered from other methodological weaknesses. For example, the one-year follow-up of the Guarino-Ghezzi and Kimball study would be considered insufficient by today's standards for examining treatment outcome (e.g., see Hanson and Bussiére, 1998). Worling and Curwen included treatment dropouts and treatment refusers in their comparison group. When results from these youth were removed from examination, the group differences (between treated youth and youth referred only for assessment) approached nonsignificance (Hanson et al., 2002; Letourneau, 2004).

Based largely on its success in treating adult sexual offenders, cognitive-behavioural approaches have proliferated in the treatment of juvenile sexual offenders. While the two studies reviewed above provide some support for cognitive-behavioural sex offender-specific treatment, there are several good reasons why such treatment may not provide the most effective treatment for juvenile sexual offenders. First, little evidence suggests that juvenile sexual offenders possess the cognitive biases and deficits that are the foci of these treatments. Second, an extensive literature in the area of delinquency and adolescent substance abuse treatment suggests that group treatment of adolescents with antisocial behaviour can be iatrogenic (Arnold and Hughes, 1999; Dishion, McCord and Poulin, 1999; Dishion, Patterson, Stoolmiller and Skinner, 1991). That is, treating delinquent youth in groups can result in higher overall rates of delinquency. This is an important consideration in light of the aforementioned findings that juvenile sexual offenders may be more similar to other juvenile offenders than not. Third, the prevailing treatment model delivered in clinic and institutional settings provides little consideration of the real world contexts in which youth develop. In fact, treatments that have been shown to be more effective in the areas of delinquency (Elliott, 1998) and adolescent substance abuse (National Institute on Drug Abuse, 1999) focus interventions on risk factors across youths' natural ecologies (i.e., family, peers, school). We discuss one such intervention model 'MST' later in this chapter.

Treatment of children with sexual behaviour problems

Two randomised controlled trials have examined treatment for children (ages 6 to 12) with sexual behaviour problems (Bonner et al., 1999; Pithers et al., 1998). In both studies, children with sexual behaviour problems were randomly assigned to receive either structured, cognitive-behavioural treatment that focused specifically on sexual behaviour problems or an alternate treatment, such as dynamic play therapy. Results from these two trials suggest that sexual behaviour problems in young children respond equally well to a variety of treatments, all of which were relatively short-term (e.g., 12 to 24 weekly sessions) and all of which included significant caregiver involvement (Bonner et al., 1999; Pithers et al., 1998). Thus, it has been suggested that caregiver involvement, rather than specific treatment methods, may be an essential component in the treatment of children with sexual behaviour problems (Chaffin et al., 2002; Pithers et al., 1998).

There are no RCTs examining treatment outcome in older children with non-criminal sexual behaviour problems. However, we later describe a study that examined the use of MST with children and adolescents who were rated by their caregivers as having sexual behaviour problems. Before describing the studies that employed MST, it is useful to describe this home-based, caregiver-focused treatment approach.

Overview of MST

MST's Theoretical Foundation

Based primarily on the work of Bronfenbrenner (1979), Haley (1976), and Minuchin (1974), MST is rooted in systems theory and social ecological models of behaviour. Within this theoretical framework, youth are viewed as embedded in multiple systems that have direct and indirect influences on the youth's behaviour. Likewise, the youth influences each of the systems.

Figure 16.1 shows the various systems in which youths are embedded and the arrows indicate the bi-directional nature of the influence. The systems are depicted as a series of concentric circles. The child is in the centre. Those systems that are closer to the child are assumed to have more relative power and influence over the child's behaviour. Following this figure, the family has the greatest influence over their child and that influence extends well into the child's adult life. When compared to systems that occur naturally (i.e., family, peers), the system that carries the least amount of influence on the child is the treatment provider. Thus, the MST model assumes that the relationship between the therapist and child is neither necessary nor sufficient to obtain favourable clinical outcomes. Although therapists should have a good working relationship with the child, the primary relationship for the therapist is with the caregiver(s) who is the manager of the child's ecology and exerts the greatest amount of influence. Thus, treatment maximises the parent's positive influence on the child by strengthening the parent's capacity to manage the problems the child is experiencing.

MST's research foundation

MST has been cited as an effective treatment of adolescent antisocial behaviour by the Surgeon General (US Public Health Service, 1999, 2001) Elliott's Blueprints Series (1998) and leading reviewers (e.g., Farrington and Welsh, 1999; Kazdin and Weisz, 1998). These distinctions are based on the outcomes of several well-controlled and scientifically rigorous studies that examined the capacity of MST to reduce behavioural difficulties and rearrest in juvenile offenders.

Three randomised controlled trials (RCT's) conducted with violent and chronic offenders in the 1990s provide the strongest evidence

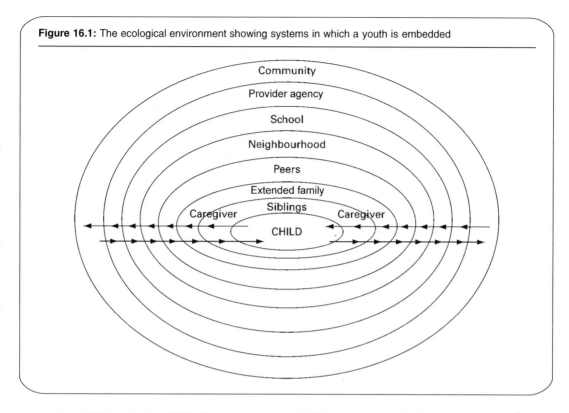

Figure 16.1: The ecological environment showing systems in which a youth is embedded

supporting MST. In the first RTC, Henggeler, Melton and Smith (1992) randomly assigned 84 juvenile offenders that were at imminent risk for out-of-home placement because of serious criminal activity to MST or usual services provided by the Department of Juvenile Justice. At post-treatment, youth that participated in MST reported less criminal activity than did youth in the usual services group; and at a 59-week follow-up, MST had reduced rearrests by 43%. In addition, usual services youth spent an average of almost three times more weeks incarcerated (average = 16.2 weeks) than MST youth (average = 5.8 weeks). Furthermore, at 2.4 years post-referral, twice as many MST youth had not been rearrested (39%) as usual services youth (20%) (Henggeler, Melton, Smith, Schoenwald and Hanley, 1993).

In the second RCT (Borduin et al., 1995), 200 chronic juvenile offenders and their families were randomly assigned to receive either MST or individual therapy (IT). Four-year follow-up arrest data showed that youth that received MST were arrested less often and for less serious crimes than youth who received IT. While youth who completed a full course of MST had the lowest rearrest rate (22.1%), those who received

MST but prematurely dropped out of treatment had better rates of rearrest (46.6%) than IT completers (71.4%), IT dropouts (71.4%) or treatment refusers (87.5%).

In the third RCT, Henggeler, Melton, Brondino, Scherer and Hanley (1997), in contrast with previous clinical trials in which the developers of MST provided ongoing clinical supervision and consultation, MST experts were not significantly involved in treatment implementation. One hundred and fifty-five chronic or violent juvenile offenders at risk of out-of-home placement were randomly assigned to receive MST or the usual services offered by DJJ. Over a 1.7-year follow-up, MST reduced rearrests by 25%, which was lower than reductions in rearrest in the previous MST studies with serious juvenile offenders. Days incarcerated, however, were reduced by 47%. Importantly, high therapist adherence to the MST treatment protocols, as assessed by caregiver reports on a standardised measure, predicted fewer rearrests and incarcerations.

Clinical description of MST

MST is an ecological treatment model that takes into account risk and protective factors occurring

Table 16.1: The nine principles of MST

Principle 1:	The primary purpose of assessment is to understand the fit between the identified problems and their broader systemic context.
Principle 2:	Therapeutic contacts emphasise the positive and use systemic strengths as levers for change.
Principle 3:	Interventions are designed to promote responsible behaviour and decrease irresponsible behaviour among family members.
Principle 4:	Interventions are present focused and action oriented, targeting specific and well-defined problems.
Principle 5:	Interventions target sequences of behaviour within and between multiple systems that maintain the identified problems.
Principle 6:	Interventions are developmentally appropriate and fit the developmental needs of the youth.
Principle 7:	Interventions are designed to require daily or weekly effort by family members.
Principle 8:	Intervention effectiveness is evaluated continuously from multiple perspectives with providers assuming accountability for overcoming barriers to successful outcomes.
Principle 9:	Interventions are designed to promote treatment generalisation and long-term maintenance of therapeutic change by empowering caregivers to address family members' needs across multiple systemic contexts.

in each of the key systems in the life of a child (e.g., family, peers, school). These factors influence the design of interventions in that interventions are tailored to the specific strengths and needs of each individual family.

In order to facilitate replication studies and the transport of MST programmes to community settings, MST implementation procedures have been operationalised and described extensively. Clinically these procedures include: a) nine principles that guide the formulation of clinical interventions; b) a family-friendly engagement process; c) a structured analytical process that is used to prioritise interventions; d) empirically-supported treatment techniques that are integrated into the MST conceptual framework; e) a home-based delivery of services that enables the provision of intensive services, f) a highly supportive supervision process; and g) a stringent quality assurance process to promote treatment fidelity.

Nine principles guide interventions. The clinical practice of MST follows nine principles (see Table 16.1). Youth outcomes have been associated with therapist adherence to these principles.

Principle 1 involves understanding the fit between identified problems and the systemic context. MST assessment identifies specific factors within the child's social ecology that appear to be driving or maintaining the problems. Principle 2 involves keeping a strengths focus. Strengths within each system are identified and used to

influence behaviour change. Principle 3 focuses on promoting responsible behaviour. Increasing responsible behaviour in caregivers is often accomplished by altering those behaviours that tend to support and sustain the problem behaviour of the child, while increasing behaviours that are considered protective. For example, weak parental supervision of a child might be changed by interventions that reduce caregiver alcohol use. Principle 4 involves clearly defining the target behaviour, determining how to measure the behaviour and change in the behaviour, and using well-defined interventions that focus on the behaviour. Consistent with systems theory, Principle 5 supports defining the sequence of behaviours and making key changes to that sequence to effectively change the behavioural outcomes. With juvenile sexual offenders, these sequences can pertain to behaviours that lead to grooming and victimising children or peers.

Principle 6 pertains to gearing interventions to the developmental needs of the youth. Developmental appropriateness refers to what an individual can handle cognitively and to where a child or parent is developmentally in the treatment process.

Principle 7 sets the expectation for designing interventions that require daily or weekly effort by family members. Doing so increases the likelihood that goal oriented behaviour change tasks will become a part of the family's repertoire. Through Principle 8, interventions effectiveness is evaluated continuously from multiple perspectives (e.g., parents, teachers, neighbours). In addition, providers assume responsibility for overcoming barriers to successful outcomes. Principle 9 speaks to generalisation of therapeutic change. When generalisation of outcomes occurs, caregivers can continue to manage the behaviour of the child in the natural ecology when the therapist is no longer present.

Family-friendly engagement process. Rather than waiting for a family to engage and closing a case due to lack of response when such does not occur in a timely fashion, with MST, the therapist and clinical team are responsible for family engagement and outcomes (Cunningham and Henggeler, 1999). Until the family is engaged, treatment can neither begin nor progress. When families are hesitant to engage in treatment, there may be many valid and understandable reasons. With juvenile sex offenders for example, family members might be embarrassed or not trust the system providing the therapy. Therapists hold the job of helping family members address these reasons.

Several characteristics of MST are designed to promote family engagement in treatment. The strength focus maintained by MST therapists contrasts favourably with the deficit focus that families may have typically experienced in their interactions with service systems. Regardless of their behaviour in the past, strengths are emphasised and efforts are made for treatment to be a collaborative process. Even when families are struggling through the engagement process, giving up on them or labelling them as 'resistant' is not done. Instead, the treatment team assumes responsibility for assessing and understanding family barriers to engagement and implementing new engagement strategies to overcome these barriers. Further, MST follows a home-based model of service delivery that helps overcome practical barriers to attending treatment, such as transportation.

A structured analytical process. The MST analytical process shown in Figure 16.2 is used to operationalise the nine treatment principles. The process starts by identifying referral behaviours from individuals in multiple systems (i.e., caregivers, youth, child protective services, probation officer, other invested parties, and official records). The referral behaviours are then consolidated to identify the key targets for change. Next, the key individuals in the child's natural ecology are identified and interviewed to gain their perspective of the problem, to identify the strengths that they bring, gain their view of the child and family strengths, and to determine from their perspective what changes will be necessary to achieve success. Third, individual goals from key participants are combined to develop the overarching goals of treatment. These goals define the scope and the end point of MST treatment. Fourth, after the overarching goals are set, the 'fit' of the problem behaviours is identified, considering factors within each of the systems. For example, the youth has touched his brother in a sexual way that led to the referral and this behaviour is the key behaviour to stop. Considering input from each of the systems and knowledge of the family based on observations, the therapist records possible factors that are driving the sexual behaviour on a 'fit circle.' She determines the following fit factors: a) youth has low skills for making friends and interacts with younger children; b) youth has been left to baby-sit his brother, so parental monitoring is low; c) the sequence of events that led up to the sexual abuse started with a physical interaction between the youth and parent (i.e., parent slapped youth); and, d) the school is using the youth as a teacher's helper in the kindergarten class.

After the fit factors have been comprehensively identified, the therapist and clinical team determine which of the factors are the primary drivers of the behaviour problems. Those factors are targeted initially for change, and those changes are defined as intermediary goals. For example, low parental monitoring might be viewed as the primary factor that gives the youth in the above example access to his brother. Thus, therapeutic attention (i.e., who will do what, when, where, and how) might initially focus on planning how the youth will be monitored and not left alone with any children. The interventions are implemented with all participants monitoring the success and providing feedback to the therapist and caregivers. If sufficient success has not been obtained, the therapist and treatment participants identify the barriers to achieving the treatment goals. This new information is then compared with or added to the current understanding of how the behaviours 'fit' within the natural ecology, and the process is reinitiated each week (i.e., fit – prioritisation – interventions – evaluation). The structured analytic process

Figure 16.2: The Multisystemic Therapy (MST) analytical process

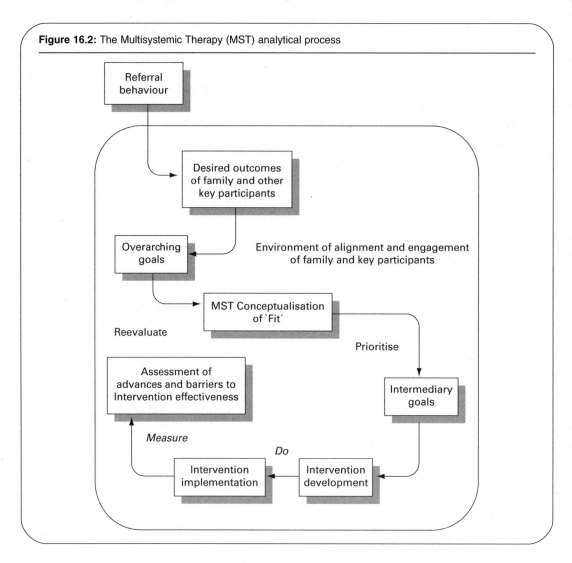

continues until such time as the overarching goals have been completed.

A core feature of the MST model is the incorporation of interventions that have empirical support, such as the cognitive-behavioural therapies, behaviour therapies, pragmatic family therapies, and certain pharmacological interventions (e.g., for attention deficit, hyperactivity disorder). There are several major differences between using these techniques within MST and using them alone. Within MST, the ecology is the client rather than the individual child or the family alone. So, in cases where the empirically supported treatments have historically focused on the youth's skill through individually therapy, MST integrates those interventions into a broad-based ecological framework that addresses a range of pertinent factors across family, peer, school, and community contexts. Second, interventions are delivered primarily by the caregivers whenever possible. For example, cognitive behavioural therapy for improving the youth's management of anger might be taught to the mother by the therapist, and the mother would then teach these skills to her son.

Home-based delivery of services. In all the MST research studies and across all the dissemination sites in the United States and internationally, MST has been delivered via a home-based model of service delivery. This delivery model removes barriers to service access and promotes the capacity of interventions to alter the youth's ecology. The way in which MST services are delivered allows intensive services to be provided. Service delivery characteristics include:

(a) Low caseloads of 3–6 families per clinician.
(b) Each therapist has a primary caseload but the therapists work within a team of 3–4 practitioners.
(c) Treatment occurs daily to several times a week, with sessions decreasing in frequency as the family progresses (i.e., titrated to family need).
(d) Treatment is time-limited and generally lasts 4–7 months depending on the seriousness of the problems and success of the interventions.
(e) Treatment is delivered in the family's natural environment; in their home, community, or other places convenient to the family.
(f) Treatment is delivered at times convenient to the family.
(g) Therapists are available to clients 24 hours per day, 7 days per week. Generally, a shared on-call system is developed for use after hours.

Highly supportive supervision process. The purpose of MST clinical supervision is to provide therapists with an understanding of the MST model, facilitate adherence to the nine treatment principles, assist in determining ways to engage families and professionals from other systems, assist in learning and implementing evidence-based techniques, and help identify barriers to the success of interventions (Henggeler and Schoenwald, 1998). MST provides a high level of weekly supervision (i.e., average two to four hours of face-to-face contact in a group format) along with supervisor availability that matches the therapist schedule – 24 hours a day, seven days a week. The clinical supervisor is available to consult with the therapist when needed and even visit the family with the therapist to address safety concerns or for clinical skill building.

Stringent quality assurance process. Significant associations between therapist fidelity to MST treatment principles and outcomes for youths (e.g., rearrest, incarceration) and families (e.g., improved functioning) have been established through several published studies (Henggeler,

Melton, Brondino, Scherer and Hanley, 1997; Henggeler, Pickrel and Brondino, 1999; Huey, Henggeler, Brondino and Pickrel, 2000; Schoenwald, Henggeler, Brondino and Rowland, 2000; Schoenwald, Sheidow, Letourneau and Liao, 2003). Based on these data, considerable attention is devoted to quality assurance for enhancing treatment fidelity. The quality assurance system includes:

(a) An orientation training week.
(b) Quarterly booster training.
(c) Weekly on-site MST supervision.
(d) Weekly consultation from an MST expert.
(e) Feedback on adherence ratings from parents and therapists; and, in MST clinical trials.
(f) Feedback via expert ratings of audiotaped therapy sessions.

Orientation training week. Prior to beginning an MST programme, therapists, supervisors, and administrators participate in an initial five-day orientation. This training provides an overview of the MST treatment model and carefully reviews the treatment manual (Henggeler, Schoenwald, Borduin, Rowland and Cunningham, 1998).

Booster training. Clinical teams participate in booster trainings on a quarterly basis. The content of that training is specific to the needs of the clinical team. Examples of the types of booster training that occur include specific techniques for treating cocaine addiction.

Weekly on-site supervision. As noted previously, weekly supervision is intensive and geared toward helping therapists achieve the overarching goals for each family and maintain high adherence to the nine principles.

Weekly consultation from an MST expert. Following the MST consultation protocol (Schoenwald, 1998), an MST consultant who is distal to the programme site provides weekly consultation to the team with the aim of promoting positive client outcomes through adherence to the MST treatment model. This consultation is over the phone and generally involves one hour per week.

Feedback via expert ratings of audiotaped sessions. In MST clinical trials, where treatment fidelity is absolutely critical for the validity of the research, therapists audiotape every treatment session. On a weekly basis, a session tape is randomly selected and rated by an expert to measure adherence to the nine principles.

New directions for treatment of sexual problems in youths

Although the scientific literature on causes and correlates of youth sexual aggression point out the multidetermined nature of sexual offending, in practice few treatments address these multiple factors. Instead, treatments continue to be implemented that address individual youth factors. As noted earlier, MST is one of the few treatments that addresses multiple determinants of delinquency and has scientific support for efficacy across two studies with JSO's. Efficacy studies offer a preliminary examination of whether a treatment works under ideal conditions, and such studies generally precede 'effectiveness' trials, where the treatment is employed in real world settings. Also described is an ongoing effectiveness trial that aims to gather data on a large sample, half of whom will be treated by MST delivered from a real world treatment centre (i.e., masters-level, full-time MST therapists and a full-time supervisor not previously connected with the development or refinement of MST). Lastly, described below is a study examining treatment outcome for delinquent youth treated with MST (Letourneau et al., 2004). A subsample of these youth was described by their caregivers as having significant sexual problems. This subsample was compared with the other delinquent youth whose caregivers indicated no minimal sexual problems. We believe this is the only published study examining the characteristics and treatment outcome for children with non-criminal sexual behaviour problems whose sample includes teenagers. There was no alternative treatment comparison group, however, so the results from this study must be considered preliminary.

MST with juvenile sex offenders

Two randomised controlled trials have provided initial evidence of the efficacy of MST for reducing sexual crime among juveniles (Borduin, Henggeler, Blaske and Stein, 1990; Borduin, Schaeffer and Heilblum, 2000; Borduin and Schaeffer, 2002). In the first study, 16 adolescents and their families were randomly assigned to home-based MST services provided by doctoral students in clinical psychology or to outpatient individual therapy provided by master's level mental health professionals in the local community. Three-year recidivism data were collected from juvenile court records, adult court records, and state police records. None of the adolescents had moved out of the area at follow-up. Recidivism for sexual offenses was 12.5% for adolescents who received MST (with a mean of 0.12 sexual arrests per adolescent) and 75% for adolescents who received individual therapy (mean of 1.62 sexual arrests per adolescent). Recidivism for nonsexual offenses was 25% for MST adolescents (mean of 0.62 arrests per adolescent) and 50% for adolescents in the individual therapy condition (mean of 2.25 arrests).

Borduin and his colleagues recently completed a larger study with a longer follow-up (Borduin et al., 2001; Borduin and Schaeffer, 2002). Forty-eight adolescents who had raped peers or adults (N=24) or had molested younger children (N=24) were randomly assigned to MST delivered by doctoral students in clinical psychology, or usual services. Adolescents in the usual services condition received court orders including one or more stipulations (e.g., individual or group therapy at local agencies, alternative schooling, curfew), and adherence to these stipulations was monitored weekly by deputy juvenile officers. At post-treatment, adolescents in the MST condition had fewer behaviour problems, less criminal offending (self-reported), more positive and less negative family relations (i.e., more warmth, less conflict) and improved peer relations (i.e., more emotional bonding with peers, less involvement with deviant peers), and better grades in school than did adolescents in the usual services condition. Parents in the MST condition reported decreased symptomatology relative to their counterparts in the usual services condition. In addition, adolescents in the MST condition spent 75 fewer days in out-of-home placements during the first year following referral to treatment than did adolescents in the usual services condition. Most importantly, an 8-year follow-up revealed that adolescents in the MST condition were less likely than their usual services counterparts to be arrested for sexual (12.5% versus 41.7%) or nonsexual (29.2% versus 62.5%) crimes and spent one third as many days incarcerated as adults. The 2-year recidivism rate was 12.5% (i.e., all sexual reoffenses occurred within the first two years) for the MST group and 37.5% for the usual services group (i.e., 96% of all sexual reoffenses occurred within the first two years (Borduin and Schaeffer, 2002). Importantly, offender type (peer/adult rapists versus child molester) did not moderate MST treatment effectiveness. For both offender types, recidivism was about three times greater for youth in the comparison group. These recent findings replicated and extended those of Borduin et al. (1990) and provide support for the efficacy of MST with juvenile sex offenders. It is now time to assess the effectiveness of MST with a more substantial sample and using practicing clinicians from a real world community mental health setting.

Ongoing research. At present, a 5-year RCT funded by the National Institute of Mental Health (NIMH) is underway, examining the effectiveness of MST with JSOs. This study expands on the two smaller efficacy studies by (a) employing a larger sample size (sample goal = 160 youth and families); (b) providing MST within a 'real-world' provider setting (versus the doctoral-level students who provided MST in the two efficacy trials); and (c) comparing MST with an outpatient, community-based, cognitive-behavioural sex offender treatment programme. For the purposes of treating JSOs and their families, MST has been adapted to address issues believed to occur more commonly among these families than among families of other juvenile delinquents. These adaptations focus on community safety, interrupting the offender's grooming process (i.e., those strategies used by some adolescents to gain access to sexual assault victims), and reducing denial, particularly in caregivers (e.g., see Swenson, Henggeler, Schoenwald, Kaufman and Randall, 1998). At present, too few participants are enrolled to provide even preliminary information on results.

MST with Children and Adolescents with Sexual Behaviour Problems

Preliminary research. Schoenwald has conducted an extensive examination on the transportability of MST to real world settings (Schoenwald and Hoagwood, 2001; Schoenwald et al., 2002). This transportability study involves 41 MST sites across 26 states and Canada. Though not intended as a study on sexual behaviour problems, the assessment protocol for the transportability study included the Child Behaviour Checklist (CBCL; Achenbach, 1991). The CBCL was used to obtain caregiver ratings of youth sexual behaviour problems (see Letourneau et al., 2004 for a description of this

subscale and scoring procedures). Comparisons of groups with no sexual behaviour problems (n = 943), low sexual behaviour problems (n = 413) and high sexual behaviour problems (n = 166) indicated that rates of sexual and nonsexual behaviour problems were significantly lower, both clinically and statistically, at immediate post-treatment for the High group, although scores remained higher for youth in this group as compared with youth in the No and Low groups. Specifically, the High group evidenced declines on CBLC internalising and externalising T scores and on a measure of behavioural functioning. More recently, criminal records have been collected for a portion of the youth in this study as part of an on-going effort to examine recidivism. Formal analyses of these data are underway. An informal examination of the data reveal only six charges for sexual crimes (at two years post-treatment), none of which were committed by youth in the High sexual behaviour problems group. This preliminary result casts doubt on the assumption that youth with sexual behaviour problems are likely to graduate into juvenile sex offenders.

Conclusions

To improve community and family safety and to promote responsible behaviour in children and adolescents, effective treatments must be applied to the problems of juvenile sexual offending and child sexual behaviour problems. Prevailing treatments for juvenile sex offenders have limited empirical support. The lack of support does not necessarily equate to ineffectiveness; rather, additional research is sorely needed in this field (c.f. Letourneau, 2004). If we are to take seriously the problem of sexual abuse, we must take seriously the scientific evaluation of treatment. Preliminary evidence supports the efficacy of both MST and SOS as used with JSOs. Likewise, preliminary evidence supports the use of several treatment modalities with children with sexual behaviour problems, all of which have substantial caregiver components. We believe that any treatment that purports to address these problems, should at minimum, address factors across a youth's ecology rather than limiting the focus exclusively (or nearly so) on individual youth characteristics. Such a strategy seems insufficient in light of the multitude of factors associated with sexual offending and with sexual behaviour problems. However, only empirically rigorous research that compares well-defined treatments is capable of answering this question. Thus, additional randomised controlled trials should compare the prevailing treatments (e.g., SOS in the case of juvenile sexual offenders) with experimental treatments (e.g., MST) and should include long-term follow up on well-defined targeted behaviours.

References

Achenbach, T.M. (1991) *Manual for the Child Behavioural Checklist and 1991 Profile.* Burlington, VT: University of Vermont Department of Psychiatry.

Ageton, S.S. (1983) *Sexual Assault Among Adolescents.* Lexington, MA: Lexington Books.

Alexander, M.A. (1999) Sexual Offender Treatment Efficacy Revisited. *Sexual Abuse: Journal of Research and Treatment,* 11, 101–16.

Arnold, M.E. and Hughes, J.N. (1999) First do no Harm: Adverse Effects of Grouping Deviant Youth for Skills Training. *Journal of School Psychology,* 37, 99–115.

Awad, G.A. and Saunders, E.B. (1989) Adolescent Child Molesters: Clinical Observations. *Child Psychiatry and Human Development,* 19, 195–206.

Barbaree, H.E. and Cortoni, F.A. (1993) Treatment of the Juvenile Sex Offender Within the Criminal Justice and Mental Health Systems, in Barbaree, H.E., Marshall, W.L. and Hudson, S.M. (Eds.) *The Juvenile Sex Offender.* New York: Guilford. 243–63.

Becker, J.V. (1998) What we Know About the Characteristics and Treatment of Adolescents Who Have Committed Sexual Offenses. *Child Maltreatment,* 3, 317–29.

Becker, J.V. and Kaplan, M.S. (1993) Cognitive Behavioural Treatment of the Juvenile Sex Offender, in Barbaree, H.E., Marshall, W.L. and Hudson, S.M. (Eds.) The Juvenile Sex Offender. New York: Guilford. 264–77.

Bischof, G.P., Stith, S.M. and Whitney, M.L. (1995) Family Environments of Adolescent Sex Offenders And Other Juvenile Delinquents. *Adolescence,* 30, 157–70.

Blaske, D.M., Borduin, C.M., Henggeler, S.W. and Mann, B.J. (1989) Individual, Family, and Peer Characteristics of Adolescent Sex Offenders and Assaultive Offenders. *Developmental Psychology,* 25, 846–55.

Boney-McCoy, S. and Finkelhor, D. (1996) Is Youth Victimisation Related to Trauma Symptoms and Depression After Controlling for Prior Symptoms and Family Relationships? A Longitudinal, Prospective Study. *Journal of Consulting and Clinical Psychology,* 64, 1406–16.

Bonner, B.L., Walker, C.E. and Berliner, L. (1999) *Children With Sexual Behaviour Problems: Assessment and Treatment* (Final report, Grant No. 90-CA-1469) Washington, DC: Administration of Children, Youth and Families, Department of Health and Human Services.

Borduin, C.M., Henggeler, S.W., Blaske, D.M. and Stein, R.J. (1990) Multisystemic Treatment of Adolescent Sexual Offenders. *International Journal of Offender Therapy and Comparative Criminology,* 34, 105–13.

Borduin, C.M., Mann, B.J., Cone, L.T., Henggeler, S.W., Fucci, B.R., Blaske, D.M. and Williams, R.A. (1995) Multisystemic Treatment of Serious Juvenile Offenders: Long-Term Prevention of Criminality and Violence. *Journal of Consulting and Clinical Psychology,* 63, 569–78.

Borduin, C.M. and Schaeffer, C.M. (2002) Multisystemic Treatment of Juvenile Sexual Offenders: A Progress Report. *Journal of Psychology and Human Sexuality,* 13, 25–42.

Borduin, C.M., Schaeffer, C.M. and Heilblum, N. (2000, May) *Multisystemic Treatment of Juvenile Sexual Offenders: A Progress Report.* Paper presented at the 6th International Conference on the Treatment of Sexual Offenders, Toronto.

Bremer, J.F. (1992) Serious Juvenile Sex Offenders: Treatment and Long-Term Follow-Up. *Psychiatric Annals,* 22, 326–32.

Bronfenbrenner, U. (1979) The Ecology of Human Development: Experiments by Design and Nature. Cambridge, MA: Harvard University Press.

Browne, A. and Finkelhor, D. (1986) Impact of Child Sexual Abuse: A Review of The Research. *Psychological Bulletin,* 99, 555–84.

Caldwell, M.F. (2002) What We do Not Know About Juvenile Sexual Reoffense Risk. *Child Maltreatment,* 7, 291–302.

Cauffman, E. and Steinberg, L. (2001) Immaturity of Judgment in Adolescence: Why Adolescents May Be Less Culpable Than Adults. *Behavioural Sciences and The Law,* 18, 741–60.

Chaffin, M., Letourneau, E.J. and Silovsky, J.F. (2002) Adults, Adolescents and Children Who Sexually Abuse Children: A Developmental Perspective, in Myers, J.E.B., Berliner, L., Briere, J., Hendrix, C.T., Jenny, C. and Reid, T.A. (Eds.) *The APSAC Handbook on Child Maltreatment* (2nd edn) Thousand Oaks, CA. Sage.

Cohen, M.A., Miller, T.R. and Rossman, S.B. (1994) The Costs and Consequences of Violent Behaviour in The United States, in Reiss, A.J. and Roth, J.A. (Eds.) *Understanding and Preventing Violence* (Vol. 4): Consequences and Control. Washington, DC: National Academy Press. 67–167.

Cunningham, P.B. and Henggeler, S.W. (1999) Engaging Multiproblem Families in Treatment: Lessons Learned Throughout The Development of Multisystemic Therapy. *Family Process*, 38, 265–81.

Daleiden, E.L., Kaufman, K.L., Hilliker, D.R. and O'Neil, J.N. (1998) The Sexual Histories and Fantasies of Youthful Males: A Comparison of Sexual Offending, Nonsexual Offending, and Nonoffending Group. *Sexual Abuse: A Journal of Research and Treatment*, 10, 195–209.

Davis, G.E. and Leitenberg, H. (1987) Adolescent Sex Offenders. *Psychological Bulletin*, 101, 417–27.

Dishion, T.J., McCord, J. and Poulin, F. (1999) When Interventions Harm: Peer Groups and Problem Behaviour. *American Psychologist*, 54, 755–64.

Dishion, T.J., Patterson, G.R., Stoolmiller, M. and Skinner, M.L. (1991) Family, School and Behavioural Antecedents to Early Adolescent Involvement With Antisocial Peers. *Developmental Psychology*, 27, 172–80.

Elliott, D.S. (1998) *Blueprints for Violence Prevention* (Series Ed.) University of Colorado, Center for The Study and Prevention of Violence. Boulder, CO: Blueprints Publications.

Farrington, D.P. and Welsh, B.C. (1999) Delinquency Prevention Using Family-Based Interventions. *Children and Society*, 13, 287–303.

Fehrenbach, P.A., Smith, W., Monastersky, C. and Deisher, R.W. (1986) Adolescent Sexual Offenders: Offender and Offense Characteristics. *American Journal of Orthopsychiatry*, 56, 225–33.

Finkelhor, D. and Dziuba-Leatherman, J. (1994) Children as Victims of Violence: A National Survey. *Pediatrics*, 94, 413–20.

Finkelhor, D. and Jones, L.M. (January, 2004) Explanations for The Decline in Child Sexual Abuse Cases. *OJJDP Juvenile Justice Bulletin*.

Ford, M.E. and Linney, J.A. (1995) Comparative Analysis of Juvenile Sexual Offenders, Violent Nonsexual Offenders, and Status Offenders. *Journal of Interpersonal Violence*, 10, 56–70.

Freeman-Longo, R.E., Bird, S., Stevenson, W.F. and Fiske, J. (1995) *1994 Nationwide Survey of Treatment Programs and Models: Serving Abuse Reactive Children, Adolescent and Adult Sex Offenders*. Brandon, VT: Safer Society.

Friedrich, W.N., Fisher, J.L., Acton, R., Berliner, L., Butler, J., Damon, L., Davies, W.H., Gray, A. and Wright, J. (2001) Child Sexual Behavior Inventory: Normative, Psychiatric, and Sexual Abuse Comparisons. *Child Maltreatment*, 6, 37–49.

Friedrich, W.N., Grambsch, P., Broughton, D., Kuiper, J. and Beilke, R.L. (1991) Normative Sexual Behaviour in Children. *Pediatrics*, 88, 456–64.

Friedrich, W.N., Grambsch, P., Damon, L., Hewitt, S.K., Koverola, C., Lang, R.A., Wolfe, V. and Broughton, D. (1992) Child Sexual Behaviour Inventory: Normative and Clinical Comparisons. *Psychological Assessment*, 4, 303–11.

Graves, R.B., Openshaw, D.K., Ascione, F.R. and Ericksen, S.L. (1996) Demographic and Parental Characteristics of Youthful Sexual Offenders. *International Journal of Offender Therapy and Comparative Criminology*, 40, 300–17.

Griffin, P., Torbet, P. and Szymanski, L. (1998) *Trying Juveniles as Adults in Criminal Court: an Analysis of State Transfer Provisions*. Washington, DC: US Department of Justice, Office of Justice Programs, Office of Juvenile Justice and Delinquency Prevention.

Guarino-Ghezzi, S. and Kimball, L.M. (1998) Juvenile Sex Offenders in Treatment. *Corrections Management Quarterly*, 2, 45–54.

Hagan, M.P., King, R.P. and Patros, R.L. (1994) Recidivism Among Adolescent Perpetrators of Sexual Assault Against Children. *Journal of Offender Rehabilitation*, 21, 127 37.

Haley, J. (1976) *Problem Solving Therapy*. San Francisco: Jossey-Bass.

Hanson, R.K. and Bussiére, M.T. (1998) Predicting Relapse: A Meta-Analysis of Sexual Offender Recidivism Studies. *Journal of Consulting and Clinical Psychology*, 66, 348–62.

Hanson, R.K., Gordon, A., Harris, A.J.R., Marques, J.K., Murphy, W., Quinsey, V.L. and Seto, M.C. (2002) First Report of The Collaborative Outcome Data Project on The Effectiveness of Psychological Treatment for Sex Offenders. *Sexual Abuse: A Journal of Research and Treatment*, 14, 169–94.

Hastings, T., Anderson, S.J. and Hemphill, P. (1997) Comparisons of Daily Stress, Coping, Problem Behaviour, and Cognitive Distortions in Adolescent Sexual Offenders and

Conduct-Disordered Youth. *Sexual Abuse: Journal of Research and Treatment*, 9, 29–42.

Henggeler, S.W., Melton, G.B., Brondino, M.J., Scherer, D.G. and Hanley, J.H. (1997) Multisystemic Therapy With Violent and Chronic Juvenile Offenders and Their Families: The Role of Treatment Fidelity in Successful Dissemination. *Journal of Consulting and Clinical Psychology*, 65, 821–33.

Henggeler, S.W., Melton, G.B. and Smith, L.A. (1992) Family Preservation Using Multisystemic Therapy: an Effective Alternative to Incarcerating Serious Juvenile Offenders. *Journal of Consulting and Clinical Psychology*, 60, 953–61.

Henggeler, S.W., Melton, G.B., Smith, L.A., Schoenwald, S K. and Hanley, J.H. (1993) Family Preservation Using Multisystemic Treatment: Long-Term Follow-Up to A Clinical Trial With Serious Juvenile Offenders. *Journal of Child and Family Studies*, 2, 283–93.

Henggeler, S.W., Pickrel, S.G. and Brondino, M.J. (1999) Multisystemic Treatment of Substance Abusing and Dependent Delinquents: Outcomes, Treatment Fidelity, and Transportability. *Mental Health Services Research*, 1, 171–84.

Henggeler, S.W. and Schoenwald, S.K. (1998) *The MST Supervisory Manual: Promoting Quality Assurance at The Clinical Level.* Charleston, SC: MST Institute.

Henggeler, S.W., Schoenwald, S.K., Borduin, C.M., Rowland, M.D. and Cunningham, P.B. (1998) *Multisystemic Treatment of Antisocial Behaviour in Children and Adolescents.* New York: Guilford Press.

Howell, J.C. (2003) *Preventing and Reducing Juvenile Delinquency: A Comprehensive Framework.* Thousand Oaks, CA: Sage Publications.

Huey, S.J., Henggeler, S.W., Brondino, M.J. and Pickrel, S.G. (2000) Mechanisms of Change in Multisystemic Therapy: Reducing Delinquent Behaviour Through Therapist Adherence and Improved Family and Peer Functioning. *Journal of Consulting and Clinical Psychology*, 68, 451–67.

Hunter, J.A., Goodwin, D.W. and Becker, J.V. (1994) The Relationship Between Phallometrically Measured Deviant Sexual Arousal and Clinical Characteristics in Juvenile Sexual Offenders. *Behavioural Research and Therapy*, 32, 533–8.

Hunter, J.A. and Santos, D. (1990) The Use of Specialised Cognitive-Behavioural Therapies in The Treatment of Juvenile Sexual Offenders. *International Journal of Offender Therapy and Comparative Criminology*, 34, 239–48.

Jacobs, W.L., Kennedy, W.A. and Meyer, J.B. (1997) Juvenile Delinquents: A Between-Group Comparison Study of Sexual and Nonsexual Offenders. *Sexual Abuse: Journal of Research and Treatment*, 9, 201–17.

Kazdin, A.E. and Weisz, J.R. (1998) Identifying and Developing Empirically Supported Child and Adolescent Treatments. *Journal of Consulting and Clinical Psychology*, 66, 19–36.

Kempton, T. and Forehand, R.L. (1992) Suicide Attempts Among Juvenile Delinquents: The Contribution of Mental Health Factors. *Behaviour Research and Therapy*, 30, 537–41.

Knopp, F.H., Freeman-Longo, R. and Lane, S. (1977) Program Development, in Ryan, G. and Lane, S. (Eds.) *Juvenile Sexual Offending: Causes, Consequences, and Correction* (2nd edn) San Francisco: Jossey-Bass.

Knopp, F.H., Freeman-Longo, R. and Stevenson, W.F. (1992) *Nationwide Survey of Juvenile and Adult Sex-Offender Treatment Programs and Models.* Orwell, VT: Safer Society.

Lab, S.P., Shields, G. and Schondel, C. (1993) Research Note: an Evaluation of Juvenile Sexual Offender Treatment. *Crime and Delinquency*, 39, 543–53.

Langstrom, N., Grann, M. and Lichtenstein, P. (2002) Genetic and Environmental Influences on Problematic Masturbatory Behaviour in Children: A Study of Same-Sex Twins. *Archives of Sexual Behaviour*, 31, 343–50.

Letourneau, E.J. (2004) A Comment on The First Report: Letter to The Editor. *Sexual Abuse: A Journal of Research and Treatment*, 16, 77–81.

Letourneau, E.J., Schoenwald, S.K. and Sheidow, A.J. (2004) Children and Adolescents With Sexual Behaviour Problems. *Child Maltreatment*, 9, 49–61.

Loeber, R. and Farrington, D.P. (Eds.) (1998) *Serious and Violent Juvenile Offenders: Risk Factors and Successful Interventions.* Thousand Oaks, CA: Sage.

Maguire, K. and Pastore, A.L. (1998) *Sourcebook of Criminal Justice Statistics 1998.* Washington, DC: US Department of Justice, Bureau of Justice Statistics. 337.

McGrath, R.J., Cumming, G.F. and Burchard, B.L. (2003) *Current Practices and Trends in Sexual Abuser Management: The Safer Society 2002 Nationwide Study.* Brandon, VT: The Safer Society Foundation.

Milloy, C.D. (1998) Specialised Treatment for Juvenile Sex Offenders: A Closer Look. *Journal of Interpersonal Violence*, 13, 653–6.

Minuchin, S. (1974) *Families and Family Therapy.* Cambridge, MA: Harvard University Press.

National Institute on Drug Abuse. (1999) *Principles of Drug Addiction Treatment: A Research-Based Guide.* NIH Publication No. 99–4180.

Pithers, W.D., Gray, A., Busconi, A. and Houchens, P. (1998) Children With Sexual Behaviour Problems: Identification of Five Distinct Child Types and Related Treatment Considerations. *Child Maltreatment*, 3, 384–406.

Saunders, B.E., Villeponteaux, L.A., Lipovsky, J.A., Kilpatrick, D.G. and Veronen, L.J. (1992) Child Sexual Assault as a Risk Factor for Mental Disorders Among Women: A Community Survey. *Journal of Interpersonal Violence*, 7, 189–204.

Schoenwald, S.K. (1998) *Multisystemic Therapy Consultation Guidelines.* Charleston, SC: MST Institute.

Schoenwald, S.K., Henggeler, S.W., Brondino, M.J. and Rowland, M.D. (2000) Multisystemic Therapy: Monitoring Treatment Fidelity. *Family Process*, 39, 83–103.

Schoenwald, SK., Henggeler, S.W. and Edwards, D. (1998) *MST Supervisor Adherence Measure.* Charleston, SC: MST Institute.

Schoenwald, S.K. and Hoagwood, K. (2001) Effectiveness, Transportability, and Dissemination of Interventions: What Matters When? *Psychiatric Services*, 52, 1190–7.

Schoenwald, S.K., Sheidow, A.J., Letourneau, E.J. and Liao, J.G. (2003) Transportability of Multisystemic Therapy: Evidence for Multilevel Influences. *Mental Health Services Research*, 5, 223–39.

Schram, D.D., Milloy, C.D. and Rowe, W.E. (1991) *Juvenile Sex Offenders: A Follow-Up Study of Reoffense Behaviour.* Olympia, WA: Washington State Institute for Public Policy.

Silovsky, J.F. and Niec, L. (2002) Characteristics of Young Children With Sexual Behaviour Problems: A Pilot Study. *Child Maltreatment*, 7, 187–97.

Sipe, R., Jensen, E.L. and Everett, R.S. (1998) Adolescent Sexual Offenders Grown Up: Recidivism in Young Adulthood. *Criminal Justice and Behaviour*, 25, 109–24.

Smets, A.C. and Cebula, C.M. (1987) A Group Treatment Program for Adolescent Sex Offenders: Five Steps Toward Resolution. *Child Abuse and Neglect*, 11, 247–54.

Smith, G. and Fischer, L. (1999) Assessment of Juvenile Sexual Offenders: Reliability and Validity of The Abel Assessment for Interest in Paraphilias. *Sexual Abuse: A Journal of Research and Treatment*, 11, 207–16.

Swenson, C.C., Henggeler, S.W., Schoenwald, S.K., Kaufman, K. L. and Randall, J. (1998) Changing The Social Ecologies of Adolescent Sexual Offenders: Implications of The Success of Multisystemic Therapy in Treating Serious Antisocial Behaviour in Adolescents. *Child Maltreatment*, 3, 330-8.

Swenson, C.C. and Letourneau, E.J. (In Press) Multisystemic Therapy With Juvenile Sex Offenders, in Schwartz, B. and Cellini, H.R. (Eds.) *The Sex Offender, Volume 5.* New York: Civic Research Institute.

US Public Health Service (1999) *Mental Health: A Report of The Surgeon General.* Rockville, MD: US Department of Health and Human Services, National Institutes of Health, National Institute of Mental Health.

US Public Health Service (2001) *Youth Violence: A Report of The Surgeon General.* Washington, DC: Author.

White, J.W. and Koss, M.P. (1993) Adolescent Sexual Aggression Within Heterosexual Relationships: Prevalence, Characteristics, and Causes, in Barbaree, H.E., Marshall, W.L. and Hudson, S.M. (Eds.) *The Juvenile Sex Offender.* New York: Guilford. 182–202.

Widom, C.S. and Morris, S. (1997) Accuracy of Adult Recollections of Childhood Victimisation: Part 2. *Childhood Sexual Abuse. Psychological Assessment*, 9, 34–46.

Worling, J.R. (1998) Adolescent Sexual Offender Treatment at The SAFE-T Program, in Marshall, W.L. Fernandez, Y.M., Hudson, S.M. and Ward, T. (Eds.) *Sourcebook of Treatment Programs for Sexual Offenders.* New York: Plenum. 353–66.

Worling, J.R. and Curwen, T. (1998) *The Adolescent Sexual Offender Project: A 10-Year Follow-Up Study.* Toronto, ON. SAFE-T Program (Sexual Abuse: Family Education and Treatment) Thistletown Regional Centre for Children and Adolescents and Probation and Community Services, Ontario Ministry of Community and Social Services.

Worling, J.R. and Curwen, T. (2000) Adolescent Sexual Offender Recidivism: Success of

Specialised Treatment and Implications for Risk Prediction. *Child Abuse and Neglect*, 24, 965–82.

Author Note

Correspondence should be addressed to Elizabeth J. Letourneau, Family Services Research Center, Department of Psychiatry and Behavioural Sciences, Medical University of South Carolina, 67 President Street – Suite CPP, PO Box 250861, Charleston, SC 29425 (letourej@musc.edu).

Preparation of this manuscript was supported by grants MH60663–01 and MH065414 01A1 from the National Institute of Mental Health.

Chapter Seventeen

Mode Deactivation Therapy: Cognitive-Behavioural Therapy for Young People with Reactive Conduct Disorders or Personality Disorders or Traits Who Sexually Abuse

Jack A. Apsche and Serene R. Ward Bailey

Introduction

The development of mode deactivation therapy (MDT) as an applied CBT methodology for young people with reactive conduct disorder or personality disorders or traits has been a challenge. The difficulty begins in the attempt to treat young people with a complicated history of abuse and neglect and multi-axial diagnoses. Many young people are victims of sexual, physical, or emotional abuse, as well as neglect. These individuals have developed personality traits as survival coping strategies. These personality disorders or traits are not true to their cluster, or cluster bound, meaning that they are translated into beliefs and schemas that are inclusive of beliefs from all three personality disorder clusters. Often it has been thought that individuals with personality disorders stay true to their cluster. This is not so, with the adolescent typology.

Often CBT, as viewed by 'arguing' the concepts of cognitive distortions, fails with these youngsters. They do not respond well to being in a one-down position, no matter how aligned they are with their therapist. Cognitive therapy as normally practiced will trigger a negative reaction by these youngsters. They perceive the therapist as another person attempting to change them from a system of defences that has been developed to protect them. CBT as normally practiced will often fail with this typology of youngster.

According to Weissberg, Kumpfer and Seligman (2003), The American Psychological Association (APA)'s Task Force on Prevention found that universal programming is not as effective as programmes which are empirically based treatment for a specific target group, such as the specific typology of adolescents described in this chapter. Weissberg et al. also indicate that empirical literature regarding this area is 'sparse' and that 'the most important advances regarding the effective implementation of empirically supported' treatment are yet to come. MDT will prove to address this need for empirically supported treatment for a specific target group. Although Weissberg et al. discuss this need in the context of prevention; MDT addresses this specific need as a methodology for adolescents both as treatment for existing problem behaviours, as well as for preventing problem behaviours by addressing the underlying beliefs.

Ollendick and King (2000), suggest guidelines for empirically supported treatments for children and young people. These guidelines are based on the 1995 Society of Clinical Psychology Task Force on Promotion and Dissemination of Psychological Procedures published report on empirically validated psychological treatments. As Ollendick and King point out, the Task Force proposed three categories of treatment efficacy one, well-established treatments, two, probably efficacious treatments and three, experimental treatments. According to their definition and criteria for these treatments, MDT has moved from experimental treatment to probably efficacious treatment. The rationale for this statement is in meeting the definition of probably efficacious treatment.

Ollendick and King (2000: p387) clarify the definitions of the three categories of efficacious treatment as; 'the primary distinction between well-established and efficacious treatments was that a well-established treatment should have been shown to be superior to a psychological placebo, pill, or another treatment, whereas a probably efficacious treatment must be shown to be superior to a waiting-list or no-treatment control only'. Furthermore, 'probably efficacious treatment may be validated through group designs in which patients would be assigned randomly to the treatment of interest, or one or more comparison conditions – or carefully controlled single-case experiments and their group analogues' (p388). MDT has been shown to be more effective than standardised normalised

CBT in a descriptive study (Apsche and Ward, 2003). MDT has also been demonstrated as effctive in a series of case studies (Apsche, Ward and Evile, 2002) (Apsche and Ward Bailey, 2003).

The early development of MDT was conceived from the need to apply the principles of CBT with complex adolescent aberrant typologies. These individuals have long histories of sexual, physical, and/or emotional abuse. Often they respond in ways that manifest in personality disorders and/or conduct disorders. These are youngsters that may respond by committing aggressive acts, and/or other aberrant behaviours. These youngsters are viewed as 'criminals' and are the underclass within our society and active within the criminal justice system. The term 'typology' refers to this specific complex adolescent with these types of histories.

The concepts of mode deactivation therapy (MDT) are derived from some aspects of functional analytic behavioural therapy (FAP), dialectical behaviour therapy (DBT), and cognitive behaviour therapy (CBT). Functional analytic behavioural therapy (FAP) (Kohlenberg and Tsai, 1993) states that reality or the perception of reality and unconscious motivations are created through past contingencies of reinforcement. Dialectical behaviour therapy (DBT) methodology validates the perception of reality, accepting an adolescent for who he is based on his beliefs. MDT stresses the importance of identifying the adolescent's beliefs and then applies the DBT concepts of validating the beliefs and then balancing the dialectical nature of the beliefs.

Along with adopting concepts from FAP and DBT, the focus of MDT is largely based on Beck's recent area of theoretical interest, the system of modes (Beck, 1996, Alford and Beck, 1997). According to Alford and Beck (1997) a comprehensive theory of personality, that includes the various systems of complex human behaviour such as behavioural, cognitive, motivational, is needed. Modes, consisting of schemas, activate survival strategies developed to protect an individual, but have become maladaptive. Beck has alluded to the need for a theory, which considers the various systems of personality and their interaction. He has also described his concept of modes, schemas which may become maladaptive. MDT developed as a theory to consider the various systems of personality and their interaction, activating modes and manifesting in aberrant behaviours. The goal of MDT is to modify the schemas, which comprise modes, thereby modifying the aberrant behaviours.

Mode deactivation therapy: functionally based treatment

Mode deactivation therapy (MDT) as an applied CBT methodology aims to address reactive conduct disorders and personality disorders or traits. MDT is based on Beck's (1996) mode model with aspects of other therapies including functional analytic psychotherapy (FAP) (Kohlenberg and Tsai, 1993) and dialectical behaviour therapy (DBT) (Linehan, 1993). Additionally, there are areas of MDT which reflect concepts of schema therapy (Young, Klosko and Weishaar, 2003). In an effort to clarify the similarities and differences between MDT and these other therapies, we present a comparison chart (see Figure 17.1). Please refer to this chart as we discuss MDT in greater detail.

The theoretical underpinnings of mode deactivation therapy are based on Beck's model of modes. In his article Beyond Belief: A Theory of Modes, Personality, and Psychopathology (1996) Beck defines modes as specific suborganisations of the basic systems of the mind. Specifically, suggesting that people learn from unconscious experiential components and cognitive structural processing components. Functional analytic psychotherapy (FAP) (Kohlenberg and Tsai, 1993) theory focuses on the deeper unconscious motivations that were formed as a result of past contingencies of reinforcement. Perception is based on past contingencies, therefore, reality and the concept of reality reflects what has been experienced in the past. Considering reinforcement history in the context of a person provides a more complete assessment of a person and specific behaviours (Kohlenberg and Tsai, 1993). Therefore, to change the behaviour of individuals there must be a restructuring of the experiential components, and a corresponding cognitive restructuring of the structural components. The dysfunctional experiential and structural learning (conscious and unconscious) develop dysfunctional schemas that generate high levels of anxiety, fear, and general irrational thoughts and feelings, as well as aberrant behaviours. This system is self-reinforcing and protected by the development of the conglomerate of the beliefs underlying the developing personality disorders. This conglomerate is comprised of multiple

Figure 17.1: Comparison of approaches

	MDT (Apsche and Ward Bailey, 2003)	CBT (Beck, et al, 1990)	DBT (Linehan, 1993)	FAP (Kohlenberg and Tsai, 1993)	Schema Therapy (Young et al., 2003)
Goal oriented treatment	Yes	Yes	Yes	Yes	Yes
Focus of treatment	Present, in-vivo work in sessions	Initially present focused	Present	Present	Present
Session structure	Yes, but flexible	Yes	Yes	Yes	Yes
Session limitation	Aims to be time limited	Aims to be time limited	Aims to be time limited		
Cognition	Unconscious and conscious	conscious	conscious	conscious	conscious
Goals for therapy	Yes – Empower patient to modify underlying beliefs to thereby change moods and behaviours (deactivate modes).	Yes – Uses variety of techniques to change thinking, moods, and behaviours.	Yes – Skills training to better manage symptoms	Yes – Uses within-session contingencies to change behaviour	Yes – Identify and modify maladaptive mode schemas
Collaboration between therapist and client	Yes	Yes	No		Yes
Therapeutic alliance important	Yes	Yes	Yes	Yes	Yes
Addresses resistance	Yes	No – Assumes patients will comply with treatment	Yes		Yes
Empowers client to be own therapist	Yes	Yes	No	No	Yes
Thoughts/beliefs as dysfunctional	No – Beliefs are not thought of as dysfunctional, which invalidates the patient's experience. Beliefs are validated as being created out of a patient's experience, then are balanced to deactivate modes.	Yes – Teach patient to identify, evaluate, and respond to their dysfunctional thoughts and beliefs with schema assumptions (scanning)	Yes – Balance through change and acceptance.	Yes	Yes – Maladaptive mode schemas

Figure 17.1: *Continued*

Cognitive distortions	No – thoughts/beliefs are not distortions since they are based on past experience	Yes	No	Yes	Yes – Maladaptive mode schemas
Dialectical thinking	Yes – Focus on balancing	No	Yes – Focus on the dialectical pattern/process	No	No
Case conceptualization	Yes – ever-evolving and drives treatment	Yes – ever-evolving formulation of the patient's problems in cognitive terms	Yes – important	Yes – case formulation	Yes
Case conceptualisation is specific typology driven	Yes	No	No	No	No
Acceptance and validation in the moment	Yes	No	Yes	No	No
Modes	Yes – Perceptions trigger physiological cues, which trigger beliefs (entire process is mode activating)	No	No	No	No
Triggers important	Yes – Learning the triggers is key to preventing activation of modes				
Client's perceptions important	Yes – Perceptions trigger modes	No – Perceptions are distorted	Yes – Perceptions are based on past experiences	No	No
Reducing anxiety, addressing trauma	Yes – Uses exposure to fear cue to decrease perception of fear	No – Focuses on thought-feeling-behaviour connection	No	No	No
Fear→avoids paradigm	Yes	No	No	No	No

clustered compound core beliefs, which are the most pronounced impediment to treatment (Beck, 1996). The compound core beliefs are systematically treated and restructured throughout mode deactivation therapy, beginning with the MDT Case Conceptualisation.

By restructuring beliefs, MDT addresses underlying perceptions that may be applicable to setting in motion the mode related charge of aberrant schemas, that enable the behaviour integration of dialectical behaviour therapy (DBT) principles (Linehan, 1993) when treating adolescents with reactive conduct disorder and personality disorders/ traits. Many of Linehan's teachings describe radical acceptance and examining the 'truth' in each client's perceptions. This methodology of finding the grain of truth in the perception of the adolescent is at the crux of MDT. We also 'borrow' radical acceptance in the form of helping the youth accept who he is based on his beliefs. The other major similarity between DBT and MDT is the use of balancing the dichotomous or dialectical thinking of the client. Just as DBT emphasises the importance of maintaining 'balance,' so does MDT.

Study of cognitive therapy emphasises the characteristic patterns of a person's development, differentiation, and adaptation to social and biological environments (Alford and Beck, 1997). Cognitive theory considers personality to be grounded in the co-ordinated operations of complex systems that have been selected or adapted to insure biological survival. These consistent co-ordinated acts are controlled by genetically and environmentally determined processes or structures termed as 'schema.' Schema are essential both conscious and unconscious meaning structures. They serve as survival functions by protecting the individual from the trauma or experience. An alternative and more encompassing construct is that of modes and suggest that the cognitive schematic processing is one of many schemas that are sensitive to change or orienting event.

Beck, Freeman and Associates (1990) suggested that cognitive, affective and motivational processes are determined by the idiosyncratic structures or schema that constitute the basic elements of personality. This is a more cognitive approach suggesting that the schema is the determinant to thoughts, moods, and behaviours.

According to Young (2003), CBT has helped many patients with Axis I disorders. However, many patients with Axis II disorders have gone largely unhelped. Using CBT alone, Axis II disordered patients continue to experience significant emotional distress and impaired functioning, especially patients with borderline personality disorder and narcissistic personality disorder. (Young, 2003) In FAP theory, contingencies of reinforcement, such as families of origin, create the perception of reality and resulting beliefs, which drives behaviours. (Kohlenberg and Tsai, 1993) Therefore, continuing to reinforce these perceptions/ beliefs thereby perpetuates the resulting aberrant behaviours. Modifying the beliefs and perceptions will in turn modify the behaviours. 'In general, it is much better for patients with borderline personality disorder not to live with or have frequent contact with their family of origin, especially in the early stages of treatment. Their family is very likely to continue reinforcing the very schemas and modes the therapist is fighting to overcome.' (Young, 2003)

Schema therapy (Young, 2003) states that internal schemas lie at the core of personality disorders and the behaviour patterns. The behaviours are what is seen and therefore are usually the basis for Axis II diagnoses. Young (2003) agrees that in order to address the underlying schemas (beliefs) and take into account the modes, a concept which Young acknowledges has been difficult to address in the past but is important. Mode oriented therapy is used when therapy seems stuck and patients are rigid, such as with personality disorders and those who display frequent fluctuations in affect (Young, 2003). Personality disordered patients present with varying symptoms, including: being highly self-punitive, self-critical, and experiencing emotional numbness. MDT is used because of the complexities of personality disorders.

Linehan (1993) sees individuals with borderline personality disorder analogous with burn victims where the slightest movement is automatic and causes extreme pain. 'Because the individuals cannot control the onset and offset of internal or external events that influence emotional response' she suggests that the experience is itself a 'nightmare of intense emotional pain' and a struggle to regulate themselves.

According to Dodge, Lochman, Harnish, Bates and Petti (1997), there are two sub-groups of aggressive conduct type youngsters; proactive, the sub-type that receives benefit and rewards from aggression and reactive, the sub-type that is aggressive due to being emotionally reactive or dysregulates. Frequently, reactive adolescents have multiple personality disorder according to Dodge et al. (1997). It appears that reactive conduct disorder adolescents emotionally dysregulate and many of their aberrant responses are results of their emotional dysregulation. Reactive conduct disorder youth tend to have a history of early life trauma, such as parental rejection, exposure to family violence, and family instability. In addition, these youth show a pattern of emotional dysregulation that includes somatisation, depressive symptoms, sleep disorder symptoms, and personality disorders (Dodge et al., 1997). Reactive conduct disorder youth demonstrate a greater tendency to interpret peers' intents as hostile, responding to their environment similarly to individuals with borderline personality disorder. They are reactive and engage in dialectical thinking that seems contradictory and often attention seeking. In reality, these youngsters often endorse dichotomous beliefs and engage in dichotomous behaviours. Often what appears to be impulsive behaviour may be their acting upon these dialectical beliefs or being reactive (Dodge et al., 1997). Reactive conduct disorder youth have difficulty regulating their emotions with incoming stimuli (Dodge et al., 1997). Koenigsberg, Harvey, Mitropoulou, Antonia, Goodman, Silverman, Serby, Schopick and Siever (2001) found that many types of aggression, as well as suicidal threats and gestures were associated with emotional dysregulation.

Reactive conduct disorder youth have greater problems than proactive conduct disorder youth in encoding relevant social cues (Dodge et al., 1997), i.e., reactive youth have difficulty with perception. As FAP theory states, perception is based on past experiences. MDT addresses reactive conduct disorder by identifying beliefs that were developed from past experiences, borrowing validation of truth of the perception from DBT, and taking it a step further by balancing the beliefs and modifying them into healthier beliefs.

In CBT theory, it is believed that aberrant behaviour is related to dysfunctional schema. CBT attempts to identify dysfunctional schemas and modify them. Beck (1996) suggested that the model of individual schemas (linear schematic processing) does not adequately address a number of psychological problems, therefore the model must be modified to address such problems. Working with adolescents who present with complex typologies of aberrant behaviours, such as anxiety or fear reactions and personality beliefs and/or disorders, it was necessary to address this typology of youngsters from a more 'global' methodology. The concept of modes provided the framework to develop such a methodology. MDT incorporates the model of individual schemas with Beck's notion of modes as integrated suborganisations of personality (1996). Modes assist individuals to adapt to solve problems, such as, the adaptation of adolescents to strategies of protection and mistrust when they have been abused. They consist of schemas (beliefs) that are activated by the fear versus avoids paradigm. To address the schema processing based on thoughts and beliefs without understanding the modes is insufficient and does not explain the specific adolescent typology referred to in mode deactivation therapy (MDT). MDT is a methodology that addresses dysfunctional schemas through systematically assessing and restructuring underlying dysfunctional compound core beliefs. MDT is applicable to adolescents with personality disorders or traits, reactive conduct disorder, and/or who engage in aggressive or delinquent behaviours.

Specifically, Beck (1996: p2) describes modes as a 'network of cognitive, affective, motivational, and behavioural components'. He further described modes as 'consisting of integrated sections or suborganisations of personality that are designed to deal with specific demands'. Beck continues to describe 'primal modes' as including the derivatives of ancient organisations that evolved in prehistoric circumstances and are manifested in survival reactions and in psychiatric disorders. Young (2003: p271) describes modes as 'the set of schemas or schema operations – adaptive or maladaptive – that are currently active for an individual'. A 'schema mode' is the 'predominant state that we are in at a given point in time' (p37). Beck also explains that the concept of charges (or cathexes) being related to the fluctuations in the intensity gradients of cognitive structures.

Alford and Beck (1997) explain that the schema typical of personality disorder is theorised to operate on a more continuous basis; the personality disorders are more sensitive to a variety of stimuli than other clinical syndromes. Since these youngsters are often personality activated, it seems that they are in continuous operation. This is one of the difficulties, they are always ready to defend and/or attack.

Modes are important to understanding this typology of adolescents in that they are particularly sensitive to danger and fear, serving to charge the modes that as multi-victims of various abuse these youngsters are sensitive to danger and fear. These fears signal danger and are activated by conscious and unconscious learned experiential fears. The unconscious refers to the cognitive unconscious as defined by Alford and Beck (1997). Abused children develop systems to adapt to their hostile environment. These systems are often manifested by personality disorders or traits (Johnson, Cohen, Brown, Smailes and Bernstein, 1999). Longitudinal studies demonstrate that abused children frequently develop personality disorders in adolescence. From the perspective of modes, these disorders are adaptations to a dangerous environment. MDT suggests that the danger produces a fear reaction that is often reactive to danger and fear. This reactivity and sensitivity do not respond to traditional CBT. The adaptation of a theory proposed by Beck (1996), on modes into the dialectical methodology of DBT, led Linehan (1993), to create the blueprint for MDT. The understanding of conscious and unconscious fears being charged and activating the mode system explains the level of emotional dysregulation and impulse control of this typology of youngsters.

Modes provide the content of the mind, which is reflected in how the person conducts their perspectives. The modes consist of the schemas (beliefs) that contain the specific memories, the system on solving specific problems, and the experiences that produce memories, images and language that forms perspectives. As Beck (1996) states disorders of personality are conceptualised simply as 'hypervalent' maladaptive system operations, co-ordinated as modes that are specific primitive strategies. Although the operation of dysfunctional modes in the present state is maladaptive, it is important to note that they were developed over time for survival and adaptation. These systems prove to become maladaptive as problematic behaviour resulting in destruction.

Underlying the MDT methodology is the MDT Case Conceptualisation. MDT Case Conceptualisation is a combination of Beck's (1995) case conceptualisation and Nezu, Nezu, Friedman, Haynes's (1998) problem solving model, with several new assessments and methodologies recently developed to address the specifics of adolescents. Conceptualising a case is a fluid and dynamic process (Beck, 1995). Many therapists 'dismiss case conceptualisation as an abstract exercise' (Friedberg and McClure, 2002). Although, as these authors have observed, conceptualising a case is 'one of the most practical tools' clinicians can use. The case conceptualisation not only helps the clinician to have a clear idea of developing a treatment plan, but it can also aid in diagnosing a client (Friedberg and McClure, 2002). The goal is to provide a blueprint to treatment within the case conceptualisation.

Case conceptualisations include the presenting problems, test data, cultural issues, history and development, cognitive issues, and behavioural issues (Friedberg and McClure, 2002). The MDT Case Conceptualisation takes conceptualising a case further. The MDT Case Conceptualisation helps the clinician examine the underlying fears of the youth. These fears serve the function of developing avoidance behaviours in the youngster. These behaviours usually appear as a variety of problem behaviours in the milieu. Developing personality disorders often surrounds underlying post traumatic stress disorder (PTSD) issues. The MDT Case Conceptualisation method has an assessment for the underlying compound core beliefs that are generated by the developing personality disorders. Thus far, preliminary results suggest that our typology of the youngsters have a conglomerate of compound core beliefs associated with personality disorders. This conglomerate of beliefs is the crux of why youngsters fail in treatment. One cannot treat specific disorders, such as aggression, without gathering these conglomerate beliefs. It is also apparent that these beliefs are not cluster specific. That is to say that the conglomerate of beliefs and associated behaviours contains beliefs from each cluster that integrate with each other. Because of this complex integration of beliefs, it makes treatment for this typology of youngster more complicated. The conglomerate of compound core beliefs represents protection for the individual from their vulnerability issues, which may present as treatment interfering behaviours. The conglomerate of beliefs and behaviours is consistent with schema therapy's categories of maladaptive modes, although acknowledges the complexities of these modes to allow for more individualised, specific identification through identifying the understanding beliefs and corresponding behaviours for the individual. The conglomerate of beliefs and corresponding behaviours serves to sort out the schemas of each individual. In contrast to Young's schema therapy, MDT does not label the client's modes. Rather, MDT recognises that modes are fluid and ever changing and therefore, they are not categorised. The attempt to use the usual didactic approaches to treatment, without addressing these beliefs amounts to treatment interfering behaviour on the part of the psychologist, or treating professional, and is not empirically supported and counter-initiated.

Mode deactivation therapy is designed to assess and treat this conglomerate of personality disorders, as well as remediate aggression and other problematic behaviours. It is important to note that mode deactivation therapy is an empirically based and driven treatment methodology.

The theoretical constructs of mode deactivation therapy are based on the mode model. Specifically, suggesting that people learn from unconscious experiential components and cognitive structural processing components. Therefore, to change the behaviour of individuals there must be a restructuring of the experiential components and a corresponding cognitive restructuring of the structural components. The dysfunctional experiential and structural learning (conscious and unconscious) develop dysfunctional schemas that generate high levels of anxiety, fear, and general irrational thoughts and feelings, as well as aberrant behaviours. This system is self-reinforcing and protected by the development of the conglomerate of the developing personality disorders. This conglomerate is comprised of multiple clustered compound core beliefs. These conglomerates of personality disorders are the most pronounced impediment to treatment, and are systematically treated throughout mode deactivation therapy, beginning with the MDT Case Conceptualisation.

Mode activation

Beck (1996) introduced the concept of modes to expand his concept of schematic processing. He suggests that his model of individual schemas (linear schematic processing) does not adequately address a number of psychological problems; therefore he suggests the system of modes. He described the network of modes as consisting of integrated sectors of sub-organisations of personality that help individuals adopt to solve problems, such as the adaptation of adolescents to strategies of protection and mistrust when they have been abused.

Beck (1996) also suggests that these modes are charged, thereby explaining the fluctuations in the intensity gradients of cognitive structures. They are charged by triggers, fears and dangers that set off a system of modes to protect the fear. Modes are activated by charges that are related to the danger in the fear versus avoids paradigm. The orienting schema signals danger, activates or charges all systems of the mode. The affective system signals the onset and increasing levels of anxiety. The beliefs are activated simultaneously reacting to the danger, fear versus avoids and physiological system. The motivational system signals the impulse to the attack and avoids (flight, fight) system. The physiological system produces changes in the heart rate or increases or lowers the blood pressure, the tightening of muscles, etc.

Mode deactivation therapy is built on a mastery system. Adolescents move through a specifically designed MDT Workbook at the rate of learning that accommodates their individual learning style. The system is designed to allow the youngster to experience success, prior to undertaking more difficult materials. Through the MDT Case Conceptualisation and MDT Workbook, the system allows the youngster to systematically address the underlying conglomerate of personality disorders, as well as the specific didactics necessary, the problem behaviours and/or anger/aggression. Mode deactivation therapy is designed to assess and treat this conglomerate of personality disorders, as well as remediate aberrant behaviours. It is important to note that mode deactivation therapy is an empirically based and driven treatment methodology. Carefully following the MDT Case Conceptualisation and methodology ensures empirically based and driven treatment (Apsche and Ward Bailey, 2003, in press).

Additionally, mode deactivation therapy (MDT) includes imagery and relaxation to facilitate cognitive thinking and then balance training, which teaches the youngster to balance his perception and interpretation of information and internal stimuli. The imagery is implemented to reduce the external stimulation of the emotional dysregulation, which is the basis for the underlying typologies of these youngsters. Many of their underlying behaviours include aggression (physical and verbal) as well as addiction and self-harm. MDT can be applied to couples and family therapy to provide a systems oriented approach.

The MDT Case Conceptualisation methodology provides the framework to assess and treat these complicated typologies of adolescents and integrates them into a functionally based treatment. The goal is to deactivate the Trigger, leading Fear to Avoids, Compound Core Beliefs mode, and teach emotional regulation through the balancing of beliefs.

Apsche, Ward and Evile (2002) have suggested that the systematic approach of MDT has had positive results in reducing aberrant behaviours and beliefs of adolescents. Apsche and Ward (2002) have also reported positive descriptive results of MDT as compared to cognitive therapy in a descriptive, empirical but not comparison study. The study compared two groups of adolescent sex offenders who received different types of therapy. One group received treatment as usual (TAU), a cognitive behaviour therapy approach, while the other group participated in MDT. These adolescents had prior unsuccessful treatment outcomes. The two groups were followed through their mean 16.36 months lengths of stay in residential treatment. At their twelfth month of treatment, both groups were tested, revealing that the group participating in MDT had lower scores on all measures than the TAU group. Groups were measured on the Child Behaviour Checklist (CBCL), Devereaux Scales of Mental Disorders (DSMD), Juvenile Sex Offender Adolescent Protocol (J-SOAP), and Fear Assessment. Groups were also measured on behaviour points earned, and need for restraints/ seclusions. MDT participants' scores on the CBCL were at least one standard deviation below the TAU group on all scales and scores on the DSMD were at or near one standard deviation below the TAU group, indicating a decrease in symptoms. The MDT group scores on the J-SOAP indicate a significantly lower level of risk to the community than the TAU group. The MDT group resulted in fewer restrictions and precautions for at-risk behaviour than the TAU group. Additionally, results indicate that the MDT group had significantly less aggressive and destructive behaviours than the TAU group.

Apsche and Ward (2002) found that MDT reduced personality disorder/trait beliefs significantly and taught the individual to self-monitor and balance their personality

disorder beliefs. The study also found a reduction of internal distress, resulting from various psychological disorders, as well as a reduction of sex offending risk in the group that participated in MDT. Overall, the study indicates that treating this typology without addressing the underlying compound core beliefs, appears to be related to recidivism.

The following case analysis represents theory integrated into practice concerning a youngster who was in numerous, seven, correctional and treatment facilities previous to this treatment. He had been removed from all facilities for aggression and he attacked staff and youths alike.

This case analysis is a step-by-step case study, with a corresponding theoretical analysis based in MDT. The methodology known as MDT suggests potential for effective treatment of youngsters with similar backgrounds as John. It is hoped that MDT will be studied in rigorous empirically based studies.

Case analysis

Consider a case of a youngster (please see the example of the mode activation from his MDT Case Conceptualisation following this case analysis). John is an adolescent who is reactive and has a conglomerate of personality disorders. He endorsed multiple Borderline Personality Disorder beliefs in various belief assessments. John was severely physically abused and perceives threats in many situations. He feels threatened by authority figures and also perceives danger in many situations, so therefore reacts to prevent re-victimisation.

If John perceives that he could be in a situation where he may be confronted or reprimanded, his anxiety would increase. For example, he can be involved in normal activities with a friend or peer, but if he notices the time getting closer to a group or meeting with 'authority figures' he feels his anxiety increasing. Even if he was not increasingly thinking about the meeting, group, etc., some kind of preconscious processing of the anticipated event is occurring and producing anxiety. The discernment that he will be involved in a situation that he perceives as confrontational has already set in motion the cognitive, affective, behavioural, and physiological processes.

Although John may not be consciously thinking about confrontation, and may be focused on the discussion or activity with a friend, an attempt to elicit his thought at this point, would generate the same information as if he were actively thinking about the anticipated event. He would express anger about the upcoming perceived 'slight' or correction and he would be able to discuss that he has a dichotomous belief in operation, such as 'whenever I am angry my emotions are extreme and out of control.' He would be able to identify the fear that was endorsed related to his anger and that he perceived physical danger from the perceived upcoming situation.

As the time of the perceived confrontation nears, feared group or meeting, he would have a conscious fear or threat of being a victim and was also fearful that he would become verbally and/or physically aggressive to protect himself. The situation appeared threatening (real or perceived) based on his life's experiences. He was fearful of his own actions in this situation and worried that he would later feel humiliated by the outcome of the situation.

At a later time when John is no longer confronted with the dangers of the situation, he is not experiencing the fears of the perceived situation. The distance from the dangerous situation represents the Woody and Rachman (1994) concept of a 'safety signal.' When the parameters of the same situation recur the pattern of fears versus avoids beliefs is repeated.

Reviewing the fear reaction pattern in John, using Beck's (1996) analysis of modes, the activating circumstances are directly related to the anticipated event and the perception of the re-victimisation of the meeting. These circumstances are processed through the orienting component of the 'primal mode relevant to danger;' the imagined risk of being victimised, beaten and letting someone else control him. As this related fear is activated, the various systems of the mode are also activated and energised. During the physiological manifestation of the activation of the mode, John becomes tense, grinds his teeth, has involuntary muscle movements, increasingly intense headaches, tightened facial muscles, his hands and legs shake, move around, anxiety increases, and his fists may tighten.

The actual progression of the mode activates as John nears the time of the group or meeting, i.e., his orienting schemas signal danger ahead. This system is based on the perception of danger of victimisation/ vulnerability and is sufficient to activate all the systems of the mode. The affective system generates rapidly increasing levels of

anxiety; the motivational system signals the impulse and the flight/fight signal, increasing the attack or avoid and the physiological system, which produces the consequent grinding of his teeth, involuntary muscle movements, heart races, etc.

John becomes aware of his distressing feelings at this point and he is often unable to activate his own cognitive controls, or 'voluntary controls' to override this 'primal' reaction to be able to mediate the conflict. Once he is able to mediate the fears and avoidance, he would be able to participate in a supportive meeting and the anxiety would begin to de-escalate.

John's interpretation of his physiological sensations magnifies his fears of the anticipated physical and psychological re-victimisation. Throughout the process of the feedback that he receives from his bodily sensations, like the flush anxious feelings, the powerful fear of loss of control and the sequel of physiological responses develops the fear of yelling and screaming and potential aggression and a disastrous situation. This fear is compounded by the events that lead to another fear, which is the fear of feeling humiliated by the perceived threat of victimisation or vulnerability and loss of control in the presence of other people.

Client summary

Brief Treatment History Prior to Current Placement

This is the first admission to this facility and second youthial placement for this sixteen-year-old boy who sexually sodomised at least one younger male friend of the family and attempted to recruit two younger cousins to perform fellatio upon him. He was treated at a youthial facility from May 1998 to May 1999, but was discharged because of chronic behavioural problems, including verbal and physical aggression and extreme oppositional and defiant behaviour, in spite of numerous attempts to intervene. Since then, John was placed at a youth detention centre until his current placement.

While at his previous placement, John was started on Prozac. He perceives no change in his mood on that medication. The discharge summary from his placement indicates that he was frequently non-compliant with treatment. At the youth detention centre, he was also placed on Wellbutrin SR 150 mg, which he took every morning in combination with the Prozac. There was no bedtime dose of Wellbutrin given, according to John and available records. John reports that he perceives no effect from the Wellbutrin either. He chose to discontinue the medication.

John has a longstanding history of sleep disturbance with mid-state wakening as well as some diurnal mood variation. He reports that he frequently has excessive energy and periodic hyposomnia, but not excessively. Rather, it is difficult for him to assess this because he was frequently awakened while in the youth detention centre. He does, however, report recurrent dreams in which he is killed either by drowning or by being shot. He associates the dreams to early physical trauma by his mother and father.

John's behavioural problems were first noted in early childhood. He has historically been an extremely aggressive child who, from age four or five, was noted to be emotionally disturbed and a serious behavioural problem. Throughout his school career, he has repeatedly been suspended because of his poor anger control. He was in several foster homes and his father, on prior occasions, refused to continue to care for him and his siblings because of the youth's behaviour.

John has no prior history of alcohol or other substance abuse, and does not smoke cigarettes.

Family history

John's mother was a physically abusive woman who ultimately was incarcerated for child abuse. His family was reported to social services as early as when John was three years old. A year later, John reportedly grabbed a teacher's leg and attempted to fondle her genitalia, stating his mother did it to him. At that time, three and a half, investigation determined that John had been exploited by an unknown perpetrator. A year later, after kicking his principal, he told his social worker that he was beaten with an electric cord and baseball bat. He and his sister were reported to be forced by his mother to sit in bleach because she perceived they were 'too dark skinned.' Five years after that, John and his siblings (sister and two brothers) were taken to live with their father when the mother was arrested. Subsequently, John and his sister and brothers were given over to their maternal aunt, where they lived, along with her boyfriend, and her own children, a total of two adults and eight children, in a two bedroom apartment.

In January 1993, a Child Protective Services therapist insisted that John's aunt could not satisfactorily care for John and his father refused to take him back. At this time, he was placed in foster care because of his behavioural and emotional problems.

Subsequently, John went to live with his father and younger sister, Sadie, and his two brothers. In 1996, his father's longstanding girlfriend left the family because she could not tolerate John's behaviour. The family moved because of financial constraints and ultimately John was sent back to live with his aunt.

In November, 1997, John was accused of sexually assaulting three children in his aunt's home, as noted above. He pleaded guilty to one count of first degree sexual assault and continued to deny the others, with the exception of the attempted grooming, as noted above. He was subsequently placed at a local locked youthial programme until his unsuccessful discharge because of his chronic behavioural problems.

There is no known or reported family history of substance abuse, serious psychiatric disturbance, or associated hospitalisations. However, John witnessed considerable physical abuse in his home, including on one occasion seeing his mother cut his father with a knife. It is known that she physically abused him with a two-by-four and extension cords, baseball bats, and belts.

Results from the Fear Assessment suggest that John is an individual who has anxiety and fear that relates to external areas or things outside of himself over which he has little or no control. His mean score of 2.51 in external related fears suggest that the focus of his Post Traumatic Stress Disorder may be his fears of external stimuli activity upon him. This appears to validate his history of perverse and severe physical abuse.

Another score that suggests concern and requires treatment is his score of 2.25 on the Environmental Sub-score of the Fear Assessment. This score suggests that the youth has anxieties and fears of certain environmental stimuli, such as closed rooms, being locked in rooms, etc. This score is also congruent of an individual who has the youth's history of neglect and abuse.

John's initial score on the Beliefs of Aggression was 78 which suggest an individual who engages in aggression frequently to resolve problems. His score on the Beliefs about Victims suggests that he understands the impact of aggression and sexual offending on others. It also suggests that he may have the capacity for empathy for his victims.

The Beliefs of Personality Disorders suggests that John has a Personality Disorder NOS – mixed features of Borderline, Dependent, Avoidant, Antisocial, and Histrionic.

John endorsed numerous beliefs of the Borderline Personality. Many of these beliefs appear to have gone untreated by the previous therapists. Previously, it was suggested that John used his aggression as an intimidation. Examining his beliefs indicates that it may be that his aggression is related to the emotional dysregulation and his dichotomous borderline beliefs.

Compound core beliefs

John endorsed the following compound core beliefs as occurring always:

- Everyone betrays my trust.
- It I trust someone today, they will betray me later.
- Whenever I hope, I will become disappointed.
- When I am angry, my emotions are extreme and out of control.
- When I hurt emotionally, I do whatever it takes to feel better.
- Life at times feels like an endless series of disappointment followed by pain.
- I try to control and not show my feelings of grieving, loss, and sadness, but eventually, it comes out in a rush of emotions.
- In relationships, if the other person is not with me, they are against me.

Diagnosis
Axis I: Posttraumatic stress disorder
           Sexual abuse of a child (victim and
           offender issues)
           Physical abuse of a child (victim issues)
           Mood disorder, NOS
           Obsessive compulsive disorder
Axis II: Personality disorder (NOS) mixed
           features of borderline, antisocial,
           dependent, and avoidant
Axis III: Exercise induced asthma
Axis IV: History reported GAF: 60
           Current GAF: 50
           Admission GAF: 43

Recommendations:
Cognitive Psychotherapy to address his underlying schema related to the borderline beliefs that he endorses (see MDT Case Conceptualisation).

Address the specific aggression that relates to his emotional dysregulation (see MDT Case Conceptualisation).

Continue Cognitive Group therapy, including conclusion of sexual offending specific therapy.

Address independent living skills to prepare youth for community placement.

Mode Deactivation Therapy: MDT Case Conceptualisation, which offers a step-by-step methodology to implement MDT.

Additionally, MDT offers specifically designed assessments, which are the basis of completing the MDT Case Conceptualisation. The MDT Case Conceptualisation then becomes the basis for implementing MDT methodology. The Fear Assessment, Compound Core Belief Questionnaire (CCBQ), and the Typology Survey are all presented in this article. All of these assessments have been tested for validity, reliability, and effectiveness. The results of statistical analysis of these assessments will be presented in future articles by the authors.

The MDT Case Conceptualisation is a schematic representation of Beck's (1996) theory of modes combined with Apsche and Ward Bailey's (2003) interpretation of the applied methodology of Linehan's (1993) DBT, and Kohlenburg and Tsai's (1993) FAP. It is intended to provide the blueprint for treatment for the youngster. The MDT Case Conceptualisation provides a functional treatment methodology that integrates into the treatment plan.

The MDT Case Conceptualisation is typology driven and individualises the treatment based on empirically based assessment. The MDT Case Conceptualisation also provides a methodology to address the reactive adolescent emotional dysregulation. The typology of adolescents often reacts aggressively and destructively through emotions to threats or perceived threats. The case provides the structure of the Conglomerate of Beliefs and Behaviours (COBB) to address the dysregulation by balancing the beliefs.

The Conglomerate of Beliefs and Behaviours (COBB) identify behaviours that correlate with beliefs and is the structure to work with the youngster. This provides a method to relate the emotional dysregulation to the beliefs. The goal is to teach the youngster to balance beliefs by recognising that they activate the emotional and behavioural dysregulation.

The MDT Case Conceptualisation also provides a methodology to address the reactive adolescent emotional dysregulation. The emotional dysregulation refers to the Linehan (1993) model of the Borderline Personality Disorder (BPD) emotional dysregulation, integrated with the Reactive Conduct Disorder (Dodge et al., 1997).

Once the information is gathered and the case is formulated, the client and the therapist develop collaboratively the Conglomerate of Beliefs and Behaviours (COBB). The completion of the COBB follows the review of the five column Triggers, (2), Fear, Avoids, Compound Core Beliefs (TFAB) and moves to this form, see Figure 6.

The Conglomerate of Beliefs and Behaviours (COBB) is the crux of treatment for the client. Once he collaboratively validates the Triggers, Fear, Avoids, Compound Core Beliefs (TFAB) and begins this form, he helps validate his behaviour responses that are congruent with his compound core beliefs.

This form, once completed, remains with him throughout treatment and is the basis for all of his work in the MDT Workbook. The client recognises that these beliefs could be activated throughout his lifetime and he continually works to deactivate his fears, avoids, and beliefs.

The MDT Case Conceptualisation is a systematic, carefully designed, sequential methodology intended to provide functionally based treatment, to complex emotional, thought and behaviour disorders. First, complete all assessments: Typology Survey, Fear Assessment, and Compound Core Belief Questionnaire (CCBQ).

Complete all assessments:
a. Typology Survey (see Appendix A):

The Typology Survey gathers information about the youth's history including: family, substance abuse, medical, educational, emotional, physiological, interpersonal relationships/social, offences, physical abuse, sexual abuse, emotional abuse, neglect, and expectations of treatment. Consult all records and parents/guardian for validation of specific responses before meeting with the youth. Explain the nature of the assessment and its purpose. Enlist the youth's co-operation by letting him know that he can help him more effectively by providing this information, as he is an expert on himself.

Maintain an open conversation while administering this assessment to encourage the youth to speak more freely. Once you begin the assessment, write down all responses in the space provided. Be sure to complete all questions, even if they seem irrelevant. This information is essential for completing your MDT Case Conceptualisation as well as providing effective therapy.

b. Fear Assessment (see Appendix B):

The Fear Assessment is a 60-question assessment exploring fears of the youth, providing insight into the youth's underlying traumas. The Fear Assessment is important and will be necessary to complete the Trigger, Fear, Avoids, and Compound Core Belief – Correlation (TFAB) component of the MDT Case Conceptualisation. It should be completed after the Typology Survey.

c. CCBQ (Compound Core Beliefs Questionnaire)(see Appendices C1 and C2):

The CCBQ (Compound Core Beliefs Questionnaire) is a 209-question assessment used to gather a succinct understanding of a youth's beliefs or thought processes. There is also a short version (96 questions) of the CCBQ, which may be more appropriate for younger and/or lower functioning youth. This worksheet offers the therapist to gather valuable information concerning beliefs endorsed by the youth. Beliefs endorsed on this assessment are necessary to complete the Triggers, Fear, Avoids, and Compound Core Belief – Correlation (TFAB) component of the MDT Case Conceptualisation.

Complete the case:
Step I: Relevant Childhood Data (Abuse History):

This section includes physical/sexual, emotional abuse, development, behavioural, aggression, suicidal, parasuicidal, substance abuse, and medication history. This information should be readily available with a completed Typology Survey. It is important to complete this review systematically to lay the foundation for your MDT Case Conceptualisation. Review the data from this case, then ask yourself; 'What do I need to know about this youngster, and how does the following information help to begin to understand this youngster?' Ask yourself, 'What do I begin to look for behaviourally?' Remember, use Socratic questioning, and ask if this is so, then what? Example:

Step II: Problem Behaviour Data:

Include all relevant information specific to the youth's problem behaviours. This should be attained from the typology survey and by working in the Mode Deactivation Therapy (MDT) Workbook.

Figure 17.2: Relevant childhood data (abuse history)

Relevant Childhood Data (Abuse History)

Date of Birth: 7/8/82

Date of Admission: 1/13/00

Physical/Emotional Abuse: Reports of physical abuse by mother. John and siblings were taken out of her custody by DYFS in 1992. John was beaten with extension cords, wire hangers, and baseball bats. Mother was arrested.

Sexual Abuse: John denies being sexually abused though there are reports that state that John was touched inappropriately by his mother at the age of 5 or 6 years old.

Developmental History (include age/date of birth, behavioural, environmental, social, and biological): John has a history of oppositional and defiant behaviour, particularly at school. At age 4, John grabbed his teacher's breast and put his fingers on her clothes, towards her vagina. At age 5, John kicked his principal. At a prior RTC, John was verbally abusive and oppositional towards staff. John has a history of aggression, both verbally and physically. John has some issues regarding the complexion of his skin being too dark.

Substance Abuse History (include drug of choice, frequency of use, familial substance abuse history, etc.): None noted

Current Medication: Zoloft 75 mg, Clarks AD 40 mg

This section also includes risk assessment instrument findings, as well as significant results from any objective measure of aberrant interests. Examine the results and include those results in this section. Example:

Step III: Diagnoses:
This is the diagnosis given by a physician or licensed clinical psychologist. It can be attained from the most recent monthly psychiatric progress note. Take notice of the concordance of Axis II diagnoses to beliefs endorsed in the CCBQ. There should be agreement between the results of the CCBQ and the diagnoses. Example:

Step IV: Triggers, Fears, Avoids, Compound Core Beliefs Correlation (TFAB):

Fears: The key to the youngster is the proper administering of the Fear Assessment. Investigate the level of trauma. Begin by identifying the fears endorsed as occurring always and/or almost always. Prioritise the fears in order of the hierarchy of treatment.

Hierarchies of Target Behaviours within Target Classes in Outpatient Individual Therapy. (Linehan, M.M. (1993). *Treating borderline personality disorder: The dialectical approach.* New York, NY: Guilford Press.)

Suicidal behaviours:
  Suicide crisis behaviours
  Parasuicidal acts

Figure 17.4: Diagnoses

Diagnoses

Axis I: 1. Posttraumatic stress disorder, chronic
2. Sexual abuse of child (victim and offender issues)
3. Physical abuse of child (victim issues)
4. Mood sisorder, NOS
5. Obsessive-compulsive disorder

Axis II: Borderline personality disorder

Axis III: None

Axis IV: Psychosocial stressors related to physical abuse, legal system involvement

Axis V: Current GAF: 43
Highest GAF past year: 60

Figure 17.3: Problem behaviour data

Problem Behaviour Data

At age 15, John had two younger male cousins – ages 3 and 7 perform oral sex on John on one occasion. One younger male family friend, age 11, 'grinds' on him on one occasion.

Intrusive suicidal urges, images, and communications

Suicidal ideation, expectations, emotional responses

Therapy-interfering behaviours:

Patient or therapist interfering behaviours likely to destroy therapy

Immediately interfering behaviours of patient or therapist

Patient or therapist interfering behaviours functionally related to suicidal behaviours

Quality-of-life interfering behaviours:

Behaviours causing immediate crises

Easy-to-change (over difficult-to-change) behaviours

Behaviours functionally related to higher-order targets and to patient's life goals

Increasing behavioural skills:

Skills currently being taught in skills training

Skills functionally related to higher-order targets

Skills not learned yet

Personal Reactive-External Fears: Personal Reactive External is a subscale of the Fear Assessment. This category represents the predominant category of fears that is the basis of treatment. Personal Reactive External is a category of fears that is internally reactive to external events. These fears are based on negative experiences that simulate the cognitive conscious and subconscious. For example, to not trust anyone there has to be a person or external stimuli to the internal fear. Personal Reactive-External Fears should be identified first in the treatment hierarchy.

The Personal Reactive-External Fears are as follows on Fear Assessment-Revised: 1, 2, 3, 4, 12, 21, 23, 24, 27, 28, 30.

The other categories of subscales of the Fear Assessment, at times, 'may' be considered for the TFAB. Though it is most likely that the treatment hierarchy of fears will be derived from the Personal Reactive External category, since it is likely that these fears will create life threatening or treatment interfering behaviours.

Avoids: You might also hypothesise that this youngster is difficult to manage; he most likely has a well-learned set of avoidance behaviours to compensate for his underlying fears.

The next step is to identify what the youth will avoid for each identified fear.

Avoids are the functional alternatives to the fears. Vulnerability is at the core of what the

---

Figure 17.5: Fear, avoids paradigm

Fear ◄──────►	Avoids
Alone in dark rooms	Bedroom
Dusk to dark	Bedtime
Sleep in room at night	Aberrant behaviours to get out of room, silly provoking other youths
Seclusion	Any behaviour to get out of seclusion, probably restrained

---

person avoids. For example, if you fear elevators you avoid elevators. And, if you fear trusting people, you avoid disclosing relationships and/or intimacy.

Think in terms of non-functional alternatives, or a sort of opposites. If your youth is afraid of being alone in dark rooms and dusk to dark, what do you think he may avoid? Dark rooms, dusk, bedtime, seclusion rooms; dusk to dark, bedtime, evening and night shift.

Ask yourself what might your youth's life look like in the youthial milieu and ask yourself, when would expect your youth to have 'behavioural' problems? Why?

This information should flow from the Fear Assessment. The fears produce avoidance. It is important to understand the functional relationship between fears and avoidance. This should be your step-wise programme to implement exposure training, as well as the basis for your MDT Case Conceptualisation.

Understanding the fear and avoidance relationship, will explain many of the problem behaviours in which the youngster engages. The youngster avoids these fears by escaping or avoiding.

Chemical Dependency and Compound Core Beliefs: Beck, Wright, Newman and Liese (1993) suggest that a major thrust of cognitive therapy of chemical dependency or abuse is to help the individual in two ways. One, reduce the intensity and frequency of the urges by understanding the underlying beliefs, and two, teach the individual, specific techniques for controlling and managing their urges.

The MDT Case Conceptualisation methodology examines substance abuse from the framework of how the underlying disorder is involved in the use of substances. It is important that there is an understanding that this discussion is focusing only on the typology of the adolescent that is represented in these methodologies.

The compound core beliefs are the activation to the pathways to a variety of drug usage. Beliefs activate behaviours, engaged to help the youth avoid related fears. Behaviours may be sleeping, arguing, etc., and may include the need or desire for drugs or alcohol, which may lead to chemical dependency or abuse. For example, beliefs such as 'whenever I hurt, I do whatever I need to do to feel better' may activate a youth to use drugs or alcohol to reduce the intensity of hurting.

Pain is an emotional trigger that activates the dysregulation of emotions, which in turn activates the need to relieve or regulate their painful and hurtful emotions. Often drugs or alcohol are used to help relieve pain and/or emotional dysregulation. Often, over doing is a method of reducing or regulating pain, therefore, drug usage is a methodology of regulating as well.

Beliefs endorsed as always or almost always from the CCBQ are used. The personality disorder beliefs are the pathways for numerous problem and aberrant behaviours, as well as emotional dys-regulation.

Identify compound core beliefs that correspond to the already identified fears and avoidance. These beliefs are identified through the CCBQ.

The identified beliefs are integrated with the fear assessment and the avoids. Remember, the avoids are the functional alternatives to the fears. If you fear trusting people, you avoid disclosing relationships and intimacy. A compound core belief that is congruent with the fear and avoids is: 'if I trust someone today, they will betray me later.'

Triggers: Triggers are anything that activates the fear, avoidance, compound core belief. They can be people, places, objects, noises, smells, sights, experiences, etc. Anything the youth may be aware of that would trigger or activate the fear, avoidance, compound core beliefs would be identified as Trigger 1 (conscious trigger).

Anything the youth is not aware of, but can be identified through observable behaviours to trigger or activate the fear, avoidance, compound core beliefs are assigned as Trigger 2 (unconscious trigger). Unconscious triggers are the many times just what it is that the youth avoids. The same trigger may be both conscious (Trigger 1) and unconscious (Trigger 2).

When you have completed this section you should understand how the youngster behaved, and be prepared to explain it to him, when he reaches the appropriate section in his MDT Workbook.

Practice this section in the MDT Workbook. This should produce a cognitive pathway to the youngster's problem behaviour(s). Example:

Step V: Conglomerate of Beliefs and Behaviours (COBB)

The conglomerate of beliefs and behaviours incorporates compound core beliefs and the corresponding behaviours. It develops as a defence to underlying trauma. It is the pathway to the complex series of moods, schemes, and behaviours. Beliefs endorsed as always or almost always from the CCBQ are used. The personality disorder beliefs are the pathways for numerous problem and aberrant behaviours, as well as emotional dysregulation.

Remember, complete the compound core belief, the cluster beliefs, and dependent personality disorders. Synthesise these four compound core beliefs on the Conglomerate of Beliefs and Behaviours form and you have your treatment interfering behaviours, as well as possibly a separate discreet personality disorder that a youngster may develop, from physical, sexual, emotional and environmental abuse. Understand that these cluster of beliefs present the most challenging part of treatment interfering behaviours. These compound core beliefs are the underlying protection to the fears, anxieties and trauma. Be complete, and do not rush through developing a treatment hypothesis. Example:

Step VI: Situational Analysis

This section requires an analysis of actual situations in which the youngster has been involved. Completing the situational analysis provides an opportunity to test the hypotheses you formulated in the Triggers, Fears, Avoids, Compound Core Belief – Correlation section.

Be sure to complete all three situations! Example:

Step VII: Mode Activation/Mode De-Activation: Mode Activation

Modes are important to the typology we serve in that they are particularly sensitive to danger and fear, serving to charge the modes. The understanding of conscious and unconscious fears being charged and activating the mode system explains the level of emotional

Figure 17.6: TFAB: Triggers, Fears, Avoids, Beliefs

Trigger 1 Conscious processing	Trigger 2 Unconscious processing	Fears	Avoids	Compound core beliefs
Unfamiliar situations	Situations that require trying, failing	Failing	Trying new behaviours	I am inadequate; I will do whatever I must to hide it
Trust versus betrayal	Situations of trust or counting on someone	Hurting someone physically	Relationships-trust	If I trust someone today, they will betray me later
Disrespect	Vulnerability	My anger	Confrontation Being a victim	Whenever I hurt emotionally, I do whatever it takes to feel better When I am angry, my emotions are extreme and out of control
Pressure situations (confrontation, consequences, anything that triggers victim stuff)	Trust	No one will believe me	Trusting others	Everyone betrays my trust In relationships, if the other person is not with me, then they are against me
Showing weaknesses	Emotions (hurt, betrayal)	Something is wrong with me	Showing emotions (especially hurt and anger)	I try to control my feelings and not show my grieving, loss, sadness; but it eventually comes out in a rush of emotions
Situations that require showing feelings to others (emotional intimacy)	Close feelings	My feelings	Close relationships	Everyone betrays my trust Whenever I hope, I will become disappointed

Figure 17.7: COBB: Conglomerate of Beliefs and Behaviours

Compound Core Belief	Corresponding Behaviours
Borderline Personality Disorder	
Everyone betrays my trust . . . always.	Doesn't trust people or engage in relationships.
If I trust someone today, they will betray me later . . . always.	Reserved, distanced, and blunted in relationships.
Whenever I hope, I will become disappointed . . . always.	Gives up and becomes negative at any 'bump' or disappointment.
When I am angry, my emotions are extreme and out of control . . . always,	Dysregulates, displays anger quickly.
When I hurt emotionally, I do whatever it takes to feel better . . . always.	Will clown or 'mess around,' or disengage.
Life at times feels like an endless series of disappointments followed by pain . . . always.	Feels and acts depressed.
I try to control my feelings and not show my grieving, loss, sadness, but eventually it comes out in a rush of emotions . . . always.	After disturbing family phone calls, becomes angry and aggressive.
In relationships, if the other person is not with me, then they are against me . . . always.	Vacillates through all or nothing thinking.
Dependent Personality Disorder	
If I am not loved, I am unhappy . . . always.	Emotion vacillates, between extremes of idealisation and devaluation..
I am helpless and cannot make it on my own . . . always	Sadness, anger.
Avoidant Personality Disorder	
I am inadequate; I will do whatever I must to hide it . . . always.	Distances self, anger and aggression.
I would rather do anything to avoid failing because I cannot succeed . . . always.	Anger, outbursts, emotional dysregulation (but accepts responsibility for his sexual offending behaviours).
Antisocial Personality Disorder	
Unless you have videotape of me, you cannot prove I did it . . . .always.	Denial of small areas of responsibilities.
If he/she can't take care of himself, they get what they deserve . . . always.	High opinion of self.
Histrionic Personality Disorder	
I am so exciting; others want to be around me . . . always.	Anger, silliness.
When I am bored, I need to become the centre of attention . . . always.	Silly in groups and other tense situations.
If I act silly and entertain people, they won't notice my weakness . . . always.	

Figure 17.8: Situations

Situation 1		Situation 2		Situation 3
Very disruptive in group, clowning affecting topics and issues.		Provoked by peer.		Confrontation with staff Told to take hat off-'did' Staff asked if he would speak to mother the way he speaks to staff.
	Fear		**Fear**	
Automatic Thought I don't want to deal with this stuff...now.		**Automatic Thought** What is his problem? He thinks he is tough.		**Automatic Thought** What did you say about my mom? Fuck you!
Cognitive Distortion Minimising	**Avoids**	**Cognitive Distortion** Jump to conclusions	**Avoids**	**Cognitive Distortion** All or nothing thinking
Meaning of Automatic Thought When I hurt emotionally I will do whatever it takes to feel better.	**CC Belief**	**Meaning of Automatic Thought** When I am angry, my emotions are extreme and out of control. If he can't take care of himself he got what he deserves.	**CC Belief**	**Meaning of Automatic Thought** If you are not with me, you are against me.
Physiological Grind teeth, involuntary movements, heart races, face tightens, legs shake, hands shake, stop listening, get antsy, fists tighten, only see darkness		**Physiological** Grind teeth, involuntary movements, heart races, face tightens, legs shake, hands shake, stop listening, get antsy, fists tighten, only see darkness		**Physiological** Grind teeth, involuntary movements, heart races, face tightens, legs shake, hands shake, stop listening, get antsy, fists tighten, only see darkness
Emotion Hurt, Sad, Numb		**Emotion** Hurt, fear, anger		**Emotion** Hurt, anger
Behaviour(s) Laughing and making sarcastic comments during group		**Behaviour(s)** Youth punches peer		**Behaviour(s)** Grabbed staff by shirt-but let go.

dysregulation and impulse control of the typology of youngsters that we treat.

To address the schema processing based on thoughts and beliefs without understanding the modes is insufficient and does not explain the specific adolescent typology referred to in mode deactivation therapy methodology.

The mode system is compounded by the charge of analogous schema once danger activates the orienting schemas. Identify the various systems of the personality at the time of the trigger, or orienting schema.

Mode De-Activation: There are four areas where a mode can be deactivated prior to an aggressive act or other forms of emotional dysregulation: orienting schema, perception or interpretation of the fear to danger activation, physiological system, and avoids. The mode deactivation system takes into account the reactive type of dysregulation, which includes parasuicidal acts, as well as aggression.

Step VIII: Functionally Based Treatment Form

The Functionally Based Treatment Development Form is the culmination of all previous components of the MDT Case Conceptualistion. This form is intended to give direction to treatment based on what has been learned about the youth through doing the case. The basis of this form is the development of a new, healthier belief system. These beliefs are healthy alternatives to the compound core beliefs identified in the Triggers, Fear, Avoid, Compound core belief Correlation (TFAB).

This is the blueprint to treatment. It takes time and thought. When you finish you should have measurable goals for your treatment plan. You also should be able to set up your programme. A rule of thumb is to set up trial groups of 10, which is congruent with a percentage score. An example of this is the scale of trust. A score of 1 indicates no trust, a score of 10 indicates total trust. You can use the scale of trust to objectively measure the level of trust your youth has for you (the therapist) and anyone else significant in his life.

The Functionally Based Treatment Form is designed to identify desired behaviours and prescribe the implementation of these new behaviours through validating, clarifying, and redirecting. It is important to continuously validate-clarify-redirect during individual therapy. Validate the grain of truth in the youth's responses. Clarify content of his responses. Redirect his responses.

Application of Validate, Clarify, and Redirect (VCR). MDT integrates with Linehan's (1993) basic premises for DBT. MDT, like DBT, uses behaviour goals, problem solving goals, reflection and radical acceptance of the client. The mode-deactivation theory (Beck, 1996) clearly delineates the truth in the client's perceptions based in their cognitive unconscious and conscious information processing that developed their perception or world view.

An integral part of MDT is the concept of validation, clarification, and redirection (VCR). Validation was defined by Linehan (1993), as the therapist's ability to uncover the validity within the client's beliefs. The grain of truth reflects the client's perception of reality. The truth in this reality needs to be validated to clarify the content of his responses; and also clarify the beliefs that are activated. It is important to understand and agree in the 'grain of truth' in the clarification.

Redirect responses to others, to other views or possibilities on his or her continuum of truths. There are numerous continuums implemented, with scales from 1 to 10 to evaluate areas such as truth, trust, fear, and beliefs. These continuums are essential to MDT in that they give both the client and the therapist an empirical measure of the client's measured perception of truth.

Teaching a client who often engages in dichotomous thinking that their perception can fall within the range of a continuum, rather than only a 1 or a 10 (all or nothing), is extremely validating and it is the basis for a positive redirection to other possibilities for the client.

Results

John reduced his aggressive outburst from an average of one per day to two per month by the sixth month of treatment. He also stopped overt physical aggression and would verbalise his anger and withdraw behaviourally from the situation. John attributed this to understanding his preconscious trigger of perceiving that he was vulnerable. This perceived vulnerability set off the entire mode system. He was able to identify situations that produced the vulnerability and to examine his cue beliefs that were part of the activation process. He began verbalising when he felt or thought he was uncomfortable. He also knew his physiological responses to the danger signal, his vulnerability and the fact they disabled John to work on balancing his belief exercises.

Figure 17.9: Mode activation

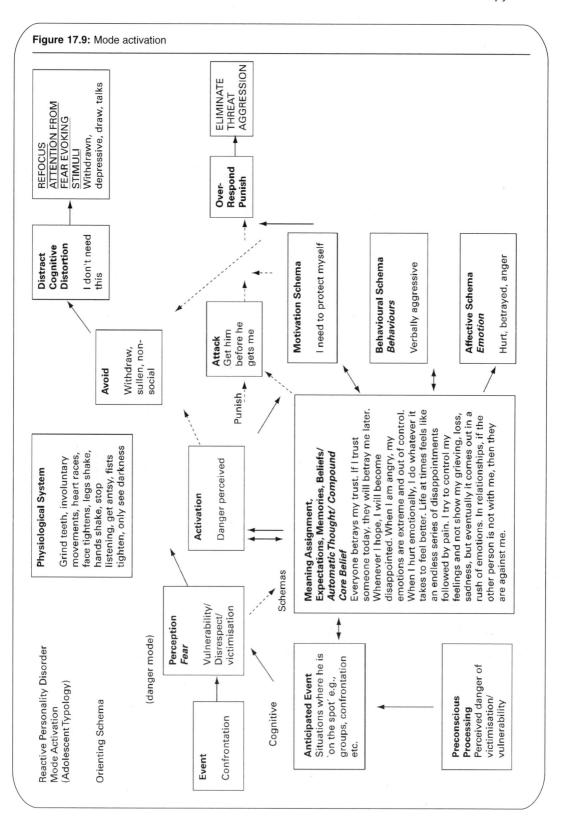

Figure 17.10: Mode de-activation

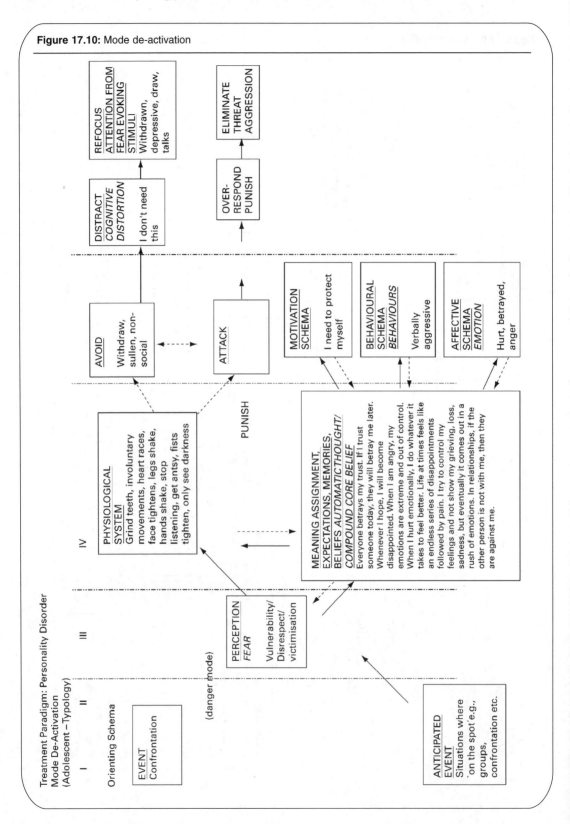

Figure 17.11: Functionally based treatment development form

Functionally Based Treatment Development Form

Identify new belief system	Identify healthy alternative thoughts	Functional alternative compensatory strategy	Functional reinforcing behaviour(s)	Specific functional treatment individual therapy to milieu	Validate/Clarify/ Redirect (VCR) Validate the grain of truth in his responses/ clarify content of his responses/ Redirect his responses
I can trust some people some times.	If others disagree, they may not be against me.	I will take small steps and measure others … trust level.	Work on scales of trust with therapist to develop alliance.	Try to trust one staff, Ms. Margaret.	It's okay to not trust some people at times, identify one person he does trust some of the time and use scale of trust to measure trust daily.
I am adequate. I can balance myself.	I can take a risk to feel.	I accept others' faults; they accept mine.	Work on balance of belief scales.	Pick one issue and take a risk one step at a time, in group.	It's okay to make mistakes, help him identify areas of adequacy and use belief scales to balance.
When I hurt (emotional) I can balance myself.	I can balance my pain.	Practice rational thought and balance.	Identify my balance thoughts.	Identify issues that cause pain and practice balance.	It's okay to feel overwhelmed by emotions, identify thoughts/ beliefs to balance emotions.
My anger can be balanced.	I can deactivate my anger.	Identify physiological triggers, rank – identify cognitions and anticipated events.	Practice through imagined exposure to all physiological and cognitive triggers.	Practice mode activation with staff in vivo. Identify when physiological triggers initiate. Identify continuum of fear activation. Identify when beliefs go out of balance.	It's okay to feel angry, identify physiological system and beliefs to slow down, prevent, or reduce escalation. Use belief scales to balance beliefs.

John was originally perceived as proactive, which would have suggested that he was aggressive due to a perceived positive outcome from the aggression. Careful analysis of his MDT Case Conceptualisation revealed that John is actually reactive, indicating an entirely different purpose for his aggression, and a need for a different focus in treatment.

Mode De-Activation

There are four areas where a mode can be deactivated prior to an aggressive act or other forms of emotional dysregulation. The mode deactivation system takes into account the reactive type of dysregulation that includes parasuicidal acts, as well as aggression.

Orienting Schema – The orienting schemas consists of the anticipation of an event. The orienting schemas in the typology of a youngster that we treat usually involves a danger or threat.

Adolescents who have been abused or deprived have developed reactions to direction or instructions that may activate the orienting schemas because of the threat or perceived threats. For example, if an authority figure gives a directive in a firm and singular fashion it may activate the orienting schemas of danger. This danger activation or change will activate the modes.

The perception is the interpretation of the fear to danger, and activation into an anxiety reaction. The perception activates the fear, anxiety that reacts to the danger activation from the orienting schema. The perception is affected by the fear and its relationship with the activated personality disorder belief. Thus a direction may activate the oriented schema and activate the fear, belief paradigm.

The validation, clarification, redirection strategy (VCR) is particularly effective at this point. Validate the grain of truth in the youth's responses. Clarify content of his responses, and then redirect his responses. It is important to validate the perception of fear or danger, as the perception of danger is as significant to the mode activation system as a real threat. Refer to VCR section of the Functionally Based Treatment Form for further explanation of the strategy.

A. The physiological system is a system that is generally involved when a fear related threat has been activated. These systems accompany states of fear and anxiety. The physiological system charges the individual for action.

B. The meaning, expectations and beliefs can be addressed by the validation, clarification and redirection strategy (VCR). The meanings and expectations are directed by the beliefs. The beliefs activate simultaneously in an alga-rhythmic fashion following the activation of the orienting schema.

The beliefs should be balanced by using the conglomerate of beliefs form and implementing the VCR methodology to balance the beliefs. The motivation, behavioural and affective schemas are directly related to the underlying fear, avoidance, compound core beliefs.

As Beck (1996) states, the motivational and behavioural systems provide the mechanism for automatic motivation of the organism for action or inaction. These systems actually incorporate the attack, avoid mode. The construct of motivation includes biological drives such as appetite and sexuality and the hunger to attack or avoid. These systems are triggers, automatically and rapidly following the change of the orienting schema.

Avoids is the last chance to deactivate the aggressive, self-destructive part of this mode. The avoids or attack modes are activated by the beliefs and physiological systems.

To deactivate the attack mode it is necessary to teach the youngster to identify the physiological system firing, by rank order. This is simply the order in which the various physiological system fires (i.e., clutches fist, clinches teeth, etc.). Once the physiological system is identified, the therapist needs to help the youngster identify the first and second physiological reaction and thus teach avoidance to the youngster.

It is imperative that the physiological be related to the compound core beliefs that are activated as they activate the physiological system.

Summary

The theoretical case analysis presented provides the framework for future investigations for alternative treatment methodologies for reactive adolescents with personality disorders or traits. MDT can be applied to treat existing problem behaviours as well as preventing future problem behaviours by addressing the underlying compound core beliefs, which drive behaviour. MDT offers new methodology specifically designed for difficult adolescents, a treatment need indicated by Weissberg et al. (2003). MDT has been shown to be effective as compared to manualised CBT in a descriptive study (Apsche and Ward, 2002). The authors are planning a randomised study, testing MDT in empirically based work.

References

Alford, B.A. and Beck, A.T. (1997) *The Integrative Power of Cognitive Therapy*. New York, NY: Guilford Press.

Apsche, J.A. (1999) *Thought Change Workbook*. Portsmouth, VA: Alternative Behavioural Services.

Apsche, J.A. and Ward, S.R. (2002) Mode Deactivation Therapy and Cognitive Behaviour Therapy: A Description of Treatment Results for Adolescents With Personality Beliefs, Sexual offending and Aggressive Behaviours. *The Behaviour Analyst Today*, 3 (4), 460–70.

Apsche, J.A., Ward, S.R. and Evile, M.M. (2002) Mode Deactivation: A Functionally Based Treatment, Theoretical Constructs. *The Behaviour Analyst Today*, 3 (4), 455–9.

Apsche, J.A. and Ward Bailey, S.R. (2003) *Mode Deactivation Therapy (MDT): Case Conceptualisation*, Unpublished.

Apsche, J.A. and Ward Bailey, S.R. (2003) Mode Deactivation Therapy (MDT): A Theoretical Case Analysis (Part I), *The Behaviour Analyst Today*, in Press.

Beck, A.T. (1996) Beyond Belief: A Theory of Modes, Personality, and Psychopathology, in Salkovaskis, P.M. (Ed.) *Frontiers of Cognitive Therapy*. New York, NY: Guilford Press. 1–25.

Beck, A.T., Freeman, A. and Associates (1990) *Cognitive Therapy of Personality Disorders*. New York: Guilford Press.

Beck, A.T., Wright, F.D., Newman, C.F. and Liese, B.S. (1993) *Cognitive Therapy of Substance Abuse*. New York: Guilford Press.

Beck, J.S. (1995) *Cognitive Therapy: Basics and Beyond*. New York, NY: Guilford Press.

Dodge, K.A., Lochman, J.E., Harnish, J.D., Bates, J.E. and Petti, G.S. (1997) Reactive and Proactive Aggression in School Children and Psychiatrically Impaired Chronically Assaultive Youth. *Journal of Abnormal Psychology*, 106 (1), 37–51.

Johnson, J.G., Cohen, P., Brown, J., Smailes, E.M. and Bernstein, D.P. (1999) Childhood Maltreatment Increases The Risk for Personality Disorders During Early Adulthood. *Archives of General Psychiatry*, 56, 600–8.

Koenigsberg, H.W., Harvey, P.D., Mitropoulou, V., Antonia, N.S., Goodman, M., Silverman, J., Serby, M., Schopick, F. and Siever, L. (2001) Are The Interpersonal and Identity Disturbances in The Borderline Personality Disorder Criteria Linked To The Traits of Affective Instability and Impulsivity? *Journal of Personality*, 15 (4), 358–70.

Kohlenberg, R.J. and Tsai, M. (1993) Functional Analytic Psychotherapy: A Behavioural Approach To Intensive Treatment, in O'Donohue, W. and Krasner, L. (Eds.) *Theories of Behaviour Therapy: Exploring Behaviour Change*. Washington, DC: American Psychological Association. 638–40.

Linehan, M.M. (1993) *Treating Borderline Personality Disorder: The Dialectical Approach*. New York: Guilford Press.

Nezu, A.M., Nezu, C.M., Friedman, S.H. and Haynes, S.N. (1998) Case Formulation in Behaviour Therapy: Problem-Solving and Functional Analytic Strategies, in Eells, T.D. (Ed.) *Handbook of Psychotherapy Case Formulation*. New York, NY: The Guilford Press. 368–401.

Weissberg, R.P., Kumpfer, K.L. and Seligman, M.E.P. (2003) Prevention That Works for Children and Youth: an Introduction. *American Psychologist, Journal of The American Psychological Association*, 58 (617), 425–32.

Woody, S. and Rachman, S. (1994) Generalised Anxiety Disorder (GAD) as an Unsuccessful Search for Safety. *Clinical Psychology Review*, 14, 743–53.

Young, J.E., Klosko, J.S. and Weishaar, M.E. (2003) *Schema Therapy: A Practitioner's Guide*. New York, NY: Guilford Press.

Appendix A: Typology Survey – © 2003 by Serene R. Ward Bailey, M.A. and Jack A. Apsche, Ed.D. ABPP

To be completed by therapist; include parent/guardian interview and chart review

Clinician: Date:

I.	Identifying Information:	Clinical Record Number:
A.	Youth Name:	
B.	Date of Birth/Age:	
C.	Ethnicity (Black, White, Asian, Native American, Latino, combination, etc.):	
D.	Date of Admission:	
E.		
F.		

	Youth Interview:	Parent/ Guardian:	Chart/Record Review:
II. Family Information:			
1. Briefly describe each member of the youth's family (please indicate who resides with the youth). Include any children with their ages and gender.			
2. Indicate all the places that the youth has lived in his life.			
3. Where does the youth plan to live after leaving The Pines?			
4. Describe the relationship of the youth's parents. (include marital status)			
5. Describe relationship between youth and mother/guardian.			
6. Describe relationship between youth and father/guardian.			
7. Describe what the youth/parent/guardian would like to see change about their relationship.			

8. Describe relationship between youth and siblings.			
9. What is the best thing and worst thing mother/guardian has ever done for/to the youth?	Best: Worst:	Best: Worst:	Best: Worst:
10. What is the best thing and worst thing father/guardian has ever done for/to the youth?	Best: Worst:	Best: Worst:	Best: Worst:
11. Is there anyone in youth's family he does not like to be with? Who and Why?			
12. Indicate whom the youth talks to when he feels worried, sad, or scared.			
13. Any other relevant information about family?			

	Youth Interview:	Parent/ Guardian:	Chart/Record Review:
III. Substance Abuse History:			
1. What drugs/alcohol have you used?			
2. If you have used, how often, and for how long?			
3. Do you believe your use of drugs/alcohol has affected your ability to function?			
4. Referral to chemical dependency counsellor?			

	Youth Interview:	Parent/ Guardian:	Chart/Record Review:
IV. Medical:			
1. Has the youth been to the hospital? If so, explain.			
2. Is the youth taking any medication? If so, for what reason?			
3. Does the youth have a history of childhood head trauma, hits to the head, or central nervous system?			

4.	Is there history of intrauterine drug or alcohol usage? Did mother use any substances prior to the birth of the child?			

	Youth Interview:	Parent/ Guardian:	Chart/Record Review:
V. Educational:			
1. What grade is the youth in? Special education?			
2. How is the youth doing in school?			
3. What are the youth's academic goals? (GED, diploma, college, technical school, etc.)			
4. Has the youth held a job? If so, when and where?			
5. Describe any previous training or preparation for vocational training and/or independent living.			

	Youth Interview:	Parent/ Guardian:	Chart/Record Review:
VI. Emotional:			
1. What is your usual mood like? (If negative, ask: When was it last good)			
2. What do you do when you are sad?			
3. Suicidal ideation. Have you ever thought of hurting yourself? How? If yes, when was the last time you felt this way? Please explain circumstances.			
4. Have you ever tried to hurt yourself in any way? (When, How, Where, What Happened)			
5. Are there any unpleasant memories that keep coming back to you? What are they?			
6. How have you been sleeping? Do you experience any of the following: Trouble falling asleep; Trouble waking in the morning; Waking in the middle of the night; Tiredness during the day; Nightmares.			

7.	Has your interest in food increased or decreased? Have you gained or lost weight recently?			
8.	Is there a history of bedwetting? Describe.			
9.	Does the youth have a history of fire setting? Describe.			
10.	Have you ever run away from home or other residence? If yes, please explain?			
11.	Describe the youth's aberrant behaviours.			
12.	Has the youth ever been in counselling before? If so, describe.			
13.	Has the youth ever been hospitalised? If so, for what and when?			
14.	Has the youth ever been in another treatment programme? If so, for what and when?			
15.	What does the youth usually do when he gets really upset or angry?			
16.	Has the youth ever intentionally harmed animals?			
17.	Has the youth ever destroyed things or hit anyone in anger? If so, tell me about it.			
18.	Homicidal ideation. Has the youth ever been so mad that he wanted to really hurt or kill someone else? If so, when, how, where, why.			

VII Physiological:

1.	Describe an incident where the youth was angry or upset.			
2.	Ask the youth for descriptions of specific physiological responses. Describe what 'my face is red,' 'my blood boils,' clinched fists, teeth and jaws feel like and what do these feelings mean? Take your time and ask about breathing; all responses.	Example: Gritting teeth Clenching fists Sweating Face and arms flush Redness of face Veins bulge	Youth's physiological responses:	Ranked physiological responses:

Rank in order the physiological responses and how the youth responds to them. Rank from first physiological response to final physiological response. (Remember, muscle tightened, stomach tightened, etc.)	Jittery Shaking Crying Frowning Heart rate increases Shortness of breath Loss or change in vocal pitch Burning in chest Stomach/ intestinal pains Cramping Exhaustion/ fatigue Nervous twitching Raised voice		

	Youth Interview:	Parent/ Guardian:	Chart/Record Review:
VIII Interpersonal Relationships/Social			
1. What did you typically do in the afternoons after school and on the weekends?			
2. What kinds of things do you do for fun?			
3. How old were you when you had your first sexual experience?			
4. Sexual Preference: (Heterosexual, Homosexual, Bisexual, Celibate)			
5. How many sexual partners have you had?			
6. What type of birth control did you use?			
7. Has any physical or emotional maltreatment occurred in any of your social relationships? If yes, please explain.			
8. Has the youth engaged in any sexual deviant behaviours? If so, has he received any type of previous treatment?			

IX. History of Other Abuse:

	Youth Interview:	Parent/ Guardian:	Chart/Record Review:
Emotional Abuse: Youth's history of emotional abuse			
1. Indicate who the perpetrator is; include relationship to youth (family member, an individual known to the family, stranger).			
2. Age of onset, duration			
3. Describe the abuse:			
4. How and when was the emotional abuse discovered (include the youth's age at the time of the discovery)?			
5. What was done about the abuse when it was discovered?			
6. Has the emotional abuse been reported? If so, what was the outcome?			
7. Is there any suggestion that the youth was subjected to emotional invalidation as a child or adolescent by primary care giver?			

	Youth Interview:	Parent/ Guardian:	Chart/Record Review:
Neglect:			
8. Describe any neglect the youth has experienced (lack of shelter, food, clothing, love, environmental deprivation, etc). Include the length of time the neglect was suffered.			
9. Describe the environment the youth was raised in. Include SES (socioeconomic status)			
10. Was either parent frequently away or out of the home at any time in the youth's life? If yes, please explain.			

Other Trauma:

11. Describe any other trauma the youth has experienced, i.e., witness the death of someone, or have their life threatened? Severity?			
12. Age of onset, frequency.			
13. Has the youth lost contact with anyone special to him (i.e. death, imprisonment, etc.)?			
14. Indicate any physical violence the youth has ever witnessed between family members? Please explain.			
15. Has the youth ever witnessed any violence? Describe.			
16. Describe family stresses at this time (i.e. financial, marital difficulties, etc.)			
17. Indicate if the youth has been involved in a gang or crew in his neighbourhood.			
18. Is there a history of group (neighbourhood) influence on his behaviour? Give details.			
19. What 'survival skills' did the youth need to survive in home environment?			

	Youth Interview:	Parent/ Guardian:	Chart/Record Review:
X Expectations of Treatment:			
1. What would the youth like to do differently when he is discharged?			
2. What are some goals the youth has for the next year?			
3. Willingness and motivation to be involved in family therapy sessions:			
4. If the youth could change anything about himself, what would he change?			

XI. Offences

Offences

Victim name/ and relationship	Youth age	Victim age	#of incidents	Describe the offence (oral, anal, vaginal, fondling, animal, digital penetration, stalking, telephone scatalogia, flashing, frottage, combination, etc.)	How did the youth get the victim to go along?	How did the youth get caught?	What are the related charges?
1 Youth interview:							
Parent/guardian:							
Chart review:							
2 Youth interview:							
Parent/guardian:							
Chart review:							
3 Youth interview:							
Parent/guardian:							
Chart review:							
4 Youth interview:							
Parent/guardian:							
Chart review:							

XI. Offences *continued*

Offences

Victim name/ and relationship	Youth age	Victim age	# of incidents	Describe the offence (oral, anal, vaginal, fondling, animal, digital penetration, stalking, telephone scatalogia, flashing, frottage, combination, etc.)	How did the youth get the victim to go along?	How did the youth get caught?	What are the related charges?
5 Youth interview:							
Parent/guardian:							
Chart review:							
6 Youth interview:							
Parent/guardian:							
Chart review:							
7 Youth interview:							
Parent/guardian:							
Chart review:							
Total number of victims:		Total number of offenses (incidents):					Total number of charges:

XII. History of Physical and Sexual Abuse

History of Physical Abuse

	Perpetrator name/and relationship	Youth age at onset	Duration	Perp's age	# of incidents	Describe the abuse (hitting, use objects, burning, etc.)	How did the perpetrator get the youth to go along?	How and when was it discovered (youth's age at the time of the discovery)	What was done about the abuse when it was discovered	Has the abuse been reported?	Outcome of reporting
1 Youth interview:											
Parent/guardian:											
Chart Review:											
2 Youth interview:											
Parent/guardian:											
Chart Review:											
3 Youth interview:											
Parent/guardian:											
Chart Review:											
4 Youth interview:											
Parent/guardian:											
Chart Review:											

XII. History of Physical and Sexual Abuse *continued*

History of Physical Abuse

Perpetrator name/and relationship	Youth age at onset	Duration	Perp's age	# of incidents	Describe the abuse (hitting, use objects, burning, etc.)	How did the perpetrator get the youth to go along?	How and when was it discovered (youth's age at the time of the discovery)	What was done about the abuse when it was discovered	Has the abuse been reported?	Outcome of reporting
5 Youth interview:										
Parent/guardian:										
Chart Review:										

Any other relevant information about history of physical abuse?

XIII. History of Sexual Abuse

	Perpetrator name/and relationship	Youth age at onset	Duration	Perp's age	#of incidents	Describe the abuse (oral, anal, vaginal, fondling, animal, digital penetration, stalking, telephone scatalogia, flashing, frottage, combination, etc.)	How did the perpetrator get the youth to go along?	How and when was it discovered (youth's age at the time of the discovery)	What was done about the abuse when it was discovered	Has the abuse been reported?	Outcome of reporting
1 Youth interview:											
Parent/guardian:											
Chart Review:											
2 Youth interview:											
Parent/guardian:											
Chart Review:											
3 Youth interview:											
Parent/guardian:											
Chart Review:											

XIII. History of Sexual Abuse *continued*

	Perpetrator name/and relationship	Youth age at onset	Duration	Perp's age	#of incidents	Describe the abuse (oral, anal, vaginal, fondling, animal, digital penetration, stalking, telephone scatalogia, flashing, frottage, combination, etc.)	How did the perpetrator get the youth to go along?	How and when was it discovered (youth's age at the time of the discovery)	What was done about the abuse when it was discovered	Has the abuse been reported?	Outcome of reporting
4 Youth interview:											
Parent/guardian:											
Chart Review:											
5 Youth interview:											
Parent/guardian:											
Chart Review:											

Any other relevant information about history of sexual abuse?

Appendix B: Strength of Fears – © 2003 by Jack A. Apsche, Ed.D, ABPP and Serene R. Ward Bailey, M.A.

Please read the statements below and circle how often you endorse each one.

	Never	Sometimes	Almost Always	Always
1. Fear of trusting anyone	1	2	3	4
2. Fear of trusting males younger, older, race _____	1	2	3	4
3. Fear of trusting females younger, older, race _____	1	2	3	4
4. Fear of trusting relative specific relative: _____	1	2	3	4
5. Fear of being home alone	1	2	3	4
6. Fear of closed rooms	1	2	3	4
7. Fear of showers or bathrooms. Be specific	1	2	3	4
8. Fear of failing. Be specific, of failing at what?	1	2	3	4
9. Fear someone will do something sexual. Who? The sexual behaviours I am afraid of are _____	1	2	3	4
10. Fear of hurting someone. Who?	1	2	3	4
11. Fear of someone hurting me or self	1	2	3	4
12. Fear that I did something wrong	1	2	3	4
13. Fear of being dumb	1	2	3	4
14. Fear of going to bed	1	2	3	4
15. Fear of being weak	1	2	3	4
16. Fear of not being masculine enough	1	2	3	4
17. Fear of being gay	1	2	3	4
18. Fear of dying. How?	1	2	3	4
19. Fear of my anger	1	2	3	4
20. Fear that someone will beat me up	1	2	3	4
21. Fear of someone knowing the secret	1	2	3	4
22. Fear that I caused the problem	1	2	3	4
23. Fear no one will believe me	1	2	3	4
24. Fear I have no one to talk to	1	2	3	4
25. Fear of the attacker; retaliation or repeat attack	1	2	3	4
26. Fear of not being strong enough to get away	1	2	3	4
27. Fear of being caught	1	2	3	4
28. Fear that people will know by looking at me, I've done something wrong	1	2	3	4
29. Fear I will live	1	2	3	4
30. Fear that I am sick and they will find out	1	2	3	4
31. Fear of a specific place. Where?	1	2	3	4
32. Fear of being emotionally intimate	1	2	3	4
33. Fear of crowds	1	2	3	4
34. Fear of being alone	1	2	3	4
35. Fear I will die young	1	2	3	4
36. Fear I will be physically hurt for no reason	1	2	3	4
37. Fear that something is wrong with me	1	2	3	4
38. Fear of never being 'normal'	1	2	3	4
39. Fear of my feelings	1	2	3	4
40. Fear I will never feel good	1	2	3	4
41. Fear of talking with someone about my sexual abuse	1	2	3	4
42. Fear of being in a crowded room	1	2	3	4

43. Fear of being touched by someone that I don't know well	1	2	3	4
44. Fear of being alone with adults that look like my abuser	1	2	3	4
45. Fear of seeing the person who abused me	1	2	3	4
46. Fear of reading about the person who abused me	1	2	3	4
47. Fear of someone coming up behind me	1	2	3	4
48. Fear of someone standing too close to me	1	2	3	4
49. Fear of seeing someone the same size and race of my abuser	1	2	3	4
50. Fear of being locked or restricted in a room	1	2	3	4
51. Fear of wearing clothes similar to those worn when I was abused	1	2	3	4
52. Fear of seeing and hearing about an assault on TV	1	2	3	4
53. Fear of having sexual contact	1	2	3	4
54. Fear of having physical contact	1	2	3	4
55. Fear of losing control	1	2	3	4
56. Fear of talking to strangers	1	2	3	4
57. Fear of going to the place where I was abused	1	2	3	4
58. Fear of confronting my abuser	1	2	3	4
59. Fear of talking to a therapist about my abuse	1	2	3	4
60. Fear that my abuser will get me again	1	2	3	4

Appendix C1: Compound Core Beliefs Questionnaire – CCBQ

Name _____   Date _____

Please read the statements below and circle how often you endorse each one.

	Never	Sometimes	Almost Always	Always
Everyone betrays my trust. I cannot trust anyone. (III)	1	2	3	4
If I am not loved, I am unhappy. (V)	1	2	3	4
Since I am afraid, I know I cannot achieve. (II)	1	2	3	4
When I see it and want it, I will take it. (IV)	1	2	3	4
I have to get what I want and need; others who are weak deserve what they get. (I)	1	2	3	4
I am special, others should get me what I want. (VII)	1	2	3	4
I am so exciting, others always want to be with me. (VI)	1	2	3	4
If I don't do it, it won't be done right. (VIII)	1	2	3	4
Rules are for others, I make my own rules. (XI)	1	2	3	4
I cannot trust others, they will hurt me. (X)	1	2	3	4
If you annoy me, I will 'go off' and let you know it.(IX)	1	2	3	4
If I trust someone today, they will betray me later. (III)	1	2	3	4
I am only fulfilled by being with a strong person. (V)	1	2	3	4
Others are critical, thereby they will reject me. (II)	1	2	3	4
Weaker people are here for the strong to prey on, using any means I need. (IV)	1	2	3	4
There is no problem if others don't know I did something. (I)	1	2	3	4
If others don't follow me, they should be punished. (VII)	1	2	3	4
My feelings are always right, thinking complicates issues. (VI)	1	2	3	4

If you are not perfect, you are terrible. (VIII)	1	2	3	4
People in authority are useless because they do not understand how special I am. (XI)	1	2	3	4
Other people have hidden motives and want something from me. (X)	1	2	3	4
Unless you agree with me, you are my enemy. (IX)	1	2	3	4
Whenever I hope, I will become disappointed. (III)	1	2	3	4
Others make better decisions than I; I can not make up my mind. (V)	1	2	3	4
When I feel, it may be unpleasant. (II)	1	2	3	4
Only I count, others are there to fill my needs. (IV)	1	2	3	4
Unless you have a videotape of me, you cannot prove I did it. (I)	1	2	3	4
If you criticise me, you are against me. (VII)	1	2	3	4
If I don't make myself known, others will not know how special I am. (VI)	1	2	3	4
If a job is not perfect, it is not complete. (VIII)	1	2	3	4
Things never work out for me, I never get a break. (XI)	1	2	3	4
If I am not on guard, others will take advantage of me. (X)	1	2	3	4
I don't need adults, rules, or regimentation; I will do what I want or need. (IX)	1	2	3	4
When I feel empty, I'll do whatever I need to do to feel better (including hurting myself).(III)	1	2	3	4
I am helpless and cannot make it on my own. (V)	1	2	3	4
I am not good enough, and others will reject me. (II)	1	2	3	4
If it makes me feel good, I do what I want. (IV)	1	2	3	4
My sexual offenses did not hurt anyone; they wanted it and will get over it. (I)	1	2	3	4
I am so brilliant and special, only a 'gifted' few understand me. (VII)	1	2	3	4
When I am bored, I need to become the centre of attention. (VI)	1	2	3	4
Without systems, everything will fall apart and there will be no order. (VIII)	1	2	3	4
Supervisors and bosses are useless and only stifle my creativity. (XI)	1	2	3	4
If I give others the chance, they will hurt me. (X)	1	2	3	4
I fulfill my own needs to amuse myself; others' needs don't mean anything to me. (IX)	1	2	3	4
When I am angry, my emotions are extreme and out of control. (III)	1	2	3	4
Others are stronger and I need them to cope. (V)	1	2	3	4
I am inadequate; I will do whatever I must to hide it. (II)	1	2	3	4
If I want sex, I'll take it, others' consent is not important. (IV)	1	2	3	4
If he wasn't so weak, I wouldn't have beaten him up. (I)	1	2	3	4
I deserve admiration and respect, whether I work for them or not, others don't deserve recognition.(VII)	1	2	3	4
My 'inner feelings' and intuition are all I need, rational thinking doesn't help.(VI)	1	2	3	4

Any flaws, defects, and mistakes are intolerable and totally invalidate any good or positive. (VIII)	1	2	3	4
I don't have to follow rules, I take care of myself. (XI)	1	2	3	4
Whenever I am alone, I cannot relax because someone is creating problems for me. (X)	1	2	3	4
Things that go wrong for me are others' fault. (IX)	1	2	3	4
When I get angry, my emotions go from annoyed to furious. (III)	1	2	3	4
I cannot think for myself, so I must find someone to take care of me. (V)	1	2	3	4
If I am afraid something will be unpleasant, I will avoid it. (II)	1	2	3	4
Others' personal property is of no concern or value to me, it's there for me to use how I choose. (IV)	1	2	3	4
If he/she can't take care of themselves, they get what they deserve. (I)	1	2	3	4
Others are unreliable, will let me down, or reject me. I need to protect myself. (III)	1	2	3	4
When others are paying attention to me, I am never bored. (VI)	1	2	3	4
People should do things my way because I know the best way to do them. (VIII)	1	2	3	4
Others may demand, but I do things my way. (XI)	1	2	3	4
If I let others know me, they will take advantage and hurt me. (X)	1	2	3	4
I know what I want and how to do everything. (IX)	1	2	3	4
When I hurt emotionally, I do whatever it takes to feel better. (III)	1	2	3	4
Being alone insures that I cannot be successful. (V)	1	2	3	4
Anything is better than feeling unpleasant. (II)	1	2	3	4
I will steal or take what I want from others, if it suits my needs. (IV)	1	2	3	4
I got hurt (victimised) before and I am strong now, so anyone I hurt will get better. (I)	1	2	3	4
If I act silly and entertain people, they won't notice my weaknesses. (VI)	1	2	3	4
Every detail is important, without completion of every detail your life will fail. (VIII)	1	2	3	4
When I tell the 'truth' I will be discounted, misunderstood, or rejected. (III)	1	2	3	4
If I let others know information about me, they will use it against me. (X)	1	2	3	4
If I fail it's because others got in my way. (IX)	1	2	3	4
When I am in pain, I'll do whatever I need to do to feel better (including hurting myself).(III)	1	2	3	4
Without another strong person, I am nothing. (V)	1	2	3	4
If others notice me, they will see my inadequacies. (II)	1	2	3	4
Truth means nothing; words are only a tool to get what I want. (IV)	1	2	3	4
Whenever I give (emotionally, physically, etc) it will be rejected. (III)	1	2	3	4
Others tend to be too casual and relaxed, and without formality and structure they will fail in life.(VIII)	1	2	3	4

People tell me or say things to me, and mean something else. (X)	1	2	3	4
If you don't do what I want, I'll get angry, and you will pay for my anger. (IX)	1	2	3	4
Life at times feels like an endless series of disappointments followed by pain. (III)	1	2	3	4
If I feel bad, I can't control it. (II)	1	2	3	4
Stealing is OK, if it fills my needs and suits my pleasure. (IV)	1	2	3	4
I can do what I want, consequences don't affect me directly unless I am caught. (I)	1	2	3	4
Any deviation from perfection means failure. (VIII)	1	2	3	4
If I am close to a person, they will betray me. (X)	1	2	3	4
If I am not perfect, I am a failure.(III)	1	2	3	4
If others criticise me, I know they are right. (II)	1	2	3	4
I cannot tolerate any rules or disagreement with my will, I will avoid these rules. (IV)	1	2	3	4
Consequences only matter when I am caught. They are for others. (I)	1	2	3	4
If I cannot be orderly, structured and perfect, I am a failure.	1	2	3	4
(VIII)	1	2	3	4
If others think they can get away with taking advantage of me, they will use me and information about me. (X)	1	2	3	4
In my living environment, often it is the social environment's fault for my failure, for any demands that are unrealistic. (III)	1	2	3	4
I would rather do anything to avoid failing because I cannot succeed. (II)	1	2	3	4
My own rules are more important than my parents or caregivers. (IV)	1	2	3	4
If I don't take what I want, I won't get what I need; and I deserve it. (I)	1	2	3	4
I try to control and not to show my grieving, loss, sadness, but eventually it comes out in a rush of emotions.(III)	1	2	3	4
If I don't think about or deal with a problem, it is not real. (II)	1	2	3	4
Only my internal rules count, any authority figures who disagree must pay, or be avoided. (IV)	1	2	3	4
In relationships, if the other person is not with me, then they are against me. (III)	1	2	3	4
People are not worth being around if they criticise me. (II)	1	2	3	4
My feelings about myself are so poor that I will do whatever I need to do to compensate for this. (III)	1	2	3	4
Problems are too big to solve; if I avoid them, they'll go away. (II)	1	2	3	4
Whenever I try to feel better, I will make things worse and feel more pain eventually. (III)	1	2	3	4
If they ask me to do something I don't want to do, I'll pay them back. (XI)	1	2	3	4

	1	2	3	4
I do it because I can, I deserve to get what I want. (I)	1	2	3	4
Only my thoughts, feelings, issues are important; others' are subservient to mine. (VII)	1	2	3	4
Whenever I need someone they are not there for me, there is no one I can count on. (III)	1	2	3	4
Rules are for others. (VII)	1	2	3	4
It is not important to keep promises unless they are to your closest friends. (I)	1	2	3	4
If people don't respond positively to me, they are not important. (VI)	1	2	3	4
I am alone if I am unattached. (V)	1	2	3	4
I need to avoid situations in which I am the centre of attention; I should be behind the scenes. (II)	1	2	3	4
I don't have to follow the rules for other people. (VII)	1	2	3	4
It is OK to do what I do as long as I get away with it. (I)	1	2	3	4
If I don't keep others focused on me, they won't like being around me. (VI)	1	2	3	4
I must always be subservient, in order to maintain relationships. (V)	1	2	3	4
I would rather not try something new than fail at something. (II)	1	2	3	4
I have every reason to expect wonderful things for myself, since I am so special. (VII)	1	2	3	4
I've been treated badly, so whatever I need to do to get what I need is OK. (I)	1	2	3	4
My 'gut' feelings tell what I need to do; that's more important than thinking through problems. (VI)	1	2	3	4
I never make decisions on my own, I always need support. (V)	1	2	3	4
Unpleasant feelings usually escalate and then get out of control . . . and get worse. (II)	1	2	3	4
My needs are more important, and others needs shouldn't interfere. (VII)	1	2	3	4
I will con people to get whatever I need; it's not a problem. (I)	1	2	3	4
I should be the centre of attention, living life up. (VI)	1	2	3	4
If I am on my own without support, something will happen to me. (V)	1	2	3	4
If people get to know me, they will know I am inferior; that is intolerable. (II)	1	2	3	4
Since I am so talented and gifted, others should promote (help) me get what I want. (VII)	1	2	3	4
Others should not criticise me; if they do it's because they usually can't understand me. (VII)	1	2	3	4
If people don't care for themselves, whatever happens to them is their problem. (I)	1	2	3	4
Circumstances dictate how I feel and behave. (VI)	1	2	3	4
When I am abandoned I feel like life is over. (V)	1	2	3	4
If people do not show me respect and give me what I am entitled to, it is intolerable for me. (VII)	1	2	3	4
Most of my relationships with people are extremely intimate, because people love to be around me or with me. (VI)	1	2	3	4

I am happiest when people pay attention to me. (VI)	1	2	3	4
I cannot handle my life without support. (V)	1	2	3	4
I am needy and weak inside, no matter what others see. (V)	1	2	3	4
Since I am so special, rules should not apply to me. (VII)	1	2	3	4
I tell a girl/boy anything I need to get sex, or what I want. (I)	1	2	3	4
I always look good and people check out what I am wearing. (VI)	1	2	3	4
I must be subservient to all in authority; I cannot make it on my own. (V)	1	2	3	4
People criticise me or annoy me because I am so special. (VII)	1	2	3	4
I don't need to work to achieve; things should come my way because I deserve it. (VII)	1	2	3	4
If he/she was in my way then I would have hurt him/her. (I)	1	2	3	4
It is easy for others to want to be sexual with me; they know how good I am. (VI)	1	2	3	4
Whenever I end a relationship I immediately find a new one. (V)	1	2	3	4
Any difficulties in a relationship mean that 'it has gone bad' and I must end the relationship. (II)	1	2	3	4
Most people are not as gifted as I am, and my behaviour lets them know it. (VII)	1	2	3	4
Whenever I am not getting attention, I am bored. (VI)	1	2	3	4
Being alone is terrible. (V)	1	2	3	4
If I don't 'take care' of them first, then they will get me. (I)	1	2	3	4
Most of my peers would rather be me . . . than themselves. (VII)	1	2	3	4
People listen to me because I impress them with my speech and language. (VI)	1	2	3	4
I cannot cope like others, I need support. (V)	1	2	3	4
Others' feelings are not as important as achieving a goal for myself. (VII)	1	2	3	4
If I don't dress well, people won't notice me. (VI)	1	2	3	4
I enjoy relationships, but I am unwilling to pay the price to remain in them. (V)	1	2	3	4
If other people get any information on me, they will use it against me. (X)	1	2	3	4
Other people expect too much from me. (XI)	1	2	3	4
My way of doing things is the best way; others do not do things as well as I do. (VIII)	1	2	3	4
If you disagree with me, you'll pay. (IX)	1	2	3	4
Stealing or breaking into someone else's house is OK if I need money (or something). (IV)	1	2	3	4
My friends will sell me out if the price is right. (X)	1	2	3	4
Rules are not important and smother. (XI)	1	2	3	4
Without details, nothing will work. (VIII)	1	2	3	4
I see their disagreement as a never-ending personal attack. (IX)	1	2	3	4

Whatever I have to say or tell others is OK as long as it gets me what I want. (IV)	1	2	3	4
If I act too friendly, others will see my weakness and exploit me. (X)	1	2	3	4
If others are too bossy and demanding, I don't have to follow them. (XI)	1	2	3	4
If I don't control my emotions, I am flawed. (VIII)	1	2	3	4
I need not respect adults; they do not know any more than I do. (IX)	1	2	3	4
I will sneak around and take or steal what I need. (IV)	1	2	3	4
Anyone who insults me, will never get a second chance, I will keep him or her away. (X)	1	2	3	4
Authority figures tend to be controlling/demanding and act like they are in control. (XI)	1	2	3	4
If people are too bossy or demanding, I do not need to listen to them. (VIII)	1	2	3	4
I only do what I choose; adult needs or requests are not important. (IX)	1	2	3	4
My priorities involve my own wants and needs at the time. (IV)	1	2	3	4
Others always have hidden motives and I cannot really trust anyone. (X)	1	2	3	4
If I don't want to do something my mood changes and I withdraw emotionally. (XI)	1	2	3	4
People in authority are too demanding, bossy, and intrusive. (VIII)	1	2	3	4
I amuse myself by any means I choose, even if I demean someone.(People are my amusement).(IX)	1	2	3	4
If parents or authority figures do not what I want, I will run away. (IV)	1	2	3	4
If I let others know 'who I am' they'll know my weaknesses and use them against me. (X)	1	2	3	4
I never like to show my anger directly but others know when I am angry. (XI)	1	2	3	4
I must do things my way or they won't work. (VIII)	1	2	3	4
Errors that I make are because of someone else's doing. (IX)	1	2	3	4
I don't need to go to school, I'd rather do what's important to me. (IV)	1	2	3	4
Others often communicate threats hidden in normal conversations. (X)	1	2	3	4
Others should not tell me what to do; I will eventually do what I want to do anyway. (XI)	1	2	3	4
I can decide what is best for me; if others do I get annoyed. (VIII)	1	2	3	4
If you mess with me I'll make you pay. (IX)	1	2	3	4
Animals do not have feelings; they are here for my use. (IV)	1	2	3	4
Those who attempt to attack me won't get a second chance, will get them. (X)	1	2	3	4
I have to keep myself from being dominated by authority figures, while gaining their acceptance and approval. (XI)	1	2	3	4

To be successful, I need organisation and control. (VIII)	1	2	3	4
Getting even is important. (IX)	1	2	3	4
Others often attempt to get over on me by exploiting or harming me in some way. (X)	1	2	3	4
I really am self-sufficient but I often need others' help to reach my goals. (XI)	1	2	3	4
Any mistakes I make are catastrophic. (VIII)	1	2	3	4
Others' mistakes have created my problems. (IX)	1	2	3	4
Authority figures usually stifle my creativity and prevent my progress toward goals. (XI)	1	2	3	4
People who annoy me get what they deserve. (IX)	1	2	3	4
Guidelines or demands are for others and are insults to me. (XI)	1	2	3	4
It is ok to bother people when I am in the mood. (IX)1	1	2	3	4

Scoring the CCBQ:

Circle all beliefs endorsed as always or 4:

I: 5, 16, 27, 38, 49, 60, 71, 88, 94, 100, 110, 114, 119, 124, 129, 135, 144, 149, 156

II: 3, 14, 25, 36, 47, 58, 69, 79, 86, 92, 98, 102, 105, 107, 117, 122, 127, 132, 152

III: 1, 12, 23, 34, 45, 56, 61, 67, 74, 77, 81, 85, 91, 97, 101, 104, 106, 108, 112

IV: 4, 15, 26, 37, 48, 59, 70, 80, 87, 93, 99, 103, 167, 172, 177, 182, 187, 192, 197

V: 2, 13, 24, 35, 46, 57, 68, 78, 116, 121, 126, 131, 137, 141, 142, 146, 151, 155, 159, 162

VI: 7, 18, 29, 40, 51, 62, 72, 115, 120, 125, 130, 136, 139, 140, 145, 150, 154, 158, 161

VII: 6, 17, 28, 39, 50, 111, 113, 118, 123, 128, 133, 134, 138, 143, 147, 148, 153, 157, 160

VIII: 8, 19, 30, 41, 52, 63, 73, 82, 89, 95, 165, 170, 175, 180, 185, 190, 195, 200, 204

IX: 11, 22, 33, 44, 55, 66, 76, 84, 166, 171, 176, 181, 186, 191, 196, 201, 205, 207, 209

X: 10, 21, 32, 43, 54, 65, 75, 83, 90, 96, 163, 168, 173, 178, 183, 188, 193, 198, 202

XI: 9, 20, 31, 42, 53, 64, 109, 162, 164, 169, 174, 179, 184, 189, 194, 199, 203, 206, 208

Circle all beliefs endorsed as almost always or 3:

I: 5, 16, 27, 38, 49, 60, 71, 88, 94, 100, 110, 114, 119, 124, 129, 135, 144, 149, 156

II: 3, 14, 25, 36, 47, 58, 69, 79, 86, 92, 98, 102, 105, 107, 117, 122, 127, 132, 152

III: 1, 12, 23, 34, 45, 56, 61, 67, 74, 77, 81, 85, 91, 97, 101, 104, 106, 108, 112

IV: 4, 15, 26, 37, 48, 59, 70, 80, 87, 93, 99, 103, 167, 172, 177, 182, 187, 192, 197

V: 2, 13, 24, 35, 46, 57, 68, 78, 116, 121, 126, 131, 137, 141, 142, 146, 151, 155, 159, 162

VI: 7, 18, 29, 40, 51, 62, 72, 115, 120, 125, 130, 136, 139, 140, 145, 150, 154, 158, 161

VII: 6, 17, 28, 39, 50, 111, 113, 118, 123, 128, 133, 134, 138, 143, 147, 148, 153, 157, 160

VIII: 8, 19, 30, 41, 52, 63, 73, 82, 89, 95, 165, 170, 175, 180, 185, 190, 195, 200, 204

IX: 11, 22, 33, 44, 55, 66, 76, 84, 166, 171, 176, 181, 186, 191, 196, 201, 205, 207, 209

X: 10, 21, 32, 43, 54, 65, 75, 83, 90, 96, 163, 168, 173, 178, 183, 188, 193, 198, 202

XI: 9, 20, 31, 42, 53, 64, 109, 162, 164, 169, 174, 179, 184, 189, 194, 199, 203, 206, 208

Circle all beliefs endorsed as sometimes or 2:

I: 5, 16, 27, 38, 49, 60, 71, 88, 94, 100, 110, 114, 119, 124, 129, 135, 144, 149, 156

II: 3, 14, 25, 36, 47, 58, 69, 79, 86, 92, 98, 102, 105, 107, 117, 122, 127, 132, 152

III: 1, 12, 23, 34, 45, 56, 61, 67, 74, 77, 81, 85, 91, 97, 101, 104, 106, 108, 112

IV: 4, 15, 26, 37, 48, 59, 70, 80, 87, 93, 99, 103, 167, 172, 177, 182, 187, 192, 197

V: 2, 13, 24, 35, 46, 57, 68, 78, 116, 121, 126, 131, 137, 141, 142, 146, 151, 155, 159, 162

VI: 7, 18, 29, 40, 51, 62, 72, 115, 120, 125, 130, 136, 139, 140, 145, 150, 154, 158, 161

VII: 6, 17, 28, 39, 50, 111, 113, 118, 123, 128, 133, 134, 138, 143, 147, 148, 153, 157, 160

VIII: 8, 19, 30, 41, 52, 63, 73, 82, 89, 95, 165, 170, 175, 180, 185, 190, 195, 200, 204

IX: 11, 22, 33, 44, 55, 66, 76, 84, 166, 171, 176, 181, 186, 191, 196, 201, 205, 207, 209

X: 10, 21, 32, 43, 54, 65, 75, 83, 90, 96, 163, 168, 173, 178, 183, 188, 193, 198, 202

XI: 9, 20, 31, 42, 53, 64, 109, 162, 164, 169, 174, 179, 184, 189, 194, 199, 203, 206, 208

Youth Name _____   Date _____

Therapist Name _____

Profile Chart

	Personality Disorder	# of 4's Endorsed	# of 3's Endorsed	# of 2's Endorsed	Total
I	Antisocial Personality Disorder				
II	Avoidant Personality Disorder				
III	Borderline Personality Disorder				
IV	Conduct Disorder				
V	Dependent Personality Disorder				
VI	Histrionic Personality Disorder				
VII	Narcissistic Personality Disorder				
VIII	Obsessive-Compulsive Disorder				
IX	Oppositional Defiant Disorder				
X	Paranoid Personality Disorder				
XI	Passive Aggressive Personality Disorder				

Appendix C2: Compound Core Beliefs Questionnaire (CCBQ)

Short Version

Name _____   Date _____

Please read the statements below and circle how often you endorse each one.

	Never	Sometimes	Almost Always	Always
Everyone betrays my trust. I cannot trust anyone. (III)	1	2	3	4
If I am not loved, I am unhappy. (V)	1	2	3	4
I am so exciting, others always want to be with me. (VI)	1	2	3	4
I cannot trust others, they will hurt me. (X)	1	2	3	4
If I trust someone today, they will betray me later. (III)	1	2	3	4
I am only fulfilled by being with a strong person. (V)	1	2	3	4
Others are critical, thereby they will reject me. (II)	1	2	3	4
There is no problem if others don't know I did something. (I)	1	2	3	4
Other people have hidden motives and want something from me. (X)	1	2	3	4
Whenever I hope, I will become disappointed. (III)	1	2	3	4
Others make better decisions than I; I can not make up my mind. (V)	1	2	3	4
When I feel, it may be unpleasant. (II)	1	2	3	4
Unless you have a videotape of me, you cannot prove I did it. (I)	1	2	3	4
If you criticise me, you are against me. (VII)	1	2	3	4
If I don't make myself known, others will not know how special I am. (VI)	1	2	3	4
Things never work out for me, I never get a break. (XI)	1	2	3	4
If I am not on guard, others will take advantage of me. (X)	1	2	3	4
I am so brilliant and special, only a 'gifted' few understand me. (VII)	1	2	3	4
When I am bored, I need to become the centre of attention. (VI)	1	2	3	4
If I give others the chance, they will hurt me. (X)	1	2	3	4
When I am angry, my emotions are extreme and out of control. (III)	1	2	3	4
Others are stronger and I need them to cope. (V)	1	2	3	4
I am inadequate; I will do whatever I must to hide it. (II)	1	2	3	4
My 'inner feelings' and intuition are all I need, rational thinking doesn't help.(VI)	1	2	3	4
When I get angry, my emotions go from annoyed to furious. (III)	1	2	3	4
If I am afraid something will be unpleasant, I will avoid it. (II)	1	2	3	4
Others are unreliable, will let me down, or reject me. I need to protect myself. (III)	1	2	3	4
When others are paying attention to me, I am never bored. (VI)	1	2	3	4

Others may demand, but I do things my way. (XI)	1	2	3	4
If I let others know me, they will take advantage and hurt me. (X)	1	2	3	4
When I hurt emotionally, I do whatever it takes to feel better. (III)	1	2	3	4
Anything is better than feeling unpleasant. (II)	1	2	3	4
If I act silly and entertain people, they won't notice my weaknesses. (VI)	1	2	3	4
If I let others know information about me, they will use it against me. (X)	1	2	3	4
If others notice me, they will see my inadequacies. (II)	1	2	3	4
People tell me or say things to me, and mean something else. (X)	1	2	3	4
Life at times feels like an endless series of disappointments followed by pain. (III)	1	2	3	4
If I feel bad, I can't control it. (II)	1	2	3	4
I can do what I want, consequences don't affect me directly unless I am caught. (I)	1	2	3	4
Consequences only matter when I am caught. They are for others. (I)	1	2	3	4
If others think they can get away with taking advantage of me, they will use me and information about me. (X)	1	2	3	4
If I don't take what I want, I won't get what I need; and I deserve it. (I)	1	2	3	4
I try to control and not to show my grieving, loss, sadness, but eventually it comes out in a rush of emotions.(III)	1	2	3	4
If I don't think about or deal with a problem, it is not real. (II)	1	2	3	4
People are not worth being around if they criticise me. (II)	1	2	3	4
My feelings about myself are so poor that I will do whatever I need to do to compensate for this. (III)	1	2	3	4
Whenever I try to feel better, I will make things worse and feel more pain eventually. (III)	1	2	3	4
If they ask me to do something I don't want to do, I'll pay them back.(XI)	1	2	3	4
I do it because I can, I deserve to get what I want. (I)	1	2	3	4
Whenever I need someone they are not there for me, there is no one I can count on. (III)	1	2	3	4
Rules are for others. (VII)	1	2	3	4
If people don't respond positively to me, they are not important. (VI)	1	2	3	4
I need to avoid situations in which I am the centre of attention; I should be behind the scenes. (II)	1	2	3	4
I don't have to follow the rules for other people. (VII)	1	2	3	4
It is OK to do what I do as long as I get away with it. (I)	1	2	3	4
I would rather not try something new than fail at something. (II)	1	2	3	4
I have every reason to expect wonderful things for myself, since I am so special. (VII)	1	2	3	4
I've been treated badly, so whatever I need to do to get what I need is OK. (I)	1	2	3	4

My 'gut' feelings tell what I need to do; that's more important than thinking through problems. (VI)	1	2	3	4
I never make decisions on my own, I always need support. (V)	1	2	3	4
Unpleasant feelings usually escalate and then get out of control . . . and get worse. (II)	1	2	3	4
My needs are more important, and others needs shouldn't interfere. (VII)	1	2	3	4
I will con people to get whatever I need; it's not a problem. (I)	1	2	3	4
Since I am so talented and gifted, others should promote (help) me get what I want. (VII)	1	2	3	4
Others should not criticise me; if they do it's because they usually can't understand me. (VII)	1	2	3	4
If people don't care for themselves, whatever happens to them is their problem. (I)	1	2	3	4
Circumstances dictate how I feel and behave. (VI)	1	2	3	4
When I am abandoned I feel like life is over. (V)	1	2	3	4
If people do not show me respect and give me what I am entitled to, it is intolerable for me. (VII)	1	2	3	4
Most of my relationships with people are extremely intimate, because people love to be around me or with me. (VI)	1	2	3	4
I am happiest when people pay attention to me. (VI)	1	2	3	4
I cannot handle my life without support. (V)	1	2	3	4
I am needy and weak inside, no matter what others see. (V)	1	2	3	4
I tell a girl/boy anything I need to get sex, or what I want. (I)	1	2	3	4
I must be subservient to all in authority; I cannot make it on my own. (V)	1	2	3	4
I don't need to work to achieve; things should come my way because I deserve it. (VII)	1	2	3	4
Whenever I end a relationship I immediately find a new one. (V)	1	2	3	4
Most people are not as gifted as I am, and my behaviour lets them know it. (VII)	1	2	3	4
Whenever I am not getting attention, I am bored. (VI)	1	2	3	4
Being alone is terrible. (V)	1	2	3	4
If I don't 'take care' of them first, then they will get me. (I)	1	2	3	4
I cannot cope like others, I need support. (V)	1	2	3	4
Others' feelings are not as important as achieving a goal for myself. (VII)	1	2	3	4
If other people get any information on me, they will use it against me. (X)	1	2	3	4
Other people expect too much from me. (XI)	1	2	3	4
If others are too bossy and demanding, I don't have to follow them. (XI)	1	2	3	4
Authority figures tend to be controlling/demanding and act like they are in control. (XI)	1	2	3	4
Others always have hidden motives and I cannot really trust anyone. (X)	1	2	3	4

If I don't want to do something my mood changes and I withdraw emotionally. (XI)	1	2	3	4
If I let others know 'who I am' they'll know my weaknesses and use them against me. (X)	1	2	3	4
I never like to show my anger directly but others know when I am angry. (XI)	1	2	3	4
Others should not tell me what to do; I will eventually do what I want to do anyway. (XI)	1	2	3	4
I have to keep myself from being dominated by authority figures, while gaining their acceptance and approval. (XI)	1	2	3	4
Others often attempt to get over on me by exploiting or harming me in some way. (X)	1	2	3	4
I really am self-sufficient but I often need others' help to reach my goals. (XI)	1	2	3	4
Authority figures usually stifle my creativity and prevent my progress toward goals. (XI)	1	2	3	4

Scoring the CCBQ:

Circle all beliefs endorsed as always or 4:

I: 8, 13 , 39, 40, 42, 49, 55, 58, 63, 66, 74, 81

II: 7, 12, 23, 26, 32, 35, 38, 44, 45, 53, 56, 61

III: 1, 5, 10, 21, 25, 27, 31, 37, 43, 46, 47, 50

IV: 2, 6, 11, 22, 60, 68, 72, 73, 75, 77, 80, 82

V: 3, 15, 19, 24, 28, 33, 52, 59, 67, 70, 71, 79

VI: 14, 18, 51, 54, 57, 62, 64, 65, 69, 76, 78, 83

VII: 4, 9, 17, 20, 30, 34, 36, 41, 84, 88, 90, 94

VIII: 16, 29, 48, 85, 86, 87, 89, 91, 92, 93, 95, 96

Circle all beliefs endorsed as sometimes or 2:

I: 8, 13 , 39, 40, 42, 49, 55, 58, 63, 66, 74, 81

II: 7, 12, 23, 26, 32, 35, 38, 44, 45, 53, 56, 61

III: 1, 5, 10, 21, 25, 27, 31, 37, 43, 46, 47, 50

IV: 2, 6, 11, 22, 60, 68, 72, 73, 75, 77, 80, 82

V: 3, 15, 19, 24, 28, 33, 52, 59, 67, 70, 71, 79

VI: 14, 18, 51, 54, 57, 62, 64, 65, 69, 76, 78, 83

VII: 4, 9, 17, 20, 30, 34, 36, 41, 84, 88, 90, 94

VIII: 16, 29, 48, 85, 86, 87, 89, 91, 92, 93, 95, 96

Circle all beliefs endorsed as almost always or 3:

I: 8, 13 , 39, 40, 42, 49, 55, 58, 63, 66, 74, 81

II: 7, 12, 23, 26, 32, 35, 38, 44, 45, 53, 56, 61

III: 1, 5, 10, 21, 25, 27, 31, 37, 43, 46, 47, 50

IV: 2, 6, 11, 22, 60, 68, 72, 73, 75, 77, 80, 82

V: 3, 15, 19, 24, 28, 33, 52, 59, 67, 70, 71, 79

VI: 14, 18, 51, 54, 57, 62, 64, 65, 69, 76, 78, 83

VII: 4, 9, 17, 20, 30, 34, 36, 41, 84, 88, 90, 94

VIII: 16, 29, 48, 85, 86, 87, 89, 91, 92, 93, 95, 96

Youth Name _____   Date _____

Therapist Name _____

Profile Chart

	Personality Disorder	# of 4's Endorsed	# of 3's Endorsed	# of 2's Endorsed	Total
I	Antisocial Personality Disorder				
II	Avoidant Personality Disorder				
III	Borderline Personality Disorder				
IV	Conduct Disorder				
V	Dependent Personality Disorder				
VI	Histrionic Personality Disorder				
VII	Narcissistic Personality Disorder				
VIII	Obsessive-Compulsive Disorder				
IX	Oppositional Defiant Disorder				
X	Paranoid Personality Disorder				
XI	Passive Aggressive Personality Disorder				

Part V

Management issues

Chapter Eighteen

The Extra Dimension: Developing a Risk Management Framework

Christine McCarlie and Ann Brady

Introduction

Approaching problem sexual behaviours and the inherent risks can invoke real anxiety in professionals involved in child protection. This often results in a lack of clarity about roles and leaves workers and carers feeling powerless to respond to their duties in the management of risk. This chapter draws on work undertaken by the Halt Project in developing a framework for managing risk. Both the authors are involved in direct practice and this chapter is written from a practitioner's perspective.

The Halt Project was established in 1994 by Social Work Services in Glasgow to work with children (13–18yrs) involved in abusive sexual behaviours. Our remit over the years has changed, reflecting the need for a service for a wider age range (5–18yrs) and recognising the presentation of different kinds of equally complex problem sexual behaviours. We now work with children who engage in a range of problem sexual behaviours, not just those with behaviour defined as abusive. In doing so this has reinforced the importance of understanding and defining different types of sexual behaviours as this has proved critical in informing the different interventions and risk management strategies required.

The Halt Project's interventions have always been placed within an overall systemic framework. However, the risk management framework has highlighted that we had been using the systems in a limited way: the main focus being restricted to significant adults helping the child through a programme of work. Developing the risk management framework caused us to reconsider the interface between the child and their environment and recognise the huge impact the environment can have in making risk more manageable.

It is now widely recognised that most children who engage in problematic sexual behaviours have themselves been victims of trauma. (Ryan et al., 1987). This is the experience of Halt and we view this as being of considerable significance in our understanding of the development of problem sexual behaviours and required interventions. Our approach is holistic and draws from our understanding of a range of theories such as sexual behaviour theories (Finkelhor, 1984; Lane, 1991), trauma (Briere, 1995; James, 1989) and attachment (Howe, 1999; Howe and Fearnley, 1999; Archer, 2000). We use cognitive and behavioural as well as psychodynamic approaches and all our work is undertaken from a child development perspective.

To help explain the different and necessary components of the work we have found it helpful to make a distinction between behaviour specific and behaviour related work with the latter focusing on the child's wider needs including trauma related issues (see Figure 18.1).

This chapter will describe how we work with systems that often struggle to work with sexual behaviour problems in an ongoing way that truly reflects the complex nature of risk. We will describe the development of the framework, how it has evolved and where it fits with our assessments and interventions. It is still a work in progress but we are clearly recognising the benefits of it in terms offering a clarity and purpose to our practice. A major strength of this framework is that it addresses risk without compromising the child's needs, recognising and utilising the integral relationship between the two.

Factors resulting in developing the framework

As practitioners we were aware that there were barriers to us working effectively with risk. By identifying what these issues were, we began the process of creating more constructive ways of working with and managing it:

Risk viewed as static

There seems to be a general lack of helpful language that allows risk to be discussed in a

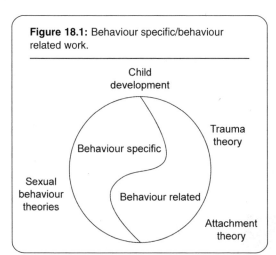

Figure 18.1: Behaviour specific/behaviour related work.

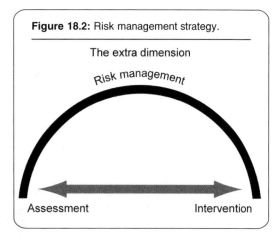

Figure 18.2: Risk management strategy.

constructive way that reflects its fluid nature. This restrictive language can lead workers to quantify risk in terms of high, medium or low. In our experience this encourages risk to be viewed in a static way, more suited to a model working with adult sex offenders.

Lack of joint ownership in the management of risk

Perhaps another consequence of the lack of helpful language is that risk is not being talked about explicitly in meetings, particularly in more complex cases where risk is evident on a day-to-day basis. As a result the accountability for holding and managing the risk can be implicitly placed or accepted by individuals within the professional group e.g., carer. This can lead to a lack of joint ownership of risk with workers feeling isolated, resulting in a fragmented professional group.

Agency responses reactive in nature

Professional systems can often be incident led in their responses. For example, where a child has previously been involved in sexually abusive behaviour followed by a settled period, the risk dimension can slowly recede. There can be an implicit assumption that the risk is reduced. This may be the case but it would not be an informed opinion evidenced, for example, by the child demonstrating insight into their behaviour or attaching some meaning to it. Alternatively, where a child's risk is at one time documented as serious, this view can remain static for years to come regardless of any change demonstrated.

The above points are based on the subjective experience of practitioners within the Halt Project and Calder (1999) in exploring 'barriers to working together', was helpful in understanding these practice points within a wider context.

Within the Halt Project there is clarity about our assessments and interventions, and the overlap between them. The above process crystallised the need for an additional dimension to our work: an overarching risk management strategy that would allow us to manage, evaluate and monitor the risk as the assessment and intervention was underway (see Figure 18.2).

The framework

Philosophy

The framework has evolved from the philosophy that underpins it and this continues to remain central to its implementation.

Three strands of the philosophy:

- Risk is a dynamic and fluid concept
- One of the main aims of the intervention is for the child to be responsible for managing their own risk. This is a process and as such, initially, this responsibility often has to be held by the adult systems.
- The child's environment has a significant impact on risk and therefore must be seen as a valuable resource.

Risk is dynamic and Fluid

It has long been acknowledged by professionals in this field that risk has to be viewed as fluid and dynamic in nature (Ryan, 1999). However, as

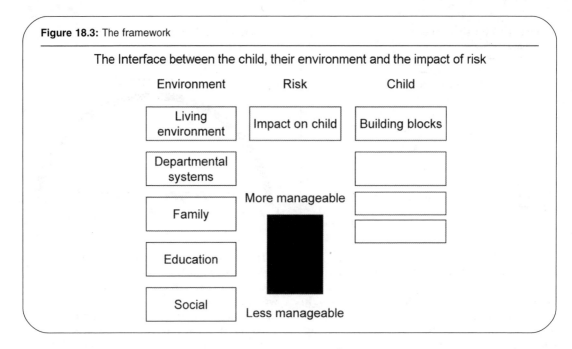

Figure 18.3: The framework

The Interface between the child, their environment and the impact of risk

social workers working within social work and related systems, it has been our experience that those systems do not lend themselves to this view. One of the challenges for us in developing the framework was to find ways to work effectively with risk that allows us to consider the ongoing internal and external influences that are continually impacting upon it.

The framework denotes risk as being more or less manageable. This leads us to an exploration and consideration of the different factors that impact upon it, naturally inviting us to explore the systems around the child, alongside considering the child's internal resources. This has resulted in risk becoming a more tangible concept with workers feeling less anxious and more able to effect some change upon it.

Responsibility

The notion of responsibility within a risk management context is in relation to the role of the systems and the child in taking responsibility for managing the risk. The overall aim of the intervention is for the young person to be responsible for managing their own risk.

In acknowledging the impact of trauma on child development (Lyons-Ruth, 1996), we would not, in the early stages of our intervention have the expectation that a child would have the capacity or internal resources to be able to take

responsibility for managing their own risk. They have to learn this skill through a process of work that may involve gaining insights, resolving past experiences, and learning new skills, all of which would have to be evidenced in a range of settings. This is different to our on-going intervention with the child where we help them to take responsibility for their behaviour, in relation to their past actions and impact on any victims.

This stance on risk necessitates a joining with the adults around the child leading to a shared consensus of viewing responsibility in this way. This process of engagement has at times been challenging, as this way of working may not naturally fit with some well-established cultures. Using a child development perspective, particularly exploring the impact of trauma on development has helped staff view, and respond to, the child in a more holistic way. From this perspective, staff move towards more realistic expectations of the child in terms of their ability to manage their own risk.

Environment

Exploring the notion of responsibility in the above way naturally moved us to look at the systems around the child in more detail. The framework allows a consideration of how all the systems impact on the risk, e.g., societal, community, caring environment. In practice this means considering how these systems interact with the child on a day-to-day basis. For example, from high risk offending community, family contact not happening, unstable children's unit, down to considering the impact and meaning of a particular remark.

As a result we now view the environment as a valuable resource, a resource with enormous potential for impacting on risk.

By being more explicit about the impact the environment has on risk it has naturally increased the demands made upon it. Where the systems do work together, are accountable and effective in their interactions with the child, the risk can become more manageable in a short space of time. For us this has been an exciting and inspiring process. Where this is not happening, the framework can be used to identify which parts of the systems are making the risk less manageable. This allows consideration of what, where and how interventions can be targeted to impact on the risk, and issues of accountability and responsibility can be explored more openly.

The framework

On the left side of the framework (Figure 18.6) would be all the systems in a child's life. The right side depicts the child's progress. Through the assessment process specific aims of intervention are formulated that would ultimately evidence the child's ability to manage their own risk. As the child engages in work the building blocks would be evidencing their progress. Risk is depicted in the centre. This reinforces symbolically that it is the interaction of the child with their environment that determines the manageability of the risk.

Managing risk: an ongoing process

The framework is a helpful means by which to organise information from a risk management perspective. The philosophy underpinning the framework brings together the systems and the child in a way that reflects the complex and dynamic nature of risk as the child goes through the process of being able to take the responsibility for managing their own risk effectively. We have found it helpful to think of this process in three phases:

- Phase One: Risk reduction has to be via the systems. Responsibility for managing the risk is owned by the systems.

- Phase Two: Risk is being reduced by engagement in work. Responsibility for managing the risk moves towards a shared ownership between the child and the systems.
- Phase Three: Risk is reduced and the child has the ability and increased awareness to manage their own risk where developmentally appropriate.

Phase one

During the initial period of contact we would be explicit that, where appropriate, the responsibility for managing the risk is owned by the adults around the child.

Aims

- Identify how the different parts of the systems are impacting on the risk, making it more or less manageable.
- Identify specific areas for intervention within the relevant systems to impact positively on the management of risk.
- Identify and formulate specific goals (predictive outcomes) of individual work with the child.

During this period staff at Halt would be working intensively with the environment. Previously we would have been providing a supportive role to the environment, predominantly focusing on the living environment. We now engage all the systems in focused work. This would include exploring what approaches are working and what needs to be changed, assessing the strengths of the different systems and identifying what areas of work need to be undertaken. Using the framework ensures all of this would be from a risk management perspective.

For example, within the living environment it could consist of:

- Exploring the impact of trauma on the child.
- Identifying specific language to use with the child.
- Creating and implementing a behaviour management strategy.
- Helping staff work out how to teach the child to link feelings to behaviours.

In the initial stages the framework can feel quite threatening particularly to the child's living environment e.g., foster carers. It has been important for us to be sensitive at this stage and it

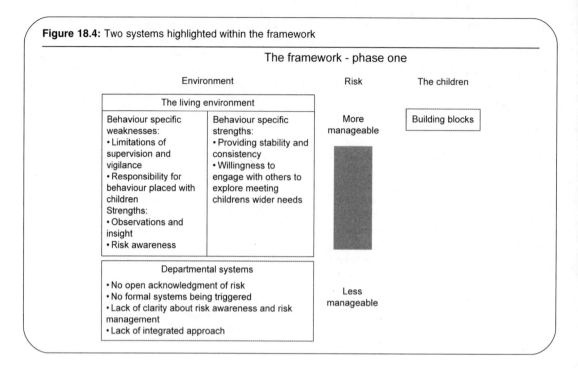

Figure 18.4: Two systems highlighted within the framework

The framework - phase one

Environment		Risk	The children
The living environment			
Behaviour specific weaknesses: • Limitations of supervision and vigilance • Responsibility for behaviour placed with children Strengths: • Observations and insight • Risk awareness	Behaviour specific strengths: • Providing stability and consistency • Willingness to engage with others to explore meeting childrens wider needs	More manageable	Building blocks
Departmental systems • No open acknowledgment of risk • No formal systems being triggered • Lack of clarity about risk awareness and risk management • Lack of integrated approach		Less manageable	

has helped to explain that sometimes looking at and changing simple systems and structures can have positive impact on making the risk more manageable.

Practice Example – Phase One

We used the framework in a recent case to highlight our concerns about risk. The case involved a sibling group in a foster placement. The children had all experienced chronic levels of neglect, deprivation and abuse in their birth family. They reported their sexual behaviours as beginning in the family home. In the foster placement they continued to display sexual behaviours mostly of an extensive mutual nature as described by Gil and Johnston (1993).The referral by the social worker was prompted by the foster carers. Due to the on going complexities of the case, risk had not until then been prioritised by the area team.

The framework was used as a basis for discussion within our team in the initial stages of our involvement to clarify our expectations of other systems and prioritise areas for intervention (see Figure 18.4). In doing this we were able to consider how the different systems were impacting on risk.

More manageable

In the school setting the children's sexual behaviours had never been identified as problematic. The children attended different schools and seemed to benefit from the activities and the structure. Staff were alerted to the behaviours and were able to offer high levels of supervision. Staff were also concerned with working with the children to enhance different skills that they were clearly deficit in e.g., social skills and problem solving.

In the foster placement the carers had a good awareness of the extent of the children's sexual behaviours. They were good at gauging situations that could provoke sexual behaviours and showed insight into some of the children's non-sexual behaviours. They seemed committed to working with Halt to increase their skills in meeting the children's needs and managing their behaviours.

Less manageable

The foster carers were lacking considerably in behaviour specific areas in relation to insight and intervention. They had unrealistic expectations of the children in terms of giving them the responsibility not to engage in the sexual behaviours. They often left them together unsupervised and the general layout of their house and grounds were not amenable to provide good enough observation and supervision.

They viewed the behaviours almost as a pass or fail of themselves as carers and had a high investment in keeping the children together. This contributed to the carers beginning not to discuss or acknowledge sexual behaviours with Halt.

The carers were being given mixed messages by the different systems involved in their lives regarding the children. Their family placement worker and Halt had differing views about risk awareness and risk management and the Area Team responsible for the case had not taken any strong view and had not utilised any formal procedures within which to frame their work with the children.

In considering risk another important factor was the children themselves. They were clearly a long way from being able to take responsibility for managing their own behaviours. In addition they were presenting with the kind of sexual behaviours that we find the most difficult to work with. These children are the most difficult to engage in a therapeutic relationship due to their deep mistrust of all adults. They are also the most difficult to motivate to change and to implement effective external controls.

In our experience when dealing with sibling sexual behaviours our own departmental systems often struggle to acknowledge and work with risk in an explicit way. This may be due to lack of clarity about who is victim and victimiser and the pervasive nature of this particular category of behaviours. This often results in the responsibility for risk being subtly placed with carers.

We went on to use the framework as a tool in the first two workers meetings in an attempt to be explicit about the different factors impacting on risk and move towards a shared view of it. Using the framework in this way highlighted the systems that were impacting positively i.e., education, and helped to identify and prioritise areas of intervention in other systems. For example by invoking Child Protection Procedures the responsibility for managing the risk was shifted from individual ownership to one that was shared within the professional group. This promoted more open discussion with the foster carers about some of the problems they were experiencing.

In this case the framework highlighted and crystallised some of the difficult dilemmas for professionals and carers living with risk where there are clear factors making it significantly less manageable.

Preparation for Phase Two

Within the individual work we differentiate for the child between phase one and two. In the early stages of phase one we are realistic in our expectations and don't necessarily talk to the child about risk in any depth. Instead risk and risk management is discussed with the external systems. However once they have engaged and are becoming more responsive to our interventions, particularly in respect of their behaviours, we would see them as nearing the end of phase one. We would then be explicit about undertaking specific preparation work for them moving to phase two where the responsibility for managing risk is a shared process. This explicitness can have a real motivational impact on them. We would now introduce the concept of risk and move towards a shared understanding of what we mean by it. If it has not already been part of the work with the child, relapse prevention techniques will be identified and rehearsed, where appropriate. These strategies will be shared and rehearsed in the child's living environment. Because of the relationship and the work already done with the child there is a real feeling of partnership and of wanting to move towards a shared responsibility for risk management.

Phase Two

By this stage the child will have engaged in work, in particular they will have been able to discuss their behaviour and risk in a meaningful way with significant others. We'll have formulated predictive outcomes. The management of their risk is becoming a shared responsibility.

Aims

- Inform what factors impact on the ongoing manageability of the risk.
- Engaging the child in work towards achieving their predictive outcomes.
- Informed increasing and decreasing of external controls.

This is a period of intensive work with the child, our interventions are more in depth and the predictive outcomes are becoming more achievable. We are gauging the effectiveness of systems and continue to be responsive to their needs. At this stage we have usually moved from an educative role to exploring complimentary and integrated approaches.

Within the living environment in particular it is anticipated that there will be a joining with the child in negotiating and making decisions about risk on a day-to-day basis from an informed perspective. This would include:

- Anticipating situations or stresses in the child's daily life and formulating opinions about the child's ability to cope.
- Formulating an opinion about how manageable the child's risk is, based on the above.
- Being inclusive with the child in discussing the above and reaching a decision about risk.
- Being confident in decisions about increasing and decreasing external controls.
- Helping the child learn during this process through reflective practice and coaching using actual situations (reactive) or through anticipating situations (proactive).

The expectations of the child are equally different from phase one. Here we would be anticipating that they are much more able to demonstrate in their day-to-day living that they are attempting to apply their learning to a more pro-social lifestyle. In particular we would be anticipating that they are able to do the following:

- Engage in discussions about their emotions and feelings and how this might impact on risk.
- Accept the fluid nature of the increase and decrease of external controls and their own internal processes.
- Use the environment proactively to help them deal with challenging situations and emotions.
- Continue to use situations as learning processes.
- Accept the guidance and controls of their environment.

Inevitably this stage will at times be tense and workers sometimes describe it like walking a tight rope, balancing awareness and insight with unforeseen setbacks. These unforeseen circumstances may adversely affect a child's coping strategies. It is therefore crucial that they are prepared for experiencing difficult times during this process and that this may include resorting to patterns in thinking and behaviours

that could lead to more problem sexual behaviours. If they, and the environment, are prepared and given strategies for dealing with setbacks they will be much less likely to get into self-defeating pattern of behaviours. Instead the child's learning will be promoted and hopefully they will be more resilient and confident in handling future situations.

The above places expectations on the systems both in terms of embracing responsibility for managing risk and taking a clear role in progressing a child through change. However there are circumstances where this is not possible such as a child who is living with their birth family where there are enmeshed, unhealthy relationships or a young person, who has exhibited sexually abusive behaviour and is residing in their own tenancy. In these cases there are fewer opportunities to influence the environment and the systems are not necessarily able to accept responsibility for managing risk to the same extent.

In these circumstances it would not be possible to utilise the environment, in particular the living environment, as intensively. We would therefore use the framework in these cases to:

- Consider to what extent and be specific about how the systems are helpful or unhelpful in managing risk.
- Identify what parts of the systems can be targeted.
- Identify realistic areas for intervention e.g., in working with birth families with complex needs the framework has been helpful in ring fencing work that specifically addresses risk.
- Identify what additional resources would be useful in managing risk.

Practice Example – Phase Two

Alan aged 14 was referred to Halt following the sexual abuse of his younger sister. His background was characterised by violence and sexual abuse. He lived in a foster placement and while there his mother died from a drug-related illness.

Following an initial period of hostility and denial, Alan began to make significant progress in his sessions at Halt particularly in his ability to discuss his sexual behaviours and his risk in a realistic way. During the individual work in phase two he disclosed sexual abuse by his father and was allowing himself to be exposed to a whole host of painful and powerful feelings.

Figure 18.5:

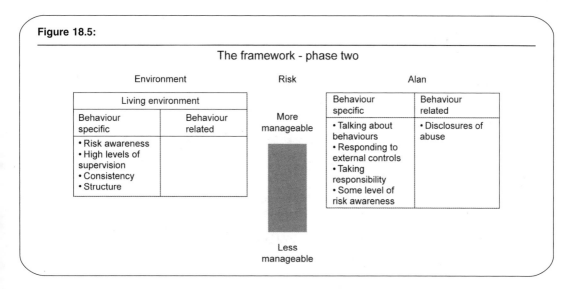

The framework - phase two

Living environment		Risk	Alan	
Behaviour specific	Behaviour related		Behaviour specific	Behaviour related
• Risk awareness • High levels of supervision • Consistency • Structure		More manageable Less manageable	• Talking about behaviours • Responding to external controls • Taking responsibility • Some level of risk awareness	• Disclosures of abuse

In these circumstances we would normally be predicting a positive outcome for such a child. However Alan's risk seemed to be becoming more unmanageable in his placement. Using the framework with his carers allowed us to explore this.

As can be seen in the framework there were many positive factors that should have been making Alan's risk more manageable.

Within his placement the carers were very behaviour focused and there was an adequate level of risk awareness and high levels of supervision. This provided Alan with the consistency and structure that he needed and benefited from. However there was a fundamental factor missing from his living environment that contributed to the carer's being unable to meet Alan's wider emotional needs. The carers were unable to view Alan holistically. Ironically, as he was making progress more demands were being made on his carers to meet these emotional needs. The more apparent their inability was becoming the less secure and contained Alan felt, so, in effect despite his progress his risk was becoming less manageable.

The framework helped the carers to explore Alan's risk in the context of their care and they were able to acknowledge that they had difficulty in seeing Alan beyond the abuse he had perpetrated. From this we were able to identify that Alan needed to move to a different placement where his wider therapeutic needs could be met.

Final phase

In this phase we would be making use of predictive outcomes, see Figure 18.6, to help us determine whether or not a child could take responsibility for managing their own risk and it would be expected that these would be evidenced within different environments. At this stage therefore the child would largely be responsible for managing his own risk as was developmentally appropriate.

Aims

- Systems to monitor and evaluate child's ability to manage their own risk.
- Systems to provide additional short-term supports as needed.
- Preparation for ending and disengagement from specialist resource.

In phase three the environment takes on a different and less interventionist role. They now have a monitoring, supportive and reflective role. This would include responding to any unforeseen stressors by reinforcing learning such as coping strategies, relapse prevention techniques etc.

Unlike in phase one the balance of responsibility has now shifted to the child. It is now expected that they can move on in their lives using the skills they have learned and retaining these and their insight to avoid further problem sexual behaviours. In particular we would anticipate that they have the following:

Figure 18.6: Example of predictive factors for child presenting with abusive sexual behaviour

Predictive outcomes

Environment	Risk	Child

Living environment	The young person	
• Monitoring • Evaluation • Observation • Reflecting • Responding	**Behaviour specific**	**Behaviour related**
	• Developed meaning to behaviours	• Demonstrates new coping strategies
Departmental systems	• Realistic appreciation of risk and risk factors	• Increased emotional awareness and self regulation
Family		
	• Accepts responsibility actions	• Increase in general empathy skills
Education		
	• Increased victim empathy awareness	• Improved social skills
Social		
	• Demonstrated use of relapse prevention strategies	• Increased ability to resolve conflict and make decisions
		• Increased self concept and self esteem

- Increased internal resources.
- An awareness that managing risk is something they may need to continue to do and that these skills are now incorporated in their lifestyle.
- A means of accessing future help from the systems around them e.g., their families or Halt.

At Halt we work hard to create an ending that facilitates the child being able to utilise relapse prevention strategies in their futures. The Project continues to be a resource through which they can action assistance if required

Conclusion

The framework has made the internal and external influences on risk more tangible, offering the opportunity to consider how the interactions of these influences impact on risk. Its application has enhanced our interventions in a number of ways:

- It clearly highlights the factors that impact on risk.
- It recognises and utilises the crucial role that meeting needs has in relation to managing risk.

- Risk is demystified and therefore naturally becomes easier to implement strategies towards a more effective management.
- It offers realistic expectations of the child and the risk they present dependant on where they are in the intervention process.
- It highlights issues of accountability and responsibility and therefore promotes a shared responsibility.
- It reduces feelings of being overwhelmed and disempowered by enabling the systems around the child.
- It naturally encourages an integrated approach.
- It is simple and easy to understand.

For the child, as a working tool it also has clear advantages:

- It helps the child understand why and what makes their risk fluctuate.
- It enhances relapse prevention work.
- It acts as a powerful motivator in the change process for the child.
- It joins the child to their significant adults that truly facilitates their change.

Overall the framework is being positively received by Glasgow City Council's Social Work

Services and we are currently presenting it on a strategic level to different managerial systems and related services. In addition to our on going interventions we are also using the framework in our consultation service, therefore social workers, residential staff and foster carers are participants in its application to practice. A recent evaluation of the project highlighted that the co-ordinated approach is viewed positively by carers and professional staff. It is hoped that Glasgow City Council will adopt the Risk Management Framework and that Area Teams will apply it when they are working with or considering children with a range of problem sexual behaviours.

The framework will continue to evolve and we would welcome any comments that will contribute to its further development.
* We have used the term 'child' throughout this chapter referring to children up to 18 years as defined in the Children (Scotland) Act 1995: s93[2][a]

References

Archer, C. (2000) *Next Steps in Parenting The Child Who Hurts*. Jessica Kingsley.

Briere, J. (1995) *Child Abuse Trauma Theory and Treatment of The Lasting Effects*. Sage Publications.

Calder, M.C. (Ed.) (1999) *Working With Young People Who Sexually Abuse: New Pieces of The Jigsaw Puzzle*. Lyme Regis, Russell House Publishing.

Finkelhor, D. (1984) *Sourcebook on Child Sexual Abuse*. Sage.

Gil, E. and Johnson, T.C. (1993) *Sexualised Children: Assessment and Treatment of Sexualised Children and Children Who Molest*. Rockville, Md, Launch Press.

Howe, D. et al. (1999) *Attachment Theory, Child Maltreatment and Family Support*, Macmillan.

Howe, D. and Fearnley, S. (1999) Disorders of Attachment and Attachment Therapy. *Adoption and Fostering*. 23: 2.

James, B. (1989) *Treating Traumatised Children New Insights and Creative Interventions*, Lexington Books.

Lane, S. (1991) *Juvenile Sexual Offending*. Ryan and Lane.

Lyons-Ruth, K. (1996) Attachment Relationships Among Children With Aggressive Behaviour Problems: The Role of Disorganised Early Attachment Patterns. *Journal of Consulting and Clinical Psychology*, 64, 64–73. Cited in Howe, D. and Fearnley, S. (1999) Disorders of Attachment and Attachment Therapy. *Adoption and Fostering*. 23: 2.

Ryan, G., Lane, S., Davis, J. and Isaccs, C. (1987) Juvenile Sex Offenders: Development and Correction. *Child Abuse and Neglect*, 385–95.

Ryan, G. (1998) Paper Presented at Nota Conference.

Chapter Nineteen

The Use of Sex Offender Registration with Young People Who Sexually Abuse

Robert E. Longo and Martin C. Calder

An overview of registration laws

In the United States of America, both convicted sex offenders and innocent citizens have experienced serious and negative consequences resulting from the implementation of the Jacob Wetterling Crimes against Children and Sexually Violent Offender Registration Act (Pub. L. 104–145,110 Stat.1345) passed in 1994, which included a national sex offender registration law and a sex offender notification law which was passed in 1996 (Megan's Law), requiring public notification of sex offender release. The Jacob Wetterling Act is a national law that is designed to protect children and was named after Jacob Wetterling, an eleven-year-old boy who was kidnapped in October 1989. Jacob is still missing. As is the case with similar laws regarding sexual offenders, this law was based upon a single horrific crime perpetrated by an adult offender.

The Sexually Violent Offender Registration Act required all states to establish stringent registration programmes for sex offenders by September 1997. However, when enacted, these laws were applicable to both adult and juvenile sexual offenders. Unfortunately, when such laws are applied to juveniles, issues regarding development, cognitive ability, and mental illness are not considered. Since the inception of these laws in the USA, similar laws have been enacted in the UK. This chapter reviews the implications and impact of these laws on juveniles in both the USA and the UK.

The first law to address the registration of sex offenders in the USA was passed in California in 1947. Presently, all 50 states have sex offender registration laws 29 states[1] require some or all juveniles adjudicated for sex offences to register

(Matson, 2002), and all 50 states have sex offender public notification laws. Most of the states that register juveniles also do some kind of notification in certain situations.[2]

Sex offender registration laws, especially those open to the public and especially through the Internet,[3] seem logical to their supporters. In the USA the number of sexual offenders who are registered continues to increase with time. For example, in April 1998 there were 263,166 sex offenders registered in the USA (US Department of Justice, 2002). By February 2002, that number had grown to 386,112 (US Department of Justice, 2002). These numbers are not broken down by adult and adolescent offenders, however, in the USA it is estimated that between 30–50% of child sexual abuse is perpetrated by juveniles and 10–20% of rapes are perpetrated by juveniles. Conservatively, this means that over 150,000 juvenile sex offenders appear on sex offender registries.

In the UK legislation has been in place since 1933 to identify offenders who have committed offences against children (includes young people) that secures them a label of being a schedule one offender for life. This basically means that when they appear in families or employment where they have access to children a risk assessment is undertaken. The enduring problem has been one of tracking their movements as there was no requirement to notify professionals of their moves unless it was a condition of their supervision.

A series of high-profile cases where children were seriously hurt and even murdered by known sex offenders (such as Sidney Cooke and Robert Oliver) provided a political incentive to introduce a new piece of legislation in the UK

---

[1] Alabama, Arizona, Arkansas, California, Colorado, Delaware, Idaho, Illinois, Indiana (age 14 or older), Iowa, Kentucky, Louisiana, Massachusetts, Michigan, Minnesota, Mississippi (if twice adjudicated for a sex offense), Montana, New Jersey, Nevada, North Carolina, Oregon, Rhode Island, South Carolina, South Dakota (age 15 or older), Texas, Vermont, Virginia, Washington, Wisconsin.

[2] California, Colorado, Idaho, Minnesota, Mississippi, Missouri, North Carolina, and South Dakota register juveniles, but do not perform notification on them.

[3] In 1999 15 states had sex offender registries maintained on websites. By 2001 29 states had sex offender registries on web sites.

that required registration and ongoing professional monitoring. The Government's proposal to create a national register of convicted sex offenders was based on three arguments: to help police identify suspects after a crime, to help prevent such crimes, and to help deter such crimes. The argument for a register appeared therefore to be that sex offenders find it difficult to change their behaviour and sex offender treatment programmes have limited success. That being the case, the offender coming out of prison may continue to pose a threat and will need close supervision by the probation service. At present, when such supervision has ended, the former offender has a free hand to go where he likes and, live where he likes. Indeed, he has all his civic rights and duties restored to him as a free citizen. If he however continues to be seen as a threat, such freedom will only enhance the potential threat.

In the UK, sex offender registration was introduced through the Sex Offender Act (1997), which came into force on the 1st September 1997. It requires those who have convictions for certain specified offences to register with the police in the area in which they live, and to provide and keep up to date information about their whereabouts. The Act's stated purpose is to ensure the accuracy of the information on sex offenders recorded on the police national computer. Prior to the introduction of the Act, this information was often limited to the address of the offender at the time of his conviction, and was therefore very often out of date.

Guidance issued in support of the Act has made it clear, however, that the purpose is not simply to record the information but to use it proactively to undertake risk assessments of all convicted sex offenders living in the community and to monitor the activities of those who are considered to represent a significant risk.

The Act is not retrospective. It applies only to persons convicted after the 1st September and those who, on the date of implementation, were serving community or custodial sentences for relevant offences (in this respect it could be said in a limited way to be retrospective). The Home Office estimated that there were around 4,000 offenders in prison on the 1st September to whom the provisions of the Act would apply.

Qualifying offences include rape, buggery and indecent assaults on adult men or women and incest, rape indecent assault and other indecency offences involving children. A complete list of all

the qualifying offences is set out in Schedule 1 of the Act. Schedule 1 of the Sex Offenders Act is substantially different from Schedule 1 of the Children and Young Persons Act 1933 in that, among other differences it includes sexual offences against adults and excludes offences involving physical assaults on children. It does attract the requirement to register, however. Unfortunately the introduction of a second 'schedule one' list is a recipe for confusion.

Those convicted of a qualifying offence after the 1st September, 1997 will be issued with a certificate by the Court in which they are convicted. This certificate provides confirmation of the conviction or finding and contains a summary of the registration requirements with which the offender must comply. A copy of the certificate is sent to the police criminal records unit, in the area in which the offender normally resides, and, where a prison sentence is imposed, to the relevant custodial establishment. The custodial establishment will inform the police of the prisoner's release date.

All those who are liable to register must, within 14 days of conviction or release:

- Inform the local police of their name(s), date of birth and current address.
- Report any subsequent change of address within 14 days of the change.
- Notify the police of any other address at which they stay or are resident for 14 days or longer in any 12-month period.

Notification may be provided in writing or by going in person to any police station in the area where the offender is living. Responsibility for registration lies with the offender himself. Supervising probation officers are expected to ensure that the offender is aware of the requirements but are not directly responsible for ensuring compliance. However, agency procedures generally require confirmation of the advice given to the offender to be provided to him in writing with a copy to the local police. The offender must register within 14 days of sentence or release. Failure to register is a criminal offence punishable by a fine and up to 6 months' imprisonment.

Offenders under 18 years cannot be sent to prison for failing to comply with the registration requirements. However, the court in which the juvenile offender is convicted can impose the notification requirement on the offender's parent or guardian. In the case of young people who are looked after, the local authority can, by order of the court imposing sentence, be made responsible for discharging the registration requirements.

The length of time for which the registration requirements apply depends upon the length of the sentence imposed for the qualifying offence or offences. In the case of young people under the age of 18 years, the period of registration is half that which would apply if an adult had received a similar sentence.

Length of sentence	Adults	Juveniles
Life imprisonment	Indefinite	Indefinite
Hospital [restriction order]	Indefinite	Indefinite
>30 months prison	Indefinite	Indefinite
6 months to 30 months	10 years	5 years
<6 months prison	7 years	3 and a half years
Hospital [no restriction order]	7 years	3 and a half years
Non custodial sentence or caution	5 years	2 and a half years

The notification period starts from the date of caution, conviction or release from sentence. When a court convicts a person of one of the qualifying offences it will issue a certificate to the offender and send a copy to the police. The police will issue a similar certificate where the offender receives a caution.

Home Office Circular 39/97 directs the police to undertake a risk assessment in respect of each offender in order to determine:

- Generally, the potential threat to the community.
- Specifically, the immediate threat to any persons with whom the offender may be having contact (including members of the same household).

The police will receive notification of an individual's requirement to register from a number of sources e.g., from courts following sentence, and from prisons prior to the offender's release. Within two weeks of notification (and regardless of actual registration) the local Crime Management Unit (CMU) must complete an initial intelligence check and risk assessment which will include:

- Details of all previous sex offences including sentences.

- Details of all offences involving violence.
- The method and pattern of the individual's offending.
- Details of any treatment received.
- Attitude towards victims/offences.
- Any significant relationships with other sex offenders.

In gathering information and undertaking the assessment of risk the CMU is expected to liaise with other police units and with other agencies that may have a contribution to make. In particular, the local probation service will be contacted in order to establish whether the offender is currently under supervision or has been known to them in the past. The probation service is itself required to undertake an assessment of the potential for harm and the risk of re-offending for all clients with whom they are involved or on whom they have prepared a pre-sentence report.

Following the completion of the initial intelligence check and risk assessment each offender will be provisionally assigned to one of the following categories:

- Screened out – low/ moderate risk.
- Screened in – offender in custody – high risk.
- Screened in – offender in community – high risk.

Where an offender is screened out this decision will be reported to other agencies and the case will be reviewed in 6 to 12 months. Where an offender is screened in, i.e., assessed as high risk, consideration will need to be given to the development of a strategy for managing the risk. This will include consideration of whether the criteria for referral to a Multi-Agency Protection Panel (MAPP) are met. All cases where there is thought to be a need for disclosure to a third party must be referred to the MAPP. Home visits by the police are considered to be an important source of information in undertaking the risk assessment and in verifying the information provided to the register by the offender.

There is another major piece of legislation in the UK that impacts directly on young people who have sexually abused. The Crime and Disorder Act (1998) signalled a more interventionist approach designed to hold offenders accountable for their behaviour. This legislation introduced a gravity matrix which allocates a number of points according to a particular offence (for example, gross indecency, two points; rape, four points). All offences are given a gravity score to aid the decision-making process. The scores range from 1 (minimum response) to 4 (always charge). Aggravating and mitigating factors are listed which could increase or decrease a gravity score, taking into consideration the circumstances of the offence. You can only increase or decrease the baseline gravity factor by one point, no matter how many of the aggravating or mitigating factors may be present. This creates immense problems as it assumes an informed decision can be taken based solely on criminogenic factors. The time frame of expecting the charge sergeant to dispose of the case within four hours is an additional problem and precludes an informed social assessment. There is a danger that an imbalanced and hasty decision will lead to more young people being charged and placed before the courts, potentially clogging up the system with young people who may not represent a huge risk for re-offending.

Accompanying this came a broader and much needed review of sex offender legislation. 'Setting the Boundaries' (Home Office, 2000: p58) acknowledged that young people do sexually abuse as well as experiment and it defines the criminal law as providing 'a remedy that can be used to deal with those children who do abuse'. They went on to note that 'a variety of suggestions have been made as to the best way to treat young abusers' and included 'that wherever possible they should be removed from the criminal justice system, and civil remedies, together with welfare support, should be used to tackle abusive behaviour'. They declined to process this further, arguing that 'the principles of the punishment or treatment of young offenders is beyond our remit, but we did consider that whatever approach was adopted needed to reflect the basic principles of protecting the community and the individual and preventing re-offending' (p59).This represents a timely rebuke and challenge to the legislation requiring sex offender registration for young people who sexually abuse.

In their recommendations, they argued that it is:

... important that these young offenders are given appropriate sentences and disposals to ensure that they do not continue to pose a risk to others, and they receive appropriate treatment. Baseline assessment of these children was important for the courts in sentencing them appropriately, and we thought it was essential that courts had available a detailed specialist assessment of the child, to inform the judges' decision on sentencing and disposal. This would need to take into

account the perceived risk that the young offender presents, which should also include situational factors such as family perceptions; collusion; denial etc, and any kind of abuse suffered by the offender ...

(p59).

Revisiting sex offender registration and notification laws

In previous publications, Calder (2001) and Freeman-Longo (1996a, 1996b, 2002) noted problems associated with sex offender registration and notification laws. Freeman-Longo and Blanchard (1998) commented that appropriate and useful legislation requires close examination of its potential effects on citizens before it is enacted. The creation of any law requires the resources to fund and uphold it. Sex offender registration laws require an understanding of how they will serve the citizens they are designed to protect.

Since the passage of the sex offender registration laws, there have been many instances of violence toward sexual offenders and innocent persons. Some states in the USA have posted registration lists on compact disks (CDs) and more recently on the Internet. Numerous problems have occurred, including, among others, innocent families being harassed, adolescents being harassed at school and in the community, families of juvenile sex offenders being harassed, victims of sexual abuse being identified, and private residences of law-abiding citizens being posted on registries and the Internet as the residences of sex offenders. Some states have applied these laws retroactively, resulting in persons charged with indecent exposure for urinating publicly being labelled as sex offenders. Other states have applied registration to young people, labelling children as sex offenders for life. The list of problems does not stop here.

In the United States, sex offender registration laws and sex offender notification laws are closely linked. Given some of the negative fallout from registration and notification laws, more challenges to these laws have been forthcoming. In November 2002 the US Supreme Court heard testimony challenging the laws. Boston Globe news reporter, Lyle Denniston (2002) noted that the Supreme Court took up two constitutional issues in the November hearings.

The first case tested whether it is a form of punishment to require convicted sex offenders who have served a sentence to register with authorities and then have their names, addresses, and sometimes pictures released to the public and, in 28 states, posted on the Internet. If that approach does amount to punishment, it cannot be imposed on individuals who were convicted before a state passed a Megan's Law. That issue arose in a test of an Alaska law.

The second case tested whether it is unconstitutional to display, on the Internet and in other public venues, the identities of convicted sex offenders without first establishing, at a hearing, that they remain dangerous. That issue was before the court in a test of a Connecticut law.

Sherry Colb (2002) also noted in relationship to these hearings:

Many states provide for a very broad dissemination of the registration data, so that information about names and locations of ex-sex offenders may, for example, be available on the Internet. Those who challenged the Connecticut and Alaska versions of the law last week asserted that notification provisions provide for punishment after the fact, in violation of the Constitution's Ex Post Facto Clause. They also argued that these provisions stigmatize people as posing a continuing danger to the public, without the benefit of a hearing.

During an exchange with one of the attorneys during oral argument, Chief Justice Rehnquist asked whether posting the names and photographs of the FBI's 'Ten Most Wanted' criminal suspects in public places violates anyone's rights. The lawyer, predictably, responded that it does not.

The lawyer's response, however, is not nearly as revealing as Rehnquist's question itself – suggesting, as it does, that Megan's Laws and 'Ten Most Wanted' lists are comparable. Consider the implicit analogy between the two . . .

. . . And that is why Megan's Laws can pose a serious threat of violence. The families that live near John Doe understandably begin to resent that he is there and that he could, in theory, strike again at any time. They assume, perhaps incorrectly, that he has not truly reformed and that their children are not safe as long as he lives in the neighbourhood. They conclude that it would be better for everyone if Doe moved away.

One method of bringing about this desired change would be to frighten Doe into moving, perhaps by leaving threatening notes or resorting to vandalism or worse. Peaceful co-existence with a person known or presumed to be dangerous to the neighbourhood children may ultimately lead to a not-so-peaceful attempt to end that co-existence.

There are 450,000 registered sex offenders in the USA. Some states consign flasher and rapist to the same Internet purgatory. About 22 states treat every sex offender as someone who was, is, and

will be forever dangerous. Linda Greenhouse (2002), a reporter for the New York Times writes:

According to the Justice Department, the number of people imprisoned for sex crimes from 1980 to 1994 grew at a faster rate than for any other category of violent crime. To cite one example of the intensity of public interest, the Web site on which Connecticut posted the whereabouts of convicted sex offenders – before the site was shut down by the court decision the state is now appealing – was visited more than 3 million times in its first five months in a state with a population of only 3.4 million people.

Connecticut is one of 25 states that publicise the whereabouts of all those who have committed particular sex offences. By contrast, other states make individual assessments of the potential dangerousness of each offender.

Dr. Robert J. McLaughlin of Texas explains:

Texas now allows judges the discretion to determine whether a juvenile must register with the state as a sex offender and whether the youth will be subject to public notification. Treatment providers in Texas have indicated the law creates new dilemmas for treatment providers.

The court is to consider two criteria pertaining to registration and public notification. First, is community safety served by the registration (and public notification) of this youth? Second, does the harm or potential harm to the youth or family due to registration (or public notification) outweigh the (presumed) increase in community safety offered by registering this youth? Judges may decide at the time of adjudication but in our jurisdiction tend to defer the decision for some period of months. Youth already registered under prior laws may file a one-time motion to the court to be 'de-registered' or at least removed from public notification.

Dr. Craig Latham of Massachusetts points out yet another dilemma with registration and notification laws:

'Providing the court information about the practical effects of registration, may keep a youth in treatment, however, youth dangerous enough to justify community notification should not be in the community in the first place.'

And Jim Grady, Executive Director of a 52-bed residential treatment programme for sexually aggressive adolescents at New Hope Treatment Centres (NHTC) in South Carolina states:

"By taking an appropriate stance (with the courts and the general public) and avoiding making narcissistic generalisations when it comes to assigning risk to kids, we move closer to the opportunity for change. The

danger out there (in the community and juvenile justice system) is that others do not necessarily take the same stance. Courts and systems get confused because for every professional who sticks to the scientific facts (or who testifies as to the absence of scientific facts) there are five others who will render a 'clinical' opinion, masked as science that meets the needs of a scared and misinformed system.

I would also note that with adolescents, 'generally accepted practice standards' are also not science. The fact remains that with these kids (adolescents) we have no valid scientific risk instrument for 'sexual offences'. and I hope we never claim to have one.

We might instead place our efforts into what makes up the most appropriate treatment model and continuum of care for kids with behavioural problems that include sexual problems. I would imagine risk decreases substantially when kids and their families work with a system that is educated, compassionate, and provides supportive and appropriate interventions.

In a recent story by Ellen Goodman of the Boston Globe, she writes:

... In Alaska, sex offenders include rapists, but they also include someone convicted of indecent exposure. They include paedophiles, but they also include 19-year-old boys who had consensual but illegal sex with 14-year-old girls ...

In Connecticut, anyone who has ever been convicted of a sexual offence goes up on the Web – for life – without a chance to prove he's no longer dangerous ...

There are 450,000 registered sex offenders in this country. Some states consign flashers and rapists to the same Internet purgatory.

Reporter Kelby Hartson Carr recently reported:

... Virginia's online sexual offender registry is being challenged in a lawsuit that alleges it is unconstitutional ...

... Other states with nearly identical registries have faced problems, including Michigan, whose site was shut down in June. Now, the nation awaits a U.S. Supreme Court decision on Connecticut's registry, which mirrors Virginia's ...

... Last month, Virginia Attorney General Jerry Kilgore filed a brief in support of Connecticut's case. A U.S. Supreme Court decision could force many states to revamp or shut down their Web sites ...

... Proponents of the registries say they give parents a tool for safeguarding their children against predators ... Those challenging the registries argue they violate offenders' rights because all violent offenders automatically must register ...

... The government should prove that an offender remains a threat after release from jail, they assert. The issue is a particularly sensitive one in the Fredericksburg, VA region ...

... The high-profile kidnappings and slayings of the young Lisk sisters and Sofia Silva in recent years made area parents hyper-aware of the potential threats from sexual predators ...

...'Everybody's comfort level changed once that happened', said Eric Olson, a Stafford County prosecutor who handles many sexual offence cases. 'We realised it's not something that just happens to other kids'. ...

... Even so, having the sexual offender registry would probably have done nothing to prevent those murders ... Local law enforcement officials believe they finally have a suspect in the slayings ... But [he] was never a registered sex offender ...

Registries nationwide have been criticised. They are self-reported, which means convicts must be trusted to provide reliable information, including all changes of address and employment ...

... The suit also argues that the registry is retroactive, which means someone who was perhaps innocent, but pleaded guilty to avoid jail time a long time ago, was not aware of this new punishment they face today. Many previous offenders are not a threat, yet they suffer the indignities of having their backgrounds online. This can be devastating, costing them jobs, forcing them to flee neighbourhoods and subjecting them to vigilantism.

... Statistics show that sexual offenders actually have among the lowest re-arrest rates. The U.S. Bureau of Justice Statistics tracked prisoners released in 1994 for the following three years. Those convicted of sexual assault and rape had among the lowest rates: 41.4% and 46%, respectively, were re-arrested in three years.

Conversely, those who committed property crimes had substantially higher recidivism rates; 78.8% of those convicted of motor vehicle theft, for example, were arrested again during the study period ...

In the UK, the registration requirement was never likely to yield the results hoped for. It has struggled to protect the community as there is no requirement to notify those living in the area that a resident is a risk to children in their community. Where word emerges of the offender then they receive undue attention every time there is an offence in their area. Since 90% of sex offenders never get prosecuted or convicted then it is likely that professionals and the community are focusing in the wrong place and this allows the 'real offender to continue their abusive behaviour. It is also a dubious proposition as to whether registers will prevent offending. Sex offenders are very careful in their planning and thus are unlikely to offend in their own neighbourhood. They may well travel between areas and unless this is managed on a 24-hour basis then the register becomes meaningless as a preventative tool. Valios (1998) reported on social work views of sex offender registration. They deemed it a flop as it did not include convictions before September 1997 and over one-third said it had made no impact on their management of sex offenders in the year since its inception. However, 60% felt as though the public debate around sex offenders was more likely to effect child protection. Half felt that the community should be told if a convicted sex offender moved into their area (a slightly smaller proportion than the public as a whole). Not all members of the public agreed that the whole community should be in the know, with 17% saying information should be restricted to local head teachers, while 4% thought that only neighbours should be told. 16% thought that headteachers and neighbours should be told. Interestingly, almost 67% of social workers thought that children and young people under 18 should be included on the sex offender register. 5% wanted children aged 10 and under to be named. The average lowest age social workers thought should be included was 15 years old.

Juvenile sex offenders and registration laws

We will focus our efforts in this chapter on the application of registration laws to juveniles. For the purposes of this chapter, we will use the term Juvenile Sex Offender (JSO), although we recognise that the terms, children with sexual behaviour problems, adolescents who sexually abuse, adolescents with sexual behaviour problems, are becoming increasing more popular and appropriate as phases used to describe young people with sexual behaviour problems. We will also use the term JSO to incorporate those unfortunate children under the age of 13 who may be subject to registration laws at an even earlier age than formal adolescence.

Our concern for writing this chapter is that while many people believe that registration laws for JSOs are useful and preventive, the contrary is generally true. There are numerous problems associated with JSO registration laws, which we will demonstrate, that include: the laws' one, are not effective at preventing future sex crimes, two, give the public a false sense of safety, and three, damage the lives of JSOs, their families, and others in a variety of ways. No law can ultimately stop behaviour. Registration laws and public notification laws, especially as applied to youth, are not going to prevent sexually abusive and/or aggressive behaviour from occurring. In fact, these laws may go on to not only damage these

young lives, but also further delay their individual potential for healthy recovery.

Schwartz et al. (1993) found that the majority of American citizens favour trying juveniles as adults for serious crimes. Such a view is associated with an increased public fear of victimisation, particularly in older citizens.

There are growing concerns about the register overall, and there are some issues particular to the juvenile population. Brown (1998) has argued that they need to be treated differently from their adult counterparts both because of their age and maturity and because of the nature of their offending behaviour. In addition, the low rate of disclosure, the high rate of denial among young people and their families and the variation across the country in the type of offence pursued by the courts or through a caution means that young people in different parts of the country are treated in a very different way.

Brown identified four potential difficulties for young people, which we have added to and expanded upon:

Disclosure and investigation: whilst we do not want to ignore sexual behaviour of concern, there is no national uniformity around how to deal with particular presenting situations. This leads to a huge inconsistency in how young people are dealt with. There is a case to be made which allows us to address the behaviour but outside the criminalisation of the activity. There should be an assessment pre-disposal in order to filter out those cases where a repetition of the sexual behaviour is considered unlikely. The standards and timescales accompanying the Crime and Disorder Act (1998) are making this almost impossible and where they are taking place, within unrealistically short timescales. At the other extreme, there is evidence of serious sexual abuse being diverted from the legal system, thus giving the message out that their behaviour is OK.

The need for a register: Registration of adults who commit sexual offences is based on a need to monitor those who may re-offend so that there is some protection for the public. Adults who have developed a pattern of offending are likely to find opportunities to re-offend. However, most young people have not been offending for long enough to develop a clear pattern of abusing and many are still very immature. With appropriate intervention, the risk of long-term offending is low for the majority of young people. Those young people who are assessed as high-risk do need to be registered as they become adults.

Issues of denial: This is a feature of most young people, largely because of fear and a lack of understanding of what is likely to happen to them as a result of their behaviour which they have not fully understood. They know what they did was sexual but they often lack the maturity to fully recognise the consequences and effects of their behaviour on others and on themselves. They are not aware of the processes, which lead to patterns of offending because no one has ever looked with them at exactly what is going on. They do not usually have any sense of their own motives and may not make any links with their own experiences as victims or have a real understanding of their own values about sexual issues. They may have been brought up with a skewed understanding about the reasons for sex and its meaning and never have had an opportunity to clarify this. There is a real need to have time to overcome denial, working through the fears and enabling the young person to become motivated to change.

Risks to the young person: one of the difficulties young people who have been involved in abusing behaviour often face is the reaction of their local community. Because of the variations in how young people are expected to report, there are still circumstances where they go to the police station, wait in a queue and announce the reason for their visit. It is hardly surprising that this information may leak out locally and cause problems. This may penalise them inappropriately and they may run the continuing risk of ostracism or actual physical violence.

There has to be some genuine concern that registration, in itself, is either helpful to the young person or the community at large. Because we are often uncomfortable with their sexuality and the ways in which it finds expression, we are at risk of treating them all like 'little adults' and ascribing to them motivations and understanding, which they have not yet developed. In doing so, we label and subscribe their behaviour so that they, their families and the other agencies involved with them, think that there is no possibility of change.

Clearly, if the registration system serves to increase the apprehensions and resistance of parents to engage in treatment work, then the potential gains will have been more than outweighed by the alienation of the group most critical to the monitoring and management of juveniles, the parents.

Professionals, educators and others need to understand that sexual behaviour is on a

continuum. Not all behaviours are the same. As Cordelia Anderson notes:

I deal so much with this issue. I spend a great deal of time in schools k-12 helping staff discern the sexual behaviour continuum and think about appropriate 'restorative interventions.' I want them to think about the slippery slope of pushing everything into legal verses educational responses. Sexual behaviours are behaviours. Sexual harm is harm. Sexual violence is violence. Our children need to learn what is appropriate and what isn't. What is expected and what isn't. What is harmful and what isn't and not just wait until we charge them with sexual harassment or criminal sexual conduct. We're piloting a whole piece on reduction of sexual harm.

Problems associated with juvenile sex offender registration laws

Freeman-Longo (1996a, 1996b, 2002) has noted that there are several potential problems that are inherent with registration laws. Many of these problems have continued to persist over time despite being pointed out to lawmakers and others, and in particular impact young people who sexually abuse when subjected to such laws.

Below is a list of problems that have been associated with these laws in the past as well as continue to be problematic in their application to youth. In some areas recent cases are cited as examples of how these laws can negatively impact young people required to comply with them, as well as how communities, families, and others can be adversely affected when subject to these laws.

Behaviour taken out of context

There are several instances when persons have been charged with behaviours that may not constitute a sexual offence but the nature of the charges resulted in the person being listed on sex offender registries. It is common to charge a person with public indecency for urinating in a public area. In many states public indecency falls under a crime that has resulted in these persons being listed on sex offender registries. In Ann Arbor, Michigan, it was a common ritual for University students to 'streak' across the campus during an annual college event. The police chief of Ann Arbor announced that anyone caught 'streaking' would be charged with public indecency and listed in the sex offender registry.

A professional who chooses to remain anonymous recounts this most recent situation that happened to her son:

I know of many horrendous cases and I also happen to have a son who is on the registry because at age 18 he had consensual over-the-clothes sexual contact with a 15 year-old. In my state, he will be on the registry for 25 years, and even if he were to move elsewhere, he will still be bound to this under this state's law. When his case came up, I informed them this 'incident' occurred in my home. I went into the room to be introduced to her, I even asked her age (she lied, and said she was 16, which is legal age of consent) but we were told none of this was relevant, and to plea to the misdemeanour since the only relevant issue was what her birth certificate said, not consent, not lying ... nothing could change the outcome. Of course, so it would still be 'just a misdemeanour,' we took the plea, not realising the punishment would last longer than most sentences for murder – complete with public shame and a constant cloud.

As you might guess, though I have been a victim advocate for years, I feel strongly this matter has gotten far out of hand. There is now a group in my state working to change the laws here. I think its called Second Chance.

Cost to the public

Sex offender registration laws (SOR) require continuous monitoring by public service agencies (police, courts, and probation agencies) to ensure offender compliance. In the USA, public/government funds have had to finance the costs of this mandated law (which did not come with funding for implementation). Some localities have reported that the initial cost of setting up registration and notification has been as high as $200,000. Additional costs are an ongoing fiscal challenge, such as those for law enforcement agencies and other agencies in the criminal justice system responsible for maintaining and updating the registries and conducting notification. Despite these costs, most states acknowledge that the registries are not accurate. Monies would be better spent on prevention (see below).

Subsequent violence

SOR has lead to further violence. Many youth who are identified as sexual offenders through SOR, have been harassed by peers and others, in their communities, and at school. In many cases the families of these targeted youth also suffer the consequences. The case of Jeff:

Jeff is a sixteen year-old male who was sent to a residential treatment facility in north-eastern USA. Jeff's mother lived in a small New England town where most people finally heard about and knew what Jeff had done. As a result, Jeff's mother slowly became an outcast in her own community and received threats of harm to both Jeff and her if she did not move. Eventually, she caved in under the pressure out of fear for her son and her own personal safety and moved to a new town.

Confidentiality

The American Psychiatric Association's Diagnostic and Statistical Manual of Mental Disorders-IV-TR classifies the sexual abuse of children under a diagnostic category known as paedophilia. Public notification laws require that this mental health/medical diagnosis be made public, while many other harmful conditions and behaviours remain private. For youth 16 years of age and older (who can be diagnosed with paedophilia) their rights to privacy from a medical and mental health standpoint are compromised.

The use of confidentiality waivers is commonplace in working with sex offenders, including JSOs. Unfortunately, when the details of their lives and crimes are posted on public registries and divulged through notification, it is not only the offenders' confidentiality that is violated. Through the misuse and abuse of these laws, the names and addresses of families and, in some cases, the victims of sexual abuse are unfortunately revealed. This is likely to happen with interfamilial sexual abuse as well.

Excessive punishment

Legal scholars and others have looked at public notification and sex offender registration laws as a form of punishment. Arguments addressing this very issue were heard in the United States Supreme Court on November 13, 2002. There are several examples of how professionals and others have used this law beyond the way it was designed.

For example, in some cases, law enforcement personnel have organised neighbourhoods to exclude sex offenders from housing. Additionally, law enforcement officers and others have released inaccurate information about registered sex offenders and those subject to notification laws (Dennis, 1999). When these laws harm sex offenders and others (e.g., their families and other community members) beyond the intent of the law, how can one not consider the impact as cruel, unusual, and excessive punishment?

Prevention

The best way to stop sexual abuse is to prevent it before it begins. Public notification laws are tertiary prevention efforts at best, and the antithesis of prevention at their worst. When laws result in a decrease in reporting of a particular crime, increased plea-bargaining, and causing harm to innocent people, they cannot be seen as preventive. The arguments used over and over again in favour of sex offender registration and public notification laws have been that if they save one child, they are worth it. But is any law worth harming others, especially innocent persons, for the sake of one?

Most public health officials believe primary prevention is much less costly and more effective than tertiary prevention. Treating sex offenders is primary prevention, especially when treatment is successful and the abuser no longer reoffends. In New Jersey, one of the side effects from Megan's Law and the sex offender registry is a reluctance to prosecute juveniles for sex offences, thus subjecting them to lifelong registration. The 'diverted' juvenile sex offenders are not getting treatment (Brieling, 1998).

Current efforts by the Centres for Disease Control and Prevention (CDC) and other professionals are looking at the method of offending, Modus Operandi (MO) in an effort to better understand why JSOs sexually abuse and how we can prevent them from abusing in the first place. Public funds would be better placed and utilised in conducting such research rather that the ongoing support of laws that have yet to be proven effective, and cause harm to the juveniles, their families, and communities.

Registration laws are virtually impossible to research regarding their efficacy. It is not possible to accurately determine that a child or adult has avoided being sexually abused, and thus an uncommitted crime not reported. We would better spending government, public and private funds (and time) on prevention efforts with young persons, early identification of young persons at risk to become sexually abusive, and education programmes to raise the public's awareness about JSOs and sexual abuse.

Kathy Lowenberg, director of a counselling programme in Iowa notes:

'I work with many young children who are 'abuse-reactive' and sexually perpetrate on younger children. They need treatment but not to be treated like hardened criminals. Education is the key. Unfortunately, at least here in Iowa, what I see is many counties without the professionals available to treat these young people, so they are simply ignored until their sexual acting out behaviours become habitual and (eventually) criminal. At that point, I see them as referrals from the Juvenile Court Services. This is a travesty for everyone involved. Foster parents, parents, case-workers, and therapists need to understand how important it is to intervene in a positive clinical way in the lives of these young abusers. Here in Iowa City, I am trying to promote the usefulness of doing Psycho-sexual evaluations on young perpetrators to ascertain exactly where the problem lies and how best to treat them. Of course, money for paying for this service remains a problem.'

A false sense of security

Public notification and sex offender registration laws are simplistic and ineffective solutions to the highly emotional issue of sexual offending. This is especially true as it pertains to JSOs. The very nature of the law leads the public to believe that by knowing where a sex offender lives, one will feel safer. By knowing a youth is sexually abusive, all persons can now avoid him or her and thus no further victims will be created. Of course, JSOs come into contact with peers and other children daily. Not all persons who come into contact with a registered juvenile sexual offender will know his or her background and thus avoid contact with that person. It is not realistic to start a school for 'normal kids' and one for dangerous kids. Safety is more than knowing information, and effective personal safety requires demonstrated use of effective prevention strategies. Some people feel more anxious knowing they now live near a convicted juvenile sex offender. Others cannot sell their homes when they want to move because known sex offenders are residing in nearby housing.

The truth of the matter is that the few published studies in the literature indicate low recidivism rates for JSOs and suggest that most are not at high risk to sexually reoffend. Furthermore, we have not yet established typologies for these young abusers. The absence of good typologies makes risk assessment more difficult. Thus, registration will not necessarily be able to determine or point out the most dangerous JSOs, and any risk assessments done to indicate a child is dangerous are not reliable nor valid. It is predicted that it will be many years before we will have reliable and valid risk assessments for JSOs, if we are able to develop such scales at all (Caldwell, 2002).

Community fears

As sex offender registration and public notification laws begin to identify an increasing number of offenders, these laws will create increasing levels of panic. One can only feel so safe knowing that there are sex offenders moving into and living in one's neighbourhood and community. In some cases there are concentrations of sex offenders living in certain neighbourhoods. As numbers increase and citizens become more concerned, more drastic measures to address the issue may result.

In one neighbourhood, a residential programme for juvenile sexual abusers has been operating for more than ten years. As a result of sex offender registration and notification laws, citizens banded together to have the programme moved, despite prior knowledge of its existence in their neighbourhood (Louks, 2000). Fear of what may happen in the future, versus looking at the absence of incidents in the past, created panic among local residents.

In New Zealand, a government-funded project to build a residential programme for JSOs was delayed by three years over community resistance to building the facility near neighbourhoods.

In England, similar community resistance is delaying the development of locating and building a residential programme for JSOs.

In South Carolina, NHTC is currently facing a battle to have one of its programmes, that has been in existence for over seven years, shut down based upon registration laws leading to community fears and panic.

Unfortunately, wealthy families and communities will be more successful in banning or diverting sexual abusers from living in their neighbourhoods, rendering these young folks and their families less options for housing, and/or driving them to poverty stricken and or high crime neighbourhoods.

Impact on victims

Public notification affects more than just juvenile sex offenders. When left to individual state

discretion, many states have carried these laws to the extreme.

In Virginia, these laws have had an impact on victims and the families of convicted sex offenders. In one case, the wife and family (including the daughter who was also the victim) were harassed when the registry went on the Internet and their address was posted, even though the offender was sentenced to prison where he will remain incarcerated for some time. Despite the offender being in prison, his family's address was posted on the Internet as the address of a convicted sex offender (O'Brien, 1999).

Impact on others

The impact of public notification goes well beyond the offender and, in some cases, even beyond the victim. Highly publicised cases have demonstrated a severe and negative impact on the victim's family and the offender's family. In other instances, innocent persons, incorrectly identified as sex offenders, have been harassed and assaulted. Now these laws can even affect the purchase and sale of real estate.

In Iowa, an 18-year-old high school student on the state's sex offender registry list had to quit school. He received death threats, and his family did not know how to protect their son.

A recent article in the Los Angeles Times, California, by reporter Michelle Hofmann describes how Megan's Law and sex offender registration laws can impact anyone trying to buy or sell a home. She reports:

> Since July 1, 1999, California law has required that purchase contracts for residential property serve as a notification to buyers of the availability of information on sex offenders. They also must include resources for information, such as county Web-based information as well as the state's Megan's Law database . . .

Because the law does not require sellers or agents to track down the number of registered sex offenders in any given area, June Barlow, vice president and general counsel of the California Assn. of Realtors, recommends that home buyers do their own research on sex offenders in an area before making a purchase.

Told by her real estate agent about the availability of such data, Schultz used the Los Angeles County Sex Offender Locator Web site and discovered there were five 'serious' sex offenders living within one-tenth of a mile of the condominium she wanted to buy and 22 within a one-half mile radius. Orange, San Diego and

Riverside counties also provide this information online. The database allows viewers to search by name, ZIP Code, county, birth date, physical description and crime. It provides details on physical appearance, ethnic background, aliases, identifying marks and tattoos, sometimes with photos. It also describes the crimes committed, using penal code sections to identify and explain the types of crimes.

For some, concerns about reduced home prices and safety issues related to living near a registered sex offender are deal breakers. Will Brown, a real estate agent at Century 21 Better Homes in Santa Monica, said one buyer backed out of a deal after the family learned that three sex offenders lived within one mile of the sale property. As with any potential problem related to purchasing a home, buyers who locate known sex offenders living close to the property during the inspection period have the right to terminate sales contracts and receive full refunds of their deposits. Today, 28 states have some kind of Web-based sex offender information.

Critics say the system represents only a fraction of the nation's actual sexual predators and does not provide accurate information on their locations although 70% to 75% of registrants are in compliance and living at their stated location.

Impact on the young person's family

Families do not ask to have children with sexual behaviour problems. Once this happens in a family there are a multitude of issues that have to be addressed in the juvenile justice system, the mental health system, within the community, and so forth. Unfortunately, registration of juvenile sexual offenders creates even more problems for these already overwhelmed families. The following direct quotations are from interviews conducted with sex offenders and their family members about their experiences with, and thoughts on, the community notification process. The interviews were conducted between August and October 2001 by Alisa Klein, Director of Public Policy, STOP IT NOW!

Sister: Where can my brother go? Who will want him? How can I advocate for him when everyone either hates him or wants to pretend that he doesn't exist? I pray for him everyday while I try to figure out how to help him.

A wife: When the notification happened, neighbours called the media – they came and blocked our driveway at the top of our property. When the media vans arrived, my 17-year-old son was home alone. They harassed him, kept ringing the doorbell and knocking on the door. He was very shaken up.

The frenzy prompted me to get a fence around our property. I took my older son with me to take measurements. As we approached one far-edge of our property, our neighbour came up to us with a gun. He thought my son was the offender. The neighbour was drunk and threatened us to get out of there or he'd shoot, even though we were on our property! Ultimately, we brought a suit against him and he was convicted.

A father: Between the ages of 16 and 18, my son served 21 months in a juvenile detention facility. When he was going to be released, I decided to pre-empt the community notification and inform our immediate neighbours and the landlord of the duplex we were living in at the time. A few days later, the landlord gave us 30 days notice and booted us. He said his wife was a child sexual abuse survivor and didn't want my son there. It was really frustrating, because I had talked to the neighbours, and they were okay with it. We had been looking to buy a house before that, but since we had to move out really soon, we settled on a place we never would have chosen if we'd had more time to look. My son's picture, history and offences were in the paper and on the news repeatedly. Our 14-year-old daughter was taunted by a few kids at school.

A mother: Once you're listed and notified upon as a SO, no context is put around it. And there is certainly no effort made to help the offender make sense of it.

A mother: (Her son was 18-years-old at the time of his offence against a 15-year-old girl. He has since been diagnosed with mental illness. He had been abducted and raped as a young child himself). The notification process is humiliating and has prevented him from getting a good job. He can barely keep it together in general, but when he moved from one apartment to another apartment three streets away, he didn't understand that he had to re-register and go through notification again. He got in trouble. It's like never getting off probation. For him in particular, as a victim of sexual abuse whose offender was never apprehended, this is an irony. Now he is the sex offender.

A mother: CN is a lie. We are being sold a lie that tells us that we're safe and that this protects our children. CN is an 'easy out' rather than the social change that needs to be done, the hard work we need to do to prevent sexual abuse.

A father: It's the families with money that can hire big-name lawyers, apply pressure that can get their kids off. Families like us have to take what we can get, depend on lousy lawyers and watch our sons get taken away from us and notified on.

A mother: The system of notification shows me the inequities of the legal system. For instance, while fathers who have abused their own kids are sometimes given custody of them, other highly vulnerable people like minorities and the mentally ill are targeted because the politicians and law enforcement need to show that they're tough on crime.

A mother: This whole process of registration and notification for my son has made me less hopeful about life and people. It is a thing that never ends. I can still sob years later because it's a never-ending pain.

A mother: My son is made to feel like he is constantly watched. It plays into his problems of paranoia and helplessness. It just isn't good for his mental health and his potential to get better.

A mother: How do they expect my son to make good with his life with that level of shame, with that tattoo on his forehead? This only locks him into that shame and makes him feel like he can never move forward.

A father: When you're being saturated with negative attitudes towards you, how can you heal in a setting like that?

Plea-bargains

Sexual offence cases are often weak in evidence, resulting in plea bargains to lesser offences. With the coming of sex offender registration and community notification laws, young persons charged with sex offences now have a greater motive to avoid prosecution and to plea-bargain their crimes to lesser, nonsexual crimes. In some cases, social workers and child protection workers are reluctant to report cases involving juvenile sexual offenders to authorities out of concern that these young persons will be subjected to sex offender registration and community notification laws (Freeman-Longo and Blanchard, 1998). In these cases many are

quietly and privately referring these young persons to sex offender treatment specialists to get them treatment without the negative consequences of the law.

Adversarial role/ethical dilemma

Professionals who treat sex offenders often do not receive professional respect from their colleagues who do not treat, or are opposed to treating, such offenders. Additionally, professionals in other disciplines often see little value in the work done by those of us who treat sexual abusers. Many of the case examples provided in this chapter have been from professional colleagues who treat sexual abusers. They have provided numerous personal accounts of how their work with other agencies and other professionals has been damaged due to their treating sex offenders.

In our travels around our respective countries, we have heard from a variety of professionals and child protection workers that they have been faced with the ethical dilemma of not reporting sex crimes perpetrated by young people who sexually abuse in order to avoid the consequences these young people face from registration and notification laws. Many have, in fact, revealed that they have not reported some cases.

Undermining treatment

The majority of juvenile sex offender treatment specialists identify mental health problems common among juvenile sex offender clients, including (but not limited to) poor anger management skills, fear, lack of trust, low self-esteem, feelings of rejection, inadequate social skills, lack of empathy, isolation from others, and poor communication skills (Calder, 2001). These skills need to be improved, and that happens when sex offenders have good community support systems and close ties in the community.

Another concern specific to JSO is that most have not completed the maturing process. Normal child and adolescent development is impacted by these laws when as outlined above, these young persons are subject to harsh and critical treatment by professionals, communities and individuals because of their crimes. Normal developmental stages such as peer relations, social skills, and individual identity are just a few areas impacted by laws that result in the stigmatisation of young people.

Another area of concern is the number of JSOs who have co-morbid/co-occurring psychiatric diagnosis in addition to their sexual behaviour problems. Many of these young people are diagnosed with PTSD, ADD, ADHD, conduct disorder, substance abuse disorders, depression, bi-polar disorder, attachment disorder, and so forth. Many of these are serious psychiatric disorders that can be further exacerbated by community harassment, peer rejection, and the other problems associated with registration laws.

Limiting of the youth's ability to function in the community

Sex offenders need to learn appropriate skills that assist them in functioning appropriately and safely in the community. In the absence of these skills they do not function well and are at greater risk of re-offending. Threats, harassment, and fear of reprisal by citizens keep the offender in a state of stress and anxiety and, thus, more likely to re-offend. Juveniles face problems with dating, being involved in peer activities, sports, and social events. To function in the community, the offender has to feel a part of the community like anyone else, and have access to schools and other public services and functions. Sex offender registration and public notification laws compromise the sex offender's ability to do so in a healthy and safe way.

Bryan Allmandinger (2002) of Iowa reports:

In our inpatient programme we have an opportunity to integrate some of the residents in public schools only after successfully completing guidelines in our programme. There has been an issue with parents in the community being concerned about having offenders in the school.

B. J. Oneal, of Renton, Washington similarly reports:

By history, our residential treatment programme has had a significant amount of resistance from the local school district to place JSO's from our treatment programme into the public schools.

Age of the offender

Registration laws often do not take into account the age of the JSO. Children and young people are often indiscriminately lumped into the general category of sexual offender under registration laws. For example, in South Carolina, a child of any age who is charged with a sexual

offence can be placed on a registration list, and here we know of at least one child registered at the age of 13. With tougher laws, laws waiving youth to adult courts, the public sentiment toward all sex offenders, and the general failure to separate different types of sex offenders by age, gender, mental illness, level of functioning, and risk, juveniles are now subject to sex offender registration and public notification laws in a growing number of states. This is being done without regard for the youth's maturity and developmental stage, or the potential long-term consequences on their lives.

In several states in the United States, young people are now listed on the Internet. In one case, an 11-year-old was listed improperly, exposing his name to other adult sex offenders who might prey on him (Grooters, 1999). In another example an 18-year-old male, who engaged in a 'senior prank' of 'mooning' the school principal was convicted of indecent exposure, had to register with the state for 25 years, and has his name, address, and crime publicly posted (Rosenberg, 2000). In yet another case, one professional had two juvenile clients who were harassed at school by classmates as a result of having their names and addresses posted on the Internet (Grooters, 1999).

The state of Texas does registration of all sex offenders, children and juveniles included. The youngest on the list is ten-years-old. The name and address of this ten-year-old and other children of the same age are now posted on the registry for anyone to see (Davis, 1999).

Cordelia Anderson of Minnesota notes:

I believe the youngest in this state was 10. I believe this is a huge issue. I talked to an official of The Minnesota Department of Corrections that coordinates sex offender registration; her take is that a high percentage of these cases (JSOs) were 'experimenters', and what I call 'bad choices' behaviour that needs to stop. Impact on the victim and others needs to be understood, but registration is not necessary, helpful or appropriate.

Kara Cornelisse from Michigan reports:

We have at least one 8-year-old registered. I believe he was adjudicated in 2000. He was registered for CSC 1st degree and will register for the duration of his life.

Dr. Frank Vandervort of the University of Michigan describes:

Michigan's sex offender registry requires that all children found responsible for sex offences be listed on the registry, most of them for life, without regard to age. When the child becomes 18 this information becomes public. These requirements led a three-judge panel of the Michigan Court of Appeals to write 'we express our concern over the draconian nature of this act.' However, the act was upheld against a constitutional challenge. I do not know the younger ages of children actually listed, although I am confident that there are children as young as 10 on the list.

Kathleen Faller of the University of Michigan, School of Social work writes:

I am in Michigan. We had a case two years ago involving siblings, an 8-year-old girl and a 9-year-old boy, who were involved in sexual activity with each other, when originally placed on the registry. As far as we could tell the brother was predatory. We also think the father was a sex offender. His goal was to get both of these children out of his home and into the institutional care system. He was successful. The girl, who was our client when she was 14–16, ended up in a series of placements: shelters, a group home, a psychiatric hospital, and a residential treatment centre. The boy was in at least three institutions, including a residential treatment programme for adolescent offenders. They both aged out of the system.

Matthew Rosenberg of Michigan reports:

In Michigan, juveniles are placed on the list upon conviction. The youngest I have worked with was 10. They will not have public notification, or be on the public list. However, depending on the type of sex crime, they will be registered (viewable by police and court only) for a minimum of 25 years, to life for the two most serious sex crimes. Upon their 18th birthday, they will be subjected to public notification for the time remaining on their registration period.

Gayle Zeller from Washington State reports:

It is very rare for any youth to be incarcerated in Washington under the age of 10 for any offence. Under the age of 12, youth would be considered sexually aggressive and treatment would be the first option. Over the age of 12, there is a greater likelihood of criminal charges, or at least waiting in detention until an evaluation is completed to determine treatment options. If the sex offence is committed by someone under the age of 15, the court can be petitioned 24 months after the conviction to remove the registration requirement, with consideration of the offence and no other problems noted during that time. If the offence is committed by someone over the age of 15, the court can be petitioned when the youth turns 18 to remove the registration requirement, again given the type of offence and no other problems occurring.

The youngest sex offender in California that went to the California Youth Authority (CYA), was an 11-year-old. Sex offenders who are released from the CYA have to register until age 25.

Mentally ill sex offenders

A small percentage of offenders sexually abuse because they suffer from a biological anomaly or a mental illness. Despite this handicap, and the need to be sensitive to people with mental illnesses, once a mentally ill sex offender is registered or subject to notification, they are treated with the same level of disrespect and disregard as other sex offenders.

It is not uncommon to find co-occurring or co-morbid disorders among JSOs. At New Hope Treatment Centres in South Carolina a good number of our patients who have sexual behaviour problems also have a psychiatric diagnosis. This diagnosis ranges from conduct disorder, PTSD, ADHD and Reactive attachment Disorder, to bi-polar disorder, depressive disorders and schizophrenia.

There is ample research that addresses the hidden effects and long-term medical consequences of childhood trauma (Dallam, 2001). Most JSOs have experienced some form of child maltreatment and many have been victims of both neglect and severe childhood abuse. The shame, and social ramifications of being on a sex offender registry are only but two of the many issues that impact children with sexual behaviour problems who have a psychiatric diagnosis and are subject to sex offender registration laws.

Intellectual deficits

Many sexual abusers are developmentally disabled. Some are mildly retarded, while others have severe learning disabilities. Like the mentally ill, they live in society with a handicap that makes their lives more difficult, and the need to adjust to society more stressful.

At NHTC, like many other programmes and residential facilities, we have a special programme for adolescent males that are lower-functioning and may have IQs as low as 46–50. When released these patients are already struggling and coping with the communities response to their lack of normal intellectual functioning. Being placed on registration lists will only serve to further their general fears of people, rejection by community members, and the other social ailments they have and will experience as a lower functioning person in a normal functioning person's world.

Female sexual abusers

Female abusers are being identified in increasing numbers. As of the writing of this paper, I have not received any cases or news stories regarding the impact of sex offender registration and Megan's Law on females who sexually abuse. In one case, the female sexual abuser was so distraught by the impact of these laws on her life that she requested that the therapist not forward any information about her case, even if made confidential. Given the absence of cases involving female sexual abusers, it may be possible that the public feels less threatened by females who sexually abuse.

None-the-less, female adolescent sexual abusers face the same problems male adolescents do in addition to the stigma and social consequences of being a female 'sexual offender'. There is so little information in the literature regarding female adolescent sexual abusers (see Chapter ten for a review), that application of registration laws to young girls is at best a social experiment that treads on extremely thin ice.

Decrease in reporting

Reports from New Jersey and Colorado, among other states, indicate that there is a decrease in the reporting of juvenile sexual offences and incest offences by family members and victims who do not want to deal with the impact of public notification on their family.

Although reported, many sex crimes are not resulting in convictions, now, or the charges are reduced to non-sexual offences through plea-bargaining. In Michigan, many judges and prosecutors are having a difficult time obtaining convictions for juvenile sex offenders because many jury members do not want to live with the guilt of ostracising a 15-year-old for the majority of his life. Moreover, the actual prosecutors, judges, and referees are reluctant to convict these juveniles for the very same reason. They are placing a growing number of juveniles under advisement status. (If the juvenile sex offender completes treatment, the juvenile record is dismissed) (Rosenberg, 2000).

In Idaho, one professional noted that since enacting the juvenile registry law, actual juvenile sex offences are down approximately 85%. Original charges are being reduced to unspecified 'battery' charges in order to avoid the registry law (Meyers, 1999).

Rethinking registration and notification requirements?

In 'Setting the Boundaries' (Home Office, 2000) certain proposals of relevance were made:

- The age of legal consent should remain at 16.
- Whatever the law says about the age of consent, children below 16 may agree to have sex. There was a case therefore for setting a lower age in law beneath which no possibility whatever of consent to sexual activity would be recognised in order to protect younger children. This lower age limit was proposed to be 13.
- There should be an offence of sexual activity between minors to apply to those aged above 16 and under 18 and those under the age of consent.
- Further attention should be given to appropriate non-criminal interventions for young people under 16 engaged in mutually agreed under-age sex who are not currently and should not in the future normally be subject to prosecution.

In the UK, the review of the Sex Offenders Act (1997) (Home Office, 2001) identified a list of concerns they had considered in relation to applying sex offender registration to young people. These included:

- Children and young people are less likely to be entrenched in their patterns of deviant behaviour than is the case of older sex offenders. This allows for the potential for change through effective interventions, reducing the need to protect the community through registration.
- There is a recognition that young people who sexually abuse have a wide range of experiences and needs in their own right that need to be addressed and registration does not, in itself, address such needs.
- Some young people have been subject to the registration requirements because of inappropriate youthful experimentation. Magistrates have expressed in a range of individual cases that they thought the circumstances of the offence did not warrant registration of the young person, which would automatically be required as a result of the sentence they passed. This was because the offence was relatively minor and the victim regarded the offending behaviour as

unwelcome and distasteful rather than frightening or distressing.

- A range of adult offenders are included within the remit of the legislation and we should differentiate young people from those more entrenched in their offending behaviour.

The question of how they should deal with the issue of children and young people who abuse caused considerable concern in the consultation groups, although no consensus was reached about the way forward. It was recognised that some of the children and young people in question posed a clear danger to others, which had to be fully considered regardless of whatever factors may have given rise to this. For them, as for adults, registration under the Act both meant that a risk assessment would be triggered and that the police would know of their whereabouts. This remained important when some young people changed addresses as they moved in and out of care establishments.

Having failed to reach any conclusion in relation to this group, the consultation document (Home Office, 2001) continued registration on an interim basis but posed a series of consultation questions in relation to the following alternatives for young people who sexually abuse:

- Continuing the present registration regime for those under 18.
- Continuing to register those over 16 as at present whilst removing the registration requirement from those under this age unless they had been sentenced to a custodial sentence of any length or admitted to hospital subject to a restriction order.
- Registering children and young people who sexually abuse with an agency other than the police who had a remit to address their abusive behaviour and their wider needs.
- Judicial discretion to require registration only in those cases where this was considered necessary after hearing the circumstances of the case.
- Continuing registration as at present but introducing provision for de-registration when the young person reached 18 if they were assessed as no longer posing a risk.

Adopting a balanced risk assessment framework

Youth Offending Teams are charged with conducting risk assessments of young people

using the ASSET forms, and social workers utilise the Assessment Framework (DoH, 2000). The police are charged with using Matrix 2000 which was designed for use exclusively with adult sex offenders when someone has been convicted of an offence requiring sex offender registration. At the earlier point in the criminal process, the police are constrained by the application of the criminal focused gravity matrix which is likely to pull in rather than divert young people where a sexual offence has been alleged. Print et al. (2001) have developed a more balanced framework for conducting assessments of young people who sexually abuse that has a clear outcome matrix that should appropriately identify those people as an ongoing risk from those that may not. This impacts positively on screening cases that should be prosecuted and thus receive registration requirements.

Rights of appeal against registration

In the UK, NACRO (1999) have recommended that local authorities actively initiate a process of exempting a young person from the consequences of schedule one registration if they have made sufficient progress following their conviction. This would mean that the schedule one status for life is deactivated and then the parallel sex offender registration would run only for the duration set down by their offence and disposal. This would allow us to focus our efforts on those who cause us the most concern and exiting those where the risk is deemed to have reduced. This is detailed in Calder (2002).

Summary

There is no doubt that unexpected problems and blatant abuses of sex offender registration and notification laws have occurred. Many of these were foreseeable and could have been avoided with more planning, research, and forethought about potential problems. The application of registration laws to young people with sexual behaviour problems creates further problems for young people that may be life long problems, and have serious impact on their psycho-social development.

We wrote this chapter to draw further attention to what we see now and foresee as the emerging problems with sex offender registration for youth with sexual behaviour problems. Until we look at them closely and research their potential effectiveness, we are concerned that laws designed to protect our citizens may, instead, do more damage than if they did not exist at all.

We believe registration should not be used with JSOs except under the most extreme conditions in which they pose a serious threat to others and the community. Proposed conditions would include the following:

The young person:

● Refuses treatment.
● Is not responding to treatment.
● Is failing in treatment.
● Dropped out of treatment.
● Was terminated unsuccessfully from treatment.

References

Allmandinger, B. Personal Communication. E-Mail 11/21/02.

Anderson, C. Personal Communication. E-Mail Dated 11/22/02.

Blassingame, G. Personal Communication. E-Mail 11/21/02.

Brieling, J. (1998, August 27) *The Association for the Treatment of Sexual Abusers List-Serve*, Public Posting.

Brown, A. (1998) The Sex Offenders Act Part 1: Issues Relating to Adolescents Convicted of a Sexual Offence. *Not A News* 27: 21–7.

Calder, M.C. (2002b) Structural Changes in the Management of Young People who Sexually Abuse in The UK, in Calder, M.C. (Ed.) *Young People Who Sexually Abuse: Building The Evidence Base for Your Practice*. Lyme Regis: Russell House Publishing, 265–308.

Calder. M.C. (2002) *Juveniles Who Sexually Abuse: Frameworks for Assessment*. (2nd Edn). Lyme Regis: Russell House Publishing.

Caldwell, M.F. (2002) What We Do Not Know About Juvenile Sex Offender Re-Offence Risk. *Child Maltreatment*, 7(4) 291–302.

Carr, K.H. (2002) Soon You May No Longer Be Able to Search Online for Violent Sexual Offenders in Your Neighbourhood. *The Free Lance-Star*. 8/4/02 Http://Fredericksburg.Com/News/Fls/2002/082002/08042002/674769

Colb, S.F. (2002) *The Supreme Court Evaluates Megan's Laws: Probably Valid But Still Wrong*. Http://Writ.News.Findlaw.Com/Colb/20021120.Html.

Dallam, S.J. (2001) The Long-Term Medical Consequences of Childhood Trauma, in

Franey, K., Geffner, R. and Falconer, R. (Eds.) *The Cost of Child Maltreatment: Who Pays? We All Do*. San Diego, Ca: Fvsai Publications. 1–14.

Davis, G. Personal Communication. November 2, 1999.

Dennis, P. (1999, October 2) *The Association for the Treatment of Sexual Abusers List-Serve*, Public Posting.

Denniston, L. (2002) *Justices Question Sex-Offender Laws: Supreme Court Hears Pros, Cons of Registry*. 11/14/2002.

Faller, K.C. Personal Communication. E-Mail 11/21/02.

Freeman-Longo, R.E. (1996a) Feel Good Legislation: Prevention or Calamity. *Child Abuse and Neglect*, 20 (2) 95–101.

Freeman-Longo, R.E. (1996b) Prevention or Problem. *Sexual Abuse: A Journal of Research and Treatment*, 8 (2) 91–100.

Freeman-Longo, R.E. (2002) Revisiting Megan's Law and Sex Offender Registration: Prevention or Problem, in Hodgson, J.F. and Kelley, D.S. (Eds.) *Sexual Violence: Policies, Practices, and Challenges in The United States and Canada*. Praeger Publishers, Westport, Ct. (Formerly Published on Line by The American Probation and Parole Association (Http://Www.Appa-Net.Org; 4/6/00)

Freeman-Longo, R.E. and Blanchard, G.T. (1998) *Sexual Abuse in America: Epidemic of The 21st Century*. Brandon, Vermont. Safer Society Press.

Goodman, E. *Not All Sex Offenders Are Dangerous to Kids*. Boston Globe 11/17/02. D11.

Grady, J. Personal Communication. E-Mail 9/3/2002.

Greenhouse, L. States' Listings of Sex Offenders Raise A Tangle of Legal Issues. *New York Times*, November 4, 2002

Grooters, R. Personal Communication. January 24, 1999 and October 22, 1999.

Hofmann, M. Megan's Law Gives Buyers Another Tool. *L. A. Times Special to The Times*, Nov 17 2002. Http://Www.Latimes.Com/Business/Realestate/Commercial/La-Re-Megan17nov17.Story

Home Office (2000) *Setting The Boundaries: Reforming The Law on Sex Offenders*. London: Home Office.

Home Office (2001) *Consultation Paper on The Review of Part 1 of The Sex Offenders Act 1997*. London: Home Office.

Http://Www.Boston.Com/Dailyglobe2/318/Nation/Justices Question Sex Offender Laws+.Shtml

Kara, C. Personal Communication. E-Mail 11/21/02.

Klein, A. and Gordon, A. (November 9, 2001) *The Impact of Sexual Offender Laws on Public Safety: What Offenders and Their Families Can Tell Us Workshop*: Atsa Conference, San Antonio Texas.

Klein, A. *Stop It Now!* Haydenville, Ma.

Latham, C. Personal Communication. E-Mail Dated 8/31/02.

Louks, R. Personal Communication. January 20, 2000.

Lowenberg, K. Personal Communication. E-Mail Dated 11/22/02.

Matson, S. Centre for Sex Offender Management. Personal Communication 8/28/2002.

McLaughlin, R.J. Personal Communication. E-Mail Dated 8/31/02.

Meyers, R. (1999, October 24) *The Association for the Treatment of Sexual Abusers List-Serve*, Public Posting.

Nacro (1999) *Young People Who Commit Schedule One Offence*. Briefing Paper. Feb. London: Nacro.

O'Neal, B.J. Personal Communication. E-Mail 11/21/02.

O'Brien, K. (1999, July 11) Mom: Sex Offender Registry Also Hurts Victims. *The Roanoke Times*.

Print, B., Morrison, T. and Henniker, J. (2001) An Inter-Agency Assessment Framework for Young People Who Sexually Abuse: Principles, Processes and Practicalities, in Calder, M.C. *Juveniles and Children Who Sexually Abuse: Frameworks for Assessment* (2nd Edn) Lyme Regis: Russell House Publishing.

Rosenberg, M.D. Personal Communication. E-Mail 11/21/02.

Schwartz, I.M., Guo, S. and Kerbs, J.J. (1993) The Impact of Demographic Variables on Public Opinion Regarding Juvenile Justice. *Crime and Delinquency* 39: 5–28.

US Department of Justice (2002) *Summary of State Sex Offender Registries, 2001. Bureau of Justice Statistics Fact Sheet; March 2002, Ncj192265.* US Department of Justice; Office of Justice Programmes.

Valios, N. (1998) Social Workers Warn Register is Flawed. *Community Care*, 27th Aug-2nd Sep, 1–2.

Vandervort, F. Personal Communication. E-Mail 11/21/02.

Zeller, G. Personal Communication. E-Mail 11/21/02.

Part VI

Outcomes

Chapter Twenty

Family Reunification in Cases of Sibling Incest

Jerry D. Thomas and C. Wilson Viar

Introduction

The subject of family reunification for neglected and abused children is a serious concern for all professionals who are faced with responsibility for making these decisions. The consequences of bad decision making can have a devastating impact on all concerned. It is for this reason that the following chapter will focus specifically upon the family reunification process in cases of sexual abuse by a young person upon a sibling, the key criteria for determining the appropriate level of reunification, or, alternately, the decision not to reunify at all.

Responsible, safe and healthy family reunification is not a job that any treatment provider tackles alone. It must be a collaborative effort that involves a number of professionals and agencies, the treatment providers, the abuser, and the family as a whole. As with the treatment of any type of child sexual abuse, family reunification in these cases also considers the family as active participating members of the treatment team.

While the first and foremost concern of family reunification in such cases is the well-being of victims – both present and future – the well-being of all family members must be seriously considered as well. What many outside the field of sexual offender treatment don't realise is that family reunification is an ideal rather than presumed goal of treatment work with young people who have sexually abused a sibling. What that means is that responsible treatment providers consider family reunification as merely the best-of-all-possible-worlds end of a continuum of potential outcomes for each and every family. Treatment will determine which outcome is realistically optimal for a family. Many government and social directives mandate family reunification as a paramount goal in all cases. Responsible treatment provision for sexually abusive youth, however, is driven first and foremost by the attempt to produce the optimal results in each individual case, based upon the particular needs of all the individuals involved, the safety of the victim, and the safety of the community.

In many cases it will become obvious very early that family reunification will never be healthy, safe, or even possible. Family Reunification Planning, however, is not about treating reunification as a measure of success. It is about all the many organisations and professionals involved in any specific case providing the victim, family and offender with whatever individual and joint services they require to come as close as possible to the optimal state of healing. It is based on the assumption that while family reunification may be the ideal level of success when speaking generally about the subject of sibling incest, the actual best measure of success with any specific victim, offender, and family will be an entirely individualised undertaking.

Basic goals

In order for the reconciliation, rejoining and reunification of families that have been separated as a result of sibling sexual abuse to take place, three basic goals must be met:

1. The abused siblings feel safe, supported and empowered not only within the treatment process, but within their family as a result of the successful treatment of all the people and dynamics which contributed to their victimisation.
2. The family has eliminated any patterns of behaviour and/ or interactions which support, encourage, permit or unwittingly allow offending to take place, and have learned how to support and encourage non-offending behaviour.
3. The sexual abuser has learned to admit responsibility for victimising another, has proved they appreciate the emotional and psychological cost of their actions on their victims and others, and has demonstrated, to the satisfaction of specially trained professionals, that they can manage their own

behaviour not just in or immediately after treatment, but over the long term.

As noted above, it may become clear early in the treatment process that full family reunification would be unhealthy or even dangerous. Yet just as clearly, any work treatment providers and the professionals collaborating with them can do to bring victim, family, and sexually abusive youth closer to meeting these goals is therapeutic. Family Reunification Planning is a step-by-step process providing a range of optimal outcomes for each youth and their family. Decision making about these goals are an ongoing part of the assessment, treatment planning, and reconstruction process for the sexually abusive youth, their family, and their victim. This is why such treatment is often called a family resolution rather than reunification process, a phrase coined some years ago by Dr Ben Sanders, Diretor of Child and Family Program of the National Crime Victims Research and Treatment Center in South Carolina and Ms Mary Meinig, Director of the Office of Family and Children's Ombudsman in the state of Washington, to emphasise that family treatment is an ongoing, continuing process. Mary Meinig was one of the first treatment providers to develop a structured approach to family reunification with adult offenders who had sexually abused within their family. The authors' own work with sexually abusive youth and their families in reunification has been inspired by Meinig's ground breaking work in this area.

It is important to remember that treatment is a process of change for all concerned, treatment providers included. The characteristics of the sexually abusive youth, their family, and their victims initially present will alter over the course of the intervention and treatment process. As well, the various professionals' perception of them should and will change as ongoing assessment reveals an ever-increasing and deepening body of information about them. Participants' suitability or unsuitability for particular treatment outcomes is something that will find its own time over the course of the process, and can't be reliably judged at the outset.

Clarification, reconciliation and reunification

The three important benchmarks of this family treatment plan and process are Clarification, Reconciliation, and Reunification. The first benchmark is the successful completion of the clarification sessions. In these meetings between the youth and all or part of his family, the sexually abusive youth is clear about the nature of the sexually abusive behaviour, honest about how it occurred, and takes full responsibility for the behaviour in a face-to-face meeting with all family members without minimisation, rationalisation, or projection of blame.

The second benchmark is the reconciliation of the family members to each other and to circumstances. Reconciliation is the therapeutic process whose outcome is a resolution or coming to terms with the occurrence of sibling sexual abuse, as well as of the problems and conflict areas that prevent the family members from maintaining healthy and safe relationships. Reconciliation may take place without reunification, but reunification cannot take place without reconciliation. Even when treatment has revealed that full reunification is not the appropriate goal of a particular case, reconciliation work is still needed if the family members are to resolve feelings of anger, hurt, and mistrust, and move on with their lives.

The third benchmark is family reunification. Reunification is the reconciliation and rejoining of a family where sexual abuse has occurred, in this case incest between siblings, children in the same home, or in the same extended family. Reunification can only take place after the sibling who has been sexually abusive has learned to manage their sexual behaviour, when the victims feels safe, supported and empowered, and after the family has eliminated and replaced any patterns of behaviour which support or encourage abusive behaviour with patterns of behaviour which support and encourage non-offending behaviour.

This chapter will focus narrowly on attempting to reach the final benchmark. It will not attempt to educate the reader on how to conduct family therapy, or suggest interventions for the family therapist to utilise given the space provided, but simply gives the treatment provider and other involved parties a tool to guide decision making.

The risks if family resolution (the reunification process) is not attempted

There are professionals in the field of child sexual abuse who do not believe in family reunification in cases of sibling sexual abuse under any circumstances. This is generally due to their lack of information about the risks to everyone involved if the process of family resolution isn't attempted. These risks, however, are very real, and include threats to the well being of the victim, the sexually abusive youth, and to the family as a whole. Undoubtedly there are also some risks in entering into the process for all involved, but they are more than outweighed by the possible detriment to all family members of failing to attempt the process, as well as the many benefits of resolution work in general.

The following are some of the risks to the sexually abused sibling if no family resolution work is incorporated into the programme:

- If there is no structured contact between abused and abusive siblings in a safe and therapeutic context, there is no opportunity to reduce the victim's fears and help them become better able to face future fears.
- The abused sibling loses the opportunity to work through and overcome their perceptions of helplessness and inability to face fearful situations.
- The victim loses their therapeutically best opportunity to work through and reduce the effects of a trauma in a safe, healing, and empowering environment.
- There is no opportunity to redirect the abused sibling's misattribution of blame from themselves to their abusive sibling, allowing self-blame to continue.
- The victim is allowed to continue to store up anger and rage, not only denying them the opportunity to redirect it to their abusive sibling where it belongs, but quite often allowing them to turn that anger upon themselves.
- The abused sibling never receives the opportunity to see and judge for themselves if and how the abusive sibling has changed, perpetuating the abusive relationship in their mind, and denying them an opportunity to observe and be reassured by the value of the treatment process and its focus upon eliminating their abusive sibling's victimising behaviour.
- The abused sibling is denied important opportunities to resolve and eliminate any loyalty dilemmas, conscious or overt, either to their abusive sibling and/or to the family that has been disrupted by the revelation that the victim has been abused.

- The victim quite often remains stuck in the dynamics of the abusive relationship when resolution work is not provided, a situation which can contribute, due to fears of the consequences of disclosure, to subsequent episodes of abuse not only by the sibling but even in the future by members of other intimate relationships.
- The abused sibling is denied the chance to see their abuser as merely another person, a person who is in treatment for the problems that they have inflicted on the victim and others, a perception which in turn empowers other types of personal decision-making.
- The victim is denied the opportunity to reach any real closure of the relationship which provided the context for their abuse.

To rephrase these risks in the form of their correlate positive benefits when the necessary work is engaged in: Family resolution is a therapeutic process which provides the victim with the opportunity to redirect anger and guilt to their abuser, to observe the same healthier attributions by their abuser and other family members, to observe and assess the purpose and effectiveness of treatment, to eliminate feelings of helplessness and perceive their abuser as someone they have the power to stand up to, and to obtain closure on the abusive relationship and develop new, healthier relationships with family members.

The primary risks to the victim of conducting family reunification work, risks which are actively addressed by all therapists working with them, are increased anxiety before, during and after encounters with the abuser (and possibly some other family members). Many also worry that this anxiety in turn will lead to regression, flashbacks and the opening of old wounds. Yet such risks are greatly ameliorated if the victim is provided the proper preparation and support, and if such encounters are structured and timed properly. Remember, the first and foremost emphasis of family reunification work is the victim. Not only are encounters with the abuser or other potentially threatening family members not conducted until the victim has reached an appropriate state of readiness within their individual therapeutic process. As well, such encounters are not allowed until the sexually abusive youth and family members have also reached a point in the therapeutic process where they are capable of contributing to the safety, empowerment, and therapeutic benefit of the victim. And they are only allowed in a safe, protective environment.

The risks to the sexually abusive youth of failing to provide family resolution work are much more obvious and generally understood. These include allowing them to continue objectifying the victim, intellectualising the abusive behaviour, and avoiding confronting and fully accepting what they have done and its impact upon the victim and others. The latter is a particular risk, since it is especially difficult for an abusive youth to experience real empathy for their victim unless they are directly confronted by the victim and observe and hear the pain, fear and trauma they have caused.

The risks of taking part in resolution work for the abusive youth revolve primarily around the skill and perspicacity of the treatment providers working with them. In addition to the potential negative impact upon the victim or other family members, if the abusive youth sabotages or otherwise acts in a contra-therapeutic manner this can stall, retard or even damage their progress. Likewise, particularly for very young abusers, being confronted too soon with the anger and pain they have caused may cause trauma or defensive regression in treatment (increased denial, etc.).

Yet these risks are minimal, and, in fact, are actually more treatment opportunities than therapeutic dangers. The victim's therapist, the offender's therapist and others will be present in any such encounters. As a result, not only will there be adequate therapeutic aid available to the offender if they were not as emotionally prepared as believed to be confronted by their victim and family. As well, there will be a wealth of support available to the victim if the offender behaves contra-therapeutically, providing an excellent opportunity for therapeutic interventions which demonstrate more clearly than a therapist's simple assertions in one-to-one sessions the support of the victim and what is expected of the offender.

Responsibilities of the family therapist in the resolution process

The family therapist has major responsibilities in family reunification. Every possible task has been considered even though not all of them may be necessary for every family treatment plan. The number of tasks depends on the individual family and level of care required:

- Engagement of the family in treatment collaboration.
- Assessment and evaluation of the family.
- Assuring that individual assessments of family members take place as indicated.
- Development of a treatment plan that outlines the steps necessary in order for clarification, reconciliation and/or reunification to occur.
- Monitoring and updating of the treatment plan.
- Co-ordination and co-operation with all other therapists and agencies involved.
- Collaborating closely with a programme treatment team, if there is one.
- Providing either individual family, subsystem or multi-family therapy if all are offered by the programme or co-ordinating these therapies.
- Providing parent education that is specific to child sexual abuse and offence specific treatment.
- Structuring and conducting critical family sessions.
- Assessment of readiness for clarification, reconciliation, and reunification.
- Monitoring and planning agency/programme visits, home visits, and community outings.
- Assessment of readiness for programme termination and community reintegration.
- Transition and discharge preparation.
- Aftercare services or referral for aftercare services.
- Monitoring outcome.

Given the huge scale of this task and the many different structures and focuses of child sexual abuser treatment agencies, it is very helpful to work in a programme where staff members can share these tasks. For example, while the family therapist provides therapy, another staff member will conduct the psycho-educational group for parents. Alternately, the family therapist might incorporate this education into family therapy. In some treatment programmes, the family therapist operates primarily as a co-ordinator melding together the work of a number of staff into an over-arcing family treatment programme. Just as every family has different strengths and needs, every programme has different resources, personnel and capabilities. There is no set formula for how the above treatment components should be delivered or assembled- be creative. The important considerations are that those who provide any given component have adequate training and supervision for their tasks, and that they work together as a team.

Collaboration with all agencies involved

A systemic approach must be developed with agencies defining their specific responsibilities and developing policy statement and child protection services. Sexually abusive behaviours require a multi disciplinary, multi model, multi system, multi theory combination of interventions. Whilst we have to create an infrastructure for the operational work I would argue that further accessible information, training, and coordinated research and using good examples of best practice are the best way forward rather than central guidance.

(Calder, 1997).

It is widely accepted that the most effective response to child sexual abuse is a multi-disciplinary, multi-agency effort. Professional organisations such as the Association for the Treatment of Sexual Abusers (ATSA) in the United States and the National Organisation for the Treatment of Abusers (NOTA) in Great Britain have all released position statements emphasising the critical importance of collaboration. The Centre for Sex Offender Management in Washington, DC has published several supporting briefs. The issues of multi-disciplinary roles and professional collaboration dominate The National Task Force Report on Juvenile Sexual Offending, published by the National Council of Juvenile and Family Court Judges in co-operation with the National Kempe Centre in Colorado.

The NOTA position paper includes the following:

Intervention with young people who sexually offend should be prompt, based on inter-agency co-operation and informed assessment and provide access to other appropriate and effective services. The constituency of an inter-agency group may vary and be dependent upon where in the process the adolescent is placed. As a general principle, an inter-agency group should comprise of all those professionals who can play a positive and helpful role in managing the young person's behaviour and in promoting change. It is likely that, at an initial assessment stage, a group centred on the constituent members of the Youth Offending Team, perhaps with the addition of a representative from the Crown Prosecution Service, would be appropriate and balanced. Intervention and management will also require work to be undertaken with the support systems of the young person, whether that is through work with birth family members, foster-carers, residential workers, schools or other community groups. Young people exist in social relationships and work which does not take this into account is likely to be much less effective in supporting behaviour changes.

The problems in developing a collaborative network

Writing about collaboration in treatment and about specific methods and examples for an audience residing in widely separated countries, states and counties is complicated by a number of factors. In the US, while the several systems involved in a case of juvenile sexual offending are generally very similar on paper from state to state, they can also often be very dissimilar in their actual operation and nomenclature. As well, systems tend to change as political and professional leadership and staff change, sometimes subtly and sometimes not. These differences are even more pronounced between different countries.

Yet the specific format or method of collaboration is not as important as the recognition of its importance, and the effort by a particular system to ensure that the appropriate collection of agencies and professionals work together with the family in the decision making involved in each particular case. In the US several states have developed standards of practice for reunification. The State of Colorado addressed this issue directly in the Multidisciplinary Team Functions section of its State treatment standards of practice:

500.00: The purpose of the multidisciplinary team is to manage and supervise the juvenile through shared information. The individualised evaluation, pre-sentence investigation, information from all caregivers, and ongoing assessments provide the basis for team decisions related to risk assessment, treatment and behavioural monitoring. Supervision and behavioural monitoring are the collaborative and co-operative responsibilities of the multidisciplinary team. The team may include the parent or caregiver, supervising officer or agent, treatment provider, human services caseworker, polygraph examiner, other clinical professionals, school personnel and guardian ad litem.

Parents shall be advised of the multidisciplinary team's expectations including the requirements of informed supervision. Parents and caregivers are recognised as having an integral role in the juvenile's development and, ultimately, community-based stability. The team may also include extended family members, law enforcement, church leaders, peers, victim therapists, victims, coaches and employers.

Discussion: *Parental involvement with the multidisciplinary team is strongly encouraged throughout the supervision and care continuum. Families provide invaluable information about the juvenile's environment and are in most cases the central support system* of the juvenile. Family involvement is required in treatment per these Standards in Section 3.140.

5.110 Each multidisciplinary team shall at a minimum consist of:

(a) *The supervising officer/agent.*
(b) *Department of Human Services caseworker, if assigned.*
(c) *The juvenile's caregiver in any out-of-home placement.*
(d) *The treatment provider.*
(e) *The polygraph examiner, when utilised.*
(f) *Victim representation (Section 8.000).*

Each team is formed around a particular juvenile and is flexible enough to include any individual necessary to ensure the best approach to managing and treating the juvenile. The multidisciplinary team members perform separate and distinct functions relative to their agency affiliations. Maintaining the integrity of the team and the specified relationship with the juvenile is crucial to the success of the team. Therefore, team members shall not perform more than one role for an individual juvenile. In smaller communities professionals may work for two agencies. In these cases their primary role must be identified. The professional may act as a secondary or co-facilitator after primary role clarification is made.

5.120 The multidisciplinary team shall be convened and co-ordinated by the supervising officer/agent, or DHS caseworker, in the absence of a supervising officer/agent, who shall facilitate team decision making regarding:

- *The members of the team beyond required membership, and members' attendance at any given meeting.*
- *The frequency of multidisciplinary team meetings which shall occur quarterly at a minimum.*
- *The content and goals of the meetings, with input from the team members.*
- *The type(s) of information required to be released.*
- *The designation of the custodian of the complete case record (supervising officer/agent, beyond their agency affiliation record keeping requirements), for data gathering purposes as required in section 16-11.7-103, C.R.S.*

Because these Standards apply to adjudicated juveniles, the final authority regarding community safety and supervision rests with the supervising officer/ agent or DHS caseworker (in the absence of a supervising officer/agent). The supervising officer has final authority in all decisions regarding conditions set by the court or parole board and regarding court orders in the delinquency action. Placement recommendations are to be made by the multidiscip-

linary team; however community placements are the responsibility of the Department of Human Services and are generally decided by the court.

Situations may arise, including emergencies that require a multidisciplinary team member to make an independent decision in order to protect victims or community safety. Independent decisions should be the exception rather than the rule. These decisions must be reviewed as soon as possible with the multidisciplinary team."

The above serves as an excellent example of what one body of standard makers accomplished for one state in the United States by meeting together and agreeing on the collaboration of each multi-disciplinary team member and how that response was to be operationalised.

Step by step reunification process

The step by step reunification process is one in which progress by abusive youth, victims and family depends upon the completion of clearly defined objectives and tasks. For the youth who has been in out of home placement and will either be returning home to live with a previously victimised sibling, non-victimised siblings, or in proximity to other potential child victims, a step-by-step plan for family reunification and reintegration into the community is crucial. This is in the best interests of the future well-being and health of the sexually abusive youth, as well as an important protection of the safety of existing and potential victims.

An outline of reunification planning

Before discussing the steps individually, the following is a basic outline of the family reunification process:

Step One: Family assessment and evaluation.
Step Two: Treatment planning.
Step Three: Family therapy in preparation for the clarification session.

- Preparing for the clarification session.

  - The tasks of the abusive sibling in preparing for the clarification session.
  - The tasks of the abused sibling in preparing for the clarification session.
  - The tasks of the family in preparing for the clarification session.
  - The tasks of the non-abused siblings in preparing for the clarification session.

- The clarification questions.
- The clarification session.

Step Four: Family therapy in preparation for supervised and unsupervised agency/programme visitation.

- Criteria for visits.
- Rules for visits.

Step Five: Family therapy in preparation for community visits.

- Criteria for community outings with the family.
- Rules for community outings with the family.

Step Six: Preparing for home visits with the family.

- Critieria for home visits.
- Rules for home visits.
- Check list of minimum criteria for community and home visitation for abusive sibling, abused sibling, non abused siblings, and parents.

Step Seven: Reunification.

- Abusive sibling's rules of conduct and relapse prevention plan.
- Family rules of conduct and safety plan.
- Abused siblings rules of conduct and safety plan.

Step Eight: Post-reunification services.

- Scheduled outpatient work.
- Follow-up evaluatory visits.
- Voluntary resources available to family (i.e., example of the programme which provides post-treatment services free to families).

Step One: family assessment and evaluation

It is extremely important that the abusive youth's family be involved in a comprehensive assessment and evaluation procedure as soon as possible after the youth's admission to the treatment programme. In fact, though a formal assessment procedure is necessary, any treatment provider's first contacts with the family should be treated as opportunities to engage, as well as gather and share information.

Assessment and evaluation are not finite procedures, but an ongoing process which spans the entire course of treatment. Information is revealed at its own pace and time throughout

treatment depending upon the particular circumstances and characteristics of each family. Stories may grow, alter, or change completely over time, and therapists should never assume that they have obtained either complete or objectively unadulterated information. For this reason it is important to begin the information exchange between therapists and family as soon as possible.

Beginning engagement work is even more vital in these initial contacts. Engagement of the family is just as essential to the assessment and evaluation process as engagement of the sexually abusive youth is to the effectiveness of their treatment. Even when family treatment is not actually performed within the same agency as the abusive youth, effective engagement will be critical both to the quality of the information gained by assessment, and to the quality of the family's support of the treatment of the abusive sibling.

Effective engagement can sometimes be a difficult process due to family denial, resistance to loss of privacy and control, and a host of other problems. As well, it can be extremely tricky to judge just how successful engagement has been. Treatment providers are all too aware of what accomplished social manipulators young people who sexually abuse can be, but there are also some parents that can be just as accomplished at misleading 'outsiders'. Particularly when the courts have mandated treatment of their involvement in the process, some families will work hard to convince therapists that they are actively engaged in the programme when in reality they are only engaged in whatever behaviours it takes to get them away from you and back to their 'normal lives' as soon as possible. This is relatively rare compared to open resistance, but it is a possibility which therapists must keep in mind.

In addition to concerns about the fullness or veracity of information received from family members at any particular time, there is the simple fact that it is a rare human being who can provide a truly objective picture of themselves or those closest to them, even when not immersed in crisis. Given the complexity of the issues involved in sibling sexual abuse, it is crucial that treatment providers avail themselves of the broadest possible body of information resources from agencies that have been involved with the family or family members in the past.

Between the importance of beginning the assessment process as soon as possible, and the need to assemble the largest and most cross-referenced body of information possible, the collaboration between all professionals and agencies involved should be established at these earliest stages as well. Family and youth treatment providers and the professionals of other agencies need not wait until their first contacts with the family members to begin working together to share information and records.

Assessment focus

Although each family is an individual entity with their own set of circumstances, traits, relationships, and structure, there are some common characteristics that are found in a great many families of sexually abusive youth. These characteristics are often the ones that may have engendered, supported, or unwittingly allowed the offending behaviour, and as a result are important to assess carefully. They include but are not limited to:

- Abuse of power within the family.
- Family isolation.
- Family denial, minimisation and projection of blame.
- Lack of empathy or unresponsiveness to another person's feelings.
- Problems in communication patterns, particularly cognitive distortions and inability to share on a feeling level.
- Blurred role boundaries.
- Emotional deprivation and neediness.
- Failure to protect.
- Failure to set appropriate limits or boundaries.

Step Two: treatment planning

The family assessment and evaluation will determine the issues to address, in what sequence, and with which family members, and this strategy is part of the family treatment plan. The plan outlines the goals and objectives of treatment, the interventions used to achieve these goals and objectives, the staff responsible for treatment modalities, and the expected time frames for completion of these objectives.

Every family system is made up of subsystems. As a result quite often the treatment plan will require the inclusion of preparatory or concurrent work with individual family subsystems in addition to therapy involving the entire family. It may be necessary for clarification or

reconciliation to take place with subsystems before they can take place with the entire family. These are clinical judgements determined by the therapist based on information gained during the assessment or initial stages of treatment.

The following are three common examples of the range of possibilities typifying this approach in cases of sibling sexual abuse:

- Subsystems of the family will work on identified treatment issues that only affect those subsystems, or that prepare those subsystems for collective family-system work.
- The abusive sibling and parents may need to work together prior to meeting with abused or non-abused siblings.
- The abusive sibling, parents, and non-abused siblings may meet together, followed by a session involving the abusive sibling, the parents, and the abused siblings prior to entire family sessions.

Obviously, in cases of multiple-sibling or intergenerational sexual abuse within the family, attention during treatment planning to family subsystem issues are even more critical, as well as more complex.

The treatment plan, developed from the assessment data, is your roadmap of treatment, complete with signposts, to tell you how much further, you have to go. With a treatment plan, no one has to wonder what the treatment is trying to accomplish because it is documented and detailed. Nothing is vague. The plan is a guide that structures the focus of treatment toward the ultimate goal, the prevention of abusive behaviour. It does so by identifying and interrupting the family patterns that may have allowed or supported abusive behaviour, replacing those with patterns that support non-abusive and pro-social behaviour, interrupting the cycle of intergenerational abuse, healing the wounds caused by family membership or non-membership, teaching self-management skills to the sexually abusive/aggressive youth, outlining the standards of care for victim clarification and family reunification, and learning what it means to be a part of a healthy family.

Step Three: the clarification session

Preparation for clarification sessions

As family reunification process begins, one of the most critical steps is preparation for the clarification session. The name clarification session is fairly self-explanatory. They are sessions conducted with the abusive youth, the abused siblings, the parents, and non-abused siblings in order to clarify what has occurred in a therapeutic and safe setting. It is the first session in which family members meet face-to-face for the purpose of honestly acknowledging the sexually abusive behaviour, the accountability of the young person who has sexually abused, and what the victim, as well as others have experienced as a consequence.

According to the needs, methods and schedules identified in treatment planning, the family members begin the initial therapy by accomplishing the tasks which must precede the clarification session. The details of the tasks which need to be completed by the family members separately and in subsystems prior to beginning clarification sessions will vary to a certain extent according to the idiosyncrasies of the family and family members. Clarification sessions are not always initially conducted with the entire family. Sometimes it is a better practice to do this in stages, with the sexually abusive youth and their parents first, then the abusive youth and his non-abused siblings, and then whatever combination the victim chooses.

Clarifications sessions are extremely important therapeutic steps for all concerned, particularly the abused and abusive siblings, and they are not attempted until everyone involved feels safe, supported, and empowered. Like family reunification, they are not conducted without the unanimous approval of all team members.

Each of the family members has therapeutic tasks that they must accomplish prior to the clarification session and each of these are equally important.

The tasks of the abusive sibling:

- To take full responsibility for their behaviour without minimisation or rationalisation.
- To demonstrate the ability to experience and express empathy.
- To write an account of the abusive behaviour from the victim's point-of-view.
- To re-establish initial contact through writing a letter of responsibility to the victim. This is a letter which, considering the age and developmental stage of the victim, does the following:

- Accepts responsibility for the abuse without minimisation, rationalisation or projection of blame.
- Acknowledges the harmfulness of the abuse to the victim and to the entire family.
- Assures their sibling that they are not to blame and that the sexually abusive sibling is solely responsible.
- Relieves the abused sibling's guilt over disclosure by telling them that 'they did the right thing to tell'.
- Says that the courageous act of telling was the reason why the abuse stopped, and was the reason they both got help.

The letter avoids the following:
- It does not ask forgiveness.
- Does not tell the abused sibling what to do about anything, or how to feel about anything.
- Does not attempt to make the abused sibling feel sorry for the abuser.
- Does not parrot the therapist but expresses genuine feelings.

Most sexually abusive youth cannot write this letter of responsibility either easily or quickly. The therapist, the treatment team and the members of the youth's offence specific group will all listen to and assess the letter for genuineness, and offer suggestions for change. Sometimes letters are rewritten many times before they pass this critical review.

The letter not only is a vehicle to re-establish contact between the siblings and to acknowledge the responsible party, but it serves as a rich therapeutic experience for the abusive youth. Being able to write the letter and accomplish all of the five requirements of the letter while avoiding all the four concerns illuminates and provides structured opportunities for the therapeutic work the offender needs to complete to accomplish important treatment goals.

The receipt of the letter by the victim is co-ordinated by the victim's therapist and the parents. Usually it is read with the therapist and parents in attendance so that feelings can be addressed and questions answered. Reactions to this letter can be very different – the victim may want to write back, may want some time to think about the letter, or may decide the offender is not sincere. Whatever the response, however, it marks the real beginning of the reunification process for the two siblings.

While this process is taking place with the abusive sibling, the other family members are simultaneously completing therapeutic tasks of their own:

The tasks of the abused sibling:

- To understand that they are in charge of the clarification session and can end it at any time.
- To choose the place for the meeting and who participates in the meeting.
- To understand that their needs are foremost.
- To participate in a child sexual abuse assessment to determine what, if any, treatment interventions are needed or recommended.
- To participate in whatever victim specific treatment is recommended.
- To resolve any acute symptoms of victimisation such as suicidal ideation, self-mutilation, anxiety, sleeplessness, night terrors, etc.
- To affirm that they feel supported and safe.

The tasks of the family:

- To resolve feelings of shock and denial.
- To understand what family patterns may have supported or facilitated the offending behaviour, even if unknowingly.
- To understand what family patterns of behaviour will support non-offending behaviour and to begin work on those changes.
- To acknowledge and accept responsibility for their failure to protect.
- To commit to be protective and supportive of the victim and all children in the family in the future.

The tasks of the non abused siblings:

- To understand why their sibling has been removed from the home and is in treatment.
- To understand the meaning of treatment.
- To understand what prevention means and how to use the tools of prevention.

The clarification sessions:

The actual face-to-face clarification session or sessions do not take place until all treatment team members believe that the above requirements have been met. This means at a minimum that all of the therapeutic tasks have been successfully completed, and that the victim has chosen a

setting which makes them feel safe. At times the participants in the session could include the two siblings, the treatment providers, the parents, other siblings, or extended family members. Or it might include just the two siblings and their therapists. The session could take place in someone's office or at home. Whatever the particular setting the most important factor is the victim understands that there has been careful planning for this session and that they have the right to stop the sessions at any point that they feel unsafe. This rarely happens since this meeting has been so carefully prepared for. In fact in the author's experience the abused sibling is generally eager for this opportunity to confront the abusive sibling.

Because the clarification session itself is built around the acceptance of accountability of the abusive sibling, and establishing the importance of supporting and helping the victim, the sessions generally revolve in large part around questions asked of the abusive youth by their victims. The importance of appropriate and genuine responses to such questions is the reason that the abuser has considered these questions as part of his therapeutic work prior to the session.

The following are some of the questions which victims commonly say they would like to ask the abuser if given the opportunity:

- Why did you molest me?
- How can you live with yourself after what you did?
- How did you trick me?
- Do you still love me even though I told?
- Are you mad at me because I told?
- Do you feel guilty about what you did?
- Is the treatment helping? How?
- What do you need to work on in treatment?
- How long will treatment take?
- Do you want to be a part of the family again?
- Will you (molest) me again?
- Why did you (interfere with) my life?
- How did you keep Mom and Dad from knowing?
- Did you ever think that I was scared?
- How did you think the abuse has affected my life?

It may take several clarification sessions before successful family resolution is accomplished. When this happens, however, it is the first benchmark of the reunification process. Indeed, clarification sessions represent a form of extremely limited, highly structured family reunification. They are, in effect, the first step in a resolution and reunification continuum that stretches from these sessions to full, permanent, unsupervised reunification of the family. Exactly where each family finds its best and safest place along this continuum is still unknown at this stage, but positively and constructively managing the clarification sessions is an extremely promising sign.

Step Four: agency/programme visitation

The next step in the reunification continuum is agency visitation. The treatment team will determine whether and how much additional group and individual therapeutic work will be required before these visits take place. This decision will be based both on the team's collective judgments about the clarification sessions, on their individual sessions with the abusive youth, the abused sibling, and the other family members afterward, and upon the results of a pre-visitation family session involving all those who will be involved.

Since clarification sessions may have begun with some parts of the family and not others, agency visitations may begin with these subsystems before the others are ready. Typically the first to visit will be the parents. As other family members complete the clarification session and pre-visitation work they will be added to the agency visitation list. Visitations are trial affairs, and the victim may end their participation in an agency visit at any time.

Agency/programme visitations are supervised, conducted according to previously discussed behavioural rules, and built around specific tasks for those involved in a particular visitation, but they are still more naturalistic interactions than normal family therapy sessions.

These visits start off brief, are processed with the family before and after each visit, and extended according to their agreed upon level of success. Visitations are important therapeutic opportunities to interact as a family according to the new patterns of behaviour and communication which all participants have learned to date. In essence, they are experiential laboratories for the exploration, practice and internalisation of what they have learned in earlier individual and family therapy sessions.

For the parents the visitations are also supervisory training sessions. With the aid of the agency/programme visitation supervisor and the examples of the supervisory behaviour of therapists in earlier family sessions, the parents begin the process of learning how to oversee a family that includes sexually abusive and abused children.

The following are the criteria for facility visitation:

- The clarification session has been successfully completed.
- All visitors state that they are comfortable meeting with the abusive sibling in this sort of setting.
- The treatment team approves an appropriate supervisor for the visits. This means that the supervisor understands and is able to confront offender dynamics, and to terminate the visit if necessary.
- The treatment team judges that the abusive sibling is ready to re-establish family contact in this sort of context.
- The abused sibling feels secure that the parent will protect them, and the family is genuinely supportive.
- The family members are able to discuss the abuse and its impact on their lives openly with the abusive sibling.
- The sexually abusive sibling has practiced role plays about realistic visitation situations and knows how to handle them.
- The family members all have an understanding of treatment, rules, etc.

The general rules for agency visitation are:

- Each visit approved by the treatment team.
- Each visit supervised until the treatment team makes another.
- The sexually abusive youth must accept any limits imposed by the supervisor or parents.
- The sexual abuse will not be discussed in detail without a therapist present.
- The sexually abusive youth may not be alone at any time with the sexually abused sibling or non-abused siblings and may not engage in disciplinary behaviour of any type.
- The sexually abusive sibling must not be in any bathroom setting with any children.
- The sexually abusive youth is not to ask for affection from the sexually abused sibling.

Step Five: community visitation

Assuming that the programme/agency visitation has taken place successfully, that any issues have been dealt with therapeutically, it is time for the next step which is community visitation. This covers an extremely broad range of possible visits between various combinations of family members with the youthful abuser in public settings such as restaurants, movies, parks, playgrounds, shopping, etc.

Criteria for Community Visits:

- The clarification step has been successfully completed.
- Agency/programme visits have been successful.
- There is a written family contract of agreement for outside visits and where they will take place in the community.
- The family understands the abusive cycles of behaviour.
- The family understands the youth's relapse prevention plan.
- The family has developed a family relapse prevention plan or safety plan.
- The family knows the high risk factors and situations of the abusive youth.
- The parents provide adequate support and supervision.
- The family recognises offending behaviour even when subtle.
- The parents are willing to limit the abusive sibling's access to the abused siblings and to other children.
- The abusive sibling is at an appropriate treatment stage for visits outside of the facility.

The range of possibilities for community visitation are as broad as the resources of the community, the imagination of the treatment team, and the collaborative agreements they can form with various community organisations. Like facility visitations, each particular community visitation must be approved by all therapists and family members involved, and discussed both before and afterward.

Also like agency visitations, community visitations progress in length of time as success in treatment progresses. As well, community visits between the parents and abusive youth are likely to precede community visits which include non-abused siblings, and, finally the victimised sibling. Unlike agency/programme visitations, however, visits in the community also progress over a wide range of levels of professional and lay supervision. Initial community visitations might be held as part of a free or paid programme conducted specifically for these families by a community organisation, and supervised passively at a relative distance by staff specially trained for the purpose. Later, according to the progress and comfort of the family and family members they might progress to meals at a restaurant, attending a school play or sporting event, a picnic in a public park, etc.

Just as with all types of visitations, community visits are conducted with the understanding that they can be ended at any time by the victimised sibling if they feel unsafe. Entrusting the family with this responsibility to place the support and emotional protection of the victim above all other considerations lies at the core of the purpose of these visitations. As such, they are not only conducted exclusively after the most rigorous consideration by all the members of the treatment team. As well, their successful completion can have an even greater therapeutic value for the victim than for any other family member. However brief or public, these are the first contacts between the abusive and abused siblings with their parents and siblings in social contexts where there is even a remote opportunity for the abusive youth or other family members to treat them inappropriately. The successful demonstration of pro-therapeutic learning and trustworthiness by the abusive sibling and other family members, and the successful demonstration of the ability to trust and face anxiety or fear in a safe structured framework can be extremely empowering and healing for all concerned.

Step Six: home visits

After the successful completion of a graduated series of community visitations and correlate work in therapy by the family, the family can progress to visits to the home by the sexually abusive sibling. With increasing lengths of time and decreasing supervision. Again, these will probably initially involve only the sexually abusive child and parents, will be relatively brief, and may involve a wide range of specifically pre-discussed and pre-approved activities. With the successful completion of these visits and the therapeutic work associated with them, the visits will increase in time and feature a gradual decrease in external supervision.

The reunification stage begins as an expansion upon the agency and community visitation. As with the initial stages of family and community visitation, the initial home visitations are brief, pre-defined interactions built around specifically discussed rules and tasks, and which are observed by either a member of the agency staff or a representative of one of the other agencies collaborating in the family's treatment.

As a way of adding an intermediate level of treatment, some treatment facilities have home-like apartments or houses on their grounds specifically for the purpose of providing -like environments for day-time and overnight visitations which offer greater actual and subjective security for family members. Some agencies or programmes have families of sibling sexual abusers who live in these apartments or cottages while the abusive child is in segregated treatment. They then, where appropriate, graduate the abuser, victim, and family through the various levels of home visitation 'on-campus' prior to attempting any level of home visitation.

As with all the other major and sub-levels of visitation, home visitations are conducted in a drawn-out, carefully monitored and discussed continuum of increasing length and independence which are based entirely upon treatment progress and the subjective comfort of all concerned.

The most important aspect of these examples when it comes to the general population of sibling sexually abusive families is that they represent an attempt by an agency to exercise imagination and creative use of available resources to meet the idiosyncratic needs of each particular family.

Just as with the previous levels of visitation, additional individual and family work may be required before any level of home visitation may be attempted. Likewise, the initial home visitations may involve family subsystems before including the entire family because of variations in the circumstances and needs of each family and its members, and differences in various family members or subsystem's progress along the continuum of reunification tasks.

Prior to the home visits the following should take place:

- The family participates actively in treatment.
- The treatment team views the parent, guardians or supervisory adults as capable of protecting children.
- The children have requested home visitation.
- Home visits are structured to meet treatment needs.
- Any other agency guidelines related to home visits also apply.

Checklist of minimum criteria for both community and home visitation (adapted from Mary Meinig)

Abusive Sibling:

- Impulsive behaviours are at a manageable level.
- Sexual behaviour and sexualised behaviour are managed.
- Is willing to plan for visits and accept supervision during visits.
- Accepts total responsibility for the abuse.
- There is no major difference between the abused sibling and the abusive sibling statement of the abuse.
- Has intellectual understanding of the impact on the victim and family.
- Has approval for visits from therapists.
- Is willing to totally accept limits on visits by family or victim.
- Emotional empathy for victim is increasing and is shown on both a behavioural and feeling level.
- Has shown willingness to disclose to others.
- Has shown ability to delay gratification.
- Has exhibited a noticeable decrease in abusive traits.
- Has completed responsibility letter.
- Has completed clarification session.
- Is cleared for visits by staff and other systems involved.
- Takes full responsibility for their offending behaviour.
- Knows their abusive cycle (chain or pattern) of behaviour and how to intervene.
- Has developed an individual and personalised relapse prevention plan.
- Has not exhibited abusive behaviour for a considerable period of time.

Abused Sibling:

- Has had a victim specific assessment to determine intervention needs.
- Is in abuse specific treatment if recommended.
- Is able to talk about the sexual abuse in a clinical setting.
- Is able to discuss the abuse with the mother or approved adult supervisor.
- Places the responsibility for the abuse on the abusive sibling.
- Is assertive enough to make needs heard.
- Knows sex offender characteristics and what is required of them in treatment.

- Is able to identify the ways in which the abuse has affected their life.
- Has completed initial clarification session with the abusive sibling.
- Understands safety and prevention information.
- Understands and can utilise family relapse prevention plan.
- Knows support system and how to use it.

Parents:

- Have developed an understanding of abusive sexual behaviours, and of abused sibling's abusive characteristics and treatment needs.
- Know the nature of the sexual abusiveness and has a willingness to know sexual history, including all past offences and abusive acts.
- Places full responsibility for the sexual abuse on the abusive sibling.
- Has a support system in the extended family and in the community.
- Can discuss the sexual abuse without minimising, rationalising or making excuses.
- Has demonstrated the ability to be supportive of the abused sibling.
- Has demonstrated an ability to identify behavioural signs which would indicate high risk behaviour of the abusive sibling, and understand the actions necessary to protect their children.

Non-Abused Siblings:

- Have been involved in family therapy.
- Are able to talk about the abuse.
- Have an understanding of the nature of the abuse.
- Have an understanding of the systems involved with the family, why they are involved, and what they are responsible for.
- Hold abusive sibling solely responsible for the abuse, and does not blame the abused sibling.
- Have an understanding of victim impact.
- Can identify ways that the abuse has impacted their lives.
- Have good information on abusive sexual behaviour and abusive behaviour in general.
- Have completed initial clarification session with the abusive sibling.

Although these are called rules of conduct, they may be called a safety plan or seen as part of a relapse prevention plan. It is helpful to practice the operationalisation of these rules through role plays prior to discharge.

Abusive Sibling's Rules of Conduct for Visits and Permanent Return to the Home (partially adapted from Mary Meinig)

Rules for the Abusive Sibling:

- Is never to be alone with the abused sibling or with other children.
- Is never to be responsible for supervising or disciplining children.
- Is never to initiate physical contact with other children.
- Is never to discuss issues of sexuality with children.
- Is never to ask for special affection from children.
- May never use alcohol or other drugs.
- Must be supervised by an adult approved by the treatment team whenever in the presence of children.
- Will only discuss abuse in the treatment setting.
- Will not sit next to children in car, restaurants, etc.
- May not have any secrets with children.
- May not give gifts to children unless approved by the parents.
- May never enter their sibling's bedrooms without an approved adult present.
- Will use separate bathroom facilities when possible. In all cases, family members should lock the bathroom door when it is in use.
- Should be within eyesight of the adult supervisor at all times during home visits, or if not within eyesight, the adult supervisor knows where they are and that they are either alone or not with anyone vulnerable to abuse.
- Should not be in control or dictate children's activities.
- Is not to confront the children about their misbehaviour.
- Is never to be involved in the physical hygiene of the children.
- Is not to criticise or compliment the children's physical appearance unless specifically asked their opinion by the child.
- Is not to engage in horseplay or tickling with other children.
- Should be fully dressed any time they are outside their bedroom or bathroom.
- May not play with other children unsupervised.

The above home rules serve as the basis for a safety plan that protects the family from further abusive behaviour. This plan often needs to be individualised in order to address the different circumstances and issues of individual families.

Step Seven: reunification

What is successful completion of treatment when reunification is the goal?

It can be very confusing for families if their expectation of treatment completion is the completion of workbooks, modules or level systems, or some finite programme schedule. In actuality, completion of treatment is the achievement of the safest and healthiest state possible along a continuum of potential goals as determined by observable behaviour. What's more, completion of treatment in a case of sibling sexual abuse is dependent upon the progress of family members individually as well as a unit. These are not measures of treatment success or completion which conform to any pre-set time-table.

Successful completion for the young person who has sexually abused must be dependant upon measurable outcomes such as decrease in sexual behaviour, increase in management of impulsive behaviour, ability to manage anger in an appropriate way, etc. Completion for the family means that they have interrupted the family patterns that allowed, supported or encouraged offending behaviour and replaced those with patterns that support non-offending behaviour. Completion for the victimised and non-victimised siblings is more problematic and the most difficult to forecast, in part because it is dependent upon the completion of treatment goals by the abusive sibling and the parents.

Ideally, everyone in the family will complete the tasks of family reunification and will continue in treatment and co-operate in post-reunification services. In reality, the further each family can progress through the reunification process in part or whole the greater the accomplishment and the greater their prospects for future health and safety.

Step Eight: post-reunification services

The family's involvement with the treatment programme and work with the treatment team does not end with discharge – particularly when the family has been reunified. More often than not, the continued work of the entire treatment team, family included, may be essential for the family and abusive youth to succeed over the long term in maintaining the behaviour and relationship patterns they have learned in treatment.

After all, even without treatment, if the abusive child is out of the home for any length of time he will come home changed, the family will undoubtedly have changed in their absence, and, as a result, the dynamics of living together will likely be different too. Since the very purpose of treatment is to substitute healthy behavioural patterns for unhealthy ones in the abusive child, family, and victim, following successful treatment the family system and members will be significantly altered by definition.

Though the purpose of the different visitation stages of the family reunification treatment process is to help all concerned gradually learn and adjust to such changes, and family reunification is not considered or allowed except under the most optimal circumstances, there is likely to be at least a significant subjective difference for family members between the lengthiest home visitations of treatment and the open-ended process of post-treatment, reunified life. If an abusive child was in residential treatment he may have lived within a structure that makes freedom a scary prospect. The parents are also likely to be scared about whether they are really prepared to cope yet. The abused sibling, however much affirmation and support they may have received within the treatment process, may naturally, at the least, have reservations about how real the changes in their abusive sibling and family will be once formal treatment is completed. The non-abused siblings may have any and all of these uncertainties, as well as others particularly their own.

In years past, it was common for agencies to mistakenly believe that treatment and therefore the treatment team's responsibility to the family, ended with 'matriculation out of the programme'. Over the last few decades we have learned the hard way that follow-up and aftercare are necessary and therefore formal aspects of a treatment plan.

Because of the different structure and resources of the agencies which may be involved in the treatment of any particular case, there are no set rules or specific requirements for treatment providers when it comes to follow-up and after-care. In the United States, there are some independent private organisations which offer voluntary aftercare services for a price. There are also some treatment and independent agencies which offer free after-care services upon request to families who have completed normal treatment programmes. The specific method or agency by which follow-up and aftercare are provided is not important. What's important is that the different agencies and professionals involved, working within the realities of their individual, collective and community resources, ensure that the parents and the family have the resources and safety net they need to assure that the positive changes they have accomplished in treatment are not just internalised, but will last.

When everything you do isn't enough

The plan for reunification is a roadmap towards a goal. In that sense it is simply a guide, and the actual circumstances and conditions you find along the way may force changes. There are times when the road is straight and the visibility fine. When this is true then a reunification plan will work like a jigsaw puzzle. When the road is rocky and mountainous and you have to take side roads to get where you want to go the trip may not turn out quite like you planned. This is also true with families. There will be times when some of the steps outlined in your reunification plan are impossible to achieve. There are reasons why reunification may not work no matter how hard everyone tries and there are contraindications to reunification. It is important to know what the bottom lines are for safety's sake. Some of the typical reasons why reunification may not work or be contraindicated are listed below:

Contraindications to reunification

- The abusive sibling has not participated in offence specific treatment.
- The family or a significant part of the family has not participated in offence specific treatment.
- The abused sibling has not participated in offence specific treatment.
- The family, abusive sibling, or abused sibling have not reached the treatment goals necessary for a safe reunification.
- The family is not agreeable to changes that support non-offending behaviour.
- The family has participated in treatment but will not provide adequate support for the abused sibling, cannot provide adequate

supervision for the abusive sibling, or is not willing to develop and practice a family relapse prevention plan.
- Parental denial of problems cannot be changed.

Reasons why reunification may not work:

- Parental problems not resolved, or number and severity of problems were underestimated.
- Parental ambivalence.
- Parents allow abusive child inappropriate contact with the victim or other children.
- Service delivery systems fail to work collaboratively or work at cross purposes, undermining treatment.
- A treatment plan process orientation instead of outcome orientation.
- Agency has resource problems that interfere with provision of services such as worker turnover or inconsistency, inexperience, excessive caseload, inadequate casework supervision, etc.
- Agency policy lacks outcome focus and there are unclear expectations about what is necessary for reunification.

Decision making if reunification fails

Rationale for removing the abusive sibling rather than the abused sibling:

- Protects the abused sibling and potential victims if the abusive sibling is placed where there are no children.
- Assigns responsibility for the abuse with the abusive sibling.
- Changes structure of the family and redefines the abused sibling as someone needing protection.
- Helps the abused sibling to see that the abusive sibling will be held accountable.
- Increases motivation for the abusive sibling in treatment if they wish to return home.

Problems inherent in removing the abused sibling from the home rather than the abusive sibling

- The abused sibling will be convinced that they are responsible for the abuse.
- Other siblings are still at risk.
- Decreases motivation for family to collaborate in treatment if the abused sibling is allowed to be perceived as the problem.

- The abused sibling will show an increase in symptoms.
- Placement maintenance of abused sibling will be difficult because of increase in symptoms.
- Gives the abused sibling all of the responsibility and no rights.
- The abused sibling will continue to see themselves as helpless.

Final steps when reunification is unworkable

Certainly family treatment can be healthy and healing even when reunification is contraindicated or unworkable. There are other very successful resolutions for many families. There is a continuum of family resolution that can go from grieving the loss of family to full family reunification. The goal is for all family members to lead a healthy and productive life and this may mean different things for individual families.

Conclusion

Ideally, everyone in the family will complete the tasks of family reunification, will continue in treatment, and will co-operate in post-reunification services. In reality, this is not always possible. Sometimes this is because of problems that arise within the family or treatment process. Sometimes it is a result of agencies, failing to understand the possibilities created by imaginative and collaborative approaches, setting arbitrary time limits on treatment for fiscal reasons. Sometimes families lose the opportunity to reach their optimal treatment outcome because of factors outside of the involved professionals' control.

Unfortunately, issues involving children, families, or sexuality alone are socially and politically volatile, and sibling incest involves all three. Currently in the US, Canada and Europe legislative bodies have enacted nation-wide policies which mandate the preservation and reunification of families. Because policies are often determined at the political rather than the informed professional level, as a result it is not rare for the decision to reunify or maintain the separation of a family to be made despite the recommendations of the trained professionals of the juvenile justice, child protective services, and/or treatment agencies involved.

This regrettable reality, however, only increases the importance of actively and conscientiously engaging in the family resolution and

reunification process. Whether the final decision about reunifying a particular family is made in concert by trained and qualified professionals or whether it is made as a result of social policy, family resolution and reunification work will result in a safer and healthier victim, family, abuser, and community at large.

References

National Standards for Offence Specific Residential Treatment Programmes for Sexually Abusive Youth (1999), Whitman Publications.

Association for the Treatment of Sexual Abusers (2001) *Practice Standards and Guidelines,* Oregon. Beaverton.

Barbaree, H., Marshall, W. and Hudson, S. (Eds.) (1993) *The Juvenile Sex Offender,* New York, NY. The Guilford Press.

Bera, W., Hindman, J., Hutchens, L., McGuire, D. and Yokley, J. (1990) *The Use of Victim-Offender Communication in the Treatment of Sexual Abuse: Three Intervention Models,* Brandon, VT. The Safer Society Press.

Burnham, J., Moss, J., Debrelle, J. and Jamieson, R. (1999) Working with Families of Young Sexual Abusers: Assessment and Intervention Issues. In Erooga, M. and Masson, H. (Eds.) *Children and Young People Who Sexually Abuse Others,* London. Routledge.

Calder, M.C. (1997) *Juveniles and Children Who Sexually Abuse: Frameworks for Assessment,* Lyme Regis. Russell House Publishing.

Carlo, P. (1991) Why a parental involvement programme leads to a family reunification: A dialogue with childcare workers, *Residential Treatment For Children and Youth,* 9(2) 37–48.

Centre for Sex Offender Management (2000) *The Collaborative Approach to Sex Offender Management,* Washington, DC. Centre for Sex Offender Management.

Garner, H. (1988) *Helping Others through Teamwork: A Handbook for Professionals,* New York, NY. Child Welfare League of America.

Gil, E. (1987) *Children Who Molest: A Guide for Parents of Young Sex Offenders,* Walnut Creek, CA. Launch Press.

Jongsma, A., Peterson, M. and McInnis, W. (1996) *The Adolescent Psychotherapy Treatment Planner,* New York, NY. Wiley and Sons.

Levenson, J.S. and Morin, J.W. (2001) *Treating Nonoffending Parents in Sexual Abuse Cases: Connections in Family Safety,* Thousand Oaks, CA. Sage Publications.

Long, P. and Jackson, J. (1994) Childhood Sexual Abuse: An Examination of Family Functioning, *Journal of Interpersonal Violence*, 9(2) 270–7.

Lundrigan, P.S. (2001) *Treating Youth Who Sexually Abuse: An Integrated Multi-Component Approach*, New York. Haworth Press.

Meinig and Bonner (1990) Returning the Treated Sex Offender to the Family, *Violence Update*.

National Adolescent Perpetrator Network (1988) Preliminary Report from the National Task Force on Juvenile Sexual Offending, *The Juvenile and Family Court Journal*, 39, 2.

O'Connell, et al. (1990) *Working With Sex Offenders: Guidelines for Therapist Selection*, Newbury Park, CA. Sage Publications.

Rich, P. (2003) *Understanding, Assessing, and Rehabilitating Juvenile Sexual Offenders*, Hoboken, NJ. John Wiley and Son.

Ryan, G. and Lane, S. (1991) *Juvenile Sexual Offending: Causes, Consequences and Correction*, Lexington, MA. Lexington Books.

Ryan, G. et al. (1999) *Web of Meaning: A Developmental-Contextual Approach in Sexual Abuse Treatment*. Brandon, VT. The Safer Society Press.

Saunders, B.E. and Meinig, M.B. (2000) Immediate Issues Affecting Long Term Family Resolution in Cases of Parent–Child Sexual Abuse, in Reece, R.M. (Ed.) *Treatment of Child Abuse: Common Ground for Mental Health, Medical, and Legal Practitioners*, Baltimore, MA, The John Hopkins University Press.

Saunders, B.E. and Meinig, M.B. (2001) *Family Resolution Therapy in Cases of Child Abuse*, Charleston, SC, Authors.

Thomas, J. (1991) The Adolescent Sex Offender's Family in Treatment, In Ryan, G. and Lane, S. (Eds.) *Juvenile Sexual Offending: Causes, Consequences and Correction*, Lexington, MA, Lexington Books. 333–76.

Thomas, J. and Viar, C.W. (2001) Family Treatment of Adult Sexual Abusers, in Mussack and Carich (Eds.) *Handbook of Sexual Abuser Assessment and Treatment*, Brandon, VT. Safer Society Press, 163–92.

Trepper, T. and Barret, M. (1988) *Treating Incest: A Multiple Systems Perspective*, Binghamton, NY. The Haworth Press.

Warsh, R., Pine, B. and Maluccio, A. (1994) *Teaching Family Reunification: A Sourcebook*, Washington, DC. Child Welfare League of America.

Wiehe, V. (1996) *The Brother/Sister Hurt: Recognising the Effects of Sibling*, Brandon, VT. The Safer Society Press.

Chapter Twenty-One

Sex Offender Treatment in a Juvenile Correctional Setting: Programme Description and Nine-Year Outcome Study

Edward Wieckowski, Dennis Waite, Relana Pinkerton, Elizabeth McGarvey and Gerald L. Brown

Introduction

This chapter describes a correctional sex offender treatment programme within the Virginia Department of Juvenile Justice in the USA. The evolution of the programme over a 14 year period and reports the effectiveness of treatment as measured by recidivism rates based on a nine-year outcome study. The results of the outcome study may provide insight into emerging characteristics of juveniles at risk for re-offending sexually and non-sexually.

Opening the sex offender treatment programme

The juvenile correctional setting has the potential to provide an effective and necessary treatment environment for the serious juvenile sexual offender. The Virginia Department of Juvenile Justice (DJJ) opened the first state-operated juvenile sex offender treatment programme in the state in 1990. It was established to meet the treatment needs of the growing population of juvenile sex offenders within the Department and to offset the high cost of private residential sex offender treatment, which was the other option. The only available, secure residential facility in Virginia at that time cost the Department $110,000 per year to treat each sex offender.

The Department took great care in opening the first sex offender unit in January 1990. All staff, including the juvenile correctional officers, participated in 40 hours of sex offender specific training in the following areas: attitudes and values about sexuality; adolescent development; psychopathology; teambuilding; sex offender aetiology; juvenile typologies; and treatment issues. In that first period of time, the Department accepted four juveniles into the treatment programme that had the capacity to provide services to 15, in order to pilot test the protocol and adequacy of training, and to establish the initial integrity of the programme. This phase of the programme allowed newly hired staff to gain experience with the intensive treatment protocol and ensured that a proper milieu was initially developed. Additional beds were gradually opened, but it was not until the second year that all 15 beds were operational. Male juveniles' ages 11 through 20 who were housed in any of the DJJ facilities and met the criteria for the programme were transferred to this unit.

An obstacle that emerged during this time period was adapting the programme appropriately to meet the needs of cognitively impaired, juvenile sex offenders. These offenders did not respond well to the treatment protocol because they had a difficult time understanding, conceptualising, and generalising the abstract concepts of the cognitive-behavioural treatment programme. In response to this situation, a separate 10 bed unit for cognitively impaired sex offenders of all ages was opened in September 1991, at a second correctional centre. These juveniles received a similar protocol addressing many of the same treatment areas, but at a more rudimentary level. In January 1992, the programme again was modified to address the differentiated needs of older juvenile sex offenders and to reduce the possibility of older juveniles intimidating and exploiting the younger juveniles on the unit. A separate 15 bed unit for older juvenile sex offenders, ranging in age from 16 through 20, was opened at a third correctional centre.

The DJJ sex offender treatment programme built a positive reputation for itself in the community and in the court system during this time. Over the years, additional units were opened to meet the demands created by the increasing number of sex offenders committed to DJJ to participate in treatment. Currently, the Department has 149 specialised treatment beds in eight units housed in four juvenile correctional centres. Two facilities (five individual units) offer services to younger juveniles, one facility (two individual units) to older juveniles, and one unit of 10 beds serves cognitively impaired juveniles of all ages.

The evaluation process

Initial Evaluation at the Reception and Diagnostic Center (RDC) for All Offenders

All juveniles committed to the Virginia DJJ first receive a standard series of evaluations at RDC. During their four-week stay at RDC, juveniles are evaluated across many domains. This assessment includes a general psychological evaluation and a mental status examination (MSE), an educational assessment, a physical health examination and review of systems, sexual history review, substance abuse and behavioural and social functioning assessments among others. All juveniles also are assigned a length of stay for incarceration by the RDC staffing team, if one had not already been given by the committing judge.

Sex offender assessment procedure

In addition to the standard initial assessment at RDC, juvenile sexual offenders also undergo a sex offender risk evaluation. The standard battery of measures a clinician uses for a comprehensive sex offender evaluation includes the following sex offender and non-sex offender specific instruments:

- A **sex offender specific interview** is performed to ascertain the sex offence dynamics and characteristics of the juvenile. The key areas addressed in the interview include: *offence dynamics* (i.e., description of the sexual acts; frequency and duration of the offences; victim's age, gender and relationship to the juvenile; use of force and aggression, degree of planning, etc.) and *characteristics of the juvenile* (i.e., degree of responsibility for the offences; level of distorted thinking; presence of remorse and/or empathy; level of conduct-disordered behaviour, indications of paedophilic or deviant sexual interests, etc.).
- The **Juvenile Violence Assessment Protocol (JVAP)** is administered and scored for evaluation purposes. The JVAP is a 37-item protocol developed by the Virginia DJJ, which includes the Juvenile Sex Offender Assessment Protocol-Second Edition (JSOAP-II, Prentky and Righthand, 2003). The JVAP was developed to meet the unique needs of the incarcerated juvenile sex offender population, and consists of four scales: Sexual Factors; Conduct Disorder-Antisocial; Treatment Response; and Projected Parole Compliance.

- **Minnesota Multiphasic Personality Inventory-Adolescent (MMPI-A) or Minnesota Multiphasic Personality Inventory-Second Edition (MMPI-2).** A standardised, well researched method of assessing an individual's personality make-up, as well as an indication if deceit were involved in test responses.
- **The Multiphasic Sex Inventory (MSI).** A method of assessing an individual's comprehensive sexual functioning, including sexually deviant behaviours, thoughts and fantasies – or – **The Sexual Adjustment Inventory for Juveniles (SAI-J)** – a 13 scale inventory that identifies and quantifies sexually deviate and paraphilic behaviour.
- Other pencil/paper tests and scales may be administered for additional information to aid in assessment and treatment planning once the juvenile is transferred to a juvenile correctional facility from RDC. These tests include measuring levels of cognitive distortions, sexual knowledge, sexual deviant fantasies, level of anger, etc.

Classification of treatment levels

Each juvenile's sex offender treatment needs are classified at RDC as either Mandatory or Recommended. This classification has a direct impact on the length of time a juvenile may remain in a correctional facility.

A **mandatory** classification is primarily assigned to juveniles who were committed to DJJ on a sex offence. It also applies to a violation of probation/parole (VOP) where the original conviction was a sex offence, or a violation of court order for sex offender treatment. This level requires a juvenile to remain incarcerated until he completes his treatment, or reaches the statutory limit of his commitment (generally up to 36 months, or in some cases up to their 21st birthday). Also, this treatment classification overrides his length of stay (LOS) (e.g., a juvenile with a 12–15 month LOS, may remain incarcerated past 15 months if he does not complete mandatory sex offender treatment). However, some high-risk juveniles receive a determinate sentence from the judge, which means that a set number of months must be served and that treatment needs cannot change the LOS. These youth are eligible to receive a 'mandatory,' but treatment cannot be required over a time period longer than that set by the committing judge.

A **recommended** classification is primarily assigned for juveniles who only have prior convictions for a sexual offence. A recommended classification encourages juveniles to participate in treatment, but they cannot be incarcerated past their late release date. For example, a juvenile with a 12–15 month LOS, may only be held a maximum of 15 months. As above, juveniles who receive a sentence from the judge also are eligible for this classification, but the judge determines the length of their stay and release date.

Treatment at the juvenile correctional centres

Programme's Philosophy

The programme offers individualised treatment specific to the juvenile's offence dynamics and offender characteristics. Juveniles are held accountable for their actions and provided the opportunity for rehabilitation. The principal aims of treatment are to reduce the juvenile's probability of re-offending once released into the community and to provide him with the skills needed to make a positive contribution to society.

Self-contained units

When the DJJ sex offender programme was first implemented, all juvenile sex offenders received treatment in a *self-contained unit*. Each specialised unit provided intensive milieu treatment to a maximum of 16 juveniles. The average length of time juveniles spent in a self-contained unit was 18–24 months. Staff in the units were involved with the juvenile throughout his stay in the programme. As mentioned earlier, all staff directly involved in treatment were trained in working with juvenile sex offenders to maximise their assessable knowledge in the fundamental treatment modalities for this population. New staff are required to attend a three-day training that consists of: Day 1 – An overview of working with juvenile sex offenders; Day 2 – Treatment techniques and methods; Day 3 – Cultural diversity, female offenders, and balancing security and treatment.

The staff in the sex offender units work as a treatment team to provide a multi-disciplinary

approach to treating juveniles in intensive milieu settings. Each treatment team typically consisted of a psychologist, clinical social worker, counsellor, and juvenile correctional officers (JCOs). Personnel from other departments/ services provide support to the programme such as medical staff (including a psychiatrist) for monitoring medications, teachers from the Department of Correctional Education, and recreational staff. The units also utilise volunteers and part-time employees from local universities who are at a graduate or undergraduate level of study. The institution superintendent, institution manager, and programme managers provide administrative support for the programmes.

A typical week for juveniles in the units consists of two group psychotherapy sessions, two psycho-educational groups, a community meeting, one individual psychotherapy session, one counselling session, and treatment team meetings. Family therapy is provided to juveniles and their families, as appropriate, by the psychologist or clinical social worker. The extent of family therapy offered by the therapist depends on the family's willingness to attend sessions, level of co-operation with treatment, and geographical distance from the facility. This milieu approach in the programme helps juveniles apply what they learn in treatment to the daily routine in the unit and at the facility, and further, to generalise this behaviour in the community.

Initially, juveniles worked toward completing the programme by addressing 15 specific treatment objectives, which included the following:

- **Autobiography**: to facilitate self-examination based on life history.
- **Disclosure of offences**: to facilitate responsibility for one's actions by self-identification and admitting sexual offences and deviant sexual behaviours.
- **Cycle of offending**: to ascertain, analyse, and chart the specifics of the offence cycle.
- **Cognitive distortions**: to become aware of, monitor and try to change thinking errors related to sex offences and everyday life.
- **Log book**: to facilitate self-awareness by maintaining a daily record of feelings, thoughts, fantasies, and cognitive distortions.
- **Feelings (power/anger/rage)**: to facilitate self-awareness and self-management by examination of the role of affect as related to sex offences.

- **Defence mechanisms**: to examine the role of defence mechanisms related to sex offences.
- **Social Skills**: to exhibit pro-social interactions with staff and peers and learn to improve decision making skills.
- **Victim empathy**: to examine the effect of offences on one's victim and victim's family, and to address the offences from the victim's perspective.
- **Personal victimisation**: to ascertain and process sexual and non-sexual victimisation of one's self.
- **Family issues**: to identify and study family problem areas that appears to have contributed directly or indirectly to the offences.
- **Fantasy and arousal**: to examine their role as related to sex offences and reduce deviant sexual urges by using techniques such as thought stopping and covert sensitisation.
- **Personal Treatment Objectives (2)**: to examine two areas specific and unique to the offender that may have contributed to the sexual offending behaviours.
- **Relapse prevention**: to understand how to cope with potential high-risk situations and lapses the juvenile may encounter at the facility and in the community. To integrate and to apply treatment issues addressed in the programme to interrupt the individual's offence cycle and to reduce the probability of re-offending.

The juveniles also participate in **psycho-educational groups**, both didactic and interactive, for addressing issues such as emotions, sexuality, sexual aggression, treatment issues, interpersonal relations, and independent living skills. Some juveniles also are referred to other specialty treatment programmes at the facility for treatment of substance abuse, or anger management.

Implementation of two-level sex offender treatment services

Over time, the number of juvenile sex offenders entering the system continued to increase, and demand for treatment exceeded capacity within two years of operation. There was a limited amount of space available in the self-contained units and numbers of juveniles were put on waiting lists. As a result, a second level of treatment was developed to help offset the growing number of sex offenders committed to DJJ.

After two years of operations, the Department began offering a two-level approach to sex offender treatment. When juveniles arrived at the correctional centres, they were assessed by either a psychologist or social worker at the JCC to determine which level of treatment was most appropriate for them. This was in addition to the assessment they received at RDC. Those needing intensive milieu treatment were placed in *self-contained units*, and the remaining juveniles received sex offender services through *prescriptive services*. Prescriptive services were offered to juveniles not meeting criteria for a self-contained unit, and if resources allowed, to juveniles on a waiting list for a self-contained unit in order to facilitate their progress in treatment once they entered a unit.

Criteria were developed, based on the known risk factors at the time, to prioritise the level of services (self-contained unit or prescriptive services) juveniles would receive. To meet criteria for placement in a DJJ self-contained-unit, juveniles had to meet three or more of the following:

1. Sexual assault with threat or force, or sadistic sexual acts in which the psychological or physical suffering or humiliation of the victim is a key feature of the offence.
2. A pattern of sexually deviant behaviour involving physical contact to one or more victims over an extended period of time.
3. Escalation and progression of sexually deviant behaviour that involved physical contact (e.g., sequence of deviant sexual fantasy, voyeurism, and frottage to sexually battery or rape).
4. Apprehended more than once for sex offences.
5. Sex offences against both males and females.
6. Sex offences against strangers.

Prescriptive services

Juveniles with less serious sex offence histories resided in the open population at the facility, but were brought together for treatment sessions. Their average time spent in treatment was about 9–15 months. Based on the treatment needs of the juvenile and/or resources at the facility, the juveniles participated in one or more of the following components: individual psychotherapy, group psychotherapy, psycho-educational groups, and family therapy sessions. They addressed nine of the 15 treatment objectives required by the self-contained units, listed above, omitting the log book, social skills, personal victimisation, fantasy/arousal, and the two personal treatment objectives. The nine were selected because they met the treatment needs of less serious sex offenders, and were still able to be properly applied in a non-milieu treatment programme.

Individualised treatment plans

In the late-1990s, the number of juvenile sex offenders in the system again increased significantly and the time juveniles spent waiting for treatment at some facilities was one year or longer. In 1999, the Department of Juvenile Justice received a grant from the Department of Criminal Justices Services (DCJS) that funded six full-time sex offender therapists and allowed three additional self-contained-units. The Department reviewed the status of the sex offender programme, and in 2001, decided to modify significantly the treatment protocol by developing individualised treatment plans (ITPs) instead of the 15 treatment objectives of the self-contained units or nine treatment objectives in prescriptive services.

The ITPs allowed the therapists at each JCC to individualise treatment for each juvenile based on his specific treatment needs as determined by the initial sex offender assessment at RDC, the therapist's preliminary sessions with the juvenile, and therapist's clinical judgment. Since the number of self-contained unit treatment beds increased and treatment was being individualised, there was no longer a need for prescriptive services. Under this new protocol, all juvenile sex offenders worked toward 10 general treatment goals, but through distinctive paths. The therapist chose which of the treatment objectives, if any, the juvenile must complete. The goal for each juvenile was to complete only those areas of treatment specific to his needs. As such, ideally the time that juveniles would spend in treatment would decrease, which would permit other juvenile sex offenders to obtain admittance to a treatment unit.

The ITPs were thought to be a move in the right direction, but two problems occurred with the implementation of this protocol. First, many therapists were hesitant to decrease the number of objectives juveniles had to complete because of the potentially harmful ramifications on society if one of their juveniles sexually re-offended after completing treatment. As a result, the average overall length of stay in treatment *increased* since many juveniles who were previously in

prescriptive services now had to complete 15 objectives. Second, there was no minimal standard for treatment because there was no requirement that juveniles had to complete certain objectives.

In the summer of 2003, the ITP protocol was revised by setting a minimal standard that applies to all juvenile sex offenders in the system. All juveniles work toward 10 general goals and complete a minimum of eight designated core treatment activities. Each of the core treatment activities consists of a worksheet with several assignments related to a specific treatment area. Additional treatment activities are developed by the therapist to meet the unique needs of the juvenile. The 10 goals are used as a starting indication to select the individualised treatment activities.

The 10 goals of the programme are:

1. Take responsibility for actions and decrease excuses, rationalisations, and projections of blame.
2. Reduce thinking that supports general or sexual criminal attitudes.
3. Understand factors that contributed to offence.
4. Manage anger and other emotions that contributed to offence.
5. Interact with others in socially acceptable ways.
6. Understand the impact of the offence on the victim, and reduce exploitation of others in sexual and non-sexual ways.
7. Understand role of own victimisation in sex offence.
8. Understand family dynamics that may have contributed to offence, and work toward improving family relations if appropriate.
9. Control own sexually deviant interests.
10. Interrupt cycle of offending by applying information learned in treatment.

The core treatment activities were developed by identifying treatment areas that are applicable to all or most sex offenders. Most juveniles incarcerated for a sex offence will likely need to complete more treatment activities, thus providing the therapist an opportunity to individualise treatment. The therapist uses the 10 goals as a starting indication to select and develop the individual treatment activities for each juvenile. At the same time, a therapist may provide only the core activities to a lower risk juvenile. The core treatment activities consist of:

1. Autobiography
2. Disclosure
3. Cycle
4. Cognitive distortions
5. Empathy
6. Family relations
7. Sexuality and arousal
8. Relapse prevention

Completing the sex offender treatment programme

To meet programme criteria for release each juvenile must complete the core treatment activities and any additional individual activities that are selected by the therapist. Advancement in treatment is measured by staff assessing the progress that the juvenile has made working toward the 10 general goals, which translates to the juvenile not only completing the treatment activities but also applying the knowledge and skills to his daily living situation. Once the juvenile meets the criteria for release, he appears before an exit panel to present his case for successfully completing the programme. The exit panel consists of the juvenile's therapists, therapists from other units, a counsellor, and a juvenile correctional officer. It may also include a teacher, treatment supervisors, and administrators. The panel reaches a consensus and either approves successful completion, or identifies additional areas the juvenile still needs to address in treatment.

Quality assurance

Programme evaluation and quality assurance are integral components of the DJJ sex offender treatment programme. The programme incorporates several means of providing oversight, guidance and supervision for the programme and its staff. Each facility has a licensed clinical psychologist who provides clinical and administrative supervision for the sex offender therapists. In addition, the Department developed two advisory committees and hired a co-ordinator of the sex offender services, which provided additional quality assurance among the sex offender units.

The treatment of adolescent sex offenders committee

The Department convened a Treatment of Adolescent Sex Offenders Committee (TASOC) in

the early 1990s to ensure consistency in the application of the sex offender treatment programme across all facilities. TASOC provides advisory input for sex offender treatment, reviews the existing sex offender treatment programme, and recommends training needs. This system of oversight maintains those treatments that are thought to be most effective from current literature assessments, and facilitates the standardisation of sex offender treatment among juvenile correctional centres. The committee consists of the following members appointed by the DJJ Deputy Director for Institutions: the DJJ Co-ordinator of Sex Offender Services, one therapist from each facility, a JCC Superintendent, a counsellor from the sex offender programme, a community services representative, the Central Office Programme Manager, a Department of Correctional Education (DCE) representative, and the DJJ Chief Psychologist. The objectives of this committee are:

- Providing advisory input on the condition and course of treatment.
- Reviewing treatment materials presented to the committee for feedback.
- Making recommendations on issues that need to be addressed by the programme.
- Disseminating information relevant to sex offender treatment.
- Encouraging assessment of the literature

The community advisory board

Since sex offender treatment is a sensitive topic and at times may include somewhat controversial treatment techniques, a community advisory board was developed by DJJ to provide advice and guidance for the programme during its initial implementation phase. The committee served as a preventative measure to assess and evaluate any possible negative reactions about the programme from the community, courts or parents. It reviewed treatment approaches, assessment instruments and the overall philosophy of treating sex offenders within the juvenile justice system. Members consisted of a juvenile judge, sheriff, community mental health treatment administrator, ethicist/minister, DJJ facility superintendent and DJJ chief psychologist.

Program supervisor of sex offender services

A program supervisor sex offender services was hired in January 2002, to co-ordinate and direct

DJJ's sex offender treatment efforts. The main objective for this position was to provide standardisation and quality assurance among the units that were distributed across four facilities. The program supervisor's duties include monitoring treatment within the programme and recommending changes in areas of programme implementation, delivery of treatment services, sex offender assessments, allocation of sex offender treatment resources, and data collection related to sex offender characteristics, quality assurance and efficacy of treatment methods. The program supervisor provides consultation, training, and technical assistance for the units; and he serves as a liaison to professional organisations, state and federal agencies.

Parole services for juveniles completing sex offender treatment

A therapeutic regime that includes strict parole rules and follow-up treatment significantly increases the likelihood that gains made during treatment will be maintained for most offenders. The majority of juveniles who complete sex offender treatment at a JCC will require additional community-based treatment, which is arranged by the juvenile's parole officer and court services unit. Juveniles leaving the correctional centre will need support as they make the transition to a less restrictive environment; they will also need monitoring to ensure they are applying what they learned in treatment. In order to facilitate a smooth transition, the juvenile's treatment team at the JCC works closely with the court services unit and parole officer from the day the juvenile enters treatment at a JCC until he is discharged. When the juvenile has completed the treatment, his treatment team will provide recommendations for continued services in the community.

Sex offender treatment programme evaluation

DJJ has historically viewed sex offender treatment as an important component of the juvenile justice system and has allocated a substantial portion of its treatment resources to this effort. The expansion of sex offender treatment services within the Virginia system since its inception in 1990 was described in some detail earlier in this chapter. By fiscal year 2002 (July 1, 2001 to June 30, 2002) the Department was allocating

approximately \$1.5 million each year for clinical services to treat sex offenders. While the average cost of confining a juvenile offender in Virginia's juvenile correctional centres was about \$72,000 for that year, the average cost of treating a juvenile sex offender was closer to \$80,000. The cost difference resulted from sex offenders being housed in smaller units with higher staff-to-youth ratios and a more intensive level of clinical services devoted to their treatment. Sex offenders averaged about two years to complete treatment in a self-contained unit; two years of such treatment would translate into approximately \$160,000 per offender assigned to this level of service at current costs.

Due to the amount of resources devoted to sex offender treatment and the cost of the treatment, available grant funds were directed toward an evaluation of the programme. The Virginia DJJ contracted with the Division of Preventative Research in the Department of Psychiatric Medicine at the University of Virginia to design and implement an evaluation of the sex offender treatment programme.

The nine-year sex offender treatment outcome study

The University of Virginia Evaluation Team, with input from the DJJ Chief Psychologist, designed an outcome study to determine the effectiveness of the treatment programme for juvenile sex offenders. The primary outcome of interest was a measure of *recidivism rates* for sexual re-offending by type of juvenile sex offender and treatment modality. As part of the study, the University Evaluation Team conducted a comprehensive review of juvenile sex offender programme evaluations nationwide.

The literature provided little information on risk factors associated with sexual recidivism, in part probably due to the low base rates of sexual recidivism. Attempts were made to identify characteristics of juvenile sex offenders (O'Brien and Bera, 1986; Knight and Prentky 1993), but these lacked empirical support. Recently, factors such as psychopath, deviant arousal, cognitive distortions, truancy, prior known sex offence, blaming the victim, and use of force or threats were empirically associated to sexual recidivism (Weinrott, 1998, as cited in Righthand, 2001: p34). Risk factors for non-sexual recidivism that were supported by the literature included anti-social personality, previous criminal involvement, negative self-image, low socio-economic status, rejection by parents, negative relationships between the parent and child, aggression, and poor social relationships (Worling, et al., 2000; Farrington, 1989; Loeber, 1990; and Moffitt, 1993).

A review of the literature on JSOs recidivism studies revealed that those few published studies assessing the effectiveness of sex offender specific treatment programmes were substantially limited in their utility by several important methodological flaws. The three most salient study design limitations included: one, small sample sizes, two, comparing outcomes between those who agree to treatment compared to those who refused treatment and three, short-follow-up periods after programme completion. The current outcome study described below has the benefit of a reasonably large sample of juveniles who committed serious sex offences, a comparison group who were assigned to a less intensive treatment protocol, and a nine-year follow-up period.

Limitations of comparing the self-contained versus prescriptive treatment programme

The primary obstacle to assessing the effect of self-contained versus prescriptive treatment on reducing recidivism is that important pre-treatment differences between juvenile sex offenders are confounded with assignment to treatment group. The most serious offenders were assigned to the most intensive treatment protocol (see specific criteria listed earlier). However, an important methodological advantage for purposes of this study was that assignment to self-contained treatment was limited by availability of self-contained dedicated beds. In the years soon after inception of the sex offender treatment programme, juveniles who would have been assigned to self-contained treatment were at that time assigned to prescriptive treatment. This historical variable allowed some opportunity for meaningful comparison groups to be identified within each treatment group. With this consideration in mind, an essential element for this study's design was to capture all available replicable and consistently measurable pre-treatment information, especially information that current research suggests may be predictive of recidivism. It was anticipated that this information would provides some ability to 'control' for pre-treatment differences when assessing post treatment outcome.

Study questions

Given the study's parameters, two questions were addressed:

Question 1: What is the base rate of recidivism for treated juvenile sexual offenders who were released from DJJ?

Question 2: Is the rate of recidivism lower among juvenile sex offenders who received intensive self-contained treatment compared to those who received prescriptive treatment?

Data collection

To complete the project, the team had to establish a reliable data set consolidated from multiple sources on all juvenile sex offenders remanded to the Virginia Department of Juvenile Justice from 1988 to 1998 and to facilitate additional coding to obtain information on treatment type that was not available in the existing computerised databases. Prior to beginning, procedures were established to ensure that all identifying information on the subjects in the study was kept strictly confidential.

DJJ staff provided blind coded data to the evaluators at the University of Virginia to ensure anonymity for the juveniles treated in the programme. All of the information on a given juvenile was combined by DJJ staff and then released to faculty at the university, for data analysis. The data file was stripped of identifying information and each juvenile was assigned a unique subject number that was matched with the identifying information on a list maintained by DJJ staff.

A final juvenile sex offender SPSS database was created for the sample that includes recidivism data, typological classification, psychological assessments and client profile data collected at RDC. The details of the requirements of assembling a complete database are described below.

Background information

Background data for each juvenile were gathered from two sources: one, client profile data that consisted of an extensive demographics database, which was collected by staff at RDC at time of the juvenile's admission into the system; and two, archival data collected by researchers through reviewing juvenile's state files. Twelve individuals coded the information, and achieved

Table 21.1: Data sources

Data sources	Variables
Client Profile Database (DJJ)	Contains over 600 variables, including: arrest record, intellectual (WISC-III, WAIS-II, WASI), behavioural and emotional assessments, school, medical and psychiatric history, as well as extensive family history (e.g., sexual/physical abuse, stability of home life, parental substance abuse and psychiatric history).
Written therapist's assessments and clinical notes, case files (DJJ).	Victim information, number of victims, age at first sex offence, and other sex offences not captured in the Client Profile Database.
The Virginia Criminal Information Network (VCIN) (Virginia State Police)	This database contains all Circuit Court records for the State of Virginia. The Criminal Justice Information Services Division provides literal charges for adult arrests with disposition by conviction and incarceration with associated dates pursuant to the Code of Virginia Section 19.2–389 for individual and agency research.
Juvenile Tracking System	This juvenile database contains the same level of detail as VCIN and is maintained by the Planning and Evaluation Unit of the Department of Juvenile Justice.
Juvenile Sex Offender Assessment Protocol (JSOAP, Prentky et al., 2000)	A modified version of Scale 2 – Impulsive/Antisocial Behaviour was used for this study.

90% inter-rater reliability. Archival data included offender type, release dates, type of treatment (self-contained versus prescriptive), prior sexual offences, age at first sex offence (including self-report and treatment records), and total number of victims.

Recidivism data

The recidivism measure for the nine-year study was based on re-arrests for criminal behaviour. This information was obtained from the Virginia DJJ Juvenile Tracking System database for subjects re-arrested as juveniles, and the Virginia Criminal Information Network (VCIN) database for subjects re-arrested as adults. Additional information regarding disposition of cases was obtained from the DJJ court services units, and sex offender registries of states in the immediate proximity of Virginia were searched to determine if any of the juveniles had been convicted of a sex offence. See Table 21.1 for a summary of all sources of data.

The arrest data was organised into three categories of arrest for predicting recidivism:

- **Sexual** – i.e, rape, child molestation, aggravated sexual battery, etc.
- **Non-sexual violence** – i.e, simple assault, felonious assault, attempted murder, murder, robbery, etc.

- **Property offence** – i.e, fraud, possession of drugs, firearm possession, breaking and entering, etc.

Many juveniles were charged with multiple offences that spanned more than one category of offence. Charges were prioritised hierarchically from least to most serious: property, non-sexual violent to sexual offending. For example, a juvenile who was charged with both non-sexual violent and property type offences would be categorised as a non-sexual violent recidivist. Sexual offence was classified as the most serious because that was the principal targeted behaviour of this study.

Final sample

The study pool consisted of 700 sex offenders who were treated in the juvenile correctional centres during this time period. However, the records for only a portion of the pool could be readily located. The final sample consisted of 253 male juvenile sexual offenders whose age range was 12–20 years old at the time they participated in treatment. The subjects in the sample were released between 1992 and 2000, with birth dates between 1974 and 1980. All subjects were between the ages of 21 and 27 at the time of data collection. The length of time subjects had been released from a juvenile correctional centre averaged 55 months and ranged from six months to over nine years.

Demographic information

Demographic data indicated that 50.0% of juveniles were African American, 42.5% White, 6.7% Hispanic, and 0.8% other ethnic groups. The most frequent sex offence convictions were for aggravated sexual battery, forcible sodomy, rape, and sexual battery in that order. The intellectual functioning of the sample averaged in the Low-Average range as measured by the Wechsler Intelligence Scale for Children-3rd Edition (WISC-III), Wechsler Adult Intelligence Scale-2nd Edition (WAIS-II), or Wechsler Abbreviated Scale of Intelligence (WASI). The mean Verbal score was 84.3 (range 56–131), Performance score was 88.6 (range 50–129), and Full Scale IQ was 85.9 (range 49–132). The subjects' living situation at time of initial incarceration was 31.0% living with mother only; 22.2% with adoptive parents, or in a foster home/group home/hospital setting or similar setting; 18.0% with both biological parents; 16.3% with a biological and step parent; 6.7% with grandparents, and 5.9% with the father only. Data on history of abuse of the juveniles themselves indicated that 20.4% had been sexually abused, 22.1% physically abused, and 9.2% both sexually and physically abused.

Sexual offence characteristics

The average age at first sexual offence, including self-reported information, was 14.4 years with a range of 8–18 years. Thirty-four percent of the subjects were classified as rapists, 41.5% child molesters, and 7.5% both, and 17% other. These classifications were based on the definitions developed by Prentky, Harris, Frizzell and Righthand (2000), where a juvenile was classified a 'child molester' if all his victims were age 11 or younger, and there was at least a 5-year age difference between him and his youngest victim. He was classified a 'rapist' if all his victims were age 12 or older and the sexual act included penetration, and there was less than a 5-year age difference between the offender and their youngest victim. The 'other' category represented sexual offences where the offender and victims were all under age 11, there was no penetration, or there was no physical contact. Data on total number of sex offence victims indicated 51.6% of the subjects had only one victim while 37.7% had two to five victims, and 10.7% had six or more victims.

Non-sexual criminal history

The subjects of this study were a highly delinquent group who engaged in a wide range of non-sexual delinquent activities. Eighty percent of the sample had 3 or more convictions for criminal activity. Over 90% had a conviction for a felony offence and two-thirds had a conviction for a felony prior to their current committing offence(s). Data obtained from file review, based on the Multiple Types of Offences section in Scale-2 of the JSOAP, indicated that 67% were involved in drug related offences, 62% for property offences, 57% for other rule breaking behaviour, 52% for conduct related behaviours, 51% for non-sexual person assaults, and 11% for serious motor vehicle violations. A full 75% of the sample had offence behaviour in three or more of these categories.

Data analysis

Kaplan-Meier survival curve analyses were used to predict the rate of recidivism, based on re-arrest, as the sample was followed over variable periods of time. The predicted survival rates were reported as the percentage of subjects likely to get re-arrested if all subjects had been tracked over the full nine-year follow-up period of the study. Pearson Chi-squares were reported when the margin of error for the Kaplan-Meier survival curves were too large to provide meaningful information.

Evaluation results

Baseline Recidivism Rates for the Entire Sample

Study Question 1: What is the base rate of recidivism for Juvenile Sex offenders released from DJJ?

Of the subjects who were arrested post release, only 11 or 4.3% were arrested for sexual offences. One was charged and incarcerated as a juvenile after only six months from release. Ten were re-arrested for sexual offences as adults although three were not convicted of the offence. A comparable 4% recidivism rate was also found for the larger sex offender pool (n = 669), from which the sample was originally drawn, but for

Table 21.2: Projected recidivism rates by treatment group

	Sexual	Non-sexual violence	Property	Any
Self-contained (*n*=142)	7.5%	31.2%	21.0%	57.2%*
Prescriptive (*n*=111)	6.9%	40.8%	22.9%	71.0%*

*Survival curve functions significantly differed *p*>0.05.

whom the authors were unable to locate records for file review.

The Kaplan Meier survival curve analyses, which are predictive statistical procedures, which were employed for the 253 sex offender subjects, produced a projected 7.7% re-arrest rate for sexual offending if the entire sample had been at risk for 9 years. The comparable projection for non-sexual violence was 36.1%, and 23.7% for a property offence. As outlined earlier, these categories are mutually exclusive. The survival curve analysis for predicting whether a subject would be re-arrested for any offence over the nine year period was 69.2%. As such, the rate of sexual recidivism among the subjects who were juvenile sex offenders was low.

Of particular interest, all juveniles released from a DJJ juvenile correctional facility in 1998 and 1999, and followed for 36 months, had mean recidivism rates for re-arrest of 75% and 74%, respectively (Virginia Department of Juvenile Justice, 2002). However, over that same time period, only 49.6% juvenile sex offenders had been arrested for any offence. Although the rate of recidivism for any type of offence appears high for juvenile sex offenders released from DJJ, their outcome is favourable compared to the recidivism rates documented for the general population of juveniles committed to DJJ correctional centres.

Recidivism rates by type of treatment

Question 2: Is the rate of recidivism lower among juvenile sex offenders who receive intensive self-contained treatment compared to those who receive prescriptive treatment?

Predicted recidivism by treatment type indicated similarly low recidivism rates for sexual re-offending, 7.5% for self-contained versus 6.9% for prescriptive. The extremely low base rate of sexual recidivism for both groups makes application of statistical tests unreliable. Table 21.2 shows recidivism rates by treatment group. The rate of property offences between the

two groups was nearly identical (21.0% for self-contained and 22.9% for prescriptive). The survival curve functions showed the prescriptive group was somewhat (9.6%) more likely to be involved in non-sexual violent offences than the self-contained group, although this difference was not statistically significant. Juveniles in the prescriptive treatment group were 24.1% more likely to get re-arrested for any offence than those in the self-contained treatment group. The predicted recidivism rates for any type of offence (i.e, sexual, non-sexual violent, and property combined) were statistically significantly different between the two groups: 57.2% for self-contained and 71.0% for prescriptive projected to nine years post release (Log Rank $\chi^2 = (1, n=253) = 7.57, p=0.01$).

Treatment group differences in type of sex offence committed

Juveniles in the self-contained group were significantly more likely to have committed offences against younger children (Pearson $\chi^2(2,253) = 31.64, p=0.001$). Nearly 60% of JSOs assigned to the self-contained treatment group had committed at least one sex offence against a child 5 years younger (i.e, Child Molester), compared to only 35% among JSOs assigned to prescriptive treatment. About 34% of JSOs in each treatment group had victimised someone their own age or older.

Type of sex offence and recidivism rates

Recidivism rates differed based on type of sex offence committed as a juvenile. See Table 21.3 for a summary of recidivism by type of sex offence.

Rapists were most likely to sexually re-offend post release, although this was not a statistically significant trend. Nineteen juveniles in this sample committed both acts of Child Molestation and Rape, and were classified as Mixed. Forty-three juveniles committed sex offences that

Table 21.3: Projected recidivism rates by type of offender

	Sexual	Non-sexual violence	Property	Any
Rapist (n=86)	8.2%	29.1%*	19.3%	59.3%*
Child molester (n=105)	4.1%	30.9%*	29.8%	65.4%*
Mixed (n=19)**	5.3%	36.8%*	10.5%	47.4%*
Other (n=43)	2.4%	53.8%*	24.1%	83.0%*

*Survival curve functions significantly differed $p> -0.05$.
**Note*: Percentages for *Mixed* are based on raw numbers due to small cell sizes.

did not fall into either the Rapist or Child Molester categories, and were designated as other type offenders. Juveniles who fell into this category committed the less serious type of offences, which included: non-contact paraphilia, frottage, indecent exposure and others. Despite having committed less serious sexual offences, this group was most likely to commit non-sexual violent type offences post release (Log Rank $\chi^2=(1, N=253)=8.86$, p=0.03), as well as to commit offences of any kind (Log Rank $\chi^2=(1, N=253)=10.73$, p=0.01).

General conclusions

The evaluation of Virginia's Department of Juvenile Justice juvenile correctional centre sex offender treatment programme indicates that contrary to the generally held belief that juvenile sex offenders go on to become adult sex offenders, the projected nine year re-arrest rate for these juvenile sex offenders is a relatively low 7.7%. This finding demonstrates that most juvenile sex offenders do not continue their sex offending behaviour, at least as demonstrated by official re-arrest rates. The evaluation of our sex offender treatment programme was never intended to be a research study but rather a systematic evaluation of the effectiveness of this treatment. However, these analyses may indicate which kinds of juveniles might be most amenable to our treatment programme. We are ethically obligated to provide what is thought to be the most appropriate treatment for the individual. We cannot give 'placebo' treatment, but we can carefully define our treatment methods and compare outcomes as well as classify incoming juveniles. As was reported earlier, this was a highly delinquent population from the onset, and the sex offender programme had only limited success in reducing general criminal behaviour. Another finding is that juveniles assigned to

self-contained sex offender treatment were less likely to be involved in later criminal activity after release.

There were several limitations to this study. The study sample consisted of high-risk sex offenders in a correctional facility and the findings may not apply to less restrictive residential programmes or community treatment settings. However, this 'restrictive' environment also serves as a kind of research control that allows more accurate interpretation of our findings. The recidivism data were based on re-arrest, which likely underestimated the rate of sexual recidivism since a significant amount of sexual abuse is unreported. The study population had a high non-sexual recidivism rate that suggested some juveniles were incarcerated, decreasing their time at-risk for sexual re-arrest. Treatment completers were not distinguished from non-completers due to lack of reliable archived data, which likely underestimated the effects of treatment. The low base rates for sexual re-offending precluded the authors from making any significant empirically based conclusions about characteristics of juveniles who are at risk to sexually re-offend.

This study made a strong argument for the positive effects of sex offender treatment for serious juvenile sex offenders, especially in a self-contained unit, within Virginia's Department of Juvenile Justice. The projected long-term recidivism rates for sexual offending by individuals who began their sexual offending as juveniles and received treatment as juveniles were comparable, if not better, than those published in the literature. Further to investigate recidivism rate differences among types of offenders, the authors are currently conducting a 10-year outcome study comparing low Impulsive/Antisocial juveniles with high Impulsive/Antisocial juveniles using Scale 2 of the JSOAP (Prentky et al., 2000).

The projected recidivism rates for non-sexual offences suggested future efforts in sex offender treatment generalise their treatment strategies to include non-sexual behaviours, since a significant amount of juvenile sex offenders exhibited nonsexual criminal behaviours before and after participating in a specialised sex offender treatment programme. Future research also is needed for empirical validation to measure the effectiveness of clinically accepted treatment areas such as victim empathy, denial, and cognitive distortions. Also, the development of an empirically sound typology for juvenile sex offenders will allow analysis for matching treatment strategy to offender type and increasing the predictive validity for current and future risk instruments.

References

Alexander, M.A. (1999) Sexual Offender Treatment Efficacy Revisited. *Sexual Abuse: A Journal of Research and Treatment*, 11, 101–16.

Becker, J.V. (1990) Treating Adolescent Sex Offenders. Professional Psychology: *Research and Practice*, 21, 362–5.

Borduin, C.M., Henggler, S.W., Blaske, D.M. and Stein, R.J. (1990) Multisystemic Treatment of Adolescent Sexual Offenders. *International Journal of Offender Therapy and Comparative Criminology*, 34, 105–13.

Brannon, J.M. and Troyer, R. (1995) Adolescent Sex Offenders: Investigating Adult Commitment Rates Four Years Later. *International Journal of Offender Therapy and Comparative Criminology*, 39, 317–26.

Bremer, J.F. (1992) Serious Juvenile Sex Offenders: Treatment and Long Term Follow-Up. *Psychiatric Annals*, 22, 326–32.

Farrington, D.P. (1989) Early Predictors of Adolescent Aggression and Adult Violence. *Violence and Victims*, 4, 79–100.

Hagan M.P. and Cho, M.E. (1996) A Comparison of Treatment Outcomes Between Adolescent Rapists and Child Sexual Offenders. *International Journal of Offender Therapy and Comparative Criminology*, 40, 113–22.

Kahn, T.J. and Chambers, H.J. (1991) Assessing Reoffense Risk With Juvenile Sexual Offenders. *Child Welfare*, 70, 333–45.

Kahn, T.J. and Lafond, M.A. (1998) Treatment of The Adolescent Sexual Offender. *Child and Adolescent Social Work*, 5, 135–48.

Knight, R.A. and Prentky, R.A. (1993) Exploring Characteristics for Classifying Juvenile Sex Offenders, in Barbaree, H.E., Marshall, W.L. and Hudson, S.M. (Eds.) *The Juvenile Sex Offender*. New York: Guilford Press. 45–83.

Lab, S.P. Shields, G. and Schondel, C. (1993) Research Note: an Evaluation of Juvenile Sexual Offender Treatment. *Crime and Delinquency*, 39, 543–53.

Langstrom, N. and Grann, M. (2000) Risk for Criminal Recidivism Among Young Sex Offenders. *Journal of Interpersonal Violence*, 15, 855–71.

Loeber, R. (1990) Development and Risk Factors of Juvenile Antisocial Behaviour and Delinquency. *Clinical Psychology Review*, 10, 1–41.

Moffitt, T.E. (1993) Adolescence-Limited and Life-Course-Persistent Antisocial Behaviour: A Developmental Taxonomy. *Psychological Review*, 100, 674–701.

National Adolescent Perpetrator Network (1993) The Revised Report From The National Task Force on Juvenile Sexual Offending. *Juvenile and Family Court Journal*, 44, 1–121.

O'Brien, M. and Bera, W. (1986) Adolescent Sexual Offenders: A Descriptive Typology. *A Newsletter of The National Family Life Education Network*, 1, 1–5.

Prentky, R. and Righthand, S. (2001) *Juvenile Sex Offender Assessment Protocol (JSOAP)*. Bridgewater, MA: Justice Resource Institute.

Prentky, R. and Righthand, S. (2002) *Juvenile Sex Offender Assessment Protocol-Second Edition (JSOAP-II)*. Bridgewater, MA: Justice Resource Institute.

Prentky, R., Harris, B., Frizzell, K. and Righthand, S. (2000) an Actuarial Procedure for Assessing Risk With Juvenile Sex Offenders. *Sexual Abuse: A Journal of Research and Treatment*, 12, 71–93.

Rasmussen, L.A. (1999) Factors Related to Recidivism Among Juvenile Sexual Offenders. *Sexual Abuse: A Journal of Research and Treatment*, 11, 69–85.

Righthand, S. and Welch, C. (2001) *Juveniles Who Have Sexually Offended: A Review of The Professional Literature*. Washington, D.C. Office of Juvenile Justice and Delinquency Prevention, US Department of Justice.

Schram, D.D., Malloy, C.D. and Rowe, W.E. (1992) Juvenile Sex Offenders: A Follow-Up Study of Reoffense Behaviour. *Interchange,* July, 1–3.

Sipe, R., Jensen, E. L. and Everett, R.S. (1998) Adolescent Sexual Offenders Grown Up: Recidivism in Young Adulthood. *Criminal Justice and Behaviour*, 25, 109–24.

Smith, W.R. and Monastersky, C. (1986) Assessing Juvenile Sexual Offenders' Risk for Reoffending. *Criminal Justice and Behaviour*, 13, 115–40.

Virginia Department of Juvenile Justice. (2002) *Data Resource Guide: Fiscal Year 2002.* Richmond, VA: The Virginia Department of Juvenile Justice Research and Evaluation Unit. 173–81.

Worling, J.R. and Curwen, T. (2000) Adolescent Sexual Offender Recidivism: Success of Specialised Treatment and Implications for Risk Prediction. *Child Abuse and Neglect*, 24, 965–82.